Basic Cost Accounting Concepts

Basic Cost Accounting Concepts

HENRY R. ANDERSON PH.D., CPA
Professor and Chairman
Department of Accounting
California State University, Fullerton

MITCHELL H. RAIBORN PH.D., CPA, CMA
Professor of Accounting
Texas Tech University

HOUGHTON MIFFLIN COMPANY
BOSTON
Atlanta   Dallas   Geneva, Illinois
Hopewell, New Jersey   Palo Alto   London

Printed in the U.S.A.

Library of Congress Catalog Card Number: 76–12017

ISBN: 0–395–20646–4

To Our Fathers

HUGO RUDOLPH ANDERSON   M. H. RAIBORN

CONTENTS

PREFACE

Basic Cost Accounting Concepts integrates relevant topics into a rigorous, comprehensive, one-semester cost accounting course. Although not essential, a prerequisite of two semesters of fundamental accounting principles provides a proper foundation for total coverage of this text in one semester. Following topic selection as discussed below, this text could also be used for an introductory managerial accounting course after a basic one-semester course in financial accounting. When combined with supplementary reading assignments, research papers, and other learning projects, this text provides a focal point of concepts for an introductory managerial accounting course at the graduate level.

Academic Preparation for Professional Accounting Careers, published by the American Institute of Certified Public Accountants, recommended that the introductory course in cost or management accounting include:

Authors' Viewpoint

1. Cost determination and analysis
2. Cost control
3. Cost-based decision making

The contents of *Basic Cost Accounting Concepts* were selected to accomplish this objective. All subjects essential to instruction of traditional cost accounting courses are included in the text. Conceptual foundations are described and related to practical applications in cost accounting. Concepts and techniques of planning, control, and decision making are also interrelated.

The sequence of chapters in *Basic Cost Accounting Concepts* reflects the authors' philosophy that the field of management accounting, encompassing all facets of managerial information needs for decision purposes, is best introduced by proceeding from cost accounting foundations to their applications. Accordingly, product cost accounting, cost behavior, cost-volume-profit analysis, and standard costing are considered essential tools for period budgeting, cost control, and short-run decision analysis. The text is designed to present concepts and techniques in this building-block fashion; when a particular subject such as cost behavior analysis is mastered by the student, this material is then related to subject matter in subsequent chapters. In our opinion, the seventeen-chapter sequence of this text provides a logical organization and approach to the study of cost accounting. Topics in cost accounting also are related to financial accounting, and this relationship is reinforced throughout the text so that students will understand that cost and management accounting are integral parts of the total accounting process.

Alternative Course Design Plans

Basic Cost Accounting Concepts contains seventeen chapters grouped into four modules. The modular organization affords considerable flexibility in course planning and desired emphasis by individual instructors. Module Two covers job order costing, overhead accounting, process costing, and accounting for joint production costs. This module is especially suited for courses that emphasize product cost determination and related accounting procedures.

For a managerially oriented course, many instructors prefer to emphasize the use of accounting information for planning, control, and decision-making purposes. Module Three provides the foundations of accounting for planning, control, and decision making, and Module Four presents related applications in cost control, responsibility accounting, period budgeting, short-run decision analysis, capital expenditure evaluation, and divisional performance evaluation.

Regardless of desired course emphasis, Module One can be used to establish the nature of cost accounting and its relationship to the field of management accounting. Topics in Module One include an overview of the management accounting cycle, organizational aspects of production activity, basic accounting procedures for a manufacturing company, and a conceptual framework of management accounting.

The text contains the following module and topic structure:

Module One—Manufacturing Environment: Management, Cost Accounting, and Production

1. Cost Accounting and Management
2. The Manufacturing Process
3. Nature and Reporting of Manufacturing Costs
4. Cost Concepts, Objectives, and Accounting Systems

Module Two—Traditional Approaches to Product Cost Accounting

5. Overhead Accounting and Job Order Cost Systems
6. Process Cost Accounting
7. Extended Practices in Process Costing
8. Analysis of Joint Production Costs

Module Three—Foundations of Management Planning and Control

9. Cost-Volume-Profit Analysis
10. Theory and Application of Direct Costing
11. Standard Cost Accounting
12. Analysis of Standard Cost Variances

Module Four—Applications of Planning and Performance Evaluation Techniques

13. Cost Control and Responsibility Accounting
14. Period Budgets and Profit Planning
15. Short-Run Operating Decisions
16. Capital Expenditure Decisions
17. Divisional Performance Evaluation

Complete modules or only selected chapters may be utilized in designing a particular course. Suggested course content is outlined below for emphasizing either a course in cost accounting or one that is managerially oriented. As illustrated, other variations are possible depending upon student needs and instructor preferences.

| TOPICS (CHAPTERS) | CLASS OF 42 HOURS THAT EMPHASIZES | | |
	Cost accounting	Managerial accounting	Cost and managerial accounting
Introduction (1 and 2)	4	4	3
Manufacturing costs (3)	3	3	3
Conceptual foundation (4)	2	3	2
Overhead accounting and job order costing (5)	3	3	3
Process costing (6 and 7)	6	–	5
Joint production costs (8)	3	1	3
Cost-volume-profit (9)	3	3	3
Direct costing (10)	3	3	2
Standard costs (11 and 12)	6	6	5
Responsibility accounting (13)	1	3	2
Period planning (14)	2	3	2
Short-run decisions (15)	2	3	3
Capital expenditure decisions (16)	3	4	3
Divisional performance (17)	1	3	3
Total hours	42	42	42

Special Organizational Format and Text Features

A unique feature of this text is the Chapter Highlights section that introduces each chapter. This section contains three specific parts:

1. *Purpose and Learning Objectives*   The purpose of each chapter is clearly stated, and learning objectives for student accomplishment are specified. Learning objectives indicate concepts and techniques that students should be able to apply upon completing the chapter.
2. *Relevant Concepts*   Concepts that are essential to an understanding of material presented in each chapter are identified and described.
3. *Chapter Summary*   A brief summary is included in the Chapter Highlights section to preview the detailed contents of each chapter.

Each chapter concludes with a Final Note, which integrates various sections of the chapter and relates this material to other parts of the text. Students then are directed to the Chapter Highlights section to review the chapter learning objectives, concepts, and summary. The authors believe this introductory Chapter Highlights section is a useful device because it provides an efficient method of surveying detailed chapter contents and assessing attainment of learning objectives.

Students beginning their study of cost accounting should have a basic knowledge of the manufacturing process. Many cost accounting concepts assume such knowledge but only a few students can actually relate to production methods. Chapter 2 is designed to bridge this gap and to provide a frame of reference for understanding cost accounting concepts and for applying cost accounting techniques. The production process of Elco Industries, Inc., Rockford, Illinois, is the focal point of the chapter.

Chapter 4 contains a unique discussion of cost concepts, objectives, and accounting systems. After a thorough analysis of these areas and of cost classification methods, the topics are interrelated to formulate the conceptual foundation for the text and for the cost accounting discipline.

To give the instructor needed flexibility, we have incorporated an extraordinary number of questions, exercises, and problems into the text. Care has been taken to make sure that every major topic is covered by at least one exercise and one problem to help reinforce the concept or technique. In addition, over seventy problems from professional accounting examinations are included in the text.

Acknowledgments

We are grateful to the following professors and professional colleagues for reviewing various drafts of the manuscript and for constructive comments that led to improvements in the text:

Thomas E. Balke	University of Nebraska, Lincoln
William B. Barrett	University of Arizona
James C. Caldwell	Texas Tech University
C. P. Carter	Northeastern University
John A. Caspari	University of Nebraska, Lincoln
Robert B. Denis	University of Connecticut
C. Willard Elliott	Louisiana State University
David E. Emerson	Highland Community College
Albert Ewald	Temple University
Joseph M. Goodman	Chicago State University
Wilber C. Haseman	University of Missouri, Columbia
Bonnie Jack	Johnson County Community College
Fred A. Jacobs	University of Tennessee, Knoxville
James W. Pattillo	University of Notre Dame
Cecily A. Raiborn	University of Texas, Arlington
Karl E. Reichardt	Institute of Management Accounting
Jack C. Robertson	The University of Texas, Austin
Kamal E. Said	University of Houston
Frank E. Watkins	University of Tennessee, Knoxville
Farouq A. Zuaiter	Chicago State University

We thank the American Institute of Certified Public Accountants and the Institute of Management Accounting for granting permission to use their problem material. In addition, we appreciate the cooperation of the National Association of Accountants, which granted permission to use information from its publications. To the management of Elco Industries, Inc., Rockford, Illinois, we owe a special debt of gratitude for allowing us to illustrate various phases of its production process and source documents.

Several former students at Southern Methodist University assisted in developing problem solutions and in reviewing manuscript drafts. Those making significant contributions include: Diane Taggart, Becky Anderson, Jackie Perkinson Krejci, Robert Crist, and Carolyn Bednarz. A special thank you is directed to our "word processors," Mary Kesner and Shelley Kessel, for their skillful and timely manuscript preparation.

To Sue Anderson, Deborah, Howard, Harold, and Hugh Anderson, and to all the Raiborns: We sincerely appreciate your encouragement and sacrifice.

HENRY R. ANDERSON
MITCHELL H. RAIBORN

Villa Park, California
Lubbock, Texas

Basic Cost Accounting Concepts

Module One

Manufacturing Environment: Management, Cost Accounting, and Production

THE PRIMARY PURPOSE of this text is to convey basic concepts of cost accounting in a meaningful, understandable manner. In addition, we hope this book will instill in students a curiosity about the dynamic management accounting field and encourage them to seek advanced courses in the area.

As a profession grows and matures, specialization becomes the dominant force pushing it toward greater horizons. The accounting profession today exemplifies this. An individual entering the profession generally chooses one of three career areas: public accounting, industrial accounting, or governmental accounting or positions with other nonprofit organizations. Each of these career opportunities is further specialized. In public accounting, for instance, a person usually specializes in one of three major areas: auditing, taxation, or management services. Even within these areas, further specialization becomes necessary. Many large CPA firms require their auditing and tax personnel to become proficient in a particular industry, such as public utilities, insurance companies, or manufacturing concerns. Management services work involves problem-solving techniques performed jointly by several specialists— engineers, mathematicians, sociologists, psychologists, and systems experts as well as accountants.

Management accounting is rapidly becoming specialized. Modern computers have freed management accountants from laborious bookkeeping duties and given them time to think about new industrial accounting concepts and techniques. Optimization methods and other quantitative models are still bringing new stature to management accountants. The flow of strategic information through highly sophisticated, refined systems was made possible by modern computer technology. Recipients of accounting reports are also being studied to determine the behavioral effect of various reports submitted to them. These recent innovations have made management accountants "information specialists."

Although cost accounting is now part of management accounting, this was not always true. Managerial or management accounting is a rather recent innovation. Historically, cost accounting dates to about the fourteenth century, when small Italian, English, Flemish, and German enterprises used costing techniques. Literature on cost accounting was scarce until the latter part of the nineteenth century. Even during the first two decades of the twentieth century, business leaders regarded internal cost accounting systems as secret tools linked to the firm's profitability. Newly developed techniques were not discussed openly.

Around 1920, cost accounting concepts and techniques began to appear in accounting literature. The first major topic to receive attention was cost allocation and cost attachment to units of production (which is still the basis of management accounting research). Many major developments took place from 1920 to 1945, including: (1) an increasing number of businesses utilizing cost accounting systems; (2) refinements in existing cost accounting approaches, techniques, and concepts; (3) a shift from product costing interests to control procedures for internal manufacturing operations; (4) development of budgeting techniques; and (5) application of cost concepts to the distribution segment of company operations.

Since 1945, emphasis in management accounting has shifted from product costing techniques and procedures to planning and control of internal operations. Decision making has become a major reason for generating information. As these changes occurred, management accounting became more dynamic and challenging. Cost accounting concepts now provide the basic framework for management accounting and are prerequisite to specialization in the field.

The chapters in Module One are designed to introduce students to the basic concepts and environmental factors underlying management accounting. Chapter 1 relates the characteristics of cost and management accounting to the functions of management, and Chapter 2 focuses on an illustrative analysis of an actual production process. Chapter 3 introduces the nature and reporting of manufacturing costs. Chapter 4 discusses the objectives of cost accounting systems and several important cost concepts.

Chapter 1: Cost Accounting and Management

Accounting is the art of recording, classifying, interpreting, and reporting financial transactions of a business entity. Many people believe that an accountant's only function is the preparation of financial statements, including the year-end statement of earnings and statement of financial position (balance sheet). This represents an incomplete view of the total accounting function.

Year-end financial statements show a composite financial picture of an enterprise's transactions for an entire year. Proper recording and classification of hundreds of daily events are necessary before financial statements can be prepared. Each financial transaction is the result of a decision. Transactions involving the purchase of a product, the sale of a product, the hiring of an employee, the purchase of a machine or a building, the acquisition of adequate insurance coverage, or the borrowing of funds are all results of management decisions. Thus, accounting is a service activity, recording past financial transactions and providing information upon which future management decisions can be based.

All activities summarized in year-end financial statements can be divided into two main categories: (1) the actual sale of a product or service and related transactions that occur after the point of sale and (2) the many events and transactions that must first occur in order to develop a salable product or service. Management accounting deals primarily with the second group of activities. It emphasizes the planning and control of internal operations, the determination of product costs, and the supplying of relevant, timely information to management for decision-making purposes.

This chapter examines the entire field of management accounting. Such broad exposure will create an awareness of the magnitude and significance of management accounting and establish a frame of reference for the entire text.

Upon completion of this chapter, students should be able to:

1. State the relationship between cost accounting and management accounting
2. Identify the differences between management accounting and financial accounting

3. Identify traditional management functions and management accounting functions and illustrate how they are interrelated
4. Distinguish between cost planning and cost control

The following basic concepts are introduced in this chapter:

Relevant Concepts

Cost accounting   Internal cost data accumulation based on a set of cost concepts and related cost accumulation and other analytical techniques necessary for transforming business data into useful information for management.

Management cycle   The collective efforts of a team of experienced business managers who together establish the objectives and goals of the organization and guide its various segments to the eventual attainment of those goals.

Management accounting cycle   An interrelated set of cost and managerial accounting concepts and techniques that aid in servicing the informational requirements of management.

Cost accounting is the segment of management accounting that consists of cost concepts, related cost accumulation methods, and analytical techniques which provide information for management decision making, forecasting, and control.

Chapter Summary

The fields of management accounting and financial accounting can be differentiated by comparison within the following areas: primary users of information, types of accounting systems, restrictive guides, units of measurement, focal points for analysis, frequency of reporting, and degree of reliability.

The general goal of management accounting is to provide relevant, timely information to management. Although relatively unrestricted in terms of report format and content, all information must be useful in response to underlying needs. Usefulness is judged by the quality of results that the information suggests or promotes.

Planning, organizing, executing, reviewing, and stewardship are the main functions of management. Through the data processing function, management accountants are expected to simulate plans utilizing various alternative courses of action, to communicate plans and expected results to managers, to accumulate data from operations as plans are executed, and to evaluate operating performance by comparing actual results with initial plans.

The terms *cost accounting* and *management accounting* have been used synonymously by many accountants in recent years. But are their accounting boundaries similar? Cost accounting initially aimed to adequately account for the resources used in the manufacturing process. Through the years, however, the subject matter of cost accounting has broadened. Many areas of study—such as computer applications, information systems approaches (MIS), quantitative methods, behavioral influences, and long-range planning techniques—have been added to courses in cost accounting. Management accountants can no longer be concerned only with techniques of product costing. Cost accounting now aids management in planning and controlling costs related to both production and distribution operations. Decision making has come to the

COST ACCOUNTING OR MANAGEMENT ACCOUNTING?

forefront of the subject area, and the complete set of subjects is called management accounting.

This relatively new field of management accounting should be distinguished from the traditional area of *cost accounting*, which Haseman defines as:

The phase of general accounting which is concerned with the recording, reporting, and analyzing of detailed cost information for internal management uses.[1]

In comparison, the Committee on Management Accounting of the American Accounting Association (AAA) developed the following definition of *management accounting*:

The application of appropriate techniques and concepts in processing the historical and projected economic data of an entity to assist management in establishing plans for reasonable economic objectives and in the making of rational decisions with a view toward achieving these objectives. It includes the methods and concepts necessary for effective planning, for choosing among alternative business actions, and for control through the evaluation and interpretation of performance. Its study involves consideration of ways in which accounting information may be accumulated, synthesized, analyzed, and presented in relation to specific problems, decisions, and day-to-day tasks of business management.[2]

Scores of other definitions could be analyzed but little would be gained. Management accounting has grown so rapidly in the last decade that authors have difficulty in agreeing upon its boundaries, much less nailing down an appropriate all-inclusive definition. In this text, management accounting is viewed as the segment of accounting described above by the AAA committee.

Cost accounting is a segment of management accounting; it consists of a set of cost concepts and related cost accumulation and other analytical techniques necessary for transforming business data into useful information for management. These cost accounting concepts are integrated into traditional cost accumulation systems and concentrate on specific data collection and reporting techniques. Once relevant information has been gathered, classified, and summarized, management accounting techniques take over.

Cost accounting emphasizes the basic terms, procedures, and techniques used by accountants in their routine cost analysis activities. Special decision approaches (simulation) and the use of highly quantitative and behavioral approaches to these decisions are areas of advanced management accounting. Exhibit 1-1 depicts the role and place of basic cost accounting concepts in the field of management accounting. The cost accounting area is limited to product costing procedures and related information processing; it appears in Exhibit 1-1 as "traditional cost classification tools and techniques." Further distillation of information requires more sophisticated management accounting practices.

MANAGEMENT VERSUS FINANCIAL ACCOUNTING

Before studying management accounting, it is important to compare it with financial accounting. Essentially, *financial accounting* involves the recording, classifying, and summarizing the balance sheet and income statement effects of internal events and external transactions. It is concerned primarily with the organization and preparation of reports on enterprise assets, equities, and net income. The traditional balance sheet, income statement, and statement of

[1] Wilber C. Haseman, *Management Uses of Accounting*, Allyn and Bacon, Boston, 1963, p. 385.

[2] "Report of Committee on Management Accounting," *Accounting Review*, 34 (April 1959), 210.

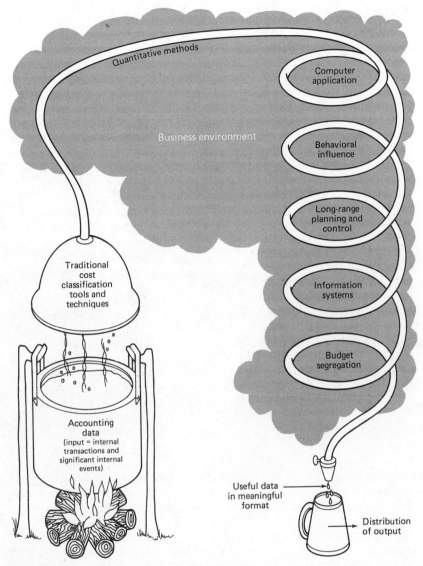

Labels within image:
Quantitative methods
Computer application
Business environment
Behavioral influence
Long-range planning and control
Traditional cost classification tools and techniques
Information systems
Budget segregation
Accounting data (input = internal transactions and significant internal events)
Useful data in meaningful format
Distribution of output

EXHIBIT 1-1
USING COST ACCOUNTING DATA

sources and uses of funds are prepared mainly for users outside the enterprise, such as present and potential stockholders, creditors, and financial analysts.

In contrast, *management accounting* is concerned with information for internal use. Most accounting principles dealing with external financial reporting have little relevance to management accounting. Although applicable to many types of organizations, management accounting usually is associated with manufacturing firms. However, all organizations can utilize some form of accounting system to generate useful data for managerial decision making.

Both management and financial accounting involve the analysis and flow of information. However, to get a proper perspective on the techniques and

EXHIBIT 1-2

COMPARISON OF FINANCIAL AND MANAGEMENT ACCOUNTING

AREAS OF COMPARISON	FINANCIAL ACCOUNTING	MANAGEMENT ACCOUNTING
1. Primary users of information	Persons and organizations outside the business entity	Various levels of internal management
2. Types of accounting systems	Double-entry system	Not restricted to double-entry system; any system that is useful
3. Restrictive guides	Adherence to generally accepted accounting principles	No guides or restrictions; only criterion is usefulness
4. Unit of measurement	Historical dollar	Any monetary or physical measurement unit that is useful—labor hour, machine hour, etc. If dollars are used, they may be historical or future dollars.
5. Focal point of analysis	Business entity as a whole	Various segments of the business entity
6. Frequency of reporting	Periodically on regular basis	Whenever needed; may not be on a regular basis
7. Degree of reliability	Demands objectivity; historical in nature	Heavily subjective for planning purposes, but objective data are used when relevant; futuristic in nature

concepts discussed in this text, students must understand the objectives and purposes of management accounting and be able to distinguish management accounting from financial accounting. Some important differences can be seen in Exhibit 1-2.

Throughout the following comparative analysis of financial and management accounting, one central theme appears. Financial accounting must operate within set boundaries, but management accounting practices are not confined to predetermined constraints. Exhibit 1-2 demonstrates this point. Management accounting has only one restriction: Reports, analyses, and related information must be *useful* and *relevant* to specific management needs. In part, this flexibility evolves from the numerous demands for information and different cost-revenue-resource analyses that management accountants must produce. In financial accounting, stewardship reporting and income determination are clearly more restricted in scope.

Primary Users of Information

The users of traditional financial accounting statements are external to the reporting entity. Although internal management is responsible for preparing the firm's periodic financial statements, these reports are used primarily to satisfy stewardship responsibilities. Because they are condensed, these statements offer little for purposes of internal analysis and decision making. External financial statements purport to show only the financial position of the enterprise at a particular point in time and the results of its operations for the period. Primary users include present and potential stockholders, creditors, financial analysts, stock exchanges, government agencies, and others outside the enterprise.

In contrast, internal reports and analyses generated by management accounting systems are used by every member of internal management. The content and scope of internal reports will vary for different levels of management, the segment or phase of operations analyzed, and the planning or control purpose underlying each report. The emphasis is on supplying relevant information to persons who are responsible for particular activities. Therefore, different information will be given to plant managers than to departmental supervisors. Examples of different types and uses of internally generated information include: (1) unit cost analyses for product costing purposes, (2) budgets for planning future operations, (3) control reports by responsibility unit for measuring performance, (4) relevant cost reports for short-run decision making, and (5) capital budgeting analyses for corporate long-term planning.

Types of Accounting Systems

External financial statements contain summarized dollar totals reflecting balances of all accounts contained in a firm's general ledger. Before financial data are entered into the general ledger, these amounts must be coded, adjusted, or translated into a form suitable for a double-entry accounting system. Journals, ledgers, and other devices used in processing financial accounting information are based upon the double-entry system.

Information flow of internal accounting data does not depend upon the double-entry framework. Data may be gathered for small or large segments of an organization and may be expressed in units other than dollars. Under these situations, the information storage and retrieval system must have greater capabilities than required for financial accounting. The only restriction upon internal systems design is that the system must be useful for satisfying the informational needs of management.

Many reports and analyses prepared for management deal with planning and control of operations. Information contained in these reports may represent estimates of future operating results (budgets for planning purposes), or the reports may contain detailed analyses of actual operating performance showing variations between actual and predicted costs. Almost all this information is for internal use only.

However, actual cost summaries and product costing analyses are part of a firm's general accounting operations. Such information must be integrated into the firm's financial statements and must be processed in double-entry form. Ending inventory values and cost of goods manufactured and sold are primary examples of such results. When appropriate internal analysis of these items has been completed, journal entries are prepared to merge the management accounting information with other financial data processed during the period. This transition is smooth and mechanical, as is illustrated throughout this text.

Restrictive Guides

Financial accounting is concerned with analyzing, recording, classifying, and reporting an enterprise's financial activities. As already indicated, the resulting financial statements are prepared primarily for external recipients. To protect the interests of various parties and to instill trust among financial statement users, accountants must adhere to generally accepted accounting principles and standards that govern the recording, measuring, and reporting of financial information. Although necessary for protective and credibility purposes, generally accepted accounting principles confine accountants to a finite number of operating practices. Examples of the restrictions placed on financial accounting are principles that involve matching revenues and expenses, stating inventories at lower of cost or market, reporting fixed assets at acquisition cost, realizing revenue in appropriate periods, maintaining objectivity, and reporting on a consistent basis.

Management accounting has only one restrictive guide: The technique or accounting practice must produce useful information. Once usefulness is defined realistically for a particular problem, the management accountant chooses the appropriate concepts, procedures, and techniques required to solve that problem. To illustrate, suppose the management of the Downes Company is deciding whether to purchase a particular piece of machinery. Return on investment information is relevant to this decision. Before return on investment can be computed, the financial effect of the new machine on company operations must be determined. This analysis requires estimates of the increase in product sales, changes in variable and fixed manufacturing costs, and changes in selling and administrative expenses. Once these amounts have been estimated, the management accountant must select an appropriate method for determining the machine's return on investment. Computing projected net income based on the estimated data is one approach. Management could then compare expected net income with the cost of the machine to arrive at a return on investment figure.

A second return on investment approach is to analyze the present value of future cash flows resulting from the use of the new machine. This type of analysis is superior to the projected net income approach because it considers the time value of money (a complete explanation of this concept is found in Chapter 16). Further refinements centering on the sensitivity and interdependency of the estimated figures are also possible. If such information is useful, it is relevant to management and should be developed if economically feasible.

Unit of Measurement

Financial accounting serves a stewardship or accountability function by providing financial information on past events of an enterprise. All information is presented in dollar amounts. To be more specific, the unit of measurement commonly associated with financial accounting is the "historical" dollar. Transactions summarized in the financial statements have already occurred, and the financial effects are objectively measurable.

While there are current movements to adjust financial statements for price-level changes, external financial statements presented on this basis are not now required by the accounting profession. Thus, assets acquired by a firm in 1965 and still in use are disclosed in the balance sheet at their undepreciated balance based on historical cost. Current replacement costs of capital facilities usually are not disclosed.

In comparison, management accountants can employ any measurement unit that is useful in a particular situation. Historical dollars may be employed in the short-run for cost control and for measuring trends used for routine planning purposes. However, most of management's decisions are based upon analyses utilizing expected "future" dollars. Both short- and long-run decisions require forecasts and projections of operating data and must be based on estimates of future dollar flows. In addition to monetary units, the management accountant may find it necessary to use such measures as labor hours, machine hours, and product units as bases for particular analyses. The common denominator underlying all measurement, reporting, and analysis activities in management accounting is usefulness to a particular situation. Historical cost and reliance upon past transactions are essential to financial accounting but may be secondary to management accounting.

Traditionally, financial accounting communicates information about the assets, equities, and net income of a business entity as a whole. Financial statements summarize and report upon the transactions of the entire enterprise. Recent concern over reporting practices of large conglomerate organizations has resulted in limited divisional and product-line reporting practices, but these advances are still developing.

Focal Point for Analysis

Management accounting analyses are directed at various segments (cost centers, profit centers, departments, divisions) of an enterprise or to some specific aspect of its operations. Management accounting, therefore, embraces many "entities." Typical reports could range from a revenue-expense analysis of an entire division to the investigation of materials used by a particular department. Further refinement could require analysis of production and operating costs for a specific machine. In developing relevant information for given purposes, management accounting serves many segments of the firm, from small cost centers to geographical divisions.

Periodicity is one of the basic accounting postulates that explain financial accounting functions. It requires that financial statements be developed and presented at regular time intervals. Corporate annual reports may be supplemented with semiannual or quarterly financial statements, but the important consideration is that they be prepared on a regular basis. Periodicity in financial accounting explains the need for end-of-period adjustments involving accrued and deferred items to measure net income properly.

Frequency of Reporting

Management accounting operates on the premise that reports are prepared whenever needed. For some reports, regularity of preparation is not essential. Reports may be prepared on a monthly, weekly, or even daily basis. Frequency of reports is determined by particular planning and control needs; a more costly item of material may require daily control reports, while other types of manufacturing costs are compared with budgeted amounts on a monthly basis. For internal reporting purposes, relevancy and timeliness override fixed periodicity as the cause of report preparation.

Objectivity, verifiability, and freedom from bias are desirable information characteristics in financial accounting, since it is concerned primarily with evaluating an enterprise's past performance. To accomplish the stewardship function, information included in external financial statements must be determined objectively and be supported by documents verifying the occurrence of each related financial transaction.

Degree of Reliability

Management accounting is concerned mainly with planning and control of internal operations. Short- and long-term planning and managerial decision making are futuristic activities. Expense and revenue transactions of the past, although useful for establishing trends, usually are not relevant to planning activities and must be replaced by subjective estimates of future events. Attempts are made to select the most reliable estimates, but predictive analyses of future operations remain highly subjective. The control function of management accounting relies on analyses of past performance. For control activities and for determination of product unit costs for inventory valuations, management accountants must use objectively determinable information.

MANAGEMENT FUNCTIONS

Management accounting provides information concerning future management actions and results of past decisions. From a management viewpoint, the accounting function serves management and responds to specific informational requests. Since management accounting personnel are part of internal management, interactions between management and accounting are important. To establish this fact, it is necessary to examine the functions of management and to relate the responsibilities of management accounting to them.

Management is expected to establish the objectives and goals of the organization and to guide its various segments to the eventual attainment of those goals. Functions of management within this process differ from company to company because of philosophical differences. For purposes of analysis, however, the traditional view of management functions includes: (1) planning future operations, (2) organizing the firm's personnel and facilities, (3) executing the plans, (4) reviewing the results of operations, and (5) reporting the results of operations to interested persons and organizations. Exhibit 1-3 depicts these management functions as an overall management control cycle. Each phase of the cycle is discussed below.

EXHIBIT 1-3
THE MANAGEMENT CONTROL CYCLE

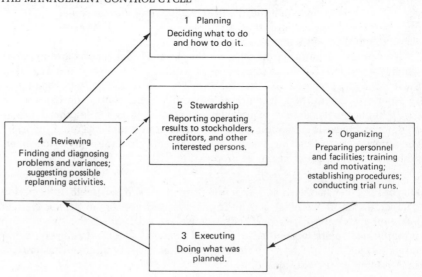

Before corporate action can be taken, management must decide what to do. Before plans can be formulated, appropriate objectives must be established. Once direction has been given to this process, various alternatives can be developed. Selecting the best course of action involves an analysis to determine the availability of resources and the economic, social, and political environments within which the plans will be executed. The formulation of goals, objectives, and corporate policies is called *strategic planning*. Annual operating plans should complement the firm's strategic plans. Once the operating plans for a period have been formed, decisions concerning various alternatives must be made. Some of these decisions are nonrecurring in nature, while others relate to periodic planning activities. The purchase of new machinery is nonrecurring, but planning a production schedule is repetitive. In summary, planning has two main parts: deciding what to do and deciding how to do it.

Planning

Planning alone does not guarantee satisfactory operating results. To put plans into action, responsibilities are assigned to various people. Personnel may need to be hired and trained. Facilities must be purchased or adjusted to fit necessary specifications. Key personnel must be motivated. Operating procedures need to be developed, and trial runs must be performed. All these events are interrelated; the efforts and abilities of people involved and the operating limits of designated facilities must be coordinated if efficient operation is to result. Selection of personnel, communication of responsibilities, preparation of facilities, and coordination of efforts related to various corporate plans are all part of the organizing function of management.

Organizing

The implementation of planned activities should begin only after plans have been developed and organized. At this point, plan directives and goals have been established, and key personnel have been notified of their responsibilities. Control of operations now becomes management's primary concern. As the implementation stage progresses, management must determine how well the various jobs are being performed. If obstacles are encountered, original plans must be revised to reflect developments that were not anticipated.

Executing

Communication of timely and relevant information is vital for controlling operations. Methods and techniques used to aid the communication process are discussed later in this chapter in connection with the management accounting cycle. When executing or implementing plans, management relies on accounting reports to monitor the progress, relative success, and results of planned actions. These reports may also be used to formulate operating changes if revisions of earlier plans become necessary. In summary, the function of executing plans centers on the implementation of a proposed project, decision, or strategy. Managerial control attempts to ensure that planned objectives are attained.

Complete implementation of plans does not guarantee that actual operating results will match those anticipated in the planning stage. The reviewing function involves a critical analysis of actual results. Problems encountered and deviations from anticipated results must be analyzed to isolate causal factors. Corrective measures should be taken as soon as possible. In addition to corrective actions for current operations, the reviewing function should supply management with suggestions for improving future planning activities.

Reviewing

Stewardship

Periodically, management is responsible for reporting the results of operations to the public. Stockholders, creditors, and others are interested in a firm's operations and are entitled to periodic summaries of past performance. Although a company's financial statements may be examined by a certified public accountant (CPA), it is management's duty to prepare the financial statements and to retain responsibility for the content of such reports.

The Management Control Cycle

The functions discussed in the preceding sections are not intended to be all-inclusive descriptions of the management process. Managements are created by people, and no two management teams act or react alike. But somewhere in the maze of daily business activity, management functions and contributes to the life of an enterprise. Achieving results through the cooperative efforts of people is the connecting thread of the management control cycle. Our analysis has chosen the functions of planning, organizing, executing, reviewing, and stewardship to represent the management control cycle shown in Exhibit 1-3. When examining this model of the management process, keep in mind that the five functions are constantly interacting and closely related. When people are involved, emotions, intuition, and ethics often dictate actions. An efficient, coordinated management team does not operate within a strictly defined set of functions, although concepts of these functions are useful learning devices.

INFORMATION REQUIREMENTS OF MANAGEMENT

Information requirements of management establish the basis for the development of an internal accounting system. Because of the individual nature of information requests, no two internal systems are identical. It would be unrealistic to describe one information system as being able to supply all management information requirements.

Conceptually, these information requirements can be placed into three main categories: (1) information for external reporting purposes, (2) information necessary for planning and controlling current operations, and (3) information that will enable the organization to plan and control unprogrammed, long-term activities. External reporting has been referred to already as the supplying of information to persons and organizations outside an organization. But how does an internal information system contribute to the external reporting function? Product costing techniques play a significant role in this process. The allocation of manufacturing costs to inventories of work in process and finished goods assists external reporting through the valuation of assets. In addition, product costing contributes to income determination by providing information about the cost of goods sold. The distinction between "period" and "product" costs significantly influences the matching of revenues with expenses.

Information for Planning and Control

Short-term planning and control include operations review and performance evaluation procedures. To properly review operations, management requires reports that direct attention to various phases of operations. After comparing actual results with planned or budgeted performance, accounting reports are condensed to highlight only the areas of exception (where budget and actual figures differ significantly). Once exceptions have been isolated, performance reports are prepared to determine the causes of variations between actual and planned results.

Information for long-term planning and control is more general in nature. Five- or ten-year plans are based on estimates of future operations. The goals and strategies of the organization influence these reports. For each annual planning period, information must be generated to assist management in analyzing unique, nonrecurring decisions.

To be useful, information must be relevant; it must satisfy the needs of a particular user. In this context, relevance also encompasses the characteristics of accuracy, reliability, and timeliness. Other characteristics of information include verifiability, freedom from bias, and quantifiability. Verifiability as applied to internal reporting differs substantially from its application in reports for external users. This point is expressed by the following statement:

> The position of the independent certified public accountant in his external reporting role is different from that of the controller reporting to his management group. Indeed, the requirement of independent certification of the external reports is indicative of a greater need externally for verifiability.[3]

Desirable Information Characteristics

Management accounting must meet the diverse information requirements of management. Each function of management demands different types of information for different purposes. In the planning phase, information must be generated that will assist in: (1) recognizing and defining operating problems, (2) searching for alternative solutions, (3) evaluating alternatives, and (4) selecting the best alternative(s). Information for control purposes should include reports of actions taken and results achieved in relation to the organizational objectives and goals. Since the functions of management form a management control cycle, management accounting activities can be illustrated by developing a management accounting cycle.

MANAGEMENT ACCOUNTING FUNCTIONS

The management accounting cycle is structured to service the multiple information needs of management and consists of the following functions: (1) simulation of preplanned activities, (2) communication of plans to key personnel, (3) accumulation of actual operating information, (4) measurement and evaluation of actual performance, and (5) processing all information generated by the organization. The management accounting cycle complements the management cycle. After discussing each segment of the management accounting cycle, this entire framework will be superimposed on the management cycle to illustrate the interaction of accounting and management.

The Management Accounting Cycle[4]

Simulation Simulation is management's method of testing proposed changes in operations through experimentation using different operating variables in repeated trials to determine optimal courses of action. It could involve planned changes in operating procedures or the introduction of a new product. Whenever plans contain uncertainties and there is a need to put interrelated

---

[3] *A Statement of Basic Accounting Theory*, American Accounting Association, Evanston, Ill., 1966, p. 53.

[4] Many ideas in this section were drawn from a series of lectures in management accounting by Professor Wilber C. Haseman. Unpublished notes, School of Accountancy, University of Missouri, Columbia, 1975. The authors are grateful to Dr. Haseman for granting permission to use this material.

variables through some "dry-run" analysis, a simulation approach is appropriate.

Methods of simulation vary significantly in degree of sophistication. The development of a master budget with accompanying cash budget and pro forma financial statements is one form of simulation. Forecasted net income and overall financial position of the firm can then be compared with desired results before deciding on future courses of action.

Systems simulation may involve the creation of a model or a set of mathematical relationships that enable experiments or repeated trials to be made of the system's projected performance. Because of its experimental ability, simulation is a useful planning technique. As an example, suppose a firm is planning to change its production process. New equipment and operating techniques are considered. First the inputs or operating variables for the proposed production process are examined in relation to other operating variables. The second step is to assign initial numerical values to these variables. With the aid of a computer, operations are then simulated or repeated numerous times to see the changes in overall profitability produced by the variables being tested. Changes in these key variables will yield different results. Simulation, then, is a trial-and-error, or heuristic, method for solving complex business problems. Although useful, a simulated solution does not yield optimal results automatically. With the aid of mathematical models, optimal solutions can be approximated.

Simulation of manufacturing and distribution operations can be attempted at any time, but it is most advantageous when associated with a firm's preplanning activities. A management accountant is called upon to assist in simulation analyses and to express and communicate probable consequences or results to management. More specifically, the accountant is asked to find alternatives, determine operating conditions, and evaluate the effects of risk and uncertainty that are inherent in tentative results. Simulation techniques used by management accountants range from traditional budgeting procedures to complex probabilistic systems models. General decision-making techniques discussed in this text include breakeven and cost-volume-profit analyses and analytical approaches to several types of alternative-choice problems such as make or buy decisions and sell or process-further decisions. More sophisticated methods— such as PERT (Program Evaluation and Review Technique), linear programming models, and probability analyses—are advanced management accounting topics and are mentioned only briefly.

Communication   An established communications system is a key to successful, efficient management. If plans are to be implemented and goals or targets are to be realized, people must be told what to do and how to do it. Once plans are communicated to operating personnel, a management accountant is expected to establish, maintain, and supervise the flow of relevant information. Managers must be told what is expected of them, how their work coordinates with other departments, and how subsequent performance will be measured and evaluated.

Responsibility accounting is the core of a smooth communication system. If managers know their responsibilities, they can plan and manage their areas more efficiently. Communicative guides, such as budgets, standard costs, operating manuals, and standard operating procedures (SOPs), are all part of a firm's communication network. Responsibility accounting is built into each of these communication guides. Through these guides, an accountant communicates areas of responsibility, overall plans of management, targets, and operating procedures to individual managers.

Accumulation One of the most significant functions of a management accountant is to maintain an established system of data accumulation. As management executes its plans, information is generated continuously. An accountant must supervise the collection and classification of this information.

To aid the accumulation of operating data, a management accountant uses various procedures and subsystems that make up the firm's accounting system. These elements include various internal control procedures, transaction documents, and subsidiary ledgers and journals that, in part, ensure quality information required to (1) regulate routine activities, (2) facilitate various product costing systems, and (3) enhance the usefulness of special decision systems. Fused into a coordinated accounting system, these devices help management accountants to perform the data accumulation function.

Performance evaluation Performance measurement is an important function of management accountants. In its narrowest interpretation, to measure performance is to gather, record, and report what has actually taken place within an enterprise during a defined period of time. The end product of the stewardship function, mentioned earlier as part of the management cycle, is a set of financial statements issued to interested sectors of the public. These statements measure past performance. For example, a firm's income statement is a summation of operations for a period of time. Revenues and expenses are shown categorically, and the resulting net income is a measure of performance.

Management accounting also includes the observation, measurement, and reporting of past performance. However, the concept of performance measurement for management use is much broader. Internally, management relies on the management accountant for performance evaluation. Information regarding results of production and distribution operations must be gathered, recorded, and reported, and the degree to which plans are being achieved must be determined. In addition, if significant variations exist between planned and actual results, the accountant is expected to help determine the causes and people responsible. Therefore, performance measurement in the management accounting context goes beyond the point of simply reporting past performance. Performance must be measured, evaluated in comparative terms, and properly reported. Tools used to aid performance evaluation include budget variance analysis, standard cost variance analysis, sales mix analysis, return on investment computations, and analysis of causes, all of which are discussed in this text.

Data processing Since the advent of computers, data processing has become centralized to serve total company needs. Although vital to the management accountant's data accumulation function, this phase of the management accounting cycle is much broader in scope. The accountant stores and retrieves information for simulation activities, budget preparation, communication, performance analysis, and evaluation. In addition to these uses, marketing, finance, and production personnel store and utilize many types of nonaccounting information. Such a centralized source of information facilitates total company operations.

Computerized data processing is responsible for major changes in the role of management accountants. The detailed tasks of posting, footing, and crossfooting journals and ledgers have been mechanized. Emphasis is now on an accountant's abilities to create and maintain information systems (before data are processed) and interpretation and evaluation of information (after data are processed). Computers have not diminished the role and importance of accountants. On the contrary, they have helped elevate accountants to top managerial status.

EXHIBIT 1-4

MANAGEMENT ACCOUNTING AND MANAGEMENT CONTROL CYCLES

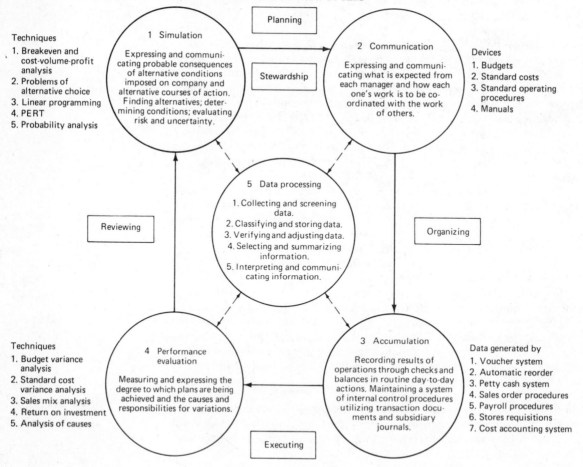

The preceding paragraphs conceptually described the various functions of management and management accountants. The management control cycle contains the functions of planning, organizing, executing, reviewing, and stewardship. Simulation, communication, accumulation, performance evaluation, and data processing are the major functions of management accountants. To be efficient, a corporation must coordinate the activities of management and accounting.

Exhibit 1-4 superimposes the management accounting cycle on the management control cycle. Simulation is shown as a preplanning activity. Communication is the catalyst that helps organize planned events. As plans are executed, the data generated from operations are accumulated. Following the accumulation of data, steps are taken to classify and analyze relevant information so that actual and planned results can be compared and evaluated. With this information, management is able to review and evaluate the degree to which plans were achieved, find and diagnose problem areas, and prescribe corrective action or replanning suggestions. If further plans are necessary, the cycles begin again. If not, management is ready to tackle new projects and plan normal operations for future periods.

Data processing is shown as a central information pool for all functions. Data from all sources, both internal and external, are stored and made available upon demand. Although shown as a management accounting function, data processing is being recognized increasingly as a separate and distinct segment of management.

Management accounting is a complex but interesting topic that is vital to an organization's success. Cost accounting concepts and techniques are used throughout the management accounting cycle to support and satisfy management information requirements. Centering on internal operations, the actions of management accountants are not hindered by external accounting restrictions. By integrating the functions of management and management accounting, the overall effectiveness of an organization is improved.

When you have completed your review of the appendix, return to the beginning of the chapter and review the highlights section before proceeding to the review questions, exercises, and problems.

APPENDIX 1-A: The Certificate in Management Accounting

In 1972, the National Association of Accountants (NAA) created the Institute of Management Accounting (IMA), a separate wing of NAA responsible for establishing and maintaining a program leading to a Certificate in Management Accounting (CMA). The program was developed because of the need to recognize professional competence in the field of management accounting. This program parallels the CPA certificate program of the American Institute of Certified Public Accountants which recognizes professional competence in the public accounting field.

As explained in Chapter 1, management accounting has come a long way since its inception as a recognized accounting discipline. As a result of these developments, management accounting can no longer be considered a minor part of the accounting profession. The management accountant has a right to be recognized, and the CMA program has been designed for this purpose. The objectives of the program clearly state this intent and are as follows:

1. To foster higher educational standards in the field of management accounting,
2. To establish management accounting as a recognized profession by identifying the role of the management accountant, the underlying body of knowledge, and by outlining a course of study by which such knowledge can be acquired, and
3. To assist employers, educators and students by establishing an objective measure of an individual's knowledge and competence in the profession of management accounting.[1]

MANAGEMENT ACCOUNTING AND THE CMA

To become a CMA, one must exhibit specific levels of proficiency in the following areas: (1) managerial economics and business finance; (2) organization and behavior, including ethical considerations; (3) public reporting standards, auditing and taxes; (4) periodic reporting for internal and external purposes; and (5) decision analysis, including modeling and information systems. At first glance, the examination coverage appears to be too broad, too all-encompassing. Many topics may seem irrelevant to the day-to-day routine of management accountants.

To fully appreciate the body of knowledge demanded of the CMA, one has to take a panoramic view of management accounting. Within our free-enterprise environment, a corporation's destiny is a function of its actions. Each action is the result of a decision. Every decision is based upon relevant information and/or management intuition (reliance on intuition tends to diminish as the business environment becomes more complex). Information supplied to management on a relevant, timely basis, then, is the key to a corporation's success.

CMA Examination Coverage

The description of the management accounting cycle in Chapter 1 facilitates the analysis of the relevance of each part of the CMA examination. "Managerial Economics and Business Finance" (part 1) is directed primarily at the environment within which the management accounting cycle operates. Decisions based upon information supplied by the accountant may have corporate, national, and even international economic repercussions. Knowledge of our free-enterprise system, of the economics of the firm (microeconomics), and of corporate capital management and capital markets is required in varying degrees in all decisions made by management. It stands to reason, then, that the supplier of the information upon which these decisions are based must be familiar with these concepts and be able to incorporate them into data-gathering and utilization techniques.

"Organization and Behavior, Including Ethical Considerations" (part 2) centers on the organization functions and hierarchy of management and the behavioral ramifications of accounting reports. To achieve its objectives, man-

[1] "Certificate in Management Accounting Established by NAA," *Management Accounting*, March 1972, p. 13.

agement must rely on the people within the organization. The goals and the steps leading to their attainment must be stated clearly and communicated articulately to the individuals responsible for each action. Performance reports generated by the management accountant should be relevant to the responsibilities of the individual, stated in explicit terms, and motivational in nature (showing successful areas as well as problem situations). Budgets and performance standards should be developed using criteria that are realistic and controllable by the people responsible for them. Using a responsibility accounting format as the basis for the flow of timely, relevant information, the management accountant should consider the recipients' receptiveness to the contents of each report as well as its quantitative accuracy.

Financial accounting cannot be ignored by the management accountant. Operational information generated for internal purposes also provides the basis for external reporting of the results of operations. For this reason, the CMA examination coverage includes "Public Reporting Standards, Auditing and Taxes" (part 3). Knowledge of the purposes and approaches to both internal and external auditing is the key to an efficient, controlled accounting system. Tax accounting is included in this area not only because of the need to compute the annual tax liability but also because the management accountant must be aware of the tax consequences inherent in management's operational decisions. Although this part of the examination appears to be a mini-CPA exam, one cannot dispute that there is a continuous interaction between the managerial and financial accounting disciplines and, therefore, a need for such coverage.

Parts 4 and 5 of the CMA examination zero in on the traditional areas of management accounting. "Periodic Reporting for Internal and External Purposes" (part 4) deals with information theory, preparation of financial statements, profit planning and budgetary controls, standard costs for manufacturing, and analysis of accounts. "Decision Analysis, Including Modeling and Information Systems" (part 5) is the quantitative section of the exam and includes such topics as fundamentals of decision processes, decision analysis, model building, and planning and control of information systems.

Careful analysis will show that the CMA examination coverage is well conceived and pertinent to the interests and responsibilities of management accountants. Some topics deal specifically with the functions outlined in the management accounting cycle. Others deal in general terms with environmental conditions within which management accountants must function. Taken together, the examination topics do indeed cover the field of management accounting.

Admission to the CMA program requires an applicant to satisfy one of the following conditions:

Admission Requirements

1. Hold a baccalaureate degree—in any area—from an accredited college or university, or
2. Achieve a score satisfactory to the Credentials Committee of the IMA on either the Graduate Record Examination (GRE) or the Graduate Management Admission Test (formerly the Admission Test for Graduate Study in Business [ATGSB]), or
3. Be a Certified Public Accountant or hold a comparable professional qualification outside the United States that is approved by the Credentials Committee.

Those who are interested in learning more about the CMA program or who wish to apply for the examination should write to:

Institute of Management Accounting
570 City Center Building
Ann Arbor, Michigan, 48108

QUESTIONS

1-1. Define and illustrate the following terms and concepts:
    a. Management cycle   e. Cost accounting
    b. Management accounting cycle   f. Performance evaluation
    c. Financial accounting   g. Simulation
    d. Management accounting

1-2. What is the difference between cost accounting and management accounting?

1-3. What are several important areas in which management accounting and financial accounting are different?

1-4. Why are restrictive guides, such as generally accepted accounting principles, essential in financial accounting? Why are management accountants not governed by the restrictive guides of accounting principles?

1-5. Historical cost is the primary unit of measure in financial accounting. Give examples of other measurement units employed by management accountants.

1-6. A principle of financial accounting is that information should be objective and verifiable. Why are management accountants permitted to use subjective estimates and futuristic information?

1-7. What are the several functions involved in the traditional view of management?

1-8. Identify the three main categories of management information requirements.

1-9. The president of Consumo Company has asked the controller to forecast the possible kinds of consumer demand for a new product. What desirable information characteristics could influence the content of this report? Assuming you are the controller, rank each of these characteristics in their order of importance in supplying the requested information.

1-10. List and briefly describe the functions within the management accounting cycle.

1-11. Two important functions in the management accounting cycle are simulation and performance evaluation. Match the following factors with the function to which each best relates:

a. Planning activities
b. Control of internal operations
c. Subjective information
d. Objective information

e. Past time periods
f. Future time periods
g. Standard cost variance analysis
h. Cost-volume-profit analysis

1-12. In planning future operations, information must be communicated throughout an organization. In what ways do budgets aid communication?

1-13. "The management accountant is an information specialist." Do you agree with this statement? Give reasons to support your conclusion.

1-14. For nonmonetary assets such as buildings and equipment, historical cost is the basis used to record initial acquisition and subsequent accounting valuations. In evaluating management decision alternatives, however, sometimes there is a need to value these assets at either cash salvage value or replacement cost. Why are valuations other than historical cost seldom used in external financial reporting?

EXERCISES AND PROBLEMS

1-15. *Types of Accounting Systems*   Many management accounting analyses are not limited by the double-entry accounting system. Two such analyses are depicted below:

a. Budgeted material purchases for January:

Copper wire	$ 40,000
Brass wire	70,000
Steel wire	250,000
Total estimated material costs	$360,000

b. Determination of likely selling price to be used for new product:

Estimated manufacturing costs per unit	$17.00
Operating expenses (10% of manufacturing costs)	1.70
Profit factor (15% of manufacturing costs)	2.55
Projected selling price	$21.25

REQUIRED:
a. Why do the above analyses not require a journal entry?
b. At what point in time will the above information enter the general ledger?

1-16. *Budgetary Disclosure*   A diversified electronics firm with annual sales of about $50,000,000 has developed a sophisticated budgeting system and has had considerable experience with annual profit planning. Company management can forecast net sales for the coming year within a variation of plus or minus 3 percent. With the exception of one year, net profit budgets have been within plus or minus 7 percent of actual results for the last ten years. The company does not publish a financial forecast or make any public disclosure of budgetary data. Discuss disclosure from the standpoint of (a) the company president, (b) current and potential stockholders, (c) the corporate controller, and (d) the company's independent auditor.

1-17. *Management Structure* The G. R. Vrana Corporation employs executives in the following positions:

Controller	Production vice president
Chairman of the board	Treasurer
Production superintendent— plant A	President
	Vice president—sales
Chief cost accountant—plant A	Chief cost accountant—plant B
Sales manager—plant A	Production superintendent— plant B
Sales manager—plant B	
Corporate legal counsel	Corporate secretary
Vice president—engineering	Corporate tax accountant
Chief engineer—plant B	Chief engineer—plant A

REQUIRED: Prepare an organization chart for the G. R. Vrana Corporation. Discuss possible alternatives.

1-18. *Product-line Information* Silvoso, Inc., is composed of two separate product divisions. Division A is engaged in retail land sales to private individuals, and Division B operates a chain of steak houses. A summary income statement for 19X7 was prepared for management review purposes.

SILVOSO, INC.
19X7 profit analysis
(Internal use only)

	TOTAL COMPANY	LAND SALES	STEAK HOUSES
Net sales	$10,000,000	$7,000,000	$3,000,000
Cost of sales	6,000,000	4,000,000	2,000,000
Gross profit	$ 4,000,000	$3,000,000	$1,000,000
Operating expenses	3,000,000	1,000,000	2,000,000
Profit (loss)	$ 1,000,000	$2,000,000	($1,000,000)
Corporate expense	(200,000)		
Income taxes	(300,000)		
Net income	$ 500,000		

The corporate annual report for 19X7 contained a balance sheet in comparative form, a funds flow statement, and an income statement showing only the total company results as disclosed above. The company president is opposed to disclosing product-line operating results. Why is the president reluctant to disclose these data and what needs would they serve for users outside the company?

1-19. *Financial Statement Users* Dunn Enterprises is a corporation that produces and distributes household cleaning products nationally. Common
and preferred stocks of the company are traded on a regional stock
exchange. There are four separate divisions in the firm, and each is
headed by a vice president. The following condensed financial statements appeared in the annual report of Dunn for 19X7:

DUNN ENTERPRISES
Balance sheet
December 31, 19X7

ASSETS			EQUITIES		
Current assets:			Current liabilities:		
Cash	$ 20,000		Accounts		
Receivables (net)	10,000		payable	$20,000	
Inventories	30,000		Accrued		
Prepaid expenses	5,000		liabilities	5,000	
Total current			Total current		
assets	$ 65,000		debt	$25,000	
Buildings and			Bonds payable	40,000	$ 65,000
equipment (net)	75,000		Preferred stock	$20,000	
Total assets	$140,000		Common stock	40,000	
			Retained		
			earnings	15,000	75,000
			Total equities		$140,000

DUNN ENTERPRISES
Income statement
For year 19X7

Net sales	$200,000
Cost of goods sold	95,000
Gross margin on sales	$105,000
Selling and administrative expenses	80,000
Operating income	$ 25,000
Interest expense	5,000
Income before taxes	$ 20,000
Income taxes	9,000
Net income ($.22 per share)	$ 11,000

Discuss the usefulness of the corporate annual report in decisions and
evaluations normally made by:

a. Holders of Dunn common stock
b. Holders of Dunn preferred
   stock
c. Potential stockholders in Dunn
   securities
d. The company president and
   board of directors
e. Company bondholders

f. Vice presidents of each division
g. Various plant superintendents
h. District sales managers
i. Cost center supervisors in each
   plant
j. Nonsupervisory salaried employees in Dunn

Chapter 2: The Manufacturing Process

Cost accounting concepts, techniques, and procedures are useful in almost every kind of financial endeavor, ranging from making up a family budget to determining whether a major corporation should expand manufacturing and sales activities to the Far East. Despite its diverse applications, cost accounting usually is associated with the manufacturing environment. And within manufacturing, it is linked most closely to the production process. Thus, despite the usefulness of cost accounting in marketing and product distribution functions, the remaining chapters of this text concentrate on its relationship to the manufacturing process.

Many students of cost accounting cannot visualize a production process in operation. Very few have toured a manufacturing plant, and only a handful have held part-time or summer jobs in a factory. Yet, knowledge of the production process is a prerequisite to understanding the various applications of management accounting concepts and techniques.

This chapter describes, in detail, one manufacturing process. Much of cost accounting focuses on and assumes knowledge of production techniques, and this chapter will give students a frame of reference for subsequent cost analyses requiring this knowledge.

Upon completion of this chapter, students should be able to:

1. Identify various phases of a production process
2. Specify the four primary resources used in production
3. Evaluate the effectiveness of product flow through the production process
4. State the relationship among the concepts of cost attachment, value added, and cost center

Relevant Concepts

The following basic concepts are introduced in this chapter:

Product design　Identification of the production phases needed to produce a product according to customer specifications.

Production flow   Arrangement of the phases of a production process to facilitate an orderly flow of goods and efficient use of available resources.

Resource allocation   Efficient resource usage to achieve cost savings while still producing a quality product.

Cost center   Any organizational segment or area of activity for which it is desirable to accumulate costs.

Value added   The concept that costs of raw materials and other manufacturing costs can be traced or allocated to a product, adding value as it progresses through the production process.

Cost attachment   The concept that direct and indirect manufacturing costs are assigned to products as manufacturing operations are performed.

Chapter Summary

A description of the fastener (bolts, screws, and nails) industry sets the stage for a thorough analysis of the production process. From the initial purchase of raw material (a coil of wire), all steps involved in manufacturing a fastener are illustrated. Included in this process are departments or work centers that head, slot, thread, point, plate, inspect, and package the fasteners.

Various resources of the company are used in its manufacturing process. For product costing purposes, these resources and their costs have to be identified, accumulated, and allocated to the units of production. Broadly classified, manufacturing resources of a firm are raw materials and supplies, personnel services, other contractual services, and tangible fixed asset usage. Resource allocation is a means of attaining efficient usage of these resources.

Plant layout is basic to the efficient use of a company's manufacturing resources. The production departments should be positioned to facilitate a smooth flow of work through the production process. Supporting service departments closely connected with the manufacturing function should be located strategically in the factory work area.

A cost center is any work center or activity area for which it is desirable to accumulate costs. With production departments serving as cost centers, manufacturing costs for each department are accumulated and allocated to the products worked on during each accounting period. As a product moves through the manufacturing process, additional costs are attached to it and represent value added to the base cost of initial raw materials. Upon completion, material, labor, and overhead costs from several cost centers have been attached to the product and now represent its complete manufacturing cost. This unit cost factor, together with the competitive factors of a free enterprise economy, helps determine the market prices of the goods we consume.

THE FASTENER INDUSTRY

The manufacturing of fasteners is not as glamorous as the production of automobiles, steel, oil, space equipment, or supersonic aircraft. But such industries depend upon an adequate supply of quality fasteners, either as components of a product or as the means to hold machines or buildings together. The desk or chair you are using is held together with some sort of fastener. Even

EXHIBIT 2-1
THE MACHINE SCREW

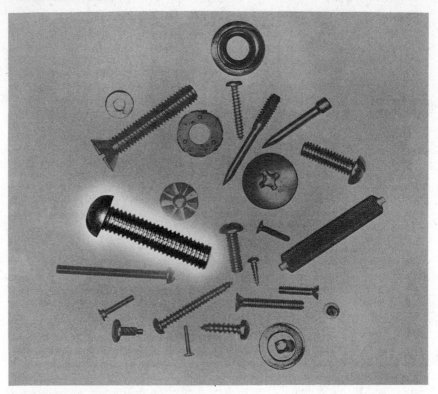

your shoes require a fastener—shoe nails. Look around you and try to imagine the world without fasteners.

Firms in the fastener industry use specific production techniques or processes to convert a coil of wire into a finished fastener. Look at the machine screw pictured in Exhibit 2-1. How did it come to be shaped that way? What would it cost to reproduce an identical machine screw? Most of us are not concerned with these questions. If we need such an item, we simply go to the hardware store and buy one. However, if we intend to produce machine screws, questions about production processes and related costs are important.

Product Characteristics   Companies in the fastener industry produce thousands of different fasteners. The machine screw in Exhibit 2-1 is but one of them. This machine screw has specific characteristics that differentiate it from other fasteners. Exhibit 2-2 summarizes these characteristics and also lists other possibilities for manufacturing various types of machine screws.

Why are such characteristics important? When one is asked to describe an automobile, the response "it's a car" is inadequate. A more meaningful answer would be, "It's a red, two-door, sports coupe with a four-cylinder engine, air conditioning, radial tires, and deluxe interior package." In the fastener indus-

EXHIBIT 2-2

MACHINE SCREW SPECIFICATIONS

PRODUCT CHARACTERISTICS	MACHINE SCREW IN EXHIBIT 2-1	OTHER POSSIBILITIES
Head style	Round head	Oval, flat, hex
Slot type	Machine slot	Philips
Diameter	⅜ inch	Various
Length	1½ inches	Various
Thread type	Roll thread, standard	Cut thread, self-threading
Thread size	18 per inch	Various
Thread length	1½ inches	Various
Material type	Steel	Aluminum, brass, stainless steel, bronze plus many different grades of steel
Plating	Cadmium	Copper, brass, galvanized, zinc

try, products are also described by product characteristics. Our particular screw is a "1½-inch, steel, cadmium-plated, round-headed machine screw with a ⅜-inch slotted head and 1½ inches of normal thread." These characteristics are important because they affect the routing of materials through various departments and ultimately determine the product unit cost.

Preproduction Design and Scheduling

Before a coil of wire can be requisitioned from the raw materials storage area so that work can begin on the fastener, the product's specifications are given to the engineering department. From this information, engineers prepare a drawing of the required fastener. Such a drawing, pictured as part of Exhibit 2-3, indicates the work to be performed by machine operators. A copy of this drawing goes with the fastener through the manufacturing process. In addition, the *routing slip,* shown in Exhibit 2-3, contains a detailed listing of the operations required to make the fastener. (Note: Machine screws of a certain size have the name *stove bolt,* as shown in the drawing.) This listing of operations is prepared by the engineer and forwarded to the production scheduling department, which coordinates all manufacturing activities and determines the actual timing of each production run.

Phases of Production Process

Blanking and heading Now that we have identified our machine screw, we can examine the manufacturing processes needed in its production. The first operation is to cut a coil of wire into short, predeterminedly sized pieces called *blanks.* Each blank is then pushed into a die to form the head of the fastener, as shown in Exhibit 2-4. In most cases, the blanking and heading operations are performed simultaneously on a machine called a *header.*

Slotting The size and type of slot in the head of a fastener varies as illustrated in Exhibit 2-2. Normally the slot is created in the heading operation as the blank is being pushed into the die to form the head shape and size. When

EXHIBIT 2-3
THE ROUTING SLIP

PART NO. 300-002-431150	CUSTOMER ELCO				PRINT NO.	DATE ISSUED	ORDER NO.
DESCRIPTION 5/16-18 X 1-1/2 ROUND HEAD STEEL STOVE BOLT						DATE WANTED	DELIVERY DATE
MATERIAL 1015 HR ROD (OH)		DIAMETER DRAW 312 TO 269		UNIT WEIGHT		QUANTITY	TOTAL WT.
WASHER				IN STOCK	ON ORDER		
TYPE OF DIE				TYPE PUNCH	FIRST BLOW	MISC. TOOLING	
PIECES BLANKED		PIECES COMPLETED		COMPLETE WEIGHT		SCRAP WEIGHT	

NO.	OPERATION	FAC.	MACH	DATE BEGIN	DATE END	INSTRUCTION & COMPLAINTS	COPY
2.5	HEAD	227		.120			TRAVEL
	WASH						PROD.
0.5	SLOT	405		.297			INSPECT
	WASH						TOOLS
1.6	ROLL THREAD	508		.201			MAT.
	WASH						COST
	PLATE	022				.00015 MIN CADMIUM PLATE	HEADING
							HEAD
	INSPECTION	099					TRIM
							SLOT
	PACKAGING	090				PACKAGE IN BUBBLE PACK WITH STANDARD CADMIUM PLATED HEX NUT.	CUT
							ROLL
							DRILL
							PRESS
							PLATE
							HT. TREAT

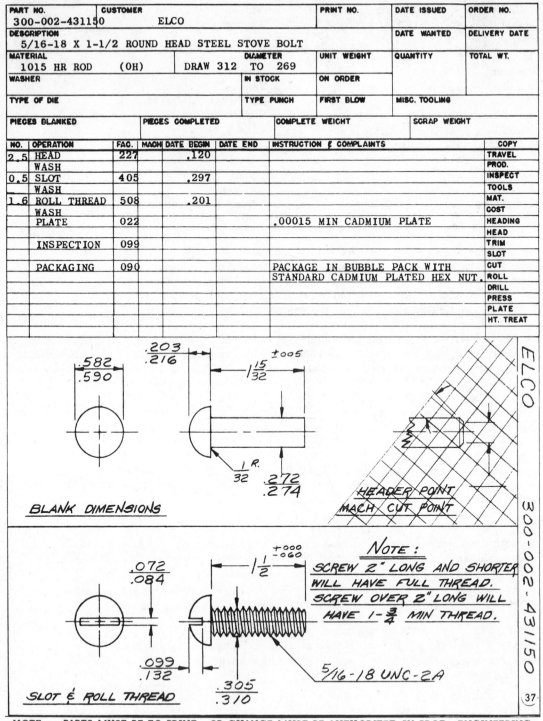

BLANK DIMENSIONS

HEADER POINT
MACH CUT POINT

ELCO

300-002-431150

NOTE:
SCREW 2" LONG AND SHORTER
WILL HAVE FULL THREAD.
SCREW OVER 2" LONG WILL
HAVE 1-3/4 MIN THREAD.

5/16-18 UNC-2A

SLOT & ROLL THREAD

NOTE -- PARTS MUST BE TO PRINT--OR CHANGE MUST BE AUTHORIZED BY PROD. ENGINEERING

EXHIBIT 2-4
THE BLANKING AND HEADING OPERATIONS

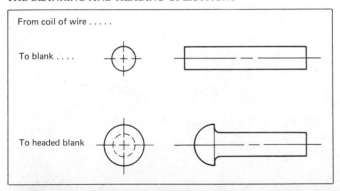

From coil of wire . . . . .

To blank . . . .

To headed blank

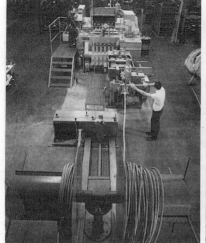

The header

specifications are more rigid, a *slotter* is used to cut a slot in the head of a fastener. This slotting operation is diagrammed in Exhibit 2-5.

Threading   Thread type and size vary with each particular fastener. Standard fasteners may be mass produced with differing thread lengths. In addition, many special-purpose or special-order fasteners are produced according to thread lengths desired by customers. The threading function can involve two different operations. In roll threading, the headed blank is rolled or pressed between a stationary die and a revolving die that displaces the material and forms the threaded portion of the fastener. But threads also can be cut into the headed blank to produce much the same result. Exhibit 2-6 shows the fastener after the threading operation.

Pointing   The pointing operation is not required on all types of fasteners. Our machine screw, for example, has a blunt end and needs no special pointing operation. However, fasteners such as wood screws and self-threading screws do require an adequate point to be functional and must be processed through a pointing operation.

EXHIBIT 2-5

THE SLOTTING OPERATION

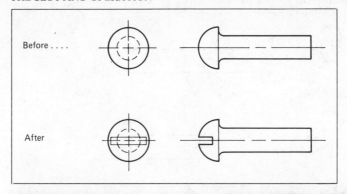

The slotter

Washing The routing slip shown in Exhibit 2-3 indicates that washing operations are common throughout the production process. Various types of lubricants are necessary for cooling and reducing friction during the production operations described. After each operation, it is necessary to remove this lubricant film before proceeding to the next operation. Each batch of fasteners is passed through a tumbling washing apparatus.

Plating Fasteners made of steel may require a resurfacing either to prevent rust or to beautify the final product. Through a chemical process, various types of rust-resistant or attractive finishes can be bonded to the steel surface of the fasteners. Examples include zinc, chrome, cadmium, and bronze finishes.

Inspection Points of inspection may occur after almost every operation described. Usually this is accomplished by sample testing, but some orders—such

EXHIBIT 2-6
THE THREADING OPERATION

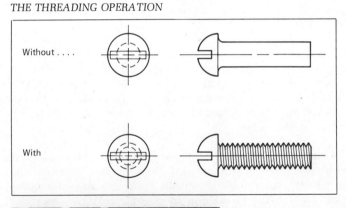

Without . . . .

With

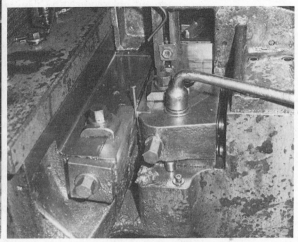

The roll threader

as government orders with rigid specifications—may entail inspection of entire batches. At a minimum, fasteners are inspected both before and after plating.

Packing   All operations now have been described for production of our single machine screw. However, firms in the fastener industry need to sell large quantities of fasteners and must be concerned with the packing function. Two general types of packaging will be described here, although specific customer packing instructions may impose different requirements. Bulk packaging is used for large quantities going to assembly operations of other companies, such as automotive assembly lines. In such situations, an attractive package is not required; thousands of fasteners can be shipped in large, plain containers.

The do-it-yourself craze forced the fastener industry to consider special packaging methods. Today, hundreds of thousands of fasteners are packaged in small polyethylene bags or other clear packaging materials. These bags are placed on racks in local hardware stores or inserted in boxes with items to be assembled at home. Such small-quantity bags entail special packaging methods that add to the cost of producing and selling fasteners.

RESOURCES USED IN PRODUCTION

Our simple machine screw has become a seemingly complicated and costly item to produce. Now that the production steps have been described, can you estimate what the screws will cost to produce? To do so, we need to review the production process in terms of resources utilized. Then we will examine the cost data required for an estimate.

Raw Materials and Supplies

The production of machine screws starts with steel wire. This wire is the raw material required for the fastener manufacturing process. The blanks cut from the coil of wire represent the principal raw material needed for our machine screws. Now think through the production process again. Were other raw materials added to the screws during production? What about the plating material (cadmium) used to coat the fasteners? It also is a form of raw material. Our order did not require any packaging materials; but if it had, the cost of those materials would also be used to calculate the complete product cost. The various lubricants used in production represent additional cost. Lubricants usually are classified as production supplies, but they constitute production costs along with all other indirect manufacturing costs.

Personnel Services

Besides raw materials and supplies, we must consider the costs of human resources used to produce our fasteners. Each machine was operated by an employee earning an hourly rate of pay. In addition, wage and salary costs were incurred for the engineer who designed the fastener, the material handling people who transferred the fasteners from process to process, the person who scheduled production time, the inspectors, the various departmental supervisors, and the plant superintendent. Each of these labor costs is part of the total cost of our fastener.

Other Contractual Services

In addition to the costs of raw materials and labor, the costs of functions needed to support the production process must be considered. The cost of our fastener includes such items as heat, light, and power costs, machine maintenance and repair costs, material ordering and receiving costs, material storage costs, tool and die making costs, and the payroll costs of the firm's top management.

Fixed Assets

Periodic depreciation of a company's fixed assets used in production is a significant manufacturing cost. We could not have produced the fasteners without the aid of the header, slotter, roll threader, and plating machinery. Then there is the building used to house the machinery. Depreciation charges for all these assets must be added to our production costs.

Cost Summary

Exhibit 2-7 itemizes the individual resource elements and the estimated cost of producing a single fastener. The costs are classified by type of resource except for Other Contractual Services, a category containing many small cost items that have been grouped for convenience under the heading Miscellaneous. The estimated cost of producing our fastener is rather crude, but it does indicate the resources and cost considerations needed to produce one machine screw.

EXHIBIT 2-7

ESTIMATED COST OF PRODUCING ONE FASTENER

Type of Resources	Estimated Cost
Raw material and supplies:	
Coil of wire	$ 47
Plating material and lubricants	21
Personnel services:	
Machine operators	35
Supporting personnel	85
Other contractual services:	
Miscellaneous	200
Fixed assets:	
Depreciation—machinery	10,000
Depreciation—building	20,000
Total manufacturing cost	$30,388
Cost per unit	$30,388

Before producing the fasteners, another alternative must be considered: Our machine screw is being sold by a firm across town for $1.75 per thousand wholesale. Do we still want to produce the machine screw?

Cost allocation   The cost shown for producing one fastener is obviously excessive. Many companies produce fasteners, and the competitive forces of supply and demand have combined to set a realistic price for consumers. Our example would be more realistic if we wanted to produce a part for a space laboratory; such items must be specifically designed and manufactured and are not readily available from local hardware stores.

   If the production of fasteners is so costly, how can firms sell them at such low prices? Look again at Exhibit 2-7. The total estimated cost changes very little if we change the production quota from 1 fastener to 10,000,000. The costs of raw materials and supplies, personnel services, and some other contractural services would increase because they vary *directly* with the number of fasteners produced. The more items produced, the more costs incurred. However, the fixed asset depreciation costs and a portion of the other contractual service costs need not increase. The same machinery and building facilities required to produce 1 fastener can also produce 10,000,000 units.

Resource allocation   The concept of resource allocation is basic to cost accounting. To be profitable and stay in business, a company must determine and control the unit cost of its products. Given appropriate cost information, pricing policies can be defined, and projections can be established for use in evaluating future product changes, selling policies, and facility expansion plans.

   Resource allocation implies efficient usage of a firm's resources. Unit production costs are minimized when efficient use is made of costly resources. Often a product's profit margin is maximized when its unit cost is minimized. Cost accounting is management's tool to determine unit costs and to identify areas that require cost reduction and control. Cost information is useful for planning and controlling a firm's operations, for valuing product inventories at the end of each accounting period, and for making decisions about future resource availability and need.

OVERVIEW OF PRODUCTION PROCESS

The production of a fastener involves more than people and machines, a few lubricants, and a coil of wire. While these resources represent a significant part of the production process, unless they are properly arranged, coordinated, and managed, little would be accomplished. To continue our analysis of machine screw production, the production phases described earlier must be organized so that products flow smoothly and efficiently.

Production Departments

Plant layout, or design of the production process, is an important factor leading to efficient manufacturing methodology and minimum material handling costs. Exhibit 2-8 illustrates a sample layout. As the production flow is discussed, try to visualize two important concepts implicit in the diagram. First, review the drawings showing the various changes as fasteners proceed from department to department. Then look at Exhibit 2-8 and try to visualize the conversion of raw materials to finished goods, in which a coil of wire becomes finished machine screws. Every manufacturing or assembly process contains a logical sequence of events, and each event adds value to the product.

Second, try to grasp how important the material handling function is to the efficient flow of products through the process. In the case of fasteners, various-sized bins containing thousands of fasteners transport the products from department to department. Handcarts and small electric carts are important in the material handling process. Notice in this example that products move from department to department in an irregular pattern. The flow of goods utilizes the same assembly-line approach to efficient production as mass production of automobiles: products move through the process on a continuous basis. To complete this tour of the fastener manufacturing process and to aid your understanding of the production flow concept, Exhibit 2-9 shows additional machines and operations keyed by letter to the plant layout in Exhibit 2-8. Most of these operations are classified as supporting service functions and are described below.

The production process begins with the receipt of raw materials. To facilitate their smooth flow through production, raw materials should be stored near the initial producing department in a manner that provides easy access. Once requisitioned and placed into production, raw materials should flow in an orderly manner and arrive in the finished product storage area ready for shipment to customers. The operations required and their normal sequence dictate the plant layout. In the case of fasteners, the normal sequence is raw material storage, blanking and heading, slotting, threading, pointing, inspection, plating, and packing.

The plant layout in Exhibit 2-8 is designed to move the fasteners through production smoothly. Numbered arrows illustrate the sequence of the flow. Notice that the finished product storage area is adequate in size and adjacent to the shipping area. To appreciate the significance of an efficient production layout, imagine the chaos and increased material handling effort that would result if the plating department were located between the raw material storage area and the heading department.

EXHIBIT 2-8

OVERVIEW OF PLANT LAYOUT

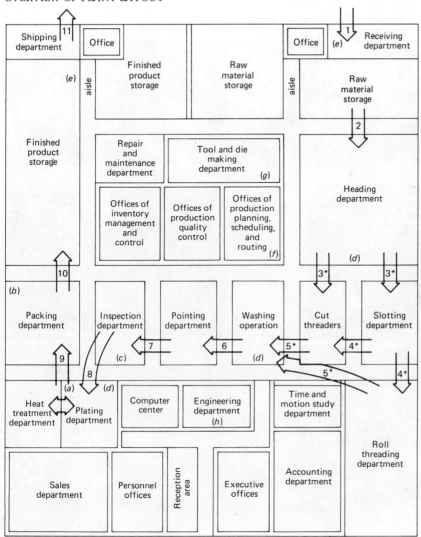

*Alternative routes

No manufacturing process can exist and function for long without supporting service departments. In a manufacturing environment, these include all necessary manufacturing activities of the firm that are indirectly connected with production. Several service functions are included in Exhibit 2-8—repair and maintenance, tool and die making, production scheduling, and quality control. Personnel activities, accounting, engineering, and time-and-motion study are other service functions that support production.

Supporting Service Departments

EXHIBIT 2-9

ADDITIONAL SEGMENTS OF THE MANUFACTURING PROCESS

(a) The plating operation

(b) The packing operation

(c) Product inspection

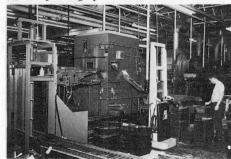

(d) The washing operation

(e) Material handling

(f) Production scheduling

(g) Tool and die making department

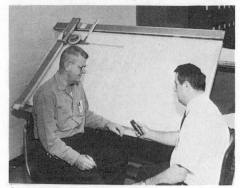

(h) Engineering department

Exhibit 2-8 shows that some supporting service functions are within the factory working area while others are adjacent to it. Logic indicates that repair and maintenance, tool and die making, production scheduling, and quality control are more effective if located where production occurs. Similarly, inventory management and control should be as close as possible to the finished product storage area. The remaining service functions are located away from the factory environment to foster productive working conditions.

There is a right and a wrong way to lay out a plant. Efficient resource utilization demands careful consideration of plant organization. Product profitability may hinge entirely on an efficient plant layout.

COST AND PRODUCTION RELATIONSHIPS

Our fastener production process has shown the different stages for converting raw materials to finished products. Various operations were performed to reshape a coil of wire into ready-to-use fasteners. As each product moves through the manufacturing cycle, it accumulates value. Until a fastener has been completed, it has no real value to anyone, except perhaps to a scrap metal dealer. However, cost accountants approach the computation of product cost from a value-added basis. The *value-added concept* holds that costs of raw materials and manufacturing operations attach to the product and add value to it as production progresses. When the final operation is completed, the product essentially has a string of costs attached to it. These costs represent its unit manufacturing cost.

Are these costs added to the product on an arbitrary basis, or are there particular points within the manufacturing process where costs "attach" themselves? Realistically, manufacturing costs are incurred in many ways: Bills may be paid at the end of the month; payroll may be distributed every Friday; or the acquisition costs of machinery may have been incurred several years earlier. The timing of cash disbursements for these costs is not important to cost accountants. They are concerned primarily with proper accumulation of manufacturing costs and with distribution of these costs to products that are manufactured with the aid of particular resources.

Manufacturing costs are accumulated first in inventory and expense accounts, such as the general ledger accounts for raw materials, labor, heat, light and power, and depreciation. Cost balances then are reclassified as material costs, labor costs, or overhead costs. Material, labor, and overhead costs represent the three elements of manufacturing cost and are analyzed in more detail in Chapter 3.

Manufacturing costs of a firm can be traced to a large division, a specific plant, or an individual department. Within a department, it even is possible to compute the costs required to operate a particular machine. Areas of operational activity—whether entire divisions, one plant, a particular department, or even one machine—are potential cost centers within a company. A *cost center* is any organizational segment or area of activity for which it is desirable to accumulate costs. For purposes of cost control, cost centers should be the *smallest* areas of activity for which costs can be accumulated and for which cost responsibility can be identified.

The concept of cost centers applies to direct and indirect manufacturing costs. Supporting service departments are also cost centers. However, for product costing purposes, costs incurred by these departments are accumulated in separate accounts, transferred to a factory overhead account, and later assigned to products.

In our fastener company, manufacturing costs are assigned to products on a departmental cost center basis. As material or labor costs are incurred, they are associated with the appropriate batch of fasteners being produced. Additional costs are attached to each batch as it progresses through each process. Overhead costs usually are assigned to products at a predetermined rate. Thus, as each manufacturing operation is performed, the material and labor costs and the related overhead costs of that operation are attached to the products.

Cost centers make it possible to accumulate manufacturing costs and redistribute them to manufactured products. As discussed in later chapters, cost accumulation also enables management to control costs by measuring the performance of individuals who are responsible for various cost centers. Our purpose here is to define a cost center and show its relevance to the cost attachment concept.

FINAL NOTE Product costing is an important part of cost accounting. Profitability is a function of a firm's ability to utilize resources efficiently and to control operating costs. The concepts of cost center, value added, and cost attachment are interrelated and assist product costing. Product design and efficient production layout also are required to conserve production resources.

Return now to the beginning of the chapter and review the highlights section before proceeding to the review questions and problems.

QUESTIONS

2-1. Define and illustrate the following terms and concepts:
  a. Production flow
  b. Resource allocation
  c. Value added
  d. Cost center
  e. Cost attachment
  f. Supporting service department
  g. Raw material
  h. Personnel services

2-2. What is meant by value added? How is the value-added concept related to the concept of cost attachment?

2-3. Why is an efficiently designed plant layout important?

2-4. List three supporting service departments that are related directly to the manufacturing process and three that are related indirectly. What similar characteristics do all six possess? What factors differentiate a directly related service function from one that is related indirectly with the production process?

2-5. What are the four primary groupings of manufacturing resources? Give examples of each.

2-6. In the manufacturing process of converting wire into a finished machine screw, what cost centers or production departments are involved? Why is it important to identify the costs incurred within each individual cost center?

2-7. What is the importance of a routing slip?

2-8. Would costs of material handling, such as wages of the truck operator and depreciation of the truck, be considered manufacturing costs? Why or why not?

EXERCISES AND PROBLEMS

2-9. *Unit Cost Determination*   A firm that produces a single product has two service departments and one production department. In January 19X7 the company produced 20,000 units of product and incurred the following costs in each department:

	FACTORY DEPARTMENTS		
COST FACTOR	*Service #1*	*Service #2*	*Production*
Materials and supplies	$10,000	$ 8,000	$22,000
Labor costs	5,000	12,000	18,000
Depreciation of equipment	1,000	3,000	4,000
Factory rental	5,000	5,000	5,000
Totals	$21,000	$28,000	$49,000

Compute the per unit manufacturing cost of production in January.

2-10. *Unit Cost Determination*   Howard Rudolph, Harold Randolph, and Hugh Roland have decided to incorporate as H. R. Toy Industries, Inc., and plan to market a doll named Debbie Kay. Mr. Rudolph, the sales manager, has conducted a market survey and has found that similar dolls sell for around $14.50. The production superintendent, Mr. Randolph, estimates that direct labor wages will be $5.00 per hour, and each doll will require one-half hour of work. Mr. Roland, the controller, has prepared the following cost estimates:

Raw materials per doll	$3.50
Direct labor (½ hour at $5/hour) per doll	$2.50
Monthly manufacturing overhead costs	$40,000

Present plant machinery has a maximum capacity of 10,000 dolls per month.

REQUIRED:

a. Compute the manufacturing cost per doll if monthly production is:
   1. 1 doll   4. 1,000 dolls
   2. 10 dolls   5. 5,000 dolls
   3. 100 dolls   6. 10,000 dolls

b. As doll production per month is increased, what happens to the unit cost? Why?

c. Of the six levels of output listed in part (a), which represents the minimum capacity that H. R. Toy Industries, Inc., must operate at to stay in business?

2-11. *Cost Estimating*   Mr. Clarence G. Avery is a cost estimator for the Orlando Fastener Company, a manufacturer of specialty fasteners. The company's price determination policy includes the following procedures:

1. Salesman receives tentative order from customer which includes complete description and specifications for the desired special fastener.
2. Details of order are given to the engineer, who prepares a drawing of the product and determines the production operations required to manufacture it.
3. The drawing and routing of operations are forwarded to the cost estimator, who determines total production cost per thousand fasteners.
4. The estimated manufacturing cost is increased by 20 percent to cover operating expenses and company profit. A bid price has been determined.
5. Salesman communicates bid price to customer, hoping it is competitive so that the company will receive the order.

REQUIRED:
a. What types of cost information will Mr. Avery require in determining the costs of manufacturing?
b. Will costs of past orders of similar products help him?
c. Should he talk to the production manager about the product?
d. What information should he seek from the purchasing agent?
e. Who should he talk to if the customer demands shipment of the order by a specific date?

2-12. *Delivery Time Policy*   Bildge Papergood Products manufactures a wide range of paper products, some of which are produced to customer specification. The sales department has just received a large order for cushioned egg cartons to have special printing, tabs, and slightly different design than normal egg cartons produced for stock purposes. In comparison with normal sales transactions, this special order is large and potentially profitable. The sales manager developed a bid price that was accepted by the customer. A delivery time of forty-five days was also promised. Upon receiving the sales memo and customer correspondence, the production manager was enraged. It seems that the sales manager forgot to include costs for the special tabs and custom printing and did not consult with the production manager concerning the backlog of production orders.

REQUIRED:
a. What primary sources of information should be used in resolving requests for product delivery time?
b. Should production managers be consulted in matters related to the timing of product delivery and special-product specifications?

c. Assume that this special order is processed on an expedited basis in accordance with the initial contract. As a result, the order is not as profitable as planned because of tab and printing costs not included in the estimate. Several additional production costs are incurred because of the rush order, special setups, and interruptions of scheduled production flow. Should these additional costs be charged to the sales department or to the production department? Defend your answer.

2-13. *Production Flow Design* The canning industry is a major contributor to our consumable food supply. Colonel Foods, Inc., is in the process of designing a production facility for canning its newest product, Mother Nature's black-eyed peas. The company envisions the following operations to be essential to the processing and packaging functions:

Cooking—heating the peas to a proper temperature so that consumers only have to reheat and serve

Inspection of raw peas—to weed out inedible peas

Canning—automatic process of putting cooked peas into cans

Labeling—placing labels on processed cans

Shelling—taking shells off raw peas

Finished goods storage—storing of canned peas awaiting shipment

Cleaning—washing operation of peas prior to processing

Receiving—central receiving area for freshly picked peas

Packing—placing labeled cans in boxes

Lid sealing—sealing lids on cans to prevent spoilage or leakage

Shipping—truck loading area where cartons are shipped according to customer demands

Bin storage—storage of raw peas prior to processing

Can inspection—to isolate improperly sealed cans

Cooling—reducing temperature of cooked peas to facilitate canning operation

REQUIRED:
a. Arrange the operations so as to structure an efficient flow of production.
b. Design a rough plant layout for Colonel Foods, Inc. (Remember that part of the process deals with a liquid. In addition, the cooking operation generates tremendous amounts of heat and humidity.)

2-14. *Production Routing* A publishing company with sixty different production departments developed a new system for tracking the progress of various printing jobs through its plant. In designing the production routing for each job, log-out cards were prepared for each department that would perform work on the order. When a department completed its work on a job, the departmental log-out card was to be signed by the department manager and placed in a pickup box. Accounting personnel collected the log-out cards weekly and tabulated these to show the location of each job, work done, and remaining work to be done. The log-out cards were key-punched data processing cards.

After eight months of trial operations, it became apparent that the new system was not functioning as planned. Some log-out cards were turned in as much as thirty days after a department worked on a job, and some cards were apparently lost or destroyed. As a result, the company could not accurately track the progress of each job or assign costs to a job on a timely basis. Both accounting and production personnel were disgusted (in different ways) with the system.

REQUIRED: Discuss possible causes and reasons for lack of success with the system.

Chapter 3: Nature and Reporting of Manufacturing Costs

As stated in Chapter 1, cost accounting includes three interrelated functions of internal accounting: determining product costs for inventory valuation, providing information for planning and control phases of internal operations, and aiding top management in decision-making activities. All these functions require cost information from past, current, and future operations.

This chapter will acquaint students with the various kinds of manufacturing costs and their classification and reporting possibilities. First, manufacturing costs are distinguished from general, administrative, and selling expenses (operating expenses) of an enterprise. Next, the three major elements of manufacturing costs—material costs, labor costs, and factory overhead costs—are identified and explored in depth. The chapter concludes with an extensive analysis of ledger accounts and accounting reports unique to a manufacturing company. A comprehensive application of cost analysis with periodic inventories is presented in Appendix 3-A.

Upon completion of this chapter, students should be able to:

1. Distinguish between manufacturing costs and operating expenses
2. Identify and account for material, labor, and overhead elements of manufacturing costs
3. Prepare journal entries for transactions related to production activities
4. Prepare supporting schedules for cost of goods manufactured and sold
5. Prepare worksheet analysis and financial statements for a manufacturing company using the periodic inventory method

The following basic concepts are introduced in this chapter:

Manufacturing costs All production costs incurred to bring manufactured products to a salable condition, including direct materials, direct labor, and indirect manufacturing (or factory overhead) costs.

Relevant Concepts

Material, labor, and factory overhead costs   The three major cost categories to which all manufacturing costs can be assigned.

Inventoriable costs   Manufacturing costs that are assigned to products and are carried from one accounting period to another in inventory accounts until the products are sold.

Periodic inventory method   A system of accounting for inventory in which costs are not routed through inventory accounts in the general ledger. Instead, end-of-period inventory values are determined from physical counts of units in storage.

Direct and indirect costs   Direct costs are those manufacturing costs directly traceable to units of output. All manufacturing costs not traceable to output are indirect costs.

Variable and fixed costs   Total variable costs for a period vary in direct proportion to units produced. Fixed costs remain constant within a specific range of output.

Manufacturing cost report   The integration of current period material, labor, and factory overhead costs with beginning and ending inventory balances to compute the Cost of Goods Manufactured and the Cost of Goods Sold for the period.

Chapter Summary   Costs incurred by manufacturing companies are classified either as manufacturing costs or as operating expenses. Manufacturing costs are treated as product costs and are included in inventory accounts when manufactured goods remain unsold at period end. Operating expenses are period costs and must be charged against revenue in the period they are incurred.

Raw material and labor costs can be either direct or indirect. Direct material and direct labor costs can be traced to specific units of output. Indirect material and indirect labor costs become part of a pool of general manufacturing costs that are not easily traced to specific units of output. This pool of costs is called manufacturing overhead.

Variable manufacturing costs vary in total with production, while fixed manufacturing costs remain constant even though production activities increase or decrease. For cost planning and control purposes, variable and fixed cost information is very useful. Certain costs have both variable and fixed components.

Manufacturing companies maintain three inventory classifications: Raw Materials, Work in Process, and Finished Goods. For each classification, physical inventory quantities must be counted and priced at year-end. Under the periodic inventory method, beginning inventory balances are carried in the general ledger throughout the year. General ledger balances are adjusted to year-end amounts through closing entries or adjusting entries.

A manufacturing company must prepare a statement of Cost of Goods Manufactured as supplemental information for the traditional year-end income statement and balance sheet. Cost of Goods Sold is computed using the period's Cost of Goods Manufactured.

Cost of goods sold is a term that was introduced in your introductory accounting course; it describes all costs associated with acquiring goods that were sold during an accounting period. Cost of Goods Sold subtracted from net sales revenue yields the firm's gross profit. Net Income Before Taxes is computed by subtracting operating expenses from gross profit. Exhibit 3-1 depicts the traditional income statement format for a merchandising company and compares it with the format for a manufacturing company's income statement.

Accounting for manufacturing firms is more complex than for merchandising operations. A typical merchandiser—such as a shoe store, a department store, or a hardware store—purchases goods that are already in salable condition. The cost of each item is its net purchase price plus freight and handling charges necessary to bring the product to a point where it is salable. A manufacturing firm's product differs in that it must be produced from raw materials. Costs of manufactured goods include all production costs incurred to bring the product to a salable condition. These production costs are used in computing Cost of Goods Sold during the period and cost of goods held in ending inventory.

EXHIBIT 3-1
INCOME STATEMENT COMPARISON

ALPHA MERCHANDISING COMPANY
Income statement
For the year ended December 31, 19X8

Sales		$740,000
Less: Cost of goods sold:		
Merchandise inventory, Jan. 1, 19X8	$ 47,540	
Plus: Purchases	409,805	
Cost of goods available for sale	$457,345	
Less: Merchandise inventory, Dec. 31, 19X8	42,345	
Cost of goods sold		415,000
Gross profit		$325,000
Less: Operating expenses		230,000
Net income before taxes		$ 95,000

EPSILON MANUFACTURING COMPANY
Income statement
For the year ended December 31, 19X8

Sales		$950,000
Less: Cost of goods sold:		
Finished goods inventory, Jan. 1, 19X8	$ 80,500	
Plus: Cost of goods manufactured*	721,000	
Cost of goods available for sale	$801,500	
Less: Finished goods inventory, Dec. 31, 19X8	84,500	
Cost of goods sold		717,000
Gross profit		$233,000
Less: Operating expenses		130,000
Net income before taxes		$103,000

* Detail provided in statement of Cost of Goods Manufactured.

Like merchandisers, manufacturers also incur operating expenses for selling and administrative functions not associated specifically with manufacturing. General and administrative expenses, expenses connected with marketing and selling products, and interest expense are not considered manufacturing costs. These items are operating expenses that are subtracted from gross profit to arrive at net income for the period.

A cost's association with the production process is the important factor in distinguishing between manufacturing costs and operating expenses. Manufacturing costs are referred to as *product costs* and are assigned to products completed during an accounting period or still in process at period end. Operating expenses are *period costs* that are incurred to maintain the enterprise's selling and administrative functions during the period. Product costs are *inventoriable*, which means that product costs attach to the products and are carried in inventory accounts from one accounting period to another until the products are sold. Period costs cannot be deferred and must be charged against revenue as an expense of the accounting period in which they are incurred.

In this chapter, the concept of product cost is explored through an examination of the elements of manufacturing costs. All manufacturing costs can be classified into one of three elements: (1) raw material cost, (2) labor cost, or (3) indirect manufacturing costs (also called manufacturing overhead, factory overhead, or burden).

ACCOUNTING FOR MATERIAL COSTS

Materials are the basic physical ingredients used in manufacturing a firm's end product. Some products, such as the machine screw in Chapter 2, have few raw materials. Others may have dozens of different raw material requirements—for example, electronic computers, telephones, and automobiles. Basic accounting for material costs is similar in all cases and should include (1) procedures to record the receipt and use of materials, (2) a network of supporting forms or source documents to verify receipt and use of materials, and (3) control devices to ensure the proper quality and quantity of material inventories.

The accounting treatment of raw material purchases and material usage is a function of the inventory system used. With a *periodic inventory system*, material costs are not routed through inventory accounts in the general ledger. This system requires that physical counts be taken at the end of each period. After pricing the quantities counted, adjusting journal entries are prepared to change beginning inventory balances to reflect end-of-period inventory costs. Under a *perpetual inventory system*, detailed inventory records are maintained and updated continuously. In the perpetual system, transactions are recorded so that material costs flow through inventory accounts. Physical counts are made only to verify the quantities of goods in ending inventory.

For control purposes, the perpetual inventory system is preferred. However, this system is expensive to install and maintain, and so many smaller companies still use periodic inventory systems. Students of cost accounting should be familiar with both methods. Journal entries and the illustrative problem in this chapter are based upon the periodic inventory system. The perpetual inventory system is introduced in Chapter 5.

Most materials used by a manufacturing company are purchased and stored for later use. Direct materials become an integral part of the end product. Other materials are used to assist production by keeping equipment and other processes running smoothly. For cost accounting purposes, the following distinction between direct and indirect material costs is important:

Direct materials Raw materials that become an integral part of the finished product and are conveniently and economically traceable to specific units of output.

Indirect materials Production supplies and other materials that cannot conveniently or economically be assigned to specific units of output.

Costs of direct material usage are accounted for separately and make up the material cost element of a product's total unit cost. Indirect material costs are accounted for as part of manufacturing overhead.

Procedures for purchasing and storing raw materials and supplies vary with the size and nature of manufacturing organizations. Control procedures are necessary to ensure that materials are purchased in proper quantities and that their use is properly recorded. An accounting system for materials includes information forms, procedures for purchasing and issuing materials, and accounting procedures for recording this information in appropriate general ledger accounts.

Material purchases The purchasing transaction begins with an approved purchase request for raw materials or production supplies. At this time, a *purchase order* is prepared as shown in Exhibit 3-2; it lists the vendor and the quantity and type of items being ordered and may include specific terms of the transaction, such as unit cost, required date of receipt, and shipping terms. The purchase order is forwarded to the supplier, and several copies are retained for the company's use. One copy usually is routed to the receiving area to verify the number of items later received from the vendor. When materials are delivered, a *receiving report* is prepared; it notes the quantity of goods received and inspection of goods received. The purchase transaction is complete when the company receives the vendor's invoice for the shipment and approves its payment. With a periodic inventory system, the following entry is required to record a purchase transaction for raw materials costing $4,000 and supplies costing $700:

Raw material purchases	$4,000	
Supplies purchases	700	
Accounts payable		$4,700

In a periodic inventory system, inventory accounts are not updated during the accounting period and *no* entry for purchase transactions is made directly to an inventory account.

Material usage and control Various means are used to safeguard raw materials and supplies stored for future use. Valuable materials may be kept under

EXHIBIT 3-2

THE PURCHASE REQUEST AND PURCHASE ORDER FORMS

QUANTITY	COMPLETE DESCRIPTION	PRICE

TO: _____

PURCHASE REQUEST

Purchase Order Number

DATE: _____

Date Needed: _____
Department: _____
Ordered By: _____

Present Inventory

ESTIMATED USAGE

This Month | Next Month | Month After

Required For: _____   Asset Number
Purchase From: _____   Asset Number
Estimated Cost: _____   Account Number

FOR PURCHASING DEPARTMENT USE ONLY

Ordered From: _____   Use Tax   ☐ YES   ☐ NO
Address: _____   For Resale   ☐ ☐

Wanted: _____   Via: _____   F.O.B. _____   Terms: _____
Approved; Superintendent: _____   Buyer: _____

Purchase request form

Purchase order form

lock and key. At least one person should be responsible for the custody of stored materials. When a production department needs items that are stored in inventory, a *materials requisition*, shown in Exhibit 3-3, is prepared; it lists the items required and their quantity, and it is signed by an authorized person in the production department. No journal entry is made to record the requisition of raw materials and supplies when a company uses a periodic inventory system. Control over materials in storage, however, is maintained by using materials requisition forms. Once materials are requisitioned, responsibility for them is transferred to the production area.

Cost of Materials Used

Under a periodic inventory system, the simplest way to determine cost of materials used during the period is to subtract the final inventory cost from cost of inventory available for use. Cost of inventory available for use is the sum of beginning inventory plus purchases. The following example illustrates this process:

Beginning raw material inventory balance	$ 20,000
Plus: Materials purchased during period	240,000
Total materials available for use	$260,000
Less: Ending raw material inventory balance	34,000
Raw materials used during the period	$226,000

The above analysis can be performed only after physically counting the items in ending inventory, selecting an inventory pricing method (FIFO, LIFO, or average cost), and attaching costs to units counted.

Physical inventory count   Taking a physical inventory at year-end is an important task for the accounting department. Care must be exercised to ensure that all items are counted accurately. Counting procedures usually involve teams of people assigned to specific sections of the plant and to inventory storage areas. Large items are counted individually, while small items may be weight-counted (quantity is determined by extending the total weight by a unit per pound factor). Counted items are tagged to prevent double counting, and

EXHIBIT 3-3
THE MATERIALS REQUISITION CARD

EXHIBIT 3-4
SAMPLE INVENTORY SHEET

Performed by _____

THE KONSTANS MANUFACTURING COMPANY
Physical inventory sheet   Page <u>4</u> of <u>15</u>
Taken on December 30, 19X7

Item's Description	Tag Number	Count	Price Per Unit	Total Cost
¼-inch sheet steel—3 × 5 feet	2503	72	$ 7.50	$ 540.00
¼-inch sheet steel—5 × 7 feet	2504	94	11.20	1,052.80
¼-inch sheet steel—3 × 5 feet (stainless)	2505	120	20.00	2,400.00
¼-inch sheet steel—5 × 7 feet	2506	47	34.40	1,616.80
⅜-inch sheet steel—5 × 7 feet	2507	90	14.70	1,323.00

Totals—this page	$10,247.40

information from the tags concerning each item's description and quantity is recorded on inventory sheets as illustrated in Exhibit 3-4.

Inventory pricing methods Inventory pricing methods are usually discussed in introductory accounting courses. The *first-in, first-out (FIFO)* method uses end-of-period purchase prices for determining costs of items in ending inventory. Initial inventory prices and beginning-of-period prices are used to determine inventory cost under the *last-in, first-out (LIFO)* method. With the *average cost* method, the beginning inventory and purchases made during the period are averaged to determine the unit cost of inventory. Before the total cost of ending inventory can be computed, an acceptable pricing method must be selected. The "price per unit" values in Exhibit 3-4 depend upon the inventory pricing method used. When inventory items have been counted, tagged, and priced, the total cost of each group of items can be "extended," or calculated. The grand total of all inventory sheets represents the ending inventory cost of raw materials.

Year-end adjusting entry When a periodic inventory system is used, the beginning inventory balance is carried in the general ledger inventory account during the entire year. In the previous example, beginning inventory was $20,000 and the final inventory balance is $34,000. The following entry would update the Raw Material inventory account in the general ledger to reflect a $14,000 increase in inventory.

Raw material inventory	$14,000	
Income summary		$14,000

As illustrated in Appendix 3-A, inventory account adjustments are usually included in closing entries. In practice, several different journal entry procedures are used. However, the basic objective is to increase or decrease the beginning inventory balance so that the year-end inventory cost appears as the balance of Raw Materials inventory.

Another element of manufacturing cost is compensation of production personnel. Wages, salaries, and various fringe benefit costs of factory personnel must be accumulated and attached to units produced. Accounting systems must satisfy two aspects of labor cost accounting:

ACCOUNTING FOR LABOR COSTS

1. Computation of gross pay, various deductions, net pay, and periodic accrual and payment of such balances
2. Accumulation of *gross* pay and related labor costs for assignment to products

Accounting for the flow of labor costs to ending inventories and cost of goods sold is distinct from the paymaster function of payroll accounting.

Manufacturing enterprises employ hundreds of people who have specific skills. Compensation for the use of these skills makes up the periodic payroll. Usually, administrative personnel receive salaries, while factory and clerical personnel earn hourly wages. To the paymaster, individual checks vary only in amount. The paymaster must compute gross wages earned and various individual deductions and then disburse a net amount to each person.

Direct and Indirect Labor

For cost accounting purposes *gross* labor costs of all factory personnel must be classified properly. Wages paid to people actually involved in shaping or processing the end product are classified as *direct labor costs;* wages and salaries paid to supporting production personnel—such as supervisors, maintenance personnel, and material handlers—are considered *indirect labor costs.* Criteria used to distinguish direct from indirect labor are defined below:

Direct labor Labor costs for specific work performed on products that are conveniently and economically traceable to end products.

Indirect labor Labor costs of production-related activities that cannot be associated with or conveniently and economically traced to end products.

Direct labor costs are accounted for separately and make up the labor cost element of total unit cost. Indirect labor costs are accounted for as part of manufacturing overhead.

Labor cost is a function of time worked and basic wage or salary rates. These two components provide the source information in accounting for labor costs. Wage and salary rates vary with an individual's skill, knowledge, and experience. In addition, wage and salary rates may be stated explicitly in union labor contracts.

Flow of Labor Cost Information

Usually, employees record their hours worked by inserting a *time card* into a clock that registers the date and times of arrival and departure. The time card is the source document for payroll; it represents the employee's attendance record. To prevent fraudulent practices, each time card usually requires the signatures of the employee and his or her immediate supervisor. Using an employee's wage rate and hours worked, the timekeeper will record gross pay earned on each time card. When all time cards are completed for a pay period, a payroll register is prepared, and individual payroll records are updated. Deductions from gross pay are made for such items as state and federal income taxes, FICA (social security) taxes, insurance premiums, government bonds, and union dues. The resulting net amount is paid to the employee, and all amounts withheld are eventually disbursed to specific companies or government agencies.

Exhibit 3-5 shows the relationship of the records used in payroll accounting. From the payroll register in Exhibit 3-5, the following journal entry would be prepared:

Direct labor	$XXX	
Indirect labor	XXX	
Sales salaries	XXX	
Office salaries	XXX	
Officers' salaries	XXX	
Federal income taxes payable		$XXX
FICA taxes payable		XXX
Government bonds payable		XXX
Union dues payable		XXX
State income taxes payable		XXX
Insurance premiums payable		XXX
Wages and salaries payable		XXX

When payroll checks are distributed, the following entry is made:

Wages and salaries payable	$XXX	
Cash		$XXX

Employer Tax Contributions

Besides state and federal taxes withheld from employees' gross earnings, employers must pay taxes for the benefit of employees. Employers are required to *match* all FICA taxes withheld from employees. Unemployment compensation (UC) taxes must be paid by the employer. Gross earnings are taxed at 3.2 percent, and the total tax is divided between state and federal unemployment agencies. In some states, the unemployment tax rate may be reduced if a firm has a stable employment record. In many states, employers also must pay workmen's compensation insurance premiums to insure employees against employment accidents and diseases. Premium payments vary with established employer risk classifications.

Overtime Premium and Shift Bonuses

Overtime premiums are commonly paid to employees who earn hourly wage rates and who work over forty hours per week. The terms *time and one-half* and *double time* represent overtime premium payments of 50 percent and 100 percent respectively, based on regular hourly wage rates. To illustrate, assume that Mr. C. Cimaglia is a machine operator for the A. G. Company and that his current wage rate is $5 per hour. During the first week of August, he worked eight hours a day Monday through Sunday, with Saturday's work being

EXHIBIT 3-5
PAYROLL DOCUMENTS AND RECORDS

PAYROLL REGISTER – – – – XYZ COMPANY – – – – WEEK ENDING JANUARY 20, 19X3

Badge	Soc. Sec. No.	Name	Total hours	Regular earnings	Overtime earnings	Night premium	Gross pay	Fed. w/h	FICA	Other w/h	Net pay
041											
047											
162											
810	000-00-0000	John Doe	42.0	$252.00	$27.00	$27.90	$306.90	$61.38	$17.58	$42.40	$185.54
890											
972											
1010											
TOTALS FOR PERIOD				$_____ . __	$_____ . __	$_____ . __	$_____ . __	$_____ . __	$_____ . __	$_____ . __	$_____ . __

Payroll register

19X4–X5   INDIVIDUAL PAYROLL RECORD   MR. JOHN DOE   Badge No. 810   Soc. Sec. No. 000-00-0000

| | | | | | | | YEAR TO DATE AMOUNTS | | | | |
Week ending	Total hours	Gross pay	Fed. w/h	FICA	Other w/h	Net pay	Gross pay	Fed. w/h	FICA	Other w/h	Net pay
Jan. 6	46.0	$323.40	$64.68	$18.75	$42.40	$197.57	$323.40	$ 64.68	$18.75	$ 42.40	$197.57
Jan. 13	40.0	283.80	56.76	16.46	42.40	168.18	607.20	121.44	35.21	84.80	365.75
Jan. 20	42.0	306.90	61.38	17.58	42.40	185.54	914.10	182.82	52.79	127.20	551.29

Individual payroll record

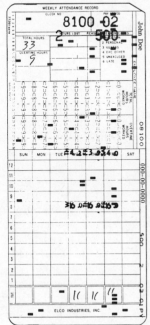

Individual time card

compensated at time and one-half and Sunday's at double time. His gross earnings for the week would be:

Regular earnings (40 hours at $5.00)	$200
Saturday: Overtime (8 hours at $5.00)	40
Overtime premium (8 hours at $2.50)	20
Sunday: Overtime (8 hours at $5.00)	40
Overtime premium (8 hours at $5.00)	40
Total earnings	$340

Notice that the overtime premium includes only the *extra* hourly earnings, not the entire amounts earned on Saturday and Sunday. If Mr. Cimaglia worked the night shift and the A. G. Company's policy was to pay a 10 percent night-shift premium, his total gross earnings for the week would be $340 plus $34 night-shift premium, or $374 total.

Accounting procedures for overtime premiums and shift bonuses vary with circumstances. If the A. G. Company is operating at full capacity when an order is accepted and if the customer agrees to pay all overtime charges, Mr. Cimaglia's entire gross earnings are accounted for as direct labor cost. If, however, Mr. Cimaglia had to work Saturday and Sunday to make up for inefficient operating results caused by management or fellow workers, all wages paid for Saturday and Sunday ($140), including overtime premium pay, would be accounted for as factory overhead.

Another common method of accounting for overtime premiums and shift bonuses is to charge all regular hourly earnings to direct labor and to charge overtime premiums and shift bonuses to factory overhead. In the case where Mr. Cimaglia worked the night shift, the $374 total labor cost is distributed as follows:

Direct labor (7 days × 8 hours × $5.00)		$280
Factory overhead (8 hours × $2.50)	$20	
(8 hours × $5.00)	40	
(Shift bonus)	34	94
Total earnings		$374

Labor-related Costs

Employee fringe benefits constitute a significant part of total labor costs. Fringe benefits and labor-related costs include paid vacations, holiday and sick pay, pension plan contributions, performance bonuses, life and medical insurance, and recreational facilities.

Vacations, holiday pay, and sick-pay benefits are costs incurred for nonproductive labor time. Labor contracts or company policy usually specify which employees are qualified to receive such payments. In accounting for vacation, holiday, and sick-pay costs, annual estimates are computed at the beginning of each year. A portion of this annual estimate is charged to the labor cost each period, and estimated liability accounts are credited. When payments are made for vacation, holiday, or sick-pay benefits, the liability account is debited. Any difference between estimated and actual costs remaining in this account at year-end is corrected by an adjusting entry.

Pension plans are complex and vary from company to company. Some pension plans require the employee to pay all contributions, some plans split the contributions between the employer and the employee, and in some cases the company pays all contributions. Employee contributions to pension plans are accounted for like other items withheld or deducted from gross earnings. Company contributions to pension plans are charged to labor costs and are credited to Employee Pensions Payable.

To reward employees for outstanding performance, performance bonuses are paid, generally at year-end. If these costs are reasonably predictable, they should be accrued during the year in a manner similar to vacation pay. Bonuses, pension contributions, and other employee fringe benefits paid by employers should be recorded as manufacturing labor costs or as selling and administrative expenses in accordance with related employee job classifications.

The following journal entry records employer payroll taxes and labor-related fringe benefits:

Direct labor	$XXXX	
Indirect labor	XXXX	
Sales salaries	XXXX	
Office salaries	XXXX	
Officers' salaries	XXXX	
FICA taxes payable (employer's share)		XXXX
Federal and state unemployment taxes payable		XXXX
Workmen's compensation insurance payable		XXXX
Accrued vacation, holiday, and sick pay		XXXX
Employee pensions payable		XXXX
Accrued performance bonuses		XXXX
Accrued health and life insurance payable		XXXX

Amounts debited to labor and salary accounts represent manufacturing labor costs and operating expenses in addition to the gross payroll earned by employees.

Labor Cost Control

Labor is a service purchased from employees. Unlike materials, labor has no physical substance and cannot be stored for future use. However, labor is as essential to production as raw materials are, and labor cost control affects a company's profitability. To control labor costs, it is necessary to design and install a labor information system. Parts of this system have been discussed already—employee time cards, time clocks, payroll registers, and employee payroll records. A widely used internal control procedure is to require the signature of an employee's supervisor on the time card. These aspects of the labor information system provide accurate measures of labor costs for payroll preparation and control.

The labor information system also should record work performed by employees on specific jobs. Product costing and control of labor costs require accurate measures of work performed by employees. Work performed on specific products or jobs is recorded on labor time tickets or *job cards;* in addition to their overall hours, employees or supervisors thus record time devoted to each job. The job-card procedure serves two purposes: (1) Employees' daily productivity can be analyzed because total time on job cards should equal total hours worked as shown on individual time cards; and (2) direct labor costs can be traced to specific jobs or products by means of the recorded job numbers.

ACCOUNTING FOR MANUFACTURING OVERHEAD

All manufacturing costs except direct material and direct labor costs are termed *manufacturing overhead* (or factory burden, factory overhead, indirect manufacturing costs). Collectively, overhead costs have the common characteristic of not being directly identifiable with or traceable to specific units of output. For example, depreciation on factory buildings and equipment benefits all production, but depreciation is not a direct cost of producing specific units. The same conclusion applies to rent, property taxes, fire insurance, utilities, equipment maintenance costs, and other overhead costs.

For product costing purposes, overhead costs must be accumulated and spread equitably over the output that benefits from these costs. The procedure by which overhead costs are attached to products is called *overhead application*. For plants with multiple products and many production processes, overhead application requires an organizational approach in which overhead costs are first identified and accumulated according to the departments where costs are incurred.

Elements of Manufacturing Overhead

Manufacturing overhead costs are a diverse collection of production-related costs that are not conveniently traceable to units of output. Costs specifically excluded from manufacturing overhead are selling expenses and all general and administrative costs. The following costs illustrate the diversity of manufacturing overhead:

EXAMPLES OF MANUFACTURING OVERHEAD COST

Depreciation on factory building	Fire insurance on factory facilities
Depreciation on factory equipment	Factory repairs and maintenance
Indirect materials	Factory heating
Indirect labor	Factory lighting and power
Rent of factory equipment	Manufacturing supervision
Property taxes on factory equipment	Factory supplies
Real estate taxes on factory building and grounds	Overtime premiums and shift bonuses
	Small tools used
Patent amortization	Production scheduling
Quality control	Engineering labor and supplies
Product inspection	Raw materials receiving department
Product storage	Material handling
Tool and die making	Product design
Factory janitorial service	Factory cafeteria

Overhead Classification

Manufacturing overhead costs can be classified according to cost behavior and traceability to specific plants and departments. For control purposes, the variable and fixed characteristics of overhead costs must be identified. For product costing and control, it is necessary to associate overhead costs with specific plants and operating departments.

Variable and fixed overhead All manufacturing costs can be classified as either variable costs or fixed costs. *Variable costs*, such as direct material and direct labor, vary in direct proportion to units produced. As production increases, variable costs tend to increase at the same rate. *Fixed costs* tend to remain constant within a specific range of output. These general comments apply to *total* variable and fixed costs for a period. When analyzing unit costs, the definitions are reversed. Variable costs are constant per unit of output. For example, if raw material is $1.00 per unit, every similar unit should contain a dollar's worth of material. Fixed costs per unit decrease as total production increases. With total fixed costs of $40,000, production of 20,000 units results in each product being assigned fixed costs of $2.00; if, however, the same plant produces 30,000 units, fixed cost per unit drops to $1.33.

Overhead costs having both variable and fixed characteristics are called *semivariable costs* (or semifixed costs). Exhibit 3-6 illustrates variable, fixed, and semivariable costs. Diagram *a* depicts a variable cost; diagram *b* shows a fixed cost; and diagrams *c* and *d* illustrate different types of semivariable costs. Examples of overhead costs within each category are (1) variable costs: production supplies, material handling costs, and product inspection; (2) fixed costs: depreciation on plant and equipment (using the straight line approach), property taxes, and rental charges; and (3) semivariable costs: utilities (heat, light, and power), tool and die usage, and product storage. Chapter 9 contains a

EXHIBIT 3-6
VARIABLE, FIXED, AND SEMIVARIABLE COSTS

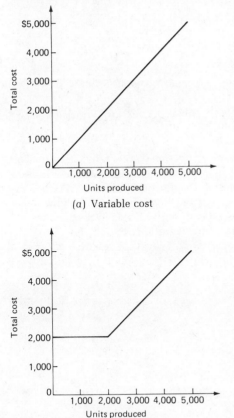

(a) Variable cost

(c) Semivariable cost

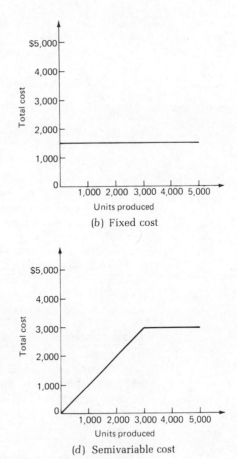

(b) Fixed cost

(d) Semivariable cost

EXHIBIT 3-7

COST CENTERS IN A LARGE COMPANY

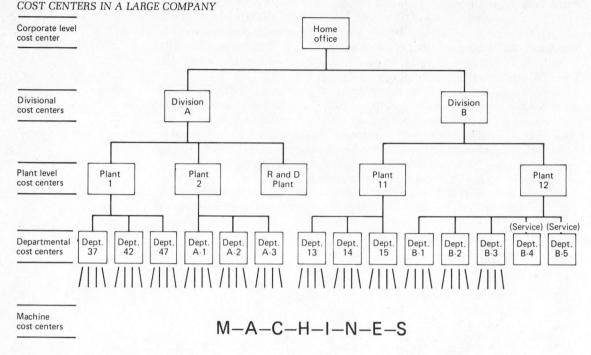

detailed analysis of variable and fixed costs and complex forms of cost behavior.

Cost centers and overhead   Manufacturing overhead costs range from the cost of equipment cleaning solvents to plant superintendents' salaries. Product costing and control require a cost center classification system in which every overhead cost is associated with a particular cost center. In Exhibit 3-7, a company organization structure illustrates different levels of cost centers. As overhead costs are incurred, they are charged initially to specific cost center accounts at divisional, plant, or departmental levels. Examples of various overhead costs and the cost center in Exhibit 3-7 to which they initially are charged are shown below:

OVERHEAD COST	COST CENTER LEVEL INITIALLY CHARGED
Division A—superintendent's salary	Division A
Plant 2—superintendent's salary	Plant 2
Depreciation of Plant 11 building	Plant 11
Depreciation of machines in Department 47	Department 47
Heat, light, and power used in departments 37, 42, and 47	Plant 1
Indirect labor in Department B-1	Department B-1
Repair crew wages in Departments 13, 14, and 15	Plant 11

If a cost can be traced to a specific department, it is charged to detailed overhead accounts for that department. If the cost is not traceable to a department, it is charged to overhead accounts at the plant level. The same concept holds at the plant level: If a division incurs a cost that jointly benefits two plants, the cost is charged initially to divisional overhead accounts.

For product costing purposes, the goal is to attach or assign all elements of manufacturing cost (material, labor, and overhead) to batches of products. All overhead costs incurred are charged first to various cost centers as described. After being classified as divisional, plant, or departmental overhead costs, they are grouped in homogeneous overhead pools and allocated to lower cost center levels. When all overhead costs have been allocated to departmental cost centers, overhead costs per unit of output can be determined. This overhead allocation process is analyzed in the illustration of product costing techniques in Chapter 5.

Overhead cost accounts   A widely used practice for general ledger purposes is to maintain separate accounts for each overhead cost. When overhead costs are incurred, they are debited to specific overhead accounts, such as Utilities, Property Taxes, Equipment Maintenance, Repairs, Equipment Rentals, and Insurance. When transactions are recorded in a cash disbursements journal, a voucher register, or a general journal, overhead costs are charged to these various accounts. Some overhead costs are recognized by adjusting entries; examples are depreciation, patent amortization, and expired insurance on factory facilities. Indirect labor costs are recorded when payrolls are journalized. Costs of indirect materials and production supplies used during a period are recorded as adjusting entries under a periodic inventory system. Separate overhead accounts can be established for costs incurred by individual cost centers. When a general ledger account is used for each overhead cost, total factory overhead incurred during a period is determined by adding all the overhead cost accounts.

MANUFACTURING INVENTORY ACCOUNTS

Accounting procedures and cost classifications for merchandising and manufacturing operations differ significantly. In manufacturing, a primary concern is accounting for the material, labor, and overhead costs. Another difference concerns the inventory accounts. Merchandising companies use a single Merchandise inventory account, but a manufacturer needs three separate inventory accounts: Raw Materials inventory, Work in Process inventory, and Finished Goods inventory.

Raw Materials Inventory

In a periodic inventory system, the year-end balance of Raw Materials inventory is computed by taking a physical count of inventory items on hand and multiplying these quantities by their respective unit costs. The year-end balance in this inventory account includes all purchased raw materials and supplies that have not been issued to production or service departments. A separate general ledger account is used for Raw Materials inventory.

Work in Process Inventory

Most manufacturing companies need considerable time to make products. The machine screw in Chapter 2 required several production processes before the screws were completed and packaged for shipment. At any one time, a factory has products that are only partially completed. At the end of each accounting period, partially completed products are classified as Work in Process inventory. The ending balance of Work in Process inventory is the amount of material, labor, and overhead costs assigned to partially completed products.

Finished Goods Inventory   The third manufacturing inventory account is Finished Goods inventory; it includes all completed products not yet shipped to customers. Like the units in ending Raw Materials and Work in Process inventory accounts, units of finished goods must be physically counted at the end of each accounting period and assigned a unit cost according to the inventory pricing methods discussed earlier. This total cost is the desired ending balance of Finished Goods inventory, and an adjusting entry is required to increase or decrease the general ledger account balance to equal this amount.

REPORTING OF MANUFACTURING COSTS   Preparing financial statements for a manufacturing company is more complex than for a merchandising concern. Not only does the balance sheet contain three inventory accounts, but each inventory account must be used to compute Cost of Goods Sold.

When ending inventory balances have been determined and all necessary general ledger adjusting entries have been recorded, the *statement of Cost of Goods Manufactured and Sold* can be prepared. Its purpose is to compute the Cost of Goods Sold amount that will appear in the income statement. Preparation of the statement of Cost of Goods Manufactured and Sold can be divided into four parts, as shown in Exhibit 3-8.

Raw Materials Used   If a company immediately uses all raw materials as they are purchased, then the cost of raw materials purchased during the period is the cost of raw materials used. However, most manufacturing companies maintain an inventory of raw materials. Beginning and ending balances of Raw Materials inventory must be considered in computing the cost of raw materials used during the period. Assume that the Kieso Fastener Company had 47 coils of wire on hand at September 1. The company purchased 110 coils during September and had 34 coils on hand on September 30. How many coils of wire were used during September? Using the formula for component A in Exhibit 3-8,

$$110 \text{ coils} + 47 \text{ coils} - 34 \text{ coils} = 123 \text{ coils used}$$

If the average cost of each coil is $180, the cost of raw materials used during September is $22,140 (123 coils × $180 per coil).

Total Manufacturing Costs   Component B in Exhibit 3-8 combines the separate cost totals for material usage, direct labor, and manufacturing overhead for the period. The sum of raw materials used, direct labor, and various manufacturing overhead costs represents the total manufacturing costs incurred during the period. If the Kieso Fastener Company paid $32,500 in direct labor costs and incurred $49,275 in overhead charges during September, total manufacturing costs for September would be $103,915 ($22,140 + $32,500 + $49,275).

EXHIBIT 3-8

COMPONENTS OF COST OF GOODS SOLD

Component A: Compute raw materials used during period

| Net raw material purchases during period | + | Beginning balance: Raw Materials inventory | − | Ending balance: Raw Materials inventory | = | Cost of raw materials used during period |

Component B: Find total manufacturing costs for period

| Cost of raw materials used during period | + | Direct labor costs for period | + | Total manufacturing overhead incurred during period | = | Total manufacturing costs for period |

Component C: Determine total cost of goods manufactured during period

| Total manufacturing costs for period | + | Beginning balance: Work in Process inventory | − | Ending balance: Work in Process inventory | = | Total cost of goods manufactured during period |

Component D: Arrive at cost of goods sold during period

| Total cost of goods manufactured during period | + | Beginning balance: Finished Goods inventory | − | Ending balance: Finished Goods inventory | = | Cost of Goods Sold during period |

Total Cost of Goods Manufactured

Total manufacturing costs are often confused with the total cost of goods manufactured. *Total Manufacturing Costs* represents the total material, labor, and overhead costs incurred during the current period. *Total Cost of Goods Manufactured* is the cost assigned to production completed during the period. Accordingly, Cost of Goods Manufactured is Total Manufacturing Costs adjusted for changes in Work in Process inventory. If the Kieso Fastener Company had a beginning balance in Work in Process inventory of $27,520 and an ending balance of $19,400, Cost of Goods Manufactured would be computed as follows:

Total manufacturing costs for September	$103,915
Plus: Work in process inventory, September 1	27,520
Total costs in process during September	$131,435
Less: Work in process inventory, September 30	19,400
Cost of goods manufactured	$112,035

Cost of Goods Sold

The computation of Cost of Goods Sold follows a pattern similar to that used to arrive at Cost of Goods Manufactured. The major difference is that interest is focused on Finished Goods inventory balances, not on balances in Work in Process inventories. Cost of Goods Manufactured is added to the beginning

EXHIBIT 3-9

STATEMENT OF COST OF GOODS MANUFACTURED AND SOLD

KIESO FASTENER COMPANY
Statement of cost of goods manufactured and sold
For month ending September 30, 19X4

Direct materials:		
Raw materials inventory, Sept. 1, 19X4		$ 8,460
Raw materials purchased (net)		19,800
Raw materials available for use		$ 28,260
Less: Raw materials inventory, Sept. 30, 19X4		6,120
Direct materials used		$ 22,140
Direct labor incurred		32,500
Manufacturing overhead costs:		
Indirect materials	$ 8,420	
Indirect labor	13,585	
Material handling—other than labor	2,750	
Heat, light, and power	3,400	
Depreciation on plant	9,500	
Depreciation on equipment	6,000	
Property taxes	2,000	
Fire insurance	1,250	
Repairs and maintenance	2,370	49,275
Total manufacturing costs for September		$103,915
Plus: Work in process inventory, Sept. 1, 19X4		27,520
Total costs in process during September		$131,435
Less: Work in process inventory, Sept. 30, 19X4		19,400
Cost of goods manufactured		$112,035
Plus: Finished goods inventory, Sept. 1, 19X4		37,450
Cost of goods available for sale		$149,485
Less: Finished goods inventory, Sept. 30, 19X4		32,725
Cost of goods sold		$116,760

balance of Finished Goods inventory to determine Cost of Goods Available for Sale. From this total, you subtract the ending balance of Finished Goods inventory. The result is Cost of Goods Sold, which represents costs attached to goods sold during the period.

Assume the Kieso Fastener Company had a beginning Finished Goods inventory of $37,450. A physical count of finished goods on hand at September 30 revealed that finished goods costing $32,725 had not been sold. Cost of Goods Sold in September is:

Cost of goods manufactured in September	$112,035
Plus: Finished goods inventory, September 1	37,450
Cost of goods available for sale in September	$149,485
Less: Finished goods inventory, September 30	32,725
Cost of goods sold	$116,760

The four components of Cost of Goods Sold for Kieso Company must be combined, and the resulting statement of cost of goods manufactured and sold appears in Exhibit 3-9. Details of the $49,275 overhead cost total are given and

EXHIBIT 3-10
INCOME STATEMENT OF MANUFACTURER

KIESO FASTENER COMPANY
Income statement
For month ending September 30, 19X4

Sales (net)		$215,740
Less: Cost of goods sold:		
Finished goods inventory, Sept. 1, 19X4	$ 37,450	
Cost of goods manufactured (from supporting		
schedule)	112,035	
Cost of goods available for sale	$149,485	
Less: Finished goods inventory, Sept. 30, 19X4	32,725	
Cost of goods sold		116,760
Gross profit		$ 98,980
Selling and administrative expenses		62,892
Net income before taxes		$ 36,088

represent specific general ledger account balances. Cost of Goods Sold of $116,760 would then be reported in the income statement for September. An alternative approach is to include part of the Cost of Goods Sold computation in the income statement. If this approach is followed, a statement of Cost of Goods Manufactured is prepared, and the end result is $112,035 for goods produced in the current period. The company's income statement under this latter approach is illustrated in Exhibit 3-10.

FINAL NOTE

For manufacturing operations, identification of raw material, direct labor, and manufacturing overhead costs is vital to effective cost accounting. Each cost category includes specific types of costs and uses various cost control procedures. An information system with related source documents makes possible the systematic flow of cost information from the beginning of the transaction to final recording in the general ledger.

Appendix 3-A is included in this chapter to illustrate a general model for developing financial statements in a cost system using periodic inventory procedures. From the analysis in Appendix 3-A, students will learn to summarize and close accounting records typically used by small and medium-sized manufacturing concerns.

When you have completed your review of the appendix, return to the beginning of the chapter and review the highlights section before proceeding to the review questions, exercises, and problems.

APPENDIX 3-A: Financial Statements: Cost Analysis with Periodic Inventories

Cost accounting systems vary with company size, type of industry, nature of products, management information requirements, and many other factors, including the use of either the periodic or perpetual inventory accounting methods. To obtain current information and to control inventories closely, a company may adopt the perpetual inventory method. This method demands additional personnel and more accounting procedures, and it is more costly.

Whatever advantages are available with the perpetual inventory method, many small and medium-sized companies do not usually use it. For their operations, an accounting system using the periodic inventory method is sufficient. Because the periodic inventory method is widely used, cost accounting students should be exposed to its accounting treatment. This appendix explains and illustrates cost analysis and financial statement preparation based on periodic inventory procedures.

PERIODIC INVENTORY METHOD

The primary difference between cost accounting with periodic inventories and perpetual inventories is the flow of costs through general ledger accounts. This cost flow is influenced by the initial recording of material purchases and other cost transactions. Resulting differences between the two methods will become apparent when perpetual inventories are studied in Chapter 5.

General Ledger Treatment

A review of journal entries used to record transactions of a manufacturing company will illustrate accounting procedures using the periodic inventory method. The analysis on the facing page concentrates on typical transactions and provides the basis for treatment of general ledger accounts.

End-of-period Costing Procedures

Costing procedures at year-end are needed to determine inventory balances following the physical count of all goods on hand. Cost of ending Raw Materials inventory is determined by multiplying *net* unit purchase price times units on hand. Costing of Work in Process and Finished Goods inventories is more complex, since they require the calculation of a unit production cost for the current period. The difference between costing work in process and finished units is that partially completed products require computation of unit costs based on different stages of completion.

Unit production cost information includes direct material, direct labor, and manufacturing overhead cost components. A typical unit cost would appear as follows:

Raw materials	$1.25
Direct labor	2.80
Manufacturing overhead (50% of direct labor cost)	1.40
Total unit cost	$5.45

Methods for determining overhead rates (here 50 percent of direct labor cost) are discussed in Chapter 5. Unit costs for raw material and direct labor components are determined by dividing total cost of materials requisitioned and total direct labor by the number of units produced during the period. Unit costs can be developed for each department or production process. When unit cost amounts have been determined, ending Work in Process and Finished Goods inventory balances can be computed. With periodic inventory procedures, unit costs and total costs of ending inventories are determined at the end of an accounting period. This procedure is called *end-of-period costing*.

Transaction Description	Journal Entry, Periodic Inventory Method	
1. Raw materials are purchased on account.	Dr.	Raw material purchases
	Cr.	Accounts payable
2. Raw materials are returned to supplier because of damage or defect.	Dr.	Accounts payable
	Cr.	Raw material purchase returns and allowances
3. Delivery costs on raw material purchases are paid by supplier and billed to company.	Dr.	Freight-in
	Cr.	Accounts payable
4. Paid account payable balance on raw materials purchased less cash discount	Dr.	Accounts payable
	Cr.	Cash
	Cr.	Purchase discounts
5. Raw materials are requisitioned from storeroom and put into production.		No entry required
6. Payroll for the period is recorded. Payroll costs are broken down into subtotals for direct labor, indirect labor, sales salaries, and administrative salaries.	Dr.	Direct labor
	Dr.	Indirect labor
	Dr.	Sales salaries
	Dr.	Administrative salaries
	Cr.	Income taxes withheld
	Cr.	FICA taxes payable
	Cr.	Sundry deductions payable
	Cr.	Wages and salaries payable
7. Payroll is distributed.	Dr.	Wages and salaries payable
	Cr.	Cash
8. Various manufacturing overhead costs are paid.	Dr.	Specific manufacturing expense accounts (heat, light, and power, property taxes, etc.)
	Cr.	Cash
9. Overhead costs are applied to units of production.		No entry required
10. Units of production are completed and transferred to Finished Goods inventory.		No entry required
11. Finished goods are sold to customers on account.	Dr.	Accounts receivable
	Cr.	Sales
12. Damaged products are returned from customers.	Dr.	Sales returns and allowances
	Cr.	Accounts receivable
13. Payments are received from customers who have taken advantage of sales discounts.	Dr.	Cash
	Dr.	Sales discounts
	Cr.	Accounts receivable
14. Inventory is physically counted at year-end; priced; and totals for Raw Materials inventory, Work in Process inventory and Finished Goods inventory are reported.		No entry required until accounts are closed

Year-end Adjusting Entries	Adjusting general ledger accounts at year-end for a manufacturing company is similar to that for a merchandising concern. Adjusting entries for depreciation, bad debt expenses, expired insurance, supplies used, accrued payroll, and other liabilities must be recorded before financial statements can be prepared. Costs such as "tools used" and "patents write-off" may be unique to manufacturers, but adjusting entry form and procedure are similar to other adjustments. Sample adjusting journal entries are shown later in the illustrative problem.

Worksheet Format

Worksheets for preparation of financial statements for manufacturing companies differ in format because space must be provided for an additional financial statement. Besides columns for Trial Balance, Adjustments, Adjusted Trial Balance, Income Statement, and Balance Sheet, columns must be provided for the statement of Cost of Goods Manufactured. When amounts in the Adjusted Trial Balance are extended to the financial statement columns, all manufacturing-related costs are entered in the two manufacturing columns. Cost of Goods Manufactured, the resulting balance of the manufacturing columns, is transferred to the Income Statement columns, much like Net Income is transferred to the Balance Sheet columns. The illustrative problem shows this procedure.

Throughout the year, *beginning* inventory balances have been carried in the Raw Materials, Work in Process, and Finished Goods inventory accounts. For worksheet purposes, the ending inventory balances are placed into the respective inventory accounts. Beginning balances of Raw Materials inventory and Work in Process inventory are shown as debit items in the manufacturing columns. Ending balances of Raw Materials and Work in Process are shown as credit entries in the manufacturing columns and as debit balances in the Balance Sheet columns. A similar approach is used for Finished Goods inventory balances in the income statement columns.

Closing Entries

Two closing entry procedures are unique to manufacturing companies. One applies to all manufacturers, while the other applies only to manufacturers using the periodic inventory method. A *Manufacturing Summary* account is used as a clearing account for all manufacturing costs. All accounts used to compute Cost of Goods Manufactured are closed to Manufacturing Summary. The balance in the Manufacturing Summary is Cost of Goods Manufactured, which then is closed to Income Summary along with other income statement accounts.

When using the periodic inventory method, beginning balances are carried in Raw Materials, Work in Process, and Finished Goods inventory accounts throughout the year. Ending balances are entered formally into the general ledger by closing entries. The beginning balances in Raw Materials and Work in Process inventories (January 1 figures) are first closed to Manufacturing Summary along with all other manufacturing costs. A second closing entry debits Raw Materials inventory and Work in Process inventory with their respective ending balances, and a credit entry is made to Manufacturing Summary for the combined total. This reduces Cost of Goods Manufactured by the costs attached to uncompleted units of production. Beginning and ending Finished Goods inventory balances are handled similarly in closing entries related to Income Summary. Formal closing entries are illustrated in the following worksheet analysis. An alternative procedure for accounting for beginning and ending inventory balances uses adjusting entries instead of closing entries. Only the closing entry procedure is illustrated here.

The trial balance of the S. K. Hedlund Manufacturing Company as of December 31, 19X7, appeared as follows:

ILLUSTRATIVE
WORKSHEET
ANALYSIS

S. K. HEDLUND MANUFACTURING COMPANY
Trial balance
December 31, 19X7

	Dr.	Cr.
Cash	$ 19,400	
Accounts receivable	21,000	
Raw materials inventory, Jan. 1, 19X7	16,750	
Work in process inventory, Jan. 1, 19X7	21,520	
Finished goods inventory, Jan. 1, 19X7	24,980	
Manufacturing supplies	5,610	
Prepaid factory insurance	4,200	
Factory machinery	194,600	
Accumulated depreciation—factory machinery		$ 80,400
Factory building	370,000	
Accumulated depreciation—factory building		115,000
Small tools	7,420	
Patents	11,675	
Common stock		200,000
Retained earnings, Jan. 1, 19X7		212,420
Sales		417,410
Raw material purchases	84,620	
Raw material purchase returns and allowances		2,860
Direct labor	102,925	
Factory supervision	15,500	
Indirect labor	24,750	
Heat, light, and power—factory	18,910	
Repairs and maintenance	3,120	
Property taxes—machinery	917	
Selling expenses—control	42,018	
Administrative expenses—control	38,175	
	$1,028,090	$1,028,090

Year-end adjustment information:

1. Depreciation—factory machinery	$11,500
2. Depreciation—factory building	24,500
3. Patent amortization	1,675
4. Factory insurance expired	2,100
5. Small tools used during period	1,670
6. Manufacturing supplies consumed	2,310
7. Accrued salaries and wages payable:	
Direct labor	1,475
Indirect labor	980
Factory supervision	525

8. Ending inventory balances:

Raw materials inventory	$19,825
Work in process inventory	22,740
Finished goods inventory	25,640

9. Accrued accounts payable:

Raw material purchases	2,205
Heat, light, and power—factory	419
10. Estimated federal income taxes	21,000

REQUIRED:

a. Prepare twelve-column worksheet and enter trial balance. Formulate year-end adjusting entries from information given, post entries to worksheet, and compute adjusted trial balance amounts.

b. Extend all amounts to proper columns for statement of Cost of Goods Manufactured, Income Statement, and Balance Sheet.

c. Complete the worksheet and prepare formal financial statements, including statement of Cost of Goods Manufactured.

d. Prepare closing entries.

Note: A complete solution to this illustrative problem follows. Schedules are keyed to specific requirements (a), (b), (c), and (d). The problem and solution represent a general model for developing financial statements in a cost system using periodic inventory procedures.

SOLUTION:

Requirement (a): First, prepare worksheet and fill in set of columns for trial balance. Next, make the following year-end adjusting entries:

1. Depreciation of factory machinery	$11,500	
Accumulated depreciation—factory		
machinery		$11,500
To record depreciation of factory machinery		
2. Depreciation of factory building	$24,500	
Accumulated depreciation—factory		
building		$24,500
To record depreciation of factory building		
3. Patent amortization	$ 1,675	
Patents		$ 1,675
To record patents write-off for period		
4. Factory insurance expense	$ 2,100	
Prepaid factory insurance		$ 2,100
To record factory insurance expired during period		
5. Small-tools expense	$ 1,670	
Small tools		$ 1,670
To record small tools used during period		
6. Manufacturing supplies expense	$ 2,310	
Manufacturing supplies		$ 2,310
To record manufacturing supplies consumed during period		

7. Direct labor	$ 1,475	
Indirect labor	980	
Factory supervision	525	
Accrued salaries and wages payable		$ 2,980
To record accrued salaries and wages		
8. Raw material purchases	$ 2,205	
Heat, light, and power—factory	419	
Accounts payable		$ 2,624
To record accrued accounts payable		
9. Federal income tax expense	$21,000	
Federal income taxes payable		$21,000
To record estimated federal income tax		

Post above entries to adjustments columns on worksheet. Requirements (b) and part of (c) are on worksheet.

Requirements (a), (b), (c): Worksheet

S. K. HEDLUND MANUFACTURING COMPANY
Worksheet
December 31, 19X7

General Ledger Account Titles	Trial Balance Dr.	Trial Balance Cr.	Adjustments Dr.	Adjustments Cr.	Adjusted Trial Balance Dr.	Adjusted Trial Balance Cr.	Statement of Cost of Goods Manuf. Dr.	Statement of Cost of Goods Manuf. Cr.	Income Statement Dr.	Income Statement Cr.	Balance Sheet Dr.	Balance Sheet Cr.
Cash	$ 19,400				19,400						$ 19,400	
Accounts receivable	21,000				21,000						21,000	
Raw materials inventory	16,750				16,750		$ 16,750	$ 19,825			19,825	
Work in process inventory	21,520				21,520		21,520	22,740			22,740	
Finished goods inventory	24,980				24,980				$ 24,980	$ 25,640	25,640	
Manufacturing supplies	5,610			(6) $ 2,310	3,300						3,300	
Prepaid factory insurance	4,200			(4) 2,100	2,100						2,100	
Factory machinery	194,600				194,600						194,600	
Accum. depr.—factory mach.		$ 80,400		(1) 11,500		$ 91,900						$ 91,900
Factory building	370,000				370,000						370,000	
Accum. depr.—factory bldg.		115,000		(2) 24,500		139,500						139,500
Small tools	7,420			(5) 1,670	5,750						5,750	
Patents	11,675			(3) 1,675	10,000						10,000	
Common stock		200,000				200,000						200,000
Retained earnings		212,420				212,420						212,420
Sales		417,410				417,410				417,410		
Raw material purchases	84,620		(8) $ 2,205		86,825		86,825					
Raw material purchase returns and allowances		2,860				2,860		2,860				
Direct labor	102,925		(7) 1,475		104,400		104,400					
Factory supervision	15,500		(7) 525		16,025		16,025					
Indirect labor	24,750		(7) 980		25,730		25,730					
Heat, light, and power—factory	18,910		(8) 419		19,329		19,329					
Repairs and maintenance	3,120				3,120		3,120					
Property taxes—machinery	917				917		917					
Selling expenses—control	42,018				42,018				42,018			
Administrative expenses—control	38,175				38,175				38,175			
	$1,028,090	$1,028,090										
Depreciation—factory machinery			(1) 11,500		11,500		11,500					
Depreciation—factory building			(2) 24,500		24,500		24,500					
Patent amortization			(3) 1,675		1,675		1,675					
Factory insurance expense			(4) 2,100		2,100		2,100					
Small-tools expense			(5) 1,670		1,670		1,670					
Manufacturing supplies expense			(6) 2,310		2,310		2,310					
Accrued salaries and wages payable				(7) 2,980		2,980						2,980
Accounts payable				(8) 2,624		2,624						2,624
Federal income tax expense			(9) 21,000		21,000				21,000			
Federal income tax payable				(9) 21,000		21,000						21,000
			$70,359	$70,359	$1,090,694	$1,090,694		$ 45,425				
Cost of goods manufactured to income statement							292,946	292,946	292,946			
							$338,371	$338,371	$419,119	$443,050	$670,424	$694,355
Net income after taxes to balance sheet									23,931			23,931
									$443,050	$443,050	$694,355	$694,355

Requirement (c)—(cont.)

S. K. HEDLUND MANUFACTURING COMPANY
Statement of cost of goods manufactured
For the year ended December 31, 19X7

Direct materials:		
Raw materials inventory, Jan. 1, 19X7		$ 16,750
Raw material purchases (net of returns and		
allowances)		83,965
Raw materials available for use		$100,715
Less: Raw materials inventory, Dec. 31, 19X7		19,825
Direct materials used		$ 80,890
Direct labor		104,400
Manufacturing overhead:		
Factory supervision	$ 16,025	
Indirect labor	25,730	
Heat, light, and power—factory	19,329	
Repairs and maintenance	3,120	
Property taxes—machinery	917	
Depreciation—factory machinery	11,500	
Depreciation—factory building	24,500	
Patent amortization	1,675	
Factory insurance expense	2,100	
Small-tools expense	1,670	
Manufacturing supplies expense	2,310	108,876
Total manufacturing costs		$294,166
Plus: Work in process inventory, Jan. 1, 19X7		21,520
Total costs in process during year		$315,686
Less: Work in process inventory, Dec. 31, 19X7		22,740
Cost of goods manufactured		$292,946

Requirement (c)—(cont.)

S. K. HEDLUND MANUFACTURING COMPANY
Income statement
For the year ended December 31, 19X7

Sales		$417,410
Less: Cost of goods sold:		
Finished goods inventory, Jan. 1, 19X7	$ 24,980	
Cost of goods manufactured		
(see supporting schedule)	292,946	
Cost of goods available for sale	$317,926	
Less: Finished goods inventory, Dec. 31, 19X7	25,640	
Cost of goods sold		292,286
Gross profit		$125,124
Operating expenses:		
Selling expenses	$ 42,018	
Administrative expenses	38,175	
Total operating expenses		80,193
Net income before taxes		$ 44,931
Federal income taxes		21,000
Net income		$ 23,931

Requirement (c)—(cont.)

S. K. HEDLUND MANUFACTURING COMPANY
Balance sheet
As of December 31, 19X7

A-S-S-E-T-S

Current Assets:		
Cash	$ 19,400	
Accounts receivable	21,000	
Raw materials inventory	19,825	
Work in process inventory	22,740	
Finished goods inventory	25,640	
Small tools	5,750	
Manufacturing supplies	3,300	
Prepaid factory insurance	2,100	
Total current assets		$119,755

Plant and equipment:			
Factory building	$370,000		
Less: Accumulated depreciation	139,500	$230,500	
Factory machinery	$194,600		
Less: Accumulated depreciation	91,900	102,700	
Total plant and equipment			333,200
Other assets			
Patents			10,000
Total assets			$462,955

L-I-A-B-I-L-I-T-I-E-S A-N-D E-Q-U-I-T-Y

Current liabilities:		
Accounts payable	$ 2,624	
Accrued salaries and wages payable	2,980	
Federal income taxes payable	21,000	
Total liabilities		$ 26,604

Stockholders' equity:			
Common stock		$200,000	
Retained earnings, Jan. 1, 19X7	$212,420		
Net income for 19X7	23,931		
Retained earnings, Dec. 31, 19X7		236,351	
Total stockholders' equity			436,351
Total liabilities and equity			$462,955

Requirement (d)

S. K. HEDLUND MANUFACTURING COMPANY
Closing entries
December 31, 19X7

Dec. 31:

Manufacturing summary	$335,511	
Raw material purchase returns and allowances	2,860	
Raw materials inventory, Jan. 1, 19X7		$ 16,750
Work in process inventory, Jan. 1, 19X7		21,520
Raw material purchases		86,825
Direct labor		104,400
Factory supervision		16,025
Indirect labor		25,730
Heat, light, and power—factory		19,329
Repairs and maintenance		3,120
Property taxes—machinery		917
Depreciation—factory machinery		11,500
Depreciation—factory building		24,500
Patent amortization		1,675
Factory insurance expense		2,100
Small-tools expense		1,670
Manufacturing supplies expense		2,310

To close manufacturing accounts to
Manufacturing Summary

Dec. 31:

Raw materials inventory, Dec. 31, 19X7	$ 19,825	
Work in process inventory, Dec. 31, 19X7	22,740	
Manufacturing summary		$ 42,565

To establish year-end balances in the
Raw Materials and Work in Process
inventory accounts and to remove
these costs from the Manufacturing
Summary account

Dec. 31:

Income summary	$419,119	
Finished goods inventory, Jan. 1, 19X7		$ 24,980
Selling expenses—control		42,018
Administrative expenses—control		38,175
Federal income tax expense		21,000
Manufacturing summary		292,946

To close income statement debit accounts
to Income Summary

Dec. 31:

Sales	$417,410	
Finished goods inventory, Dec. 31, 19X7	25,640	
Income summary		$443,050

To close sales to Income Summary and
to set up ending balance in Finished
Goods inventory

Requirement (d)—(cont.)

S. K. HEDLUND MANUFACTURING COMPANY
Closing entries
December 31, 19X7

Dec. 31:

Income summary	$ 23,931	
Retained earnings		$ 23,931
To close Income Summary account		
and transfer balance to Retained		
Earnings		

QUESTIONS

3-1. Define and illustrate the following terms and concepts:

a. Manufacturing cost	j. Inventoriable cost
b. Periodic inventory method	k. Product cost
c. Direct materials	l. Period cost
d. Indirect materials	m. Material requisition
e. Direct labor	n. Overtime premium
f. Indirect labor	o. Raw material inventory
g. Manufacturing overhead	p. Work in process inventory
h. Fixed cost	q. Finished goods inventory
i. Variable cost	r. Overhead allocation

3-2. What are the major differences between income statement formats for a merchandising firm and a manufacturing firm?

3-3. Selling commissions are not classified as an inventoriable cost. What criteria are used to identify inventoriable costs? Why are selling commissions not considered an inventoriable cost?

3-4. What criteria are used to distinguish between direct and indirect material costs?

3-5. Why are indirect material costs accounted for as part of manufacturing overhead?

3-6. Explain the origin and purpose of the (a) purchase order, (b) receiving report, (c) purchase request, (d) material requisition.

3-7. Arrange the documents listed in question 3-6 in a sequence that corresponds with the actual flow of transactions and information.

3-8. Under the periodic inventory method, physical counts of inventory items are required in order to prepare financial statements. Why are physical inventory counts also necessary under perpetual inventory methods?

3-9. Identify three inventory pricing methods and explain how each is different in its assumptions and application.

3-10. What criteria are used to distinguish between direct and indirect labor costs?

3-11. Distinguish between gross earnings and net earnings of factory employees. Which of these costs is used to determine Cost of Goods Manufactured?

3-12. Explain the origin and purpose of the (a) payroll register, (b) employee time card, (c) job time card, (d) individual payroll record.

3-13. What is the proper cost classification for employer payroll taxes, pension plan contributions, and other fringe benefits for factory personnel?

3-14. What three areas should be emphasized in an accounting system if labor costs are to be properly controlled? Discuss the main points of concern in each area.

3-15. Indirect manufacturing costs are referred to as *manufacturing overhead*. What other terms are used to describe this group of costs?

3-16. What is the purpose of an overhead allocation system?

3-17. "Variable manufacturing costs are constant per unit of output, but fixed manufacturing costs per unit vary with the level of output." Explain this statement.

3-18. "Rent on factory buildings is controllable at the plant level, and direct labor cost is controllable at the level of departmental cost centers." Explain the meaning of this statement.

3-19. Define and distinguish among (a) Total Manufacturing Costs for a period, (b) Cost of Goods Manufactured, and (c) Cost of Goods Sold.

3-20. Material, labor, and overhead costs incurred during a period were $100,000, $150,000, and $250,000 respectively. During the period, Work in Process inventory increased $25,000 in relation to its balance at the start of the period. What effect does this inventory change have on the computation of Cost of Goods Manufactured?

EXERCISES

3-21. *Accounting for Labor Costs*   The following summary information was taken from the August 14–27, 19X9, payroll register of the U. M. S. Corporation:

Sales salaries	$ 22,450
Officers' salaries	41,500
Factory administration salaries	20,750
Factory wages	110,645

Gross salaries and wages	195,345
Federal income taxes withheld	35,162
FICA taxes withheld	11,721
Government bonds	1,875
Health insurance premiums	2,450
Union dues	1,240
Net salaries and wages	142,897

REQUIRED:

a. Prepare a journal entry to record the payroll liability for period ending August 27, 19X9.

b. Assuming 20 percent of factory wages are indirect labor, prepare a journal entry to distribute payroll for period.

c. Assuming all salaries and wages listed above are subject to FICA and federal and state unemployment compensation (U.C.) taxes and that the federal U.C. rate is 0.5 percent and the state U.C. rate is 2.7 percent, prepare an entry to record employer payroll taxes.

3-22. *Overtime Premium* Payroll records of the Nif-Tie Corporation produced information on the following employees for the week ended February 29, 19X0:

EMPLOYEE	HOURS WORKED	HOURLY PAY RATE	GROSS EARNINGS
C. Snorek	44	$7.50	$ 345.00
S. Dewey	50	6.80	374.00
C. Goodwin	48	5.20	270.40
S. Higgins	42	8.70	374.10
C. Newkirk	46	5.40	264.60
			$1,628.10

REQUIRED:

a. Compute the amount of overtime premium included in gross earnings above.

b. Identify the three methods of accounting for overtime premiums and explain the circumstances supporting the use of each method.

3-23. *CPA Problem—Cost of Goods Sold* The Sanyo Company, a wholesaler, budgeted the following sales for the indicated months:

	JUNE 19X1	JULY 19X1	AUGUST 19X1
Sales on account	$1,500,000	$1,600,000	$1,700,000
Cash sales	200,000	210,000	220,000
Total sales	$1,700,000	$1,810,000	$1,920,000

All merchandise is marked up to sell at its invoice cost plus 25 percent. Merchandise inventories at the beginning of each month are at 30 percent of that month's projected Cost of Goods Sold.

Cost of sales + Markup = Sales
c/s + 25% c/s = $1,700,000

$$\frac{1,700,000}{1.25} = \$1,360,000$$

REQUIRED:

1. The Cost of Goods Sold for the month of June 19X1 is anticipated to be:
   - a. $1,530,000
   - b. $1,402,500
   - c. $1,275,000
   - d. $1,190,000
   - e. None of the above

   $\left(\dfrac{1,920,000}{1.25}\right) \times .30$

2. Merchandise purchases for July 19X1 are anticipated to be: *c/s = I Beg. + Pur + I ending.*
   - a. $1,605,500
   - b. $1,474,400
   - c. $1,448,000
   - d. $1,382,250
   - e. None of the above

   1,448,000 = 4? 04+1,447,40?+$460,800

(AICPA adapted)

3-24. *Cost Classification*   Edwards Toy Company operates a production plant in western Kentucky. An administrative office building is adjacent to the plant; sales personnel and executive offices occupy this building. The company produces small toy items that are individually boxed, crated in large volume, and shipped to wholesalers.

REQUIRED: For each item listed below, indicate whether the cost is a manufacturing cost (product cost) or an element of selling and administrative expenses (period cost).

ITEMS TO BE CLASSIFIED	PRODUCT COST	PERIOD COST
a. Machinery repairs		
b. Advertising		
c. Patent amortization		
d. Direct labor		
e. Sales salaries		
f. Freight-out		
g. Small tools		
h. Plastics and metal		
i. Glue and paint		
j. Federal income taxes		
k. Depreciation—offices		
l. Fire insurance		
m. Boxes for products		
n. Shipping crates		
o. Property taxes		
p. Legal fees		
q. Obsolete inventory		
r. Power costs		
s. Audit fees		
t. Depreciation—plant		

3-25. *CPA Problem—Cost of Goods Sold*   The following inventory data relate to the Shirley Mistaken Company:

INVENTORIES	ENDING	BEGINNING
Finished goods	$95,000	$110,000
Work in process	80,000	70,000
Direct materials	95,000	90,000

Costs incurred during the period

Cost of goods available for sale	$684,000
Total manufacturing costs	584,000
Factory overhead	167,000
Direct materials used	193,000

REQUIRED:

1. Direct materials purchased during the year were:
   a. $213,000   d. $188,000
   b. $198,000   e. None of the above or not determinable
   c. $193,000   from the facts
2. Direct labor costs incurred during the period were:
   a. $250,000   d. $224,000
   b. $234,000   e. None of the above or not determinable
   c. $230,000   from the facts
3. Cost of Goods Sold during the period was:
   a. $614,000   d. $589,000
   b. $604,000   e. None of the above or not determinable
   c. $594,000   from the facts

(AICPA adapted)

3-26. *Components of Cost of Goods Sold*   Electronic calculators are the primary products of the M. & J. Heyd Electronics Company. The following information was taken from the company's adjusted trial balance for June 19X5:

Raw materials inventory—June 1, 19X5	$120,400
Work in process inventory—June 1, 19X5	235,650
Finished goods inventory—June 1, 19X5	174,210
Raw material purchases	742,900
Direct labor	372,500
Indirect materials	17,400
Repairs and maintenance	29,620
Heat, light, and power	72,825
Indirect labor	125,120
Supervisors' salaries	71,450
Raw materials inventory—June 30, 19X5	185,720
Work in process inventory—June 30, 19X5	247,300
Finished goods inventory—June 30, 19X5	164,780

REQUIRED: Compute the cost of materials used during June.

3-27. For question 3-26, determine the total manufacturing costs for June.

3-28. For question 3-26, derive the cost of goods manufactured in June.

3-29. For question 3-26, what is the total cost of goods sold during June?

3-30. *Cost Classification*   Costs may be classified differently depending on various circumstances. Direct labor, for instance, is both a direct cost and a variable cost. For each of the costs listed below, indicate if it is a direct (D) or indirect (I) manufacturing cost and whether it is a variable (V) or fixed (F) cost:

a. Screws for a chair
b. Electric power
c. Supervisor's salary
d. Transistors in a radio
e. Overtime premium
f. Factory insurance premium
g. Tool and die costs
h. Property taxes—factory
i. Depreciation—machinery
j. Machine operator's wages
k. Payroll taxes
l. Lubricating oils
m. Plating material
n. Labels for canning operation
o. Inspection costs
p. Tires on a new automobile
q. Material handling labor
r. Factory maintenance labor
s. Cost accountant's salary
t. Engineering labor

3-31. *Cost Estimates*   The power plant at Swyers, Inc., generates steam used by several producing departments. Natural gas is purchased from local utility firms at the rate of $.40 per 1,000 cubic feet. This rate applies to the first 10,000 cubic feet of gas used each month, but thereafter the rate is $.60 per 1,000 cubic feet. About 500 cubic feet of gas are needed to generate 1 MCF (1,000 cubic feet) of steam. Water is also purchased from a local utility. The rate per 100 gallons is $.10 for any usage under 1,000 gallons per month. The usage of 2,000 gallons or less per month, the rate is $.09 per 100 gallons. Similar rate decreases apply for each 1,000 additional gallons of monthly usage until the minimum cost of $.05 for 100 gallons is reached. Approximately 100 gallons of water are needed to produce 1 MCF of steam. Depreciation of power department equipment is $6,000 per month. Salaries and wages in the power department are approximated by $3,000 per month plus $.40 per 1,000 cubic feet of steam generated. Seasonal demands vary the monthly power department production from a low of 100,000 cubic feet of steam to a high of 500,000 cubic feet.

REQUIRED:
a. Prepare separate monthly cost behavior graphs for gas, water, depreciation, and salaries incurred by the power department. Let the vertical axis represent total monthly cost. For depreciation and salaries, the horizontal axis should represent steam generated. For gas and water, use quantities of these items to represent volume (MCF of gas and water in 100 gallons).

b. Prepare an estimate of the various costs to be incurred and their total if the power department produces the following amounts of steam in a given month: 100 MCF; 200 MCF; and 300 MCF.

3-32. *Statement of Cost of Goods Manufactured* The Hugo Corporation manufactures bathroom scales. Their fiscal accounting period ends on January 31. From the following information, prepare a Cost of Goods Manufactured statement for the year ended January 31, 19X8:

Raw materials inventory, Feb. 1, 19X7	$ 47,650
Work in process inventory, Feb. 1, 19X7	64,200
Finished goods inventory, Feb. 1, 19X7	28,745
Purchases of raw materials	254,810
Sales (net)	1,425,500
Direct labor	205,240
Indirect labor	79,050
Small tools	24,925
Fire insurance—factory	2,450
Supervision—factory	70,340
Purchase returns and allowances	3,820
Purchase discounts	4,970
Depreciation—machinery	37,770
Depreciation—factory building	52,500
Accounts payable, Jan. 31, 19X8	72,640
Raw materials inventory, Jan. 31, 19X8	42,920
Work in process inventory, Jan. 31, 19X8	67,840
Finished goods inventory, Jan. 31, 19X8	32,135

3-33. *CPA Problem—Labor Costs* An important function of cost accounting is accounting for labor costs and related fringe benefits.

REQUIRED:
a. Define direct labor and indirect labor.
b. Discuss three reasons for distinguishing between direct and indirect labor.
c. Give three costing methods of accounting for the premium costs of overtime direct labor. Under what circumstances would each method be appropriate?
d. Your newly acquired client, the Lilla-Tex Manufacturing Corporation, has in prior years followed the practice of accounting for employee's vacation pay as an operating expense. What changes would you suggest to the corporate management? List reasons to support your conclusions.

(AICPA adapted)

3-34. *Journal Entries—Periodic Inventory Method* Prepare all necessary journal entries for the following transactions of the Zero Corporation assuming that they use a periodic inventory method:

April 1—Raw materials priced at $137,500 were purchased on account, terms 3/10, N/30.

April 4—Raw materials purchased on April 1 were received.

April 8—Raw materials purchased on April 1 were paid for.

April 16—Payroll liability for period April 1–14 was recorded.

Gross wages	$13,500
Income taxes withheld	1,500
FICA taxes withheld	6% of gross earnings

April 17—Payroll checks were distributed to employees.

April 17—$1,700 of raw materials purchased on April 1 were returned to vendor.

April 18—Factory utilities bill of $1,925 was paid.

April 18—Machine costing $42,000 was purchased, paying $10,000 in cash and assuming a note for the difference.

April 19—Requisition was made for $17,000 of material from stores into production.

April 20—Units of production costing $75,000 were completed and transferred to Finished Goods inventory.

April 24—Large sales order was completed and shipped to customer: selling price, $105,000; cost, $90,000; terms 2/10, N/30.

April 29—Payment for order shipped on April 24 was received.

3-35. *Statement of Cost of Goods Manufactured and Sold*   The following data are from the accounting records of Campbell Company for the year ended December 31, 19X6:

INVENTORIES	JAN. 1, 19X6	DEC. 31, 19X6
Raw materials	$ 30,000	$40,000
Work in process	15,000	20,000
Finished goods	65,000	50,000

Raw material purchases	$200,000
Indirect material	15,000
Direct labor	180,000
Indirect labor	50,000
Sales salaries	90,000
Factory power and utilities	45,000
Advertising expenses	30,000
Depreciation—factory	50,000

Production in 19X6 was 15,000 units, involving 50,000 direct labor hours.

REQUIRED: Prepare a statement of Cost of Goods Manufactured and Sold.

3-36. *Systems for Material Control*   Siebel Enterprises uses the periodic inventory method of accounting for inventory costs in its general ledger. Perpetual inventory records are maintained in terms of unit data for control purposes. Purchase requisitions are initiated by the stores clerk. The purchasing officer reviews the requisitions and issues a purchase order to the appropriate supplier. When the ordered goods arrive, the receiving dock supervisor prepares a receiving report and forwards it to accounts payable. Vendor invoices received by mail are sent to the accounts payable clerk. Production supervisors fill out a materials requisition for all units taken out of the stockroom. Accurate physical inventories are taken at the close of each month, and raw material inventories are priced on a FIFO cost basis. A summary of the documents involved in this system is shown below in relation to employee functions. Numbers in parentheses indicate the sequence of procedures for each document.

	SHIPPING DOCK	PURCHASING DEPARTMENT	STOCK ROOM	PRODUCTION	ACCOUNTS PAYABLE
Purchase requisition (P/R)		(2) Approve P/R ←	(1) Prepare P/R		
Purchase order (P/O)		Prepare P/O			
Vendor invoice (V/O)					File V/O for payment
Receiving report (R/R)	(1) Prepare R/R →		(2) File copy of R/R →		(3) Compare V/O and R/R
Material requisition (M/R)			(2) File M/R ←	(1) Prepare M/R	

In recent months, it became apparent that the system for raw material accounting had several bad points. The stockroom clerk was unable to keep track of items ordered. Accordingly, some stock items were frequently out, while others were on hand in excess. Another problem is that invoices frequently were paid, only to learn that the materials were never ordered. Production supervisors usually request an excess amount of materials for each job to avoid the clerical problem of filling out another requisition if additional materials are needed. As a result, unused materials are located in various production areas. Some items are obsolete, and production personnel usually cannot recall the jobs for which excess materials were requested.

REQUIRED:

a. What changes in the present system are needed to remedy the situations described above?

b. How do factory organization and cost accounting have an impact on financial accounting?

3-37. *Physical Inventory Corrections* Pattillo Carton Company uses the periodic inventory method to account for its Finished Goods inventory. Items in inventory consist of crates and cartons of various sizes produced for stock purposes. On May 31, 19X7, a physical count of finished goods was supervised by plant superintendent W. Ross. After double counts and adjustments to secure an accurate count, inventory tags were pulled from the various stocks of cartons. Tags were sent to the accounting department for tabulation, pricing, and extension. The completed inventory tabulation appears below:

PATTILLO CARTON COMPANY
Physical inventory summary
May 31, 19X7

TAG No.	PRODUCT DESCRIPTION	COUNT	COST PER 100 ITEMS	AMOUNT		
001	057 stock cartons	~~10,000~~ 100,000	$ 5	$ ~~500~~ 5,000	+	4,500
002	728 cushion crates	30,000	~~8~~ 9	~~2,400~~ 2,700	+	300
003	139 lined cartons	16,000	10	~~160~~ 1,600	+	1,440
004	032 super cushions	28,000	5	14,000 1,400	−	12,600
873	407 folding cartons	25,000	$ 4	1,000		
			Grand total	$800,000		<6,360>

$793,640

In reviewing counts, pricing, and extensions, you have noted that tag 001 covered 100,000 stock cartons. The unit cost per 100 items of 728 cushion crates is $9. You also selected tags 003, 004, and 873 for review of extensions.

REQUIRED:

a. With the given data, test the accuracy of listed tag counts, pricing, and extensions. Note any errors you detect and determine the necessary dollar amount of any corrections.

b. What type of adjustment or correction is necessary if the inventory of $800,000 has already been recorded and the accounts have been closed?

{ Dr. P/E − 6,360
{ CR. F/G Inv. 6,360

c. What type of adjustment or correction is necessary if the May 31 inventory has not yet been recorded in the accounts?

Dr. Finished Goods Inv. − 793,640
Cr. I/C Summary 793,640

3-38. *Worksheet analysis* The unadjusted trial balance of Reeves Production Company at September 30, 19X7, has been tabulated on the following page for your analysis and completion:

REEVES PRODUCTION COMPANY
General ledger trial balance
September 30, 19X7

	TRIAL BALANCE	
LEDGER ACCOUNTS	Dr.	Cr.
Cash	$ 16,000	
Accounts receivable	30,000	
Raw material inventory	42,000	
Work in process inventory	17,400	
Finished goods inventory	52,700	
Production supplies and tools	8,600	
Land	200,000	
Factory building	400,000	
Factory equipment	250,000	
Sales warehouse	148,000	
Accumulated depreciation—building		$ 110,000
Accumulated depreciation—equipment		72,000
Accumulated depreciation—warehouse		35,000
Patents	27,300	
Accounts payable		19,800
Accrued property taxes		12,000
Income taxes payable		50,000
Common stock		460,000
Retained earnings		300,000
Sales		761,200
Raw material purchases	218,000	
Direct labor	114,000	
Indirect labor—factory	81,000	
Sales salaries	74,000	
Repairs and maintenance	38,000	
Sales commissions	17,200	
Freight-out on sales	10,300	
Insurance expense	50,000	
Rent expense	25,500	
	$1,820,000	$1,820,000

To complete the worksheet, you have assembled the following data:

Inventories,
Sept. 30, 19X7

		Depreciation expense	
Raw materials	$51,000	Building	$4,000
Work in process	22,500	Equipment	3,000
Finished goods	61,800	Warehouse	5,000

Accrued salaries		*Other data*	
Direct labor	$3,700	Tools and supplies, Sept. 30, 19X7	$6,200
Indirect labor	2,500	Patent amortization required	2,100
Sales salaries	1,800	Property tax accrual	2,500

The rent expense item is for administrative offices of the sales staff. Prepaid insurance on September 30 was $8,000. Both insurance expense and property taxes are allocated equally to manufacturing operations and to sales-administration. The estimated accrual for income taxes is $25,000.

REQUIRED:

a. Transfer the unadjusted trial balance to a worksheet and enter the necessary adjusting entry data.
b. Extend the adjusted trial balance amounts to columns for Manufacturing Statement, Income Statement, and Balance sheet.
c. Prepare a formal income statement and a statement of Cost of Goods Manufactured.
d. Prepare adjusting and closing entries to be posted to the general ledger.

3-39. *Comprehensive Worksheet Problem* All transactions for the period February 1, 19X8, to January 31, 19X9, have been posted to the general ledger of Fukuda's Fashions, Inc., a dress-making company. The trial balance as of January 31, 19X9, appeared as follows:

FUKUDA'S FASHIONS, INC.
Trial balance
January 31, 19X9

Cash	$ 4,680	
Accounts receivable	27,940	
Allowance for uncollectible accounts		$ 2,450
Raw materials inventory, Feb. 1, 19X8	9,870	
Work in process inventory, Feb. 1, 19X8	11,470	
Finished goods inventory, Feb. 1, 19X8	5,990	
Prepaid factory insurance	1,620	
Cutting tools	2,740	
Factory machinery	240,000	
Accumulated depreciation—machinery		40,000
Patterns and designs	22,400	
Common stock		100,000
Retained earnings, Feb. 1, 19X8		120,856
Sales		240,500
Raw material purchases	52,700	
Raw material discounts		1,054
Direct labor	36,220	
Factory rent	18,000	
Repairs and maintenance	2,960	
Heat, light, and power	3,110	
Factory supervision	12,000	
Sales commissions	26,500	
Administrative salaries	25,000	
Miscellaneous factory expenses	1,660	
	$504,860	$504,860

Year-end adjustment information:

1. Patterns and designs write-off	$4,700
2. Depreciation on machinery for year	20,000
3. Factory insurance expired	810
4. Cutting tools write-off	800
5. Accrued salaries and wages:	
Direct labor	1,400
Factory supervision	650
Administrative salaries	1,000
Sales commissions	1,100
6. Ending inventory balances:	
Raw materials	11,710
Work in process	10,890
Finished goods	7,425
7. Estimated that 10 percent of year-end accounts receivable balance is uncollectible	
8. Estimated federal income taxes	10,200

REQUIRED:

a. Prepare a twelve-column worksheet and enter the trial balance. Formulate year-end adjusting entries from information given, post entries to the worksheet, and compute adjusted trial balance amounts.

b. Extend all amounts to proper columns for statement of Cost of Goods Manufactured, Income Statement, and Balance Sheet.

c. Complete the worksheet and prepare formal financial statements, including statement of Cost of Goods Manufactured.

d. Prepare closing entries.

Chapter 4: Cost Concepts, Objectives, and Accounting Systems

This chapter presents a general structure of cost accounting concepts, objectives, classifications, and systems. Each of these elements has a special role in cost accounting theory and practice, and an appreciation of their interrelationships will simplify your study of concepts and techniques in later chapters.

Upon completion of this chapter, students should be able to:

1. Identify the concepts being implemented through product cost accounting procedures
2. Specify cost accounting objectives as they relate to different information needs of management
3. Distinguish different types of costs based upon the several characteristics they possess
4. Recognize the principal features of different cost accounting systems

Although a procedural approach is used in most chapters of this text, concepts and cost accounting theory are the principal subjects of this chapter. Accordingly, concepts are discussed in detail and are not distilled from illustrated procedures. For this reason, the following outline does not include explanations of each concept; instead, each concept and its use are explained in the chapter.

Basic cost concepts   (four elements that explain cost analysis procedures)

1. Cost composition
2. Cost attachment
3. Cost flow
4. Cost formulation

Cost accounting objectives   (three phases of management information needs)

1. Product costing
2. Planning and control
3. Decision information

Cost classification methods   (five different "types" of cost groups)

1. Object and function classification
2. Product and period costs
3. Direct and indirect costs
4. Fixed and variable costs
5. Differential (incremental) costs

Cost accounting systems   (based on four principal features)

1. Integration with financial accounting
2. Basis for accumulating costs
3. Objectivity of product costs
4. Inclusiveness of product costs

Chapter Summary

Management accounting is a technical discipline based on an organized body of concepts, objectives, terminology, and cost accounting systems. Each of these elements is discussed in this chapter to establish a conceptual framework for subjects presented in later chapters. To accomplish their role on the management team, accountants provide information for product costing, planning and control of recurring business activities, and analyses for special decisions. In developing required information, accountants must integrate cost concepts and related analysis techniques. Cost concepts are abstract ideas, generalizations, and theoretical considerations that guide the selection of techniques. Like all technical disciplines, cost accounting involves terminology that must be mastered.

Relationships among concepts, objectives, and techniques are important because they guide an accountant's thinking and job performance. Objectives are derived from basic information needs of management and specify the desired analysis or report to be developed. Concepts provide a general statement about how the end results (objectives) can be achieved. Techniques or procedures are the cost measurement and analysis methods that actually achieve the objectives. Given a particular objective, concepts guide the selection of techniques to be applied. To accomplish the product cost accounting objective, several alternative techniques can be applied. A given combination of these cost accounting procedures is called a cost accounting system.

BASIC COST CONCEPTS

In accounting, *cost* is defined as the price paid or the fair value of other consideration given to acquire resources or services. Cost is an economic sacrifice measured by the monetary value of an exchange transaction. Accounting traditionally has relied upon objective measures of historical cost as the primary basis for asset valuation. Familiar examples of this cost basis are the valuations of inventories, intangible assets, permanent investments, and fixed assets such as buildings, equipment, and land. Cost is the initial value at which these assets are recorded at the time of acquisition. Subsequent accounting for these acquisition costs involves several important cost concepts.

Cost concepts are abstract generalizations about particular cost characteristics and permissible accounting operations using cost data. In part, concepts are theoretical approaches to the following practical questions:

1. How may costs be grouped or accumulated?
2. How are costs assigned to products?

3. By what process do costs ultimately appear as expenses in the income statement?
4. What are the different types of costs, and how are these classifications used?

Each question suggests a procedure, mathematical operation, or manipulation of cost data. Cost concepts provide answers to each question and are the foundation of cost accounting procedures and practice.

Four concepts are identified below and matched with the accounting activities to which they relate. Each concept is then discussed separately.

ACCOUNTING ACTIVITY OR PROCEDURE	RELATED COST CONCEPT
1. Aggregating or accumulating costs	Cost composition
2. Determining unit costs	Cost attachment
3. Identifying periodic expenses	Cost flow
4. Using cost information	Cost formulation

Cost Composition Concept

Costs have the basic characteristic of being additive. Dollar measurements of cost may be added, subtracted, or divided as in the process of computing unit costs. Cost composition expresses the idea that costs of different types and from diverse origins may be accumulated to represent a new cost measure. In essence, several costs can be combined to create a new and different cost measure. In creating a new cost, the individual cost elements being combined lose their individual identity.

For example, the cost of a fixed asset is assumed to contain the following elements;

Invoice cost of machinery	$100,000
Freight and handling cost	2,000
Installation and setup costs	4,000
Cost of engineering test runs	5,000
Total cost of equipment	$111,000

As the fixed asset is used in production, a portion of the $111,000 aggregate cost will be allocated to each year of the equipment's useful life. If the asset has a ten-year useful life, then annual straight-line depreciation cost is $11,100 ($111,000 ÷ 10). The depreciation cost will be combined with other manufacturing costs, assigned to units of product, and eventually end up in the income statement as part of cost of goods sold. During this reclassification process, elements of the initial equipment cost assumed several new identities. Asset cost became depreciation cost; depreciation cost became a part of product unit cost and was classified as a current asset while attached to work in process or finished goods inventory; inventory costs finally became expenses when the goods were sold.

Accountants often refer to the "cost" of a product, operation, or service. They recognize, however, that the separate identity of individual cost elements is lost when several costs are accumulated, reclassified in the accounts, and ultimately charged to periodic operating expenses. The *cost composition concept* describes the overall process by which costs of different types and from diverse origins may be accumulated to represent a new cost measure.

Cost Attachment Concept
Computing the unit cost of products involves dividing accumulated production costs by a measure of completed output or production. A basic objective of any cost accounting system is to determine the unit cost of various products. Complex manufacturing operations have numerous processes that must be completed before raw materials emerge as finished products. As a practical matter, accounting systems are designed to measure and accumulate the costs related to each production process so that unit costs can be determined on a step-by-step basis.

The *cost attachment concept* is a fundamental idea that direct and indirect manufacturing costs are assigned to products as manufacturing operations are performed. Products may be thought of as porous blocks or sponges that emerge from production soaked with the various cost items that have been attached or applied to the units. The cost attachment concept is important because many costs cannot be assigned directly to individual units.

Indirect costs, such as all elements of manufacturing overhead, must be attached to specific products in order to permit unit cost measurement. The cost attachment concept explains the purpose of many cost accounting procedures. Overhead costs are accumulated, allocated among cost centers or departments, and in some systems attached to units on a formula basis using predetermined overhead rates. The cost attachment concept explains the need for all these procedures.

Cost Flow Concept
Measuring periodic expenses to be matched with revenues in the income statement involves two basic problems:

1. Identification of costs that have expired and are deductible from current period revenues
2. Identification of costs that properly may be deferred and assigned to revenues in future periods

Assets such as inventories, patents, machinery, and buildings represent future benefits and service potential. Costs attached to those assets will be charged to expenses when related benefits are received. Expenses are *expired costs* from which current period operations have benefited in some way. The *cost flow concept* expresses the general idea that all costs progress toward an ultimate destination as expenses in the income statement.

The operations of transforming costs into expenses are documented by cost flows between general ledger accounts. In cost accounting systems, material, labor, and overhead costs are accumulated and attached to products. Until the related products are sold, these attached costs are classified as inventory, which is an asset. When the products are sold, inventory costs (an asset) expire and are transferred to cost of goods sold (an expense).

In addition to the cost expiration idea, cost flow has another general meaning. In this view of cost flow, costs are accumulated and attached to products as various manufacturing operations take place. In parallel with physical production processes, costs are grouped and transferred within general ledger accounts to reflect those production activities. Cost attachment occurs within the Work in Process account as shown in Exhibit 4-1. Cost flow describes the movement of cost amounts from one account to another.

Cost flow also involves a time dimension in that inventory costs may be classified as an asset in one time period and assigned to the expense classifica-

EXHIBIT 4-1

COST FLOW PATTERN

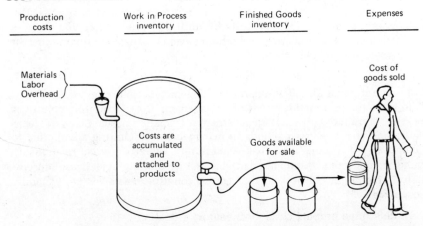

| Production costs | Work in Process inventory | Finished Goods inventory | Expenses |

tion in a later time period. The cost of units produced in 19X6 that remain unsold at year-end are classified as unexpired costs or assets; if the units are sold in 19X7, costs attached to the units are recognized as expenses for 19X7. The flow of costs is accomplished by journal entries that transfer cost amounts from one general ledger account to another.

The concepts of cost composition, cost attachment, and cost flow provide the general framework for product costing techniques. However, management has several other objectives that require cost information, such as planning routine operations, controlling operating efficiency, evaluating financial performance, and making choices in short- and long-run decisions. Each objective requires cost information tailored to the particular problem and circumstances.

Costs have several different characteristics, but reports to management for a specific purpose must emphasize the proper cost characteristics. Traditional product cost data used for inventory valuation purposes cannot satisfy all these information needs. Different types of costs must be formulated in response to management information requirements. The *cost formulation concept* indicates that costs must be identified, measured, and analyzed according to one or more particular cost characteristics. These characteristics identify different types of costs that are useful in satisfying particular management information needs.

Planning of routine operations requires an estimation of costs to be incurred at various activity levels. *Variability with volume* in this case is the important cost characteristic because management needs to know which costs will change as volume increases or decreases. Some costs, such as depreciation, tend to remain constant in total over wide ranges of activity. Other costs, such as materials and hourly labor costs, vary in total with the level of activity involved. Fixed costs and variable costs are thus formulated from these characteristics.

In the case of profit budgets, basic information needs key on cost variability; the cost formulation concept directs that fixed and variable costs be identified,

Cost Formulation Concept

measured, and analyzed to provide the basic information needed. Other cost characteristics will be identified and explained throughout this text. With practice, you will be able to analyze the information needs of a particular problem and select the types of costs to fulfill that need. First, however, the application of cost formulation and other concepts requires additional insight into cost accounting objectives.

COST ACCOUNTING OBJECTIVES

Cost accounting, as an integral part of management accounting, exists primarily to serve the information needs of management. Cost accounting objectives are derived from the different management information needs. Likewise, techniques and cost analysis methods in management accounting are applied to accomplish a particular objective. Accordingly, there is a direct relationship among management information needs, cost accounting objectives, and cost analysis techniques. The following cost accounting objectives are generally recognized:

1. To determine product costs for inventory valuation
2. To facilitate planning and control of recurring activities
3. To supply special analyses for short- and long-run decisions

Product Costing Objective

Cost accounting procedures historically were developed because of the need to determine product unit costs. Unit cost data have always been useful for pricing decisions, inventory valuation, and financial analysis by management. *Product costing* is the entire cycle of accumulating and assigning manufacturing costs to work in process and finished goods inventories. This cycle involves numerous procedures and alternative systems for recording journal entries, computing unit costs, and presenting reports to management. Concepts provide the foundations of these procedures, and the concepts of cost composition, cost attachment, and cost flow are relevant to accomplishing the product costing objective.

The most widely used basis for inventory valuation is historical cost. Alternative valuation bases include selling prices, net realizable value, and the lower of cost or market. If historical cost is used to value inventories, an inventory pricing method must be selected to implement the cost flow concept. This relationship between the cost flow concept and a pricing method has been emphasized in financial accounting:

Cost for inventory purposes may be determined under any one of several assumptions as to the flow of cost factors (such as first-in first-out, average, and last-in first-out); the major objective in selecting a method should be to choose the one which, under the circumstances, most clearly reflects periodic income.[1]

With the product costing objective, there is an important relationship between cost accounting and financial accounting. Cost accounting systems, concepts, and procedures influence the asset values and profits reported by business enterprises. Since unit costs, asset valuation, and profits are interrelated, cost accounting significantly affects financial accounting practice.

Planning and Control Objective

Another important cost accounting objective is the formulation of appropriate cost information to support all phases of planning and control by management.

[1] Committee on Accounting Procedure, AICPA, *Accounting Research Bulletin*, No. 43 (1961), 29.

The concept of cost formulation is related directly to this objective; the cost formulation concept holds that costs must be identified, measured, and analyzed according to the cost characteristics that are most useful for particular management activities and decisions. To apply the cost formulation concept, you must understand the process of planning and control and recognize the information requirements of each activity.

Planning function   In planning routine operations, management establishes goals, targets, and desired objectives for short-run performance. Coordination of sales, production, purchasing, inventories, and fixed asset utilization is necessary to attain the desired goals. The cost and profit effects of various management plans must be determined, and management accounting is responsible for this function. Budgeting or profit planning systems are devised to help plan and coordinate future business activities. In particular, these systems should be designed to:

1. Provide quantitative expressions of costs and revenues based upon forecasts, estimates, and projections
2. Distribute planning information throughout an organization to achieve coordination and to promote desired performance

In providing budget information for planning purposes, both quantitative and behavioral objectives must be satisfied. An objective of cost accounting is to produce cost analyses, reports, and futuristic information that satisfy both purposes.

Control function   The purpose of management control over recurring activities is to secure conformity between actual and planned results. Performance is evaluated, remedial measures are applied, and feedback provides the link for continuous planning and control cycles. By signaling the existence of both operating problems and superior performance, accounting information is essential to management control. Properly designed cost systems facilitate control by:

1. Comparing actual operating performance with estimates of what related costs and revenues should have been
2. Analyzing these comparisons, by areas of management responsibility, in a manner that promotes identity of cause and effect relationships
3. Supplying managers with measures of their individual performance and with reports upon performance of their subordinates

In the traditional sense, accounting information for control purposes is remedial in nature. Ideally, control should prevent undesirable results, but this ideal state is seldom achieved. Recurring activities are analyzed after the fact with accounting reports that compare actual costs and revenues with estimates of what these actual amounts should have been. The frequency and timing of this comparative analysis are critical control factors. Some processes and costs are analyzed daily and weekly, while others are reviewed on a monthly basis. Control results from whatever actions are prescribed by management. Cost information is an important element of management control, since measurement precedes evaluation and corrective action.

Decision Information Objective	An important purpose of internal accounting systems is to provide special analyses for short- and long-run decision alternatives of a nonrecurring nature. These decisions and related information requirements usually differ from analysis of recurring activities in that decision alternatives could:

1. Involve high cost commitments, such as buildings and equipment to be used for several years
2. Represent unique opportunities, such as the possibility of developing new products
3. Require selection of mutually exclusive factors, such as whether to retain or eliminate an unprofitable division

In general, planning and control of recurring activities occur within an environment that was established by many prior management decisions. Products are selected and promoted, and others are perhaps discontinued. Capacity must be provided to meet expected sales growth, and lease versus purchase decisions must be analyzed. Other problems of alternative choice must be continuously resolved during the course of a year's operations.

Appropriate cost information must be assembled to facilitate a wide variety of short- and long-run decisions. The concept of cost formulation is relevant to these matters in that no single type of cost information can satisfy all decision problems confronting management. Accordingly, different types of cost measures are formulated to correspond with the objectives of a problem situation and to ensure proper direction in selecting alternatives. The major cost accounting objectives are to supply useful information for product costing, for planning and control activities, and for special decisions. To satisfy each information need, you must understand the different types of costs and know the cost characteristics that are useful in particular problems.

COST CLASSIFICATION METHODS

The concept of cost formulation indicated that costs frequently must be identified, grouped, and analyzed by concentrating upon particular cost characteristics. Management accountants are confronted with a variety of problems having different information requirements. In providing competent analyses for these different problems, several classifications, based upon specific cost characteristics, have emerged.

The resulting cost classifications emphasize cost characteristics that are used to provide management with needed information. A given cost, such as annual depreciation of factory equipment, may fall into several cost classifications, depending upon the particular information need. The cost classification methods discussed below are pertinent to your understanding of cost accounting concepts, objectives, and procedures.

Object and Function Classification

All costs may be described initially by reference to the object acquired with particular expenditures. Costs are incurred to acquire materials, labor, equipment, or particular services such as insurance coverage or legal consultation. An *object classification* is used to structure a chart of accounts and to define the expenditures to be included under each account title. The object classification describes the basic nature of what is obtained in exchange for cash disbursements or liabilities incurred. Examples of costs classified by object include rent, equipment repairs, water, power, salaries, selling commissions, and taxes.

In measuring net income, expenses are usually classified by function in that operating expenses are grouped under the headings of manufacturing, selling, and administrative activities. A *functional classification* emphasizes the business purpose for which costs were incurred. Labor costs of different types—initially classified in the accounts by object—can be grouped according to whether manufacturing, selling, or administrative purposes were served by each cost. Manufacturing costs consist of materials, labor, and overhead charges directly or indirectly related to production activities. Selling and administrative charges may be recorded as expenses when incurred or charged to prepaid expense accounts such as Prepaid Insurance.

Functional and object classifications are simple, yet important. Costs are controlled by concentrating on individual costs in their *object* category. Manufacturing costs are the only costs that flow through the Work in Process inventory account. The functional classification is also important because it relates to the timing of cost flows into an expense category.

Cost and expense are technical accounting terms that have distinctly different meanings. *Costs* attach to assets such as inventories, equipment, and buildings that have future usefulness. These attached costs are reflected as assets in the balance sheet. As the usefulness of assets expires, the related costs become expenses that are properly deductible from revenues. *Expenses* are expired costs.

Product and Period Costs

Expiration of costs may occur immediately or over several time periods. For instance, administrative salaries and selling commissions are recognized as expenses when paid or accrued because related services and benefits have been received already. Cost expiration in this case is immediate. The cost of an administrative office building, however, expires gradually, and periodic depreciation charges measure the annual expense.

The expiration of manufacturing costs is caused by the sale of finished products. All manufacturing costs flow through Work in Process inventory and attach to units of product. These attached costs expire when related goods are ultimately sold. Cost of Goods Sold is a summary expense category that includes all expired manufacturing costs. Unexpired production costs appear in the balance sheet attached to assets; expired production costs appear in the income statement as Cost of Goods Sold.

Expired and unexpired manufacturing costs actually involve the cost flow concept. Two additional terms are integral parts of the cost flow concept—period cost and product cost. *Period cost* is the general description of all expenses reported in the income statement. If an expenditure on research programs is to be treated as a period cost, it will be recorded in an expense account. All expenses are period costs and appear in the income statement as charges against revenues of a particular accounting period.

Product costs are properly included as increases in manufacturing inventory accounts (Materials, Work in Process, or Finished Goods). All manufacturing costs are product costs, and this classification governs how the costs will be recorded initially in the accounts. Product costs are also called *inventoriable costs*, since they are admitted into the flow of costs through Work in Process inventory. When product costs expire, they become period costs and appear as expenses in the income statement.

Direct and Indirect Costs   In achieving the objectives of product costing and planning and control, management accountants are concerned with costs specifically related to products, to segments of a company, and to actions of particular managers. A basic problem in accounting is to determine the costs that are clearly applicable to a costing object, such as units of product, company segments, or some other area that is important to management.

Depending upon the nature of the costing object, costs must be traced either to their source or to their ultimate disposition. There are two sources, or points of origin, for costs: (1) actions, decisions, and authorization; and (2) a certain organizational unit, or segment, of company operations. The disposition or destination of manufacturing costs is their ultimate attachment to products. Thus, certain overhead costs will originate in operating a company power plant, but the disposition of these costs is allocation to production departments and attachment to products. There are two points of interest for these overhead costs: (1) point of origin in the power plant and (2) final destination as part of product unit costs.

Costs may be classified according to how they are associated with products, company segments, or managerial authority. Products, segments, and authority are the three aspects for which *ease of association* is important. We have already discussed direct material and direct labor. *Direct* indicates that the related material and labor costs are clearly traceable to particular product batches. Overhead is applied to products in some overall manner because these costs are indirect with respect to particular output units. In product costing, *direct* and *indirect* specify the ease with which costs are associated with output units.

Costs also may be direct or indirect with respect to particular company segments. A *segment* is a geographical division, a product line, an operating department, or any activity for which specifically associated costs must be determined. If a company has three separate divisions and a corporate headquarters group, each of these four segments will have costs related specifically to its activities. Division A will have salary payments, occupancy costs, and advertising outlays that are traceable to its operations. The direct, or traceable, costs of Division A can be identified specifically from source documents and accounting records. However, what portion of the corporate headquarters expenses should be assigned to Division A? Since the president's salary and other headquarters' expenditures benefit all three operating divisions, a specific part of these outlays cannot truthfully be associated with any division. The president's salary and similar charges are *joint costs* not specifically traceable to the various divisions. Joint costs can be associated with divisional operations only by allocation involving some formula or percentage approach.

In evaluating the performance of the Division A manager, the question arises about costs that the manager can control. In making decisions, ordering corrective measures, implementing plans, and approving certain expenditure requests, the manager controls or regulates a number of costs in the division and is responsible for them. Items subject to control are termed *controllable costs* and are used to evaluate the manager's performance. Other costs may be traceable to the division but controlled by decisions of higher-level company officials. If the company president contracts for advertising of Division A products, this cost is traceable to Division A but it is not controllable by its manager.

Direct costs, joint costs, and controllable costs must be identified and used in order to accomplish particular cost accounting objectives. Direct or joint costs in product costing have an effect on how the accounting system is designed. Direct cost information is used in many decision problems about eliminating product lines. And controllable costs are the basis of responsibility accounting used to evaluate management performance.

Cost variability with changes in input-output activity or volume must be determined for a number of planning and control reasons. Variability describes the behavior of costs as volume changes. *Fixed costs* remain constant in total regardless of changes in volume. *Variable costs* in total vary in proportion to volume changes.

Consider a manufacturing department having a potential volume range from 10,000 to 14,000 direct labor hours per month. Depreciation of equipment and supervisory salaries remain constant each month and therefore are fixed costs. In total, these two costs remain unchanged even though production volume might increase from 10,000 to 14,000 labor hours between successive months. If direct labor employees are paid five dollars per hour, the total direct labor cost depends entirely on volume and is a variable cost.

Cost behavior patterns refer to the fixed or variable characteristics of particular costs. These patterns must be determined before accurate cost estimates for budgeting can be assembled. Fixed-variable cost identity is essential to any problem in which the cost effects of management decision alternatives must be evaluated. In fact, knowledge of cost variability finds important applications in all three cost accounting objectives—product costing, planning and control, and special decision analyses. Analysis of cost behavior patterns will be covered in later chapters.

Decision making is basically a selection process. Alternative courses of action are evaluated, and the most desirable alternative is selected. Selection criteria may be increased profits or the least costly alternative. If management is evaluating alternatives X and Y, the decision analysis will eventually concentrate upon costs that differ between the two proposals. If alternative X is to continue a company's manual accounting procedures, the costs of this alternative must be determined. Alternative Y might be to lease computer facilities and eliminate certain manual procedures. A simplified decision analysis would involve these assumed cost comparisons:

TOTAL ANNUAL COST	KEEP MANUAL SYSTEMS	LEASE COMPUTER FACILITIES	BENEFIT (COST) OF LEASING
Clerical salaries	$20,000	-0-	$20,000
Controller's salary	18,000	$18,000	-0-
Computer rental	-0-	10,000	(10,000)
Accounting supplies	2,000	4,000	(2,000)
	$40,000	$32,000	$ 8,000

The $8,000 annual savings available through leasing is a *differential,* or *incremental, cost;* it is the difference between total costs to be incurred under each alternative. Note that the controller's salary remains the same in either case and is not a relevant cost factor in this analysis. The differential costs include $10,000 computer rental (a fixed cost); $20,000 of salaries (fixed costs); and $2,000 for supplies (a variable cost).

In preparing cost analysis to support management decisions, accountants capitalize upon many cost characteristics. One analysis may concentrate on cost variability, while another depends upon costs traceable to a specific division. Our manual/computer alternative requires identification of differential costs—a classification that includes costs that can be classified in many other ways.

Knowledge of cost characteristics and classifications is essential to an understanding of cost accounting. All basic management accounting objectives involve cost analysis. Cost analysis involves concepts, techniques, and specialized terminology. The cost accounting terms presented in this chapter will be repeated, but this early introduction should improve your grasp of concepts and techniques that are presented in more detail later.

COST ACCOUNTING SYSTEMS

Cost accounting applies to a broad range of business activities. In addition to its use for manufacturing, cost accounting is also used for distribution activities and in service industries such as banking, health care, professional sports, and hotel management. Distribution cost accounting is concerned with costs of promotion, physical distribution, alternative sales channels, and other phases of product marketing. Some problem applications in these areas are covered in this text. Cost accounting for service industries, however, is not extensively treated here because each industry has special characteristics, costs, and accounting objectives. This text is concerned primarily with cost accounting as it applies to firms that produce tangible products, but the same general concepts and procedures also apply to cost accounting in service industries.

Different systems and detailed procedures are applied in industry to account for manufacturing costs. Even between similar companies, cost systems will vary in the manner that material, labor, and overhead are accumulated and attached to products. Our cost characteristics and basic concepts apply to all these systems, however. Accordingly, it is desirable to explore the several alternatives that can be selected to implement the basic cost concepts. Cost accounting systems are designed by selecting alternative procedures within each of the following areas:

1. Integration with financial accounting
2. Basis for accumulating costs
3. Objectivity of product costs
4. Inclusiveness of product costs

Discussion of the possible alternatives under each area will reveal the extent to which accounting practices can vary among companies.

Integration with Financial Accounting

Many cost accounting systems are supplemental in their relation to financial accounting. In a *supplemental system*, the flow of manufacturing costs is not documented by general ledger control accounts, subsidiary ledgers for details, and perpetual inventories. Supplemental systems must rely on physical inventory counts to determine quantities of materials, work in process, and finished goods. Balance sheet and income statement information pertaining to product costs cannot be extracted from the general ledger accounts. Inventory quantities must be counted and unit costs determined before periodic financial statements can be assembled. A supplemental system is based on the periodic inventory method.

An *integrated system* remedies the lack of coordination between financial accounting and cost accounting. General ledger accounts with current balances are maintained for materials, work in process, and finished goods inventories. The physical flow of production and related manufacturing costs are recorded in accounts that are supported by subsidiary ledgers. Subsidiary ledgers summarize the input-output quantities and costs for the many types of raw materials and finished goods. The inventory accounts are perpetual in that on-hand balances and costs are readily available. An integrated cost system also maintains an updated general ledger account for Cost of Goods Sold. Financial statements may be prepared without the necessity of physical inventory counts.

Integrated systems are comparatively more sophisticated, more costly, and more conducive to cost control than supplemental systems. Important differences between supplemental and integrated cost systems concern the design of journals, ledgers, business documents, and daily accounting procedures.

A fundamental characteristic of any system is the basis for accumulating manufacturing costs. *Basis* in this case means the document, device, or approach used to accumulate costs that will be attached to products. Unit costs result from dividing properly accumulated costs by related unit output. Costs may be accumulated by individual *jobs* (job order cost system) or by manufacturing departments or *processes* (process cost system).

Basis for Accumulating Costs

A *job order cost system* has the unique feature of accumulating manufacturing costs separately for each product batch or job. A job order cost sheet is established for each job, and related costs are summarized on this document. In a printing plant, for example, a particular batch of books may be routed through only certain departments. The job routing will depend on special work to be performed, customer requirements, and paper quality. Material, labor, and overhead from each department performing work on the job are added to the job order cost sheet. When a job is completed, unit costs are determined by the total costs and quantities summarized in this document. Job order systems are best suited for products that must conform to customer specifications and that are unique in some way from other product batches. Machinery, printing, and furniture industries often meet these criteria.

In contrast, many products are of standard design and are manufactured continuously, such as paper, chemicals, fiber goods, and many oil products. With a *process cost system*, costs are accumulated by process or department. For each accounting period, accumulated costs within each department are divided by output to yield unit cost data. These unit cost amounts are then compiled for the numerous departments through which products pass. Cost of production reports are prepared for each process in the plant. These periodic reports provide the information needed to determine ultimate unit costs for finished products. A process cost system is best suited for standard products that are manufactured continuously.

Process cost systems and job order cost systems may be supplemental or integrated in relation to financial accounting. The relationship depends upon whether perpetual or periodic inventory records are used.

Objectivity of Product Costs

Our discussion to this point has assumed that actual or historical costs are accumulated and attached to products. For several reasons, cost estimates are desirable and are employed in cost systems. With *historical costs*, actual costs incurred for a period are used to compute product costs. One deviation from this approach is the use of overhead application rates. While direct material and direct labor can be computed promptly, it may be desirable to estimate the overhead element of product costs.

Overhead costs are often applied on the basis of machine hours or labor hours devoted to a product batch. In these cases, the overhead cost per machine hour or labor hour is usually based on annual budget data. Predetermined overhead rates are established by using budgetary data that are assembled before a year's operations actually begin.

Estimated overhead rates can be illustrated easily. Assume a single production plant that estimates total factory overhead for 19X2 at $500,000. The controller also estimates that in 19X2 the plant will operate a total of 200,000 direct labor hours. Our predetermined overhead rate to be used in 19X2 is

$$\text{overhead rate} = \frac{\text{estimated overhead}}{\text{estimated labor hours}} = \frac{\$500,000}{200,000} = \$2.50 \text{ per direct labor hour}$$

In a job order system, overhead would be applied to each job at the rate of $2.50 for every direct labor hour worked. Note that the $2.50 rate is estimated; actual costs and hours for 19X2 may differ from the anticipated amounts. With predetermined overhead rates, the overhead element of unit costs is an estimate. A system using actual material cost, actual labor cost, and estimated overhead is called a *normal cost system*. The distinctive feature is that the overhead cost element is not actual or historical in nature.

Complete departure from the objectivity of historical costing is found in a *standard cost system*. Standard costs are carefully predetermined estimates of what material, labor, and overhead costs should be on a per unit basis, given product specifications and desired operating efficiency. Standard costs may be developed from a review of past performance after adjustments to eliminate inefficiencies and to reflect expected future labor and material prices. Alternatively, engineering specifications and time-and-motion studies may yield more precise standards.

Standard costs are very useful in management control, but they also provide a basis for product costing. The important point is that standard costs involve estimates for all three elements of product costs—material, labor, and overhead; normal costs have one estimated element; and historical costs involve no estimated elements. You should recognize, however, that estimates are inherent in the accounting process. Even historical costs must rely upon the estimated useful lives of fixed assets to determine periodic depreciation charges.

Inclusiveness of Product Costs

So far we have seen that any two cost systems may differ regarding integration with financial accounting, basis for accumulating costs, and objectivity of product costs. One final variation concerns the inclusiveness of product costs. Previous discussion indicated that all manufacturing costs were to be accumulated and attached to products. This approach is traditional and is accepted by the accounting profession as an appropriate method for measuring net income and financial position. Under this traditional approach, all manufacturing costs—regardless of variability with volume—are assignable to products. This method is called *absorption costing*, or *full costing*, because fixed costs are absorbed by units produced. Supervisory salaries, depreciation, taxes, insurance, and utilities are fixed costs that remain relatively constant over wide ranges of production. As production levels increase, fixed costs per unit decrease as equal amounts of cost are spread over more units. Advocates of absorption costing contend that fixed manufacturing costs are properly assignable to units of production because production would be impossible without the benefits provided by these costs.

An alternative viewpoint is that only variable manufacturing costs should be attached to products. Fixed manufacturing costs are incurred to provide capacity to produce, and these costs will be incurred every year regardless of a plant's actual production volume. A *direct costing*, or *variable costing*, system operates as follows:

1. Only variable manufacturing costs are accumulated and attached to products.
2. Fixed manufacturing costs are recorded as expenses of the accounting period.

The inclusiveness of product costs depends upon whether absorption or direct costing is being applied. The arguments for each system are explored in later chapters. Because of the usefulness of fixed-variable cost information, direct or variable costing is generally more desirable for internal management accounting purposes.

Potential Cost Systems

Based upon the four principal features of cost systems discussed above, and the possible alternatives for each feature, there are twenty-four possible combinations of cost system characteristics. These basic features and alternatives are summarized in Exhibit 4-2.

To explain an existing cost system, select one method for applying each of the basic features listed in Exhibit 4-2. The procedures applied by a particular company could yield an (1) integrated (2) job order system using (3) historical (4) absorption costs. Another company might employ a (1) supplemental (2) process cost system with (3) standard (4) direct costs. While cost accounting procedures would differ between the two firms, the general cost accounting concepts (composition, attachment, flow, and formulation) are implemented within each system. Different procedures, however, may serve one of the cost

EXHIBIT 4-2
COST SYSTEM CHARACTERISTICS

PRINCIPAL FEATURE OR CHARACTERISTIC	ALTERNATIVE METHODS FOR APPLYING EACH FEATURE
1. Integration	Periodic inventories or perpetual inventories
2. Cost accumulation basis	Job order system or process system
3. Cost objectivity	Historical, normal, or standard costs
4. Cost inclusiveness	Absorption costing or direct costing

accounting objectives better than others. For instance, direct costing is generally acknowledged as better serving the planning and control needs of management.

FINAL NOTE   All concepts, objectives, cost definitions, and systems presented in the preceding sections will be expanded in later chapters. The material is introduced here to provide a conceptual foundation for cost accounting. As you learn to apply specific procedures, it is desirable that you also understand how different procedures and systems are related and reasons underlying the "how to do it" aspects of cost accounting.

Return now to the beginning of the chapter and review the highlights section before proceeding to the review questions and problems.

QUESTIONS

4-1. Define and illustrate the following terms and concepts:

a. Cost composition	j. Normal cost
b. Cost flow	k. Standard cost
c. Cost formulation	l. Absorption costing
d. Differential cost	m. Direct costing
e. Incremental cost	n. Perpetual inventory method
f. Object cost classification	o. Predetermined overhead rate
g. Function cost classification	p. Joint cost
h. Job order cost accounting	q. Cost behavior
i. Process cost accounting	r. Cost attachment

4-2. Define and state the purpose of cost accounting concepts.

4-3. Cost accounting objectives are derived from basic management information needs. In fulfilling these needs, indicate the importance of cost accounting concepts and cost accounting techniques.

4-4. What cost concept describes the overall process of forming new costs from a combination of several cost elements? Give an example of this cost concept.

4-5. "Manufacturing costs cling to units of productive output." What type of procedure is implied by this statement?

4-6. Prepaid advertising costs expire when the services are rendered. Does the same concept hold true for prepaid factory insurance? What about depreciation of factory building?

4-7. "Costs frequently must be identified, measured, and analyzed according to one or more particular cost characteristics." Identify the cost concept implied by this statement.

4-8. Traditional product cost data are developed primarily for inventory valuation purposes. Why will these costs not satisfy all management information needs regarding products?

4-9. Identify the three primary information needs of management and translate these into cost accounting objectives.

4-10. For product costing purposes, should a cost accounting system employ an object or a functional classification system? Give reasons to support your answer.

4-11. The salary of a departmental supervisor is a direct cost of that department. However, this same cost is considered to be indirect for product costing purposes. Explain this apparent lack of consistency.

4-12. If management is evaluating alternatives X and Y, why are differential costs important in the decision analysis?

4-13. Under what circumstances should a firm use a job order cost system?

4-14. What is the most important difference between absorption costing and direct costing?

4-15. There are twenty-four possible combinations of cost system characteristics. In reality, however, thousands of different cost accounting systems exist. Why are no two cost systems exactly alike?

EXERCISES

4-16. *Overhead Budgeting* A computer-controlled production process has been developed by Gregnolds, Inc., for use in its Atlanta plant. Overhead costs are being analyzed so that budgets can be developed. The fixed and variable characteristics of overhead costs are identified as follows:
   a. Production supplies—$.25 per unit produced
   b. Material handling—$.03 per unit plus $30,000 a year
   c. Repairs and maintenance—$.40 per unit plus $80,000 a year
   d. Depreciation expense—$200,000 a year
   e. Supervisory salaries—$10,000 for 50,000 units or less; $20,000 for production over 50,000 units but less than 100,000; $30,000 for production over 100,000 units but less than 150,000.
   f. Computer rental—$300 per hour for any usage of 100 hours or less; $250 per hour for usage in excess of 100 hours. Each unit of product requires approximately .002 hours of computer time.

   REQUIRED: Complete the schedule of overhead cost estimates on page 106 at potential annual production levels of 50,000 units; 100,000 units; and 150,000 units.

	ANNUAL PRODUCTION VOLUME IN UNITS		
ANNUAL OVERHEAD COST	50,000	100,000	150,000
Production supplies			
Material handling			
Repairs and maintenance			
Depreciation expense			
Supervisory salaries			
Computer rental			
Total overhead budget			

4-17. *Direct and Absorption Costing* In producing its special Marko ball-point pen during 19X2, Quill Products incurred $214,000 for direct material and $186,000 for direct labor. Factory overhead associated with this one product has been analyzed into fixed cost and variable cost classifications as follows:

	OVERHEAD COSTS FOR 19X2	
	Variable	Fixed
Tools and supplies	$115,000	-0-
Depreciation—equipment	-0-	$ 75,000
Repairs and maintenance	65,000	205,000
Property taxes	-0-	32,500
Salaries—supervisory	-0-	177,500
Labor—material handling	20,000	10,000
Total overhead	$200,000	$500,000

Production volume in 19X2 was 2,000,000 units.

REQUIRED:
a. Compute the absorption unit cost of production for 19X2.
b. Compute the unit product cost for 19X2 under direct costing.
c. Under direct costing, what is the accounting treatment of variable overhead? Fixed overhead?

4-18. *Differential Cost Analysis* The R. S. Larson Machine Tool Company is planning to lease a machine that will be used in manufacturing specialty tools. The Delta Omega Nu Leasing Company has provided the president, Mr. Larson, with information on two machines that will satisfy the monthly production requirements of the company, as follows:

1. *Augu machine:* A fully automatic machine requiring the services of only one operator. Monthly operating costs are $250. Monthly lease expense is $1,000.
2. *Stana machine:* A semiautomatic machine that requires the services of one operator and a setup staff of two. Monthly operating costs are $200. Monthly lease expense is $600.

Mr. Larson has gathered the following additional information:

Monthly machine operator's wages	$1,000
Monthly setup wages per person	$ 400
Depreciation on factory building	$1,200
Monthly capacity of each machine	400 units

REQUIRED: In good form, prepare a decision analysis for Mr. Larson that indicates the differential cost of the two alternatives. Which machine should he lease? net 350⁰⁰

4-19. *Predetermined Overhead Rates* A firm with perpetual inventory records uses predetermined overhead rates to assign overhead costs to production. In Department 43, estimated overhead costs for 19X9 consist of the following items:

COST FACTOR	19X9 ESTIMATE
Supervisory labor	$210,000
Tools and supplies	90,000
Depreciation of equipment	140,000
Factory rental—allocated	60,000
Machine supplies	20,000
Repairs and maintenance	80,000
Estimated overhead	$600,000

Based on budgeted production volume, estimated direct labor hours for 19X9 are 300,000, and the estimated direct labor cost is $1,200,000.

REQUIRED (Assume absorption costing is used):
a. Compute the predetermined overhead rate for 19X9 using direct labor hours as a volume base. 300,000 = $2⁰⁰ per hr.
b. Compute the predetermined overhead rate for 19X9 using direct labor cost as a volume base. 1,200,000 = .50 per $
c. Explain in general terms how the rate computed in part (a) will be used for cost accounting.

4-20. *Normal and Standard Costs* One plant at Ming Ho Products is used exclusively to produce pocket-sized electronic calculators. In prior years, the company has employed periodic inventory procedures with historical costing for Finished Goods inventories. All parts and components for the calculators are purchased from outside suppliers. In 19X7, the company produced 400,000 calculators and incurred actual production costs of $2,000,000 for direct materials; $3,200,000 for direct labor; and $4,800,000 for factory overhead. Budgeted overhead costs for 19X8 are $5,200,000, and the expected production volume is 400,000 units.

REQUIRED:
a. For 19X7, compute the average historical cost per unit, showing material, labor, and overhead unit costs that support the complete unit cost.

b. Given 19X8 budget data, compute the predetermined overhead rate that could be used for cost accounting purposes.

c. Assume that unit costs for direct material and direct labor in 19X7 are reasonable estimates of these cost factors under efficient operating conditions. Compute the standard unit cost of production that could be used to evaluate 19X8 operations.

PROBLEMS

4-21. *Cost System Description*   Watkin's Paper Company has retained you to analyze its accounting system for Finished Goods and Work in Process inventories. Your first step is to survey the existing system and document its characteristics and how it works. Physical inventories of finished goods and work in process are counted at the end of each month and summarized in working papers so that their total cost can be determined. Total inventory costs determined in this way are used in monthly closing entries to update the general ledger accounts for inventories.

Unit costs for each product have been carefully analyzed into components for material, labor, and overhead. Management generally looks upon these unit costs as amounts that should be incurred under efficient operating conditions. Physical quantities of different products are extended at these cost estimates to secure a total inventory value each month.

Manufacturing overhead costs are separated into fixed and variable elements for planning purposes, but all overhead costs are included in developing the unit cost data used for inventories. Watkin's Company produces a basic grade of paper in large volume that requires production phases in several different departments. Production is for inventory purposes, and customer orders are filled from available stock.

REQUIRED: Using appropriate cost accounting terminology, describe the cost accounting system you have surveyed in relation to (a) integration with financial accounting, (b) basis or device for accumulating production costs, (c) inclusiveness of unit product costs, and (d) objectivity of unit product costs.

4-22. *CPA Problem—Inventory Valuation*   Several, Inc., consists of several subsidiary companies, each of which is engaged in a separate business. One subsidiary, Art Company, deals in a single product. Inventory at December 31, 19X7, amounted to $240,000. Inventory quantities on December 31, 19X7, and December 31, 19X8, were 800,000 units and 1,000,000 units, respectively. Purchases made during 19X8 were:

	QUANTITY	COST
January	600,000	$210,000
April	500,000	200,000
September	1,000,000	246,000
November	400,000	160,000

REQUIRED:

a. Prepare a schedule computing the 19X8 ending inventory valuation at weighted average cost.

b. Assume that units are sold in the order they are purchased so that inventories usually consist of the items last purchased. Compute the ending inventory valuation for 19X8 if a FIFO (first-in, first-out) cost flow is assumed.

c. Compare the valuations computed in parts (a) and (b). What is the income statement effect of using FIFO instead of average cost?

(AICPA adapted)

4-23. *CPA Problem—Inventory Valuation* The Haag Company produces custom-made components for computers. When manufacturing an order, the company makes extra components primarily to replace defective items that customers can return within a one-year warranty period. Sometimes the company receives orders that can be filled from units still on hand from prior production runs. When scheduling an order, the number of extra units produced is the sum of (a) the estimated number of replacements and (b) the estimated number that can be sold to other customers. Material, labor, and overhead costs on each production order are charged to Cost of Goods Sold when the first customer's order is shipped. Extra components on hand are not assigned a value in the accounts. Perpetual inventory records are maintained.

REQUIRED:

a. Explain the meaning of Finished Goods inventory.

b. What are the possible balance sheet classifications for the extra components produced on each order?

c. What are the possible cost valuations related to your answers for part (b)?

d. Evaluate the propriety of the company's current accounting practice for "extra" units.

(AICPA adapted)

4-24. *Absorption Versus Direct Costing* James Galley, controller of Quad-Cities Industries, Inc., is in the process of preparing the corporation's first set of annual financial statements. Organized in late 19X6, the corporation began operations on January 2, 19X7, specializing in the production of home electric organs.

A summary of cost data for year 19X7 is presented below:

Variable costs and expenses per unit:	
Raw materials	$ 275
Direct labor	300
Variable factory overhead	150
Selling expenses (per unit sold)	100
Fixed costs and expenses:	
Factory overhead (approximately	
$175 per finished unit)	$190,000
General and administrative expenses	105,000
Selling expenses	75,000

During 19X7, the corporation manufactured 1,000 complete organs, selling 900 of them for $1,500 each. Raw material purchases for the year totaled $330,000, of which $27,500 worth of materials remained in Raw Materials inventory at year-end.

Work in Process inventory at December 31, 19X7, consists of 100 organs, with the average partial cost of completion of each being:

Raw materials	$275
Direct labor	250
Variable factory overhead	125
Fixed factory overhead	150
	$800

REQUIRED:
a. Prepare a statement of Cost of Goods Manufactured and Sold assuming the corporation follows the absorption costing system.
b. Prepare a statement of Cost of Goods Manufactured and Sold assuming the corporation uses a direct costing system.
c. What would be the corporation's net profit before taxes if: (1) The absorption costing system is used? (2) The direct costing system is used? Why is there a difference in the net profit figures?

4-25. *Unit Cost Determination*   Except for the analysis of inventories, Kon-stans Greek Curios, Inc., has entered all adjusting entry data in a columnar worksheet from which the adjusted trial balance appears below:

KONSTANS GREEK CURIOS, INC.
Adjusted trial balance
March 31, 19X3

	Dr.	Cr.
Cash	$ 8,000	
Accounts receivable	16,000	
Raw materials	–0–	
Work in process	–0–	
Finished goods	–0–	
Buildings and equipment	400,000	
Accumulated depreciation		$ 80,000
Accounts payable		9,000
Bonds payable		100,000
Common stock		150,000
Retained earnings		45,000
Sales		600,000
Raw material purchases (net)	240,000	
Direct labor	140,000	
Factory overhead—control	80,000	
Selling expense—control	43,000	
Administrative expense—control	57,000	
	$984,000	$984,000

The company produces a variety of Greek urns, all of which require the same processing time and input of materials. Because of a recent materials shortage, there were no beginning inventories for March 19X3. During March, 20,000 urns were sold at $30 each, and 2,000 units were on hand on March 31 as Finished Goods inventory. There was no Work in Process on March 31, but the ending Raw Materials inventory amounted to $20,000.

REQUIRED:

a. Compute the average unit cost of urn production during March. _$20⁰⁰
b. Determine the total cost of the finished goods inventory on March 31.
c. Enter the adjusted trial balance in a financial statement worksheet, enter appropriate cost amounts for inventories, and complete the worksheet. Use sets of columns for Cost of Goods Manufactured, Income Statement, and Balance Sheet. $440,000

Module Two

Traditional Approaches to Product Cost Accounting

THE FOUR CHAPTERS in Module One introduced management accounting, the design and operation of an actual manufacturing process, accounting for manufacturing costs with periodic inventory procedures, and a conceptual framework for cost accounting systems and analysis. Module Two discusses and illustrates the traditional approaches to product cost accounting. Traditional approaches include job order cost systems and process cost systems. Cost allocation and related accounting procedures for joint products and by-products are also presented.

Job order and process cost systems are traditional in that they commonly are found in practice and usually are presented in the first-semester cost course. Each chapter in Module Two assumes the use of absorption costing. Direct or variable costing is illustrated in Module Three in connection with cost behavior analysis and cost-volume-profit relationships.

Job order cost accounting is presented in Chapter 5 with emphasis on cost flow, perpetual inventory systems, source documents, underlying journal entries, and summary worksheet analysis. The computation and use of predetermined overhead rates also are illustrated. The section on predetermined overhead rates demonstrates methods to reapportion or allocate service department overhead costs. Service department overhead allocation is essential to an understanding of overhead accounting and formulation of predetermined overhead rates. The worksheet analysis in Appendix 5-A shows that job order cost accounting is an integral part of the financial accounting process.

Process cost accounting is illustrated in Chapters 6 and 7. Chapter 6 introduces the simpler forms of departmental cost of production reports, emphasizing basic concepts of equivalent production and unit cost determination. Chapter 7 then explores the more complex aspects of process costing, such as accounting for prior department costs, spoilage, and added units.

Module Two concludes with a chapter on allocation of joint production costs and by-product accounting procedures. In general, this four-chapter module presents the typical systems, procedures, and concepts applied to inventory valuation under absorption costing. An exposure to product cost accounting procedures will help students understand subsequent topics on cost analysis for planning, control, and decision making. For these purposes, cost analysis requires knowledge of cost accumulation procedures and an ability to recognize the limitations of unit costs computed for inventory valuation purposes.

Chapter 5: Overhead Accounting and Job Order Cost Systems

Determining product unit cost is a major goal of cost accounting. Two traditional cost accounting systems—job order costing and process costing—are designed to meet this objective. Specific production characteristics dictate which method is more appropriate for a particular manufacturing operation. Besides promoting product cost control, determination of product unit cost facilitates the pricing of orders and the valuation of ending Work in Process and Finished Goods inventories.

This chapter illustrates the concepts and procedures underlying a job order cost accounting system. It introduces the traditional cost accounting systems by comparing the characteristics of job order and process costing. Cost flow using perpetual inventories in the job order system is discussed, and there is a detailed analysis of manufacturing overhead rate computation and use. The complete job order cost system is then illustrated and analyzed.

Upon completion of this chapter, students should be able to:

1. Distinguish the characteristics of a job order cost system from those of a process cost system
2. Describe the flow of manufacturing costs through the general ledger accounts
3. Implement the concepts of manufacturing overhead rates and overhead application
4. Journalize all manufacturing cost transactions involving a job order cost system that uses the perpetual inventory method
5. Compute product unit costs and values for ending Work in Process and Finished Goods inventories

The following basic concepts are introduced in this chapter:

Job order cost system A product costing system applicable to unique or special order products in which material, labor, and manufacturing overhead costs are assigned to specific job orders or batches of products.

Perpetual inventory method A system of accounting in which inventory accounts are updated continuously for units purchased, manufactured, and sold.

Cost flow A process of cost reclassification through journal entry cost transfers between general ledger accounts to facilitate product costing and inventory valuation procedures.

Overhead rate An estimated factory overhead cost factor to be used for overhead cost assignment to specific units or jobs.

Overhead cost reapportionment The redistribution of supporting service department overhead costs to production departments for purposes of computing predetermined overhead rates.

Chapter Summary

Cost accounting systems differ because of production environment differences. Job order costing is used for special-order products or for the production and assembly of large units of output. Continuous or long-run production processes lend themselves to process costing.

Job order cost flow generally is based upon the perpetual inventory method. Unlike the periodic method, perpetual inventory account balances are updated continuously. When several Raw Materials, Work in Process and Finished Goods inventory accounts are maintained, control accounts are used for general ledger purposes and are supported by detailed subsidiary ledgers for specific inventory items.

Use of predetermined overhead rates is common in a job order cost system. To compute these rates, overhead costs are estimated for each department. Overhead costs of all supporting service departments then are reapportioned or allocated to production departments. Resulting departmental cost totals then are divided by a specific allocation base to compute predetermined departmental overhead rates. At period-end, actual overhead costs and overhead applied to products may differ. Under- or overapplied overhead usually is written off to Cost of Goods Sold.

A job order cost system requires the use of special transaction documents for materials usage and direct labor cost. Manufacturing costs assigned to particular jobs are accumulated on job order cost sheets. Cost summaries from these documents provide information for unit cost computations and inventory valuation.

JOB ORDER COSTING VERSUS PROCESS COSTING

Job order cost systems and process cost systems have the same basic objective: to develop product unit costs for purposes of inventory valuation and income determination. Unit costs applicable to products sold during the period represent Cost of Goods Sold, an important part of the income statement. Ending values for Work in Process and Finished Goods inventories are also computed with unit cost data. Beyond this common objective, the two systems differ in approach, structure, and detailed operation. The following definitions present the characteristics of each:

Job order cost system A product costing system applicable to unique or special-order products in which material, labor, and manufacturing overhead costs are assigned to specific job orders or batches of products. Unit cost is computed by dividing total manufacturing costs per job order by the number of good units produced.

Process cost system A product costing system applicable to production situations involving a large volume of similar products or a continuous production flow where manufacturing costs are accumulated by department or process rather than by batches of goods. Material, labor, and manufacturing overhead costs are assigned to cost centers (departments), and an average unit cost is computed by dividing total manufacturing costs in each department by its equivalent production for the period.

A closer look at each system will indicate several important differences. Job order and process costing are contrasted in the following summary:

1. *Cost accumulation*

   In a job order cost system, manufacturing costs are accumulated for particular jobs or batches of products.

   In a process cost system, manufacturing costs are accumulated for entire departments or processes, and no effort is made to find the cost of particular jobs or batches of products.

2. *Time-period consideration*

   In a job order cost system, costs are accumulated for particular quantities of goods without primary regard given to the period of time it takes to produce them.

   In a process cost system, costs are accumulated for specific departments, and production is measured for specific time periods.

3. *Work in Process inventory account(s)*

   In a job order cost system, *one* Work in Process (control) account is maintained and is supported by a subsidiary ledger comprised of job order cost sheets.

   In a process cost system, individual Work in Process accounts are established for *each* production department to accumulate manufacturing costs by process. The number of Work in Process accounts will vary depending on the number of production processes required.

These characteristics will become more apparent as each system is discussed. Job order costing, as presented in this chapter, is distinctly different from process costing procedures (discussed in Chapter 6). The nature of cost flow and perpetual inventory records serve to introduce job order cost accounting.

COST FLOW AND PERPETUAL INVENTORIES

With the periodic inventory method, material purchases are recorded in a separate account, and manufacturing costs are assigned initially to individual labor accounts and various overhead accounts in the general ledger. Inventory balances in the general ledger remain unchanged during the period. At period end, Raw Materials, Work in Process, and Finished Goods inventory accounts are adjusted to reflect the costs determined for ending balances of goods on hand. Under the *perpetual inventory method*, manufacturing costs are assigned initially to individual general ledger accounts, but Raw Materials, Work in Process, and Finished Goods inventory accounts are updated continuously as transactions and production occur. Manufacturing costs *flow* through the Work in Process inventory account as goods and services are used in the production process.

Cost Flow Network Job order costing is best accomplished by using the perpetual inventory method. The underlying cost flow is pictured in Exhibit 5-1. Labor and manufacturing overhead costs are incurred by (1) cash payments for goods and services, (2) incurrence of liabilities (accounts payable) for goods and services, (3) depreciation of fixed assets related to factory operations, and (4) expiration of prepaid expenses such as insurance. Initially, raw material purchase costs are charged to the Materials Inventory account; direct labor costs are charged to the Direct Labor account, and manufacturing overhead costs are charged to various overhead accounts.

When raw materials are requisitioned into production, the Raw Materials inventory account is reduced by the cost of materials issued, and the Work in Process account is increased by the same amount. Direct labor costs ultimately are charged to Work in Process inventory, and the Direct Labor account is credited for its current balance. Manufacturing overhead costs must be assigned to specific jobs by some indirect method. One procedure is to compute the ratio of total overhead costs for a period to direct labor costs. The portion of actual overhead costs assigned to each job is equal to this percentage times the labor cost of each job. A single journal entry is then prepared to debit Work in Process inventory and to credit each overhead account.

The use of predetermined overhead rates is a better method of assigning overhead costs to jobs. This approach is based on two important factors, an overhead rate and an application base. Although explained more fully later, a simple example will illustrate cost flow using a predetermined overhead rate.

EXHIBIT 5-1

PERPETUAL INVENTORY COST FLOW

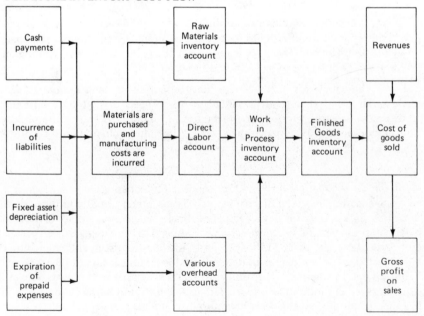

Based on past experience, the Alice Company estimates that $275,000 in manufacturing overhead costs will be incurred in 19X9. The controller selected direct labor dollars as the overhead application base and expects 19X9 direct labor costs to be $550,000. In this case, the predetermined overhead rate is 50 percent of direct labor cost ($275,000/$550,000 = 50 percent). Using this rate, a job order requiring $4,000 of direct labor will be charged $2,000 for manufacturing overhead costs ($4,000 × 50 percent). By using a predetermined overhead rate, the cost of completed jobs can be determined as they are finished rather than at the end of the month.

The Work in Process inventory account collects all costs of goods being manufactured. A subsidiary ledger is maintained to accumulate costs for specific job orders. When a particular job order is completed, the goods are transferred to the finished goods storage area, and its costs are transferred to the Finished Goods inventory account. To conclude the cost flow network, as finished goods are shipped to customers, the manufacturing costs associated with these goods are charged to the Cost of Goods Sold account.

Continuous cost flow through Raw Materials, Work in Process, and Finished Goods inventory accounts is a basic feature of the perpetual inventory method. Accounting journal entries are used to record this flow of manufacturing costs. Chapter 3 presented journal entries for the periodic inventory method. To show the accounting differences between periodic and perpetual inventory methods, the following comparative analysis of journal entries under both methods is presented, using the same transactions described in Chapter 3. Journal entries for the perpetual inventory case assume the use of predetermined overhead rates. In this system, Factory Overhead Control is the general ledger control account to which all actual overhead costs are charged. Overhead costs assigned to specific jobs are credited to Factory Overhead Applied. These two accounts are discussed further following the comparative journal entry presentation below:

Journal Entries for Perpetual Inventories

Comparative journal entry analysis

JOURNAL ENTRIES FOR PERIODIC INVENTORY METHOD	TRANSACTION DESCRIPTION	JOURNAL ENTRIES FOR PERPETUAL INVENTORY METHOD
Dr. Raw material purchases Cr. Accounts payable	1. Raw materials are purchased on account.	Dr. Raw materials inventory Cr. Accounts payable
Dr. Accounts payable Cr. Raw material purchase returns and allowances	2. Raw materials are returned to supplier because of damage or defect.	Dr. Accounts payable Cr. Raw materials inventory
Dr. Freight-in Cr. Accounts payable	3. Delivery costs on raw material purchases are paid by the supplier and billed to the company.	Dr. Raw materials inventory Cr. Accounts payable
Dr. Accounts payable Cr. Cash Cr. Purchase discounts	4. Paid account payable balance on raw materials purchased less cash discount.	Dr. Accounts payable Cr. Cash Cr. Raw materials inventory (for cash discount)
No entry required	5. Raw materials are requisitioned from storeroom and put into production.	Dr. Work in process inventory Cr. Raw materials inventory

(continued)

JOURNAL ENTRIES FOR PERIODIC INVENTORY METHOD	TRANSACTION DESCRIPTION	JOURNAL ENTRIES FOR PERPETUAL INVENTORY METHOD
No entry required	6. Excess raw materials requisitioned are returned to storeroom.	Dr. Raw materials inventory Cr. Work in process inventory

Dr. Direct labor
Dr. Indirect labor
Dr. Sales salaries
Dr. Administrative salaries
Cr.   Income taxes withheld
Cr.   FICA taxes payable
Cr.   Other deductions payable
Cr.   Accrued payroll
	7. Payroll for the period is recorded. Payroll costs are broken down into subtotals for direct labor, indirect labor, sales salaries, and administrative salaries.	Dr. Work in process inventory
		    (direct labor)
		Dr. Factory overhead control
		    (indirect labor)
		Dr. Sales salaries
		Dr. Administrative salaries
		Cr. Income taxes withheld
		Cr. FICA taxes payable
		Cr. Other deductions payable
		Cr. Accrued payroll

Dr. Accrued payroll Cr. Cash	8. Payroll is distributed.	Dr. Accrued payroll Cr. Cash

Dr. Specific manufacturing
    Expense accounts
    (heat, light, and power,
    property taxes, etc.)
Cr.   Cash
Cr.   Accumulated depreciation
    (only when depreciation is
    recorded during period.)
	9. Various manufacturing overhead costs are paid. (Depreciation may be included here or in adjusting journal entries.)	Dr. Factory overhead control
		Cr. Cash
		Cr. Accumulated depreciation
		    (only when depreciation
		    is recorded during period.)

No entry required	10. Overhead costs are applied to production.	Dr. Work in process inventory Cr. Factory overhead applied
No entry required	11. Units of production are completed and transferred to Finished Goods inventory.	Dr. Finished goods inventory Cr. Work in process inventory
Dr. Accounts receivable Cr. Sales	12. Finished goods are sold to customers on account.	Dr. Accounts receivable Cr. Sales Dr. Cost of goods sold Cr. Finished goods inventory
Dr. Sales returns and allowances Cr. Accounts receivable	13. Products shipped in error are returned by customers.	Dr. Sales returns and allowances Cr. Accounts receivable Dr. Finished goods inventory Cr. Cost of goods sold
Dr. Cash Dr. Sales discounts Cr. Accounts receivable	14. Payments are received from customers who have taken advantage of sales discounts.	Dr. Cash Dr. Sales discounts Cr. Accounts receivable

No entry required
  until books are closed
	15. Inventory is physically counted at year-end, priced, and totals for Raw Materials, Work in process, and Finished Goods are reported. These totals differ slightly from those shown in perpetual inventory balances.	Dr. Inventory losses
		Cr. Raw materials inventory
		Cr. Work in process inventory
		Cr. Finished goods inventory
		    (All inventory accounts
		    here are assumed to
		    have been over the amounts
		    shown by physical counts.)

Cost incurrence throughout an operating year normally is not constant. Some months involve more overhead costs than others. The variable portion of total manufacturing costs increases or decreases in proportion to production volume. For product costing purposes, variable costs do not distort unit cost computations, since variable costs are constant per unit. Fixed manufacturing costs do not vary proportionately with production volume. Some fixed costs are incurred monthly, while others are seasonal in nature and are incurred once or twice a year. Total manufacturing costs for months in which seasonal costs are incurred are high in comparison with production and prior-month cost totals. If actual overhead costs were assigned to products on a month-by-month basis, unit costs would be unreasonably high in months when seasonal fixed costs are incurred. One reason for using predetermined overhead rates is to avoid unit cost fluctuations caused by seasonal overhead costs.

The primary objective of predetermined overhead rates is to provide a reasonably constant unit cost that is free of distortions caused by seasonal cost fluctuations, changes in volume, or accounting methods. Instead of charging actual overhead to products, the basic approach is to develop an overhead application rate that closely approximates the amount of manufacturing overhead cost which should be charged to individual units of output. Predetermined overhead rates also make possible the immediate costing of job orders completed during the month.

As illustrated earlier, overhead rate determination has two primary components:

$$\frac{\text{total estimated manufacturing overhead costs}}{\text{application base}} = \text{predetermined overhead rate}$$

This overhead rate equation is a simplified illustration of a complex problem. The entire process for computing predetermined overhead rates involves the following sequence: (1) develop and accumulate overhead cost estimates, (2) reapportion service department costs to production departments, and (3) select an application base in each production department and compute overhead rates. A single, plantwide overhead rate is an alternative to using departmental rates. The following sections describe each phase of overhead rate computation.

Development and accumulation of cost estimates   Techniques for developing estimates of future overhead costs range from quick and intuitive approaches to methods involving highly sophisticated mathematical models. The approach described here is a compromise between the extremes. To provide realistic overhead rates, estimated costs should consider both past period costs and expected future production volume.

To illustrate this estimation procedure, assume Incobrables Fastener Company is in the process of estimating its manufacturing overhead costs for 19X9. The company specializes in one type of fastener, and the only required production processes are heading and roll threading. Finished products are bulk-packed, and customers perform plating and heat treating operations. The plant operates with three supporting service departments: repairs and maintenance, tool and die, and inspection. Production volume for 19X8 was 40,000M fasteners (M = thousands), and 42,000M are expected to be produced in 19X9. Actual

Predetermined Overhead Rate Determination

costs incurred in 19X8 are summarized in Exhibit 5-2. In addition to the 19X9 production volume estimate, the controller predicts that all costs will rise 10 percent in 19X9, except depreciation, property taxes, and fire insurance. All supporting service department costs are fixed in relation to volume. In the two production departments, variable costs fluctuate with production as measured in thousands of units.

Based on this information, estimated costs for 19X9 can be computed. Costs of depreciation, property taxes, and fire insurance will remain constant, and 19X8 costs in Exhibit 5-2 are carried over to the "estimated cost" column for 19X9. All other nonvariable costs are shown in the 19X9 columns as 19X8 amounts plus a 10 percent increase. Variable costs in the production departments require additional explanation. Indirect wages for the Roll Threading Department are estimated to be $6,930 for 19X9, which is more than a 10 percent increase. Variable costs in total are affected by changes in production volume and by price changes. Therefore, the computation of estimated 19X9 indirect wages for Roll Threading involves two steps:

Step 1: $6,000 ÷ 40,000M = $.15/M for 19X8 (unit variable cost)
Step 2: [$.15/M + (10%)($.15/M)] × 42,000M
$$= \$.165/M \times 42,000M = \underline{\$6,930} \text{ (19X9 estimate)}$$

The remaining variable cost estimates are computed using the same approach. Estimated 19X9 departmental overhead costs indicate the following totals for each department:

Repairs and maintenance	$ 27,520
Tool and die	61,600
Inspection	20,550
Heading	48,535
Roll threading	41,795
Estimated 19X9 manufacturing overhead	$200,000

EXHIBIT 5-2
DEPARTMENTAL OVERHEAD COST FORECAST, 19X9
INCOBRABLES FASTENER COMPANY

	Repairs and maintenance			Tool and die		
	19X8		19X9	19X8		19X9
Cost description	Actual cost	Var. rate	Estimated cost	Actual cost	Var. rate	Estimated cost
Indirect wages	$12,000		$13,200	$24,000		$26,400
Supervision	6,000		6,600	10,000		11,000
Indirect materials	1,500		1,650	9,000		9,900
Small tools	1,000		1,100	3,000		3,300
Heat and light	700		770	2,000		2,200
Depreciation—equipment	2,500		2,500	5,000		5,000
Property taxes	400		400	700		700
Factory rent	1,000		1,100	2,500		2,750
Fire insurance	200		200	350		350
	$25,300		$27,520	$56,550		$61,600

Reapportionment of supporting service department costs   Our goal is to compute an overhead rate that will apply total manufacturing overhead costs to units produced. The $200,000 estimated overhead costs for Incobrables Fastener Company includes costs of supporting service departments and production departments. Although production units do not flow through the supporting service departments, costs of such services are necessary to efficient operation of the production departments; service department overhead costs must be included in the overhead element of product unit cost.

In order to assign supporting service department costs to products, the estimated costs of service departments are allocated or reapportioned to production departments. When overhead rates are computed for each production department, these rates will include a portion of the service department overhead costs. In the case of Incobrables Fastener Company, estimated costs of Repairs and Maintenance Department ($27,520), Tool and Die Department ($61,600), and Inspection Department ($20,550) must be transferred to the Heading and Roll Threading Departments. This process is called *reapportionment of supporting service department costs*. The complete flow of overhead cost allocation among departments and its application to products are shown in Exhibit 5-3.

There are two generally recognized methods for reapportioning supporting service department costs to production departments, the *step method* and the *direct method*. The *step method* is employed when the services of one service department are used by other service departments as well. With the *direct method*, service department costs are allocated only to producing departments. Rather than using a single method for the entire reapportionment process, the ideal approach is to combine the methods; with this combined approach, the step method is used for service departments benefiting all departments, and the direct method is used for service departments that benefit only production departments. All three approaches will be illustrated after discussing alternative bases for overhead allocation.

Inspection			Heading			Roll threading		
19X8		19X9	19X8		19X9	19X8		19X9
Actual cost	*Var. rate*	*Estimated cost*	*Actual cost*	*Var. rate* *	*Estimated cost*	*Actual cost*	*Var. rate* *	*Estimated cost*
$10,000		$11,000	$ 8,000	.20	$ 9,240	$ 6,000	.15	$ 6,930
4,000		4,400	12,000		13,200	11,000		12,100
500		550	2,000	.05	2,310	1,700	.04	1,848
400		440	3,000	.075	3,465	2,400	.06	2,772
1,000		1,100	4,000	.10	4,620	4,000	.10	4,620
1,500		1,500	7,500		7,500	6,000		6,000
485		485	1,800		1,800	1,800		1,800
750		825	5,000		5,500	4,500		4,950
250		250	900		900	775		775
$18,885		$20,550	$44,200		$48,535	$38,175		$41,795

* Rate per thousand (M) units.

EXHIBIT 5-3

OVERHEAD COST ALLOCATION AND OVERHEAD APPLICATION

INCOBRABLES FASTENER COMPANY

	SUPPORTING SERVICE DEPARTMENTS			PRODUCTION DEPARTMENTS	
	Department 1	Department 2	Department 3	Department A	Department B
Estimated overhead costs	$XXXX	$XXXX	$XXXX	$ XXXXX	$ XXXXX
				XXX	XXX
Allocation of service department costs to production departments				XXX	XXX
				XXX	XXX
		Total estimated overhead		$XXXXXX	$XXXXXX
		÷ estimated volume		XXX	XXX
Application of overhead costs to products		Predetermined overhead rate		$ XX	$ XX*
		Product(s)			

* Example: If total estimated overhead of Department B is $2,000,000 and estimated volume is 500,000 direct labor hours, then the predetermined overhead rate for this department is $4 per direct labor hour. The overhead rate is used to assign overhead to specific jobs.

Before service department costs can be allocated, an allocation basis must be selected for each service department. The objective is to find the allocation base that best measures the causal or beneficial relationship between the department whose costs are being reapportioned and the departments receiving the service. Typical service departments and examples of bases that could be used for cost reapportionment purposes are listed below:

SUPPORTING SERVICE DEPARTMENT	POSSIBLE ALLOCATION BASES
Inspection (5, 9, 12)	1. Machine hours
Repairs and maintenance (13, 15)	2. Direct labor hours
Tool and die (1, 5, 15)	3. Direct labor dollars
Building and grounds (14)	4. Engineering hours
Engineering (4, 13, 15)	5. Units produced
Receiving and shipping (9, 10)	6. Number of requisitions
Power (1, 11)	7. Number of employees
Material handling (9, 12, 13)	8. Total labor hours
Cafeteria (7)	9. Units handled
Personnel (7, 12, 13)	10. Number of receiving tickets
Cost accounting (2, 3, 8)	11. Kilowatt, horsepower, or metered hours
Production control (1, 2, 8, 13)	12. Percentage of service costs
	13. Number of service requests
	14. Square footage
	15. Direct charges

In parentheses beside each department are the possible bases that could be used to reapportion its overhead costs. Although several different bases are appropriate for some departments, care should be exercised in finding the *one* that best expresses the causal or beneficial relationship involved. The objective in cost allocation is to recognize cause-and-effect relationships and to achieve reasonable accuracy.

Reapportionment of estimated service department overhead costs using the combined method (using both step and direct approaches) is shown in Exhibit 5-4. Estimated 19X9 overhead costs for each department of Incobrables Fastener Company are entered in the first line. Repairs and Maintenance Department costs benefit all departments, and its estimated costs are allocated to the other four departments. The selected basis for allocation is *number of service requests*. During the year, 2,752 service requests are anticipated (based on past experience), which results in reapportioned costs to other departments as follows:

DEPARTMENT	NUMBER OF REPAIR REQUESTS	PORTION OF TOTAL REQUESTS	×	COST TO BE ALLOCATED	=	REAPPORTIONED COST
Tool and die	640	640/2752	×	$27,520	=	$ 6,400
Inspection	145	145/2752	×	$27,520	=	$ 1,450
Heading	1,164	1,164/2752	×	$27,520	=	$11,640
Roll threading	803	803/2752	×	$27,520	=	$ 8,030
Total requests	2,752					$27,520

The reapportioned costs are added to the initial estimate of overhead costs for each of the remaining four departments. Of course, allocation would be easier in the Repairs and Maintenance example using $10 per request ($27,520/2,752); in this case, repair costs are allocated to the other departments at the $10 rate. Either approach yields the same results.

The remaining service departments in Exhibit 5-4 are reapportioned using the direct method. With this approach, service department costs are allocated only to the production departments. Number of machine hours is the allocation basis for Tool and Die costs, and number of units produced is used to allocate Inspection costs. The end result is that all estimated overhead costs have been accumulated in the production departments. As a procedural check, note that the total direct and reapportioned overhead costs in the producing departments must equal the total of the beginning balances in all departments.

Exhibit 5-5 illustrates supporting service department reapportionment using the step method. Notice that the Tool and Die column and the Inspection column have been reversed. For step method computations, service departments have to be arranged in *descending* order with regard to the number of other departments serviced. In this illustration, a convenient departmental sequence has been established so that no department receives a cost allocation after its cost total has been allocated to other departments. If this procedure were not used, department cost balances in the allocation worksheet would never go to zero unless a simultaneous equation approach was taken. The department serving the largest number of other departments is allocated first. For materiality reasons, actual practice seldom demands such a sophisticated approach. Allocation procedures in Exhibit 5-5 follow those explained in Exhibit 5-4 with number of service request, percentage of service costs, and number of machine hours being used as bases for cost reapportionment of

EXHIBIT 5-4
REAPPORTIONMENT OF SERVICE DEPARTMENT COSTS (COMBINED METHOD)
INCOBRABLES FASTENER COMPANY

BASES FOR REAPPORTIONMENT	SUPPORTING SERVICE DEPARTMENTS			PRODUCTION DEPARTMENTS		TOTALS
	Repairs and maintenance	Tool and die	Inspection	Heading	Roll threading	
Estimated 19X9 manufacturing overhead	$27,520	$61,600	$20,550	$48,535	$ 41,795	$200,000
Repairs and maintenance (number of service requests)	(27,520)	6,400	1,450	11,640	8,030	
	$ -0-	$68,000	$22,000			
Tool and die (number of machine hours)		(68,000)		27,200	40,800	
		$ -0-				
Inspection (number of units produced)			(22,000)	11,000	11,000	
			$ -0-	$98,375	$101,625	$200,000
Detail of bases selected:						
Number of service requests	640		145	1,164	803	2,752
Number of machine hours				54,400 (40%)	81,600 (60%)	136,000 (100%)
Number of units produced				42,000 M (50%)	42,000 M (50%)	42,000 M (same products through both departments)

EXHIBIT 5-5
REAPPORTIONMENT OF SERVICE DEPARTMENT COSTS (STEP METHOD)
INCOBRABLES FASTENER COMPANY

	SUPPORTING SERVICE DEPARTMENTS			PRODUCTION DEPARTMENTS		
BASES FOR REAPPORTIONMENT	Repairs and maintenance	Inspection	Tool and die	Heading	Roll threading	TOTALS
Estimated 19X9 manufacturing overhead	$27,520	$20,550	$61,600	$48,535	$ 41,795	$200,000
Repairs and maintenance (number of service requests)	(27,520) / $ -0-	1,450 / $22,000	6,400 / $68,000	11,640	8,030	
Inspection (percentage of service costs)		(22,000) / $ -0-	1,100 / $69,100	8,800	12,100	
Tool and die (number of machine hours)			(69,100) / $ -0-	27,640 / $96,615	41,460 / $103,385	$200,000
Detail of bases selected: Number of service requests		145	640	1,164	803	2,752 ($10 per request)
Percentage of service costs			5%	40%	55%	100%
Number of machine hours				54,400 (40%)	81,600 (60%)	136,000 (100%)

EXHIBIT 5-6
REAPPORTIONMENT OF SERVICE DEPARTMENT COSTS (DIRECT METHOD)
INCOBRABLES FASTENER COMPANY

	SUPPORTING SERVICE DEPARTMENTS			PRODUCTION DEPARTMENTS		
BASES FOR REAPPORTIONMENT	Repairs and maintenance	Tool and die	Inspection	Heading	Roll threading	TOTALS
Estimated 19X9 manufacturing overhead	$27,520	$61,600	$20,550	$48,535	$ 41,795	$200,000
Repairs and maintenance (number of service requests)	(27,520) $ -0-			16,292	11,228	
Tool and die (number of machine hours)		(61,600) $ -0-		24,640	36,960	
Inspection (number of units produced)			(20,550) $ -0-	10,275	10,275	
				$99,742	$100,258	$200,000
Detail of bases selected:						
Number of service requests				1,164 (59.2%)	803 (40.8%)	1,967 (100%)
Number of machine hours				54,400 (40%)	81,600 (60%)	136,000 (100%)
Number of units produced				42,000 M (50%)	42,000 M (50%)	42,000 M (same products through both departments)

Repairs and Maintenance, Inspection, and Tool and Die departments, respectively. The basis used for reapportioning Inspection costs is different since units of productive output are not applicable for allocation of one service department cost to another.

The direct method is presented in Exhibit 5-6. Service department costs are assigned only to the producing departments. Otherwise, the format and procedures are similar to those already described. The direct method is used most widely because it is the easiest method to apply and because differences among the results of each method are immaterial and do not warrant the additional effort. Amounts of estimated overhead costs assigned to the production departments under each allocation method are compared below:

	COMBINED METHOD	STEP METHOD	DIRECT METHOD	MAXIMUM DIFFERENCE
Heading department	$ 98,375	$ 96,615	$ 99,742	$3,127
Roll threading department	101,625	103,385	100,258	$3,127
	$200,000	$200,000	$200,000	

Under each method, $200,000 ultimately will be allocated to units of production. When the $3,127 difference is reduced to a per-unit amount (remember that 42,000M fasteners will be produced), it will have little effect on departmental unit costs.

Application bases for overhead rates   After estimating departmental overhead costs and reapportioning supporting service department costs to production departments, the third step in computing predetermined overhead rates is to select the bases upon which overhead rates will be applied in assigning overhead costs to products. Direct labor hours, machine hours, units produced, and direct labor cost are used to apply manufacturing overhead costs to products. Each potential application basis is described below.

1. *Direct labor hours*   One measure of overall production effort is the number of direct labor hours worked by each production department. Emphasis is placed on the *time* required for producing a product. Many manufacturing overhead costs such as depreciation, indirect labor, and manufacturing supplies are related to required production time. By using direct labor hours as the application basis, a time relationship connects overhead costs with units of output. The predetermined overhead rate is computed as follows:

$$\frac{\text{estimated departmental overhead costs}}{\text{estimated direct labor hours (DLH)}} = \begin{array}{l}\text{predetermined departmental}\\ \text{overhead rate}\end{array}$$

2. *Machine hours*   Machine hours is another time-related overhead application basis. It is appropriate when the production process is machinery dominated (capital intensive) and involves only a few employees. Under these circumstances, machine hours is a better measure of productive effort than direct labor hours. With machine hours as the application basis, overhead rates are expressed as $X per machine hour.

3. *Units produced*   When a single (or several very similar) product type is produced and required production operations are nearly identical, overhead

costs can be applied to products on the basis of total units produced. The units produced application basis is reasonable if each unit receives similar productive effort. With this application basis, the predetermined overhead rate is computed by dividing total estimated overhead costs by estimated units of production.

4. *Direct labor cost*   Direct labor cost is not as good a measure of productive effort as direct labor hours. Two workers may be equally efficient, but their pay rates may be different. If overhead is applied on direct labor cost basis, the jobs completed by higher-paid employees receive a larger share of overhead costs. Direct labor cost should be used as an allocation basis only when uniform pay rates exist for similar labor operations. Direct labor cost basis is used widely in practice because the amount of labor cost assignable to each job is readily available.

Combining the three steps described above, the complete predetermined overhead rate determination schedule for the Incobrables Fastener Company is presented in Exhibit 5-7. This analysis uses the direct method to reapportion supporting service department costs and direct labor hours as an application basis for computing the predetermined overhead rates.

The resulting departmental overhead rates in Exhibit 5-7 are $1.83 per direct labor hour in the Heading Department and $7.37 per direct labor hour in the Roll Threading Department. The roll threading rate is over four times as much as the rate in the heading operation. For every direct labor hour in the Heading Department, $1.83 of overhead costs will be added to a specific job. In Roll Threading, $7.37 of overhead cost will be assigned to a job for every direct labor hour worked. Note that these rates do not indicate that the Roll Threading Department is less efficient than the Heading Department. Efficiency is not measured by overhead rates. The large difference in departmental overhead rates is linked to the ratio between worker and machine:

	WORKER/MACHINE RATIO
Heading department:	
54,400 DLH/54,400 machine hours	1:1 ratio
Roll threading department:	
13,600 DLH/81,600 machine hours	1:6 ratio

The Roll Threading Department is a more *capital-intensive* operation (one employee runs six machines simultaneously) than is the Heading Department (one employee operates only one machine). Therefore, less labor hours are required, and the overhead rate in Roll Threading is comparatively higher.

Plantwide overhead rate   One additional point concerning predetermined overhead rate computation is important. Most of our analysis has centered on departmental overhead rates. Plantwide rates also are used in practice, and such a rate is shown in Exhibit 5-7. Using total manufacturing overhead and total estimated direct labor hours, the plantwide rate is $2.94 per direct labor hour. If this rate is used, $2.94 of overhead costs are added to a job for each DLH of production time. When compared with the departmental rates, the plantwide rate overstates the cost of heading operations and understates the cost of roll threading operations. Although easier to compute and use,

EXHIBIT 5-7
PREDETERMINED OVERHEAD RATE DETERMINATION SCHEDULE
INCOBRABLES FASTENER COMPANY

	SUPPORTING SERVICE DEPARTMENTS			PRODUCTION DEPARTMENTS		
	Repairs and maintenance	Tool and die	Inspection	Heading	Roll threading	TOTALS
Step 1: Estimated costs						
Indirect wages	$13,200	$26,400	$11,000	$ 9,240	$ 6,930	
Supervision	6,600	11,000	4,400	13,200	12,100	
Indirect materials	1,650	9,900	550	2,310	1,848	
Small tools	1,100	3,300	440	3,465	2,772	
Heat and light	770	2,200	1,100	4,620	4,620	
Equipment depreciation	2,500	5,000	1,500	7,500	6,000	
Property taxes	400	700	485	1,800	1,800	
Factory rent	1,100	2,750	825	5,500	4,950	
Fire insurance	200	350	250	900	775	
Estimated 19X9 manufacturing overhead	$27,520	$61,600	$20,550	$48,535	$ 41,795	$200,000
Step 2: Reapportionment of supporting service departments						
Repairs and maintenance (number of service requests)	(27,520) / $ -0-			16,292	11,228	
Tool and die (number of machine hours)		(61,600) / $ -0-		24,640	36,960	
Inspection (number of units produced)			(20,550) / $ -0-	10,275	10,275	
Total production department overhead				$99,742	$100,258	$200,000
Step 3: Overhead rate determination						
Direct labor hours				54,400 DLHs	13,600 DLHs	68,000 DLHs
Predetermined overhead rate per direct labor hour				$1.8335	$7.37191	$2.9412 ← Plantwide rate
Detail of reapportionment bases selected:						
Number of service requests				1,164 (59.2%)	803 (40.8%)	1,967 (100%)
Number of machine hours				54,400 (40%)	81,600 (60%)	136,000 (100%)
Number of units produced				42,000 M (50%)	42,000 M (50%)	42,000 M (same products through both departments)

plantwide overhead rates should be employed only when departmental rates are approximately equal or when every product follows an identical production sequence through all departments.

General Ledger Overhead Accounting

Under the periodic inventory method described in Chapter 3, overhead costs are classified by specific cost type, and a separate general ledger account is maintained for each element of overhead cost. If a company uses predetermined overhead rates and perpetual inventory procedures, it still is necessary to charge overhead costs to individual ledger accounts to account for actual overhead costs incurred.

With predetermined overhead rates, overhead costs are charged to specific jobs on an estimated basis. The amount of overhead applied to production must be accounted for in the general ledger. Systems with predetermined overhead rates generally require two general ledger overhead accounts, Factory Overhead Control, and Factory Overhead Applied. The term *control* in an account title means that the account balance is a summary of several similar costs. *Factory Overhead Control,* then, contains many types of *actual* manufacturing overhead costs. Each control account should be supported by a subsidiary ledger that contains individual cost balances. The subsidiary ledger for Factory Overhead Control is made up of a detailed listing of actual overhead costs charged to the general ledger control account.

Overhead cost flow using Factory Overhead Control and Factory Overhead Applied is diagrammed in Exhibit 5-8. Two types of journal entries are required to account for actual and applied overhead costs. One entry records actual costs incurred in the Factory Overhead Control account. In addition to recording actual overhead costs in the Factory Overhead Control account, individual amounts for factory rent, indirect labor, manufacturing supplies, property taxes, utilities, and other costs are posted to subsidiary ledger accounts. At any time, balances in the subsidiary ledger accounts in total must equal the balance in Factory Overhead Control. In the second type of entry, overhead costs applied to specific products or jobs are debited to Work in Process inventory and credited to *Factory Overhead Applied.* This journal entry records the assignment of overhead costs to products.

Recognition and Disposition of Over- or Underapplied Overhead Costs

Using predetermined overhead rates to apply overhead to Work in Process inventory does facilitate product costing. But, as shown in Exhibit 5-8, the amount of factory overhead costs applied usually does not equal the amount of actual overhead costs incurred during the period. Overhead rates are based on estimates, and some difference between actual overhead and applied overhead balances is to be expected. At the end of an accounting period, overhead costs may be overapplied or underapplied. These terms describe the net balance obtained when Factory Overhead Applied is compared with Factory Overhead Control. *Overapplied overhead* means that overhead costs assigned to goods worked on during the period exceed the actual overhead costs. *Underapplied overhead* means that overhead costs applied to production are less than actual overhead costs for the period. In either case, the amount of overhead costs charged to production is different from actual overhead costs, and an adjusting journal entry is required.

In Exhibit 5-8, overhead costs are underapplied by $300, since Factory Overhead Applied is less than Factory Overhead Control. Assuming these overhead balances are year-end amounts, an adjustment is needed to charge

EXHIBIT 5-8

GENERAL LEDGER OVERHEAD ACCOUNTING

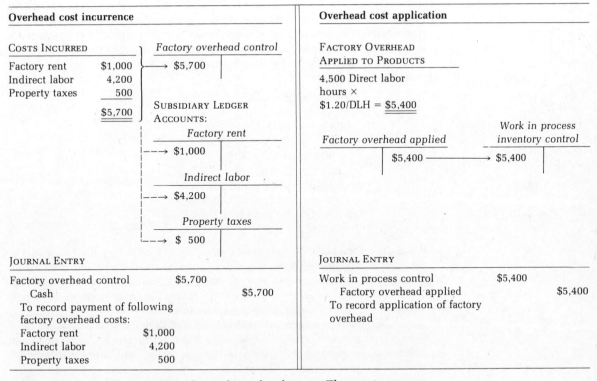

units produced with $300 of additional overhead costs. The most common accounting treatment is to close the two overhead accounts and charge (or credit) the difference to Cost of Goods Sold. The entry for our illustration would be:

Factory overhead applied	$5,400	
Cost of goods sold	300	
Factory overhead control		$5,700

To close out the applied and control
accounts and to charge difference
to Cost of Goods Sold

Closing the net balance of overhead accounts to Cost of Goods Sold is acceptable if most of the products worked on during the period were sold during the same period. Assume that during the year, work was performed on 100,000 units of product. At year-end, the status of these products is:

	Units	Percent
Completed and sold	95,000	95
Completed and in finished		
goods inventory	2,000	2
In process at period end	3,000	3
	100,000	100

Since all 100,000 units had overhead costs applied to them, the $300 amount of underapplied overhead could be allocated only to Cost of Goods Sold, as shown above, or to Cost of Goods Sold, Finished Goods inventory, and Work in Process inventory. Since 95 percent of the products have been sold, this percentage of underapplied overhead should be charged to Cost of Goods Sold. Using this approach, the $300 should be assigned to all units worked on during the year. Based on the percentage figures shown above, the entry to allocate underapplied overhead is:

Factory overhead applied	$5,400	
Cost of goods sold ($300 × .95)	285	
Finished goods inventory ($300 × .02)	6	
Work in process inventory ($300 × .03)	9	
Factory overhead control		$5,700

To close out the applied and control accounts and proportionately charge the difference to Cost of Goods Sold, Finished Goods, and Work in Process inventories

If the difference between overhead control and overhead applied accounts is significant at year-end, this allocation procedure should be followed when closing overhead accounts to prevent unit cost distortion. Allocation of the net overhead balance is an attempt to charge actual overhead costs to units produced during the period. The net balance can be allocated on the basis of total production costs or total overhead costs related to the unadjusted balances of Cost of Goods Sold, Finished Goods, and Work in Process. If the net overhead balance is immaterial, allocation is not necessary, and the entire amount should be closed to Cost of Goods Sold.

For monthly or other interim financial statements, the net overhead balance may be charged or credited to Cost of Goods Sold if the adjustment is not significant in amount. If significant, the net overhead balance should be deferred in interim statements. Deferral means that Factory Overhead Control and Factory Overhead Applied account balances will not be adjusted and closed until year-end.

THE JOB ORDER COST SYSTEM

The job order cost system is designed to compute the unit cost of each product manufactured by a company. Job order costing is useful when individual products or batches of similar products are easily identifiable. Examples include the production of a large machine, jet airplanes, or a special order of several products manufactured to customer specifications. The job order cost system requires special transaction documents that provide cost flow information used to prepare journal entries.

Transaction Documents

An information system, such as a job order cost system, requires documentation of transactions. Several documents are common to most accounting systems, including sales invoices, purchase requisitions, purchase orders, receiving reports, vendor invoices, and employee time cards. Additional documents support the flow of material, labor, and overhead costs in a job order cost system. Job time tickets, material requisitions, and job order cost sheets are the primary documents.

EXHIBIT 5-9

THE JOB TIME TICKET

			F	
CLOCK NO.	NAME		S	

ACCOUNT NO.	DETAIL		F	
			S	
MACH. NO. (ASSET)	TOOLING OR REPAIR ORDER NO.		F	
			S	
DO NOT WRITE BELOW THIS LINE			F	
TOTAL HOURS			S	
			F	
			S	
RAMAC	LABOR	BURDEN	TOT L&B	NAME	F	
					S	

ELCO TOOL AND SCREW CORPORATION — JOB TICKET

YR MO. CLOCK NO. ACC NO & DETAIL MACH. NO. TOOLING ORD. TOT HRS

0 0 0 0 0 0 0 0 0 0 0 0 0 0 0 0 0 0 0 0 0 0 0 0 0 0 0 0 0
1 1 1 1 1 1 1 1 1 1 1 1 1 1 1 1 1 1 1 1 1 1 1 1 1 1 1 1
2 2 2 2 2 2 2 2 2 2 2 2 2 2 2 2 2 2 2 2 2 2 2 2 2 2 2 2 2
3 3 3 3 3 3 3 3 3 3 3 3 3 3 3 3 3 3 3 3 3 3 3 3 3 3 3 3 3
4 4 4 4 4 4 4 4 4 4 4 4 4 4 4 4 4 4 4 4 4 4 4 4 4 4 4
5 5 5 5 5 5 5 5 5 5 5 5 5 5 5 5 5 5 5 5 5 5 5 5 5 5 5 5 5
6 6 6 6 6 6 6 6 6 6 6 6 6 6 6 6 6 6 6 6 6 6 6 6 6 6 6 6 6
7 7 7 7 7 7 7 7 7 7 7 7 7 7 7 7 7 7 7 7 7 7 7 7 7 7 7 7 7
8 8 8 8 8 8 8 8 8 8 8 8 8 8 8 8 8 8 8 8 8 8 8 8 8 8 8 8 8
9 9 9 9 9 9 9 9 9 9 9 9 9 9 9 9 9 9 9 9 9 9 9 9 9 9 9 9 9

PRINTED IN U.S.A.   UNIVAC   P-153356   767814-0

Job time tickets Besides daily time cards to indicate total hours worked, machine operators and other direct labor employees must complete job time tickets showing the hours they worked on particular jobs. This double accounting for hours worked has two purposes: (1) Time tickets that record total time per job can be used to verify total time shown on clock cards; and (2) labor hours and labor cost can be accumulated on a job order basis. Job time tickets provide the necessary information to determine labor cost for each job order. In many cases, labor information is also the basis for application of overhead costs. The sample job time ticket in Exhibit 5-9 has spaces for the employee's name, clock number, account number of job, machine identification, starting (S) and finishing (F) times, and total hours worked.

Materials requisition card When raw materials and supplies are issued from the storeroom into production, a properly authorized materials requisition card is required. In Chapter 3, a sample materials requisition form is shown in Exhibit 3-3. With a perpetual inventory system, the cost of materials issued is recorded on one copy of the requisition form. The forms are prenumbered documents that also identify the job number for which materials are being issued. Copies showing the cost of materials issued are used to prepare a materials requisition journal. This journal or listing provides the total credit entry to Materials inventory and the debit to Work in Process inventory. Cost of materials issued for specific jobs can be posted to job order cost sheets from the materials requisition journal or from separate copies of the costed material requisition forms.

Job order cost sheet The focal point of a job order cost system is the job order cost sheet. These documents accumulate the total costs assigned to each job, and they serve as the *subsidiary ledger* for the Work in Process inventory control account. A job order cost system uses only one Work in Process inventory account, and the details of costs assigned to each job are important. The job order cost sheet, shown in Exhibit 5-10, has spaces for job order number; customer and product information; material, labor, and overhead costs by department; a summary of costs; and unit cost data. When a job is completed, the job order cost sheet is removed from the subsidiary ledger file. A listing of completed job order cost sheets provides the cost total for a journal entry that debits Finished Goods inventory and credits Work in Process inventory.

Unit cost computation   For job order costing purposes, product unit cost is an average unit cost based on total job costs and number of units produced. From cost data compiled on job order cost sheets, product unit costs are computed as follows:

$$\frac{\text{total manufacturing costs for Job XY}}{\text{number of good units produced}} = \text{cost per unit on Job XY}$$

Unit cost data are used to measure Cost of Goods Sold and the cost of ending Finished Goods inventory.

EXHIBIT 5-10
JOB ORDER COST SHEET

LI-ABEL COMPANY	Date _____ Job order no. _____		
Produced for:	Product description _____		
Stock _____ No. _____	Selling price _____ Total cost _____		
Customer name_____	Cost per unit _____		
	Department 10	Department 20	Department 30
Materials: Date(s) Requisition no. Amount			
Labor: Date(s) Job time card no. Amount			
Overhead: Rate/Basis Amount applied			
Cost summary:	Dept. 10 Dept. 20 Dept. 30 Total		
Material Labor Overhead Total			
Units completed	_____ Date completed _____ Shipped _____		

A job order cost accounting system normally uses perpetual inventory procedures. General ledger control accounts are maintained for Raw Materials, Work in Process, and Finished Goods inventories and for Factory Overhead Control, which contains actual factory overhead costs. Supporting each of these four accounts is a separate subsidiary ledger. Instead of maintaining general ledger accounts for each overhead cost, the individual overhead accounts make up the subsidiary ledger for Factory Overhead Control. The Materials subsidiary ledger consists of individual stores cards for all raw materials and supplies; the Work in Process subsidiary ledger contains job order cost sheets for all jobs in process; and the subsidiary ledger for Finished Goods inventory is an itemized file of finished goods stock cards.

Job Order Transaction Analysis

Accounting procedures in a job order cost system are designed to maintain current balances in the various subsidiary ledgers and to record journal entries that update control account balances in the general ledger. If a company has a computerized accounting system, both accounting procedures could be performed daily. With manual or partially automated systems, subsidiary ledger balances are adjusted to reflect current balances, and month-end summary journal entries are prepared to update control account balances.

Exhibit 5-11 illustrates job order cost flows through both the general ledger and the subsidiary ledger accounts. Assume the Taggart Company has posted all daily transactions to subsidiary ledgers for September 19X8 and is ready to prepare month-end journal entries. As these entries are prepared and illustrated below, trace the posting of each entry to the general ledger accounts in Exhibit 5-11.

Raw material and supplies purchases   During September, the following items were purchased:

Factory supplies	$14,000
Material X25	24,000
Material Y42	14,000
Material Z39	11,000
Total	$63,000

Journal entry 1

Materials inventory control	$63,000	
Accounts payable		$63,000
To record raw material and supplies purchases for September		

Raw materials and supplies requisitioned   A summary of requisitions for direct materials ($45,000) and supplies ($11,000) during September follows:

Factory supplies	$11,000
Material X25	22,000
Material Y42	12,000
Material Z39	11,000
Total	$56,000

EXHIBIT 5-11
JOB ORDER COST FLOW—TAGGART COMPANY

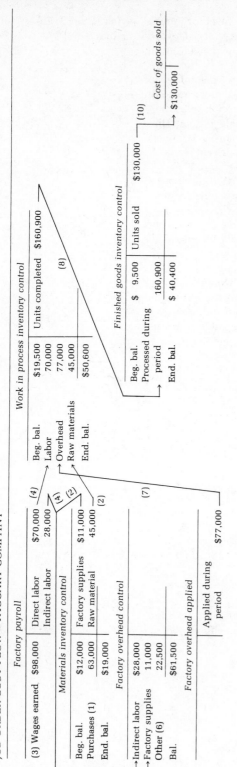

Factory payroll

(3) Wages earned $98,000	Direct labor	$70,000 (4)
	Indirect labor	28,000

Materials inventory control

Beg. bal.	$12,000	Factory supplies	$11,000 (2)
Purchases (1)	63,000	Raw material	45,000 (2)
End. bal.	$19,000		

Factory overhead control

Indirect labor	$28,000
Factory supplies	11,000
Other (6)	22,500
Bal.	$61,500

Factory overhead applied

	Applied during period $77,000

(4) (4) (2) (2) (7)

Work in process inventory control

Beg. bal.	$19,500	Units completed	$160,900 (8)
Labor	70,000		
Overhead	77,000		
Raw materials	45,000		
End. bal.	$50,600		

Finished goods inventory control

Beg. bal.	$ 9,500	Units sold	$130,000 (10)
Processed during period	160,900		
End. bal.	$ 40,400		

Cost of goods sold

$130,000	

Subsidiary ledgers

MATERIALS LEDGER

Factory supplies

Beg. bal.	$ 2,000	Used	$11,000
Purchases	14,000		
End. bal.	$ 5,000		

Material X25

Beg. bal.	$ 4,000	Used	$22,000
Purchases	24,000		
End. bal.	$ 6,000		

Material Y42

Beg. bal.	$ 3,000	Used	$12,000
Purchases	14,000		
End. bal.	$ 5,000		

Material Z39

Beg. bal.	$ 3,000	Used	$11,000
Purchases	11,000		
End. bal.	$ 3,000		

JOB ORDER COST SHEETS

Job 10A

Beg. bal.	$19,500
Direct labor	26,000
Factory overhead	28,600
Raw materials	6,200
Completed cost	$80,300

Job 20B

Direct labor	$26,000
Factory overhead	28,600
Raw materials	26,000
Completed cost	$80,600

Job 30C

Direct labor	$18,000
Factory overhead	19,800
Raw materials	12,800
End. bal.	$50,600

Labor time tickets

Overhead rate of 110% of direct labor cost

Raw material requisitions

FINISHED STOCK LEDGER

Product A

Beg. bal.	$ 2,000	Sold	$64,900
Mfg.	80,300		
End. bal.	$17,400		

Product B

Beg. bal.	–0–	Sold	$63,600
Mfg.	80,600		
End. bal.	$17,000		

Product C

Beg. bal.	$7,500	Sold	$1,500
Mfg.	–0–		
End. bal.	$6,000		

Note 1: Accounts Payable and other ledger accounts are not shown here.

Note 2: Cost flows are number-keyed to relate diagram to journal entries presented in text.

Journal entry 2

Work in process inventory control	$45,000	
Factory overhead control	11,000	
Materials inventory control		$56,000
To record raw materials and supplies		
requisitioned during September		

Monthly payroll accrual   Gross wages of $98,000 were earned by factory employees in September. Total gross wages and salaries of all employees were:

Machine operators	$ 70,000	(Factory payroll of $98,000)
Indirect factory employees	28,000	
Sales commissions	30,000	
Administrative salaries	44,000	
Total	$172,000	

From this total, $30,000 of federal income taxes, $12,000 of FICA taxes, $2,000 of United States government bonds, and $3,500 of union dues were withheld.

Journal entry 3

Factory payroll	$98,000	
Sales commissions	30,000	
Administrative salaries	44,000	
Federal income taxes withheld		$30,000
FICA taxes payable		12,000
United States government bonds withheld		2,000
Union dues payable		3,500
Accrued payroll		124,500
To record accrued payroll for September		

Journal entry 4

Work in process inventory control	$70,000	
Factory overhead control	28,000	
Factory payroll		$98,000
To reclassify factory payroll as direct		
and indirect labor and to distribute to		
control accounts		

The direct labor costs added to Jobs 10A, 20B, and 30C in Exhibit 5-11 are determined by a summary of job time tickets not presented here.

Journal entry 5

Accrued payroll	$124,500	
Cash		$124,500
To record payment of payroll		

Incurrence of factory overhead   In addition to indirect materials and indirect labor, the following overhead costs were incurred during September:

Factory rent	$14,000
Heat, light, and power	4,500
Repairs and maintenance	3,700
Property taxes	300
Total	$22,500

Note that Factory Overhead Control in Exhibit 5-11 shows $22,500 as other factory overhead costs. Additional overhead costs for machinery depreciation, fire insurance, and small-tool cost will be recognized by separate month-end adjusting journal entries. These adjusting entries are presented in Appendix 5-A which illustrates the preparation of financial statements for Taggart Company. Subsidiary ledger accounts for Factory Overhead Control are not shown in Exhibit 5-11.

Journal entry 6

Factory overhead control	$22,500	
Accounts payable		$22,500
To record overhead costs incurred during September		

Overhead application   A predetermined overhead rate equal to 110 percent of direct labor cost is used to apply factory overhead to units in process.

Journal entry 7

Work in process inventory control	$77,000	
Factory overhead applied		$77,000
To record overhead applied to units in process ($70,000 of direct labor × 110 percent)		

Cost of Goods Manufactured   During September, Jobs 10A ($80,300) and 20B ($80,600) were completed and transferred to the finished goods storeroom. The following entry recognizes cost of goods completed during the period as an addition to Finished Goods inventory.

Journal entry 8

Finished goods inventory control	$160,900	
Work in process inventory control		$160,900
To record jobs completed during September		

Cost of Goods Sold   Sales for September were $290,000, and the cost of products sold was:

Product A	$ 64,900
Product B	63,600
Product C	1,500
Total	$130,000

Journal entry 9

Accounts receivable	$290,000	
Sales		$290,000
To record September sales		

Journal entry 10

Cost of goods sold	$130,000	
Finished goods inventory control		$130,000
To record cost of products sold		

The fundamental operation of a job order cost system was illustrated by the preceding series of journal entries with related control accounts and subsidiary ledgers shown in Exhibit 5-11. The use of predetermined overhead rates is necessary if overhead costs are to be applied to products prior to the end of the accounting period. With job order costing, appropriate unit costs are computed for valuing ending inventory accounts and Cost of Goods Sold. This information is required to prepare financial statements for a manufacturing firm. Appendix 5-A illustrates the integration of job order costing with financial accounting in the preparation of financial statements.

When you have completed your review of the appendix, return to the beginning of the chapter and review the highlights section before proceeding to the review questions, exercises, and problems.

FINAL NOTE

APPENDIX 5-A: Financial Statements: Job Order Cost System with Perpetual Inventories

The last section of Chapter 5 illustrated the job order cost system used by Taggart Company. Journal entries were prepared for September transactions, and the flow of costs through general ledger accounts was shown in Exhibit 5-11. This appendix continues the Taggart Company case and illustrates the integration of job order costing with financial statement preparation.

After posting September journal entries, the trial balance for Taggart Company at September 30, 19X8, was prepared as shown in Exhibit 5-A-1. Subsidiary ledgers for inventories were reconciled with general ledger control accounts as follows:

	MATERIAL INVENTORY CONTROL	WORK IN PROCESS INVENTORY CONTROL		FINISHED GOODS INVENTORY CONTROL	
Factory supplies	$ 5,000	Job 30C	$50,600	Product A	$17,400
Material X25	6,000			Product B	17,000
Material Y42	5,000			Product C	6,000
Material Z39	3,000				
		Balance,		Balance,	
Balance, Sept. 30, 19X8	$19,000	Sept. 30, 19X8	$50,600	Sept. 30, 19X8	$40,400
Physical count of inventories at year-end revealed the following balances:	$18,700		$50,600		$40,400

In computing Cost of Goods Manufactured and Sold (formal statements), the following beginning inventory balances are required: Raw Materials, $12,000; Work in Process, $19,500; and Finished Goods, $9,500. Purchases of raw materials and supplies in September were $63,000, and issues to production were $56,000. Issues of $56,000 include $11,000 of factory supplies charged to Factory Overhead Control.

EXHIBIT 5-A-1

TAGGART COMPANY
Trial balance
September 30, 19X8

	Dr.	Cr.
Cash	$ 16,400	
Accounts receivable	290,000	
Materials inventory control	19,000	
Work in process inventory control	50,600	
Finished goods inventory control	40,400	
Prepaid factory insurance	25,200	
Small tools	26,400	
Factory machinery	720,000	
Accumulated depreciation—factory machinery		$ 120,000
Office equipment	94,000	
Accumulated depreciation—office equipment		42,600
Accounts payable		22,500
Income taxes withheld		30,000
FICA taxes payable		12,000
United States government bonds payable		2,000
Union dues payable		3,500
Common stock		750,000
Retained earnings, Aug. 31, 19X8		205,600
Sales		290,000
Cost of goods sold	130,000	
Factory overhead control	61,500	
Factory overhead applied		77,000
Sales commissions	30,000	
Administrative salaries	44,000	
Rent—office building	7,500	
Property taxes—office	200	
	$1,555,200	$1,555,200

The subsidiary ledger for overhead costs contains the following items supporting the September 30 unadjusted balance of Factory Overhead Control:

Indirect labor	$28,000
Factory supplies	11,000
Factory rent	14,000
Heat, light, and power	4,500
Repairs and maintenance	3,700
Property taxes	300
Balance, Sept. 30, 19X8	$61,500

After adjusting entries are posted, the difference between Factory Overhead Control and Factory Overhead Applied is closed to Cost of Goods Sold.
Information for September 30 adjusting entries includes:

1. Depreciation—factory machinery	$12,000
2. Depreciation—office equipment	4,400

3. Factory insurance expired in September		2,100
4. Small tools used in September		2,400
5. Estimated federal income taxes for the period		32,600

Given the Taggart Company trial balance and supplementary information, you are to prepare financial statements following the below requirements. You should then examine the solution that follows the stated requirements.

REQUIRED:

a. Enter the trial balance in a ten-column worksheet. Formulate month-end adjusting entries from information given, post entries to worksheet, and compute adjusted trial balance amounts.

b. Extend all adjusted trial balance amounts to proper columns for Income Statement and Balance Sheet and complete the worksheet.

c. Prepare formal financial statements, including statement of Cost of Goods Manufactured for September 19X8.

d. Prepare closing entries in general journal form.

SOLUTION:

Requirement (a):   Month-end adjusting journal entries

1. Factory overhead control	$12,000	
Accumulated depreciation—factory machinery		$12,000
To record depreciation on factory machinery for September		
2. Depreciation expense—office equipment	$ 4,400	
Accumulated depreciation—office equipment		$ 4,400
To record depreciation on office equipment for September		
3. Factory overhead control	$ 2,100	
Prepaid factory insurance		$ 2,100
To record factory insurance expired during month		
4. Factory overhead control	$ 2,400	
Small tools		$ 2,400
To record small tools used during period		
5. Inventory losses	$ 300	
Materials inventory control		$ 300
To record loss due to inventory shortage		
*6. Factory overhead applied	$77,000	
Cost of goods sold	1,000	
Factory overhead control		$78,000
To close out Factory Overhead Control and Applied accounts and charge Cost of Goods Sold with underapplied overhead for month		

* Factory overhead control, Sept. 30, 19X8	$61,500
Plus adjustments: (1) depreciation	12,000
(3) insurance	2,100
(4) small tools	2,400
Factory overhead control as adjusted	$78,000
Factory overhead applied	(77,000)
Underapplied factory overhead	$ 1,000

7. Federal income tax expense $32,600

     Federal income taxes payable $32,600

     To record estimated federal income taxes for September

Post above journal entries to Adjustments column on worksheet. See worksheet for requirements (a) and (b).

Requirements (a) and (b):   Worksheet

TAGGART COMPANY
Worksheet
September 30, 19X8

GENERAL LEDGER ACCOUNT TITLES	TRIAL BALANCE Dr.	TRIAL BALANCE Cr.	ADJUSTMENTS Dr.	ADJUSTMENTS Cr.
Cash	$ 16,400			
Accounts receivable	290,000			
Materials inventory control	19,000			(5) $ 300
Work in process inventory control	50,600			
Finished goods inventory control	40,400			
Prepaid factory insurance	25,200			(3) 2,100
Small tools	26,400			(4) 2,400
Factory machinery	720,000			
Accumulated depreciation—factory machinery		$120,000		(1) 12,000
Office equipment	94,000			
Accumulated depreciation—office equipment		42,600		(2) 4,400
Accounts payable		22,500		
Income taxes withheld		30,000		
FICA taxes payable		12,000		
United States government bonds payable		2,000		
Union dues payable		3,500		
Common stock		750,000		
Retained earnings		205,600		
Sales		290,000		
Cost of goods sold	130,000		(6) $ 1,000	
Factory overhead control	61,500		(1) 12,000 (3) 2,100 (4) 2,400	(6) 78,000
Factory overhead applied		77,000	(6) 77,000	
Sales commissions	30,000			
Administrative salaries	44,000			
Rent—office building	7,500			
Property taxes—office	200			
	$1,555,200	$1,555,200		
Depreciation expense—office equipment			(2) 4,400	
Inventory losses			(5) 300	
Federal income tax expense			(7) 32,600	
Federal income taxes payable				(7) 32,600
			$131,800	$131,800
Net income after taxes—to balance sheet				

	Adjusted Trial Balance		Income Statement		Balance Sheet	
	Dr.	Cr.	Dr.	Cr.	Dr.	Cr.
	$ 16,400				$ 16,400	
	290,000				290,000	
	18,700				18,700	
	50,600				50,600	
	40,400				40,400	
	23,100				23,100	
	24,000				24,000	
	720,000				720,000	
		$ 132,000				$ 132,000
	94,000				94,000	
		47,000				47,000
		22,500				22,500
		30,000				30,000
		12,000				12,000
		2,000				2,000
		3,500				3,500
		750,000				750,000
		205,600				205,600
		290,000		$290,000		
	131,000		$131,000			
	-0-					
		-0-				
	30,000		30,000			
	44,000		44,000			
	7,500		7,500			
	200		200			
	4,400		4,400			
	300		300			
	32,600		32,600			
		32,600				32,600
	$1,527,200	$1,527,200	$250,000	$290,000	$1,277,200	$1,237,200
			40,000			40,000
			$290,000	$290,000	$1,277,200	$1,277,200

Requirement (c):   *Cost of goods manufactured*

TAGGART COMPANY
Statement of cost of goods manufactured
For the month ended September 30, 19X8

Direct materials used:

Materials inventory control, Sept. 1, 19X8	$12,000	
Materials and supplies purchased	63,000	
Materials available for use	$75,000	
Materials inventory control, Sept. 30, 19X8	(18,700)	
Total usage plus inventory losses	$56,300	
Less: Inventory losses for September	(300)	
Supplies charged to overhead	(11,000)	
Direct materials used		$ 45,000
Direct labor		70,000
Factory overhead applied	$77,000	
Plus: Underapplied factory overhead	1,000	
Overhead costs charged to current production		78,000*
Total manufacturing costs		$193,000
Plus: Work in process inventory, Sept. 1, 19X8		19,500
Total costs in process during month		$212,500
Less: Work in process inventory, Sept. 30, 19X8		(50,600)
Cost of goods manufactured		$161,900

* The Work in Process inventory control account will disclose only the $77,000 of overhead costs applied to production in September. The $1,000 of underapplied overhead is added to Cost of Goods Sold as shown by adjusting entry 6 in the worksheet. In preparing a schedule to support the Cost of Goods Sold amount, underapplied overhead may be included in Cost of Goods Manufactured, as above, or added directly to Cost of Goods Sold.

Requirement (c): Balance sheet

TAGGART COMPANY
Balance sheet
September 30, 19X8

A-S-S-E-T-S

Current assets:			
Cash		$ 16,400	
Accounts receivable		290,000	
Materials inventory control		18,700	
Work in process inventory control		50,600	
Finished goods inventory control		40,400	
Prepaid factory insurance		23,100	
Small tools		24,000	
Total current assets			$ 463,200
Machinery and equipment:			
Factory machinery	$720,000		
Less: Accumulated depreciation	132,000	$588,000	
Office equipment	$ 94,000		
Less: Accumulated depreciation	47,000	47,000	
Total machinery and equipment			635,000
Total assets			$1,098,200

L-I-A-B-I-L-I-T-I-E-S   A-N-D   E-Q-U-I-T-Y

Liabilities:			
Current liabilities:			
Accounts payable		$ 22,500	
Income taxes withheld		30,000	
FICA taxes payable		12,000	
United States government bonds payable		2,000	
Union dues payable		3,500	
Federal income taxes payable		32,600	
Total liabilities			$ 102,600
Stockholders' equity:			
Common stock		$750,000	
Retained earnings, Sept. 1, 19X8	$205,600		
Net income, Sept. 19X8	40,000		
Retained earnings, Sept. 30, 19X8		245,600	
Total stockholders' equity			995,600
Total liabilities and equity			$1,098,200

Requirement (c): Income statement

TAGGART COMPANY
Income statement
For the month ended September 30, 19X8

Sales		$290,000
Less: Cost of goods sold:		
Finished goods inventory, Sept. 1, 19X8	$ 9,500	
Plus: Cost of goods manufactured (see schedule)	161,900	
Cost of goods available for sale	$171,400	
Less: Finished goods inventory, Sept. 30, 19X8	40,400	
Cost of goods sold		131,000
Gross profit		$159,000
Operating expenses:		
Sales commissions	$30,000	
Administrative salaries	44,000	
Rent—office building	7,500	
Property taxes—office	200	
Depreciation expense—office equipment	4,400	
Inventory losses	300	
Total operating expenses		86,400
Net income before taxes		$72,600
Federal income taxes		32,600
Net income		$40,000

Requirement (d): Closing entries

TAGGART COMPANY
Closing entries
September 30, 19X8

1. Income summary	$250,000	
Cost of goods sold		$131,000
Sales commissions		30,000
Administrative salaries		44,000
Rent—office building		7,500
Property taxes—office		200
Depreciation expense—office equipment		4,400
Inventory losses		300
Federal income tax expense		32,600
To close Cost of Goods Sold and operating expenses to Income Summary		
2. Sales	$290,000	
Income summary		$290,000
To close Sales to Income Summary		
3. Income summary	$40,000	
Retained earnings		$40,000
To close Income Summary account and transfer balance to Retained Earnings		

5-1. Define and illustrate the following concepts and terms:
   a. Job order cost accounting   e. Allocation base
   b. Cost reapportionment   f. Job time ticket
   c. Applied factory overhead   g. Materials requisition
   d. Over- or underapplied overhead   h. Job order cost sheet

5-2. What are the primary differences between job order and process cost accounting?

5-3. What is the relationship between the Work in Process inventory control account and job order cost sheets?

5-4. Identify the internal events or transactions that require journal entries under the perpetual inventory method but not under the periodic method.

5-5. List the advantages of using a perpetual method of accounting for inventories.

5-6. Delivery costs of raw materials are charged to Freight-in under a periodic inventory method and to Raw Materials inventory under the perpetual method. Explain why this procedural difference exists.

5-7. What are the primary objectives for using predetermined overhead rates in job order cost accounting?

5-8. Identify the components and explain the general formula used to compute a predetermined overhead rate.

5-9. "Estimated (projected) costs should be a function of both past period costs and expected future production volume." Explain this statement.

5-10. Why are estimated supporting service department costs reapportioned to production departments when computing predetermined overhead rates?

5-11. Distinguish the step method from the direct method of reapportioning supporting service department costs.

5-12. What are the factors to consider in selecting an allocation base for supporting service department overhead costs?

5-13. Direct labor hours and direct labor dollars are both bases used for overhead cost allocation. Under what circumstances would both bases produce the same results?

5-14. What is meant by capital-intensive and labor-intensive departments? What influence do such considerations have on the decision to use plant-wide or departmental overhead rates?

5-15. What are some possible causes for an overapplied overhead condition to exist for a particular accounting period?

5-16. Identify the accounting alternatives for disposing of over- or under-applied overhead balances at period-end. Under what circumstances is each appropriate?

EXERCISES

5-17. *Predetermined Overhead Rate* The following equation is the basis for computing a predetermined overhead rate:

$$\frac{\text{estimated departmental overhead cost}}{\text{basis for allocation}} = \text{predetermined overhead rate}$$

Outline the relevant accounting analyses required in determining the numerator and denominator of the equation.

5-18. *Product Costing* The C. M. Downes Company applies overhead to production orders using predetermined overhead rates. Overhead is applied on a labor cost basis for Department H and on a machine hour basis for Department K. The company made the following estimates for the year beginning January 1,19X9:

	DEPARTMENT H	DEPARTMENT K
Machine hours	1,000 hrs.	20,000 hrs.
Direct labor hours	16,000 hrs.	5,000 hrs.
Direct labor cost	$20,000	$10,000
Factory overhead cost	$30,000	$50,000

REQUIRED:

a. What predetermined overhead rate would be used in: Department H? Department K?

b. The cost sheet for Job 380 shows the following for the month of March:

	DEPARTMENT H	DEPARTMENT K
Materials cost	$2 per unit	$10 per unit
Direct labor cost	$5 per unit	$ 7 per unit
Direct labor hours	4 per unit	3 per unit
Machine hours	2 per unit	8 per unit

How much overhead cost should be applied to each product in job 380?

c. Assuming that Job 380 (as explained above) consists of fifty units of product, what is the total cost of the job?

5-19. *Overhead Application* Budgeted overhead costs and volume estimates of S. D. Reed Printing Company for 19X3 are given below:

19X3 Budget		19X3 Budget	
Variable overhead	$200,000	Direct labor hours	100,000
Fixed overhead	$160,000	Machine hours	320,000

REQUIRED:

a. Assume that the company uses absorption costing and that overhead is applied on the basis of direct labor hours. The overhead rate to be used in 19X3 is:
   1. $3.60   3. $1.60
   2. $2.00   4. $.50

b. Assume that the company uses variable costing and that overhead is applied on the basis of direct labor hours. The overhead rate to be used in 19X3 is:
   1. $3.60   3. $1.60
   2. $2.00   4. $.50

c. Assume that the company uses absorption costing and that fixed overhead is applied on the basis of machine hours, while variable overhead is applied on a direct labor hour basis. On December 31, 19X3, only Job 3102 remained incomplete. Direct materials of $10,000 and direct labor of $15,000 had been charged to the job. As of December 31, the job had required 5,000 direct labor hours and 8,000 machine hours. The balance of Work in Process inventory on December 31, 19X3, should be:
   1. $35,000   3. $29,000
   2. $39,000   4. $25,000

5-20. *Accounting for Overhead*   The following data were assembled from the accounting records of Galley Company for the year ended December 31, 19X2:

INVENTORIES	DEC. 31, 19X2	DEC. 31, 19X1
Materials and supplies	$40,000	$30,000
Work in process	20,000	15,000
Finished goods	50,000	65,000

Additional information for 19X2 included the following:

Materials and supplies purchased	$200,000
Issues of direct material	174,000
Direct labor	180,000
Indirect labor	51,000
Sales salaries	90,000
Factory power	45,000
Advertising expenses	33,000
Factory depreciation	48,000

Overhead was applied to production using a predetermined rate of $3 per direct labor hour. Production in 19X2 was 15,000 units, which involved 50,000 direct labor hours and 17,000 indirect labor hours.

REQUIRED:
a. Cost of Goods Manufactured in 19X2 is:
   1. $509,000   3. $514,000
   2. $499,000   4. $493,000
b. At year-end, the balance of Factory Overhead Applied is closed to Factory Overhead Incurred. After posting this entry for 19X2, the balance of Factory Overhead Incurred is:
   1. $6,000 overapplied   3. $10,000 underapplied
   2. $17,000 underapplied   4. $57,000 overapplied
c. Assume that factory overhead was overapplied by $50,000 and that the unadjusted balance of Cost of Goods Sold is $430,000. Overapplied factory overhead is to be allocated to Cost of Goods Sold, Work in Process, and Finished Goods. After this adjustment, the balance of Cost of Goods Sold is:
   1. $380,000   3. $430,000
   2. $473,000   4. $387,000

5-21. *Products and Cost Systems*   For each of the following products or industrial processes, indicate whether a job order system or process cost system would best apply to required cost accounting operations:
   a. Bricks for home construction
   b. Flour milling
   c. Textbook printing
   d. Aircraft production
   e. Theatre chairs
   f. Beer brewery
   g. Custom interoffice communications systems
   h. Potato chips
   i. Vegetable canning
   j. Special line of brief cases
   k. Men's shirts

PROBLEMS

5-22. *Journal Entry Analysis*   Record in general journal entry form the following transactions. Assume each transaction is independent unless you are asked to refer to a previous transaction. Also assume perpetual inventories.
   a. Raw materials were purchased—$5,000 on account.
   b. Twenty units of Job 352 were spoiled in the assembly department. Costs to point of spoilage for each unit were: material, $40; conversion costs, $5. The cause of the spoilage was traced to a recent change in the assembly technique that was specifically requested by the customer for Job 352. Assume these items have a sales value of $20 each; give the entry to transfer these units to an inventory account.
   c. Record the payroll liability if gross earnings amounted to $10,000; FICA at 4 percent on the full amount; income tax withheld, $1,000; union dues checked off, $150; and employees share of health insurance premium withheld, $200. Assume the full amount is factory pay, but only $8,200 can be traced conveniently to specific jobs.
   d. Distribute the payroll in part (c).
   e. Raw materials were issued for specific jobs—$3,000.

f. An additional $750 of material was issued to replace items costing the same amount that were spoiled or ruined on a job. This spoilage is generally expected on this job. (Record spoilage and issue.) *{add to Work in Process Inv.}*

g. A physical count of certain materials shows $500 more than the stores ledger card. Adjust stores to the physical inventory.

h. During May, the Work in Process account was charged with $1,000 of labor costs that represented overtime premium pay and that had not been anticipated. The entire $1,000 was traced to Job 742, and it was found that slow scheduling on the part of the company had caused the overtime. Make an entry to charge the overtime pay properly. *{factory overhead}*

i. Factory overhead was applied to completed jobs—$3,000.

j. Several jobs were completed and transferred to the finished goods warehouse. The total of the cost elements are: material, $5,000; labor, $6,000; and factory overhead, $12,000.

5-23. *Job Cost Analysis* Scanlan Printing Company uses a periodic inventory system to account for its custom printing operations. Since jobs are produced under contract specifications, the cost of completed jobs is immediately included in Cost of Goods Sold. Overhead is applied to each job at 200 percent of direct labor charges. Work in Process on November 1, 19X3, consisted of the following job analysis:

JOB	DIRECT MATERIALS	DIRECT LABOR	OVERHEAD APPLIED	TOTAL WORK IN PROCESS
B-743	$ 430	$207	$ 414	$1,051
P-418	125	150	300	575
D-017	350	250	500	1,100
A-411	240	175	350	765
	$1,145	$782	$1,564	$3,491

During November, a tabulation of materials requisition forms and labor time tickets showed costs for individual jobs as follows:

REQUISITION	JOB	MATERIAL COST	TIME TICKET	JOB	LABOR COST
1101	B-743	$ 120	2001	D-017	$ 190
1102	D-017	150	2002	A-411	270
1103	A-411	260	2003	D-017	100
1104	R-218	318	2004	B-743	348
1105	C-100	474	2005	P-418	200
1106	F-041	230	2006	C-100	350
1107	A-415	319	2007	R-218	420
1108	G-200	450	2008	F-041	230
1109	P-504	618	2009	P-504	429
1110	X-219	144	2010	X-219	237
1111	Z-001	275	2011	F-400	820
1112	F-400	760	2012	A-415	560
		$4,118	2013	G-200	910
					$5,064

On November 30, jobs Z-001, A-415, and X-219 were incomplete. All remaining jobs were delivered to customers at cash prices equal to 150 percent of assigned costs. Actual overhead costs for the month were $11,500.

REQUIRED:

a. Prepare a schedule to compute the Work in Process inventory balance at November 30.
b. Prepare a schedule to compute Cost of Goods Sold for November, including any amounts of underapplied or overapplied overhead.

5-24. *Reciprocal Overhead Allocation* Andborn Company is evaluating alternative methods of allocating service department overhead costs to producing departments for the purpose of computing predetermined overhead rates. The controller recommends that reciprocal relationships among service departments be recognized in the allocation. Accordingly, annual estimates of direct overhead costs for each department and percentage allocation figures were collected for your analysis:

ESTIMATED DIRECT ANNUAL OVERHEAD	SERVICE DEPARTMENTS			PRODUCTION DEPARTMENTS	
	MAINTENANCE	PERSONNEL	POWER	GRIND	POLISH
Salaries	$130,000	$ 80,000	$200,000	$300,000	$400,000
Supplies	70,000	10,000	100,000	60,000	70,000
Depreciation	50,000	10,000	100,000	90,000	30,000
Total	$250,000	$100,000	$400,000	$450,000	$500,000
Allocation basis for overhead of:					
Maintenance (M)	—	10%	30%	40%	20%
Personnel (P)	25%	—	15%	30%	30%
Power (PW)	20%	10%	—	20%	50%

REQUIRED: Let M, P, and PW represent the total costs to be allocated *from* the respective service departments. Formulate the three equations necessary to recognize reciprocal relationships among the service departments. (Hint: The equation for maintenance cost to be allocated is $M = 250,000 + .25P + .20PW$).

5-25. *Overhead Reapportionment* Haseman Company uses the step method of allocating service department overhead costs to its producing departments. There are three producing departments: Grinding, Polishing, and Finishing. The four service departments are to be allocated in the following order: (a) Plant Safety, (b) Repairs and Maintenance, (c) Building Service, and (d) Production Planning. Allocation base data and estimates of direct overhead costs to be incurred by each department in 19X8 are:

Department	Overhead	(1)* Labor Hours	(2)* Employees	(3)* Square Feet
Grinding	$100,000	3,000	100	3,000
Polishing	40,000	2,000	125	2,000
Finishing	60,000	4,000	75	2,000
Plant safety (2)	30,000	1,000	10	500
Repairs and maintenance (1)	50,000	5,000	80	1,500
Building service (3)	70,000	6,000	20	1,000
Production planning (1)	20,000	3,000	90	500
	$370,000			

* Allocation base for each department is shown by the number that corresponds with (1) labor hours, (2) employees, or (3) square feet.

REQUIRED: Prepare an overhead reapportionment schedule to allocate service department overhead costs in the described sequence.

5-26. *Cost of Goods Manufactured* The following data are from the accounting records of CAB Company for the year ended December 31, 19X1.

Inventories	Jan. 1, 19X1	Dec. 31, 19X1
Raw materials	$ 35,000	$25,000
Work in process	20,000	30,000
Finished goods	65,000	50,000

Raw materials purchases	$300,000
Direct labor	200,000
Indirect labor	50,000
Sales salaries	80,000
Factory power	55,000
Advertising expenses	30,000
Depreciation on factory	60,000
Income taxes	70,000
Equipment repairs	25,000

Overhead was applied to products using a predetermined overhead rate of $4 per direct labor hour. There were 50,000 direct labor hours in 19X1.

REQUIRED:
a. Prepare a statement of Cost of Goods Manufactured and Sold for 19X1.
b. Compare actual overhead costs with applied overhead and label the net balance appropriately.

5-27. *Journal Entry Analysis* Prepare entries in general journal form for the following transactions of the Pearson Manufacturing Company. This concern records all invoices at net (less discount assuming that all cash discounts will be taken), maintains perpetual inventory records, and uses a separate Work in Process account for material, labor, and overhead.

 a. Record factory payroll liability. Total earnings amount to $10,000; income tax withheld $1,000; union dues withheld $100; FICA tax at an assumed 5 percent rate on all earnings.

 b. Purchased $100,000 of materials and supplies on account; terms 1/10, N/30.

 c. Paid the payroll recorded in part (a) and entered the employer's payroll tax on the books. Federal unemployment rate is 0.4 percent, and the state rate is 2 percent.

 d. Received a vendor's credit memo for $10,000 for purchases returned to him for the order in part (b). Paid balance of account payable in part (b) before discount period had ended.

 e. Distribute payroll cost recorded in part (a); $8,000 can conveniently be traced to specific jobs. Included in the $8,000 is a $200 charge for additional labor required on Job 146 because the customer changed specifications after the job was started.

 f. Record a materials requisition of $20,000. Of these materials, $3,000 are low unit-value items and are not charged to any particular job order.

 g. Received and paid an invoice of $500 for repairs to factory equipment.

 h. Applied factory overhead of $10,000 to completed jobs.

 i. Sent a check for $600 to the union's treasurer for dues withheld from employee's pay.

 j. Received and paid an invoice for an item of new factory equipment costing $200,000.

 k. Billed a customer $3,000 for an order that cost $2,000 to produce.

 l. Material worth $100, requisitioned and charged to Job 160, was not needed to complete the job; instead of being returned to the storeroom, the material was moved to Job 165 to replace material damaged by "horseplay" and carelessness of two employees.

 m. A job cost sheet shows 400 units completed with the following costs: material $400; labor $1,200; overhead $800. Of the 400 units, 10 are imperfect and will be sold as "seconds" at $2 each. Show with journal entries, two methods of transferring these 10 defective units to an inventory account.

 n. Several jobs are completed and transferred to finished goods warehouse. The totals of the cost elements are: materials, $8,000; labor, $5,000; and overhead, $7,000.

 o. Close out the Applied Factory Overhead account. Assume it now has a $70,000 balance.

 p. Assume that the total actual overhead is $75,000. Considering your entry in part (o), close the under- or overapplied overhead. (Clear or close the Factory Overhead Control account.)

5-28. *CPA Problem—Job Order Cost Analysis* The president of Small Corporation has requested your assistance in reconstructing a summary of factory operations during April for a job order cost system that has been maintained inadequately since the bookkeeper left for another position early in the month.

The corporation's cost system includes a general ledger and a factory production ledger with reciprocal control accounts. A trial balance of the factory production ledger at April 1, 19X6, showed the following:

	DEBITS	CREDITS
Raw materials	$30,000	
Store supplies inventory	10,000	
Work in process	20,000	
General ledger control		$60,000
	$60,000	$60,000

After reviewing the work done up to April 1, you gathered information for the month of April from the sources indicated on the columnar analysis on the following page. (*Note:* The general ledger contains an account—Factory Ledger—that should have a debit balance of $60,000. Journal entries for production activity should include debits and credits to General Ledger when detailed accounts are not maintained in the production area.)

REQUIRED: Prepare a summary worksheet for the month ended April 30, 19X6, to compute:

a. Direct, indirect, and total costs that should be debited to Work in Process for the month.
b. The distribution of service department costs.
c. The April 30, 19X6, balances of the following accounts in the factory production ledger:
   1. General ledger control
   2. Raw materials
   3. Store supplies
   4. Work in process

(AICPA adapted)

Sources of information	GENERAL LEDGER CONTROL	RAW MATERIALS	STORE SUPPLIES	TOTAL	Work in process			
					SERVICE DEPARTMENTS		PRODUCING DEPARTMENTS†	
					Power Plant	General Plant*	Pattern Foundry	Machine Shop
From voucher register:								
Purchases	$(27,150)	$20,000	$ 7,150					
Direct labor	(6,150)			$ 6,150	$300	$ 350	$ 2,200	$ 3,300
Direct manufacturing expenses	(2,300)			2,300	50	175	730	1,345
Assets acquired	(9,400)							
Prepaid insurance	(3,000)							
From general ledger entries:								
Depreciation	(1,100)			1,100	140	80	‡	‡
Property taxes	(250)			250	40	20	‡	‡
Expired insurance	(500)			500	100	25	‡	‡
Repairs to power plant	(320)			320	320			
From requisitions:								
Raw materials		(27,000)		27,000	500	1,000	15,500	10,000
Store supplies	150		(15,150)	15,000	150	1,350	9,000	4,500
From cost of finished jobs report:								
Shipped to customers	45,000			(45,000)				
For company's own use	2,460			(2,460)				
Bases for distribution of costs:								
Power plant						50%	50%	50%

* General plant—store supplies issued to producing departments.
† Indirect costs of producing departments—direct labor costs of each department.
‡ Balance to be distributed on basis of direct labor costs (debit/credit).

5-29. *Overhead Rate Determination* The Anderson Milling Machine Company manufactures small milling machines used by various types of manufacturing companies. Mr. Hugo R. Anderson, president of the company, has requested that the controller develop predetermined overhead rates for the year 19X7. In 19X6, the company produced 1,200 milling machines, each selling for an average price of $20,000. Mr. Anderson predicts that 1,300 machines will be manufactured in 19X7.

Operating data for 19X6 are summarized below:

OVERHEAD COSTS (VARIABLE OR FIXED)	PRODUCTION DEPARTMENTS		SERVICE DEPARTMENTS	
	Milling	Assembly	Cutter maintenance	Machine maintenance
Indirect labor (V)	$ 480,000	$ 240,000	$ 60,000	$120,000
Supplies (V)	300,000	660,000	90,000	30,000
Heat, light, and power (V)	60,000	36,000	12,000	12,000
Machinery depreciation (F)	200,000	60,000	30,000	20,000
Tools (V)	72,000	120,000	24,000	24,000
Rent—factory building (F)	100,000	80,000	25,000	25,000
Factory insurance (F)	5,000	4,000	2,000	2,000
Plant supervision (F)	22,000	18,000	14,000	12,000
Totals	$1,239,000	$1,218,000	$257,000	$245,000

Indirect labor, supplies, heat, light, and power, and tools expenses vary directly with number of units produced. Price increases are expected for 19X7 as follows:

Supplies—10 percent increase
Other variable costs—5 percent increase
Rent and depreciation—to remain at 19X6 amounts
Factory insurance—10 percent increase
Plant supervision—5 percent increase

Service department costs are reapportioned to production departments as follows:

Machine maintenance—to *all* other departments on the basis of number of service requests. In 19X6, the following number of requests were made and the number is not expected to change materially in 19X7:

Milling department	1,365
Cutter maintenance department	819
Assembly department	546

Cutter maintenance—all costs charged directly to Milling Department.

In computing predetermined overhead rates for the production departments, the following information is relevant:

DEPARTMENT	BASIS	19X7 PROJECTED HOURS
Milling	Machine hours	472,250 MH
Assembly	Direct labor hours	290,970 DLH

REQUIRED:

    a. Prepare a schedule for projected overhead costs for each production and service department for 19X7.

    b. Reapportion service department costs to the production departments.

    c. Compute predetermined overhead rates for 19X7 for each production department.

5-30. *Comprehensive Worksheet Problem* The Maruzak Manufacturing Company has completed all recording procedures for 19X9. The company employs a job order costing system utilizing perpetual inventories. The trial balance for the Maruzak Manufacturing Company as of December 31, 19X9, is shown below:

MARUZAK MANUFACTURING COMPANY
Trial balance
December 31, 19X9

	Dr.	Cr.
Cash	$ 25,450	
Accounts receivable	142,240	
Allowance for uncollectible accounts		$ 7,420
Materials inventory control	20,900	
Work in process inventory control	55,660	
Finished goods inventory control	44,440	
Prepaid expenses	27,720	
Small tools	29,040	
Factory machinery	792,000	
Accumulated depreciation—factory machinery		132,000
Office equipment	103,400	
Accumulated depreciation—office equipment		46,860
Accounts payable		31,540
Employee income taxes withheld		32,500
FICA taxes payable		14,100
Union dues payable		5,100
Common stock		825,000
Retained earnings (as of Jan. 1, 19X9)		43,150
Sales		319,000
Cost of goods sold	143,000	
Factory overhead control	55,550	
Factory overhead applied		72,600
Sales commissions	33,000	
General and administrative expenses	48,400	
Rent—office building	8,250	
Property taxes—office	220	
Totals	$1,529,270	$1,529,270

Additional information:

a. Depreciation of factory machinery, 19X9	$13,200
b. Depreciation of office equipment, 19X9	4,840
c. Small tools used, 19X9	2,640
d. Accounts receivable balance at year-end contains an estimated 6 percent of uncollectible accounts	
e. Prepaid expenses that have *not* expired at year-end	22,000
f. Inventory balances disclosed by year-end physical count	
Materials inventory	20,900
Work in Process inventory	55,100
Finished Goods inventory	45,200
g. Estimated federal income taxes for 19X9	36,000

REQUIRED:

a. Prepare a ten-column worksheet and enter the trial balance. Formulate year-end adjusting entries from information given, post entries to worksheet, and compute adjusted trial balance amounts.

b. Extend all amounts to proper columns for Income Statement and Balance Sheet.

c. Complete the worksheet and prepare formal financial statements for 19X9.

d. Prepare closing entries.

Chapter 6: Process Cost Accounting

Process cost accounting is a traditional approach to product costing that is used in many industries. The basic procedure in process costing is to compute product unit costs in each production department. Unit costs are computed in departmental cost of production reports, and unit cost information is used to value Work in Process inventories. Cost of production reports summarize production activity and related costs for a fixed time period such as one month.

This chapter illustrates the cost analysis techniques used in a process costing system. In preparing a cost of production report, there are four phases of analysis:

1. Accumulate material, labor, and overhead costs incurred by each production department
2. Summarize the flow of physical units for each production department
3. Measure the number of equivalent whole units produced during a specific time period
4. Prepare departmental cost of production reports to compute unit costs for inventory valuation purposes

Each phase requires a computational schedule, and procedures for preparing these schedules are developed in separate chapter sections.

Upon completion of this chapter, students should be able to:

1. Prepare a quantity schedule to summarize the flow of physical units
2. Prepare an equivalent production schedule
3. Develop a cost assignment schedule and prepare a complete departmental cost of production report
4. Compute unit costs in a process cost system using either FIFO or average cost methods.

Relevant Concepts   The following basic concepts are introduced in this chapter:

Departmental cost accumulation The process cost system is designed to identify the manufacturing costs incurred by each production department.

Continuous production flow Products completed by one department are transferred to a subsequent department for additional processing, but all departments are simultaneously engaged in production activity.

Equivalent production In measuring the number of units produced during a period, credit is allowed for partially processed units. Thus, 200,000 fully completed units plus 80,000 units only 40 percent processed are treated as the production of 232,000 *equivalent units.*

Conversion costs Manufacturing labor and factory overhead costs incurred by a production department are treated as a single cost group called *conversion costs.*

Prior department costs With continuous production flows, costs of completed products in one department are transferred to the Work in Process inventory account of the next department. In the subsequent department, the transferred-in costs of preceding departments are called *prior department costs.*

Chapter Summary

Process cost systems are used for production operations with sequential product flows in which materials move continuously from one department to the next. Process costing is suitable for liquid products such as paint, petroleum, and chemicals and for other standardized products produced in large volume with continuous production runs. Lumber milling, brick production, and food processing involve standard products for which process costing is useful.

Process cost accounting is a system for accumulating and reporting manufacturing costs for individual production departments. A separate Work in Process inventory account is used for each production department; material, labor, and factory overhead costs are charged to these general ledger accounts. At the end of each accounting period, it is necessary to measure the number of equivalent units produced by individual departments. The typical accounting period is one month. Unit costs are computed for each department based on production costs for the period and equivalent units produced.

The computation of unit costs is presented in a departmental cost of production report. These monthly reports are prepared for each production department. Cost of production reports measure the total cost of ending Work in Process inventories and the total cost of goods transferred among departments or to Finished Goods inventory. Journal entries are prepared at the end of each month to record the flow of production costs among departments.

NATURE OF PROCESS COST SYSTEMS

As defined in Chapter 5, process cost accounting is a product costing system that applies to manufacturing operations involving a large volume of similar goods with continuous production flow. Material, labor, and manufacturing overhead costs are assigned to production departments. The term *process costing* refers to the use of departments or production processes as the primary basis for accumulating manufacturing costs. Unit costs are computed by dividing total manufacturing costs of each department by equivalent units produced during a particular time period. Two important phases of process cost accounting are to (1) trace manufacturing costs to production departments and (2) measure equivalent production volume in each department.

A process cost system has the following distinctive characteristics:

Cost accumulation   Manufacturing costs are accumulated for each production department or process. Since a specific product is produced in large volume, the system is *not* designed to compute the cost of specific jobs or product batches.

Volume–time period consideration   Manufacturing costs are accumulated by department for specific time periods. The typical accounting period is one month, and the system is designed to measure equivalent units produced during this time period.

Work in Process accounts   Separate Work in Process inventory accounts are maintained in the general ledger for each production department.

These characteristics indicate that production departments are a key factor in process cost systems.

Departmental Organization   In a process costing system, production departments are the center of attention. This departmental orientation is best suited to standardized products and continuous production processes. For instance, flour mills, steel foundries, oil refineries, chemical processing, and brick manufacturing are characterized by continuous production of standardized products. In comparison, job order cost accounting traces manufacturing costs to each separate batch of products because of the special characteristics and product specifications of every job order. Although job order or process cost accounting could be applied to any particular manufacturing activity, process costing is used in continuous production industries because it best satisfies their information and reporting needs.

A department may contain several distinct cost centers for different labor operations or for machine groups that are identified for cost control reasons. For cost accounting purposes, a production department is an organizational unit having identifiable inputs and outputs of materials that are being converted into finished products. Initial raw material inputs may flow through several departments before the final product is completed. The finished product of Department 1 may be the raw material input for Department 2. Unit costs are computed periodically in each department and therefore increase as the initial raw material progresses through each department.

The flow of raw materials and production costs through several different departments is often difficult for students to visualize. However, the ability to diagram materials and cost flow is a key factor in solving process cost problems. Raw material usage, production costs, and equivalent production for a period must be associated with specific departments. A diagram of the production process should be prepared before computing equivalent production and unit costs.

Diagrams of three different production processes are illustrated in Exhibit 6-1. Similar diagrams can be prepared for any process cost system given a description of the particular departmental organization. In example one, the complete production system requires the sequential processing of material A in three departments. The finished production of Department 1 is transferred to Department 2, and the finished production of Department 2 becomes the 'raw material' for processing in Department 3. The completed production of Department 3 is transferred to Finished Goods inventory.

A more complex system is shown in example two of Exhibit 6-1. Output of Department 1 is the input for Departments 2 and 3. Departments 1, 2, and 5

EXHIBIT 6-1

EXAMPLES OF PROCESS COSTING SITUATIONS

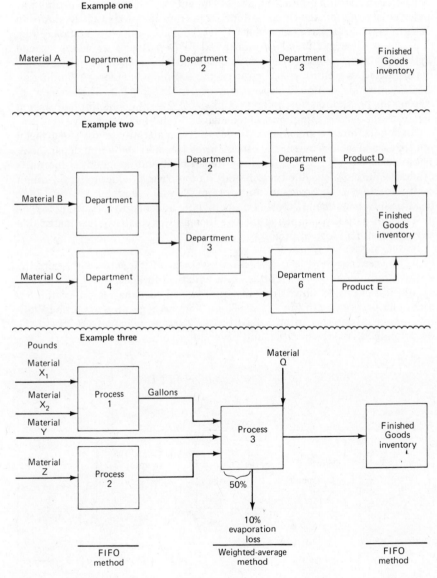

form a series of production processes that create product D. Department 6 uses the completed production of Departments 3 and 4 to manufacture product E.

The production diagram in example three includes the following factors that affect departmental cost of production reports: (1) conversion from pounds to gallons within processes 1 and 2; (2) loss of units because of evaporation in process 3; (3) use of FIFO and average cost methods to value inventories; (4) material Q is added at the end of process 3. Accounting procedures for these complex situations are discussed in Chapter 7. At this point, you should recognize that a production diagram is a useful method to organize data for process costing analysis.

Continuous production flow To illustrate the continuous production flow concept, consider the production process for automobile fenders. The only raw material is sheet metal, which is transferred from Raw Material inventory to Department 1. In Department 1, sheet metal is cut according to specific product dimensions. The cut metal is transferred to Department 2, where special equipment molds or shapes the product. Molded fenders then are transferred to Department 3, which trims and polishes the completed fenders. A production diagram for this complete process appears in Exhibit 6-2. The concept of *continuous production flow* refers to a physical flow of goods through several departments that are simultaneously engaged in production activity.

Our fender production process involves raw material cost for sheet metal plus labor and factory overhead costs incurred by each production department. These costs must be accumulated by department and assigned to the units produced during a specific time period. As the basic product moves through each department, the average unit cost of a single fender increases. Each department incurs manufacturing costs that are attached to the products. The unit cost of partially completed fenders increases as the basic raw material is converted into a finished product.

Basic process cost analysis Process cost systems must identify and record the flow of production costs that corresponds with the physical flow of production. To illustrate this cost flow, study the summarized cost analysis in Exhibit 6-3 for fender production in July, 19X7. There were no beginning or ending Work in Process inventories in any department. Assume that you are given the material, labor, overhead costs, and production volumes.

EXHIBIT 6-2

CONTINUOUS PRODUCTION FLOW—FENDER PRODUCTION

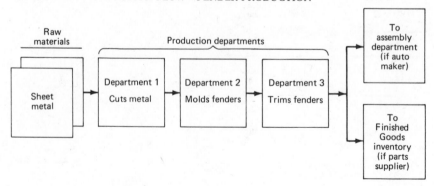

As Exhibit 6-3 shows, 5,000 fenders were started in Department 1 and were completely processed through all departments. After each department completed its work on particular units, the completed units were transferred to the next department. Production activity and movement of products between departments were continuous and occurred uniformly during the month. The *continuous production flow* concept describes this type of manufacturing activity.

Note that the average unit cost increased as the fenders moved through each department. As the manufacturing operations were performed, costs were incurred that attach to the products. Departmental unit costs are also computed in Exhibit 6-3; these amounts represent the unit cost of manufacturing operations in each department. The average unit cost of completed fenders transferred to Finished Goods is ten dollars. This cost represents the sum of unit costs in all departments:

$6 (Department 1) + $3 (Department 2) + $1 (Department 3) = $10

When there are no beginning or ending Work in Process inventories, process cost accounting is as simple as our fender production example. Production volume and manufacturing costs for a fixed time period, such as a month, are summarized by department, and unit costs are computed in departmental cost of production reports. In simple cases, a report similar to Exhibit 6-3 is an adequate cost of production report.

The fender production case also illustrates *end-of-period cost analysis*, which is typical of process cost systems. Unit costs are computed at the end of an accounting period in cost of production reports. Based upon these reports, journal entries are prepared to record the transfer of production costs between departmental Work in Process inventory accounts. Exhibit 6-3 indicates that

EXHIBIT 6-3

DEPARTMENTAL COST SUMMARY—FENDER PRODUCTION, JULY 19X7

	FENDER PRODUCTION, JULY 19X7		
	Department 1 (cutting)	Department 2 (molding)	Department 3 (trimming)
Cost and volume			
a. Cost of materials used	$10,000	None	None
b. Labor and overhead cost	20,000	$15,000	$ 5,000
c. Prior department costs	None → Cost flow →	30,000 → Cost flow →	45,000
d. Total costs (a + b + c)	$30,000	$45,000	$50,000
e. Units produced	5,000 → Product flow →	5,000 → Product flow →	5,000*
Cost per unit:			
Departmental [(a + b) ÷ e]	$6	$3	$ 1
Average (d ÷ e)	$6	$9	$10
Unit cost summary			
Costs added per department	$6	$3	$ 1
Costs of prior department	–0– →	6 →	9
Average unit cost	$6 →	$9 →	$10

* Completed production of Department 3 is transferred to Finished Goods.

$30,000 of Department 1 costs should be transferred to Department 2. This transfer is accomplished by the following journal entry on July 31:

Work in Process—Department 2	$30,000	
Work in Process—Department 1		$30,000

Similar journal entries are required to record cost flows between other departments.

End-of-period cost analysis actually simplifies the use of perpetual inventory records. During the month, material usage and transfers of production between departments can be recorded in subsidiary ledgers using unit data. Summary journal entries then are prepared at month-end to update general ledger control accounts for the total cost of material usage and departmental production transfers. Information flow in a process cost system involves general ledger accounts, subsidiary ledgers, cost of production reports, and periodic journal entries. All of these factors are illustrated and explained in the sections that follow.

Process Costing Objectives and Reports

In a process cost system, the primary cost accounting objective is to determine the costs of completed production and ending Work in Process inventories. The accounting report that accomplishes this objective is the *departmental cost of production report*. A cost of production report is prepared for each production department at specified dates on a monthly basis. The reports can be prepared more frequently, but the important idea is that they concern production activity during a fixed time interval.

The report for each department summarizes its production volume, transfers to other departments, Work in Process inventory levels, productions costs incurred, and unit cost computations. Cost analysis in these reports provides data for month-end journal entries that record departmental cost transfers. The reports also compute the cost of ending Work in Process inventories and provide support for the general ledger cost balances of Work in Process for each department.

When monthly production activity is summarized, some partially completed units usually are found in each department at month-end. These partially completed units compose the ending Work in Process inventory. Work in Process inventory is included in departmental cost of production reports, and the units are assigned an appropriate share of production costs for the period. Our fender production example is used to demonstrate process cost analysis for a department having an ending Work in Process inventory. As shown in Exhibit 6-2, Department 1 receives sheet metal from raw materials storage and cuts the metal to required size. Given the data below, an August cost of production report will be prepared for Department 1.

During August 19X7, Department 1 started 6,000 fenders, transferred 5,000 to Department 2, and had an ending Work in Process inventory of 1,000 units on August 31. The 1,000 partially completed units have gone through only 50 percent of the cutting operation. Each partially completed unit should therefore be assigned 50 percent of the labor and factory overhead costs appliable to one fully completed unit. Cost of materials issued to Department 1 is $12,000, and conversion costs (labor plus applied overhead) for August are $22,000.

Based upon this information, the August cost of production report for Department 1 is prepared in three distinct stages:

Stage 1: Prepare a quantity schedule to summarize the flow of physical units
Stage 2: Prepare an equivalent production schedule to measure the number of equivalent whole units produced
Stage 3: Prepare a cost assignment schedule to compute unit costs and determine the cost of ending Work in Process inventory and transfers to other departments

Each stage of process cost analysis is illustrated below, and the separate analyses then are combined to present the desired departmental cost of production report. When solving similar process cost problems, remember these two points:

1. The three stages described above must be completed for every production department.
2. Stages 1 and 2 deal only with units of product. Manufacturing costs are analyzed on stage 3.

Stage 1: Prepare a quantity schedule This schedule summarizes the flow of physical units (fenders) through Department 1 for August. The percentage or degree of completion for units in Work in Process inventory is not considered at this point. In terms of physical units, the report shows initial Work in Process inventory, units started during August, final Work in Process inventory, and number of units transferred out of Department 1.

Department 1
Quantity schedule

AUGUST OPERATIONS	PHYSICAL UNITS
Units started	6,000
Plus: Initial inventory, August 1	–0–
Units accountable for	6,000
Less: Final inventory, August 31	(1,000)
Units transferred out	5,000

The schedule summarizes input, output, and Work in Process inventory balances of Department 1 in terms of physical units. A quantity schedule is the starting point in preparing a cost of production report.

Stage 2: Prepare an equivalent production schedule This schedule measures the number of equivalent whole units produced by Department 1 during August. To compute unit costs of production, manufacturing costs incurred during the month are divided by the number of units produced. In measuring the number of units produced, a department counts the number of units fully completed during the period plus a fraction of the partially completed units. The resulting measure is *equivalent units* produced during the period. The concept of equivalent production allows all units worked on during the month to be included in the analysis. The number of equivalent units produced by Department 1 in August is computed in the following table.

Department 1
Equivalent production schedule

NUMBER OF EQUIVALENT UNITS	UNITS RECEIVING MATERIAL COSTS	UNITS RECEIVING CONVERSION COSTS
Transferred out	5,000	5,000
Plus: Final inventory		
(1,000 at 100% and 50%)	1,000	500
Total equivalent units	6,000	5,500
Less: Initial inventory (none)	–0–	–0–
Equivalent units produced	6,000	5,500

An equivalent production schedule has several important features. The order or sequence of items appearing in the schedule is exactly the reverse order of the quantity schedule presented in stage 1. In the equivalent production schedule, physical units in the final Work in Process inventory are multiplied by the percentage completion factor applicable to these units at month-end. Separate equivalent production computations are required for material costs, labor costs, and factory overhead costs if partially completed units have different percentages of completion for each cost factor.

In our example, all units worked on by Department 1 are 100 percent complete regarding material costs. Since all materials were introduced at the start of operations, all completed units and all units in the final Work in Process inventory have 100 percent of the material content that these units will receive. Accordingly, all units in Department 1 are 100 percent complete regarding material costs. Units in the final Work in Process inventory on August 31 had received only 50 percent of the required cutting operations. These units are therefore considered 50 percent complete with regard to labor and overhead costs.

The basic formula or schedule used in this text to compute equivalent production for material costs and conversion costs is:

UNIT DATA FROM QUANTITY SCHEDULE	NUMBER OF UNITS
Units transferred out	X
Plus: Final inventory: physical units	
times percentage completion	X
Total equivalent units	XX
Less: Initial inventory: physical units	
times percentage completion	(X)
Equivalent units produced	XX

The quantity schedule provides required information for physical units transferred out and Work in Process inventories. Physical units in the final Work in Process inventory are multiplied by their percentage of completion at month-end. Physical units in the initial Work in Process inventory are multiplied by their percentage of completion at the start of the period. The reason for subtracting initial Work in Process inventory is explained in a later section.

Stage 3: Prepare a cost assignment schedule This schedule computes product unit costs, the total cost of ending Work in Process inventory, and the total cost of units transferred to other departments. All unit data appearing in this schedule are equivalent units computed in stage 2. The cost assignment schedule is arranged to match equivalent units with related production costs. Units produced and the initial Work in Process inventory are added; equivalent units in the final Work in Process inventory are subtracted from this total to yield the number of completed units transferred to other departments. Units appearing in the cost assignment schedule follow the reverse order shown in the equivalent production schedule.

For Department 1 in August, the cost of material issues was $12,000, and conversion costs were $22,000. The cost assignment schedule uses this cost information and equivalent units shown in stage 2.

Department 1
Cost assignment schedule

	RAW MATERIALS			CONVERSION COSTS			
	Equivalent units	Unit cost	Amount	Equivalent units	Unit cost	Amount	TOTAL COSTS
Units produced	6,000		$12,000	5,500		$22,000	$34,000
Plus: Initial inventory	-0-		-0-	-0-		-0-	-0-
Total	6,000	$2	$12,000	5,500	$4	$22,000	$34,000
Less: Final inventory	(1,000)	$2	(2,000)	(500)	$4	(2,000)	(4,000)
Transferred out	5,000		$10,000	5,000		$20,000	$30,000

Separate unit costs are computed for materials and conversion costs. The unit cost of materials is computed on the "total" line of the cost assignment schedule by dividing 6,000 units into $12,000. This $2 unit cost is then used to value the ending Work in Process inventory. For conversion costs, the $4 unit cost also is computed on the "total" line by dividing 5,500 equivalent units into $22,000.

The cost of a fully completed unit is $6, which includes $2 for materials and $4 for conversion costs. Units transferred to Department 2 are assigned $30,000 of production costs (5,000 units × $6). Costs assigned to the final Work in Process inventory are $4,000. Note that separate analyses are required for material costs and conversion costs because different equivalent production measures apply to these cost categories.

Cost of production report In practice, there is no standard format for a cost of production report. The report may contain an orderly arrangement of all schedules developed in stages 1, 2, and 3. An illustrative cost of production report for Department 1 of fender production is presented in Exhibit 6-4. This report contains the essential elements of our three-stage approach and is fairly simple since there was no beginning Work in Process inventory.

Regardless of specific report format, there are three distinct phases to apply in process cost analysis: (1) summarize physical product flows, (2) measure equivalent production, and (3) compute unit costs for Work in Process inventory and transfers to other departments. Each phase requires certain

EXHIBIT 6-4

COST OF PRODUCTION REPORT, AUGUST 19X7
(DEPARTMENT 1: UNITS = NUMBER OF FENDERS)

1. UNITS STARTED, TRANSFERS, AND INVENTORIES (PHYSICAL UNITS)

Units started during August	6,000
Plus: Inventory in process, August 1	-0-
Units accountable for	6,000
Less: Inventory in process, August 31	(1,000)
Transferred to Department 2	5,000

2. EQUIVALENT PRODUCTION AND COSTS INCURRED

	Materials	Labor and overhead
Units transferred out	5,000	5,000
Inventory, August 31:		
1,000 × 100% complete	1,000	
1,000 × 50% complete		500
(a) Equivalent units produced	6,000	5,500
(b) Costs incurred during August	$12,000	$22,000
Cost per unit (b ÷ a)	$2.00	$4.00

3. PRODUCTION COST SUMMARY

Cost of initial inventory on August 1			$ -0-
Costs of current operations:			
Materials issued		$12,000	
Labor and overhead costs		22,000	34,000
Total costs accountable for			$34,000
Total costs assigned to:			
Transfers to Department 2: 5,000 units × $6 =		$30,000	
Work in process inventory, August 31:			
Materials: 1,000 units × $2	$ 2,000		
Conversion costs: 500 units × $4	2,000	4,000	
Total costs assigned			$34,000

computations that can be performed in the formal schedules illustrated for fender production: quantity schedule, equivalent production schedule, and cost assignment schedule. The departmental cost of production report summarizes the contents of these schedules. Cost of production reports provide detailed information that supports the cost balances of general ledger Work in Process accounts; the reports also provide cost data for month-end journal entries that record the flow of production costs through the cost accounting system.

Flow of Production Costs   In a process cost system with perpetual inventory records, there is a separate Work in Process account in the general ledger for each production department. Monthly departmental cost of production reports determine the cost of ending

Work in Process inventories and the cost of units transferred between departments. Based upon this end-of-period cost analysis, journal entries are prepared to record the cost of units transferred among various departments. Journal entries are also required during the period to record the issuance of raw materials and incurrence of labor and factory overhead costs. These journal entries trace the flow of production costs through the manufacturing system.

Fender production in Department 1 during August 19X7 is used to illustrate journal entries in a process cost system. Raw materials issued to Department 1 were $12,000, and conversion costs for the period were $22,000. Conversion costs charged to the department include manufacturing labor of $8,000 and Factory Overhead Applied of $14,000. This separation of conversion costs was not explained earlier, but the company uses a predetermined overhead rate equal to 175 percent of labor cost. Actual overhead costs incurred by Department 1 in August were $5,000 for depreciation of equipment, $2,000 of expired insurance premiums, and $9,000 of repairs paid in cash. The general ledger account for Work in Process inventory of Department 1 is shown below as it appears on August 31, 19X7:

Work in process inventory—Department 1

Balance, August 1	$ -0-		
(1) Raw materials	12,000	(4) Transfers	$30,000
(2) Factory labor	8,000		
(3) Overhead applied	14,000		
Balance, August 31	$ 4,000		

Four journal entries were recorded during August and posted to the Work in Process account. These entries are presented below in general journal form and are keyed to the Work in Process account:

1. Work in process—Department 1 $12,000
     Raw material inventory $12,000
     Materials issued to production
2. Work in process—Department 1 $ 8,000
     Factory payroll $ 8,000
     Labor cost for August
3. Work in process—Department 1 $14,000
     Factory overhead applied $14,000
     Overhead applied = 175% × $8,000 labor cost
4. Work in process—Department 2 $30,000
     Work in process—Department 1 $30,000
     Cost of units transferred to Department 2

Journal entry 4 is prepared at month-end from the cost of production report described in Exhibit 6-4.

Factory Overhead Applied in entry 3 is based on a predetermined overhead rate equal to 175 percent of departmental labor cost. When predetermined overhead rates are used, actual overhead costs incurred during the period are charged to departmental Factory Overhead Control accounts. Journal entry 5 records the $16,000 of actual overhead costs incurred during August:

5. Factory overhead control—Department 1 $16,000
        Accumulated depreciation $5,000
        Prepaid insurance   2,000
        Cash (for repairs)   9,000
    Actual overhead costs for August

The diagram of transactions and related general ledger accounts in Exhibit 6-5 illustrate the cost flow pattern of a process cost system. Cost amounts in the diagram are keyed to journal entries 1 through 5.

In Chapter 3, you prepared a formal statement to determine Cost of Goods Manufactured. With process costing and perpetual inventory records, the statement of Cost of Goods Manufactured is simply a summary of the Work in Process account for a particular department. In Exhibit 6-5, the Work in Process account for Department 1 shows that $30,000 is transferred to Department 2. This $30,000 is Cost of Goods Manufactured by Department 1 during August 19X7. Cost of Goods Manufactured for the entire company is determined by summarizing data from all Work in Process accounts.

PROCESS COST ACCOUNTING PROCEDURES

In a process cost system, specific accounting procedures are required to accumulate production costs by department, to summarize physical product flows, to measure equivalent production, and to compute unit costs. The fender production example with Department 1 illustrated these procedures. This example did not explain the treatment of initial Work in Process inventories or the difference between FIFO and average costing procedures. Process cost analysis involving initial inventories and different cost flow assumptions is described in this section. Operation of the accounting system to record material, labor, and overhead costs is also explored in more detail.

Material and Labor Costs

Material requisitions or bills of material authorize the issuance of materials to production departments. The cost of materials issued is recorded on one copy of the requisition, and a materials requisition journal summarizes the cost of materials issued to various departments during the month. Using cost totals from this journal, month-end journal entries are prepared to debit Work in Process accounts and credit Raw Materials inventory control in the general ledger.

In process cost systems, the distinction between direct and indirect materials is not very important. The basis for accumulating costs is the production department, not a specific order or product batch. If materials are issued to a particular department, the departmental Work in Process account is debited for this cost. Accordingly, materials issued to a department are a *direct* cost of that department.

Manufacturing labor costs that are traceable to each department are debited to the respective Work in Process inventory accounts. Labor costs related to specific departments are determined by analysis of employee gross earnings for a period. The gross labor cost of employees assigned to a particular department is debited to the Work in Process account of that department. Salaries of supervisory personnel can be allocated to several departments. Direct and indirect labor classification with regard to products is not important in process cost systems. The objective is to assign labor costs to specific departments.

EXHIBIT 6-5

COST FLOW PATTERN—PROCESS COST SYSTEM

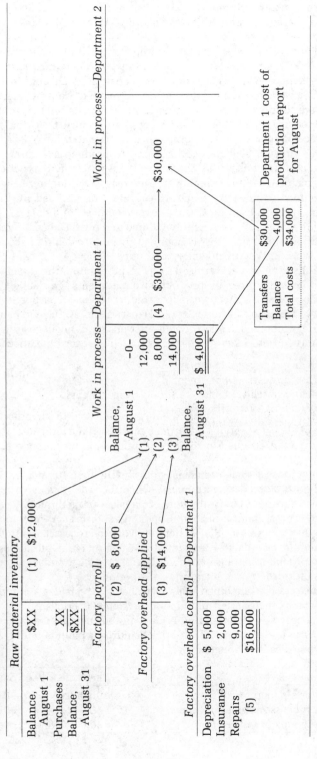

Raw material inventory

Balance, August 1	$XX	(1)	$12,000
Purchases	XX		
Balance, August 31	$XX		

Factory payroll

(2)	$ 8,000

Factory overhead applied

(3)	$14,000

Factory overhead control—Department 1

Depreciation	$ 5,000
Insurance	2,000
Repairs	9,000
(5)	$16,000

Work in process—Department 1

Balance, August 1	-0-		
(1)	12,000	(4)	$30,000
(2)	8,000		
(3)	14,000		
Balance, August 31	$ 4,000		

Transfers	$30,000
Balance	4,000
Total costs	$34,000

Department 1 cost of production report for August

Work in process—Department 2

$30,000

Accounting for Overhead Costs

If predetermined overhead rates are used in a process cost system, overhead costs are charged to production by debiting Work in Process and crediting Factory Overhead Applied. As explained in Chapter 5, a budgetary process is required to develop predetermined overhead rates. Budgeted overhead costs of service departments are allocated to production departments, and overhead rates are computed for each production department. During the year, actual overhead costs are charged to Factory Overhead Control, and subsidiary ledgers are used to record the actual overhead costs related to each department. Accounting for under- or overapplied factory overhead follows the same procedures used in a job order costing system.

In some process cost industries, monthly production volume and actual overhead costs are fairly constant during the year. Under these circumstances, it is acceptable to charge actual overhead costs to production instead of using predetermined overhead rates. Overhead rates are designed to eliminate unit cost fluctuations caused by seasonal overhead costs and changes in monthly production volume. When monthly volume and overhead costs are constant, a reasonably uniform unit cost is obtained by simply debiting actual overhead costs to Work in Process inventory accounts.

When charging actual overhead costs to production, the direct or traceable overhead costs incurred by production departments are debited to Work in Process accounts. Overhead costs incurred by service departments are debited to Factory Overhead Control—Service Departments. At the end of each month, a schedule is prepared to allocate actual service department costs to production departments. A journal entry then is prepared to record the allocation:

Work in process—Department A	$XX	
Work in process—Department B	XX	
Factory overhead control—Service Departments		$XX

The total overhead costs of Department A include its direct overhead costs plus its share of allocated service department costs. Total overhead costs of Department A then are assigned to equivalent production for the month.

Combined Quantity Schedules

In solving process cost problems, you should first summarize the flow of physical units by preparing a quantity schedule. Comprehensive analysis often requires a schedule to trace the flow of physical units through Raw Materials, Work in Process, and Finished Goods inventories. A *combined quantity schedule* has columns for Raw Materials, Work in Process, and Finished Goods. The schedule records the sequential flow of material purchases, materials issued to production, transfer of completed products to finished goods storage, and sale of finished products during the period.

To illustrate the combined quantity schedule, consider a company with a single process that started production on 200,000 bricks during September, 19X5. The only raw material used is clay, and the company purchased 570,000 pounds of it in September. Each brick requires 3 pounds of clay. Initial and final inventories for September were:

PHYSICAL INVENTORY	SEPTEMBER 1	SEPTEMBER 30
Raw materials (pounds of clay)	100,000	70,000
Work in process (number of bricks)	40,000	80,000
Finished goods (number of bricks)	50,000	5,000

EXHIBIT 6-6

COMBINED QUANTITY SCHEDULE

RAW MATERIALS, WORK IN PROCESS, AND FINISHED GOODS

PHYSICAL UNITS	RAW MATERIALS (POUNDS)	WORK IN PROCESS* (BRICKS)	FINISHED GOODS (BRICKS)
Units started†	570,000	200,000	160,000
Plus: Inital inventory	100,000	40,000	50,000
Units accountable for	670,000	240,000	210,000
Less: Final inventory	(70,000)	(80,000)	(5,000)
Transferred out	600,000‡	160,000	205,000

* Equivalent production computations use data from the Work in Process column.

† *Units started* is interpreted as follows: for Raw Materials, pounds of clay purchased; for Work in Process, number of bricks started in production; for Finished Goods, number of bricks received from production.

‡ Conversion to units of product: 600,000 lbs. ÷ 3 lbs. = 200,000 bricks.

Given only these data, a combined quantity schedule is prepared in Exhibit 6-6 to compute pounds of material issued to production, number of bricks transferred to Finished Goods, and number of bricks sold during September. The quantity schedule for materials uses pounds of clay as the physical unit. Flow of products through Work in Process and Finished Goods is measured by number of bricks. Equivalent production for the month is computed by analyzing the quantity schedule for Work in Process.

In practice, combined quantity schedules are required only when periodic inventory systems are used in process costing. With periodic inventory procedures, physical inventory counts are necessary to determine ending inventory quantities. The combined quantity schedule then is prepared to compute quantities of materials used, products transferred to Finished Goods, and products sold during the period. A process cost system based on periodic inventory procedures still uses general ledger accounts for Raw Materials, Work in Process, and Finished Goods, but no subsidiary ledgers document the flow of units and inventory balances.

After preparing a quantity schedule, the next step in process cost analysis is to measure the number of equivalent whole units produced during the period. An *equivalent production schedule* is prepared by analyzing unit data in the quantity schedule for Work in Process. This analysis also requires information concerning the percentage completion of initial and final Work in Process inventories. The following example explains the effect of initial Work in Process inventory on computing equivalent production.

In a certain chemical processing department, materials are added to production evenly throughout the process. Conversion costs are also incurred uniformly during production. Accordingly, a single percentage of completion estimate is developed for Work in Process inventories, and this percentage applies to material costs and conversion costs. The following information summarizes operations of the chemical department during March 19X8:

Equivalent Production Analysis

QUANTITY SCHEDULE	PHYSICAL UNITS	PERCENT COMPLETE AT INVENTORY DATE
Units started	200,000	
Plus: Initial inventory, March 1	40,000	30
Units accountable for	240,000	
Less: Final inventory, March 31	(80,000)	40
Transferred out	160,000	

At the start of operations on March 1, the initial inventory of 40,000 physical units was 30 percent complete with regard to material, labor, and overhead costs. Each unit contained 30 percent of the total material requirements and had received 30 percent of the processing operations necessary to produce a completed product. The initial Work in Process inventory is equivalent to 12,000 whole units (40,000 × 30 percent). These 12,000 equivalent units were included in the equivalent production measure for the preceding month (February 19X8). During March 19X8 the remaining 70 percent of required materials and processing operations will be completed on these 40,000 physical units. Completion of these units is therefore equivalent to the production of 28,000 whole units (40,000 × 70 percent). Equivalent production for March must include these 28,000 equivalent units. Equivalent production can be computed by the transferred-out method or the units started and completed method. Each method is illustrated and explained by using the chemical department example.

Transferred-out Method   An equivalent production schedule computes the number of equivalent whole units produced during a specific time period. The *transferred-out method* begins with the number of units transferred to Finished Goods (or to another department) and considers the percentage completion of Work in Process inventories at the beginning and end of the period. This procedure was illustrated for fender production in an earlier example.

Equivalent production schedule Chemical Department, March 19X8		
Transferred out	160,000	
Plus: Final inventory (80,000 × 40%)	32,000	
Total equivalent units	192,000	
Less: Initial inventory (40,000 × 30%)	(12,000)	
Equivalent units produced	180,000	

The transferred-out approach reverses the order of items appearing in the quantity schedule. Units transferred out (160,000) are 100 percent complete and include the 40,000 physical units that were in process on March 1. Equivalent units in the initial inventory on March 1 (12,000) are subtracted in order to determine the number of equivalent whole units produced during March.

Units started and completed method   The *units started and completed method* is an alternative procedure for computing equivalent production. With this method, the number of equivalent units produced is determined by adding three separate measures:

1. Physical units in the initial inventory are multiplied by the remaining percentage of work to be done on these units.
2. The number of units started *and* completed during the current period is determined.
3. Physical units in the final inventory are multiplied by the percentage completion of these units at the end of the period.

Units started and completed during the period are determined from physical unit information in the quantity schedule. Units started and completed equal the number of units started minus physical units in the ending Work in Process inventory. Using our chemical department data, units started and completed (USC) are:

$$USC = \text{units started} - \text{final inventory}$$
$$USC = 200{,}000 - 80{,}000 = \underline{120{,}000 \text{ units}}$$

During March, the department began production operations on 200,000 units, and the final inventory represents 80,000 units that were not finished. The difference of 120,000 units is the number of products both started *and* completed during March. Equivalent production is computed with the following schedule:

Equivalent production schedule
Chemical Department, March 19X8

1. Initial inventory (40,000 physical units 30% completed on March 1) 40,000 × 70% work done in March ~~80 × 50%~~	28,000 *40,*
2. Units started and completed (200,000 − 80,000) ~~600 − 50~~	120,000 *550*
3. Final inventory (80,000 physical units 40% completed on March 31) 80,000 × 40% work done in March ~~50 × 50%~~	32,000 *25*
Equivalent units produced (1 + 2 + 3)	180,000 *615*

The number of equivalent units produced is 180,000 regardless of the computational procedure used. The transferred-out method is convenient when developing a cost of production report in the three-stage sequence illustrated for fender production earlier in this chapter. Cost of production reports also can be developed by using the units started and completed procedure. Cost analysis with both methods is explained in the following sections.

After the equivalent production schedule is prepared, the cost of ending Work in Process inventory and cost of units transferred out can be determined. There are two groups of production costs to consider:

1. Costs incurred in the last period that were assigned to the initial Work in Process inventory of the current period
2. Material, labor, and overhead costs related to production activity in the current period.

Average Cost Method

With end-of-period costing procedures, the approach is to compute a unit cost that applies to units in the ending Work in Process inventory. The total cost of ending inventory is then subtracted from the sum of cost groups 1 and 2 in order to determine the total cost of units transferred out. With the *average cost method*, the unit cost of ending inventory is computed by dividing total equivalent units into total costs accountable for (sum of cost groups 1 and 2).

The average cost method of pricing ending inventory is illustrated in Exhibit 6-7 using our chemical department example for March 19X8. Assume for this illustration that costs assigned to initial inventory on March 1 were $21,600; and that material, labor, and overhead costs charged to the chemical department in March were $381,600 in total.

The cost assignment schedule in Exhibit 6-7 shows the computation of average unit cost, which is $2.10 per equivalent whole unit. This unit cost is a weighted average based on total equivalent units in process for the period (192,000) and on total costs of beginning inventory and current production

EXHIBIT 6-7

MARCH COST OF PRODUCTION REPORT—CHEMICAL DEPARTMENT
AVERAGE COST METHOD

STAGE 1: QUANTITY SCHEDULE

	Physical units
Units started	200,000
Plus: Initial inventory	40,000
Units accountable for	240,000
Less: Final inventory	(80,000)
Transferred out	160,000

STAGE 2: EQUIVALENT PRODUCTION SCHEDULE

Transferred out	160,000
Plus: Final inventory (80,000 units × 40%)	32,000
Total equivalent units	192,000
Less: Initial inventory (40,000 × 30%)	(12,000)
Equivalent units produced	180,000

STAGE 3: COST ASSIGNMENT SCHEDULE

	Equivalent units	Average unit cost	Total cost
Equivalent units produced	180,000		$381,600
Plus: Initial inventory	12,000		21,600
Total equivalent units and costs	192,000	$2.10*	$403,200
Less: Final inventory	(32,000)	$2.10	(67,200)
Transferred out	160,000		$336,000

* Average unit cost = $403,200 ÷ 192,000 = $2.10.

activity ($403,200). Cost of the final inventory is 32,000 equivalent units times average cost of $2.10 per unit.

While most firms use the average cost method, valuation of Work in Process inventories at FIFO unit cost is also an acceptable practice. First-in, first-out (FIFO) is a cost flow assumption for pricing inventories. The use of FIFO in process cost analysis requires the valuation of ending Work in Process inventory at the unit cost of current production for the period. The unit cost of current production is computed by dividing the number of equivalent units produced into production costs incurred during the current period. Using data from Exhibit 6-7, a cost assignment schedule with the FIFO cost method is presented below:

FIFO Cost Method

Cost assignment schedule
FIFO cost method

	EQUIVALENT UNITS	FIFO UNIT COST	TOTAL COST
Equivalent units produced	180,000	$2.12	$381,600
Plus: Initial inventory	12,000		21,600
Total equivalent units and costs	192,000		$403,200
Less: Final inventory	(32,000)	$2.12	(67,840)
Transferred out	160,000		$335,360

The FIFO unit cost of $2.12 represents the unit cost of production during the current period. Material, labor, and overhead costs charged to the department in March ($381,600) are divided by the number of equivalent units produced (180,000). Cost of the initial inventory on March 1 ($21,600) and related equivalent units (12,000) have no effect on the FIFO unit cost. The ending Work in Process inventory of 32,000 equivalent units is valued at $2.12 per unit under the FIFO cost method.

For control purposes, the FIFO unit cost is useful in evaluating the efficiency of current operations. Our $2.12 cost is the unit cost of *current* production and is unaffected by initial inventory costs carried forward from the preceding period. General cost control procedures compare the FIFO unit cost with the standard unit cost and require corrective actions for excessive cost incurrence.

In our chemical department examples, material, labor, and overhead costs were combined for cost analysis purposes. This combination simplified our examples and was possible only because material costs and conversion costs were incurred uniformly throughout the production process. Separate equivalent production and unit cost computations are required for each cost element having a different percentage completion factor for Work in Process inventories.

If a material is introduced at the start of a process, all units in process are 100 percent complete regarding this particular material cost. If a second material is added at the end of processing, then Work in Process inventories are 0 percent complete regarding this material cost, since partially completed units contain none of the second material. The complexity of process cost analysis depends on the production process involved. Labor and overhead costs usually are combined and analyzed as conversion costs. In most cases, conversion costs are assumed to be incurred uniformly so that a single percentage completion factor applies to these costs.

ALTERNATIVE COST ANALYSIS PROCEDURE

All process cost analysis can be performed by using the procedures illustrated in this chapter. Cost of production reports contain a quantity schedule, an equivalent production schedule, and a cost assignment schedule. Illustrations so far have emphasized the transferred-out method for computing equivalent production and use of unit costs to value ending Work in Process inventory.

An alternative method of process cost analysis emphasizes the units started and completed method of computing equivalent production and uses an entirely different form of cost assignment schedule. This method identifies and assigns production costs to :

1. Initial inventory based on work necessary to complete these units in the current period
2. Units started and completed during the period
3. Final inventory based on work performed on these units during the period

Accordingly, the cost assignment schedule follows the same sequence used to measure equivalent production under the units started and completed method. The next example illustrates this alternative cost analysis procedure.

The following quantity schedule and other data were assembled for the Milling Department after the close of operations on April 30, 19X2.

QUANTITY SCHEDULE	PHYSICAL UNITS	PERCENTAGE COMPLETION FOR Materials	Conversion costs
Units started	200,000		
Plus: Initial inventory, April 1	40,000	100	30
Units accountable for	240,000		
Less: Final inventory, April 30	(80,000)	100	40
Transferred out	160,000		

	SUMMARY OF PRODUCTION COSTS		
	Material costs	Conversion costs	Total costs
Inventory on April 1	$ 20,800	$ 25,800	$ 46,600
Production costs for April	100,000	378,000	478,000
Total accountable for	$120,800	$403,800	$524,600

Using the FIFO cost method, determine the cost of ending Work in Process inventory and the cost of units transferred to the next department.

The following equivalent production analysis uses the units started and completed procedure:

EQUIVALENT PRODUCTION SCHEDULE	MATERIAL COSTS	CONVERSION COSTS
1. Initial inventory (40,000 units times percentage work done in April)	–0–	28,000
2. Units started and completed in April (200,000 − 80,000)	120,000	120,000
3. Final inventory (80,000 units times percentage work done in April)	80,000	32,000
Equivalent units produced (1 + 2 + 3)	200,000	180,000

FIFO unit costs for materials and conversion costs are computed by dividing number of equivalent units produced into current costs charged to the department in April.

	UNITS RECEIVING	
	Material costs	*Conversion costs*
Costs incurred during April	$100,000	$378,000
÷ equivalent units produced	200,000	180,000
Cost per equivalent unit (FIFO cost)	$.50	$2.10

The cost of a unit started and completed in April is $2.60 ($.50 + $2.10). Conversion costs were incurred to complete the units in beginning Work in Process inventory; material and conversion costs were incurred to process units in the ending inventory. Costs are therefore assigned to all elements appearing in the equivalent production schedule.

Cost assignment schedule
FIFO cost method

1. Initial inventory (40,000 physical units):		
Inventory cost on April 1	$46,600	
Costs to complete: 28,000 × $2.10 =	58,800	$105,400
2. Units started and completed: 120,000 × $2.60 =		312,000
Cost of 160,000 units transferred out (1 + 2)		$417,400
3. Final inventory (80,000 physical units):		
Materials cost: 80,000 × $.50	$40,000	
Conversion costs: 32,000 × $2.10	67,200	107,200
Total costs assigned (1 + 2 + 3)		$524,600

Final Work in Process inventory of the Milling Department is $107,200 at FIFO cost. Cost of units transferred out is $417,400, and this amount is used to credit

Work in Process—Milling Department and debit Finished Goods or Work in Process of another department. Cost analysis with the units started and completed method provides the same result as using the transferred-out procedures. The two methods are closely related, although they differ in procedure and format.

FINAL NOTE Appendix 6-A provides an opportunity to apply most of the material covered in this chapter. A complete solution is also presented in the appendix. Quantity schedules, equivalent production, and cost assignment schedules are the foundations of process cost analysis. The next chapter applies these fundamental procedures to complex process cost situations.

When you have completed your review of the appendix, return to the beginning of the chapter and review the highlights section before proceeding to the review questions and problems.

APPENDIX 6-A: Comprehensive Process Cost Illustration

The Balke Company manufactures product Z by continuous processing in a single department. All materials are introduced at the beginning of production, and each final product requires one unit of raw material. Labor and overhead costs are incurred uniformly during the process, and the company charges actual monthly overhead costs to production. The weighted average cost method is used for all inventories. In addition, Balke Company uses perpetual inventory records with end-of-period costing procedures for all inventories.

During July 19X9, Balke Company purchased 20,000 units of raw material at $2.20 per unit. A journal entry is required at July 31 to record the following overhead costs for the month:

Supplies and tools	$3,500	
Water and power	4,000	
Repairs and maintenance	5,000	
Total cash payments		$12,500
Accrued payroll taxes—employer		1,500
Accrued property taxes		2,500
Expired insurance premiums		2,000
Depreciation of fixed assets		3,000
Patent amortization		500
Actual overhead costs		$22,000

Gross salaries and wages of production personnel were $46,000. During July, 22,000 units of product Z were started, and 18,000 units were transferred to Finished Goods. Inventory data are summarized on the next page:

	Inventory on July 1			Inventory on July 31	
	Units	Cost	Percent complete	Units	Percent complete
Raw materials	8,000	$12,000		6,000	
Finished goods	5,000	$26,360		2,000	
Work in process	4,000	(1 + 2)		8,000	
(1) Material costs		$ 6,000	100		100
(2) Conversion costs		$ 4,000	25		75

Based upon the above information, prepare the following schedules and analyses:

1. Combined quantity schedule for Raw Materials, Work in Process, and Finished Goods
2. Schedule computing the cost of materials issued to production in July (Note: Determine units available and related total cost; compute average unit cost; and price ending inventory at this unit cost.)
3. Equivalent production schedules for July
4. Cost assignment schedule for Work in Process
5. Schedule computing Cost of Goods Sold for July (Note: Determine units available for sale and related total cost; compute average unit cost; and price ending inventory at this unit cost.)
6. Statement of Cost of Goods Manufactured and Sold (This statement is a formal summary of cost information from schedules 2, 4, and 5. Include a detailed listing of overhead costs in the statement.)
7. Journal entries for all transactions and adjustments

These seven requirements take you through the complete cycle of a process cost system. Develop the required schedules and check your work against the following solution. Review appropriate sections in Chapter 6 as necessary to complete your understanding of the solution.

BALKE COMPANY SOLUTION

1. Combined quantity schedule

	Raw Materials	Work in Process	Finished Goods
Units started*	20,000	22,000	18,000
Plus: Initial inventory	8,000	4,000	5,000
Total	28,000	26,000	23,000
Less: Final inventory	(6,000)	(8,000)	(2,000)
Transferred out	22,000	18,000	21,000

* Purchased for Raw Materials; completed production for Finished Goods.

2. Cost of materials issued (average cost method)

	Units	Unit Cost	Total Costs
Units purchased	20,000	$2.20	$44,000
Plus: Initial inventory	8,000		12,000
Total	28,000	$2.00	$56,000
Less: Final inventory	(6,000)	$2.00	(12,000)
Transferred out	22,000		$44,000

3. Equivalent production schedule

	Material Costs	Conversion Costs
Transferred out	18,000	18,000
Plus: FI* (8,000 at 100% and 75%)	8,000	6,000
Total equivalent units	26,000	24,000
Less: II† (4,000 at 100% and 25%)	(4,000)	(1,000)
Equivalent units produced	22,000	23,000

* FI = final inventory.
† II = initial inventory.

4. Cost assignment schedule—Work in process (unit data from schedule 3)

EQUIVALENT UNITS	RAW MATERIALS Units	Unit cost	Amount	CONVERSION COSTS Units	Unit cost	Amount	TOTAL COSTS
Units produced	22,000		$44,000	23,000		*$68,000	$112,000
Plus: Initial inventory	4,000		6,000	1,000		4,000	10,000
Total	26,000	$1.92	$50,000	24,000	$3	$72,000	$122,000
Less: Final inventory	(8,000)	$1.92	(15,360)	(6,000)	$3	(18,000)	(33,360)
Transferred out	18,000		$34,640	18,000		$54,000	$ 88,640

* Conversion costs for July = labor $46,000 + overhead $22,000.

5. Schedule of cost of goods sold (average cost method)

FINISHED GOODS	Units	Unit Cost	Total Costs
Completed units received	18,000		$ 88,640
Plus: Initial inventory	5,000		26,360
Total	23,000	$5	$115,000
Less: Final inventory	(2,000)	$5	(10,000)
Transferred out (sold)	21,000		$105,000

6. Statement of cost of goods manufactured and sold

Raw materials:		
Inventory on July 1	$12,000	
Purchases	44,000	
Cost of materials available	$56,000	
Inventory on July 31	(12,000)	
Materials issued to production (schedule 2)		$ 44,000
Manufacturing labor cost		46,000
Factory overhead costs:		
Employer payroll taxes	$ 1,500	
Property taxes	2,500	
Expired insurance	2,000	
Depreciation	3,000	
Patent amortization	500	
Supplies and tools	3,500	
Water and power	4,000	
Repairs and maintenance	5,000	22,000
Total Manufacturing Costs Incurred in July		$112,000
Plus: Work in Process, July 1		10,000
Total Costs Accountable For		$122,000
Less: Work in Process, July 31		(33,360)
Cost of goods manufactured (schedule 4)		$ 88,640
Plus: Finished Goods, July 1		26,360
Cost of Goods Available for Sale		$115,000
Less: Finished Goods, July 31		(10,000)
Cost of Goods sold (schedule 5)		$105,000

7. Journal entries for July

	DEBIT	CREDIT
1. Material inventory	$ 44,000	
Accounts payable		$ 44,000
Purchased 20,000 units at $2.20— schedule 2		
2. Work in process	$ 44,000	
Material inventory		$ 44,000
Cost of materials issued—schedule 2		
3. Work in process	$ 46,000	
Factory payroll		$ 46,000
Gross salaries of production personnel		
4. Factory overhead control	$ 22,000	
Employer payroll taxes payable		$ 1,500
Property taxes payable		2,500
Prepaid insurance		2,000
Accumulated depreciation		3,000
Patents		500
Cash		12,500
Overhead costs incurred in July		

5. Work in process	$ 22,000	
Factory overhead control		$ 22,000
Charge actual overhead to production		
6. Finished goods	$ 88,640	
Work in process		$ 88,640
Cost of completed production—		
schedule 4		
7. Cost of goods sold	$105,000	
Finished goods		$105,000
Cost of units sold—schedule 5		

QUESTIONS

6-1. Define and illustrate the following terms and concepts:
 - a. Process cost accounting
 - b. Physical unit flow
 - c. Equivalent production
 - d. Conversion costs
 - e. Prior department costs
 - f. Continuous production flow concept
 - g. Quantity schedule
 - h. Cost assignment schedule
 - i. Departmental cost of production report

6-2. In process cost systems, why is there a "departmental orientation" in the accumulation and analysis of production costs?

6-3. What are the principal components of a departmental cost of production report?

6-4. How does the general ledger treatment for Work in Process inventories differ between job order and process cost systems?

6-5. In sequential order, identify the three phases of departmental process cost analysis.

6-6. How do the existence of beginning and ending Work in Process inventories add to the complexity of process cost analysis?

6-7. Department X had 1,000 units in process at the start of June that were 35 percent complete with regard to conversion costs. What is the equivalent production (FIFO flow) for this group of units during June?

6-8. Department M had 8,000 units in process at the end of August that were 40 percent complete with regard to labor and overhead. What is the equivalent production for this group of units during August?

6-9. Under what circumstances in process costing is it acceptable to charge actual overhead costs to production?

6-10. Why would a firm select FIFO cost flow over the average cost method for use in a process cost system?

6-11. "The presence of initial Work in Process inventories in a department makes necessary the use of a particular cost flow assumption, such as FIFO or average cost." Explain this statement.

6-12. A departmental cost of production report at May 31 discloses a final inventory of $67,800 and cost of transfers from the department of $812,000. What accounting use is made with each of these cost amounts?

6-13. *Quantity Schedules* Complete the following quantity schedules by computing the missing data elements.

	CASE 1	CASE 2	CASE 3	CASE 4
Units started	100,000	?	300,000	?
Initial inventory	?	40,000	15,000	–0–
Units accountable for	?	240,000	?	?
Final inventory	30,000	?	10,000	8,000
Transferred out	120,000	190,000	?	102,000

6-14. *Inventory Groups* A department with no initial Work in Process inventory on January 1 started 400,000 units during the month. Materials are introduced at the start of operations. The final Work in Process inventory consisted of several inventory batches with degree of completion for conversion costs shown in parenthesis: 10,000 units (80 percent); 5,000 (60 percent); 12,000 (50 percent); 10,000 (10 percent); 5,000 (40 percent). Prepare equivalent production schedules for material and conversion costs.

6-15. *Degree of Completion* Production of a chemical involves material and conversion costs that are incurred uniformly throughout processing. Several alternatives exist for measuring degree of completion for Work in Process inventories: engineering estimates; consistent use of 50 percent; ignoring inventories completely. For each case below, prepare the related equivalent production schedule.

	PHYSICAL UNITS	PERCENTAGE COMPLETION		
		Case 1	Case 2	Case 3
Units started	300,000	301,500	285,000	270,00
Initial inventory	20,000	20	50	0
Units accountable for	320,000			
Final inventory	50,000	70	50	0
Transferred out	270,000			

6-16. *Equivalent Production*   A department that introduces material at the start of operations started 600,000 units in December. Initial and final inventories were 80,000 and 50,000 units, respectively. Degree of completion for conversion costs is always estimated at 50 percent. Prepare equivalent production schedules assuming use of (a) the units started and completed approach and (b) the transferred-out approach.

6-17. Refer to exercise 6-16. What is the denominator for computing average unit cost? What is the denominator for computing FIFO unit cost? What is the number of equivalent units produced during December?

6-18. *FIFO and Average Cost*   For departmental operations in July, you have prepared an equivalent production schedule and summary of costs accountable for, as shown below. Material costs and conversion costs are incurred uniformly.

	EQUIVALENT UNITS	COSTS ACCOUNTABLE FOR	
Transferred out	240,000	Incurred in July	$840,000
Final inventory	60,000	Inventory, July 1	30,000
Total	300,000	Total costs	$870,000
Initial inventory	(20,000)		
Equivalent units produced	280,000		

Prepare a cost assignment schedule using (a) the average cost method and (b) the FIFO cost method.

6-19. *Use of Cost Reports*   A departmental cost of production report for March concludes with the following three lines:

	EQUIVALENT UNITS	PRODUCTION COSTS
Total equivalent units	400,000	$600,000
Final inventory	(20,000)	(30,000)
Transferred out	380,000	$570,000

What is the unit cost used in the analysis? With perpetual inventories, what journal entry does the schedule support?

PROBLEMS

6-20. *Multiple Choice*   Tap Company produces a single product in one continuous operation. Since materials are added throughout the process, only one percentage completion factor is estimated for materials, labor, and overhead. The company uses a rather simple actual cost system without perpetual inventories. Material cost and conversion costs are combined and referred to as production costs. Production costs incurred during December were $910,000. Units started in December were 12,000, and the final inventory was 3,000 units. On December 1, there were 6,000 units in process that were 50 percent complete regarding production costs. Costs assigned to these units as of December 1 were $130,000. Degree of completion for the final inventory was estimated at one-third.

REQUIRED:

a. The number of units transferred out of the process during December was:

1. 12,000   3. 13,000
2. 15,000   4. 16,000

15,000

b. The number of equivalent units produced for the month was:

1. 16,000   3. 13,000
2. 12,000   4. 15,000

c. With weighted average procedures, the unit cost of the final inventory is:

1. $43   3. $58
2. $70   4. $65

d. Using the FIFO cost flow assumption, the unit cost of the final inventory is:

1. $43   3. $58
2. $70   4. $65

e. With the FIFO cost flow assumption, the total cost assigned to units transferred out of the process is:

1. $1,050,000   3. $1,040,000
2. $970,000   4. $975,000

6-21. *FIFO/Average Cost* The accounts of Griffin Corporation contain the following information:

MIXING PROCESS	
Inventory, Nov. 1, 19X6	20,000 units
Cost of above:	
Direct materials (100% completed)	$4,000
Conversion costs (40% completed)	$16,400
Started in November 19X6	100,000 units
Current charges for November 19X6:	
Direct materials	$21,000
Conversion costs	$204,000
Completed and transferred to the boiling process	95,000 units
Inventory, Nov. 30, 19X6 (100% completed as to	
materials, 50% completed as to conversion costs)	25,000 units

In order to prepare process cost reports for November, you are presented with the following *correct* information:

Units to be accounted for   120,000

Unit cost denominator for November:

	Materials	Conversion costs
Weighted-average method	120,000 units	107,500 units
FIFO method	100,000 units	99,500 units

REQUIRED: Use good form and show all computations.
1. Using the above information and the average cost method:
   a. Compute unit costs for November.
   b. Prepare a schedule showing cost of units transferred to the Boiler Department during November.
   c. Prepare a report showing cost of the Work in Process inventory on Nov. 30, 19X6. (Show breakdown of material and conversion costs.)
2. Using the above information and the FIFO cost method:
   a. Compute unit costs for November.
   b. Prepare a schedule showing costs of units transferred to the Boiler Department during November. #214,525
   c. Prepare a report showing cost of the Work in Process inventory on Nov. 30, 19X6. (Show breakdown of material and conversion costs.)

6-22. *Average Cost Method*   The Hillman Processing Company had Work in Process at the beginning and end of 19X8 as follows:

	PERCENTAGE	COMPLETION
	Materials	Conversion costs
Jan. 1, 19X8—3,000 units	40	10
Dec. 31, 19X8—2,000 units	80	40

The company completed 40,000 units during 19X8. Manufacturing costs incurred during the year were: materials, $242,600; conversion costs, $445,200. Inventory on January 1, 19X8, was carried at a cost of $10,600 (materials, $7,000; conversion costs, $3,600).

REQUIRED: Using the average cost method:
a. Compute the equivalent production in 19X8 for (1) materials and (2) labor and overhead.
b. Compute the total cost to be transferred to Finished Goods inventory for the year.
c. Compute the cost of the ending Work in Process inventory.

6-23. *FIFO Cost Method*   The Johnson Manufacturing Company prepares a monthly cost of production report for its one-department processing plant. It uses the FIFO method of costing Work in Process inventories. For the month of March 19X9, the following production and cost data have been accumulated:

PRODUCTION DATA

Work in process—Mar. 1, 19X9: materials 70% complete; labor and overhead 25% complete	16,000 units
Units put into production during March	50,000 units
Units transferred to finished goods during March	60,000 units
Work in process—Mar. 31, 19X9: materials 80% complete; labor and overhead 40% complete	6,000 units

COST DATA

	Material	Labor	Overhead	Total
Work in process	11,200	4,000	4,000	
Mar. 1, 19X9	$17,920	$ 3,120	$ 1,400	$ 22,440
Costs for				
March 19X9	$98,720	$46,800	$23,560	$169,080
				$191,520

REQUIRED: Show and label all computations. $184 .80

a. Determine the FIFO unit cost in March for (1) materials, (2) labor, and (3) overhead. .40

b. Compute the total cost of production transferred to Finished Goods during March.

mat $8832 00
    1 920 00
oH   960 00
      11712

c. Compute the total cost of ending Work in Process inventory.— 2

6-24. *CPA Problem—FIFO Cost Analysis* Bisto Corporation manufactures valves and pumps for liquids. On December 1, 19X4, Bisto paid $25,000 to the Poplen Company for the patent for its Watertite valve. Bisto planned to carry on Poplen's procedure of having the valve casing and parts cast by an independent foundry and doing the grinding and assembling in its own plant.

Bisto also purchased Poplen's inventory of the valves at 80 percent of its cost to Poplen. The purchased inventory comprised the following:

	Units
Raw material (unfinished casings and parts)	1,100
Work in process:	
Grinding (25% complete)	800
Assembling (40% complete)	600
Finished valves	900

Poplen's cost accounting system provided the following unit costs:

	Cost per Unit
Raw materials (unfinished casings and parts)	$2.00
Grinding costs	1.00
Assembling costs	2.50

Bisto's cost accounting system accumulated the following costs for the month of December that do not include cost of the inventory purchased from Poplen:

Raw material purchases	
(casings and parts for 5,000 units)	$10,500
Grinding costs	2,430
Assembling costs	5,664

Bisto's inventory of Watertite valves on December 31, 19X4, follows:

Raw material (unfinished casings and parts)	2,700
Work in process:	
Grinding (35% complete)	2,000
Assembling (33⅓% complete)	300
Finished valves	2,250

No valves were spoiled or lost during the manufacturing process.

REQUIRED   (Bisto uses the process costing method in its accounting system):

a. Prepare a schedule to compute the equivalent units produced and FIFO unit costs for the month of December 19X4.
b. Prepare a schedule of inventories on the FIFO basis as of December 1 and 31, 19X4, setting forth by layers the number of units, unit costs, and amounts. Show all supporting schedules in good form.

(AICPA adapted)

6-25. *Consecutive Time Periods*   The Graber Metal Products Company produces small metal-cutting tools with a sequence of four processes (forging, grinding, polishing, and heat treating). The following data relate to only the grinding process for the months of January and February:

UNIT DATA	JANUARY	FEBRUARY
Beginning work in process inventory	-0-	10,000
Transferred in	58,000	60,000
Transferred out	48,000	55,000
Ending work in process inventory	10,000	15,000

COST DATA	JANUARY	FEBRUARY
Cost of beginning work in process:		
Transferred in from preceding process	-0-	?
Conversion costs (labor and overhead)	-0-	?
Costs added during the month:		
Transferred in from preceding process	$145,000	$146,500
Conversion costs	$ 58,300	$ 59,500

Units transferred in from the forging process are entered at the beginning of the grinding process. Conversion costs are incurred uniformly throughout the process. Assume that January's ending Work in Process inventory is one-half complete, while February's ending Work in Process inventory is two-thirds complete.

REQUIRED: Using the average cost method, compute the following:

a. For January, (1) unit conversion costs and (2) total cost of ending Work in Process inventory.
b. For February, (1) unit conversion costs, and (2) total cost of ending Work in Process inventory.

6-26. *Processing in Two Departments*   The Elliott Tool Company manufactures on a continuous basis a single electrical product that goes through two manufacturing departments, Machining and Assembly; output of the Machining Department is transferred to Assembly.

During the month of May, production records for Machining disclosed the following:

Units put into production	200,000
Units completed and transferred out	160,000
Units in process 100% complete regarding material, but 25% complete regarding labor and overhead	40,000

The costs of manufacturing for May in the Machining Department were:

Material costs	$240,000
Labor costs	135,150
Manufacturing overhead costs	114,750

In the Assembly Department, 120,000 units were completed and transferred to the finished stock room; 40,000 units were in process, 100 percent complete regarding material but two-thirds complete regarding labor and manufacturing overhead.

Costs of manufacturing for May in Assembly were:

Material costs (new materials added to product)	$153,600
Labor costs	163,145
Manufacturing overhead costs	49,795

There was no Work in Process inventory in either department at the beginning of the month of May.

REQUIRED: Prepare schedules using the average cost method to determine the:

a. Unit cost of goods transferred out of the Machining Department
b. Unit cost of goods transferred out of the Assembly Department
c. Cost of ending inventory in the Assembly Department
d. Is the choice between FIFO and average cost methods important in this particular problem?

6-27. *CPA Problem—Cost Control Report* The Dopern Company employs departmental budgets and performance reports in planning and controlling its process costing operations. Department A's budget for January was for the production of 1,000 units of equivalent production, a normal month's volume.

The following performance report was prepared for January by the company's accountant:

	BUDGET	ACTUAL	VARIANCE
Variable costs			
Direct material	$20,000	$23,100	$3,100 (unfavorable)
Direct labor	10,000	10,500	500 (unfavorable)
Indirect labor	1,650	1,790	140 (unfavorable)
Power	210	220	10 (unfavorable)
Supplies	320	330	10 (unfavorable)
Total	$32,180	$35,940	$3,760
Fixed costs			
Rent	$ 400	$ 400	—
Supervision	1,000	1,000	—
Depreciation	500	500	—
Other	100	100	—
Total	2,000	2,000	—
Grand total	$34,180	$37,940	$3,760

Direct material is introduced at various stages, and all conversion costs are incurred uniformly throughout the process. Because production fluctuates from month to month, the fixed overhead is applied at the rate of two dollars per equivalent unit of direct labor. Variable costs are applied monthly as incurred.

There was no opening inventory on January 1. Of the 1,100 new units started during January, 900 were completed and shipped. There was no finished goods inventory. The units in process on January 31 were estimated to be 75 percent complete regarding direct materials and 80 percent complete regarding conversion costs. There is no shrinkage, spoilage, or waste of materials.

REQUIRED:
a. Prepare a schedule of equivalent production for January.
b. Prepare a schedule computing the amount of under- or overapplied overhead on January 31.
c. Prepare a schedule computing the cost of goods shipped and the cost of the work in process inventory on January 31 at actual cost.
d. Comment on the performance report in 150 words or less. What specific conclusions, if any, can be drawn from the report?

(AICPA adapted)

6-28. *Processing in Two Departments* The Kesner Company has a two-process factory in which all materials are placed in production in Department A at the start of processing, and semifinished products are transferred to Department B for completion. No additional materials are introduced in Department B. The following data relate to the month of June:

Department A
Beginning inventory (50 units, one-fourth completed):
   materials, $50; processing costs, $50
Raw materials received during month (100 units), $115
Processing costs incurred during month, $390
Ending inventory: 60 units, one-third completed

Department B
Beginning inventory (40 units, one-half completed): materials,
   $217; processing costs, $150
Processing costs incurred during month, $540
Ending inventory: 45 units, two-thirds completed

REQUIRED: Prepare schedules under the average cost method to determine the:
a. Unit cost of goods transferred out of Department A
b. Unit cost of goods transferred out of Department B
c. Ending inventory for materials cost in Department B
d. Ending inventory for conversion costs in Department B

6-29. *Processing in Two Departments* The Tuff Kitty Company had the following inventory on January 1, 19X7:

WORK IN PROCESS	PERCENTAGE COMPLETION	COSTS
Machining Department: 1,000 units:		
Material	80	$6,400
Conversion costs	40	4,800
Assembly Department: 3,000 units:		
Material	100	66,000
Conversion costs	40	4,800

During 19X7, 5,000 units were transferred from Machining to Assembly, and 6,000 units were transferred from Assembly to Finished Goods. The company uses the weighted average cost method. Inventory on December 31, 19X7, was as follows:

WORK IN PROCESS	PERCENTAGE COMPLETION
Machining Department: 1,500 units:	
Material	20
Conversion costs	70
Assembly Department: 2,000 units:	
Conversion costs	50

The following amounts were placed into production in the Machining Department during the period: material, $40,240; conversion costs, $75,060. No material is added to production in the Assembly Department, but transfers from Machining to Assembly (prior department costs) are considered as material. During the period, $37,200 of conversion costs were added in the Assembly Department.

REQUIRED:
a. Prepare a quantity schedule for each department.
b. Prepare an equivalent production schedule for each department.
c. Compute costs per unit and total costs of:
1. Transfers from machining to assembly
2. Ending inventory—machining
3. Transfers from Assembly to Finished Goods
4. Ending inventory—Assembly

Chapter 7: Extended Practices in Process Costing

Purpose and Learning Objectives

The basic procedures for unit cost determination and inventory valuation in a process cost accounting system were described in Chapter 6. This chapter introduces process costing situations that involve costs transferred from previous departments, lost units caused by spoilage or evaporation, additional raw materials used, and added units caused by new materials.

Upon completion of this chapter, students should be able to:

1. Compute equivalent production, unit costs, and ending inventory values for process costing departments that experience (a) costs transferred from previous departments, (b) units lost due to spoilage or evaporation, (c) additional raw materials put into process, and (d) added units caused by introducing new materials
2. Distinguish between and properly account for issued but unprocessed raw materials, partially processed units, and units completed but not transferred out at period end
3. Describe and apply the various inventory valuation and cost flow assumptions commonly associated with process cost accounting

Relevant Concepts

The following basic concepts are introduced in this chapter:

Spoiled units   The concept that accountability for units and production costs is adjusted to recognize the loss of units resulting from evaporation, shrinkage, or detection and removal of unsuitable products.

Added units   The concept that accountability for units and production costs is adjusted to recognize an increase in products caused by adding new materials during processing operations.

Inventory valuation   The process of selecting and applying a particular basis for measuring inventories in monetary terms.

Inventory cost flow   The use of FIFO, LIFO, or average cost procedures to represent the assumed flow of production costs through Work in Process and other inventory accounts.

The foundations of process cost accounting were established in Chapter 6. For process cost systems using historical or normal absorption costing, you learned the basic procedures for:

1. Accumulating costs by department
2. Summarizing the flow of physical units
3. Measuring equivalent production
4. Computing unit costs for inventories

These four basic procedures must be applied in all process costing systems.

Several additional features of process costing systems make cost analysis more complex in practice. These features include:

1. Prior department costs transferred to subsequent departments
2. Lost units caused by spoilage or evaporation
3. Additional raw materials added to a process
4. Added units caused by introducing new materials
5. Issued but unprocessed raw materials
6. Units completed but not transferred out of production departments

In simple process costing situations, units accountable for always equals the sum of units started (US) plus initial inventory (II). The final inventory (FI) plus units transferred out (TO) also equals units accountable for, so that US + II = FI + TO. Unit accountability, however, is affected by other factors. Spoilage causes a loss of units such that US + II − spoilage = FI + TO. If new materials cause an increase in units held by a department, then unit accountability is affected since US + II + added units = FI + TO. As indicated in this chapter, spoilage, added units, and other complex process costing features can be properly analyzed by making minor adjustments to the set of schedules described in Chapter 6.

ACCOUNTING FOR PRIOR DEPARTMENT COSTS

With sequential product flows, costs incurred by one department normally are transferred to the Work in Process account of a second department. In the second department, these transferred-in costs are called *prior department costs*. The second department will account for prior department costs in the same manner as if raw materials were being added at the beginning of its operations. In computing equivalent production, the degree of completion for prior department costs is always 100 percent. The following illustration demonstrates accounting for prior department costs.

A chemical product is produced by two sequential processes, mixing and cooking. Quantity reports for March show the following production activity:

Physical Units	Mixing	Cooking
Units started	22,000	18,000
Initial inventory	4,000	6,000
Total	26,000	24,000
Final inventory	(8,000)	(4,000)
Transferred out	18,000	20,000

The cost of production report for the Mixing Department disclosed the following cost summary:

March Cost Summary	Mixing Department
Units produced in March	$112,000
Initial inventory	10,000
Total	$122,000
Final inventory (average cost)	(33,360)
Transferred out (18,000 units)	$ 88,640

On the basis of this cost summary, the following journal entry was prepared:

1. Work in process—Cooking Department $88,640
         Work in process—Mixing Department $88,640

During March, the Cooking Department incurred $75,000 of conversion costs, consisting of $38,000 in labor and $37,000 of applied overhead. No additional materials are added during cooking operations. Final inventory was 25 percent complete regarding conversion costs. Cooking Department initial inventory was 33 percent complete regarding conversion costs on March 1 and carried the following costs:

Prior department costs	$31,360
Conversion costs	9,000
Initial inventory cost, March 1	$40,360

You are required to prepare equivalent production and cost assignment schedules for the Cooking Department as of March 31.

In the following sections, prior department costs are noted as *PDC*. Final inventory and initial inventory are noted as *FI* and *II*, respectively.

Schedule 1

COOKING DEPARTMENT	EQUIVALENT PRODUCTION IN MARCH	
	PDC	Conversion costs
Transferred out	20,000	20,000
Plus: FI (4,000 at 100% and 25%)	4,000	1,000
Total equivalent units	24,000	21,000
Less: II (6,000 at 100% and 33%)	(6,000)	(2,000)
Equivalent units produced	18,000	19,000

Schedule 2: Weighted average cost analysis for Cooking Department (all unit data from schedule 1)

EQUIVALENT UNITS	PDC			CONVERSION COSTS			TOTAL COSTS
	Units	Unit cost	Amount	Units	Unit cost	Amount	
Units produced	18,000		$ 88,640	19,000		$75,000	$163,640
Initial inventory	6,000		31,360	2,000		9,000	40,360
Total	24,000	$5	$120,000	21,000	$4	$84,000	$204,000
Final inventory	(4,000)	$5	(20,000)	(1,000)	$4	(4,000)	(24,000)
Transferred out	20,000		$100,000	20,000		$80,000	$180,000

The following journal entries are required at March 31 for Cooking Department operations:

2. Work in process—cooking $ 38,000
       Factory payroll $ 38,000
     To record factory labor costs in March
3. Work in process—cooking $ 37,000
       Factory overhead applied $ 37,000
     To charge overhead costs to Cooking
     Department
4. Finished goods $180,000
       Work in process—cooking $180,000
     To record cost of units transferred to
     Finished Goods

After posting journal entries 1 to 4, the departmental Work in Process account appears as follows:

Work in process—Cooking Department

	Balance, March 1	$40,360			
(1)	Prior department costs	88,640	(4)	Transfers	$180,000
(2)	Factory labor	38,000			
(3)	Factory overhead	37,000			
	Balance	$24,000			

As the preceding illustration shows, there is not much difference between accounting for prior department costs and the cost of a material introduced at the start of processing. In departmental cost of production reports, it is best to analyze prior department costs separately since they are not controllable by succeeding department managers.

In all preceding examples of process cost analysis, there was no spoilage or product loss caused by shrinkage or evaporation. Basic problem situations are structured so that units started plus initial inventory equal the sum of final inventory plus units transferred out, or US + II = FI + TO. Many processes involve the element of spoilage or lost units attributable to one of the following reasons:

ACCOUNTING FOR SPOILED UNITS

1. Physical units are damaged or otherwise found unsuitable for processing and are removed from the process.
2. The basic process causes shrinkage or evaporation of the materials used so that completed output measures a smaller volume than the total of basic inputs.

The terms *spoilage* and *lost units* are used to describe product loss caused by either of the two conditions described above. With *normal spoilage*, or unavoidable spoilage, related costs are accounted for as product costs, and the cost of spoiled units is assigned to the remaining good units produced. Costs attached to abnormal spoilage should be computed and charged to the current period as a loss. *Abnormal spoilage* is defined as unusually high spoilage in relation to expected or past spoilage experience.

The difference between normal and abnormal spoilage is seen in our next example. San Angelo Corporation normally experiences a spoilage rate equal to 10 percent of units placed into production. During June, 300,000 units were started into production, but only 200,000 good units were produced. Assume that an average production cost of ten dollars was incurred for each unit placed into production and that inspection (hence spoilage detection) took place at the end of the process. There were no beginning or ending Work in Process inventories. The following cost analysis is appropriate under these given conditions:

UNITS COMPLETED AND TRANSFERRED TO FINISHED GOODS INVENTORY

Cost attached to good units completed (200,000 units × $10)	$2,000,000
Costs attached to normal spoilage (30,000 units × $10)	300,000
Cost of 200,000 units completed and transferred	$2,300,000*

Abnormal spoilage:

100,000 units (total spoilage)	
− 30,000 units (normal spoilage)	
70,000 units (abnormal spoilage) × $10	700,000
Total production costs for June	$3,000,000

---

* Note that the new unit cost is $11.50 ($2,300,000/200,000 units).

The following journal entry is required on June 30:

Finished goods inventory	$2,300,000	
Loss from abnormal spoilage	700,000	
Work in process inventory		$3,000,000

To transfer cost of good units produced to Finished Goods inventory and to record loss from abnormal spoilage during June

As shown in the above cost analysis, the basic effect of spoilage is that there are fewer good units to which the costs of a producing department can be assigned. Accounting methods for cost assignment differ depending upon where in the production process spoilage takes place. Actually, spoilage can occur and be detected at any point in the production process. For practical purposes, accountants normally use the costing procedures for initial or terminal spoilage, whichever most clearly applies. If spoilage occurs at the start of operations, it is called *initial spoilage*, and costs of the spoiled units are allocated to good production and units remaining in the final inventory. If spoilage occurs at the end of operations, this condition is called *terminal spoilage*, and costs of the spoilage are allocated only to the units transferred out of the department. Thus, spoilage occurring at the point 20 percent through a process is usually treated as though spoilage occurred at the start of operations. If spoilage occurs when processing is 75 percent complete, it is convenient to account for this event as though spoilage occurred at the end of processing. The two spoilage methods produce different cost assignment results and are analyzed in the following sections. Note that each case analyzed below assumes only normal spoilage incurrence.

For convenience, initial spoilage means spoilage that occurs at or near the start of processing in a particular department. With initial spoilage, the accounting objective is to allocate the cost of spoiled units to units transferred out *and* to units remaining in the final Work in Process inventory. Since all units started into production are either processed or spoiled immediately, all units to be accounted for (both finished and in process) should absorb part of the spoilage cost. This objective can be accomplished through our process cost accounting schedules with or without actually measuring the cost of lost units. Spoiled units are noted in the quantity schedule, which summarizes physical units. Equivalent production schedules and cost analysis then are based on good units only. Since spoilage appears only as reconciling data in the quantity report, the accounting method for initial spoilage is sometimes called "the method of neglect."

Spoilage at Start of Process

To illustrate accounting for initial spoilage, consider a chemical department that blends materials throughout a mixing operation and uses a single percentage completion for both materials and conversion costs. In February, the department started 210,000 units and transferred 160,000 units to Finished Goods. The initial Work in Process inventory of 40,000 units carried a cost of $21,600 and was 30 percent complete on February 1. The final Work in Process inventory of 80,000 units was 40 percent complete. During the month, $381,600 of material, labor, and overhead costs were charged to the department. Given these facts, you are to prepare (1) a quantity schedule, (2) an equivalent production schedule, and (3) a cost assignment schedule using the average cost method.

As the three schedules in Exhibit 7-1 show, cost accounting for initial spoilage is handled with one simple adjustment in the quantity schedule. All other computations are performed as though 200,000 units (210,000 − 10,000) were started during the period. Note that the cost of spoiled units is not identified in Exhibit 7-1, but the costs related to spoiled units simply are assigned to the remaining good units.

Since material was added gradually in our example, spoilage probably occurred sometime during the process rather than at the start. The only way to measure the cost of spoiled units in this case is to analyze comparatively the cost assignment that would be made if spoilage had not occurred. Without spoilage, the units transferred out would be 170,000 instead of 160,000, and the average unit cost would be $1.996, computed as follows:

	UNITS
Transferred out	170,000 (assuming no spoilage)
Plus: FI (80,000 at 40%)	32,000
Total equivalent units	202,000 (assuming no spoilage)
Current production costs	$381,600
Initial inventory costs	21,600
Costs accountable for	$403,200
Average cost denominator	÷ 202,000
Average cost, assuming no spoilage	$1.996
Spoilage cost: 10,000 units × $1.996 =	$ 19,960

EXHIBIT 7-1

PROCESS COSTING WITH INITIAL SPOILAGE

1. Quantity schedule

	PHYSICAL UNITS
Units started	210,000*
Less: Initial spoilage	(10,000)
Net units available	200,000
Initial inventory	40,000*
Units accountable for	240,000
Final inventory	(80,000)*
Transferred out	160,000*

* Given data.

Note that the 10,000 spoiled unit amount was not given but can be determined by preparing the quantity schedule and working backward from Transferred Out to Units Started. Equivalent production then is based on good units only, and the units of spoilage are ignored from this point on.

2. Equivalent production schedule

	ALL COST FACTORS
Transferred out	160,000
Plus: FI (80,000 at 40%)	32,000
Total	192,000
Less: II (40,000 at 30%)	(12,000)
Equivalent units produced	180,000

3. Cost assignment schedule (unit data from schedule 2)

	EQUIVALENT UNITS	UNIT COST	AMOUNT
Equivalent units produced	180,000		$381,600
Initial inventory	12,000		21,600
Total	192,000	$2.10	$403,200
Final inventory	(32,000)	$2.10	(67,200)
Transferred out	160,000		$336,000

The $19,960 cost of normal spoilage is allocated to the final inventory and actual transfers of 160,000 units as follows:

SPOILAGE LOSS ALLOCATION	TRANSFERRED OUT	FINAL INVENTORY	TOTAL COSTS
(1) Actual equivalent units	160,000	32,000	
(2) Unit cost assuming no spoilage	× $1.996	× $1.996	
(3) Costs before spoilage loss	$319,360	$63,872	$383,232
(4) Loss per unit: $19,960 ÷ 192,000 =	$ .104	$ .104	
(5) Allocated loss (1 × 4)	$ 16,640	$ 3,328	$ 19,968
Total costs (3 + 5)	$336,000	$67,200	$403,200

If it is desirable for management reporting purposes to measure the cost of spoiled units, any approach that produces the desired result is satisfactory. The effect on unit costs in our example above is:

Unit cost excluding spoilage	$1.996
Spoilage loss per good unit	.104
Average unit cost (per Exhibit 7-1)	$2.100

Note also that our process cost schedules in Exhibit 7-1 accomplish the desired product costing objectives without specifically identifying the cost attributable to spoiled units.

For problem situations in which materials are introduced at the start of processing, the spoilage loss is computed only for raw material cost. In this way, material cost is allocated to the remaining good units, while labor and overhead costs are related to the good units worked on during the period. With materials introduced at the start of a process, labor and machine time would not have been devoted to units spoiled at the beginning of operations.

Spoilage that occurs at or near the end of a process is referred to as *terminal spoilage*. The most common example of terminal spoilage is the inspection of products and rejection of defective items at the *end* of a process. If the spoilage rate is normal, then costs related to spoiled units remain product costs and are assignable to good units produced. Accounting for terminal spoilage has the objective of allocating spoilage loss entirely to units transferred out of the department. Unlike initial spoilage, terminal spoilage is detected only after production is completed. Cost of terminal spoilage should not be allocated to any item still in process. Final Work in Process inventories are valued at unit costs that do not contain a spoilage cost element. In concept, all spoilage loss is allocated to units transferred out. The final Work in Process inventory probably contains some spoiled items that will be detected when production is completed. The three basic process costing schedules are easily modified to accomplish this desired objective.

Spoilage at End of Process

As an example of terminal spoilage and related costing procedures, assume the same operating data used in Exhibit 7-1. A department starts 210,000 units during a period in which there were initial and final Work in Process inventories of 40,000 and 80,000 units, respectively. Stage of completion on these inventories for all cost factors is 30 percent at start of the period and 40 percent at end of the period. Costs charged to the department during the month are $381,600, and the initial Work in Process inventory cost was $21,600. Inspection at the end of processing detected 10,000 spoiled units during the period. From this information, we should prepare (1) a quantity schedule, (2) an equivalent production schedule, and (3) a cost assignment schedule.

These schedules are presented in Exhibit 7-2. The quantity schedule is prepared in a manner that clearly distinguishes between initial and terminal spoilage. When this difference is properly noted, equivalent production schedules can be completed in a way that simplifies the required cost assignments. The necessary adjustment for terminal spoilage is to determine units completed as well as units transferred out.

Exhibit 7-2 measures equivalent production as though no spoilage had occurred. In this way, unit costs for the final Work in Process inventory are unaffected by any spoilage loss that occurred. Accordingly, the final inventory will not carry any part of the spoilage loss. Such loss is assignable entirely to units transferred out, as shown in schedule 3 of Exhibit 7-2. Except for the number of spoiled units, all unit data in the cost assignment analysis are equivalent units from schedule 2.

Schedule 3 assigns the entire spoilage loss (10,000 units at $1.996, which is included in the $339,328 amount) to units transferred out. Accordingly, the basic accounting objective is accomplished, and the final Work in Process

EXHIBIT 7-2
PROCESS COSTING WITH TERMINAL SPOILAGE

1. Quantity schedule

	PHYSICAL UNITS
Units started	210,000
Less: Initial spoilage	None
Net units available	210,000
Initial inventory	40,000
Units accountable for	250,000
Final inventory	(80,000)
Units completed	170,000
Less: Terminal spoilage	(10,000)
Transferred out	160,000

When the quantity schedule is assembled as shown in schedule 1, equivalent production calculations should begin with units completed, as done in schedule 2.

2. Equivalent production schedule

	ALL COST FACTORS
Units completed	170,000
Plus: FI (80,000 at 40%)	32,000
Total	202,000
Less: II (40,000 at 30%)	(12,000)
Equivalent units produced	190,000

3. Cost assignment schedule (average cost method)

	EQUIVALENT UNITS	UNIT COST	AMOUNT
Equivalent units produced	190,000		$381,600
Initial inventory	12,000		21,600
Total	202,000	$1.996	$403,200
Final inventory	(32,000)	$1.996	(63,872)
Units completed	170,000		$339,328
Less: Terminal spoilage	(10,000)		—
Transferred out	160,000		$339,328

inventory is valued at $1.996 per equivalent unit, which includes no part of the spoilage loss.

Accounting for initial and terminal spoilage assumes that (1) lost units are caused by evaporation or some other cause which produces an actual loss of units or that (2) spoiled units are identified by inspection and removed from the production process. In the second case, the spoiled units physically exist and could be scrapped or sold for residual value. Proceeds from scrap sales can be treated as miscellaneous revenues or as a cost recovery. If classified as a cost recovery, proceeds from scrap sales are credited to Work in Process inventory, which reduces the costs assignable to good units produced. For example, in our case of terminal spoilage, assume that the 10,000 spoiled units are sold for $5,000 cash. The bottom portion of the cost assignment schedule would then show:

Partial Cost Schedule	Equivalent Units	Unit Cost	Amount
Units completed	170,000		$339,328
Terminal spoilage	(10,000)		(5,000) (sales proceeds)
Transferred out	160,000		$334,328

If the sales value of spoiled units is not significant, then the cost recovery procedure shown above is acceptable. Unit costs and the matching process in financial accounting would be distorted by large sales of spoiled units at significant amounts. When this occurs, the recommended procedure is to credit production for the net realizable value of spoiled units in current production and to establish inventory procedures for the subsequent sale of spoiled items. For initial spoilage, sales proceeds usually are credited to raw material costs or to prior department costs of the department in which spoilage occurred.

The preceding sections illustrated accounting procedures for initial and terminal spoilage when only one type of spoilage was involved. The three process cost schedules can accommodate the occurrence of both initial and terminal spoilage. Using the same basic data as before, assume a department starts 210,000 units and has initial and final inventories of 40,000 and 80,000 units, respectively. Initial spoilage is 10,000 units, and terminal spoilage is also 10,000 units. The three process costing schedules required in this case are presented in Exhibit 7-3.

Initial and Terminal Spoilage

The schedules in Exhibit 7-3 accomplished two objectives: (1) The cost of initial spoilage was allocated to the final inventory and units transferred out; and (2) the cost of terminal spoilage was allocated only to units transferred out. Recognize that a single percentage completion factor for inventories was used only because both material costs and conversion costs were incurred uniformly throughout the process. Separate equivalent production and cost assignment schedules are required for every cost element having a different percentage completion factor. Using a single stage of completion for all cost elements simplified the examples. However, the basic three-schedule approach to process cost accounting applies equally well to complex situations. In the next section, this three-schedule approach will be applied to situations in which raw materials are added at various stages of the production process.

EXHIBIT 7-3

PROCESS COSTING WITH INITIAL AND TERMINAL SPOILAGE

1. Quantity schedule

	PHYSICAL UNITS
Units started	210,000*
Less: Initial spoilage	(10,000)*
Net units available	200,000
Initial inventory (30% complete)	40,000*
Units accountable for	240,000
Final inventory (40% complete)	(80,000)*
Units completed	160,000
Less: Terminal spoilage	(10,000)*
Transferred out	150,000

* Given data.

Since terminal spoilage is present, start the equivalent production schedule with *units completed* and ignore initial spoilage completely.

2. Equivalent production schedule

	ALL COST FACTORS
Units completed	160,000
Plus: FI (80,000 at 40%)	32,000
Total	192,000
Less: II (40,000 at 30%)	(12,000)
Equivalent units produced	180,000

3. Cost assignment schedule (average cost method)

	EQUIVALENT UNITS	UNIT COST	AMOUNT
Equivalent units produced	180,000		$381,600
Initial inventory	12,000		21,600
Total	192,000	$2.10	$403,200
Final inventory	(32,000)	$2.10	(67,200)
Units completed	160,000		$336,000
Less: Terminal spoilage	(10,000)		—
Transferred out	150,000		$336,000

ACCOUNTING FOR ADDITIONAL RAW MATERIALS

New raw materials can be added to a process without changing the number of physical units being manufactured. For example, if units of product are painted, there is an additional raw material cost for paint but no change in the number of physical product units. Likewise, electrical tubes, wiring, and cabinets can be added in the production of radios without changing the number of units (radios) in the process. Additional raw materials that do not change the number of physical units being manufactured have no effect on equivalent production schedules for other cost factors. However, an equivalent production schedule must be prepared for additional raw materials added during production.

The degree of completion for determining equivalent production for additional materials depends upon when the new materials enter the production process. If a material is added at the start of processing, its degree of completion is 100 percent. If a material is added as the final step in a process, its degree of completion is 0 percent for all units in Work in Process inventories, because partly finished units contain none of the final material. If materials are added at various stages of production, their degree of completion is either 100 percent or 0 percent, depending upon whether the material is contained in the partially processed units composing the Work in Process inventory.

Consider a department in which a raw material is added when processing is 60 percent complete (such as after six hours in a ten-hour production process). If Work in Process inventory is 80 percent processed at the end of a period, the percentage of completion for this material is 100 percent; all units in the final Work in Process inventory contain the raw material that was added when units were 60 percent through the process. However, if the Work in Process inventory is only 20 percent processed at month end, then the degree of completion for this material is 0 percent, since partly processed units do not yet contain any of the material. It is important to determine the degree of completion correctly because this factor affects equivalent production and related cost assignment schedules. To illustrate this point, study the next illustration.

Kyle Company produces its only product in a single department that uses three different raw materials. Raw material 1 (RM1) is added at the start of processing; RM2 is added when processing is 60 percent complete; and RM3 is added as the final production step. Labor and overhead costs are incurred uniformly. For the month of May, the company's final inventory on May 31 was 20 percent processed, and the initial inventory was 80 percent processed as of May 1. Also furnished is a summary of initial inventory costs and costs charged to the department for May operations. (Labor and overhead are noted as L & OH.)

Costs Accountable for	RM1	RM2	RM3	L & OH
Work in process, May 1	$ 22,000	$ 41,000	$ -0-	$ 66,000
Costs incurred in May	98,000	139,000	45,000	$318,000
Total costs	$120,000	$180,000	$45,000	$384,000

Exhibit 7-4 contains the three-schedule solution to this problem including (1) a quantity schedule, (2) an equivalent production schedule, and (3) a cost assignment schedule using the average cost method. Review the percentage completion factors for initial and final inventories in schedule 1 to be certain that you understand how the amounts were determined. Then follow each cost factor listed in Exhibit 7-4 through schedules 2 and 3. Notice that the format of the cost assignment schedule was changed to easily accommodate four cost

EXHIBIT 7-4

PROCESS COSTING WITH SEVERAL RAW MATERIALS

1. Quantity schedule (physical unit data are given)

	PHYSICAL UNITS	PERCENTAGE COMPLETION FOR			
		RM1	RM2	RM3	L & OH
Units started	100,000				
Initial inventory (80% processed)	20,000	100	100	0	80
Units accountable for	120,000				
Final inventory (20% processed)	(30,000)	100	0	0	20
Transferred out	90,000				

2. Equivalent production schedule

	COST FACTORS			
	RM1	RM2	RM3	L & OH
Transferred out	90,000	90,000	90,000	90,000
Plus: FI (30,000 at 100%, 0%, 0%, 20%)	30,000	-0-	-0-	6,000
Total (average cost denominator)	120,000	90,000	90,000	96,000
Less: II (20,000 at 100%, 100%, 0%, 80%)	(20,000)	(20,000)	-0-	(16,000)
Equivalent units produced	100,000	70,000	90,000	80,000

3. Cost assignment schedule (all unit data from schedule 2)

	RM1	RM2	RM3	L & OH	TOTAL COSTS
(a) Equivalent units produced	100,000	70,000	90,000	80,000	
(b) Initial inventory	20,000	20,000	-0-	16,000	
(c) Total equivalent units	120,000	90,000	90,000	96,000	
(d) Costs accountable for	$120,000	$180,000	$45,000	$384,000	$729,000
(e) Average cost denominator	120,000	90,000	90,000	96,000	
(f) Average unit cost (d ÷ e)	$1.00	$2.00	$.50	$4.00	
(g) Final inventory in equivalent units	30,000	-0-	-0-	6,000	
(h) Average unit cost (f)	$1.00	$2.00	$.50	$4.00	
(i) Final inventory cost (g × h)	$ 30,000	$ -0-	$ -0-	$ 24,000	($ 54,000)
(j) Transferred out (d − i)	$ 90,000	$180,000	$45,000	$360,000	$675,000

factors, but it accomplishes the same role as schedules presented in earlier illustrations. With practice, you can find several shortcuts to process cost solutions, and several columns are saved by the arrangement in schedule 3. With the average cost method, total costs are divided by the sum of equivalent units produced plus equivalent units in the initial inventory. The average unit cost then is multiplied times equivalent units in the final inventory. Cost of units transferred out is determined residually by subtracting the final Work in Process inventory cost from total costs accountable for.

In many processes, the addition of a new raw material will change the number of physical units to be accounted for. This is particularly true if units of product are measured by volume or weight, such as gallons of product X and pounds of product Y. The addition of a fluid raw material to a liquid product can increase the number of units produced. The increase in units accountable for caused by the addition of raw materials is called *added units*.

If the additional raw material is placed in process at the start of a department's operations, then added units affect equivalent production, and costs of the raw material are assignable to the final Work in Process inventory and to units transferred out. If a new material is introduced and added units occur at the end of a process, then costs of the new material are assigned only to the units transferred out of the department. In some respects, the accounting methods for added units are similar to the procedures used for initial and terminal spoilage. With added units, however, there is an increase in the number of physical units and a potential decrease in unit costs. For cases of spoilage, we considered a decrease in number of units with a potential increase in unit costs.

Consider a liquid product that is produced by consecutive processing operations in two departments. Raw materials in liquid form are introduced at the start of Department 1 operations. Additional materials are placed in process at the start of Department 2 operations, and these new materials cause an 80 percent increase in the number of units received from department one (that is, 100 gallons of transferred-in units become 180 gallons because of the new material).

During June 19X3, Department 1 transferred 100,000 units to Department 2 at a cost of $359,500. Material XY was issued to Department 2 at a cost of $182,000. During the month, Department 2 incurred conversion costs of $127,000 and transferred 150,000 units to Finished Goods inventory. Cost and inventory data are summarized below for Department 2:

Department 2 cost summary

	PDC	MATERIAL XY	L & OH	TOTAL COSTS
Costs incurred in June	$359,500	$182,000	$127,000	$668,500
Initial inventory on June 1	40,500	18,000	9,000	67,500
Costs accountable for	$400,000	$200,000	$136,000	$736,000

Department 2 inventory data

	PHYSICAL UNITS	PERCENTAGE COMPLETION		
		PDC	Mat XY	L & OH
Initial inventory	20,000	100	100	50
Final inventory	50,000	100	100	40

Exhibit 7-5 presents the cost of production report for Department 2, consisting of (1) a quantity schedule, (2) an equivalent production schedule, and (3) a cost assignment schedule using average costs.

ACCOUNTING FOR
ADDED UNITS

Added Units at Start of
Process

EXHIBIT 7-5

PROCESS COSTING WITH ADDED UNITS AT START OF PROCESS

1. Quantity schedule

	PHYSICAL UNITS
Units started (received from Department 1)	100,000
Added units (80% of units started)	80,000
New units placed in process	180,000
Initial inventory	20,000
Units accountable for	200,000
Final inventory	(50,000)
Transferred out	150,000

2. Equivalent production schedule

	PDC	MATERIAL XY	L & OH
Transferred out	150,000	150,000	150,000
Plus: FI (50,000 at 100%, 100%, 40%)	50,000	50,000	20,000
Total equivalent units	200,000	200,000	170,000
Less: II (20,000 at 100%, 100%, 50%)	(20,000)	(20,000)	(10,000)
Equivalent units produced	180,000	180,000	160,000

3. Cost assignment schedule (average cost method)

EQUIVALENT UNITS	PDC AND MATERIAL XY			L & OH			TOTAL COSTS
	Units	Cost	Amount	Units	Cost	Amount	
Units produced	180,000		$541,500	160,000		$127,000	$668,500
Initial inventory	20,000		58,500	10,000		9,000	67,500
Total	200,000	$3	$600,000	170,000	$.80	$136,000	$736,000
Final inventory	(50,000)	$3	(150,000)	(20,000)	$.80	(16,000)	(166,000)
Transferred out	150,000		$450,000	150,000		$120,000	$570,000

In the quantity schedule, notice that initial and final inventories consist of units containing material XY; that is, the inventories are "units after addition." The only "units before addition" are the 100,000 units transferred in from Department 1. Accordingly, when material XY is introduced at the beginning of Department 2, there are 80,000 added units to account for (100,000 × 80% = 80,000 unit increase caused by adding material XY). With this one adjustment in the quantity schedule, equivalent production can be measured in the usual way.

Since the equivalent production schedules for prior department costs and costs of material XY are identical, these cost factors can be combined to simplify the cost assignment schedule. Combined cost amounts are shown on the following page as used in the cost assignment schedule of Exhibit 7-5:

	PDC	Cost of Material XY	Combined Amount
Costs incurred in June	$359,500	$182,000	$541,500
Inventory, June 1	40,500	18,000	58,500
Total costs	$400,000	$200,000	$600,000

A summary of the Department 2 Work in Process account is presented below as it would appear after posting journal entries for June:

Work in process—Department 2

Balance, June 1	$ 67,500	(4) $570,000
(1)	359,500	
(2)	182,000	
(3)	127,000	
Balance, June 30	$166,000	

Journal entry explanations:

1. Costs of Department 1 for 100,000 units transferred to Department 2 (prior department costs).
2. Costs of material XY added to process at start of production in Department 2.
3. Labor and overhead costs (conversion costs) incurred by Department 2 in June.
4. Cost of units transferred to Finished Goods as computed in schedule 3 of Exhibit 7-5.

Added Units at End of Process

When added units result from new materials introduced at the end of a process, the accounting objective is to assign the cost of new materials entirely to units transferred out of the department. Only the units transferred out contain the added units and related cost of additional materials. Work in Process inventories at the beginning and end of the period would be stated on a "units before addition" basis.

To illustrate this process costing feature, assume that the preceding illustration involves material XY being added at the end rather than at the beginning of processing in Department 2. Addition of the material to completed production in Department 2 causes an 80 percent increase in physical units of output. A diagram of the revised production process is shown in Exhibit 7-6. The resulting three-schedule cost of production report is illustrated in Exhibit 7-7.

When added units occur at the end of a process, Work in Process inventories are 0 percent complete with regard to the new material cost. Since the new material is introduced at the end of processing, partially processed units contain none of material XY. Revised data for this illustration are:

| | Units Before | Percentage Completion | | |
	Addition	PDC	Material XY	L & OH
Department 2				
Initial inventory	20,000	100	0	50
Final inventory	50,000	100	0	40

EXHIBIT 7-6

FLOW DIAGRAM—ADDED UNITS AT END OF PROCESS

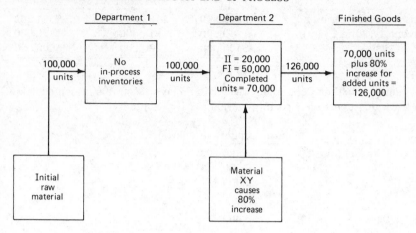

Initial inventories also would not include any cost for material XY. A summary of costs accountable for under the revised assumptions is presented below:

DEPARTMENT 2 COST SUMMARY	PDC	MATERIAL XY	L & OH	TOTAL COSTS
Costs incurred in June	$359,500	$182,000	$127,000	$668,500
Initial inventory	40,500	N. A.	9,000	49,500
Costs accountable for	$400,000	$182,000	$136,000	$718,000

Based upon the percentage completion factors given above, equivalent production is computed in schedule 2 of Exhibit 7-7. Note that equivalent production calculations start with *units completed* as shown in the quantity schedule. In this way, unit costs for the final inventory will not be affected by the added units that come into existence at the end of processing. The similarity between this procedure and the method of accounting for terminal spoilage should be apparent as you study the cost assignment schedule in Exhibit 7-7.

As shown in schedule 3, the entire cost of material XY is assigned to units transferred out of Department 2, which include 70,000 completed units plus added units of 56,000 (80 percent of 70,000) caused by adding the new material. The final inventory of $196,885 contains only prior department costs and conversion costs. The completed cost of production report supports the journal entry below:

Finished goods inventory $521,115

     Work in process inventory—Department 2 $521,115

To record cost transfer from Department 2 to
Finished Goods inventory for June

If new materials cause added units to occur at some point during a process, it is convenient to treat the situation as though added units occur either at the start or at the end of processing, whichever most clearly represents the physical processing involved. It is essential that units in initial and final Work in

EXHIBIT 7-7

PROCESS COSTING WITH ADDED UNITS AT END OF PROCESS

1. Quantity schedule

	PHYSICAL UNITS
Units started (from Department 1)	100,000
Initial inventory	20,000
Units accountable for	120,000
Final inventory	(50,000)
Units completed	70,000 (before addition)
Added units (80% increase)	56,000 (added by material XY)
Transferred out	126,000 (after addition)

2. Equivalent production schedule

	PDC	MATERIAL XY	L & OH
Units completed (before addition)	70,000	70,000	70,000
Plus: FI (50,000 at 100%, 0%, 40%)	50,000	–0–	20,000
Total equivalent units	120,000	70,000	90,000
Less: II (20,000 at 100%, 0%, 50%)	(20,000)	–0–	(10,000)
Equivalent units produced	100,000	70,000	80,000

3. Cost assignment schedule (average cost method)

EQUIVALENT UNITS	PDC Units	Cost	Amount	MATERIAL XY COSTS Units	Cost	Amount	L & OH Units	Cost	Amount	TOTAL COSTS
Units produced	100,000		$359,500	70,000		$182,000	80,000		$127,000	$668,500
Initial inventory	20,000		40,500	–0–		–0–	10,000		9,000	49,500
Total	120,000	$3.333	$400,000	70,000		$182,000	90,000	$1.511	$136,000	$718,000
Final inventory	(50,000)	3.333	(166,665)	–0–		–0–	(20,000)	$1.511	(30,200)	(196,885)
Units completed	70,000		$233,335	70,000		$182,000	70,000		$105,780	
Added units	56,000		—	56,000		–	56,000		–	–
Transferred out	126,000		$233,335	126,000		$182,000	126,000		$105,780	$521,115

Process inventories be stated on the same basis (before addition or after addition).

Accurate and conceptually sound cost assignments can be determined by analyzing inventories and production according to the actual point at which added units occur. The additional accuracy in unit costs in most cases would not warrant the complex analyses required. Accordingly, in all problem situations you should use the procedures outlined for added units at start of process or added units at end of process.

UNPROCESSED MATERIALS AND DELAYED TRANSFERS

All preceding illustrations have assumed that (1) work was begun immediately on raw materials issued to a department and that (2) units completed were transferred immediately to subsequent departments or to Finished Goods. In many instances, producing departments hold inventories of unprocessed raw materials and units completed but not transferred out. Accounting for production department costs in these cases requires a proper analysis of the *three* inventories involved: (1) unprocessed materials, (2) partially processed units, and (3) completed units not yet transferred out. Cost accounting in this situation is simplified by using a three-part quantity schedule that summarizes the flow of physical units through each inventory group. This technique is demonstrated in the following example.

Edwards, Inc., manufactures product AB in a single department. During October 19X4, 300,000 units of material were issued from Raw Materials inventory into production. One unit of raw material constitutes one unit of final product. Partially processed units at the end of a period contain all raw materials and are assumed to be 50 percent complete regarding conversion costs. Initial and final inventories in the production department for October were:

| | WORK IN PROCESS INVENTORIES | |
PHYSICAL UNITS	October 1	October 31
Unprocessed (not yet started)	10,000	40,000
Partially processed	20,000	30,000
Completed (not yet transferred)	5,000	15,000

The company uses an estimated cost system to value inventories. A complete unit is estimated to contain $3 of material cost and $4 of conversion costs. A cost of production analysis using the $7 estimated unit cost is illustrated in Exhibit 7-8.

EXHIBIT 7-8
PROCESS COSTING WITH UNPROCESSED MATERIALS AND DELAYED TRANSFERS

1. Quantity schedule

| | PHYSICAL UNITS CLASSIFIED AS | | |
	Unprocessed	Partially processed	Completed
Units started	300,000*	270,000	260,000
Initial inventory	10,000*	20,000*	5,000*
Units accountable for	310,000	290,000	265,000
Final inventory	(40,000)*	(30,000)*	(15,000)*
Transferred out	270,000	260,000	250,000

* Physical unit data are given.

2. Equivalent production schedule
   (based on partially processed units)

PARTIALLY PROCESSED UNITS	MATERIALS	L & OH
Transferred out	260,000	260,000
Plus: FI (30,000 at 100%, 50%)	30,000	15,000
Total equivalent units	290,000	275,000
Less: II (20,000 at 100%, 50%)	(20,000)	(10,000)
Equivalent units produced	270,000	265,000

EXHIBIT 7-8 (cont.)

3a. Cost of unprocessed units at estimated material cost of $3
(unit data from schedule 1)

UNPROCESSED UNITS	PHYSICAL UNITS	TOTAL COST
Units started	300,000	$900,000
Initial inventory	10,000	30,000
Total	310,000	$930,000
Final inventory	(40,000)	(120,000)
Transferred out	270,000	$810,000

3b. Cost of partially processed units at estimated cost
(unit data from schedule 2)

EQUIVALENT UNITS	MATERIAL COSTS (ESTIMATED = $3)		CONVERSION COSTS (ESTIMATED = $4)		TOTAL COSTS
	Units	Amount	Units	Amount	
Units produced	270,000	$810,000	265,000	$1,060,000	$1,870,000
Initial inventory	20,000	60,000	10,000	40,000	100,000
Total	290,000	$870,000	275,000	$1,100,000	$1,970,000
Final inventory	(30,000)	(90,000)	(15,000)	(60,000)	(150,000)
Transferred out	260,000	$780,000	260,000	$1,040,000	$1,820,000

3c. Cost of completed units at estimated cost of $7
(unit data from schedule 1)

COMPLETED UNITS	PHYSICAL UNITS	TOTAL COST
Units started	260,000	$1,820,000
Initial inventory	5,000	35,000
Total	265,000	$1,855,000
Final inventory	(15,000)	(105,000)
Transferred out	250,000	$1,750,000

The *unprocessed units* contain only material costs and have received no processing at all. No equivalent production schedule is needed for these units. The *completed units* are 100 percent finished in all respects and require no equivalent production schedule. *Partially processed units* involve a 50 percent degree of completion for conversion costs and must be analyzed for equivalent production purposes. Cost assignment schedules for three types of inventories located in the production department use unit data from the following sources:

TYPE OF INVENTORY	SOURCE OF UNIT DATA for COST ASSIGNMENT SCHEDULE
Unprocessed units	Quantity schedule (physical units)
Partially processed units	Equivalent production schedule
Completed units	Quantity schedule (physical units)

A cost assignment schedule for each type of inventory using estimated costs is assembled in schedules 3a, 3b, and 3c of Exhibit 7-8.

A summary of estimated costs chargeable to the department is presented below, and cost amounts are keyed to the related Work in Process account shown following the summary.

Initial inventories:

Unprocessed units (10,000 at $3)	$ 30,000	
Partially processed (see schedule 3b)	100,000	
Completed units (5,000 at $7)	35,000	$ 165,000 (1)
Materials issued during October (300,000 at $3)		900,000 (2)
Labor and overhead costs (schedule 3b)		1,060,000 (3)
Total costs accountable for		$2,125,000

Final inventories:

Unprocessed units (40,000 at $3)	$120,000	
Partially processed (schedule 3b)	150,000	
Completed units (15,000 at $7)	105,000	375,000 (4)
Transferred to finished goods (250,000 at $7)		$1,750,000 (5)
Total costs assigned		$2,125,000

Using summarized data for inventories, the department's Work in Process account would appear as follows after posting October journal entries:

Work in process—Production Department

(1)	Balance, October 1	$ 165,000	
(2)	Materials issued	900,000	(5) $1,750,000 to finished goods
(3)	Labor & overhead	1,060,000	
(4)	Balance, October 31	$ 375,000	

Note that estimated costs were charged and credited to the Work in Process account. Differences between actual costs and estimated costs are called *variances*. Variances are recorded in separate accounts as explained in Chapters 11 and 12 on standard cost accounting systems.

INVENTORY COST FLOW ASSUMPTIONS

All illustrations in this chapter applied the weighted average cost method in assigning production costs to final inventories. In concluding your study of process cost accounting, it is desirable to review the topics of inventory valuation and cost flow assumptions.

The entire process of assigning dollar quantities to inventories is called *inventory valuation*. Two phases of inventory valuation are: (1) selecting a basis for valuation and (2), if some measure of cost is used, selecting a pricing method to approximate the assumed flow of cost factors. Previous chapters indicated that historical cost is the primary basis for valuing inventories. Other valuation bases include:

1. Market selling prices of finished goods
2. Net realizable value, which is expected selling price less estimated cost of completion and disposal
3. Replacement cost
4. Absorption or direct costing with possible applications of historical, normal, or standard costs
5. Lower of cost or market

If historical or normal costing is selected, a cost flow assumption must be applied. FIFO, LIFO, and average cost flow assumptions can be applied at end-of-period or currently as issues and receipts of inventory items take place. If unit prices remain constant, then all three cost flow procedures produce identical results. For process costing systems, cost assignment schedules facilitate any cost flow assumption selected. The following example demonstrates FIFO, average, and LIFO cost flow procedures (inventory pricing) for Work in Process inventories.

Assume that quantity schedules and equivalent production have been analyzed and that the following partial cost assignment schedule was prepared for Work in Process inventory in a producing department:

EQUIVALENT UNITS	UNITS	UNIT COST	TOTAL COST
(1) Equivalent units produced	100,000	(FIFO cost)	$200,000
(2) Initial inventory	40,000	(LIFO cost)	85,600
(3) Total equivalent units	140,000	(Average cost)	$285,600
Final inventory	(20,000)		?
Transferred out	120,000		?

Average Cost Method

The weighted average unit cost for Work in Process is computed from line (3) of the schedule: $285,600 ÷ 140,000 = $2.04. The average unit cost is then applied to the final inventory:

Cost accountable for	$285,600
Final inventory (20,000 × $2.04)	(40,800)
Cost of transfers (also at $2.04)	$244,800

FIFO Cost Method

Since first-in, first-out describes the *flow* of costs, final inventory is valued at the most recent unit cost. For our Work in Process account, FIFO unit cost is the unit cost of current production computed from line (1): $200,000 ÷ 100,000 = $2. The FIFO unit cost is then applied to the final inventory:

Costs accountable for	$285,600
Final inventory (20,000 × $2.00)	(40,000)
Cost of transfers (by subtraction)	$245,600

Note that the department receiving 120,000 units at $245,600 would account for these units at their average unit cost ($245,600 ÷ 120,000 = $2.047) instead of trying to identify the FIFO layers being transferred out by the preceding department. Thus, the FIFO application is really to determine unit costs of a department's final inventory.

LIFO Cost Method

With an assumed last-in, first-out flow of costs, any final inventory carries the oldest unit cost, which is the initial inventory cost computed from line (2): $85,600 ÷ 40,000 = $2.14. If the final inventory is less than the initial inventory (no increase in inventory), the LIFO unit cost is applied to the entire final inventory:

Costs accountable for	$285,600
Final inventory (20,000 × $2.14)	(42,800)
Cost of transfers (by subtraction)	$242,800

If there is an increase in Work in Process inventory, then LIFO layers must be determined with any inventory increase carrying the unit cost of current production. If the final inventory were 50,000 units, its LIFO cost would be:

Base layer (40,000 units at $2.14)	$ 85,600
Additional layer (10,000 units at $2.00)	20,000
Work in process (50,000 units at LIFO cost)	$105,600

LIFO inventory procedures are seldom applied to Work in Process inventories, but LIFO procedures can be applied using the cost assignment schedules illustrated in this text. Physical units of product must flow in a FIFO manner through actual production processes. The assumed flow of production costs, however, is not required to correspond with physical production flows.

FINAL NOTE   This chapter on extended practices in process cost accounting should enable you to analyze reasonably complex inventory valuation and product costing problems in practice and on professional accounting examinations. You should recognize, however, that many firms avoid all the complexities of process costing by simply ignoring Work in Process inventories. In this case, all departmental production costs are assigned to units transferred out. Obviously, this expedient practice is acceptable only if inventories are not significant.

Return now to the beginning of the chapter and review the highlights section before proceeding to the review questions, exercises, and problems.

QUESTIONS

7-1. Define and illustrate the following terms and concepts:

a. Lost units
b. New materials
c. Defective units
d. Added units
e. Inventory valuation concept
f. Normal spoilage
g. Abnormal spoilage
h. Initial spoilage
i. Terminal spoilage
j. Spoilage loss

7-2. "Prior department costs are accounted for much like the cost of new materials introduced at the start of a process." Explain this statement.

7-3. In the production of lids for aluminum cans, a stamping operation cuts the lids out of aluminum sheets. The process automatically generates scrap trimmings, the cost of which is included in the cost of lid production. Identify four other industrial processes which also generate scrap as an inherent part of operations.

7-4. Identify two different causes of spoiled units in the production of a liquid product.

7-5. What different accounting treatments apply to normal and abnormal spoilage and why?

7-6. Discuss the propriety of ignoring unavoidably spoiled units in the computation of equivalent production for developing per unit costs. Consider in your discussion the possibility that the point of inspection, and hence the identification of spoiled units, occurs:
   a. At the end of the processing sequence in the department
   b. At the beginning of the processing sequence in the department
   c. Throughout the processing sequence in the department

(AICPA adapted)

7-7. What is the objective of accounting procedures used for spoilage that occurs at the start of a process?

7-8. What is the objective of accounting procedures used for spoilage that occurs at the end of a process?

7-9. Describe the effect of terminal spoilage on the computation of equivalent production.

7-10. Identify an industrial process that corresponds with each of the following situations:
   a. Addition of materials that do not increase units processed
   b. Addition of materials that increase units processed

7-11. For each situation in question 7-10, what is the effect of new materials on equivalent production?

7-12. "If the 'method of neglect' is used to account for terminal spoilage, unit costs for final Work in Process inventories are overstated." Explain this statement.

7-13. The producing departments in Y Company frequently have custody of unprocessed materials and completed production not yet transferred out of the departments. Evaluate this situation from the standpoints of control and proper inventory classification.

7-14. How do the cost flow assumptions of LIFO, FIFO, and average cost relate to the process of inventory valuation?

EXERCISES

7-15. *Equivalent Units—Terminal Spoilage* The following unit figures were taken from the cooking process of the Fisher Corporation for the month of June. Materials are added at the beginning of the process.

Beginning work in process inventory (30% complete)	1,200
Units started during June	36,000
Ending work in process inventory (40% complete)	2,400
Spoiled during June (normal)	1,000

Inspection takes place at the end of the process.

REQUIRED: Compute equivalent production for materials and conversion costs for June using (a) the transferred-out method and (b) the units started and completed method.

7-16. *Cost Flow Diagram* The Ewald Corporation manufactures a chemical fertilizer called Growy. Five chemicals are used in the process. Chemicals A and B enter production in Department 1 at the beginning of the process; 90 percent of the finished product of Department 1 is transferred to Department 3, and the remainder is waste. Chemicals C and D enter production in Department 2 at the beginning of its process; 100 percent of the finished goods from Department 2 are transferred to Department 3. Chemical E is placed directly into the process of Department 3; 75 percent of the finished product from Department 3 represents Growy, and the remainder is waste.

REQUIRED: Draw a diagram representing the flow of materials through the production process.

7-17. *Equivalent Units—Initial Spoilage* Rework exercise 7-15 assuming that spoilage took place at the beginning of the process.

7-18. *Accounting for Spoilage Costs* The following data are from a recent period of operations in a production department:

Total units worked on during the period	5,000 units
Total cost related to these units	$40,000
Normal spoilage during the period	120 units
Abnormal spoilage during the period	280 units

REQUIRED: Which of the following journal entries would remove spoilage costs from Work in Process *and* reallocate these costs as product costs and period costs? There were no beginning or ending Work in Process inventories.

1. Finished goods control	$40,000	
Work in process control		$40,000
2. Finished goods control	$36,800	
Factory overhead control	960	
Work in process control		$37,760
3. Finished goods control	$37,760	
Loss from abnormal spoilage	2,240	
Work in process control		$40,000
4. Finished goods control	$36,800	
Factory overhead control	3,200	
Work in process control		$40,000
5. Finished goods control	$36,800	
Cost of spoiled goods	3,200	
Work in process control		$40,000

7-19. *Accounting for Prior Department Costs* Eiteman Enterprises, Inc., produces skin cream for men. Three departments, Mixing, Heating, and Settling, comprise the production process with all products flowing through each department. All raw materials are added in Mixing, with only conversion costs being incurred in Heating and Settling. Conversion costs are applied uniformly to production. Operating data for the Heating Department during August are shown below:

Initial inventory: 3,000 gallons, 60% complete
   Costs attached:
Prior department costs	$ 9,900
Conversion costs	$ 3,330

Current period production: 40,000 gallons were received from Mixing during August.
   Current period costs:
Costs transferred-in from Mixing	$129,850
Conversion costs for August	$ 72,270

Product disposition: During August, 38,000 gallons were transferred to Settling, and 5,000 gallons remained in process at month-end, 80% complete.

REQUIRED: If the company uses the weighted average costing method, prepare the following August reports for the Heating Department:
a. Quantity schedule
b. Equivalent production schedule
c. Cost assignment schedule

7-20. *Prior Department Costs*   The following quantity schedule was prepared for operations of the Assembly Department during December 19X9:

ASSEMBLY DEPARTMENT	PHYSICAL UNITS	PERCENTAGE COMPLETION
Units started	400,000	
Initial inventory	50,000	80
Units accountable for	450,000	
Final inventory	(60,000)	50
Transferred out	390,000	

Cost of the initial inventory on December 1 included $75,000 of prior department costs and $80,000 of conversion costs added by the Assembly Department. Assembly receives plastic radio cabinets from the Cabinet Department and electrical components from the Wiring Department. Wired components are placed in cabinets, and completed pocket-sized radios are tested in the Assembly Department.
   Costs charged to Assembly in December were:

400,000 cabinets received	$ 200,000
400,000 wired component units	400,000
Labor and overhead in Assembly	760,000
Total costs in December	$1,360,000

REQUIRED: Prepare a December cost of production report for the Assembly Department using the average cost method.

7-21. *Accounting for Additional Raw Materials*   Carlton Process Company produces a product requiring three different raw materials that are added to the churning process at different times. Material Y is added at the beginning of the process; Material I at the 20 percent completion point; and Material L at the 60 percent completion point. Materials Y, I, and L are powders and, when added to a liquid base, do not cause an increase in the number of units being produced. Conversion costs in the churning process are incurred uniformly.

DATA FOR OCTOBER	MAT. Y	MAT. I	MAT. L	L & OH
Costs accountable for				
Initial inventory	$ 7,550	$ 6,100	$ -0-	$ 5,000
Costs incurred, October	67,450	56,400	21,000	87,000
Total costs	$75,000	$62,500	$21,000	$92,000
Units accountable for				
Initial inventory	2,500 units (40% processed)			
Started during month	22,500 units			
Total	25,000 units			

On October 31, 4,000 units in final Work in Process inventory were 50 percent completed, and no units were lost during the month. The weighted average costing method is used by the company.

REQUIRED: Prepare a quantity schedule, an equivalent production schedule, and a cost assignment schedule.

7-22. *Added Units and Spoilage*   The Cutting Department in Sacha Pipe Company receives 30-foot pipe sections from the Forging Department. In Cutting, each 30-foot length of pipe is cut into three equal sections. The 10-foot pipe lengths are then trimmed, smoothed, and inspected at the end of operations in the Cutting Department. Defective units are removed from the process before good units are transferred to Finished Goods.

During May 19X3 the Forging Department transferred 200,000 of the 30-foot pipes to Cutting. Work in Process inventories of the Cutting Department are summarized below, along with percentage completion factors for prior department costs (PDC) and conversion costs (CC):

		PERCENTAGE COMPLETION	
WORK IN PROCESS	10-FOOT UNITS	PDC	CC
May 1, 19X3	60,000	100	30
May 31, 19X3	40,000	100	50

The Cutting Department transferred 610,000 inspected pipe sections to Finished Goods during May.

REQUIRED: For Cutting Department operations in May:
a. Prepare a quantity schedule.

b. Prepare equivalent production schedules for prior department costs and conversion cost elements.

7-23. *Added Units—End of Process* "Paint to match any sample" is the slogan of the Odelson Paint Company. The main production process makes a white base paint from a base compound added at the beginning of the process. Coloring liquid is added at the end of the process to produce the made-to-order colors. Normally, the quantity is increased by 20 percent when the coloring liquid is added. Conversion costs are added uniformly. The information below relates to February operations:

Initial inventory	1,000 gallons (60% complete)
Final inventory	2,000 gallons (80% complete)

There was no spoilage or lost units during the period, and units started during the period were 46,000 gallons. The cost summary for February follows:

	WHITE BASE COMPOUND	COLORING LIQUID	CONVERSION COSTS
Initial inventory	$ 3,750	$ -0-	$ 2,700
Cost incurred in February	172,500	67,500	211,660
Costs accountable for	$176,250	$67,500	$214,360

REQUIRED: Assuming the company uses a weighted average cost method, prepare a cost of production report for October.

7-24. *Unprocessed Materials and Delayed Transfers* The Printing Department of Abilene Paper Company receives completed box forms from the Folding Department. Boxes are printed by machine operation using plates specially designed for each customer. Since the printing operation is similar regardless of box size or design to be printed, process costing is used in the Printing Department.

In January 19X4, the Printing Department received 800,000 unprinted boxes from the Folding Department and transferred 770,000 printed boxes to Finished Goods. Most boxes require two or more printing runs before the product is completed and ready for shipment. On January 1, 80,000 boxes were partially printed and averaged 60 percent complete. On January 31, the Work in Process inventory was 40,000 boxes averaging 20 percent complete. Inventories of unprinted box forms and fully printed boxes held by the Printing Department are summarized below:

UNITS IN INVENTORY	UNPRINTED BOXES	PRINTED BOXES
January 1	100,000	50,000
January 31	200,000	20,000

REQUIRED:
a. Prepare a quantity schedule showing flow of physical units for unprinted boxes, partially printed boxes, and printed boxes.
b. Prepare an equivalent production schedule for January.

7-25. *Several Raw Materials*   The Fair Company manufactures a product known as 2X74 in a single unified sequence of processing operations. Production costs for the month of January follow:

Materials issued to production:	
A—10,000 pounds	$ 20,800
B—1,000 gallons	5,200
C—20,000 pounds	27,300
D—1,100 dozen	3,300
Labor	15,000
Other processing costs	33,000
Total cost	$104,600

Materials A, B, and C are mixed together at the start of processing. Material D is added at the very end of processing, whereupon the finished product is transferred immediately to the shipping department.

During January, 48,000 units of 2X74 were finished, packed, and sent to the shipping department. On January 31, 4,000 units were still unfinished, but approximately one-half the necessary labor had been performed. Other processing costs vary with labor cost. There was no Work in Process on January 1.

REQUIRED:

a. Compute the cost per unit of 2X74 for the month of January.
b. Compute the total cost assigned to the units finished during the month.
c. Compute the total cost assigned to the units still in process at the end of the month.

7-26. *Allocating Spoilage*   The Almostover Company uses a process cost system for one of its products. During a recent period, 3,850 units were put into production and 3,000 finished units were completed. Inspection of this product occurs at the halfway point in the process. Normally, rejects would amount to 10 percent of the 3,500 good units inspected. The Inspection Department informs us that the process did in fact function normally during the period. The department supervisor estimates that units still in process are on the average two-thirds complete. All, however, are at least one-half done.

Costs for the period were:

Material	$38,500	Applied at the beginning of the process
Conversion costs	35,080	Applied uniformly during the process
	$73,580	

REQUIRED: Determine the cost of goods completed and the cost of the ending Work in Process inventory. Assume that there were no beginning inventories.

7-27. *Normal and Abnormal Spoilage* The Antonio Chemical Company produces a chemical compound that is sold to oil refineries for use in the production of high-octane gasoline. Operations take place in two departments, Mixing and Blending.

On December 1, 19X9, the Work in Process inventories in the manufacturing departments showed:

	MIXING	BLENDING
Cost of preceding department	–0–	$10,620
Materials cost	$4,000	–0–
Labor cost	$950	$1,550
Factory overhead	$450	$430
Number of units in process	1,500 gals.	1,800 gals.

In the Mixing Department, in addition to the Work in Process inventory, 11,500 gallons were placed in production. Of this amount, 10,200 gallons were completed and transferred to the Blending Department; 2,200 gallons were only partially complete (all materials had been added, but only one-half the labor and factory overhead had been applied); and 600 gallons were lost (this is 200 gallons over the normal gallons lost).

In the Blending Department, 9,000 gallons were completed and transferred to finished stock; 2,700 gallons were still in process, for which 40 percent of labor and overhead had been applied; and 300 gallons were lost. Normally, only 250 units have been lost in a batch of this size.

Departmental reports showed the following costs for December:

	MIXING	BLENDING
Materials	$54,500	–0–
Labor	12,140	$16,090
Factory overhead	7,880	4,610

Units lost cannot be detected until the end of each process.

REQUIRED: For December, prepare a cost of production report for each department. Use the average cost method.

7-28. *CPA Problem—FIFO Cost Analysis* In the course of your examination of the financial statements of the Zeus Company for the year ended December 31, 19X1, you have ascertained the following concerning its manufacturing operations:

Zeus has two production departments (Fabricating and Finishing) and a service department. In the Fabricating Department, polyplast is prepared from miracle mix and bypro. In the Finishing Department each unit of polyplast is converted into six tetraplexes and three uniplexes. The service department provides services to both production departments.

Fabricating and Finishing both use process cost accounting systems. Actual production costs, including overhead, are allocated monthly.

Service department expenses are allocated to production departments as follows:

EXPENSE	ALLOCATION BASE
Building maintenance	Space occupied
Timekeeping and personnel	Number of employees
Other	One-half to Fabricating, one-half to Finishing

Raw Materials inventory and Work in Process are priced on a FIFO basis.

The following data were taken from the Fabricating Department's records for December 19X1:

Quantities (units of polyplast):	
In process, December 1	3,000
Started in process during month	25,000
Total units to be accounted for	28,000
Transferred to finishing department	19,000
In process, December 31	6,000
Lost in process	3,000
Total units accounted for	28,000
Cost of work in process, December 1:	
Materials	$ 13,000
Labor	17,500
Overhead	21,500
	$ 52,000
Direct labor costs, December	$154,000
Departmental overhead, December	$132,000

Polyplast Work in Process at the beginning and end of the month was partially completed as follows:

	MATERIALS	LABOR AND OVERHEAD
December 1	66⅔%	50%
December 31	100%	75%

The following data were taken from Raw Materials inventory records for December:

	MIRACLE MIX		BYPRO	
	Quantity	Amount	Quantity	Amount
Balance, December 1	62,000	$62,000	265,000	$18,550
Purchases:				
December 12	39,500	49,375		
December 20	28,500	34,200		
Fabricating Department usage	83,200		50,000	

Service department expenses for December (not included in departmental overhead above) were:

Building maintenance	$ 45,000
Timekeeping and personnel	27,500
Other	39,000
	$111,500

Other information for December 19X1 is presented below:

	SQUARE FEET OF SPACE OCCUPIED	NUMBER OF EMPLOYEES
Fabricating	75,000	180
Finishing	37,500	120
	112,500	300

REQUIRED:
a. Compute the equivalent number of units of polyplast, with separate calculations for materials and conversion costs (direct labor plus overhead) manufactured during December.
b. Compute the following items to be included in the Fabricating Department's production report for December 19X1, with separate calculations for materials, direct labor, and overhead. Prepare supporting schedules.
  1. Total costs to be accounted for
  2. Unit costs for equivalent units manufactured
  3. Transfers to Finishing Department during December and Work in Process at December 31. Reconcile your answer to part (b)1.

(AICPA adapted)

7-29. *CPA Problem—Initial Spoilage* Ballinger Paper Products manufactures a high-quality paper box. The Box Department applies two separate operations—cutting and folding. The paper first is cut and trimmed to the dimensions of a box form by one machine group. One square foot of paper is equivalent to four box forms. The trimmings from this process have no scrap value. Box forms then are creased and folded (i.e., completed) by a second machine group. Any partially processed boxes in the department are cut box forms that are ready for creasing and folding. These partly processed boxes are considered 50 percent complete regarding labor and overhead. The Materials Department maintains an inventory of paper in sufficient quantities to permit continuous processing, and transfers to the Box Department are made as needed. Immediately after folding, all good boxes are transferred to the Finished Goods department.

During June 19X1 the Materials Department purchased 1,210,000 square feet of unprocessed paper for $244,000. Conversion costs for the month were $226,000. A quantity equal to 30,000 boxes was spoiled during paper cutting, and 70,000 boxes were spoiled during folding. All spoilage has a zero salvage value, is considered normal, and cannot be reprocessed. All spoilage loss is allocated between the completed units and partially processed boxes. Ballinger applies the weighted average cost method to all inventories. Inventory data for June are given below:

INVENTORY	PHYSICAL UNIT	JUNE 30, 19X1 Units on hand	JUNE 1, 19X1 Units on hand	JUNE 1, 19X1 Cost
Materials Department:				
Paper	Square feet	200,000	390,000	$76,000
Box Department:				
Boxes cut, not folded	Number	300,000	800,000	$55,000*
Finished Goods Department:				
Completed boxes on hand	Number	50,000	250,000	$18,000

* Materials	$35,000
Conversion cost	20,000
	$55,000

REQUIRED: Prepare the following for the month of June 19X1:
a. A report of the cost of paper used by the Materials Department.
b. A schedule showing the physical flow of units (including beginning and ending inventories) in the Materials Department, in the Box Department, and in the Finished Goods Department.
c. A schedule showing the computation of equivalent units produced for materials and conversion costs in the Box Department.
d. A schedule showing the computation of unit costs for the Box Department.
e. A report of inventory valuation and cost of completed units for the Box Department.
f. A schedule showing the computation of unit costs for the Finished Goods Department.
g. A report of inventory valuation and cost of units sold for the Finished Goods Department.

(AICPA adapted)

7-30. *Process Costing—Added Units and Lost Units*   A hair spray is the main product of Istvan Cosmetics, Inc. The manufacturing process involves two departments, the Heating and Mixing Department and the Blending Department.

Heating and Mixing: Water is introduced at the beginning of the process. At the 25 percent completion point, one pound of material H is added for each gallon of water started into process. At the 50 percent completion point, the solution reaches 100° Celsius (the boiling point). At this point, total mixing takes place, and 20 percent of the solution is lost through evaporation. The remaining solution then is cooled and transferred to the Blending Department.

Blending: Material J is added at the beginning of the blending process. For each gallon of solution received from the Heating and Mixing Department, *one-half* gallon of material J is added. Material J is an oil-based drying compound. At the end of the blending process, the solution is placed in pressurized pint-sized cans. No loss or spoilage normally occurs in the Blending Department.

In both departments, labor and overhead costs are applied to production on a uniform basis. The company employs a weighted average process costing method. Dollar and unit statistics for August 19X6 are presented below:

	Heating/Mixing			Blending		
		Costs			Costs	
	Units (GALS.)	Material	Conv. costs	Units (GALS.)	Material	Conv. costs
Beginning work in process inventories:						
Heating/Mixing: 40% complete	2,000	$ 2,000	$ 800			
Blending: 25% complete				1,500	$42,000	$ 1,600
Started during August	20,000	$20,000	$22,000			
Received during August				?	?	$18,000
Ending work in process inventories:						
Heating/Mixing: 80% complete	4,200	?	?			
Blending: 60% complete				1,600	?	?

Additional information:

a. Transferred-in costs attached to beginning Work in Process inventories of the Blending Department: $3,340
b. Cost of each pint-sized can: 20¢
c. Cost of a gallon of material J: $2

REQUIRED:

a. Compute the cost of ending Work in Process inventories for the Heating and Mixing Department and for the Blending Department.
b. Compute the total cost of completed units transferred to Finished Goods inventory from the Blending Department.
c. What was the average unit cost of a completed can of hair spray during August?
d. Prepare journal entries to transfer costs of completed units for August.

7-31. *CPA Problem—Terminal Spoilage* The Mantis Manufacturing Company manufactures a single product that passes through two departments: Extruding and Finishing/Packing. The product is shipped at the end of the day on which it is packed. The production in the Extruding and Finishing/Packing departments does not increase the number of units started.

The cost and production data for the month of January are as follows:

	Extruding Department	Finishing/Packing Department
Work in process, January 1:		
Cost from preceding department	-0-	$60,200
Material	$ 5,900	-0-
Labor	1,900	1,500
Overhead	1,400	2,000
Costs added during January:		
Material	20,100	4,400
Labor	10,700	7,720
Overhead	8,680	11,830
Percentage completion of work in process:		
January 1:		
Material	70%	0%
Labor	50%	30%
Overhead	50%	30%
January 31:		
Material	50%	0%
Labor	40%	35%
Overhead	40%	35%
January production statistics:		
Units in process, January 1	10,000	29,000
Units in process, January 31	8,000	6,000
Units started or received from preceding department	20,000	22,000
Units completed and transferred or shipped	22,000	44,000

In the Extruding Department materials are added at various phases of the process. All lost units occur at the end of the process when the inspection operation takes place.

In the Finishing/Packing Department the materials added consist only of packing supplies. These materials are added at the midpoint of the process, when the packing operation begins. Cost studies have disclosed that one-half the labor and overhead costs apply to the finishing operation and one-half apply to the packing operation. All lost units occur at the end of the finishing operation, when the product is inspected. All work in process in this department on January 1 and 31 was in the finishing operation phase of the manufacturing process.

The company uses the average costing method in its accounting system.

Required:

a. Compute the units lost, if any, for each department during January.
b. Compute the output divisor for the calculation of unit costs for each department for January. (Output divisor is used in the average costing method as equivalent production is used in the FIFO costing method.)

c. Prepare a cost of production report for both departments for January. The report should disclose the departmental total cost and cost per unit (for material, labor, and overhead) of the units (1) transferred to the Finishing/Packing Department and (2) shipped. Assume that January production and costs were normal. Submit all supporting computations in good form.

(AICPA adapted)

7-32. **CPA Problem—Spoilage and Prior Department Costs** Crews Company produces a chemical agent for commercial use. The company accounts for production in two cost centers: Cooking and Mix/Pack. In the first cost center, liquid substances are combined in large cookers and boiled; the boiling causes a normal decrease in volume from evaporation. After the batch is cooked, it is transferred to Mix/Pack, the second cost center. The batch then has a quantity of alcohol added equal to its liquid measure; the batch is mixed and bottled in one-gallon containers.

Material is added at the beginning of production in each cost center, and labor is added equally during production in each cost center. Overhead is applied on the basis of 80 percent of labor cost. The method of neglect is used in accounting for lost units (that is, all costs are allocated only to equivalent good units); the process is "in control" so long as the yield ratio for the first department is not less than 78 percent.

The FIFO method is used to cost Work in Process inventories, and transfers are at an average unit cost (the total cost transferred divided by the total number of units transferred).

The following information is available for the month of October 19X7:

COST INFORMATION	COOKING	MIX/PACK
Work in process, Oct. 1, 19X7:		
Materials	$ 990	$ 120
Labor	100	60
Prior department cost		426
Month of October:		
Materials	39,600	15,276
Labor	10,050	16,000

Inventory and production records show that Cooking had 1,000 gallons 40 percent processed on October 1 and 800 gallons 50 percent processed on October 31; Mix/Pack had 600 gallons 50 percent processed on October 1 and 1,000 gallons 30 percent processed on October 31.

Production reports for October show that Cooking started 50,000 gallons into production and completed and transferred 40,200 gallons to Mix/Pack; Mix/Pack completed and transferred 80,000 one-gallon containers of the finished product to the distribution warehouse.

REQUIRED:

a. Prepare in good form a quantity report for the Cooking cost center and for the Mix/Pack cost center, accounting for both actual units and equivalent unit production.

b. Prepare in good form a production cost report for each of the two cost centers, computing total cost and cost per unit for each element of cost in inventories and October production. Total cost and cost per unit for transfers should be computed also.

c. Compute the <u>yield ratio</u> for the Cooking Department and state whether or not the process was "in control" during October.

(AICPA adapted)

80.4%

Chapter 8: Analysis of Joint Production Costs

Accounting for joint production costs requires cost assignment procedures for joint products and by-products. These products involve a single material or several common materials that are converted into two or more separate products. Joint products have a major revenue generating ability, while by-products involve a comparatively lower total sales value. This chapter illustrates and explains various accounting procedures for joint production costs.

Upon completion of this chapter, students should be able to:

1. Identify joint or common costs incurred to produce multiple products
2. Apply cost allocation methods and compute unit costs for joint products
3. Analyze cost recovery methods of by-product accounting
4. Develop appropriate information to guide sell or process-further decisions.

The following basic concepts are introduced in this chapter:

Joint cost A cost that collectively applies or relates to several products or costing objects and that can be assigned to those costing objects only by means of arbitrary allocation.

Split-off point The stage in a joint production process where separate products are first identifiable.

Incremental cost analysis The difference between total costs and revenues of separate decision alternatives.

The point in a production process when separate products emerge from common material inputs is called the split-off point. Material, labor, and overhead costs accumulated prior to this point are joint costs, or common costs. Costs incurred prior to split-off are joint costs, since the total amount collectively relates to several different products.

Since unit costs for each product are needed for accounting purposes, joint product costs must be allocated to various joint products. Often, the relative sales value method is used for this allocation problem; using this method, joint costs are assigned to products in proportion to their relative sales values at the split-off point. In by-product accounting, the conceptually preferable method is to treat the net realizable value of by-products produced as a reduction of manufacturing costs applicable to main products.

Whether a product is sold at split-off or processed further requires an analysis of incremental revenues and incremental costs. If the expected increase in revenue potential exceeds the separable costs of additional processing, then additional processing is desirable. Joint costs incurred before split-off and allocations of these costs should be ignored in analyzing sell or process-further decisions.

NATURE OF JOINT PRODUCTION COSTS

An important characteristic of costs is their traceability to particular costing objects, such as divisions of a company, particular departments, or batches of product. As discussed in Chapter 4, direct costs are traceable to a costing object without arbitrary allocation. In job order cost accounting, direct materials and direct labor involve costs that are specifically traceable to certain products. Joint costs can be assigned to particular costing objects only by means of arbitrary allocation. If a cost or group of costs cannot be associated directly with a given costing object, the costs are joint, or common, with respect to the particular costing object.

In product costing, the overhead costs of service departments are joint costs of the various producing departments. All factory overhead costs are joint costs in relation to units of production. In both cases, joint costs must be assigned to specific costing objects, and allocation or reapportionment procedures are needed to accomplish the task. Accordingly, overhead reapportionment schedules are used to assign service department overhead costs to producing departments, and predetermined overhead rates are developed to assign overhead costs to products.

Cost allocation procedures are also necessary when material, labor, and overhead costs are incurred to produce several products that emerge from a single process. In this case, joint manufacturing costs must be allocated to several products. For example, consider a process in which material Z is converted into products A and B. Material, labor, and overhead costs are incurred and must be assigned to the units of each product that emerge from the process. The point at which the products come into existence is called the split-off point; manufacturing costs incurred before this point are joint product costs. Joint production costs and split-off are shown in Exhibit 8-1.

If products A and B in Exhibit 8-1 have major revenue producing potential, they are termed joint products. The cost accounting objective for joint products is to allocate joint production costs to each separate product group and to determine unit costs for inventory valuation purposes. If product A has an insignificant total sales value in comparison with product B, then product A is a by-product. Cost accounting objectives and procedures for by-products differ from joint product accounting. The relative sales value of a product determines whether it is a joint product or a by-product for cost accounting purposes. Since selling prices may change, the joint product or by-product classification for a specific product is also subject to change.

EXHIBIT 8-1

SPLIT-OFF POINT AND JOINT COSTS

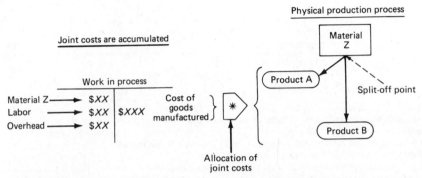

* A schedule is prepared to allocate production costs to each product.

Many industrial processes produce joint products and by-products. Joint products are found in petroleum refining, metal smelting, meat processing, and chemical production. Examples of by-products include sawdust in lumber mills, tar in petroleum refining, and mill ends in textile production.

The cost accounting objective for joint products is to determine unit costs for inventory valuation purposes. This objective requires procedures that:

1. Allocate joint production costs incurred prior to the split-off point
2. Identify the production costs incurred to process joint products beyond the split-off point

Since joint products often are processed beyond the split-off point, the production costs of additional processing also must be attached to the products involved. If a product is sold immediately after split-off, its unit cost consists solely of allocated joint product costs. If a joint product is processed beyond split-off, its unit cost will contain allocated joint costs plus the material, labor, and overhead costs of additional processing. In either case, joint production costs must be allocated to joint products using either (1) the physical volume method or (2) the relative sales value method.

ACCOUNTING FOR JOINT PRODUCTS

The *physical volume method* of allocating joint product costs concentrates on the volume of products produced. These physical measures could use pounds, gallons, board feet or any measure common to all products involved. To illustrate this method of cost allocation, assume that material Z is processed in a single department and that products A and B emerge at the end of processing. Also assume that there are no initial or final Work in Process inventories in the department. For June 19X7, the following data were accumulated:

Allocation Based on Volume Measures

Costs Incurred		Units Produced	
Material Z	$200,000	Product A	200,000 lbs.
Labor	300,000	Product B	400,000 lbs.
Overhead	100,000		
Total	$600,000		

EXHIBIT 8-2

JOINT PRODUCT COST ALLOCATION

PHYSICAL VOLUME METHOD

Product	Pounds Produced	Allocation Ratio*	Joint Costs†	Unit Cost‡
A	200,000	⅔, or ⅓	$200,000	$1
B	400,000	⅘, or ⅔	400,000	$1
	600,000		$600,000	

* Pounds of each product are divided by total pounds produced to determine the proportion represented by each product. Allocation ratio can be expressed in fraction or percentage form.
† Total joint costs of $600,000 are given. Total costs are allocated to each product by multiplying $600,000 times the allocation ratio for products A and B.
‡ Unit cost of each product is allocated joint cost divided by production volume: product A: $200,000 ÷ 200,000 = $1; product B: $400,000 ÷ 400,000 = $1. Note that unit cost of each product is equal, which is a characteristic of the volume-based allocation procedure. This schedule approach to cost allocation is more useful when sales values are the allocation basis.

Exhibit 8-2 shows the procedure for allocating joint production costs on the basis of physical measures, which in this example are pounds of each product.

With pounds as the allocation base, product A receives two-sixths the joint costs, and four-sixths of the $600,000 joint cost total is allocated to product B. Unit costs are computed from the costs allocated to each product. Note that cost allocation is based on production volume, not units sold during the period. In a process costing system, the cost allocation schedule in Exhibit 8-2 would accompany the departmental cost of production report and support journal entries to record cost of units transferred to other departments or Finished Goods. Journal entries for June and a departmental Work in Process account for the joint cost allocation example follow:

1.	Work in process	$200,000	
	Material inventory		$200,000
	Material Z issued to production department		
2.	Work in process	$300,000	
	Factory payroll		$300,000
	Labor costs of production department		
3.	Work in process	$100,000	
	Factory overhead applied		$100,000
	Charge overhead costs to production		
4.	Finished goods, product A	$200,000	
	Finished goods, product B	400,000	
	Work in process		$600,000
	Cost of goods manufactured per Exhibit 8-2		

Work in process (June 19X7)			Finished goods	
(1) Materials $200,000	(4) Units		→ $200,000	
(2) Labor 300,000	completed $600,000		(product A)	
(3) Overhead 100,000				
Balance,			→ $400,000	
June 30 -0-			(product B)	

To simplify joint cost allocation problems, Work in Process inventories usually are ignored when summarizing departmental operations. In many practical situations, Work in Process inventories should be included in the analysis. Procedures to determine the cost of Work in Process inventories depend upon the particular cost system and the nature of products involved. In a job order system, job order cost sheets are summarized to determine the cost of Work in Process inventory. In process cost systems, the procedures you learned in Chapters 6 and 7 are applied to Work in Process inventories at any stage prior to the split-off point.

If Work in Process inventory in a particular department contains materials at a stage prior to split-off plus units of joint products not completely finished, then the joint cost allocation would be part of the Work in Process cost analysis. The important fact is that split-off point will not always correspond with the end of operations in a particular department. If split-off of joint products occurs about midway through processing in a given department, this situation could require rather complex cost analysis for Work in Process inventories. The illustration in Exhibit 8-2 assumes no beginning or ending Work in Process inventories.

Returning to our example for products A and B, assume that production, sales volume, and unit selling price data for June were as follows:

Product-line Income Statements

PRODUCT	PRODUCTION VOLUME	SALES VOLUME	FINAL INVENTORY	SELLING PRICE	UNIT COST
A	200,000 lbs.	180,000 lbs.	20,000 lbs.	$3.00	$1.00
B	400,000 lbs.	350,000 lbs.	50,000 lbs.	$ .50	$1.00

Unit costs were computed in the allocation schedule in Exhibit 8-2. Assuming there were no initial Finished Goods inventories of either product, product-line income statements for June are presented in Exhibit 8-3.

EXHIBIT 8-3
PRODUCT-LINE INCOME STATEMENTS, MONTH OF JUNE 19X7

	PRODUCT A	PRODUCT B	COMBINED
Sales volume	180,000 lbs.	350,000 lbs.	
Selling price	$3.00	$.50	
Total sales	$540,000	$175,000	$715,000
Cost of goods sold (see *)	(180,000)	(350,000)	(530,000)
Gross profit (loss)	$360,000	($175,000)	$185,000
COST OF GOODS MANUFACTURED AND SOLD			
Work in process, June 1	-0-	-0-	-0-
Allocated production costs	$200,000	$400,000	(See Exhibit 8-2)
Work in process, June 30	(-0-)	(-0-)	(-0-)
Cost of goods manufactured	$200,000	$400,000	$600,000
Finished goods, June 1	-0-	-0-	-0-
Goods available for sale	$200,000	$400,000	$600,000
Finished goods, June 30:			
Product A: 20,000 × $1	(20,000)		(70,000)
Product B: 50,000 × $1		(50,000)	
* Cost of goods sold	$180,000	$350,000	$530,000

The product-line income statements highlight the biggest disadvantage of cost allocations based on physical product measures. Product B has a market price of $.50 per pound, yet the allocated joint cost is $1.00 per pound. In this example, the physical volume method of cost allocation does not produce a reasonable unit cost in relation to market selling price. If product A is steak and product B is hamburger, the fallacy of this cost allocation is even more evident. Joint cost allocations based on physical measures often produce unit costs that have no meaningful relationship with product sales value. If management expects to earn a reasonable gross profit on every product, joint cost allocation should consider the revenue potential of individual joint products.

Allocation Based on Sales Value

The relative sales value method is often used to allocate joint product costs because it avoids the unreasonable allocations and unit costs resulting from allocations based on physical product measures. With the *relative sales value method*, joint production costs are assigned to products in proportion to their relative sales values at split-off. If joint products are salable immediately after split-off, cost allocation by the sales value method will result in an equal gross profit percentage on all joint product sales. Using our product A and B example, joint product costs for June are allocated by the relative sales value method in Exhibit 8-4.

To explain Exhibit 8-4, recall that June production was 200,000 pounds of product A and 400,000 pounds of product B. Joint production costs incurred during the month were $600,000. The sales value of production at the split-off point is computed in column 3. These sales values are used to compute the allocation ratio in column 4, which shows that product A represents three-fourths the total sales value ($600,000 ÷ $800,000) and that product B represents one-fourth the total sales value ($200,000 ÷ $800,000). Product A is allocated three-fourths the total joint costs, and the remaining one-fourth of total costs is assigned to product B. The basic concept of the relative sales value method is that production costs are allocated in proportion to revenue potential. Product A represents three-fourths the total sales value, and so it is allocated three-fourths of total joint costs. Cost allocations in column 5 of Exhibit 8-4 are used to compute unit costs shown in column 6.

One criticism of the relative sales value method is that the resulting percent-

EXHIBIT 8-4
JOINT PRODUCT COST ALLOCATION
RELATIVE SALES VALUE METHOD

PRODUCT	(1) POUNDS PRODUCED	(2) SELLING PRICE	(3 = 2 × 1) SALES VALUE AT SPLIT-OFF	(4) ALLOCATION RATIO*	(5) JOINT COSTS†	(6 = 5 ÷ 1) UNIT COSTS
A	200,000	$3.00	$600,000	6/8, or 3/4	$450,000	$2.25
B	400,000	$ .50	200,000	2/8, or 1/4	150,000	$ .375
	600,000		$800,000		$600,000	

* Allocation ratio for each product is its sales value at split-off divided by total sales value of all products.
† Joint cost allocation to each product is $600,000 total production costs times the respective allocation ratios of products A and B.

age of gross profit on sales is equal for all products. The following gross profit analysis is based on Exhibit 8-4:

	PRODUCT A	PRODUCT B	COMBINED (A + B)
Selling price	$3.00	$.500	$3.500
Unit cost	2.25	.375	2.625
Gross profit	$ .75	$.125	$ .875
Profit on sales	25%	25%	25%

Since joint costs are allocated in proportion to revenue generating ability, equal gross profit percentages always will result when products are salable at split-off. Equal gross profit rates are possibly an advantage if they prevent managers from thinking that one product is more profitable than others. As a later section explains, allocated joint costs are not useful for product pricing decisions and choices between selling a product at split-off or processing it further.

In the preceding example, products A and B were sold immediately after split-off, and their respective selling prices were used in applying the relative sales value method of cost allocation. Many products require additional processing beyond the split-off point. In some instances, the product cannot be sold at split-off because there simply is no market for it. Other products can be sold immediately after split-off, or they can be processed further and then sold at higher prices. If a joint product is processed beyond split-off, any material, labor, and overhead costs incurred for additional processing must be assigned to the product.

Processing Beyond Split-off

If a product is not salable at split-off, a computed value at split-off must be determined so that costs incurred before split-off can be reasonably allocated to all joint products. The usual procedure for products not salable at split-off is to determine their ultimate sales value after additional processing and to deduct from this value all costs incurred for additional processing. The resulting "value" is fictitious, since no market exists for the product at split-off. The adjustment procedure gives each product a split-off point value so that joint cost allocations are equitable. When this adjustment procedure is used, the cost allocation method is called the *approximated sales value method*.

Our example with products A and B is revised to illustrate the approximated sales value method. Assume that material Z is introduced at the start of operations in Department 1, which produces products A and B. Product A is not salable at split-off and requires additional processing in Department 2. After additional processing, product A is sold for $5.00 per unit. Product B is salable immediately after split-off for $.50 per unit. A production diagram and operating data for July are presented in Exhibit 8-5, and cost allocation with the approximated sales value procedure is illustrated in Exhibit 8-6.

The cost allocation schedule in Exhibit 8-6 is similar to previous examples except that a sales value at split-off must be computed for product A. Product A is not salable at split-off and must be processed through Department 2, which incurs additional costs of $200,000. A hypothetical sales value at split-off is computed for product A by deducting $200,000 of additional processing costs from the $1,000,000 ultimate sales value. Without this adjustment, too much of the joint production costs would be allocated to product A.

EXHIBIT 8-5

PRODUCTION DIAGRAM AND OPERATING DATA

MONTH OF JULY 19X7

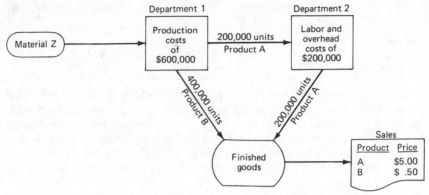

EXHIBIT 8-6

JOINT PRODUCT COST ALLOCATION

APPROXIMATED SALES VALUE METHOD

PRODUCT	POUNDS PRODUCED	SELLING PRICE	ULTIMATE SALES VALUE*	ADDITIONAL PROCESSING COSTS	APPROXIMATED SALES VALUE AT SPLIT-OFF†	ALLOCATION RATIO‡	JOINT COSTS§
A	200,000	$5.00	$1,000,000	($200,000)	$ 800,000	⁸⁄₁₀, or ⅘	$480,000
B	400,000	$ .50	200,000	–0–	200,000	²⁄₁₀, or ⅕	$120,000
	600,000				$1,000,000		$600,000

* *Ultimate sales value* uses the selling price at which the product is actually sold.
† Approximated split-off values are ultimate sales values less additional processing costs. Product B is included in all columns; but note that its ultimate sales value and approximated sales value are equal; product B is salable at split-off and receives no additional processing.
‡ Allocation ratios are computed from approximated sales value data.
§ Total joint costs of $600,000 are given. Allocations to each product are computed as $600,000 times the allocation ratios for products A and B.

Joint costs were allocated to products A and B in Exhibit 8-6, but the additional processing costs for product A must also be considered in computing unit costs. This additional step could be included in the cost allocation schedule as summarized below:

PRODUCT	POUNDS PRODUCED	ALLOCATED JOINT COSTS	+	ADDITIONAL PROCESSING COSTS	=	TOTAL COSTS	UNIT COST
A	200,000	$480,000		$200,000		$680,000	$3.40
B	400,000	120,000		–0–		120,000	$ .30
		$600,000		$200,000		$800,000	

Unit costs of $3.40 for product A and $.30 for product B are used to compute Cost of Goods Sold and ending inventory values.

When joint products are processed beyond split-off, the ultimate gross profit percentage on each product will be different. However, the approximated sales

EXHIBIT 8-7

IMPLIED AND ACTUAL GROSS PROFIT WITH PROCESSING BEYOND SPLIT-OFF

	GROSS PROFIT RELATED TO		
PRODUCT A	*Computed value*	*Actual value*	INCREASE
Sales value	$800,000	$1,000,000	$200,000
Product costs:			
Allocated joint costs	(480,000)	(480,000)	–0–
Additional processing	–0–	(200,000)	(200,000)
Gross profit	$320,000	$ 320,000	$ –0–

Note: As discussed in Exhibit 8-6, product A is not salable at split-off and is processed further in Department 2. This schedule shows that costs incurred beyond split-off are recovered from the increase in revenues, but that gross profit is not increased. If product A *could* be sold at split-off, the company would report the same gross profit of $320,000 regardless of the action it takes.

value procedure implicitly assumes that additional processing costs are recovered without generating any contribution to profits. This assumption may seem unrealistic if a product, which can be sold at split-off, is processed further. This point is emphasized in Exhibit 8-7.

Management usually incurs production costs with the expectation of recovering these amounts *plus* a reasonable contribution to profits. As shown in Exhibit 8-7, cost allocations with the approximated sales value method assume that additional costs beyond split-off are recovered but that no additional profit contribution is earned. All joint cost allocation methods have certain weaknesses and limitations. Cost allocation is an arbitrary procedure that is necessary for product cost accounting. No allocation procedure is conceptually perfect, but a particular method is accepted if resulting product unit costs are reasonable.

To select a price or value for use in joint cost allocations, the following checklist is helpful:

GUIDELINES FOR SELECTING UNIT PRICE FOR JOINT COST ALLOCATION PROCEDURES

Joint product circumstances	*Actual sales value of product at split-off*	*Computed sales value or "approximated value"*
1. Product is salable only at the split-off point.	✓	
2. Product is salable at split-off but is processed further.	✓	
3. Product is not salable at split-off and must be processed further.		✓

Approximated sales value should be computed only for products that are processed beyond split-off because they are not salable in their initial split-off condition. In all other cases, the market selling price at split-off gives an objective measure that should be used in joint cost allocations. This guideline should be followed even when a product that is salable at split-off is processed further.

ACCOUNTING FOR BY-PRODUCTS

In comparison with joint products, by-products emerge from the processing of common material inputs, but they represent a smaller potential sales value. If the salability of by-products is not certain or if their sale is sporadic, many firms simply account for by-product revenues and make no attempt to assign values to by-product inventories. Under this approach, by-product revenues could be accounted for as one of the following:

1. Credits to other income or revenue accounts
2. Credits to cost of goods sold
3. Credits to Work in Process accounts containing accumulated costs of main products

These *revenue methods* of accounting for by-products concentrate on by-product sales, not production. In some cases, these methods may be acceptable if the by-products are similar to scrap resulting from manufacturing operations. Materiality in financial accounting and proper control in cost accounting are the criteria for selecting by-product accounting methods.

If the total value of by-product production is significant,[1] then the cost recovery method of by-product accounting is warranted. This approach is recommended for by-products that are processed beyond the split-off point. Cost recovery is emphasized in this method because the net realizable value of by-products manufactured is treated as a reduction of costs applicable to the production of main products. Net realizable value is defined as selling price less estimated costs of completion and disposal. Accordingly, the cost recovery method does not allocate manufacturing costs to by-products; instead, the net realizable value of by-products reduces the manufacturing costs applicable to the main products.

To illustrate the cost recovery method, assume that joint products JP1 and JP2 are manufactured in a single process that also creates by-product BP. Costs incurred before the split-off point of all products are $1,500,000 for the current month. Currently, BP sells for $1.20 per unit less packing costs and freight charges of $.10 and $.05 per unit, respectively. Assuming that 40,000 units of BP were produced, the *by-product credit* for the current period is computed as follows:

	By-Product Credit
Selling price	$ 1.20
Less: Packing cost	(.10)
Freight-out	(.05)
Net realizable value	$ 1.05
Current production of BP	× 40,000
Credit to main product (40,000 × $1.05)	$42,000

[1] The relative significance or materiality of by-product values depends upon judgment in each case. Revenue methods are acceptable in some cases; others warrant cost recovery accounting procedures. When the value of by-product production becomes sufficiently material, the products should be accounted for as joint products.

If an inventory account is maintained in the general ledger for this by-product, the by-product credit schedule supports a journal entry to reduce production costs assignable to the two joint products:

By-product inventory	$42,000	
Work in process—Department X		$42,000

Joint costs remaining for allocation to joint products are $1,458,000.

Prior to split-off costs (material labor, and overhead common to JP1, JP2, BP)	$1,500,000
Less: Net realizable value of by-product produced in current period	(42,000)
Joint costs allocable to JP1 and JP2	$1,458,000

The relative sales value method could be used to allocate $1,458,000 of net production costs to products JP1 and JP2.

Several general ledger treatments can be used to account for by-products under the cost recovery method. Account titles and journal entry details may differ under each method. In general, the cost accounting objectives are to (1) reduce main product costs by the net realizable value of by-products produced and (2) state by-product inventories in the balance sheet at net realizable value. With end-of-period costing procedures and stable selling prices, by-product accounting usually will not show a gain or loss on by-product production and sales.

Perpetual inventory case   Assume the initial inventory of by-product BP is 5,000 units stated at net realizable value of $1.05 per unit. By-product production in July is 40,000 units, and the final inventory is 2,000 units. Sales of 43,000 units and related expense items involved cash transactions. Journal entries for by-product transactions and adjustments are explained below:

JOURNAL ENTRIES—PERPETUAL INVENTORIES			DESCRIPTION
1. By-product summary	$ 5,250		To transfer initial inventory cost to Summary
By-product inventory		$ 5,250	account (5,000 units at $1.05)
2. By-product summary	$42,000		Credit main product costs for net realizable
Work in process		$42,000	value of BP production, 40,000 × $1.05
3. By-product summary	$ 4,300		Packing costs of $.10 per unit on sales of
Cash		$ 4,300	43,000 units
4. By-product summary	$ 2,150		Freight-out of $.05 per unit on sales of
Cash		$ 2,150	43,000 units
5. Cash	$51,600		Sale of 43,000 units at $1.20 each
By-product summary		$51,600	
6. By-product inventory	$ 2,100		Recognize final inventory of 2,000 units at $1.05
By-product summary		$ 2,100	

This method of accounting is suitable for a system using perpetual inventory records without a detailed costing of by-products sold.

The By-product Summary is basically an Income Summary account for by-product transactions as pictured on the next page:

By-product summary

(1) Initial inventory	$ 5,250	(5) Sales		$51,600
(2) Current production	42,000	(6) Final inventory		2,100
(3) Packing costs	4,300			
(4) Freight-out	2,150			
	$53,700			$53,700

If selling prices change frequently and if by-product credit schedules are prepared several times during a period, the By-product Summary account may have an ending balance. Any balance in the account should be treated as a gain or loss in the income statement of the current period.

Periodic inventory case   With periodic or physical inventory systems, it is still possible to use a By-product Summary account. In this case, however, an entry is not required during the period to record the net realizable value of by-product production. Transactions in the perpetual inventory example are used below to illustrate journal entries under a periodic inventory system:

JOURNAL ENTRIES—PERIODIC INVENTORIES			DESCRIPTION
1. By-product summary	$ 5,250		Close out initial inventory carried forward from
By-product inventory		$ 5,250	prior period
2. By-product summary	$ 4,300		Packing costs of $.10 per unit on sales of
Cash		$ 4,300	43,000 units
3. By-product summary	$ 2,150		Freight-out of $.05 per unit on sales of
Cash		$ 2,150	43,000 units
4. Cash	$51,600		Sale of 43,000 units at $1.20 each
By-product summary		$51,600	
5. By-product inventory	$ 2,100		Final inventory recognized by adjusting entry
By-product summary		$ 2,100	
6. By-product summary	$42,000		Balance of By-product Summary transferred to
Manufacturing summary		$42,000	Manufacturing Summary (a closing entry)

The trial balance amount for By-product Summary at month end is $42,000 credit. Following the worksheet procedures described in Appendix 3A, this amount should be extended to the manufacturing columns of the financial statement worksheet. Note that $42,000 represents the net realizable value of current by-product production, or 40,000 units at $1.05. When placed in the credit column of the manufacturing statement, the $42,000 credit reduces the production costs assignable to inventories and Cost of Goods Manufactured. A closing entry is prepared for all account balances that appear in the manufacturing columns of the worksheet. Journal entry 6 closes the By-product Summary account and places a $42,000 credit in the Manufacturing Summary account.

SELL OR PROCESS-FURTHER DECISIONS

A decision-making application concerning joint products is the choice between selling a product at split-off or processing it further. In practice, this decision is complex because it involves many variables such as capital facilities, opportunity costs, customer demand, and interrelated effects on producing other products. The basic nature of this decision is important because it reveals the limitations of unit costs computed for inventory valuation purposes.

Whether a joint product is sold at split-off or processed further generally rests upon an analysis of *incremental* or *differential* costs and revenues. Additional processing adds value to a product and increases its selling price above the amount for which it could be sold at split-off. The decision to process further depends upon whether the increase in total revenue potential exceeds the additional costs incurred to process the product beyond split-off. Costs incurred for production prior to split-off have no effect on the decision.

Consider the following decision analysis for joint product XY. A company produces 200,000 units of product XY each year; it is salable for $3 per unit at split-off. Joint production costs allocated to product XY by the relative sales value method are $450,000. After split-off, the product is processed through a second department and then sold for $5 per unit. Variable costs of material, labor, and overhead incurred for additional processing of XY are $300,000 per year. Is the decision to process further financially desirable?

To evaluate the existing policy of processing further, comparative income statement effects for each alternative are presented in Exhibit 8-8. Incremental costs and revenues are disclosed in a separate column. Exhibit 8-8 indicates that further processing of product XY increases profits by $100,000 over profits of $150,000 if the product were sold at split-off. This profit increase is evident since incremental revenue of $400,000 exceeds incremental costs of $300,000.

If incremental processing costs for product XY were $500,000, the company would still have a $50,000 profit from processing further—$1,000,000 of sales less additional costs of $500,000 and $450,000 of joint costs. However, larger profits then could be realized by selling at split-off. In general, analysis of sell or process-further decisions should concentrate on total revenues and total costs with emphasis on incremental measures. Refer to Exhibit 8-8 and change the joint cost allocation to any amount, say $800,000. This change will not affect the decision, since the joint cost allocation is the same in both decision alternatives. Critical factors influencing the decision are incremental revenues and incremental costs.

Several technical problems are involved in measuring incremental costs incurred for additional processing beyond split-off. Some incremental costs are explicitly traceable to the product, such as costs of additional materials and direct labor. Variable overhead costs are incremental since these costs are caused by additional processing. However, supervisory salaries, property taxes, insurance, and other fixed costs that will be incurred regardless of the

EXHIBIT 8-8

INCOME STATEMENT ANALYSIS FOR SELL OR PROCESS-FURTHER DECISION ALTERNATIVES

ANNUAL VOLUME OF 200,000 UNITS	DECISION ALTERNATIVES		INCREMENTAL REVENUE OR COSTS
	Sell at split-off	*Process further*	
Revenues (at $3, $5)	$600,000	$1,000,000	$400,000
Joint cost allocation	(450,000)	(450,000)	–0–
Additional processing costs	–0–	(300,000)	(300,000)
Profit contribution	$150,000	$ 250,000	$100,000

production decision are not incremental costs. Incremental costs of additional processing should include all production costs that will be incurred only if a product is processed beyond split-off. Fixed overhead costs that are common to other production activity must be excluded from the decision analysis.

As a frame of reference for cost analysis, there are two general conditions under which a sell or process-further decision could occur:

1. The company already processes a product beyond split-off and has invested in the equipment and required personnel, or
2. The company is evaluating the possibility of processing beyond split-off and must incur certain equipment costs and other fixed costs if additional processing is to occur.

In condition 1, certain fixed costs such as supervisory salaries are related to additional processing. If production salaries would be discontinued by selling products at split-off, these costs are incremental and should be included in the decision analysis. If salaried personnel would be assigned other duties in the company when additional processing is discontinued, then salary costs are not incremental because the costs are incurred under either decision alternative. As explained in Chapter 15, depreciation expense is not an incremental cost and should be excluded from the analysis of short-run operating decisions. The principal objective under condition 1 is to select a policy that best utilizes existing capacities. Depreciation of existing equipment is not a relevant cost factor since this cost will be incurred regardless of the processing alternative selected. The principal test in identifying incremental costs is whether a certain cost factor will be incurred only if additional processing takes place. This test is difficult to answer in many cases, and the decision analysis then must incorporate reasonable assumptions or rely on existing management policies.

Condition 2 is really a capital budgeting problem. If a company must expand its physical capacity to allow additional processing, it is not sufficient to determine whether incremental revenues exceed incremental costs. Since new investments in machinery and buildings are involved, rate of return on this new investment must be considered. In general, condition 1 is a problem of how to best use existing facilities; condition 2 is a problem requiring rate of return analysis on new investment opportunities. Capital budgeting is explained in Chapter 16.

FINAL NOTE In cost accounting for joint products, the term *separable costs* is often used to describe the manufacturing costs clearly associated with additional processing of a joint product. Problems usually assume that all separable processing costs are variable. As described in the preceding section, sell or process-further decisions usually are complex and seldom involve separable processing costs that are entirely variable with production volume.

Analysis of joint production costs involves product costing and decision-making applications. Allocation of joint costs is necessary for cost accounting purposes, but the resulting unit costs are not useful in decision analysis.

Return now to the beginning of the chapter and review the highlights section before proceeding to the review questions, exercises, and problems.

8-1. Define and illustrate the following concepts and terminology:
   a. Joint cost
   b. Joint products
   c. By-product
   d. Split-off point
   e. Relative sales value method
   f. Net realizable value
   g. Separable costs

8-2. Identify and discuss the two main cost accounting objectives for joint products.

8-3. "The allocation of joint costs using physical product measures fails to allocate costs to products in relation to their revenue-producing ability." Discuss this statement.

8-4. What are some criticisms directed at the relative sales value method of allocating joint costs? Are they valid?

8-5. Under what circumstances is it necessary to use the approximated relative sales value method of allocation?

8-6. The approximated relative sales value method of allocation assumes that processing costs beyond split-off are recovered without generating any contributions to profits. How could you modify the procedure to correct this situation?

8-7. What is the role of reasonableness in decisions to select cost allocation procedures and techniques?

8-8. What distinguishes a by-product from a joint product?

8-9. What are the alternative *revenue* methods of accounting for by-products? Under what circumstances is each acceptable?

8-10. Describe the theoretically correct method of accounting for by-products.

8-11. What is the role of incremental or differential costs in sell or process-further decisions?

8-12. Joint product costs make up 90 percent of the total costs of manufacturing three joint products. Are the joint costs relevant to a decision to sell the products at split-off or process them further?

8-13. *Process-further Decision* The Inisroc Company produces three products (A, B, and C) as a result of a particular joint process. The joint costs amount to $6,000 and have been allocated equally to A, B, and C. Each

$3,700

product may be sold at the point of split-off or processed further. The sales values and costs for the two alternatives are given below:

| | | | SALES VALUES AND COSTS IF PROCESSED FURTHER | |
PRODUCT	AMOUNT OF ALLOCATED JOINT COSTS	SALES VALUE AT SPLIT-OFF	Sales	Added costs
A	$2,000	$2,700	$4,200	$900
B	2,000	4,000	4,500	800
C	2,000	2,400	3,200	900

REQUIRED:

a. What product(s) should be processed further? A

b. What is the maximum profit that this firm can achieve? 3900

8-14. *Joint and By-products* Orwell Company's plant production for March amounts to 8,000 units of Product X; 12,000 units of Product Y; and 4,000 units of Product Z. The total costs of production amounted to $58,000. The value of X is $10.00 a unit; Y sells for $12.00 a unit; and Z sells at $.50 a unit.

Z is by product
sales value is not added
to sales value
x + y $224,000

REQUIRED: Determine which of the products should be considered by-products and which should be main or joint products. Using the cost recovery method for by-products, allocate the net cost to the main or joint products by the relative sales value method. A 56,000 joint cost ÷ X+y.

8-15. *Processing Beyond Split-off* The Depressed Company produces two joint products, A and B. During August, $24,000 of joint costs were incurred. Costs after split-off were $30,000 for product A and $7,500 for product B. After additional processing, product A sells for $50 per unit, and B sells for $25 per unit.

Joint cost $4,800

REQUIRED: If the company produces 1,000 units of A and 500 units of B, determine the proper amount of joint cost that should be allocated to each product. (Assume that the approximated sales value method for allocating joint costs is used.)

8-16. *Joint Product Inventories* A and B are joint products. Their cost for the period up to the point of separation was $30,000. There were no costs beyond this point. The production of A was 20,000 units. The production of B was 40,000 units. A's selling price is $5. B's selling price is $.20.

REQUIRED: If the ending inventory is 10,000 units of A and 10,000 units of B, what is the valuation of A for balance sheet purposes? The valuation of B? Use the relative sales value method.

8-17. *Joint Product Inventories* A poultry dresser buys chickens and processes them into three joint products. Operations for July 19X2 are summarized as follows:

	EQUIVALENT OUTPUT, JULY	SALES VALUE
Grade A (legs and breasts)	10,000 lbs.	$ .40 per lb.
Grade B (wings, backs, etc.)	8,000 lbs.	.20 per lb.
Feathers	500 lbs.	1.00 per lb.

The following costs were incurred in July:

Primary processing, all products	$2,970
Secondary processing, Grade A	800
Secondary processing, Grade B	800
Secondary processing, feathers	100

There were no beginning inventories; ending inventories were:

Grade A (1,000 lbs.)	$_____
Grade B (1,000 lbs.)	$_____
Feathers (100 lbs.)	$_____

REQUIRED: Compute the values that should be assigned to these ending inventories. Defend or justify your valuation method.

PROBLEMS

8-18. *Process-further Decision*   From a particular joint process, Watkins Company produces three products: X4, Y5, and Z6. Each product may be sold at split-off or may be processed further. Additional processing requires no special facilities, and production costs of further processing are entirely variable and traceable to the products involved. In 19X2, all three products were processed beyond split-off. Joint production costs for the year were $60,000. Sales values and costs needed to evaluate the company's 19X2 production policy follow:

a) unit prod. cost $ 4.00

			SALES VALUES AND ADDITIONAL COSTS IF PROCESSED FURTHER	
PRODUCT	UNITS PRODUCED	SALES VALUE AT SPLIT-OFF	Sales value	Added costs
X4	6,000	$25,000	$42,000	$9,000
Y5	4,000	41,000	45,000	7,000
Z6	2,000	24,000	32,000	8,000 ÷ 2000 = $4.00

Joint costs are allocated to the products in proportion to the relative physical volume of output.

REQUIRED:
a. For units of Z6, compute the unit production cost that is most relevant to a sell or process-further decision. $ 4.00

b. To generate the maximum net contribution to profits, determine the products that should be subjected to additional processing. *X Y only, 8,000 Profit*

8-19. *Process-further Decision* The Mizzou Corporation has asked you to determine the most profitable course of action regarding point of sale for each of their products. Mizzou may either sell their products at split-off or process them further at additional cost.

In analyzing the decision problem, you prepared the following two reports:

Process beyond split-off

PRODUCT	EXPECTED SALES VALUE	RELATIVE SALES VALUE AT SPLIT-OFF*	ALLOCATION OF JOINT COSTS	NET PROFIT
X	$120,000	$ 60,000	$36,000	$24,000
Y	30,000	10,000	6,000	4,000
Z	40,000	20,000	12,000	8,000
Q	10,000	10,000	6,000	4,000
	$200,000	$100,000	$60,000	$40,000

* Expected sales value minus costs beyond split-off.

Sell at split-off

PRODUCT	SALES VALUE AT SPLIT-OFF†	ALLOCATION OF JOINT COSTS	NET PROFIT
X	$40,000	$30,000	$10,000
Y	6,000	4,500	1,500
Z	24,000	18,000	6,000
Q	10,000	7,500	2,500
	$80,000	$60,000	$20,000

† Actual sales offers for products at point of split-off.

REQUIRED: Using these reports, prepare an analysis that will recommend the most profitable course of action, specifying the disposition of each product. (Assume that the given reports are correct.)

8-20. *CPA Problem—Joint Costs and Sales Mix Decision* The Harbison Company manufactures two sizes of plate glass that are produced simultaneously in the same manufacturing process. Since small sheets of plate glass are cut from large sheets that have flaws in them, the joint costs are allocated equally to each good sheet—large and small—produced. The difference in costs after split-off for large and small sheets is material.

In 19X6 the company decided to increase its efforts to sell large sheets because they produced a larger gross margin than small sheets. Accordingly the fixed advertising budget devoted to large sheets was increased, and the amount devoted to small sheets was decreased. However, no changes in sales prices were made.

By midyear the production scheduling department had increased the monthly production of large sheets in order to stay above the minimum inventory level. However, it also had cut back the monthly production of small sheets because the inventory ceiling had been reached. At the end of 19X6 the net result of the change in product mix was a decrease of $112,000 in gross margin. Although sales of large sheets had increased by 34,500 units, sales of small sheets had decreased by 40,200 units.

REQUIRED:

a. Distinguish between joint costs and
   1. Costs after split-off
   2. Fixed costs
   3. Prime costs
   4. Indirect costs
b. Discuss the propriety of allocating joint costs for general purpose financial statements on the basis of
   1. Physical measures, such as weights or units
   2. Relative sales, or market value
c. In the development of weights for allocating joint costs to joint products, why is the relative sales value of each joint product usually reduced by its costs after split-off?
d. Identify the mistake that the Harbison Company made in deciding to change its product mix and explain why it caused a smaller gross margin for 19X6.

(AICPA adapted)

8-21. CPA Problem—Cost Effects of Processing Alternatives The McLean Processing Company produces a chemical compound, Supergro, that is sold for $4.60 per gallon. The manufacturing process is divided into the following departments:

1. Mixing Department. Raw materials are measured and mixed in this department.
2. Cooking Department. Mixed materials are cooked for a specified period in this department. In the cooking process there is a 10 percent evaporation loss in materials.
3. Cooling Department. After cooked materials are cooled in this department under controlled conditions, the top 80 percent in the cooling tank is syphoned off and pumped to the Packing Department. The 20 percent residue, which contains impurities, is sold in bulk as a by-product, Groex, for $2 per gallon.
4. Packing Department. In this department special 1-gallon tin cans costing 60¢ each are filled with Supergro and shipped to customers.

The company's Research and Development Department recently discovered a new use for the by-product if it is further processed in a new Boiling Department. The new by-product, Fasgro, would sell in bulk for $5 per gallon.

In processing Fasgro, the top 70 percent in the cooling tank would be syphoned off as Supergro. The residue would be pumped to the Boiling Department, where ½ gallon of raw material, SK, would be added for each gallon of residue. In the Boiling Department process there would be a 40 percent evaporation loss. In processing Fasgro, the following additional costs would be incurred:

Material SK	$1.10 per gallon
Boiling Department variable processing costs	$1.00 per gallon of input
Boiling Department fixed processing costs	$2,000 per month

In recent months, because of heavy demand, the company has shipped Supergro and Groex on the same day that their processing was completed. Fasgro would probably be subject to the same heavy demand.

During the month of July 19X3, a typical month, the following raw materials were put into process in the Mixing Department:

Material FE 10,000 gallons at $ .90 per gallon
Material QT 4,000 gallons at $1.50 per gallon

July processing costs per gallon of departmental input were:

Mixing Department 40¢
Cooking Department 50¢
Cooling Department 30¢
Packing Department 10¢

For accounting purposes, the company assigns costs to its by-products equal to their net realizable value.

REQUIRED: Prepare a statement computing total manufacturing costs and gross profit for the month of July that compares (1) actual results for July and (2) estimated results if Fasgro had been the by-product.

(AICPA adapted)

8-22. CPA Problem—Analysis of Joint Cost Allocation

Part I. By-products that require no additional processing after the point of separation are often accounted for by assigning them a value of zero at the point of separation and crediting cost of production as sales are made.

REQUIRED: Justify the above treatment and discuss its possible shortcomings.

Part II. The LaBreck Company's joint cost of producing 1,000 units of product A, 500 units of product B, and 500 units of product C is $100,000. The unit sales values of the three products at split-off are: product A, $20; product B, $200; and product C, $160. Ending inventories include 100 units of product A, 300 units of product B, and 200 units of product C.

REQUIRED:

a. Compute the amount of joint cost that would be included in the ending inventory valuation of the three products (1) on the basis of their relative sales value and (2) on the basis of physical units.

b. Discuss the relative merits of each of these two bases of joint cost allocation (1) for financial statement purposes and (2) for decisions about the desirability of selling joint products at split-off or processing them further.

(AICPA adapted)

8-23. *CPA Problem—Unit Cost Computations* In its three departments Amaco Chemical Company manufactures several products:

1. In Department 1 the raw materials amanic acid and bonyl hydroxide are used to produce Amanyl, Bonanyl, and Am-Salt. Amanyl is sold to others who use it as a raw material in the manufacture of stimulants. Bonanyl is not salable without further processing. Although Am-Salt is a commercial product for which there is a ready market, Amaco does not sell this product, preferring to submit it to further processing.

2. In Department 2 Bonanyl is processed into a marketable product, Bonanyl-X. The relationship between Bonanyl used and Bonanyl-X produced has remained constant for several months.

3. In Department 3 Am-Salt and the raw material colb are used to produce Colbanyl, a liquid propellant which is in great demand. As an inevitable part of this process, Demanyl is also produced. Demanyl was discarded as scrap until discovery of its usefulness as a catalyst in the manufacture of glue; for two years Amaco has been able to sell all its production of Demanyl.

Colbanyl cost per lb.
$32.57

In its financial statements Amaco states inventory at the lower of cost (on a FIFO basis) or market. Thus, unit costs of the items most recently produced must be computed. Costs allocated to Demanyl are computed so that after allowing for packaging and selling costs of 4¢ per pound no profit or loss will be recognized on sales of this product.

Certain data for October 19X2 follow:

RAW MATERIALS	POUNDS USED	TOTAL COST
Amanic acid	6,300	$5,670
Bonyl hydroxide	9,100	6,370
Colb	5,600	2,240

CONVERSION COSTS (LABOR AND OVERHEAD)	TOTAL COST
Department 1	$33,600
Department 2	3,306
Department 3	22,400

PRODUCTS	POUNDS PRODUCED	INVENTORIES, POUNDS		SALES PRICE PER POUND
		September 30	October 31	
Amanyl	3,600			$ 6.65
Bonanyl	2,800	210	110	
Am-Salt	7,600	400	600	6.30
Bonanyl-X	2,755			4.20
Colbanyl	1,400			43.00
Demanyl	9,800			.54

REQUIRED: Prepare for October 19X2 the schedules listed below. Supporting computations should be prepared in good form. Round answers to the nearest cent.

a. Cost per pound of Amanyl, Bonanyl, and Am-Salt produced; use relative sales value method.

b. Cost per pound of Amanyl, Bonanyl, and Am-Salt produced; use average unit cost method.

c. Cost per pound of Colbanyl produced. Assume that the cost per pound of Am-Salt produced was $3.40 in September 19X2 and $3.50 in October 19X2.

(AICPA adapted)

8-24. *By-product Accounting*   Gossett, Inc., uses the cost recovery method of accounting for by-products and allocates net joint product costs by the relative sales value method. The company produces two joint products (J1 and J2) and one by-product (A17). Operating data for September 19X9 are summarized below:

INVENTORIES, SEPTEMBER 1			SEPTEMBER PRODUCTION	
Product	Units	Value	Units	Product
J1	40,000	$36,000	200,000 lb.	J1
J2	20,000	30,000	400,000 lb.	J2
A17	4,000	3,800	80,000 lb.	A17

The joint products are sold after split-off for unit prices of $4.00 (J1) and $6.00 (J2). Product A17 sells for $1.10 per pound. Packing costs and freight on the by-product are $.12 and $.03 per unit, respectively. Joint production costs in September were $120,000 for materials, $210,000 for labor, and $400,000 for factory overhead. During September, unit sales were: 230,000 pounds of J1; 390,000 pounds of J2; and 82,000 pounds of A17. Selling expenses related to the joint products were $200,000, divided equally between J1 and J2. By-product freight charges and packing costs required cash disbursements.

REQUIRED:

a. Prepare a by-product credit schedule and a summary of cost allocations to joint products produced.

b. Journalize all transactions for September assuming the use of perpetual inventories.
c. Prepare income statements for each product line and for combined company operations during September.

Module Three

Foundations of Management Planning and Control

BASIC COST ACCOUNTING concepts are an integral part of management planning and control functions and are vital to cost accumulation and analysis activities. The traditional product cost accounting systems described in Module Two concentrate on the processing of actual manufacturing costs incurred by a company. These same systems can be used as bases for planning costs of future accounting periods and for controlling costs through performance measurement techniques.

Module Three introduces concepts and techniques for cost planning and control. When integrated with an existing cost accounting system, these concepts and techniques are used to develop reports which facilitate cost planning and control activities. Chapter 9 presents an in-depth study of cost-volume-profit analysis. Cost behavior is an important factor in most cost planning and control activities and various methods of identifying cost behavior are analyzed in this chapter. The contribution approach to income determination is also discussed in Chapter 9.

In Chapter 10, the contribution approach is expanded to provide the basis for a cost accounting method known as direct costing. Based on the concepts of cost-volume-profit and contribution margin, direct costing utilizes a cost reporting format which distinguishes between variable costs and fixed costs. Direct costing differs from the conventional absorption costing approach in that fixed manufacturing overhead costs are not assigned to products.

Standard cost accounting is introduced in Chapter 11. As a refinement of cost accounting procedures found in systems using historical costs, standard costs are also useful for cost planning and cost control purposes. Standard costs are predetermined estimates of material, labor, and overhead costs that should be incurred to manufacture particular products.

Cost control in standard cost systems begins with an analysis of variances between actual costs and standard costs. In Chapter 12, methods of variance analysis for raw material, direct labor, and factory overhead costs are discussed and illustrated. Chapter 12 also considers the disposition and reporting of cost variances for financial accounting purposes.

In Chapters 9 through 12, there is a logical sequence of subject material. Cost behavior is the foundation of cost-volume-profit analysis, contribution reporting, and direct costing. Cost behavior analysis and flexible budgets are utilized to develop standard cost information. Module Three follows a building-block approach since concepts and techniques developed in each chapter are used in subsequent chapters.

Chapter 9: Cost-Volume-Profit Analysis

The foundations of planning and control through management accounting include cost behavior analysis, cost-volume-profit (CVP) relationships, flexible budgeting, direct costing, and standard cost systems. Cost behavior analysis is an integral part of all these foundations. Accordingly, this chapter introduces the analysis of cost behavior patterns and the use of contribution margin techniques in CVP analysis.

Upon completion of this chapter, students should be able to:

1. Identify and define various forms of cost behavior
2. Use regression analysis to analyze semivariable costs
3. Construct several types of CVP graphs
4. Apply breakeven and related CVP techniques in algebraic form

The following basic concepts are introduced in this chapter:

Cost behavior   The manner in which costs respond to changes in volume or activity.

Relevant range   A band or range of potential volume levels within which actual operations are likely to occur.

Contribution margin   The excess of revenues over all variable costs related to the particular sales volume.

Contribution approach   A technique for measuring profits in which contribution margin is considered a balance available to recover fixed costs and generate profits.

Cost-volume-profit (CVP) analysis involves a number of analytical procedures based upon knowledge of fixed and variable cost characteristics for a particular company. Given such cost behavior information, it is possible to determine breakeven sales volume, to compute the sales level needed to generate desired

Relevant Concepts

Chapter Summary

profits, and to supply answers to many "what if" questions that arise in the course of management planning.

Identification and analysis of cost behavior patterns are prerequisites to reliable CVP analysis. Several types of complex cost behavior patterns are caused by contractual agreements and technological relationships. Semivariable costs contain both fixed and variable components that must be identified by regression analysis or by less formal methods such as the high-low procedure. In general, cost behavior identity involves estimation, and the resulting fixed-variable cost information is usually not precise.

The contribution approach provides an income statement format that is consistent with CVP logic and formulas. Contribution margin, the excess of revenues over all variable expenses of the related sales volume, is the key concept. Using two general formulas, it is possible to determine the cost and profit effects of many decision alternatives:

(1)   sales in units $= \dfrac{\text{fixed costs} + \text{desired profits}}{\text{contribution margin per unit}}$

(2)   sales in dollars $= \dfrac{\text{fixed costs} + \text{desired profits}}{\text{contribution margin ratio}}$

Several assumptions underlie the use of CVP techniques. If the assumptions are reasonably valid in a particular case, then CVP techniques constitute a general model of company activities that can be used to provide useful information for planning and control.

NATURE OF COST-VOLUME-PROFIT ANALYSIS

Cost-volume-profit analysis (CVP) includes a number of techniques and problem-solving procedures structured upon knowledge of a firm's cost behavior patterns. A basic application of CVP analysis is the determination of *breakeven volume*, which is the sales volume at which revenue equals all costs and profits are zero. CVP techniques express relationships among revenue, sales mix, cost, volume, and profits. These expressed relationships provide a general model of company financial activity that is useful for short-range planning, performance evaluation, and analysis of decision alternatives.

Cost behavior analysis is an integral part of all CVP applications. *Cost behavior* describes the manner in which costs respond to changes in selected measures of activity or volume. Thus, fixed and variable cost information is essential in CVP analysis. Semivariable costs and other complex behavior patterns for particular costs must be resolved into fixed and variable components before CVP analysis can be applied. With reasonable estimates of cost behavior, CVP techniques are used to measure the cost and profit effects of decision alternatives, short-run plans, and completed activities.

Elements of CVP Analysis

Basic CVP relationships can be expressed and analyzed graphically. Consider a single-product firm that sells its product for $10. Total annual fixed costs for production and distribution are $48,000. Variable costs for production, selling, and administration are $4 per unit. Basic CVP relationships for this firm are shown graphically in Exhibit 9-1.

EXHIBIT 9-1
BASIC CVP RELATIONSHIPS

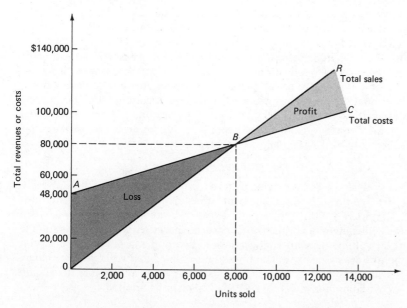

Lines for total sales and total costs are plotted in Exhibit 9-1 by locating two points for each factor and drawing a straight line between the points. For sales, we used $0 at sales of zero units and $100,000 at sales of 10,000 units. For costs, one point is $48,000 of fixed costs at zero unit sales; another point is 8,000 unit sales, where total costs are $80,000 ($48,000 fixed costs + $4 × 8,000 units). The total revenue and total cost lines intersect at the breakeven point, which is 8,000 units or $80,000 of sales. Profits are earned when sales volume is greater than 8,000 units, as noted by the shaded profit area, *RBC*. Below 8,000 units, operating losses occur as measured by the vertical distance within the loss area, *OBA*. Alternative methods of graphical analysis are presented later in the chapter.

The graph in Exhibit 9-1 is a basic CVP model; it portrays the revenue, cost, volume, and profit elements of company operations. Similar analysis can be applied to multiproduct divisions or companies as long as a given sales mix of various products is assumed. The CVP model is a useful device because it provides a general overview of company financial operations. Note also that the model is based upon a set of fixed relationships. If unit costs, prices, fixed costs, operating efficiency, or other operating factors change, the model must be revised to reflect the new relationships.

Role of CVP Analysis

With graphic analysis, algebraic computations, and reports in income statement format, basic CVP logic can be applied to measure the effects of management decision alternatives. These alternatives include possible changes in selling prices, changes in variable or fixed costs, expansion or contraction of sales volume, or other changes in operating methods or policies. Cost-volume-profit analysis is useful for problems of product pricing, sales-mix management, adding or deleting product lines, and accepting special orders. In summary, various applications of CVP analysis can provide information needed for effective planning and control.

Successful CVP applications are based on fixed and variable cost information. Identity of various cost behavior patterns is therefore a key factor. A study of cost behavior develops the cost information used in CVP analysis. In using this cost behavior information, accountants should recognize that estimates, assumptions, and generalizations are involved. Cost behavior patterns are estimated and are seldom precise; CVP analysis also involves certain assumptions that must not be grossly violated; and generalizations, such as straight-line relationships, are used if they are reasonably accurate. When assumptions and generalizations are valid and appropriate, CVP analysis provides a rather simple means to deal with complex problems.

STRUCTURE OF COST BEHAVIOR PATTERNS

A proper analysis of cost behavior patterns is the foundation of all CVP techniques. In relation to cost behavior analysis, fixed and variable cost classifications are basically two polar extremes. Some costs remain fixed in total over wide ranges of volume; other costs are perfectly variable in relation to a particular volume measure. Between these two pure classes of cost behavior are numerous costs that exhibit combinations of fixed and variable cost characteristics. Complex cost behavior patterns must be resolved into fixed and variable cost components before CVP analysis can be applied.

Variable Cost Behavior

Variable costs *in total* change in direct proportion to changes in volume or activity. For instance, the total cost of raw material usage is variable in relation to units produced. If material cost per unit of product is eight dollars, then total material cost changes in direct proportion to changes in production volume. This example of pure variable cost behavior is shown in graph *a* of Exhibit 9-2. Notice that *total* material cost is variable, but unit material cost remains constant at eight dollars per unit of product.

In classifying a particular cost as variable, the related volume or activity measure is extremely important. Consider machinery setup costs that are $500 for each production run. In total, setup costs are variable in relation to the number of setups required during a time period. For a particular production run, however, the setup cost is fixed in relation to the number of units produced. In this case, fixed or variable behavior depends upon the volume measure selected. Effects of this choice between volume measures are demonstrated in graphs *b* and *c* of Exhibit 9-2.

The general guide for selecting a volume base is to relate costs to their most logical and causal factor. Accordingly, setup costs should be considered variable in relation to the number of machinery setup operations performed. With this classification, setup costs can be budgeted and controlled more easily. Each cost with variable behavior characteristics should be related to an appropriate measure of production or sales volume. Thus, direct labor costs should be related to direct labor hours or unit production volume. Sales commissions, as another example, can usually be related to dollar sales on a percentage basis.

There are two reasons for careful analysis in selecting a volume measure for variable costs. First, each variable cost should be related to a volume base that permits planning and control of the particular cost. Second, it is necessary to combine or aggregate many different variable costs to perform CVP analysis for

EXHIBIT 9-2

EXAMPLES OF VARIABLE COST BEHAVIOR

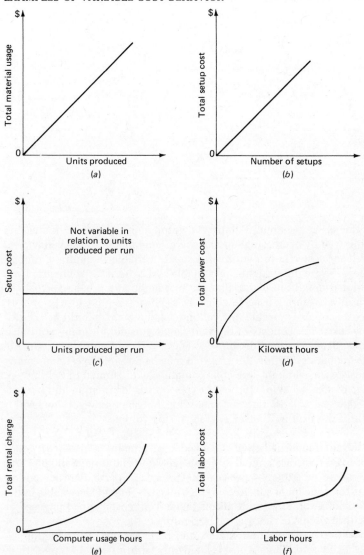

an entire company. This aggregate analysis usually considers sales volume as the measure of activity. Therefore, care must be exercised to determine that a variable cost based on machine hours or indirect labor hours is also reasonably variable with production or sales volume.

Many costs vary with volume in a nonlinear fashion, as indicated by graphs *d*, *e*, and *f* in Exhibit 9-2. Graph *d* shows the behavior of power costs when unit cost of power consumption declines as usage increases. Graph *e* reflects the behavior pattern of computer cost when each additional hour of usage costs

EXHIBIT 9-3

RELEVANT RANGE AND LINEAR APPROXIMATION

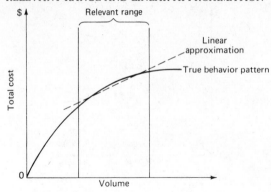

more than the previous hour. Finally, in graph *f* the effects of increasing efficiency followed by decreasing efficiency are shown to affect the behavior of a particular labor cost. These nonlinear costs are variable in nature, although they are different from the straight-line variable cost pattern shown in graph *a*.

The traditional definition of variable costs contemplates a behavior pattern like that for raw material usage, which is a linear relationship (graph *a*). Nonlinear costs are also variable in relation to volume and should be considered variable costs. The concept of relevant range is useful for many nonlinear cost functions. *Relevant range* is the segment or range of volume in which a firm expects to operate. Within this range, it may be possible to estimate many nonlinear costs with a straight-line approximation as illustrated in Exhibit 9-3. The objective of cost behavior studies is to permit cost estimation and budgeting. Knowledge that a particular cost is nonlinear at some low-volume level is hardly useful if the firm will never operate at this volume.

Fixed Cost Behavior   Within a relevant range of activity, a fixed cost remains constant *in total*. Examples of fixed costs are annual straight-line depreciation of $400,000 and supervisory salaries of $200,000 per year. Reference to a particular time period is essential to the concept of a fixed cost since all costs tend to be variable in the long run. This long-run viewpoint means that a fixed cost can be increased or decreased within whatever time period is required to increase or decrease plant capacity, machinery, labor requirements, and other factors of production associated with fixed costs. Thus, a cost is fixed only within a certain time period. For planning purposes, management usually considers an annual time period and the costs expected to be fixed within this period.

A fixed cost remains constant in total, but the unit fixed cost decreases as volume increases. Unit fixed costs therefore vary inversely with volume. To illustrate this point, consider the fact that annual depreciation of $400,000 is $2 per unit if 200,000 units are produced; the unit cost becomes $1 per unit at a volume of 400,000 units. Total and per-unit behavior patterns of fixed costs are shown in graphs *a* and *b* of Exhibit 9-4. Since the unit fixed cost depends upon a particular level of volume, most CVP applications deal with total fixed costs because these amounts will remain constant within a relevant range.

EXHIBIT 9-4

GRAPHS OF FIXED COST BEHAVIOR

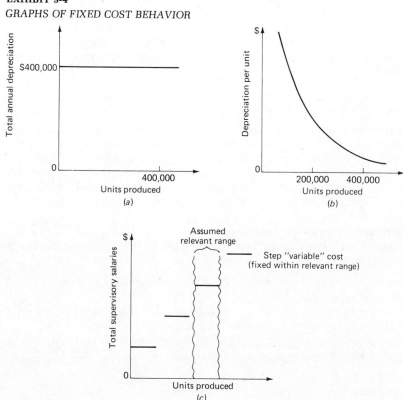

The concept of relevant range is very important in defining fixed cost behavior patterns. As an example, supervisory salaries are fixed costs at particular volume levels, but these costs increase if volume expansion requires more supervisory personnel. A steplike behavior pattern such as graph *c* (Exhibit 9-4) applies to costs of this type.

Step-cost functions as shown in graph *c* usually are called *step-variable costs*. Is the cost fixed or variable? The answer depends on the volume range under consideration. Over wide volume ranges, the step-cost does vary or change in relation to volume changes. Within a narrow range of planned volume, however, the step-cost most likely will remain constant, and it should be budgeted as a fixed cost. The important point is not whether the cost is called fixed or variable but how the cost will behave over the relevant range of activity. The ability to estimate and predict the cost of supervision is the objective, regardless of the label attached to the behavior pattern. For practical purposes, supervisory salaries are considered fixed costs within the volume range that is relevant to future operations.

Fixed costs are classified as either capacity costs or discretionary costs. *Capacity costs* are committed costs that include depreciation of fixed assets, insurance, property taxes, rental charges, and supervisory salaries. These costs must be incurred if a company continues to use its existing capacities to produce and sell. *Discretionary costs*—such as advertising, product development, basic research, and employee training—are incurred because of policy decisions by management. Discretionary costs are subject to periodic review and can be changed more easily than capacity costs. Thus, fixed costs incurred during a prolonged strike could be substantially different from the fixed costs incurred at typical volume levels.

Other Cost Behavior Patterns

A common form of cost behavior is the *semivariable*, or *mixed*, *cost*, which demonstrates both fixed and variable characteristics. This pattern often results when several different cost factors are charged to a single general ledger account such as Machinery Repairs, Factory Maintenance, Factory Power, or Supervisory Salaries. Analysis of costs recorded in past periods usually will produce a cost curve that intersects the vertical axis and yet has a positive slope, such as graph *a* in Exhibit 9-5. Semivariable costs of this form must be separated into their fixed and variable components as illustrated later in this chapter.

Some costs have unique behavior patterns because of contractual agreements that determine the total cost. Refer to Exhibit 9-5 for the behavior pattern of the following costs:

1. *Bonus cost* is incurred at the rate of $X per hour after a given volume is attained (graph *b*).
2. *Factory rental* has a basic cost of $500,000 per year less $.50 per payroll labor hour; the annual cost cannot go below $80,000 (graph *c*).
3. Cost of annual *equipment maintenance* by an outside firm is incurred at the rate of $X per service hour up to a maximum annual cost of $50,000 (graph *d*).

EXHIBIT 9-5
OTHER FORMS OF COST BEHAVIOR

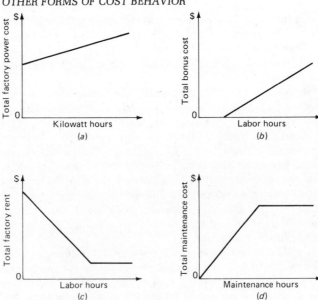

It is difficult to label the costs in graphs b, c, and d as either fixed or variable. Their behavior over wide ranges of volume is determined by a contractual formula. For budgetary planning purposes, the important point is to know how the costs will change as selected volume measures change and what volume level management expects for the normal planning period of one year. If a cost is expected to remain constant in relation to potential volume levels during a particular period, then the cost should be considered fixed for purposes of CVP analysis.

IDENTITY OF COST BEHAVIOR PATTERNS

A variety of cost behavior patterns are found in accounting practice. Several methods can be used to identify the behavior of specific cost items. Costs that are purely variable or purely fixed can be identified graphically. Behavior patterns determined by contractual agreements can be expressed in formula or algebraic style. Cost records for past periods, management policy on discretionary costs, and contractual agreements help to define the behavior patterns of specific costs. A general and rather unsophisticated approach is the *chart of accounts method,* in which all costs are classified as fixed or variable based upon the judgment and experience of the person reviewing each general ledger account.

When there is doubt about the behavior pattern of a particular cost, it is helpful to prepare a scatter diagram of cost amounts and related volume measures for past time periods. In particular, this approach should be used for costs that are thought to have a semivariable behavior pattern. The scatter diagram indicates whether a linear relationship exists between the cost item and the related volume measure. If a linear relationship appears reasonable, a cost line can be fit to the data either by visual means or by statistical analysis.

Linear Regression Analysis

Assume that a company wishes to determine the cost behavior pattern of Factory Power. A single general ledger account is used to record all costs related to power generation, including equipment depreciation, salaries, and related supplies. Power is consumed by producing departments that involve machinery-related operations. During the past year, total power costs and total machine hours were:

MONTH	POWER COST	VOLUME IN MACHINE HOURS
1	$19,000	2,000
2	20,000	2,500
3	22,000	3,000
4	23,000	3,300
5	25,000	4,100
6	26,000	5,000
7	29,000	6,000
8	27,000	5,000
9	25,000	4,500
10	24,000	4,000
11	21,000	3,500
12	20,500	3,000

EXHIBIT 9-6

SCATTER DIAGRAM OF POWER COSTS AND MACHINE HOURS

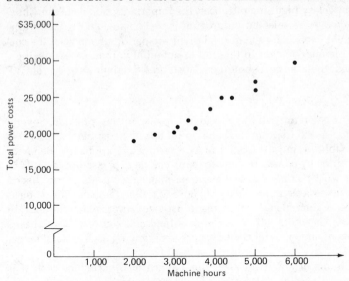

The scatter diagram in Exhibit 9-6 plots each pair of cost and volume observations. The remaining task is to fit a line to the plotted data.

Simple linear regression analysis is a statistical method for fitting a straight line to paired observations of an independent variable (volume) and a dependent variable (power cost). This line-fitting procedure is called the *least squares method* because the statistical computations result in a cost line for which the squared differences between each cost observation and the cost line are a minimum sum.[1] With regression analysis, information needed to construct the cost line is provided by solving two equations:

$$(1) \quad a = \frac{\Sigma Y}{N} - \frac{b(\Sigma X)}{N}$$

$$(2) \quad b = \frac{N\Sigma XY - \Sigma X \Sigma Y}{N\Sigma X^2 - (\Sigma X)^2}$$

where X = values of the independent variable, volume
Y = values of the dependent variable, power cost
a = value of Y where cost line intersects vertical axis
b = slope of the line or variable cost rate
Σ = summation sign
N = number of paired observations for X and Y

Thus, regression analysis provides numerical values for elements a and b such that the cost curve is a straight line of the general form $Y = a + bX$. Solving the equations requires the data computation shown in the following partial table:

---

[1] A description of the least squares criterion and derivation of equations for elements a and b is available in most textbooks on elementary statistics.

X (Machine Hours)	Y (Power Cost)	XY	X²
2,000	$ 19,000	38,000,000	4,000,000
2,500	20,000	50,000,000	6,250,000
3,000	22,000	66,000,000	9,000,000
—	—	—	—
—	—	—	—
—	—	—	—
3,000	20,500	61,500,000	9,000,000
Σ → 45,900	$281,500	1,114,900,000	190,450,000

In solving the two equations for a and b, we have:

(2) $\quad b = \dfrac{N\Sigma XY - \Sigma X \Sigma Y}{N\Sigma X^2 - (\Sigma X)^2} = \dfrac{12(1,114,900,000) - [(45,900)(281,500)]}{12(190,450,000) - [(45,900)(45,900)]}$

$\quad b = \dfrac{457,950,000}{178,590,000} = \$2.56$ variable cost per machine hour

(1) $\quad a = \dfrac{\Sigma Y}{N} - \dfrac{b(\Sigma X)}{N} = \dfrac{281,500}{12} - 2.56\left(\dfrac{45,900}{12}\right)$

$\quad a = \$13,666$ fixed cost per month

The complete regression equation for power cost is:

$$Y = \$13,666 \text{ per month} + \$2.56 \text{ per machine hour}$$

This equation represents the approximate monthly fixed cost ($13,666) and the variable cost per machine hour ($2.56) of the semivariable cost, Factory Power.

It is possible to fit a line to semivariable cost observations by simply analyzing the paired data for low cost, low volume and high cost, high volume. This method is statistically less accurate than regression analysis, but it is easier to apply. Our power cost example involved high-low volume and cost data as follows:

High-Low Method

	High	Low	Change
Power cost	$29,000	$19,000	$10,000
Machine hours	6,000	2,000	4,000

The variable cost element is measured by the slope of a line that could be drawn between the two points selected for analysis. In other words, only the variable cost element would cause a change in total cost between 2,000 and 6,000 machine hour activity levels. Variable cost per machine hour is determined by relating change in total cost to change in machine hours, or

$$\text{variable cost} = \dfrac{\Delta \text{ cost}}{\Delta \text{ volume}} = \dfrac{\$10,000}{4,000} = \$2.50$$

Once the variable cost of $2.50 per hour is estimated, the total cost is separated into fixed and variable portions as follows:

	HIGH VOLUME (6,000 HOURS)	LOW VOLUME (2,000 HOURS)
Total power cost	$29,000	$19,000
Less: Variable costs:		
(6,000 and 2,000 at $2.50)	(15,000)	(5,000)
Fixed cost	$14,000	$14,000

Only one fixed cost computation is necessary, but both are shown to prove that estimated total fixed costs under this approach are $14,000.

Note that the equation and resulting cost curve for power costs differ with the method of analysis used:

regression analysis: power cost = $13,666 + $2.56 per machine hour
high-low method: power cost = $14,000 + $2.50 per machine hour

In this case, either formula will provide satisfactory results for budgeting or CVP applications. Regression analysis involves several technical assumptions and requisite conditions for proper use. Analysis of these factors is beyond the scope of this text. Most statistical methods have certain limitations, and their solutions should be reviewed for reasonableness. In the power cost example, the high-low solution confirms the reasonableness of the regression results. Graphic analysis is also a good confirmation test.

CONTRIBUTION APPROACH TO CVP ANALYSIS

When fixed and variable cost information for a company has been measured properly, graphic and algebraic forms of CVP analysis are then possible. For total company operations or individual segments such as product lines, the excess of revenues over all related variable costs is termed *contribution margin* (CM). It is useful to think of contribution margin as a balance that serves two purposes, recovering fixed costs and generating profits. Your understanding of CVP analysis will be improved if you visualize the following process:

1. Revenues are generated by sale of products.
2. Revenues are applied to the recovery of all variable costs (variable costs are deducted from revenues).
3. Contribution margin (step 1 less step 2) is applied to the recovery of all fixed costs, and any residual balance is profit before taxes.

The cost recovery sequence described above is called the *contribution approach* to income determination. This approach emphasizes cost behavior and is the foundation of CVP logic and related techniques. The following data for Example Company are used to demonstrate the analytical ability inherent in the contribution approach. Example Company in 19X4 produced and sold 10,000 units of a single product with operating results shown in the following income statement:

EXAMPLE COMPANY
Contribution income statement
For year 19X4

Sales (10,000 units at $10)		$100,000
Variable expenses:		
Manufacturing	$30,000	
Selling and administrative	10,000	40,000
Contribution margin (60% of sales)		$ 60,000
Fixed expenses:		
Manufacturing	$37,000	
Selling and administrative	11,000	48,000
Income before taxes		$ 12,000

Notice that the order or sequence of expense deductions is determined by variable and fixed cost classifications. Contribution margin is *not* the same as gross profit or gross margin computed in traditional income statements.

With contribution margin information, analytical procedures are available with both percentage and per unit data, as shown below:

Algebraic CVP Analysis

	PER UNIT	PERCENTAGE
Sales	$10	100
Variable expenses	(4)	(40)
Contribution margin	$ 6	60

The contribution margin per unit (CM_u) is $6. This means that each unit sold provides $6 toward the recovery of fixed costs. How many units must be sold to exactly recover the $48,000 of fixed costs? The answer to this question is breakeven volume in units (BE_u):

$$BE_u = \frac{\$48,000}{\$6} = \underline{8,000}$$

How many units must be sold to generate before-tax profits of $12,000?

$$\text{units} = \frac{\$48,000 + \$12,000}{\$6} = \underline{10,000}$$

Contribution margin per unit is used in formula 1 below to compute breakeven volume or the unit sales volume required to generate a desired level of profits:

$$(1) \quad \text{units} = \frac{\text{fixed costs} + \text{desired profit}}{CM_u}$$

In percentage form, the contribution margin ratio (CM%) is equal to contribution margin divided by sales dollars. The contribution margin ratio of 60 percent for Example Company indicates that 60 percent of each sales dollar is available to recover fixed costs and provide profits. How many sales dollars are needed to breakeven for Example Company? Let X represent required sales dollars. Since 60 percent times X sales dollars = $48,000 of fixed costs, then .60X = $48,000 and X = $48,000/.6 = $80,000. The breakeven volume can be verified as follows:

Sales (computed above)	$80,000
Variable expenses (40% of sales)	(32,000)
Contribution margin (60% of sales)	$48,000
Fixed expenses	(48,000)
Income before taxes	$ -0-

To determine the dollar sales required to generate a desired level of profits, use the following general formula:

$$(2) \quad \text{dollar sales} = \frac{\text{fixed costs + desired profits}}{\text{CM\%}}$$

Sales dollars needed to produce an income before taxes of $12,000 for Example Company are:

$$\text{dollar sales} = \frac{\$48,000 + \$12,000}{60\%} = \$100,000$$

Validity of the $100,000 amount is provided by the income statement of Example Company in 19X4.

The two general formulas 1 and 2 can be used to evaluate various alternative plans of management. The following cases are solved using the two CVP formulas and data from Example Company.

Case A What sales volume is necessary for Example Company to generate $15,000 of income before taxes?

$$\text{dollar sales} = \frac{\$48,000 + \$15,000}{.60} = \frac{\$63,000}{.60} = \$105,000$$

or

$$\text{units} = \frac{\$63,000}{\$6} = 10,500$$

Case B If the tax rate is 48 percent, what sales volume is needed to generate after-tax profits of $10,400? (Let X represent income before taxes.)

$$\text{Step 1: } \$10,400 = X - .48X; \ X = \frac{\$10,400}{.52} = \$20,000$$

$$\text{Step 2: Dollar sales} = \frac{\$48,000 + \$20,000}{.60} = \$113,333$$

Case C What sales volume is required to earn a 10 percent profit margin on sales? (Income before taxes is 10 percent of sales.)

Step 1: Compute "contribution
to fixed costs" per unit:

Sales price	$10
Variable expenses (40%)	(4)
Profit margin (10%)	(1)
Contribution to fixed costs	$5

$$\text{Step 2: Units} = \frac{\$48,000}{\$5} = \underline{\underline{9,600}}$$

Case D The company produced and sold 10,000 units in 19X4. For 19X5, labor costs will increase so that variable expenses per unit will be $6. What sales volume is required in 19X5 to earn the same profit as in 19X4? (Income before taxes in 19X4 was $12,000; contribution margin per unit in 19X5 will be $10 − $6 = $4.)

$$\text{units} = \frac{\$48,000 + \$12,000}{\$4} = \underline{\underline{15,000}}$$

Cases A to D are sufficient to demonstrate that many "what if" questions can be answered quickly by using basic CVP formulas. Solutions are developed in dollar sales or units depending upon the desired information. A solution in sales dollars can be converted to units by dividing unit selling price into sales dollars. The basic relationships used in the contribution approach can also be demonstrated graphically, as described in the next section.

The simplest form of graphic CVP presentation involves one line for total revenue and another line for total costs. An example of this form was given in Exhibit 9-1. Another method of graphic presentation includes a line for total variable costs. This form is shown in Exhibit 9-7 using the basic relationships for Example Company: total fixed costs of $48,000; unit selling price of $10; and variable costs per unit of $4. The three lines in Exhibit 9-7 are constructed by locating two points on the graph for total sales, total variable costs, and total costs. Then a straight line is drawn between the two points for each item. An advantage of the graph in Exhibit 9-7 is that it shows contribution margin as the area ROV. Fixed costs are not shown explicitly, but the vertical distance between the total cost line and the variable cost line represents the fixed costs of $48,000.

Graphic CVP Analysis

EXHIBIT 9-7
CVP ANALYSIS—EXAMPLE COMPANY

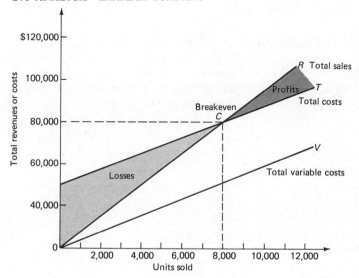

EXHIBIT 9-8

PROFIT-VOLUME GRAPH—EXAMPLE COMPANY

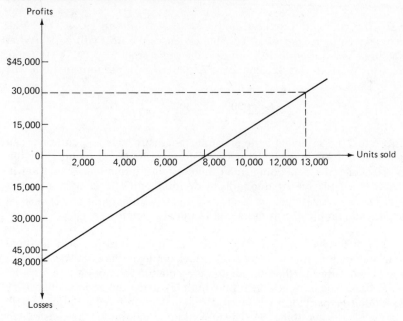

Another useful technique for presenting CVP relationships is the profit-volume graph shown in Exhibit 9-8. This graph simplifies all the relationships by using one line to show before-tax profits in relation to sales volume. To construct this graph for Example Company, we located two points of profit and related volume. At zero unit sales, fixed costs will still be incurred, and a loss of $48,000 is noted on the graph. The breakeven point is 8,000 units, at which volume the profit is zero, as indicated where the profit line crosses the horizontal axis. By connecting these two points with a straight line, we can read profits at different volume levels. For example, a profit of $30,000 is expected at a sales volume of 13,000 units, as shown by the broken lines in Exhibit 9-8.

Sales Mix Analysis

For multiproduct companies, *sales mix* refers to the relative proportions of different products that comprise total sales. If units are comparable in physical measures, sales mix indicates the percentage of physical sales volume accounted for by each product. Sales mix also can be computed on the basis of dollar sales. Consider the following case of products X and Y:

| | | | SALES MIX PERCENTAGE | |
PRODUCT	UNITS	SALES	Physical	Dollars
X	10,000	$60,000	20	75
Y	40,000	20,000	80	25
	50,000	$80,000	100	100

When several products are involved, CVP analysis is performed using an *average* contribution margin ratio for a given sales mix or an *average* contribution margin per unit. If breakeven volume is computed in sales dollars, the sales of each product composing this total are determined by using the sales-mix percentages based on dollar sales. If breakeven volume is computed in units, the units of each separate product composing this total are computed by using the sales-mix percentage based on physical sales volume. The following illustration demonstrates these procedures.

A company with three separate products reported the following operating results for 19X7:

PRODUCT	UNIT SALES	SALES	CONTRIBUTION MARGIN	
			Dollars	CM%
A	10,000	$100,000	$ 80,000	80%
B	30,000	120,000	60,000	50%
C	20,000	180,000	100,000	55.6% or 5/9
	60,000	$400,000	$240,000	
		Total fixed costs	(120,000)	
		Income before taxes	$120,000	

Assume that products A, B, and C will continue to be sold in the 19X7 sales mix. Compute breakeven volume in sales dollars and in units.

Analysis in sales dollars   Compute breakeven volume based on the average contribution margin ratio ($\overline{CM}$%) for the given sales mix. Distribute the breakeven sales dollars to each product according to the percentage of actual dollar sales represented by A, B, and C.

(1) $\overline{CM}\% = \dfrac{\$240,000}{\$400,000} = 60\%$

(2)
PRODUCT	SALES, 19X7	DOLLAR MIX
A	$100,000	25%
B	120,000	30%
C	180,000	45%
	$400,000	100%

(3)   Breakeven $= \dfrac{\$120,000}{.60} = \$200,000$

(4)   Distribution of breakeven sales: $200,000
- (A = 25%) $ 50,000
- (B = 30%) $ 60,000
- (C = 45%) $ 90,000
- $200,000

(5) Proof of breakeven:

PRODUCT	BREAKEVEN SALES	CM%	TOTAL CM
A	$50,000	80%	$ 40,000
B	60,000	50%	30,000
C	90,000	55.6% or 5/9	50,000
			$120,000
		Fixed costs	(120,000)
		Profit	$ -0-

Notice that $200,000 of total sales represents the breakeven volume for the entire firm. Fixed costs were not allocated or otherwise associated with separate products. All fixed costs were considered joint with respect to products A, B, and C. While it is possible to identify fixed costs related to each product and compute product-line breakeven points, the sum of these separate breakeven points would not equal the company-wide breakeven volume unless all fixed costs are traceable to products.

Analysis in units   Compute breakeven volume using the average contribution margin per unit $(\overline{CM_u})$ for the given sales mix. Determine the total units of each product comprising breakeven volume by reference to physical sales mix percentages.

(1) $\overline{CM_u} = \dfrac{\$240,000}{60,000} = \$4$ average contribution margin per unit

(2)

PRODUCT	UNIT SALES, 19X7	PHYSICAL MIX
A	10,000	1/6
B	30,000	3/6
C	20,000	2/6
	60,000	6/6 (100%)

(3) Breakeven $= \dfrac{\$120,000}{\$4} = 30,000$ units

(4) Distribution of breakeven sales: 30,000 units

$(A = 1/6)$ 5,000
$(B = 3/6)$ 15,000
$(C = 2/6)$ 10,000
               30,000 units

(5) Proof of breakeven:

PRODUCT	BREAKEVEN UNITS	CM_u	TOTAL CM
A	5,000	$8	$ 40,000
B	15,000	$2	30,000
C	10,000	$5	50,000
			$120,000
		Fixed costs	(120,000)
		Income before taxes	$ -0-

In using CVP analysis in multiproduct situations, the key is sales mix percentage. If you compute a breakeven volume or required sales volume in units, distribute this total to each product based on the physical sales mix. If you compute breakeven sales dollars, distribute this total to each product based on the dollar sales mix percentages.

BASIC ASSUMPTIONS IN CVP ANALYSIS

Underlying all the illustrations of CVP analysis in this chapter are certain basic assumptions. These assumptions and conditions are important because the usefulness and accuracy of CVP analysis depend upon their validity in specific circumstances. If certain assumptions are not valid in a particular situation, then the resulting CVP analysis will not be reliable. The principal assumptions and required conditions underlying CVP analysis are:

1. Fixed and variable cost behavior is accurately determined.
2. Linear approximations for cost and revenue functions are reasonably accurate.
3. Efficiency and productivity do not change in relation to volume.
4. Total fixed costs, selling prices, and unit variable costs will remain unchanged during the planning period.
5. Product sales mix will remain unchanged during the planning period.
6. Production and sales volume are approximately equal (no significant change in inventory levels).

Most of these factors relate to the lack of precision in CVP analysis and the need for estimates and approximations in assembling necessary data. CVP models are static and deterministic. If prices, unit costs, sales mix, operating efficiency, or other relevant factors change, then the overall CVP relationships also must be modified. Assumption 6, concerning inventory changes, is probably the most restrictive condition. Our examples in this chapter assumed that production and sales volume were approximately equal. When this condition does not hold, CVP computations and profits actually recorded by a firm using absorption costing can differ significantly. Chapter 10 explores further this topic.

FINAL NOTE

CVP analysis is a useful planning device, but it generally lacks the accuracy and precision that its computations imply. If the basic assumptions of CVP techniques are recognized and tested for reasonableness in particular situations, valid CVP analysis can provide the information needed by management. Such analysis requires fixed and variable cost information that must be developed by cost behavior studies. This cost behavior analysis classifies costs according to both fixed and variable characteristics. Foundations of management planning and control include flexible budgets, standard costs, and direct costing; cost behavior information is important in each of these areas.

Return now to the beginning of the chapter and review the highlights section before proceeding to the review questions, exercises, and problems.

9-1. Define and illustrate the following terms and concepts:
   a. Cost behavior
   b. Relevant range
   c. Contribution margin
   d. Contribution approach
   e. Breakeven point
   f. Fixed cost
   g. Variable cost
   h. Mixed cost
   i. Nonlinear cost behavior
   j. Step-variable cost
   k. Discretionary costs
   l. Capacity costs
   m. Linear regression analysis
   n. High-low analysis
   o. Algebraic CVP analysis
   p. Graphic CVP analysis
   q. Sales-mix analysis
   r. Linear approximation

9-2. What is the importance of cost behavior information in CVP analysis?

9-3. Discuss the uses of CVP analysis and its significance to management.

9-4. "Variable costs are fixed per unit, while fixed costs per unit vary with productive output." Discuss this statement.

9-5. "The concept of a relevant range is basic to CVP analysis." Explain this statement.

9-6. How is the concept of relevant range applied in analyzing nonlinear cost functions?

9-7. "In classifying a particular cost as fixed or variable, the volume or activity level is extremely important." Discuss and illustrate this statement.

9-8. Why is reference to a particular time period essential to the concept of a fixed cost?

9-9. Is a step-cost variable or fixed in nature? Explain your reply.

9-10. Contractual agreements often cause semivariable or mixed cost behavior. Explain and give examples of such costs.

9-11. Under what circumstances is it useful to prepare a scatter diagram for determination of cost behavior?

9-12. What is the objective of using regression analysis to analyze a specific type of cost?

9-13. For cost estimation purposes, what are the advantages and disadvantages of using the high-low method versus a linear regression approach?

9-14. "The contribution approach is the foundation of CVP logic and related techniques." Discuss this statement.

9-15. What principal assumptions and required conditions underlie CVP analysis?

9-16. In dealing with cost behavior, what is the danger of ignoring the underlying assumptions of CVP analysis?

9-17. *CVP Analysis and Budgeting*   Avery Corporation has just been formed and is the sole distributor of product Y. During the first year of operations, plant capacity will be 9,000 units, which corresponds with expected sales volume. Planned cost data include:

Direct labor	$2.50 per unit
Raw materials	$ .50 per unit
Other variable costs	$1.00 per unit
Fixed costs	$30,000

REQUIRED:

a. If the company wishes to earn a before-tax profit of $24,000 the first year, compute the required selling price and total contribution margin.

b. The company has an opportunity to expand capacity in its second year. Annual fixed costs will increase $20,000, and total plant capacity will expand to 30,000 units. Assume that the selling price per unit is $8 and that the desired before-tax profits are $36,000. Compute the required sales volume in Avery Corporation's second year.

9-18. *Breakeven Analysis*   Henzer Corporation produces and distributes door knobs. The present annual sales volume is 500,000 units, and the current selling price is $1.00 per unit. Variable expenses amount to $.60 per unit. Fixed expenses are $100,000 per year.

REQUIRED   (Consider each case separately):

a. 1. What is the present annual total profit?
   2. What is the present breakeven point in dollars? In units?

b. Compute the new profit for each of the following changes (consider each situation independently):
   1. A per-unit increase of two cents in variable expense
   2. A 10 percent decrease in fixed expenses and a 10 percent increase in sales volume
   3. A 20 percent increase in fixed expenses, a 20 percent decrease in selling price, a 10 percent decrease in variable expenses per unit, and a 30 percent increase in units sold

c. Compute the new breakeven point *in units* for each of the following changes:
   1. A 10 percent decrease in fixed expenses
   2. A 10 percent increase in selling price and a $25,000 increase in fixed expenses

9-19. *Product Pricing and CVP*   The Grand Rapids Furniture Company produces bridge tables and chairs for department and furniture stores. The current selling prices are $8 per chair and $16 per table. Based on these prices, the company is able to break even by selling 12,000 chairs and 3,000 tables. The estimated cost of each is:

	CHAIRS	TABLES
Variable costs:		
Materials	$2.50	$ 7.50
Labor	1.00	2.00
Variable factory overhead	.50	2.50
Variable selling expenses	.40	.40
	$4.40	$12.40

Fixed costs:	
Manufacturing	$37,500
Selling and administrative	16,500
	$54,000

The company's competitors have recently reduced prices on similar items of equal quality to $7.50 for a chair and $15 for a table.

REQUIRED: Assuming the same ratio of four chairs to one table, how many units of each would the company have to sell to meet competitors' prices and still make a profit of $51,000?

9-20. *CVP and Pricing Policy* Able Company has a plant capacity of 100,000 units per year, but the 19X6 budget indicates that only 60,000 units will be produced and sold. The entire 19X6 budget is as follows:

Sales revenues (60,000 units at $4)		$240,000
Less: Cost of goods produced		
(based on production of 60,000 units):		
Materials (variable)	$60,000	
Labor (variable)	30,000	
Variable manufacturing costs	45,000	
Nonvariable manufacturing costs	75,000	
Total cost of goods produced		210,000
Gross margin		$ 30,000
Less: Selling and administrative expenses:		
Selling (10% of sales)	$24,000	
Administrative (nonvariable)	36,000	
Total selling and administrative expenses		60,000
Loss from operations		$ (30,000)

REQUIRED:

a. Given the budgeted selling price and cost data, how many units would Able have to produce and sell in order to break even?

b. Market research indicates that if Able were to drop its selling price to $3.80 per unit, it could sell 100,000 units in 19X6. Would you recommend the drop in price? Indicate the new profit or loss figure.

9-21. *CVP and Equipment Alternatives* A doughnut company is evaluating two mutually exclusive investment alternatives for equipment. Machine

A involves monthly fixed costs of $15,000 and variable costs per gross package of $8. A gross package is sold by the firm for $12. Machine B will incur monthly fixed costs of $9,000 and variable costs of $9 per package.

REQUIRED:
a. The breakeven point in units for machine A is:
   1. 3,000   3. 1,875
   2. 3,750   4. 1,000
b. The contribution margin ratio for machine B is:
   1. 75 percent   3. 25 percent
   2. 33 percent   4. 67 percent
c. If machine B is selected, a monthly sales volume of 8,000 packages will produce a margin of safety (the excess of actual or budgeted sales over breakeven sales) of:
   1. $60,000   3. $24,000
   2. $15,000   4. $51,000
d. Machine A and machine B are equally profitable at a unit sales volume of:
   1. 4,000   3. 3,750
   2. 6,000   4. 3,000

9-22. CMA Problem—Profit-Volume Graph

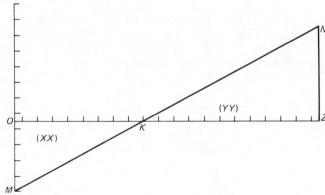

REQUIRED:
a. Based on the profit-volume graph above, select the true statement:
   1. Areas XX and YY and point K represent profit, loss, and volume of sales at breakeven, respectively.
   2. Line OZ represents the volume of sales.
   3. Lines OM and NZ represent fixed costs.
   4. Line MN represents total costs.
   5. None of the above is true.
b. The vertical scale represents:
   1. Volume of sales   4. Contribution margin
   2. Units produced   5. None of the above
   3. Profit above zero and
      loss below zero   (IMA adapted)

9-23. *Graphical CVP Analysis*

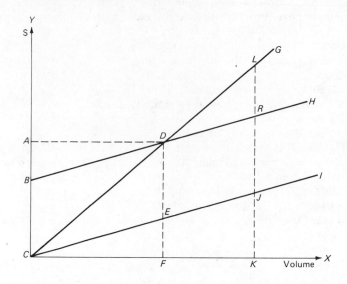

REQUIRED: Identify the appropriate point, line segment, or area of your cost-volume-profit graph that corresponds with the related questions below:

a. The maximum possible operating loss is:
   1. AB   3. BC
   2. DF   4. EF

b. Breakeven volume in sales dollars is:
   1. CF   3. AD
   2. DE   4. AC

c. At volume CK, total contribution margin is:
   1. JK   3. RJ
   2. LJ   4. LR

d. Profits are represented by area:
   1. GDH   3. BDC
   2. GCI   4. ICX

e. At volume CK, total fixed costs are represented by:
   1. JK   3. RJ
   2. RK   4. LR

f. If volume increases from CF to CK, the change in total costs is:
   1. RJ–DE   3. LK–DF
   2. JK–EF   4. LJ–DE

9-24. *CVP and Profit Goals*   Wrigley Company has a maximum capacity of 200,000 units per year. Variable manufacturing costs are $12 per unit.

Fixed factory overhead is $600,000 per year. Variable selling and administrative costs are $5 per unit, whereas fixed selling and administrative costs are $300,000 per year. Current sales price is $23 per unit.

REQUIRED: Consider each situation independently and show all computations in good form.
a. What is the breakeven point in (1) units and (2) dollar sales?
b. How many units must be sold to earn a target net income of $240,000 per year?
c. Assume that the company's sales for the year just ended totaled 185,000 units. A strike at a major supplier has caused a material shortage, so that the current year's sales will reach only 160,000 units. Top management is planning to slash fixed costs so that the total for the current year will be $59,000 less than last year. Management also is thinking of either increasing the selling price or reducing variable costs or both in order to earn a target net income that will be the same dollar amount as last year's. The company already has sold 30,000 units this year at a sales price of $23 per unit with costs per unit unchanged. What contribution margin per unit is needed on the remaining 130,000 units in order to reach the target net income?

9-25. *Graphical CVP Analysis*

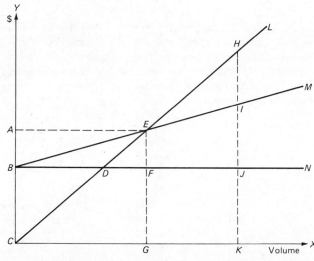

REQUIRED: Identify the appropriate point, line segment, or area of your cost-volume-profit graph that corresponds with the related questions below:
a. Total revenue at any volume is represented by:
   1. BM   3. BN
   2. CL   4. CY

b. Total costs at any volume are represented by:
   1. CL   3. BM
   2. CB   4. BN
c. Maximum possible total loss is represented by:
   1. BN   3. AB
   2. EF   4. BC
d. Breakeven point in units is represented by:
   1. CA   3. CG
   2. BE   4. EG
e. At volume CK, total variable costs are:
   1. IJ   3. JK
   2. HI   4. IK
f. At volume K, total variable profits are:
   1. HI   3. HK − HI
   2. HI + JK   4. None of the above
g. Losses are represented by area:
   1. LEM   3. BEC
   2. AEC   4. BEG
h. The incremental or differential costs of increasing volume from G to K are:
   1. CK − CG   3. IK − BC
   2. IJ − EF   4. EG + JK

9-26. *Regression Analysis* Sacks-Shapiro Sound Company is preparing a budget for 19X7. Many overhead costs can be classified easily as being either variable with a specific base or fixed per time period. However, the company's electricity cost is a mixed cost, having both variable and fixed components. The following data represent last year's cost incurrence and related machine hour usage:

Month	Machine Hours (X)	Electricity (Y)	XY	X^2
January	1,200	$ 5,400		
February	1,120	5,000		
March	1,340	5,900		
April	1,500	5,690		
May	1,600	6,100		
June	1,740	5,710		
July	1,910	6,600		
August	2,100	6,740		
September	2,050	6,600		
October	1,870	6,020		
November	1,910	6,100		
December	1,930	6,400		
Totals	20,270	$72,260		

REQUIRED: Using the regression analysis approach, fill in the columns for XY and X^2 and compute the fixed portion of monthly utility cost and the variable cost per machine hour.

9-27. *CMA Problem—Profit Planning* Mr. Calderone started a pizza restaurant in 19X0. For this purpose a building was rented for $400.00 per month. Two women were hired to work full time at the restaurant, and six college students were hired to work thirty hours per week delivering pizza. An outside accountant was hired for tax and bookkeeping purposes. For this service, Mr. Calderone pays $300 per month. The necessary restaurant equipment and delivery cars were purchased with cash. Mr. Calderone has noticed that expenses for utilities and supplies have been rather constant. Between 19X0 and 19X3, business has increased; profits have more than doubled. Mr. Calderone does not understand why profits have increased faster than volume.

A projected income statement for 19X4 has been prepared by the accountant and is shown below:

CALDERONE COMPANY
Projected income statement
For the year ended December 31, 19X4

Sales		$95,000
Cost of goods sold	$28,500	
Wages and fringe benefits, restaurant help	8,150	
Wages and fringe benefits, delivery staff	17,300	
Rent	4,800	
Accounting services	3,600	
Depreciation of delivery equipment	5,000	
Depreciation of restaurant equipment	3,000	
Utilities	2,325	
Supplies (soap, floor wax, etc.)	1,200	$73,875
Net income before taxes		$21,125
Income taxes		6,338
Net income		$14,787

Note: The average pizza sells for $2.50. Assume that Mr. Calderone pays out 30 percent of income in income taxes.

REQUIRED:
a. What is the breakeven point in number of pizzas that must be sold?
b. What is the cash flow breakeven point in number of pizzas that must be sold?
c. If Mr. Calderone withdraws $4,800 for personal use, how much cash will be left from 19X4 income-producing activities?
d. Mr. Calderone would like an after-tax net income of $20,000. What volume must be reached in number of pizzas in order to obtain the desired income?
e. Briefly explain why profits have increased at a faster rate than sales.
f. Briefly explain why the cash flow for 19X4 will exceed profits.

(IMA adapted)

9-28. *Various CVP Applications* Gonzales Gear Company manufactures a special gear for automatic transmissions that it sells to automobile manufacturers. The gear sells for $28 and the company normally produces and sells approximately 500,000 gears annually. The cost per gear, based upon the 500,000 volume, is:

Direct material	$6
Direct labor	6
Variable costs:	
Manufacturing	2
Selling and administrative	4
Fixed costs:	
Manufacturing	6
Selling and administrative	2

REQUIRED: Provide supporting computations for your answer to each of the following questions:

a. The company's total annual fixed costs are:
   1. $1,000,000   3. $4,000,000
   2. $3,000,000   4. $6,000,000
b. The company's variable cost per unit is:
   1. $6   3. $14
   2. $12   4. $18
c. The company's breakeven point in units is:
   1. 100,000   3. 400,000
   2. 300,000   4. 600,000
d. If the company values its inventory using the direct costing concept, the cost per gear assigned to the ending inventory would be:
   1. $12   3. $18
   2. $14   4. $20
e. If the company values its inventory using the full or absorption costing concept, the cost per gear assigned to the ending inventory would be:
   1. $14   3. $20
   2. $18   4. $26
f. The company's anticipated net income per year, before taxes, is:
   1. ($1,000,000)   3. $5,000,000
   2. $1,000,000   4. $6,000,000
g. The company's present tax rate is 40 percent. If the company wishes to earn a profit after taxes of $1,500,000, its sales would have to equal:
   1. 500,000 units   3. 650,000 units
   2. 600,000 units   4. 750,000 units
h. The company's present margin of safety is:
   1. $2,800,000   3. $8,400,000
   2. $5,600,000   4. $11,200,000
i. The company would like to increase its sales price to $30 per gear. If this increase is undertaken, sales volume would probably decline by 5 percent and:
   1. Sales would increase by $250,000, thereby increasing profits by $250,000.
   2. Fixed costs would decline to $3,800,000.

3. Contribution margin would increase by $700,000.
4. Profits would decline by $150,000.

j. The company has received an offer from a European automobile manufacturer to purchase 25,000 of its gears. The domestic sales will be unaffected by this offer. Variable distribution costs on these gears will increase by $1.50 because of shipping, insurance, and import duties. The cost per gear that should be considered when quoting the foreign manufacturer a price would be:

1. $18.00   3. $25.50
2. $19.50   4. $27.50

k. The company has some gears in inventory that are several years old and cannot be sold to regular customers. The gears are carried in inventory at $24 each. Which of the following alternatives would be most advantageous for the company:

1. Sell the gears to a junk dealer for $2 each.
2. Rework the gears at a cost of $2 each so that they are exactly like the current gear and sell them through normal channels.
3. Throw the gears away.
4. Melt the gears down at a cost of 50¢ each and use the material to manufacture new gears.

9-29. *CPA Problem—Change in Labor Cost*   The president of Beth Corporation, which manufactures tape decks and sells them to producers of sound reproduction systems, anticipates a 10 percent wage increase on January 1 of next year to the manufacturing employees (variable labor). No other changes in costs are expected. Overhead will not change as a result of the wage increase. The president has asked you to assist in developing the information needed to formulate a reasonable product strategy for next year.

You are satisfied by regression analysis that volume is the primary factor affecting costs and have separated the semivariable costs into their fixed and variable segments by means of the least-squares criterion. You also observe that the beginning and ending inventories are never materially different. Below, current year data are assembled for your analysis:

Current selling price per unit	$80
Variable cost per unit:	
Material	$30
Labor	12
Overhead	6
	$48
Annual sales volume	5,000 units
Fixed costs	$51,000

REQUIRED: Provide the following information for the president using cost-volume-profit analysis:

a. What increase in the selling price is necessary to cover the 10 percent wage increase and still maintain the current contribution margin ratio of 40 percent?

b. How many tape decks must be sold to maintain the current net income if the sales price remains at $80 and the 10 percent wage increase goes into effect?

(AICPA adapted)

9-30. *CMA Problem—Advertising Expenses* Ro Company, maker of quality handmade pipes, has experienced a steady growth in sales for the last five years. However, increased competition has led Mr. Ro, the company president, to believe that an aggressive advertising campaign will be necessary in 19X4 to maintain the company's present growth.

To prepare for the 19X4 advertising campaign, the company's accountants have prepared and presented Mr. Ro with the following data based on 19X3 operations:

VARIABLE COSTS (PER PIPE)		ANNUAL FIXED COSTS	
Direct labor	$ 8.00	Manufacturing	$ 25,000
Direct materials	3.25	Selling	40,000
Variable overhead	2.50	Administrative	70,000
	$13.75		$135,000

Sales volume in 19X3 was 20,000 units at $25 per pipe. Target sales volume for 19X4 is $550,000, or 22,000 units. Assume a 40 percent tax rate.

REQUIRED:
a. Compute the 19X3 after-tax net income.
b. Compute the breakeven volume in units for 19X3.
c. Mr. Ro believes an additional selling expense of $11,250 for advertising in 19X4, with all other costs remaining constant, will be necessary to achieve the sales target. Compute the after-tax net income for 19X4 assuming the target sales volume and expenditure for advertising occur as planned.
d. Compute the breakeven volume in dollar sales for 19X4 assuming the additional $11,250 is spent for advertising.
e. If the additional $11,250 is spent for advertising in 19X4, what is the 19X4 dollar sales volume required to earn the 19X3 after-tax net income?
f. At a 19X4 sales level of 22,000 units, what is the maximum amount that can be spent on advertising if an after-tax profit of $60,000 is desired?

(IMA adapted)

9-31. *Sales-mix Analysis* Walker Toy Company produces four dolls that are marketed under the trade names of Charlie, Bill, Carol, and Martha. Each doll is designed for a different age group, is handled by different types of retail establishments, and, hence, is priced differently in both retail and wholesale markets. Walker Company sells only to wholesale outlets. Despite these market differences, each doll is produced by similar operations using common plant facilities. During 19X0, Walker Company operated at 80 percent of maximum potential manufacturing volume with operating results as indicated on the next page:

TOTAL 19X0 OPERATIONS		PRODUCT NAME	PERCENTAGE OF TOTAL DOLLAR SALES	CONTRIBUTION MARGIN RATIO
Sales	$2,000,000	Charlie	30	40%
Expenses	2,150,000	Bill	25	30%
Net loss	$ (150,000)	Carol	35	50%
		Martha	10	60%

REQUIRED:
a. With the 19X0 sales mix, determine the company's breakeven point in dollar sales and as a percent of maximum capacity.
b. For 19X1, Walker Company has budgeted sales of $2,400,000. Fixed costs are budgeted at $1,160,000. What overall contribution margin ratio must be achieved to earn net income of $40,000 before taxes?

9-32. *CVP and Budgeting* The Standard Division of Anders Company desires a 25 percent annual rate of return on average total assets. The unit selling price of the division's only product is therefore adjusted annually in view of expected costs, sales volume, and assets to be employed. Budgeted operating data for 19X2 disclose:

Variable costs	$800 per unit
Annual fixed costs	$20,000,000
Expected sales volume	100,000 units
Average total assets	$40,000,000

REQUIRED:
a. Determine the unit selling price required to produce the desired rate of return in 19X2.
b. Assume that the unit selling price is $1,200 and that budgeted sales are expected to occur uniformly in 19X2. What is the annual breakeven volume in units and in what month will this sales level be reached?
c. Assume that the unit selling price is $1,500. Determine the unit sales volume required to produce a 10 percent profit margin on sales (profits = 10 percent of sales dollars).

9-33. *Sales-mix Analysis* Gomez Division produces and sells three broad product lines, A, B, and C. Individual products within each line are comparable and the firm uses average selling prices and variable costs within each product line for budgeting purposes. Representative averages for the most recent year were:

PRODUCT	SALES PRICE	VARIABLE COSTS	PERCENTAGE OF TOTAL DOLLAR SALES
A	$30	$15	10
B	$20	$12	50
C	$40	$30	40

Estimated total fixed costs for the division are $700,000.

REQUIRED:
a. Compute the division's annual breakeven volume in sales dollars, showing required sales dollars for each product line and for the division in total. Fixed costs are common to all products and accordingly should not be allocated in the solution.
b. Assume that the average contribution margin ratio for the division as a whole is 40 percent. Determine the total dollar sales required to generate an after-tax profit of $250,000. Assume a 50 percent tax rate.

9-34. *CPA Problem—Product-line Analysis* The officers of Bradshaw Company are reviewing the profitability of the company's four products and the potential effect of several proposals for varying the product mix. An excerpt from the income statement and other data follow:

	TOTALS	PRODUCT P	PRODUCT Q	PRODUCT R	PRODUCT S
Sales	$62,600	$10,000	$18,000	$12,600	$22,000
Cost of goods sold	44,274	4,750	7,056	13,968	18,500
Gross profit	18,326	5,250	10,944	(1,368)	3,500
Operating expenses	12,012	1,990	2,976	2,826	4,220
Income before taxes	$ 6,314	$ 3,260	$ 7,968	$ (4,194)	$ (720)
Units sold		1,000	1,200	1,800	2,000
Sales price per unit		$10.00	$15.00	$7.00	$11.00
Variable cost of goods sold per unit		$2.50	$3.00	$6.50	$6.00
Variable operating expenses per unit		$1.17	$1.25	$1.00	$1.20

REQUIRED: Each of the following proposals is to be considered independently of the other proposals. Consider only the product changes stated in each proposal; the activity of other products remains stable. Ignore income taxes.
a. If product R is discontinued, the effect on income will be:
   1. $900 increase   4. $1,368 increase
   2. $4,194 increase   5. None of the above
   3. $12,600 decrease
b. If product R is discontinued and a consequent loss of customers causes a decrease of 200 units in sales of Q, the total effect on income will be:
   1. $15,600 decrease   4. $1,250 decrease
   2. $2,866 increase   5. None of the above
   3. $2,044 increase
c. Part of the plant in which product P is produced can easily be adapted to the production of product S, but changes in quantities may make changes in sales prices advisable. If production of product P is reduced to 500 units (to be sold at $12 each) and production of product S is increased to 2,500 units (to be sold at $10.50 each), the total effect on income will be:
   1. $1,765 decrease   4. $1,515 decrease
   2. $250 increase   5. None of the above
   3. $2,060 decrease

d. If the sales price of product R is increased to $8 with a decrease in the number of units sold to 1,500, the effect on income will be:
1. $2,199 decrease
2. $600 decrease
3. $750 increase
4. $2,199 increase
5. None of the above

e. The plant in which product R is produced can be utilized to produce a new product, T. The total variable costs and expenses per unit of T are $8.05, and 1,600 units can be sold at $9.50 each. If T is introduced and R is discontinued, the total effect on income will be:
1. $2,600 increase
2. $2,320 increase
3. $3,220 increase
4. $1,420 increase
5. None of the above

f. Production of product P can be doubled by adding a second shift, but higher wages must be paid, increasing variable cost of goods sold to $3.50 for each of the additional units. If the 1,000 additional units of P can be sold at $10 each, the total effect on income will be:
1. $10,000 increase
2. $5,330 increase
3. $6,500 increase
4. $2,260 increase
5. None of the above

(AICPA adapted)

9-35. *Various CVP Applications* The condensed 19X2 income statement of Baxter Sales Division is presented below. The division handles a single product, and in 19X2 the sales volume was 10,000 units. Data for 19X2 follow:

Sales	$200,000	
Cost of sales	40,000	
Gross profit on sales		$160,000
Operating expenses:		
Fixed	$ 40,000	
Variable	70,000	
Semivariable	30,000	140,000
Income before taxes		$ 20,000

Cost of Sales is entirely variable with sales volume. Semivariable expenses include $20,000 of fixed charges.

REQUIRED:

a. The fixed-variable cost structure of the division in 19X2 may be expressed as:
1. Profits equal 10 percent of sales
2. $60,000 plus 60 percent of sales
3. $120,000 plus 30 percent of sales
4. $200,000 minus $180,000

b. Variable expenses per unit in 19X2 were $12. If sales volume in 19X3 increases from 10,000 to 15,000 units, unit variable expenses will be:
1. $ 8
2. $10
3. $12
4. Some other amount

c. The breakeven sales volume in units for 19X2 was:
1. 7,500
2. 5,000
3. 3,000
4. Some other amount

d. If fixed expenses in 19X3 increase by $16,000, to maintain income before taxes at $20,000, sales volume must increase by:
   1. $16,000   3. $20,000
   2. $40,000   4. $32,000
e. The number of units that must be sold to earn income before taxes of $60,000 is:
   1. 12,000   3. 15,000
   2. 7,500   4. None of the above
f. If the tax rate is 40 percent, the number of units that must be sold to earn income after taxes of $60,000 is:
   1. 20,000   3. 13,333
   2. 26,250   4. None of the above

9-36. *CPA Problem—Cost Behavior Identity*

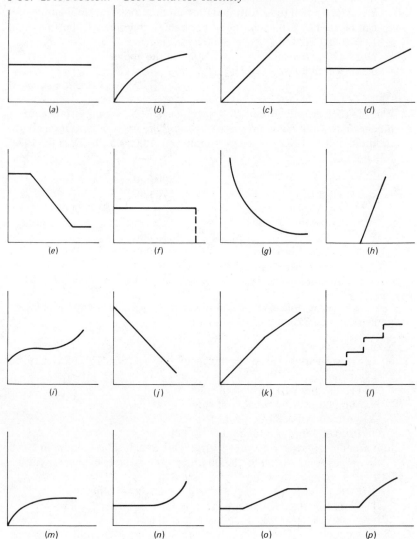

REQUIRED: Identify the graph that best represents the cost behavior patterns described below. Vertical axes represent total dollar cost, and horizontal axes represent production volume or other appropriate activity base.

a. Utility cost: a fixed cost plus a variable cost that applies only after a certain number of kilowatt hours are used.

b. Labor bonus cost: incentive wage plan that is variable with production; the plan is operative only after a certain volume is produced.

c. Rent expense: payment of $100,000 less $1 for each labor hour worked in excess of 200,000 hours, with minimum required payment of $20,000.

d. Water bill: cost per gallon is $.006 for any usage up to 100,000 gallons and $.004 per gallon thereafter.

e. Computer terminal: a fixed cost plus a variable cost per usage hour. The variable cost is a surcharge that applies to usage exceeding 100 hours. Maximum cost per time period is $8,000.

f. Depreciation of equipment computed by means of the machine-hours method.

g. Cost of machine lubricants where the cost per unit decreases with each pound of lubricant used. For example, total cost for 1 pound is $10.00; for 2 pounds, $19.95; for 3 pounds $29.90.

h. Depreciation of equipment computed by means of the straight-line method.

i. Cost of direct materials used.

j. City water bill computed as follows:

First 1,000,000 gallons or less	$1,000
Next 10,000 gallons	$.003 per gallon
Next 10,000 gallons	$.006 per gallon
Next 10,000 gallons	$.009 per gallon

k. Salaries of repair personnel; one staff member is needed for every 1,000 hours of machine time.

(AICPA adapted)

9-37. *Regression Analysis* Hawg Warsh Products began operations in 19X4 and manufactures a single product line consisting of men's shave cream and after-shave lotion. During 19X4, all semivariable or mixed production costs were charged to a single general ledger control account. These costs include indirect labor costs, repairs and maintenance, and factory power. A summary of monthly charges to this control account during 19X4 along with total labor hours is presented below:

MONTH	TOTAL COST	LABOR HOURS	MONTH	TOTAL COST	LABOR HOURS
January	$130,000	12,000	July	$160,000	13,500
February	135,000	12,100	August	158,000	13,400
March	141,000	12,700	September	152,000	13,000
April	149,000	12,800	October	148,000	12,900
May	156,000	13,000	November	149,000	13,000
June	158,000	13,300	December	141,000	12,800

REQUIRED:
a. Prepare a scatter diagram that shows the movement of semivariable costs in relation to labor hours.
b. Compute a cost behavior equation for the semivariable costs using linear regression analysis.
c. Compare your cost equation from part (b) with results obtained by using the high-low analysis method.

Chapter 10: Theory and Application of Direct Costing

Direct costing is an approach to product cost accounting that relies heavily upon cost behavior analysis and the contribution approach to income determination. Under direct costing, fixed manufacturing overhead costs are recorded as expenses of the accounting period. Product unit costs contain only direct material, direct labor, and variable manufacturing overhead. This chapter explains the concept of direct costing and illustrates its use in product costing and income determination.

Upon completion of this chapter, students should be able to:

1. Determine inventory valuation under direct costing
2. Measure net income under direct costing
3. Reconcile profit differences between direct and absorption costing approaches
4. Identify the major changes necessary to convert a cost accounting system to direct costing

The following basic concepts are introduced in this chapter:

Direct costing   An approach to product costing in which only variable manufacturing costs are accumulated and attached to products.

Absorption costing   Traditional approach to product costing in which all manufacturing costs, regardless of variability with volume, are treated as product or inventoriable costs.

Normal costing   An approach to cost accounting for products in which factory overhead costs are charged to Work in Process by using a predetermined overhead rate.

Direct costing was developed in response to management needs for useful and understandable information. By treating all fixed overhead costs as expenses when they are incurred, direct costing generates unit product costs and income measures that are consistent with results of cost-volume-profit analyses developed for planning purposes. Net income under direct costing is a function of sales volume, but net income under absorption costing depends partly on the level of production. Between consecutive years having the same sales volume, net income under absorption costing can be increased simply by increasing the production level in the second year.

Direct costing is a valuable tool for management planning and control, but absorption costing is the required procedure for external financial reporting purposes. Companies can use direct costing for internal reporting purposes, but their annual financial statements must be adjusted to approximate absorption costing. Absorption costing is required in annual reports to stockholders, in filings with the Securities and Exchange Commission (SEC), and in determining income tax liabilities.

NATURE OF DIRECT COSTING

Cost-volume-profit analysis, the contribution approach to income reporting, and direct costing are interrelated techniques that use cost behavior information. *Direct costing* extends the contribution approach into the area of cost accounting for products; as a cost accounting procedure, direct costing excludes fixed manufacturing overhead costs from the product cost classification. Unit product costs therefore consist of direct material, direct labor, and variable manufacturing overhead. Since only the variable production costs are assigned to products, direct costing is also called *variable costing* or *marginal costing*. Fixed manufacturing overhead costs—such as depreciation, supervisory salaries, and property taxes—are treated as period costs under direct costing. These fixed costs are accounted for as operating expenses and are deducted from revenues in the income statement.

Concepts of Product Cost

In earlier chapters on job order and process cost accounting, all manufacturing costs were accumulated and attached to products. *Absorption costing* is an approach to product costing in which all manufacturing costs, regardless of variability with volume, are assignable to products. In absorption costing, *product cost*, *manufacturing cost*, and *inventoriable cost* all have the same meaning and are used to describe production costs that flow through the Work in Process inventory account. The term *period cost* describes all expenses reported in the income statement.

One alternative in cost accounting systems concerns the definition and inclusiveness of product costs. In the traditional absorption costing, all manufacturing costs are product costs. Direct costing is an alternative approach in which only variable manufacturing costs are assigned to products. Advocates of direct costing contend that fixed manufacturing overhead is incurred to provide the capacity to produce. Since these fixed costs are incurred every year and are not a function of production volume, only variable production costs should be included in unit product cost. A cost accounting system based on direct costing operates as follows:

1. Only variable manufacturing costs are accumulated and assigned to products.
2. Fixed manufacturing overhead costs are recorded as expenses of the accounting period.

The definition of product cost and related cost accounting procedures therefore depends upon whether it is direct costing or absorption costing that is being considered.

Concepts and definitions of product cost are important since they govern the accounting procedures applied under direct and absorption costing. The critical difference between direct costing and absorption costing is the accounting treatment of fixed factory overhead. To show the effect of this difference, consider the example of Bryan Company, which manufactures a single product. Estimated annual production volume is 10,000 units, and the company has developed the following cost estimates for overhead rate determination:

Accounting for Fixed Overhead

	ANNUAL OVERHEAD COSTS		
ANNUAL ESTIMATE FOR	Fixed	Variable	Total
Depreciation of plant	$ 9,000	—	$ 9,000
Supervisory salaries	10,000	—	10,000
Factory power	7,500	$ 4,000	11,500
Property taxes	3,000	—	3,000
Insurance	2,500	—	2,500
Equipment repairs	4,000	3,000	7,000
Indirect labor	—	8,000	8,000
	$36,000	$15,000	$51,000
Overhead per unit (÷ 10,000)	$3.60	$1.50	$5.10

In addition to the overhead cost data, assume that raw material unit cost is $.50 and that unit direct labor cost is $1.00. Estimated unit costs for inventory valuation purposes are assembled as follows:

UNIT COST ELEMENT	ABSORPTION COSTING	DIRECT COSTING	COST BEHAVIOR
Raw materials	$ .50	$ .50	Variable
Direct labor	1.00	1.00	Variable
Variable overhead	1.50	1.50	Variable
Fixed overhead	3.60	None	Fixed
Inventory cost per unit	$6.60	$3.00	

In accounting for factory overhead, the predetermined overhead rate for direct costing is $1.50 per unit produced as compared with $5.10 per unit under absorption costing. For plants producing several products, the predetermined overhead rate can be measured in relation to labor hours, machine hours, or direct labor cost. In direct costing, it is important to realize that variable overhead is still an indirect cost that must be attached to products by using a predetermined overhead rate. In this respect, the term *variable costing* is really a more accurate description than *direct costing*.

EXHIBIT 10-1

COMPARATIVE JOURNAL ENTRIES FOR BRYAN COMPANY DIRECT COSTING AND ABSORPTION COSTING

TRANSACTION OR ADJUSTMENT	DIRECT COSTING PROCEDURE		ABSORPTION COSTING PROCEDURE	
1. Purchase raw materials on credit for $8,000	1. Material inventory Accounts payable	$ 8,000 $ 8,000	1. Same entry	
2. Issue $5,000 of materials to produce 10,000 units	2. Work in process Material inventory	$ 5,000 $ 5,000	2. Same entry	
3. Incur $10,000 of direct labor cost	3. Work in process Factory payroll	$10,000 $10,000	3. Same entry	
4. Incur actual overhead costs: variable, $15,000; fixed, $36,000	4. Variable overhead control Fixed overhead control Credit various accounts	$15,000 36,000 $51,000	4. Factory overhead control Credit various accounts	$51,000 $51,000
5. Apply overhead costs based on production of 10,000 units	5. Work in process Variable overhead applied (10,000 units at $1.50)	$15,000 $15,000	5. Work in process Factory overhead applied (10,000 units at $5.10)	$51,000 $51,000
6. Transfer completed production to finished goods	6. Finished goods Work in process (sum of entries 2, 3, 5)	$30,000 $30,000	6. Finished goods Work in process (sum of entries 2, 3, 5)	$66,000 $66,000
7. Record sale of 9,000 units at $10.00	7. Cash Sales	$90,000 $90,000	7. Same entry	
8. Record cost of goods sold	8. Cost of goods sold Finished goods (9,000 units at $3.00)	$27,000 $27,000	8. Cost of goods sold Finished goods (9,000 units at $6.60)	$59,400 $59,400
9. Close factory overhead accounts; note that actual overhead equals overhead applied	9. Variable overhead applied Variable overhead control	$15,000 $15,000	9. Factory overhead applied Factory overhead control	$51,000 $51,000

Journal entries for overhead cost transactions differ between direct and absorption costing. In absorption costing, actual overhead costs should be debited to Factory Overhead Control when these costs are incurred. In direct costing, two control accounts should be used for recording actual overhead costs—Variable Overhead Control and Fixed Overhead Control. At the end of each accounting period, the balance of Fixed Overhead Control is reported as an expense in the income statement. In both systems, appropriate accounts for Factory Overhead Applied are credited for the overhead costs charged to Work in Process inventory. Debits to Work in Process are computed with the predetermined overhead rate applicable to each particular system.

To illustrate alternative overhead accounting procedures, assume that Bryan Company produced 10,000 units during 19X4 and that actual costs for the year were exactly equal to the estimated costs given above. There were no beginning or ending Work in Process inventories in 19X4. Journal entries under direct and absorption costing are compared in Exhibit 10-1.

Based upon the journal entries in Exhibit 10-1, Work in Process and Finished Goods general ledger accounts appear as presented below:

Comparative Financial Statements

DIRECT COSTING

Work in process

(2) Materials	$ 5,000	(6) $30,000	
(3) Labor	10,000		
(5) Variable overhead	15,000		
Balance	$ -0-		

Finished goods

(6) $30,000	(8) $27,000		
Balance	$ 3,000		

Cost of goods sold

(8) $27,000	

ABSORPTION COSTING

Work in process

(2) Materials	$ 5,000	(6) $66,000	
(3) Labor	10,000		
(5) Overhead	51,000		
Balance	$ -0-		

Finished goods

(6) $66,000	(8) $59,400		
Balance	$ 6,600		

Cost of goods sold

(8) $59,400	

In this example, there is no initial or final balance in Work in Process inventory, and overhead costs incurred are equal to overhead applied. In both direct and absorption costing, any balance of underapplied or overapplied factory overhead is usually closed to Cost of Goods Sold when preparing annual financial statements.

Cost of Goods Manufactured A statement of Cost of Goods Manufactured is prepared from summarized information contained in the Work in Process inventory account. The following comparative statements for Bryan Company disclose important differences between direct and absorption costing:

COST OF GOODS MANUFACTURED	DIRECT COSTING	ABSORPTION COSTING
Beginning work in process	-0-	-0-
Raw materials used	$ 5,000	$ 5,000
Direct labor cost	10,000	10,000
Overhead applied	15,000	51,000
Costs accountable for	$30,000	$66,000
Ending work in process	-0-	-0-
Cost of goods manufactured	$30,000	$66,000
Unit cost (÷ 10,000 units)	$3.00	$6.60

Cost of Goods Sold Bryan Company had no beginning Finished Goods inventory in 19X4, and 9,000 units of current production were sold. Comparative Cost of Goods Sold schedules are presented below:

COST OF GOODS SOLD	DIRECT COSTING	ABSORPTION COSTING
Beginning finished goods	-0-	-0-
Cost of goods manufactured	$30,000	$66,000
Cost of goods available	$30,000	$66,000
Ending finished goods:		
1,000 units at $3.00	(3,000)	
1,000 units at $6.60		(6,600)
Cost of goods sold	$27,000	$59,400

Income statements Assume that 19X4 selling and administrative expenses for Bryan Company were $12,000, all of which are fixed costs. The following comparative income statements indicate a $3,600 difference in net income under direct costing and absorption costing:

INCOME STATEMENT	DIRECT COSTING	ABSORPTION COSTING
Sales (9,000 at $10.00)	$90,000	$90,000
Cost of goods sold (9,000 at $3.00 and $6.60)	(27,000)	(59,400)
Contribution margin (Gross profit*)	$63,000	$30,600*
Selling and administrative expenses	(12,000)	(12,000)
Fixed factory overhead	(36,000)	N.A.
Net income (ignoring taxes)	$15,000	$18,600
	(Difference = $3,600)	

Fixed overhead accounting causes the $3,600 difference in profits. Under direct costing, $36,000 of actual fixed overhead costs are deducted from sales. With absorption costing, only $32,400 of fixed overhead is included in the $59,400 amount for Cost of Goods Sold. The initial overhead rate computation showed that fixed overhead cost per unit in absorption costing is $3.60. This amount is attached to each unit sold and to each unit in the Finished Goods inventory. In absorption costing, total fixed overhead is accounted for thus:

ACCOUNT LOCATION OF FIXED OVERHEAD	AMOUNT
Cost of goods sold (9,000 units at $3.60)	$32,400
Final inventory (1,000 units at $3.60)	3,600
Total fixed factory overhead	$36,000

Analysis of fixed overhead accounting explains the profit difference between direct and absorption costing. Of the $36,000 of fixed overhead costs, $3,600 was assigned to the ending Finished Goods inventory in absorption costing and will be recognized as an expense when related goods are sold. Final inventory with direct costing is $3,000 (1,000 units at $3.00); final inventory with absorption costing is $6,600 (1,000 units at $6.60). In the Bryan Company example, the difference between profits under the two costing techniques can be reconciled as follows:

profit difference = unit change in inventory × fixed overhead per unit

$3,600 = 1,000 units × $3.60

The Finished Goods inventory increased 1,000 units during 19X4. The effect of this change is that $3,600 of current fixed overhead costs were assigned to the ending Finished Goods inventory under absorption costing procedures. Whenever production and sales volume are not equal, profits reported under direct and absorption costing will differ.

History of Direct Costing

In the comparative analysis for Bryan Company, which measure of net income is correct? While several advantages can be cited for both direct and absorption costing, it is not possible to say that either profit measure is correct. In the United States, accountants and managers began to experiment with direct costing in the 1930s. Since then, many firms have adopted direct costing for internal accounting purposes.

Direct costing is preferred by many companies because of certain advantages that are not available with absorption costing. These advantages include:

1. Accounting records in direct costing will contain fixed and variable cost data that are useful for CVP analysis.
2. Profits under direct costing are a function of sales volume; with absorption costing, profits are affected also by inventory changes and production levels.
3. Managers can more easily understand direct costing profit reports.
4. Direct costing for products is compatible with flexible budgeting, CVP analysis, and other tools used for planning, control, decision making, and performance evaluation.

Many published papers in accounting journals and descriptions of actual accounting practice since 1950 attest to the managerial usefulness of direct costing. The direct costing controversy centers on the acceptability of direct costing for external reporting purposes. For the most part, these arguments involve issues in accounting theory, such as proper definition of assets, the matching concept, and alternative views concerning the proper timing of fixed overhead cost expiration. Direct costing can provide useful data for internal management decisions, but it is not currently acceptable for external financial reporting. A company using direct costing for internal accounting must adjust its annual financial statements to approximate absorption costing results.

BASIC DIRECT COSTING PROCEDURES

Direct costing omits fixed overhead costs from Work in Process and Finished Goods inventory accounts. These fixed overhead costs include such items as depreciation, property taxes, casualty insurance, supervisory salaries, and to some extent, factory power and machinery repairs. Properly identified fixed overhead costs are accumulated in a separate control account and are deducted from revenues in the direct costing income statement.

Proper segregation and identity of fixed and variable overhead costs are clearly essential to the valid use of direct costing. Direct costing requires a detailed accounting system designed to classify and record fixed and variable cost information. Because of its emphasis on cost behavior information, direct costing is closely related to CVP analysis and contribution reporting.

Integration with Existing Systems

As a characteristic of cost accounting systems, direct costing concerns only the inclusiveness of product costs. Unit product costs in direct costing contain only direct material, direct labor, and variable manufacturing overhead. If a company uses direct costing, it must be integrated properly with other cost

EXHIBIT 10-2
FLOW CHART OF DIRECT COSTING SYSTEM
PERPETUAL INVENTORIES AND PREDETERMINED OVERHEAD RATES

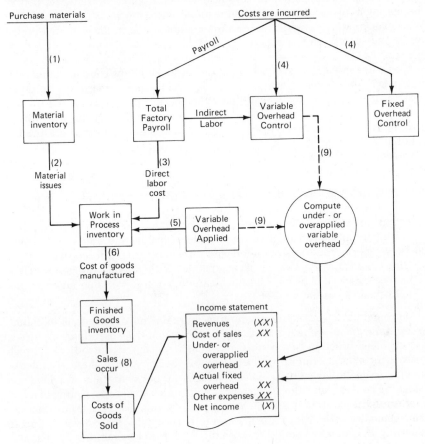

Note: Cost flows are number-keyed to the journal entries in Exhibit 10-1.

accounting system characteristics. Examples of cost accounting systems that incorporate direct costing include:

1. Direct costing with either job order or process costing
2. Direct costing with either periodic or perpetual inventory records
3. Direct costing with historical costs, normal costs, or standard costs

Use of direct costing in any accounting system simply dictates the cost elements to be attached to products. Accounting records and journal entries then are designed to achieve the desired results. For instance, a direct costing system using predetermined overhead rates for variable overhead is diagrammed in Exhibit 10-2. This flow chart corresponds with the direct costing illustration for Bryan Company in which journal entries and financial statements were presented.

In Exhibit 10-2, predetermined overhead rates are used only for variable manufacturing overhead. Any under- or overapplied variable overhead must be properly accounted for. The flow chart depicts a direct costing system using predetermined overhead rates (normal costs) and perpetual inventory records. This system could involve job order or process cost accounting.

Direct costing distinguishes between fixed and variable costs and is an approach to product costing that is compatible with contribution reporting. The contribution approach is a technique for reporting profits that emphasizes contribution margin. *Contribution margin* is the excess of revenues over *all* variable expenses related to the particular sales volume. Variable selling and administrative expenses must be deducted to compute contribution margin, but these variable operating expenses are not assigned to units of production under direct costing.

Income and Inventory Analysis

To illustrate this point, consider Car Company, which manufactures a single product and has annual fixed overhead costs of $36,000. Fixed selling and administrative expenses are $12,000 a year, and variable selling expenses average $1.00 per unit sold. Variable selling expenses include packing costs, shipping charges, and royalty expenses, which are incurred only for units sold. Variable manufacturing costs are $.50 a unit for direct material and $1.00 per unit for direct labor. The predetermined overhead rate for variable overhead is $1.50 per unit. There was no beginning Finished Goods inventory for 19X5; the company produced 10,000 units in 19X5 and sold 8,000 units at $15.00 each. Actual variable overhead for the year was $17,000.

Based on Car Company data, a contribution approach income statement and supporting computations are presented in Exhibit 10-3. Note that only variable costs related to the sales volume of 8,000 units are deducted from revenues. Variable Cost of Goods Manufactured is $30,000, but $6,000 of this amount represents the ending balance of the Finished Goods inventory account. The unit product cost for inventory purposes is $3, consisting of direct material, direct labor, and applied variable manufacturing overhead. Variable selling expenses of $1 per unit sold are *not* inventoriable and do not form part of the unit cost for inventory purposes. However, these variable selling expenses are deducted from revenues to measure contribution margin.

Overhead accounting in Exhibit 10-3 follows the general guidelines specified in the direct costing flow chart (Exhibit 10-2). Actual fixed overhead costs of $36,000 are deducted as an expense in the income statement. Actual variable overhead costs incurred during the period were $17,000. These transactions were recorded as debits to the Variable Overhead Control account and credits

EXHIBIT 10-3

CONTRIBUTION APPROACH INCOME STATEMENT
CAR COMPANY, 19X5

Sales (8,000 units at $15)		$120,000
Variable expenses:		
Cost of goods sold (8,000 units at $3.00)	$24,000 (1)	
Selling expenses (8,000 units at $1.00)	8,000	
Underapplied variable overhead	2,000 (2)	34,000
Contribution margin		$ 86,000
Fixed expenses:		
Selling and administrative	$12,000	
Factory overhead	36,000	48,000
Net income (ignoring taxes)		$ 38,000

1. *Cost of goods sold computation*

Materials used (10,000 at $.50)	$ 5,000
Direct labor (10,000 at $1.00)	10,000
Variable overhead applied (10,000 at $1.50)	15,000
Current manufacturing costs	$30,000
Change in work in process inventory	–0–
Cost of goods manufactured	$30,000 (÷ 10,000 units = $3.00)
Finished goods, Jan. 1, 19X5	–0–
Finished goods, Dec. 31, 19X5	(6,000) (2,000 units at $3.00)
Cost of goods sold (8,000 at $3.00)	$24,000

2. *Underapplied variable overhead*

Actual variable overhead (debits to variable overhead control)	$17,000
Variable overhead applied (10,000 units at $1.50)	(15,000)
Underapplied variable overhead	$ 2,000*

* Underapplied variable overhead is charged to Cost of Goods Sold in this illustration. As an alternative, $400 could be allocated to Finished Goods inventory and $1,600 to Cost of Goods Sold based on the fact that 20 percent of current production is unsold at year-end.

to accounts such as Cash or Accounts Payable. Variable Overhead Applied is $15,000 based on production of 10,000 units multiplied by the predetermined variable overhead rate of $1.50. The following journal entries are presented to support variable overhead costs that appear in Exhibit 10-3:

1. Variable overhead control	$17,000	
Cash		$ XX
Accounts payable		XX
Factory payroll and other accounts		XX
To record actual costs incurred		
2. Work in process	$15,000	
Variable overhead applied		$15,000
To apply variable overhead:		
10,000 units at $1.50		
3. Underapplied variable overhead	$ 2,000	
Variable overhead applied	15,000	
Variable overhead control		$17,000
To close variable overhead accounts		

This complete illustration of direct costing procedures can be simplified by preparing a more concise solution for the income statement. For example, the average variable production cost of $3 can be used to determine Variable Cost of Goods Sold (8,000 units at $3 = $24,000). The Cost of Goods Manufactured schedule is not really necessary if there are no Work in Process inventories. The adjustment for underapplied or overapplied variable overhead is necessary only if predetermined overhead rates are used.

An important reason for using direct costing is that it produces income measures that are consistent with CVP computations in management planning. Depending upon production levels, absorption costing may reflect profits that differ from management expectations. To show the relationship between direct costing and CVP analysis, the Car Company example is continued.

Direct Costing and CVP Analysis

In 19X6, Car Company expects to sell 10,000 units, although the level of production could vary from 8,000 to 12,000 units, depending upon labor relations and availability of raw materials. For competitive reasons, the company is forced to reduce its selling price to ten dollars in 19X6. For simplicity, actual costs incurred are assumed to correspond with estimated costs for the year. Relevant cost data are:

VARIABLE COSTS	UNIT COST	
Direct materials	$ .50	
Direct labor	1.00	
Variable overhead	1.50	
Variable production cost	$3.00	(per unit produced—a product cost)
Variable selling cost	$1.00	(per unit sold—a period cost)
Variable cost per unit sold	$4.00	

ANNUAL FIXED COSTS, 19X6	
Factory overhead	$36,000
Selling and administrative	12,000
Total fixed costs	$48,000

Expected actual production volume is 10,000 units. The fixed overhead rate in absorption costing is therefore $3.60 per unit produced ($36,000 ÷ 10,000). Unit costs for inventory purposes under direct and absorption costing are computed as follows:

INVENTORY COST PER UNIT	DIRECT	ABSORPTION	
Direct materials	$ .50	$ .50	
Direct labor	1.00	1.00	
Variable overhead	1.50	1.50	(or $5.10 combined)
Fixed overhead	None	3.60	
Unit cost for inventory	$3.00	$6.60	

Given these cost estimates and revised product selling price, the following cost-volume-profit analysis is performed to determine breakeven volume and expected profits for 19X6:

1. Breakeven volume $= \dfrac{\$48,000}{\$10 - \$4} = \underline{\underline{8,000}}$ units of sales

Proof:

Sales (8,000 at $10)	$80,000
Variable expenses (8,000 at $4)	32,000
Contribution margin	$48,000
Total fixed costs	(48,000)
Profit	$ -0-

2. Expected profit for 19X6:

Sales (10,000 at $10)	$100,000
Variable expenses (10,000 at $4)	40,000
Contribution margin	$ 60,000
Total fixed costs	(48,000)
Net income	$ 12,000

At sales volume of 8,000 units, all fixed costs for 19X6 will be recovered, and profit is zero. At the expected sales volume of 10,000 units, sales volume will exceed the breakeven point by 2,000 units and will provide profits of $12,000 (2,000 units at $6 unit contribution margin).

Car Company management was pleased with these plans until the projected profits to be reported under absorption costing were presented as shown in Exhibit 10-4. While the CVP computations indicate a $12,000 profit at sales volume of 10,000 units, the profit to be reported under absorption costing depends on the actual production volume for 19X6. With a constant sales volume, profits under absorption costing increase as the production level increases. As indicated in Exhibit 10-4, absorption costing profits at a sales volume of 10,000 units can range from $4,800 to $19,200.

To clarify the situation for company management, Car Company accountants produced the direct costing income statements shown in Exhibit 10-5. The following comparison was used to reconcile and explain the profit differences between direct and absorption costing where P is production volume and S is sales volume in units of product:

	CONDITION 1: $S > P$	CONDITION 2: $P = S$	CONDITION 3: $P > S$
Profits computed by:			
Direct costing	$12,000	$12,000	$12,000
Absorption costing	(4,800)	(12,000)	(19,200)
Profit difference	$ 7,200	$ -0-	$ (7,200)
Fixed factory overhead deducted from sales under:			
Direct costing	$36,000	$36,000	$36,000
Absorption costing	(43,200)	(36,000)	(28,800)
Expense difference	$ (7,200)	$ -0-	$ 7,200

With this comparison, it is evident that actual fixed overhead costs of $36,000 are deducted from revenues under direct costing regardless of production volume. When sales volume is greater than production (condition 1), fixed overhead costs deducted from sales under absorption costing exceed

EXHIBIT 10-4

CAR COMPANY PROFITS UNDER ABSORPTION COSTING
19X6 ALTERNATIVE PRODUCTION PLANS

	CONDITION 1	CONDITION 2	CONDITION 3
Units to be produced	8,000	10,000	12,000
Expected sales volume in units	(10,000)	(10,000)	(10,000)
Increase (decrease) in finished goods	(2,000)	-0-	2,000
Sales (10,000 units at $10.00)	$100,000	$100,000	$100,000
Cost of goods sold (10,000 units at $6.60)	$ 66,000	$ 66,000	$ 66,000
Variable selling expenses (10,000 units at $1.00)	10,000	10,000	10,000
Fixed operating expenses	12,000	12,000	12,000
Under- (over-)applied overhead (computed below*)	7,200	-0-	(7,200)
Total expenses	$ 95,200	$ 88,000	$ 80,800
Net income (ignoring taxes)	$ 4,800	$ 12,000	$ 19,200

Under- (over-)applied overhead:

Actual overhead costs incurred:			
Variable ($1.50 per unit produced)	$12,000	$15,000	$18,000
Fixed overhead	36,000	36,000	36,000
Actual overhead costs incurred	$48,000	$51,000	$54,000
Overhead applied ($5.10 per unit produced)	(40,800)	(51,000)	(61,200)
Under- (over-)applied overhead (all fixed costs)	$ 7,200	$ -0-	$ (7,200)

The following fixed overhead analysis is used to explain profit
differences between absorption costing and direct costing.

Fixed overhead deducted from sales:			
Cost of goods sold (10,000 units at $3.60)	$36,000	$36,000	$36,000
Under- (over-)applied fixed overhead (see above)	7,200	-0-	(7,200)
Fixed overhead deducted from sales	$43,200	$36,000	$28,800

EXHIBIT 10-5

CAR COMPANY PROFITS UNDER DIRECT COSTING
19X6 ALTERNATIVE PRODUCTION PLANS

	CONDITION 1	CONDITION 2	CONDITION 3
Units to be produced	8,000	10,000	12,000
Expected sales volume in units	(10,000)	(10,000)	(10,000)
Increase (decrease) in finished goods	(2,000)	-0-	2,000
1. Sales (10,000 units at $10)	$100,000	$100,000	$100,000
Variable expenses:			
Cost of goods sold (10,000 units at $3)	$ 30,000	$ 30,000	$ 30,000
Selling expenses (10,000 units at $1)	10,000	10,000	10,000
2. Total variable expenses	$ 40,000	$ 40,000	$ 40,000
3. Contribution margin (1 − 2)	$ 60,000	$ 60,000	$ 60,000
Fixed expenses:			
Selling and administrative	$ 12,000	$ 12,000	$ 12,000
Fixed factory overhead	36,000	36,000	36,000
4. Total fixed expenses	$ 48,000	$ 48,000	$ 48,000
Net income (3 − 4)	$ 12,000	$ 12,000	$ 12,000

Note: Profits under direct costing for a sales volume of 10,000 units are $12,000 regardless of production volume.

the fixed overhead costs incurred for the current year. This difference in fixed overhead costs deducted from sales explains the profit difference between direct and absorption costing. When production is greater than sales (condition 3), absorption costing charges a portion of current fixed overhead costs to the Finished Goods inventory. In condition 3, only $28,800 of current fixed overhead costs appear in the absorption costing income statement, while $7,200 of current fixed overhead costs are added to the Finished Goods inventory account.

The Car Company example shows that CVP analysis based on absorption costing information is valid only if sales volume and production volume are equal (condition 2). Approximate equality of production and sales was listed in Chapter 9 as a restrictive condition of CVP analysis. Notice that this restriction does not apply if a company uses direct costing. Cost-volume-profit analysis is concerned with the recovery of all fixed costs *incurred* during a particular period. In direct costing, all fixed costs incurred are charged to expense accounts in the income statement. If direct costing is used, measures of net income will correspond with related CVP computations.

Based on the Car Company illustrations, the following generalizations apply to comparative analysis in direct and absorption costing:

1. When production is greater than sales volume, profit under absorption costing is larger.
2. When sales volume is greater than production, profit under direct costing is larger.
3. When sales volume and production are equal, profits under both costing methods are equal.
4. Profits under direct costing are dependent upon sales volume, not production volume.
5. Profits under absorption costing can be altered by changes in production volume.
6. If production volume is constant, profits under both costing methods move in the same direction as sales volume.

ACCOUNTING SYSTEMS FOR DIRECT COSTING

Examples in the previous section illustrated single-product companies. This situation simplifies the comparative analysis required to master the basics of direct costing. The natural question following these examples is whether direct costing can be applied in multidepartment plants that manufacture many products. Use of direct costing in these complex situations requires proper attention to conversion procedures, revision of overhead accounting methods, and analysis of factory overhead cost behavior patterns.

Conversion to Direct Costing

If a company is using absorption costing, the change to direct costing will require several modifications in accounting procedure. A thorough analysis of fixed and variable cost behavior is essential. Every manufacturing cost and operating expense must be classified as fixed, variable, or semivariable in behavior. The cost behavior analysis methods described in Chapter 9 must be applied to determine the fixed and variable cost information required for direct costing. Cost behavior studies may dictate changes in the chart of accounts to provide separate control accounts for expenses that currently have fixed and variable elements charged to a single account.

Most companies will continue to use absorption costing for external reporting purposes. The use of direct costing in this case involves no change in accounting principle, but simply a revision of internal accounting procedures and reporting practices for management. When direct costing is adopted, it is necessary to restate the initial Work in Process and Finished Goods inventories on a direct costing basis. This downward adjustment in inventory values will eliminate the fixed factory overhead costs contained in these accounts.

For example, assume that Adams Company wishes to adopt direct costing in 19X7. Inventories at absorption cost as originally reported on January 1, 19X7, are compared with computed estimates of inventories under direct costing:

INVENTORIES, JANUARY 1, 19X7	FINISHED GOODS	WORK IN PROCESS
1. Absorption costing	$4,800,000	$1,100,000
2. Direct costing	3,900,000	800,000
Adjustment (1 − 2)	$ 900,000	$ 300,000

The following journal entry is required to record the reduction in beginning inventory values:

Allowance to state inventory		
at absorption cost	$1,200,000	
Finished goods		$900,000
Work in process		300,000
To record reduction of inventories		
to direct costing basis		

Separate Allowance accounts can be maintained for Work in Process and Finished Goods if desired. The Allowance account is a debit balance adjustment account that is added to the general ledger balances for Work in Process and Finished Goods when preparing a balance sheet. By using the allowance account procedure, inventory accounts can be maintained on a direct costing basis, and the debit balance Allowance account permits reporting of inventories and operating results on an absorption costing basis when necessary.

To restate the initial inventories on a direct costing basis, some companies revise prior-year overhead rates to eliminate fixed manufacturing overhead. The computed variable overhead rates then are used to determine inventory valuations under direct costing. An alternative approach is to identify total variable overhead and total fixed overhead incurred in the year before direct costing is adopted. For groups of similar inventory items, a ratio is computed by comparing total fixed overhead to total cost of goods manufactured at absorption cost. This ratio is the percentage reduction necessary to reduce absorption costing inventory balances to estimated direct cost. Detailed perpetual inventory records also must be adjusted to reflect the lower unit cost computed for direct costing purposes.

Overhead Accounting Procedures

Transactions and journal entries required in a direct costing system have been illustrated already. Fixed manufacturing overhead costs should be charged to a separate account, Fixed Overhead Control. These costs will be reported as expenses in the direct costing income statement and are best controlled if they are not charged to an account that also contains variable costs. Recording transactions in separate control accounts requires no special procedures for many fixed and variable overhead costs. Initial recording of overhead costs is primarily a problem for semivariable costs that are not purely fixed or variable in behavior.

For example, assume that monthly power costs have been estimated as $12,000 fixed plus a variable cost equal to 5¢ per kilowatt hour. Several items of power cost were incurred in November, including equipment depreciation, salaries, repairs, and supplies. If total power costs for the month amount to $18,100, some procedure is required to determine the fixed and variable components. The best procedure in this case is to record all elements of power cost in the Fixed Overhead Control account. An adjusting entry is prepared at month-end to transfer the estimated variable power costs to Variable Overhead Control. Journal entries related to power costs in November are:

1. Fixed overhead control $18,100
       Accumulated depreciation $ XX
       Salaries payable   XX
       Other accounts   XX
   Effect of several journal entries related
   to power cost
2. Variable overhead control $ 6,100
       Fixed overhead control $6,100
   Transfer estimated variable expenses
   to Variable Overhead Control:
   $18,100 total – $12,000 fixed estimate

Another important phase of overhead accounting involves allocation of service department costs. Overhead cost allocations from service departments to producing departments are simplified by use of direct costing. There is no need to allocate fixed overhead costs incurred within the service departments. However, the variable costs incurred by service departments still must be reapportioned to producing departments. This allocation is required when analyzing estimated costs to develop variable overhead rates. Actual variable costs incurred by service departments are allocated to producing departments also, so that accurate measures of under- or overapplied variable overhead can be determined for each producing department at the end of an accounting period.

Financial Statement Adjustments

To restate direct costing results to approximate results under absorption costing, assume that Elmo Products disclosed the following inventory data in its January 1, 19X7, balance sheet:

Finished goods (at direct cost)	$300,000
Allowance to state inventory at absorption cost	72,000
Finished goods (at absorption cost)	$372,000

During 19X7, inventories of the company's various products increased (production was greater than sales). On December 31, 19X7, the balance of Finished Goods inventory at direct cost was $900,000. Variable overhead costs incurred during 19X7 were $8,264,000; actual fixed overhead costs were $9,916,800. An adjustment to the financial statements is necessary to permit external financial reporting on the basis of absorption costing.

The ratio of actual fixed overhead to variable overhead for the year is $9,916,800 ÷ $8,264,000 = 120 percent. This ratio can be used as a supplementary overhead rate to determine the necessary fixed overhead content of the ending Finished Goods inventory. The final inventory at direct cost is found to consist of:

INVENTORY, DECEMBER 31, 19X7	AMOUNT
Material and labor	$ 720,000
Variable overhead	180,000
Direct costing valuation	$ 900,000
Fixed overhead (120% × $180,000)	216,000
Absorption costing valuation	$1,116,000

The fixed overhead assignable to inventories at year-end indicates that the Allowance account requires an ending balance of $216,000. The unadjusted balance of the allowance account is $72,000; an adjusting entry of $144,000 is required at year-end.

Required balance in allowance	$216,000
Balance, Jan. 1, 19X7	(72,000)
Required adjustment	$144,000

The related adjusting entry on December 31, 19X7, is:

Allowance to state inventory at absorption cost	$144,000	
Fixed overhead control		$144,000

Internal management reports can be based on direct costing, but external financial reporting must reflect the absorption costing basis. After posting the adjusting entry for $144,000, the Allowance account balance is $216,000; this amount plus the $900,000 balance of Finished Goods computed under direct costing yields the absorption costing inventory amount of $1,116,000. Since inventories increased during 19X7, the adjusting entry transferred part of current fixed overhead costs to the Finished Goods inventory account. If inventories had decreased during the year, a reduction in the Allowance account would be necessary.

DIRECT COSTING AND ACCOUNTING THEORY

Since direct costing is consistent with CVP applications, the approach has considerable merit because it produces useful information for management. Financial accounting theory considers this advantage as well as arguments concerning the propriety of asset valuation and income determination with direct costing. Proponents of direct costing argue that fixed overhead costs are incurred regardless of production volume. These fixed charges provide the capacity to produce, but they represent no expected future benefits and should be recorded as period expenses. Variable production costs, however, are incurred because units are produced; these variable costs should be classified as an asset that will expire when related products are sold. Absorption costing advocates assert that fixed overhead costs should be allocated to units produced because each unit benefits from the capacity provided by fixed costs.

The real issue in these arguments concerns the period in which fixed overhead costs are charged to expenses: (1) in the period incurred (direct costing) or (2) in the period when manufactured goods are sold (absorption costing). Debate on this issue raged throughout the 1950s, but no distinct winner emerged. Arguments about proper matching, deferring costs that provide future benefits, and similar thoughts produced no solid conclusions. The current situation remains about the same as twenty years ago: Use absorption costing for external reporting in accordance with generally accepted accounting principles; use direct costing if desired for internal management reporting.

FINAL NOTE   Concepts and techniques of direct costing provide an important foundation of management planning and control. Direct costing, CVP analysis, and the contribution approach have several applications. The contribution approach to income determination is expanded in Chapter 17. Analysis for short-run decisions of alternative choice also will use the concepts involved in direct costing. Flexible budgeting, developed in Chapter 11, is an integral part of direct costing applications.

Return now to the beginning of the chapter and review the highlights section before proceeding to the review questions, exercises, and problems.

QUESTIONS

10-1. Define and illustrate the following terms and concepts:
  a. Normal costing
  b. Cost behavior
  c. Contribution margin
  d. Absorption, or full, costing
  e. Direct, or variable, costing
  f. Period cost
  g. Product cost

10-2. Describe the distinctive features of direct costing.

10-3. What is the relationship between the contribution approach and direct costing?

10-4. What unique information is available to management with a direct costing system?

10-5. Why would a company use absorption costing for external reporting purposes but use a direct costing format to maintain its internal information and reporting system?

10-6. How are cost-volume-profit analysis, the contribution approach, and direct costing interrelated?

10-7. What are the three principal components of product unit cost under direct costing?

10-8. Does direct costing eliminate the use of predetermined overhead rates? Defend your response.

10-9. Under direct costing, do the terms *product cost*, *inventoriable cost*, and *manufacturing cost* have the same meaning? Support your position.

10-10. What reasons are given by advocates of direct costing to support its use as an approach to product costing and inventory valuation?

10-11. What effect on net income will direct costing have, in comparison with absorption costing, when production volume exceeds sales volume? When sales volume exceeds production volume?

10-12. A company using absorption costing incurred $500,000 of fixed factory overhead during a year in which production volume was greater than sales volume. Assuming a FIFO flow of costs, in which financial statement(s) and specific account(s) would fixed factory overhead be contained?

10-13. If the company in question 10-12 used a direct costing approach, would your answer be the same? Explain.

10-14. Why is direct costing appropriate for pricing special orders but not useful as a basis for general pricing structure of a company's products?

10-15. With absorption costing, breakeven volume is computed under the assumption that production volume and sales volume are equal. Is this assumption necessary when computing breakeven volume under direct costing? Defend your answer.

10-16. Using good accounting theory, support the position of those who defend the use of absorption costing versus direct costing.

10-17. I. M. Loud, president of the Ter Ific Company, made the following comment concerning direct costing: "Net income determined by the use of direct costing procedures will always be less than net income determined under absorption costing procedures." Do you agree with this statement? Support your position.

EXERCISES

10-18. *Unit Cost Determination* In producing its special Marko ball-point pen during 19X2, Quill Products incurred $214,000 for direct material and $186,000 for direct labor. Factory overhead associated with this one product has been analyzed into fixed cost and variable cost classifications as follows:

| | OVERHEAD COST, 19X2 | |
	Variable	Fixed
Tools and supplies	$115,000	—
Depreciation—equipment	—	$ 75,000
Repairs and maintenance	65,000	205,000
Property taxes	—	32,500
Salaries—supervisory	—	177,500
Labor-material handling	20,000	10,000
Total overhead	$200,000	$500,000

Production volume in 19X2 was 2,000,000 units.

REQUIRED:
a. Compute the absorption unit cost of production for 19X2.
b. Compute the unit product cost for 19X2 under direct costing.

10-19. *Comparative Inventory Valuation* As part of its investigation regarding the possible adoption of direct costing, the management of Lost Nations Company asked the controller what effect the adoption of such procedures would have on inventories. In developing a reply to this request, the following figures representing operations of the past year are available:

Units:	
Produced	100,000
Sold	80,000
Beginning finished goods inventory	$ –0–
Direct material costs	250,000
Direct labor costs	300,000
Factory overhead costs:	
Variable	100,000
Fixed	250,000

REQUIRED: Indicate the value to be assigned the 20,000 units in ending inventory using (a) absorption, or full, costing and (b) direct, or variable, costing.

10-20. *Pricing Marginal Output* Harris Company normally operates at 90 percent of productive capacity, producing 9,000 typewriters per month. The total manufacturing costs for a normal month are as follows:

Direct materials	$180,000
Direct labor	162,000
Variable factory overhead	72,000
Fixed factory overhead	90,000
Total production costs	$504,000

The company has been invited by a governmental agency to submit a bid for 1,000 typewriters to be delivered within a month. If the contract is obtained, it is anticipated that the additional activity will not interfere with normal production and will not increase selling or administrative expenses.

REQUIRED:
a. Compute the absorption unit cost for production of 9,000 units per month.
b. Compute the unit cost under direct costing when monthly production is 9,000 units.
c. Compute the minimum unit price the Harris Company should bid on this contract.
d. Could the company increase its net income by accepting a special contract such as this one at a price that is less than the normal absorption unit cost? Explain your answer.

10-21. *Comparative Income Analysis* Dewey Manufacturers opened its Lankton operation in early January. One product was manufactured during the year. The relevant data follow:

Sales ($10 per unit)	50,000 units
Production (no spoilage incurred)	60,000 units

	VARIABLE COSTS		FIXED
	Per unit	Total	COSTS
Costs and expenses:			
Direct materials	$1.00	$60,000	
Direct labor	1.50	90,000	
Maintenance labor	.25	15,000	$ 9,000
Packaging cost	.10	6,000	
Production supervision			30,000
Depreciation:			
Production department			45,000
Other departments			5,000
Insurance on equipment:			
Other departments			2,000
Miscellaneous manufacturing overhead	.20	12,000	15,000
Selling and administrative expenses	.75	37,500	60,000

REQUIRED:
a. Compute the ending inventory valuation under absorption costing.
b. Compute the ending inventory valuation under direct costing.
c. Compute net income under the two costing methods and provide a reconciliation of net income between the two methods.

10-22. *CVP and Direct Costing* During 19X4, Rayson Corporation manufactured 7,500 units of product Z14 and sold 8,000 units at $12 each. The company has used absorption costing for several years and applies a FIFO assumption for cost flow purposes. The company's 19X4 income statement is summarized below:

Sales (8,000 units at $12)	$96,000
Cost of goods sold (schedule 1)	38,600
Gross margin on sales	$57,400
Selling and general expenses (fixed = $12,000)	20,000
Income before taxes	$37,400

Schedule 1 (all inventories are finished goods)

	UNITS	TOTAL COST	UNIT COST COMPOSITION
Initial inventory	2,000	$ 8,600	VC = $3.50; FC = $.80
Units produced	7,500	37,500	VC = $4.00; FC = $1.00
Goods available	9,500	$46,100	
Final inventory	(1,500)	(7,500)	$5 per unit under FIFO
Units sold	8,000	$38,600	

REQUIRED:

a. Prepare a schedule showing net income under direct costing using the FIFO cost flow assumption.
b. Compute the company's breakeven volume in units.
c. Using CVP logic and the contribution approach, what net income should result from 8,000 units of sales? Why is this amount different from the absorption costing net income shown by the company in 19X4?

10-23. *Overhead Rate Computation* Storevik Crane Company manufactures overhead cranes and uses a direct costing approach for product costing purposes. Mr. Terry, controller, is in the process of computing a factory overhead rate. The following information pertains to estimates for the year 19X4 (V = variable; F = fixed):

Direct labor hours to be worked	18,000
Indirect manufacturing costs:	
Indirect labor (V)	$15,660
Indirect materials (V)	7,740
Depreciation—plant (F)	41,000
Depreciation—equipment (F)	27,000
Property taxes (F)	4,000
Maintenance and repair (⅓ V)	5,400
Heat, light, and power (½ V)	8,640
Plant superintendent (F)	18,000
Total	$127,440

REQUIRED: Compute the predetermined factory overhead rate for the Storevik Crane Company for 19X4.

10-24. *Application of Overhead Rates* Lilla Company employs a job order costing system that is based on direct costing. During July 19X3, the following transaction summaries appeared on the records:

Purchased raw materials	$ 74,000
Raw materials requisitioned into production	62,000
Direct labor costs	47,000
Indirect labor costs (V)	12,000
Indirect material costs (V)	7,000
Other variable overhead costs	9,400
Depreciation—plant and equipment (F)	24,000
Other fixed overhead costs	11,000
Costs transferred to finished goods	124,000
Costs transferred to cost of goods sold	119,000

The company applies overhead costs to Work in Process inventory using a variable overhead rate of sixty cents per direct labor dollar.

REQUIRED:

a. Prepare journal entries for the above transaction summaries including overhead application.

b. Close overhead control account(s) to overapplied or underapplied overhead.

c. Prepare a journal entry to close the over- or underapplied overhead account.

10-25. *Flexible Budget Analysis*   Equipment maintenance costs in a particular plant are semivariable, or mixed, in behavior. Through regression analysis, monthly maintenance costs are estimated to be $30,000 fixed plus $1.05 per machine hour in the producing departments. During August 19X7, producing departments worked 50,000 machine hours, and $109,000 of maintenance costs were debited to Fixed Overhead Control.

REQUIRED:

a. Assuming the use of direct costing, prepare an adjusting entry to transfer estimated variable maintenance costs to Variable Overhead Control.

b. Identify the alternative measures for variable costs in part (a) and justify your choice.

PROBLEMS

10-26. *CMA Problem—Contribution Approach to Pricing*   E. Berg and Sons build custom-made pleasure boats that range in price from $10,000 to $250,000. For the past thirty years, Mr. Berg, Sr., has determined the selling price of each boat by estimating the costs of material, labor, a prorated portion of overhead, and adding 20 percent to these estimated costs. For example, a recent price quotation was determined as follows:

Direct materials	$ 5,000
Direct labor	8,000
Overhead	2,000
	$15,000
Plus 20%	3,000
Selling price	$18,000

The overhead figure was determined by estimating total overhead costs for the year and allocating them at 25 percent of direct labor.

If a customer rejected the price and business was slack, Mr. Berg, Sr., would often be willing to reduce the markup to as little as 5 percent over estimated costs. Thus, average markup for the year is estimated at 15 percent.

Mr. Ed Berg, Jr., has just completed a course on pricing and believes the firm could use some of the techniques he learned. The course emphasized the contribution margin approach to pricing, and Mr. Berg, Jr., feels such an approach would be helpful in determining the selling prices of the boats.

Total overhead, which includes selling and administrative expenses for the year, has been estimated at $150,000; $90,000 of this is fixed, and the remainder is variable in direct proportion to direct labor.

REQUIRED:

a. Assume the customer in the example rejected the $18,000 quotation and also rejected a $15,750 quotation (5 percent markup) during a slack period. The customer countered with a $15,000 offer.
1. What is the difference in net income for the year between accepting or rejecting the customer's offer?
2. What is the minimum selling price Mr. Berg, Jr., could have quoted without reducing or increasing net income?

b. What advantages does the contribution margin approach to pricing have over the approach used by Mr. Berg, Sr.?

c. What pitfalls are there, if any, to contribution margin pricing?

(IMA adapted)

10-27. *CPA Problem—Direct Costing and Breakeven Analysis* Metal Industries, Inc., operates its production department only when orders are received for one or both of its two products, two sizes of metal discs. The manufacturing process begins with the cutting of doughnut-shaped rings from rectangular strips of sheet metal; these rings are then pressed into discs. The sheets of metal, each 4 feet long and weighing 32 ounces, are purchased at $1.36 per running foot. The department has been operating at a loss for the past year as shown below:

Sales for the year	$172,000
Expenses	(177,200)
Net loss for the department	$ (5,200)

The following information is available:

a. Ten thousand 4-foot pieces of metal yielded 40,000 large discs, each weighing 4 ounces and selling for $2.90, and 40,000 small discs, each weighing 2.4 ounces and selling for $1.40.

b. The corporation has been producing at less than "normal capacity" and has had no spoilage in the cutting step of the process. The skeletons remaining after the rings have been cut are sold for scrap at $.80 per pound.

c. The variable conversion cost of each large disc is 80 percent of the disc's direct material cost, and variable conversion cost of each small disc is 75 percent of the disc's direct material cost. Variable conversion costs are the sum of direct labor and variable overhead.

d. Fixed costs were $86,000.

REQUIRED:

a. For each of the parts manufactured, prepare a schedule computing:
1. Unit material cost after deducting the value of salvage
2. Unit variable conversion cost
3. Unit contribution margin
4. Total contribution margin for all units sold

b. Assuming you computed the material cost for large discs at eighty-five cents each and for small discs at fifty-one cents each, compute the number of units the corporation must sell to break even based on a normal production capacity of 50,000 units. Assume no spoiled units and a product mix of one large disc to each small disc.

(AICPA adapted)

10-28. *Conversion to Absorption Costing*   Tide Company follows a strict policy of producing 200,000 units a year in order to stabilize employment and to minimize labor turnover costs. The firm relies upon an aggressive sales force to prevent inventories from increasing significantly above the base inventory of 60,000 units. For the year 19X3, the following estimated direct costing income statement was developed in connection with other budget procedures:

Sales (206,000 units)	$1,854,000
Less variable costs:	
Cost of goods sold ($6/unit)	(1,236,000)
Selling and general ($1/unit)	(206,000)
Contribution margin	$ 412,000
Less fixed costs:	
Manufacturing overhead	(100,000)
Selling and general	(40,000)
Net income before taxes	$ 272,000

REQUIRED: Assume that the current estimate of fixed overhead is the same as actual fixed overhead in 19X2. Convert the budgeted operating results to absorption costing and present a formal income statement on that basis for the budget year 19X3. Prepare a reconciliation of the difference in net income under each approach.

10-29. *CMA Problem—Comparative Income Analysis*   Robertson, Inc., uses direct costing for internal management reporting purposes and converts these results to absorption costing for annual external reporting requirements. At the end of 19X1, management expected a 20 percent increase in sales volume during 19X2. Production in 19X2 was therefore increased from 20,000 units to 24,000 units to meet expected demand. Because of several conditions that developed in 19X2, actual sales volume was 20,000 units, the same as in 19X1. Selling prices and other data for the two years appear below:

	19X1	19X2
Selling price per unit	$30	$30
Sales (units)	20,000	20,000
Beginning inventory (units)	2,000	2,000
Production (units)	20,000	24,000
Ending inventory (units)	2,000	6,000

Actual variable costs per unit for 19X1 and 19X2 were:

Labor	$ 7.50
Materials	4.50
Variable overhead	3.00
	$15.00

Annual fixed costs for 19X1 and 19X2 (budgeted and actual) were:

Production	$ 90,000
Selling and administrative	100,000
	$190,000

The overhead rate under absorption costing is based upon capacity of 30,000 units per year. Under- or overapplied factory overhead is allocated entirely to Cost of Goods Sold. Assume that the company uses an allowance account procedure in making the annual adjustment from direct to absorption costing.

REQUIRED:
a. Prepare the 19X2 income statement based on direct costing.
b. Prepare the 19X2 income statement based on absorption costing.
c. Prepare the adjusting entry necessary on December 31, 19X2, to reflect the ending inventory at absorption cost in the general ledger.

(IMA adapted)

10-30. *Absorption Versus Direct Costing*   James Galley, controller of Quad-Cities Industries, Inc., is in the process of preparing the corporation's first set of annual financial statements. Organized in late 19X6, the corporation began operations on January 2, 19X7, specializing in the production of electric organs for the home. A summary of cost data for the year 19X7 is presented below:

Variable costs and expenses per unit:	
Raw materials	$275
Direct labor	300
Variable factory overhead	150
Selling expenses (per unit sold)	100
Fixed costs and expenses:	
Factory overhead (approximately $175 per finished unit)	$190,000
General and administrative expenses	105,000
Selling expenses	75,000

During 19X7, the corporation manufactured 1,000 complete organs, selling 900 of them for $1,500 each. Raw material purchases for the year totaled $330,000, of which $27,500 worth of materials remained in Raw Materials inventory at year-end. Work in Process inventory on December 31, 19X7, includes 100 organs; the average partial cost of completion of each unit is:

Raw materials	$275
Direct labor	250
Variable factory overhead	125
Fixed factory overhead	150
	$800

REQUIRED:

a. Prepare a statement of Cost of Goods Manufactured and Sold assuming the corporation uses an absorption costing system.
b. Prepare a statement of Cost of Goods Manufactured and Sold assuming the corporation uses a direct costing system.
c. Determine the corporation's net profit before taxes if (1) absorption costing is used and if (2) direct costing is used. Reconcile the difference in net profit figures.

10-31. *CPA Problem—Direct Costing Analysis* The following annual flexible budgets have been prepared for production and sales possibilities of product X:

Units produced and sold	150,000	200,000	250,000
Sales	$1,500,000	$2,000,000	$2,500,000
Manufacturing costs:			
Material and labor	$ 150,000	$ 200,000	$ 250,000
Variable overhead	450,000	600,000	750,000
Fixed overhead	200,000	200,000	200,000
Operating expenses:			
Variable (per unit sold)	300,000	400,000	500,000
Fixed	160,000	160,000	160,000
Total period expenses	$1,260,000	$1,560,000	$1,860,000
Net income	$ 240,000	$ 440,000	$ 640,000

The 200,000 unit budget has been adopted for 19X2 and will be used for applying manufacturing overhead costs to production of product X. All fixed costs are incurred uniformly during the year, and all fixed costs incurred correspond with budget estimates. Over- or underapplied overhead is deferred and charged to Cost of Goods Sold at year-end. During the first nine months, 120,000 units were produced and 80,000 units were sold.

REQUIRED:

a. Parts 1 through 5 are to be answered assuming the company uses absorption costing procedures. Prepare schedules and computations as necessary to provide the following information:
   1. The total amount of factory overhead applied to production during the first nine months
   2. The amount of fixed factory overhead applied to production during the first nine months
   3. The Cost of Goods Sold for the first nine months
   4. For inventory purposes, the unit cost of product X
   5. Total operating expenses for the first nine months

b. Parts 6 through 10 are to be answered assuming the company uses direct costing procedures. Prepare schedules and computations as necessary to provide the following information:
   6. The total amount of factory overhead applied to production during the first nine months
   7. The amount of fixed factory overhead applied to production during the first nine months
   8. The total contribution margin reported for the first nine months
   9. For inventory purposes, the unit cost of product X
   10. The annual breakeven point in units of product X

(AICPA adapted)

10-32. *Journal Entry Preparation*   Cecil Enterprises manufactures a diverse line of industrial products and uses a perpetual inventory system. Overhead is applied on the basis of direct labor hours. For 19X8, the predetermined overhead rate is $6 per hour, which includes a variable cost portion of $2. The fixed portion of the overhead rate was determined by using average monthly capacity of 150,000 labor hours. General ledger balances on February 1, 19X8, were: Raw Materials, $10,000; Work in Process, $5,000; Finished Goods, $8,000. Transactions during February included the following events:

> Purchased raw materials on credit for $15,000
> Issued $20,000 of raw material to production area
> Direct labor payroll for 120,000 hours was $400,000
> Incurred variable overhead costs of $300,000
> Incurred fixed overhead costs of $580,000
> Credit sales for the month were $2,000,000

Inventories on February 28 were $45,000 for Work in Process and $108,000 for Finished Goods. Under- or overapplied factory overhead is deferred in monthly financial statements.

REQUIRED:
a. Assume that given inventory valuations were determined under direct costing. Prepare journal entries for February transactions, including overhead application and other adjusting entries you consider necessary.
b. Assume that given inventory valuations were determined under absorption costing. Prepare journal entries for February transactions, including overhead application and necessary adjustments, to the extent that there is any difference between direct and absorption costing.
c. For the absorption costing case, prepare a schedule of Cost of Goods Manufactured and a partial income statement.

10-33. *Direct Costing—Overhead Rate Determination*   The manufacturing operation of the Emerson Company is made up of two producing departments, Molding and Trimming, and three service departments, Repairs and Maintenance, Inspection, and Material Handling. The following schedule represents actual overhead costs incurred in 19X6:

| | SERVICE DEPARTMENTS | | | PRODUCING DEPARTMENTS | | |
	Repairs and maintenance	Inspection	Material handling	Molding	Trimming	TOTAL
Indirect labor (V)	$12,500	$19,000	$16,400	$ 24,000	$ 32,000	$103,900
Indirect materials (V)	7,400	6,000	2,700	32,000	12,000	60,100
Heat, light, and power*	8,000	6,000	4,500	36,500	38,000	93,000
Supplies (V)	2,400	3,100	2,700	4,500	6,200	18,900
Depreciation (F)	7,000	10,000	32,000	75,000	67,000	191,000
Factory insurance (F)	200	300	400	1,000	1,500	3,400
Plant supervision (F)	9,200	16,500	14,700	34,500	36,000	110,900
	$46,700	$60,900	$73,400	$207,500	$192,700	$581,200

* 40 percent variable cost.

All variable costs are expected to increase by 10 percent in 19X7. Fixed costs will remain unchanged.

For reapportionment purposes, all service department costs are allocated directly to producing departments (direct method): three-fifths are charged to Molding and two-fifths are charged to Trimming.

During 19X7, the Molding Department expects to use 45,000 direct labor hours, and the Trimming Department will use 73,750 machine hours.

REQUIRED: Compute predetermined overhead rates for 19X7 for the Molding and Trimming departments using direct labor hour and machine hour bases, respectively. Assume the use of direct costing.

10-34. *Restatement of Inventories* Perkinson Industries, Inc., maintains Work in Process and Finished Goods inventory account balances on a direct costing basis, using an allowance account to accumulate fixed manufacturing costs applicable to these inventory accounts. On December 31, 19X8, these account balances were:

Work in process inventory	$ 746,500
Finished goods inventory	1,247,800
Allowance to state inventories at full cost	672,700
Total inventories (at absorption cost)	$2,667,000

During 19X9 Perkinson Industries, Inc., underestimated consumer demand for their products; the result was that the Finished Goods inventory balance on December 31, 19X9, was down by 55 percent from the previous year-end balance. Work in Process inventory on December 31, 19X9, on the other hand, was up 10 percent from the prior year's balance. Variable manufacturing overhead costs included in the December 31, 19X9, inventory balances are:

| Work in process | $164,230 |
| Finished goods | 112,302 |

Fixed manufacturing overhead costs incurred in 19X9 were $4,257,344, while $2,475,200 of variable manufacturing overhead was recorded during the same period. No adjustments have been made to the Allowance account during 19X9.

REQUIRED:

a. Compute the December 31, 19X9, balances of Work in Process and Finished Goods inventory accounts.

b. Prepare a breakdown of the balances in part (a) showing the prime cost and variable manufacturing overhead costs in each account on December 31, 19X9.

c. Compute the ratio of actual fixed overhead to variable overhead for 19X9 and prepare the adjusting entry required to update the allowance account on December 31, 19X9.

d. What are the December 31, 19X9, balances of the Work in Process and Finished Goods inventory accounts stated on an absorption costing basis?

10-35. *Conversion to Direct Costing*   In March 19X9, Drew Products management decided to adopt direct costing for internal reporting purposes. The company has used absorption costing since its formation twelve years ago and will continue to use this basis in all external reporting situations. The company manufactures a complete line of folding and setup boxes and related paper products. Cost of Goods Manufactured and Sold during the preceding year is summarized below:

DREW PRODUCTS
Production cost summary
Year ending December 31, 19X8

Materials issued to production		$ 300,000
Direct labor incurred		500,000
Overhead applied (200% of labor)		' 1,000,000
Current production costs		$1,800,000
Work in process:		
Jan. 1, 19X8	$100,000	
Dec. 31, 19X8	(300,000)	(200,000)
Cost of goods manufactured		$1,600,000
Finished goods:		
Jan. 1, 19X8	$ 80,000	
Dec. 31, 19X8	(180,000)	(100,000)
Cost of goods sold (normal cost)		$1,500,000
Plus: Underapplied overhead		30,000
Cost of goods sold (actual)		$1,530,000

Based upon cost variability studies, it was determined that overhead applied included $800,000 of fixed manufacturing overhead.

REQUIRED:

a. Compute the percentage relationship of fixed factory overhead to Cost of Goods Manufactured and to Current Production Costs.

b. Determine the approximate direct costing valuation of Work in Process and Finished Goods on December 31, 19X8.

c. Prepare the adjusting entry as of January 1, 19X9, to adopt the direct costing valuation.

10-36. *Direct Costing and CVP Analysis* Gronk Metal Parts uses periodic inventory procedures to account for its production activities. The company manufactures a limited line of components for airplane engines. Inventory items are numerous and of small value. Accordingly, production output is measured simply in tons of output. At year-end, there is never any Work in Process inventory, and predetermined overhead rates are not employed. An absorption costing income statement for 19X7 appears below:

GRONK METAL PARTS
Income statement
Year ending December 31, 19X7

Sales (6,000,000 tons at $5)		$30,000,000
Cost of goods produced:		
Raw materials	$ 2,000,000	
Direct labor	3,000,000	
Variable overhead	2,000,000	
Fixed overhead	7,000,000	
Total output (7,000,000 tons)	$14,000,000	
Finished goods:		
Jan. 1, 19X7	–0–	
Dec. 31, 19X7 (1,000,000 tons)	(2,000,000)	
Cost of goods sold		12,000,000
Gross margin on sales		$18,000,000
Selling and general expenses:		
Fixed	$11,000,000	
Variable (related to sales volume)	6,000,000	17,000,000
Income before taxes		$ 1,000,000

REQUIRED:

a. Apply direct costing procedures to the valuation of Finished Goods inventory on December 31, 19X7.

b. Using the results from part (a), prepare a contribution approach income statement under direct costing.

c. Based on unit contribution margin, determine the annual breakeven sales volume in units.

d. Compare your solution to part (c) with the absorption costing income statement given in the problem; write a brief explanation of any apparent inconsistencies between 19X7 absorption costing profits and the breakeven volume computation.

Chapter 11: Standard Cost Accounting

Purpose and Learning Objectives

Standard cost accounting is an important foundation of managerial planning and control. The development and use of standard costs increase cost consciousness among management and employees and can improve company profits. Standard costing demands internal management cooperation and increases overall operating efficiency by providing a vehicle for performance evaluation. This chapter introduces the concepts and basic procedures of standard cost accounting.

Upon completion of this chapter, students should be able to:

1. Formulate standard costs for raw materials, direct labor, and factory overhead
2. Relate standard cost accounting to budgetary control
3. Apply the concepts of capacity levels and flexible budgeting to standard costing
4. Distinguish among ideal standards, basic standards, and currently attainable standards
5. Prepare journal entries to record transactions in a standard cost system

Relevant Concepts

The following basic concepts are introduced in this chapter:

Standard cost accounting   The use of realistic predetermined unit costs to facilitate product costing, cost control, cost flow, and inventory valuation.

Budgetary control   The process of planning a company's operating activities and the control of operations to aid in attaining those plans.

Capacity level   The level of productive output that can be expressed in varying amounts depending upon operating conditions and intended use.

Flexible budget   A summary of estimated costs to be incurred at various levels of productive activity.

Standard cost flow The integration of standard costs and actual costs for the same transactions into the cost accounting system and the isolation and disposition of resulting cost variances.

Standard costs are introduced into a cost accounting system to facilitate the budgetary control process. Standard costs are realistically predetermined costs that usually are expressed as a cost per unit of finished product. Standard costs are used to formulate operating budgets, to promote cost control, and to simplify cost accounting for inventories. At the end of an accounting period, standard costs are compared with actual costs, and the resulting variances help to pinpoint ineffective operating areas within a company. Such analyses lead to better cost control and smoother planning activities in the future.

The concepts of capacity levels and flexible budgeting are basic to the structure and operation of a standard cost system. There are several different measures of capacity, and this chapter describes the potential usefulness of each measure in a standard cost system. In many cases, total capacity is far greater than that actually used for current production needs. Measuring performance against a level of output known to be too high is meaningless. For this reason, normal capacity is used commonly and is stated in terms of current market demand weighted by a company's present productive capacity.

A flexible budget is a summary of estimated costs that is geared to changes in the level of productive activity and is prepared for a range of activity levels. Flexible budgets are used to prepare cost control reports and to determine standard fixed overhead rates. In evaluating performance with standard cost information, managers must consider employee motivation and behavioral response in addition to technical cost analysis procedures. Currently attainable standard costs reflect these considerations most closely.

A standard cost accounting system uses material, labor, and overhead cost standards. Each standard is developed through a thorough analysis utilizing information from all relevant functional areas of a company. The cost accounting area coordinates information flow from purchasing, engineering, sales, and production departments and is responsible for calculating the cost standards. Separate measures are developed for material price standards, material quantity standards, labor time standards, labor rate standards, as well as standard variable and fixed overhead rates.

Standard cost accounting systems involve several procedures that differ from traditional cost accounting systems. Raw Materials inventory, Work in Process inventory, Finished Goods inventory, and Cost of Goods Sold are the accounts affected by standard cost accounting. Journal entries for manufacturing activities are modified to recognize variance accounts at the time of recording material, labor, and overhead transactions. This procedure allows only standard product costs to flow through inventory accounts.

Cost accounting systems, concepts, and procedures discussed in prior chapters have centered on actual costs incurred by a company. Job order costing, process costing, and joint product costing assumed the use of actual or historical costs. *Standard costs*, however, are realistically predetermined costs that usually are expressed as a cost per unit of finished product. Standard costs are projections of what actual costs should be; they are used to prepare cost budgets for management planning and to promote cost control in current operations.

INTRODUCTION TO STANDARD COSTS

**Standard Costs and
Budgetary Control**

Budgetary control involves the successful planning of a company's operating activities and the control of operations to aid in attaining those plans. In cost accounting terms, the objectives of budgetary control are:

1. To aid in establishing procedures for preparing a company's planned costs and revenues
2. To aid in coordinating and communicating these plans to various levels of management
3. To formulate a basis for effective cost control

Standard costs play a major role in the budgetary control process. Standard material, labor, and manufacturing overhead costs are useful in projecting anticipated cost incurrence for a future period. For example, assume that Grisham Company estimates that it will manufacture 125,000 products during the upcoming year. Each product requires 2½ hours of labor (labor time standard) at a cost of $5.50 per hour (standard labor rate per hour). Planned labor costs for the year for this product would be:

$$125,000 \text{ products} \times 2.5 \text{ hours} \times \$5.50 = \$1,718,750$$

This example involves estimates of number of products, standard labor hours per product, and standard labor cost per hour. Such information facilitates the planning process by coordinating plans throughout the enterprise and by communicating information to those managers who are responsible for production volume and factory labor. The estimate of 125,000 products provides the production superintendent with an output goal for the year. Production personnel know that these 125,000 units should be produced by using an average of 2½ labor hours on each unit with an average labor rate of $5.50 per hour.

At year-end, assume the Grisham Company had incurred actual labor costs of $1,947,400 to manufacture this product. In standard costing terms, a variance has been incurred:

or
$$\text{actual cost} - \text{standard cost} = \text{variance}$$
$$\$1,947,400 - \$1,718,750 = \$228,650(U)$$

A *variance* is the difference between actual results and related standard or anticipated results. In our example, actual costs exceeded standard costs, which resulted in an *unfavorable* variance. An unfavorable variance is designated by the symbol (U). If actual costs are less than standard costs, the variance is *favorable* and is noted by the symbol (F).

Variance analysis is used in the cost control phase of the budgetary control process. With the aid of standard costs, variances are computed and analyzed. When the causes of a variance have been determined, corrective measures are implemented to prevent nonstandard performance in future periods.

What caused the Grisham Company to incur $228,650 more labor cost than was anticipated? From the information given, no single reason or cause can be isolated. The following list of possible causes indicates the types of factors that should be investigated to obtain an appropriate explanation:

1. The company produced more than 125,000 products during the year.
2. More than 2½ labor hours were used per product.
3. The average labor rate exceeded the standard labor rate of $5.50.
4. The variance resulted from a combination of factors included in items 1, 2, and 3.

In general, standard cost variances measure the degree of nonstandard performance, and additional information must be obtained to identify the related causes of such performance.

In summary, standard costs are useful for planning purposes and also provide excellent performance goals or targets for managers. Without comparisons of actual and standard costs, management would have limited information regarding the effectiveness of individual managers. Standard costs are useful in pinpointing efficiencies or inefficiencies in company operations. Analysis and investigation of variances force management to recognize operational problem areas. Control problems then are reviewed with individual managers who are responsible for these areas. By continuous review of operational problems, management can reduce costs and improve operating performance. The development and successful use of standard costs require appropriate measures of plant capacity and flexible budgets for overhead costs.

Capacity is defined as the total productive ability of a company for a specific time period; it is measured in terms of potential output or by input factors such as labor hours. In measuring capacity, it is important to distinguish between the company's ability to produce and its plans to produce. The production capacity of a company can be expressed in terms of (1) what it can produce or (2) what it will produce. Using this classification scheme, specific measures can be developed for the following capacity levels:

Measures of Plant Capacity

1. What can be produced: (a) theoretical capacity; (b) practical capacity
2. What will be produced: (a) normal capacity; (b) expected annual capacity

Theoretical capacity Theoretical, or ideal, capacity of a company or a department is maximum productive output assuming that all facilities operate at optimum speed without production interruptions. This level of capacity does not include time allowances for machine downtime, retooling, maintenance, or employee work breaks. Market demand, inventory levels, and storage problems are not considered as limiting factors since the objective is to measure total possible production capability. Theoretical capacity is an engineering concept.

Practical capacity Practical capacity also measures what can be produced, but this measure gives consideration to expected work stoppages. *Practical capacity* is theoretical capacity reduced by allowances for unavoidable facility downtime resulting from anticipated machine repairs, retooling, and other stoppages caused by employee, raw material, or power failure. Practical capacity is a reasonable measure of productive capability, but it does not consider limiting factors such as market demand for products.

Normal capacity When capacity is predicted for a future time period, external and environmental factors should be considered along with physical production capabilities. It serves no useful purpose to produce at full capacity if market demand does not match productivity, since risk of obsolescence and storage costs of unsold inventory items would be excessive. For these reasons, normal capacity is often used to express a firm's production intentions for future planning and cost allocation purposes. This capacity level requires an estimate of what will be produced with a company's productive facilities and manpower. *Normal capacity* is the average annual level of productive activity that will satisfy anticipated sales volume based upon consideration of seasonal factors and cyclical business fluctuations. Normal capacity is an average annual measure based on three- to five-year projections.

Expected annual capacity   If three- to five-year projections are not feasible, a company may use expected annual capacity. This short-range approach to measuring productive capacity is useful when market forces cause estimates for longer periods to be unreliable. *Expected annual capacity* is the budgeted production level expected to occur in the succeeding year.

Selecting a Capacity Level

If demand factors indicate less than full-capacity usage, it is unrealistic to compare actual productive output or plant utilization with some measure of what can be produced. Capacity based on product demand is realistic and provides a good base for measuring predetermined overhead rates used in standard cost analysis. If a company utilizes all available productive resources, normal capacity and practical capacity will be identical. However, many companies maintain idle facilities, or *idle capacity*, to be used only during peak production periods or during repair stoppages of similar equipment. In comparison, *excess capacity* represents production capability that will not be utilized in the foreseeable future. In measuring normal capacity or expected annual capacity, expected usage of idle facilities is included.

Capacity levels are the basis for many planning activities. Cost-volume-profit relationships are based on specific levels of productive capacity, and capacity levels provide important profit planning information as described in Chapter 14. Capacity levels also are used in calculating predetermined overhead rates. Chapter 5 illustrated the determination of predetermined overhead rates, which are used to apply fixed and variable overhead costs to units produced. In calculating those rates, total estimated departmental overhead costs were divided by a specific base such as direct labor hours, units of output, or machine hours. The base used in computing overhead rates is a capacity measure.

In standard cost systems, a capacity level must be selected in order to compute standard overhead costs per unit of product. Standard overhead cost per unit involves the same computation procedures as the determination of overhead rates. Estimated overhead costs are divided by a selected capacity level. Flexible budgets are used to estimate the overhead costs to be incurred at various capacity levels.

Nature and Use of Flexible Budgets

A *flexible budget* is a summary of estimated costs that is geared to changes in the level of productive activity and is prepared for a range of activity levels. These budgets are used to compute overhead unit costs, to forecast overhead costs in budgeting, and to develop a comparative basis for performance evaluation and cost control reports.

In the Grisham Company example presented above, the company anticipated production of 125,000 products and had estimated direct labor costs based on this production level. When actual labor costs exceeded planned costs, one possible cause of the resulting variance was that more than 125,000 products were produced. In the original estimate, planned labor costs were based on a *static budget* that considered only a single level of activity.

It is unrealistic to compare planned or standard costs based on one level of activity with actual costs resulting from a different level of activity. Exhibit 11-1 illustrates the need for adjusting budgeted costs to the actual level of

EXHIBIT 11-1

USE OF FLEXIBLE BUDGET AND STATIC BUDGET TO COMPUTE LABOR COST VARIANCE

STATIC BUDGET BASED ON NORMAL CAPACITY (125,000 UNITS)*	FLEXIBLE BUDGET BASED ON ACTUAL UNITS PRODUCED (141,630 UNITS)†	ACTUAL COSTS INCURRED	VARIANCE
125,000 units × 2.5 labor hours × $5.50 per hour = $1,718,750 ────────────→		$1,947,400 ──→	$228,650(U)
	141,630 units × 2.5 labor hours × $5.50 per hour = $1,947,412.50 ──────→	$1,947,400 ──→	$ 12.50(F)

* The original budget based on normal capacity is static because only the estimated production of 125,000 units was considered in preparing the labor cost budget. The original production estimate corresponds with normal capacity only by coincidence.
† The flexible budget based on actual volume is prepared at the end of an accounting period, when actual production volume is known. This budget indicates the labor costs that should have been incurred to produce 141,630 units of product.

output when evaluating performance. Assume that normal capacity for the Grisham Company is 125,000 units and that actual production was 141,630 units. The labor cost variance resulting from comparing standard costs based on normal capacity ($1,718,750) with actual costs ($1,947,400) is $228,650(U). Since the actual number of units produced was 141,630, actual labor costs should exceed the cost budget based on 125,000 units. Each product still requires 2½ labor hours at an average labor rate of $5.50 per labor hour; to manufacture 141,630 products, then, the cost should be $1,947,412.50 (141,630 × 2.5 × $5.50).

The flexible budget computation shows a favorable labor cost variance of $12.50 and generally indicates that labor costs were controlled properly during the period. The computations and explanatory notes in Exhibit 11-1 illustrate the basic concept of a flexible budget. In this case, a flexible budget was used to analyze labor costs. The most common use of flexible budgets is for factory overhead costs.

The preparation of a flexible budget for overhead costs uses the cost behavior patterns discussed in Chapters 9 and 10. As the number of units to be produced increases, total variable costs will increase proportionately. Total fixed costs will remain constant as long as production activity remains within the relevant range. A *relevant range* is an interval of activity levels within which total fixed costs will remain constant. If production volume exceeds the limits of a relevant range, total fixed costs will usually increase.

Exhibit 11-2 presents an example of a flexible budget for overhead costs. All semivariable, or mixed, costs have been separated into variable and fixed components. This flexible budget discloses estimated costs at four potential levels of output. In this example, capacity is measured in direct labor hours rather than units produced. Variable cost behavior is shown as follows:

VARIABLE COST	COST PER DIRECT LABOR HOUR
Indirect labor	$ .70
Supplies	3.00
Other variable costs	1.40
Variable cost per hour	$5.10

For every hour of direct labor worked, variable overhead costs will increase by $5.10.

Since all levels of capacity in Exhibit 11-2 are within the assumed relevant range, total fixed costs are shown to remain constant. Fixed and variable cost behavior in a flexible budget can be reduced to a formula that is useful for computing total overhead costs at different volume levels. Using direct labor hours as a basis, the *flexible budget formula* is constructed as follows:

$$\begin{array}{c}\text{total budgeted}\\ \text{overhead cost}\end{array} = \left(\begin{array}{c}\text{variable cost per}\\ \text{direct labor hour}\end{array} \times \begin{array}{c}\text{number of direct}\\ \text{labor hours}\end{array}\right) + \begin{array}{c}\text{budgeted fixed}\\ \text{overhead costs}\end{array}$$

The flexible budget formula for the example shown in Exhibit 11-2 is:

total budgeted overhead cost = ($5.10 × direct labor hours) + $12,000

Flexible budgets are useful in any situation related to cost control and performance evaluation. Operating performance evaluation begins by comparing actual costs with comparable budgeted costs. By applying the flexible budget formula to actual volume, a cost budget is prepared that is comparable to actual operating costs. This flexible budget information is essential if mean-

EXHIBIT 11-2
THE FLEXIBLE OVERHEAD BUDGET

MONA LISA JANSSON CLOTHING, INC.
Budgeted overhead costs
For month ending December 31, 19X7

	CAPACITIES (DIRECT LABOR HOURS)				COST PER HOUR
	3,000	4,000*	5,000	6,000	
Overhead costs:					
Variable:					
Indirect labor	$ 2,100	$ 2,800	$ 3,500	$ 4,200	$ .70
Supplies	9,000	12,000	15,000	18,000	3.00
Other variable costs	4,200	5,600	7,000	8,400	1.40
Total variable costs	$15,300	$20,400	$25,500	$30,600	$5.10
Fixed:					
Superintendent's salary	$ 3,000	$ 3,000	$ 3,000	$ 3,000	
Other fixed costs	9,000	9,000	9,000	9,000	
Total fixed costs	$12,000	$12,000	$12,000	$12,000	
Total budgeted overhead costs	$27,300	$32,400	$37,500	$42,600	

Flexible budget formula:
Total costs = ($5.10 × direct labor hours) + $12,000

* Assumed normal capacity level.

ingful conclusions are to be derived from comparisons of actual and budgeted costs.

To illustrate this concept, assume that Mona Lisa Jansson Clothing, Inc., had the following actual operating results for December 19X7:

Actual direct labor hours	4,750
Actual overhead costs:	
Variable:	
Indirect labor	$ 3,305
Supplies	14,450
Other	6,680
Fixed:	
Superintendent's salary	3,000
Other	9,000
Total overhead costs, December 19X7	$36,435

Which level of capacity in the flexible budget schedule in Exhibit 11-2 should be used to evaluate operating performance for December? Normal capacity is 4,000 direct labor hours (DLHs) but the 5,000 hours more closely correspond with actual labor hours for the month. The 5,000-hour budget could be used to approximate the costs that should be incurred at 4,750 hours. An alternative is to use the flexible budget formula to prepare a budget based on 4,750 actual hours.

	ACTUAL COST	BUDGET BASED ON ACTUAL DLHs	VARIANCE
Variable costs:			
Indirect labor	$ 3,305	$ 3,325 (4,750 × $ .70)	$ 20 (F)
Supplies	14,450	14,250 (4,750 × $3.00)	200 (U)
Other	6,680	6,650 (4,750 × $1.40)	30 (U)
Fixed costs:			
Superintendent's salary	3,000	3,000	–0–
Other	9,000	9,000	–0–
Total overhead costs	$36,435	$36,225	$210 (U)

Only by adjusting budgeted costs to correspond with actual capacity levels can meaningful comparisons be made with actual costs. In the above example, indirect labor was $20 under budget, while supplies and other variable overhead costs were over budget by $200 and $30 respectively.

The flexible budget is a useful tool to assist management in isolating areas of excessive cost incurrence within operating departments. However, the preceding example does not identify those managers responsible for the unfavorable cost variances. Variance computations are only the first step in evaluating operating performance. By combining the application of the flexible budget with standard cost variance analysis (discussed in Chapter 12), causes of cost variations—and those managers responsible for the causes—can be identified.

STANDARD COST DETERMINATION

Throughout the introductory pages of this chapter, standard costs have been used synonymously with planned or budgeted costs. This section will illustrate vividly that the development of standard costs is more rigorous than the formulation of budgeted or estimated costs. However, standard costs are excellent amounts to use in assembling corporate budgets and, used in this manner, have characteristics similar to those of estimated costs.

Estimated Costs Versus Standard Costs

The basic difference between an estimated cost and a standard cost is depth of analysis and amount of effort put forth to develop cost information. *Standard costs* are realistically predetermined costs. Standards are compiled from engineering specifications, time-and-motion studies, selected measures of plant capacity, and cost behavior analysis supporting flexible budgets. *Estimated costs* are derived from projections based on past trends of actual costs and generally involve averages of past cost performance. Estimated costs can be employed in much the same manner as standard costs. Since standards involve more operations analysis and comprehensive review of cost factors, they are more reliable measures for product costing, planning, and cost control purposes.

Behavioral Effects of Standards

A standard cost should be viewed as a target cost by managers who are responsible for each area of manufacturing operations. The operating objective is to achieve the standard performance target in terms of material usage and costs, labor time and costs, and overhead costs incurred to produce a given volume of products. Standard costs are carefully determined, but they are seldom precise measures since estimates are required in their computation. In evaluating operating performance of managers, standards should be considered a reasonable measure of desired performance. When actual costs are compared with related standards, variances should be expected. Significant or large variances pinpoint operating efficiencies or inefficiencies.

If standard costs are to be accepted as targets or cost performance goals, managers and employees must consider the standards reasonable and must be able to attain the standard performance levels. Standards that are not attainable will soon be recognized, and they will cease to inspire operating efficiency. Therefore, a successful standard cost system must include motivational considerations in the development of standard costs. All managers and employees should be advised of their specific areas of responsibility and take part in the development of related standards and budget targets. Basing standard costs upon motivational factors as well as upon efficient operating considerations will assist management in reaching the overall corporate objectives.

Types of Standard Costs

Standard costs generally are classified as ideal standards, basic standards, or currently attainable standards. Each type of standard cost is useful, but ideal standards and basic standards require certain adjustments before they are acceptable for performance evaluation and inventory valuation purposes.

Ideal standards Ideal standards (also called *theoretical* or *perfection standards*) allow minimum materials, labor time, and cost constraints for manufacturing each product. Performance equivalent to ideal standards is only rarely accomplished. Standards based on this maximum efficiency approach are effective only when operating personnel are made aware of this factor and are rewarded for performing at a percentage of standard, say 85 or 90 percent of standard.

As an example of ideal standards, assume that machine 707 can produce 600 units per hour, which is standard. U. Believit, operator of the machine is told by the supervisor that the target is to average 540 units per hour, even though the ideal standard is 600 units per hour. By adjusting ideal standards downward, realistic operating goals can be communicated to employees in order to promote employee motivation. Ideal standards are based on theoretical capacity and represent minimum unit costs of production.

Basic standards   Basic standards seldom are revised or updated to reflect current operating costs and price level changes. *Basic standards* are used primarily to measure trends in operating performance. Although useful, basic standards also must be adjusted before they can be used for performance evaluation purposes. Basic standards are characterized by their infrequent revision. They can be based upon any desired capacity level that is selected initially to formulate the standards.

Currently attainable standards   Standard costs that are updated periodically to reflect changes in operating conditions and current price levels for materials, labor, and overhead costs are called *currently attainable standards.* Unlike ideal standards, currently attainable standards measure reasonable performance under average operating conditions assuming normal efficiency. Under these conditions, labor standards include allowances for recurring machine downtime and work stoppages by employees. Material standards are based on current market prices and include allowances for normal scrap and spoilage losses.

Currently attainable standards are acceptable for product costing, performance evaluation, planning, and employee motivation. Unless otherwise indicated, the remaining illustrations and problems in this text assume the use of currently attainable standards. Currently attainable standards also yield inventory valuations that closely approximate actual unit costs and are acceptable for external financial reporting purposes.

In the following illustration, currently attainable standard costs are developed for a specific product. The resulting standard cost per unit includes separate measures of standard material costs, standard labor costs, and standard overhead costs.

Material, Labor, and Overhead Standards

Standard material cost   The standard material cost per unit of finished product is computed by multiplying the standard price of raw material inputs times the standard quantity of raw materials used. *Standard material cost* per unit includes *material price standards* and *material quantity standards.* To illustrate, assume that in the manufacturing of a filing cabinet, the Fancy Furniture Company has developed the currently attainable standard material costs shown in Exhibit 11-3. Standard material cost for a filing cabinet consists of five material quantity standards and five material price standards. For filing cabinet 4H-51974, standard material cost is computed as follows:

MATERIAL	STANDARD QUANTITY	STANDARD PRICE	COST PER CABINET
Sheet steel	5 sheets	at $5.00/sheet	$25.00
Handles	2 handles	at $2.00/pair	2.00
Rollers	8 rollers	at $ .75/pair	3.00
Guides	4 guides	at $3.00/pair	6.00
Paint	1 pint	at $6.00/gallon	.75
Standard material cost per cabinet			$36.75

Standard labor cost Standard labor cost per unit of finished product is determined by multiplying standard labor time by standard labor rate. A *labor time standard* is the labor time required to produce a unit of product. A *labor rate standard* is the standard dollar-per-hour rate paid for various labor operations.

For Fancy Furniture Company, assume that filing cabinet 4H-51974 requires the labor operations listed on the following page.

EXHIBIT 11-3
STANDARD MATERIAL COSTS

The Fancy Furniture Company
Filing cabinet #4H-51974

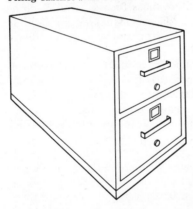

RAW MATERIAL REQUIREMENTS AT STANDARD:

Required raw materials	Material quantity standards	Material price standards
4′ × 5′ sheets (12 gauge steel)	5	$5.00/sheet
Drawer handles	2	$2.00/pair
Drawer rollers	8	$ .75/pair
Drawer guides	4	$3.00/pair
Paint	1 pint	$6.00/gallon

Sheet metal stamping operator	.5 hour	at $4.50/hour	$2.25
Cabinet assembly worker	1.2 hours	at $4.00/hour	4.80
Painting	.1 hour	at $6.00/hour	.60
Standard labor cost per cabinet			$7.65

Each cabinet requires labor operations in the Stamping Department, the Assembly Department, and the Painting Department. Standard labor hours for each operation are multiplied by standard labor rates to determine standard labor cost per cabinet of $7.65.

Standard overhead cost Standard overhead cost per unit is not broken down into the various elements of manufacturing overhead cost. Standard overhead cost per unit is computed using predetermined overhead rates similar to the illustrations in Chapter 5. Since overhead costs cannot be traced directly to specific products, these costs are allocated to units by using standard overhead rates. When cost behavior analysis is used to separate overhead costs into fixed and variable costs, a standard overhead rate is computed for each cost category. Multiplying the *standard variable overhead rate* and *standard fixed overhead rate* by a predetermined allocation basis (such as direct labor cost, direct labor hours, or units of output) will yield the *standard overhead cost* of finished products.

The Fancy Furniture Company employs the following set of standard variable and fixed overhead rates based on direct labor hours (DLH):

	VARIABLE +	FIXED =	ABSORPTION COSTING OVERHEAD RATE
Stamping department	$2/DLH	$5/DLH	$7/DLH
Assembly department	$3/DLH	$1/DLH	$4/DLH
Painting department	$1/DLH	$1/DLH	$2/DLH

Standard overhead cost per unit involves the following calculations:

	STANDARD DLH	STANDARD OVERHEAD RATE	STANDARD COST
Stamping department	.5 hour	at $7/DLH	$3.50
Assembly department	1.2 hours	at $4/DLH	4.80
Painting department	.1 hour	at $2/DLH	.20
Standard overhead cost per cabinet			$8.50

Standard cost per product The standard cost per unit of finished product is the sum of the standard unit costs computed for standard material costs, standard labor costs, and standard overhead costs. In the Fancy Furniture Company example, the standard cost of filing cabinet 4H-51974 is:

Standard material cost	$36.75
Standard labor cost	7.65
Standard overhead cost	8.50
Total standard cost per cabinet	$52.90

The standard unit cost of $52.90 is used to value inventories of Finished Goods and Work in Process and to evaluate the efficiency of production operations.

Developing Standard Costs

Procedures for developing standard costs differ among companies, but certain technical aspects are common to most approaches. As illustrated in the Fancy Furniture Company example, standard cost per unit of product is a function of several elements:

> Material price standard(s)
> Material quantity standard(s)
> Labor time standard(s)
> Labor rate standard(s)
> Standard variable overhead rate(s)
> Standard fixed overhead rate(s)

The development process for these standards requires information from several functional areas of a company. The cost accounting department must determine the various informational needs, coordinate the processing of required information, and compute standard unit costs for each product. Procedures used to develop the component standards listed above are discussed in the following paragraphs.

Material price standards   To be currently attainable, material price standards must reflect current market prices. Standards are predetermined costs or predictions of costs that will be incurred in future time periods. Since raw material prices are subject to sudden change, current material price standards are often established at a level that anticipates price increases. The company's purchasing agent is responsible for providing information used in setting material price standards. The price standard for each raw material should reflect expected unit purchase prices during the next twelve-month period. If actual and standard material prices differ during the year, the purchasing agent is held accountable for explaining the causes of such variances.

Material quantity standards   Material usage depends on factors such as machines used, quality and experience of workers, and types and quality of basic raw materials. Old equipment, inexperienced workers, and inferior grades of materials tend to produce larger amounts of scrap and spoilage, which increase total raw material usage. In developing material quantity standards, all these factors are considered. The primary responsibility for developing material quantity standards is assigned to the production superintendent, various departmental supervisors, and production engineers. By considering the views of experts in all areas related to raw materials usage, quantity standards can be developed that incorporate expected losses from anticipated, or "normal," spoilage and machine failure. The objective is to establish currently attainable quantity standards that express expected normal usage of raw materials.

Labor time standards   Like material quantity standards, labor time standards are developed from information received from several sources. A *labor time standard* is a realistic estimate of the labor time required to complete each specific phase in manufacturing a product. In the Fancy Furniture Company example, the stamping operation requires one-half standard hour of direct labor. This time standard is based on the hourly capacity of stamping machines in use and the average skill of machine operators. The machine can produce a specific number of filing cabinet housings per hour, but actual time required per unit of output is affected by the skill of production personnel and machine operators. The skill and efficiency of machine operators can be measured by *time-and-motion study* procedures, in which manufacturing operations are timed by taking samples of work effort from several employees at varying times and under different work conditions; then, using average production time figures, currently attainable time standards are established that indicate the processing time which should be required to produce one unit of product.

Labor rate standards   Pay rates vary according to employees' skills, experience, and seniority. In addition, labor union contracts often state specific pay rates for each job category in a company. If labor contracts are in force, labor rate standards are obtained from union wage schedules. If the company is not under a labor union contract, average hourly pay rates should be computed for each labor operation required to manufacture a product. *Labor rate standards* express the estimated hourly labor cost expected to prevail during the next twelve-month period.

Standard overhead rates   Standard variable and fixed overhead rates are developed from a schedule of budgeted or planned manufacturing overhead costs for an accounting period. The standard variable overhead rate is the sum of all unit variable cost components in this budget. If a breakdown of the variable cost components is not available, the standard variable overhead rate can be computed as follows:

$$\frac{\text{standard variable}}{\text{overhead rate (SRv)}} = \frac{\text{total budgeted variable overhead costs}}{\text{application base}}$$

As discussed in Chapter 5, several different application bases are available for use. Direct labor hours was used in the Fancy Furniture Company example. The standard variable overhead rate is also the unit variable cost factor used in the flexible budget formula described earlier in this chapter.

A specific capacity level must be selected to compute the standard fixed overhead rate. Since the fixed rate will be different as capacity is increased or decreased, one measure of capacity must be selected to serve as the goal of annual production. Normal capacity is a good measure because it represents average annual capacity utilization expected during the next three- to five-year period. Expected annual capacity is also a satisfactory measure. Once a capacity measure has been determined and total anticipated fixed overhead costs are known, the standard fixed overhead rate used in absorption costing is computed as follows:

$$\frac{\text{standard fixed}}{\text{overhead rate (SRf)}} = \frac{\text{total budgeted fixed overhead costs}}{\text{normal or expected annual capacity}}$$

Updating and Maintaining Standards	Currently attainable standards will not remain currently attainable unless they are reviewed and updated periodically. Changing prices, new personnel, new machinery, changing quality of raw materials, and new labor contracts all tend to make currently attainable standards obsolete. Obsolete standards lead to unrealistic budgets, poor cost control, and unreasonable unit costs for inventory valuation.

To prevent standards from becoming obsolete, a company should install a program designed to update standards and to maintain them at currently attainable levels. If labor rates are increased, then labor rate standards should be adjusted immediately. If a new, more efficient piece of machinery is purchased to replace a relatively inefficient machine, labor time standards and material quantity standards should be updated. In addition to these obvious adjustments, a system for revising standard costs should require that every standard be analyzed for adequacy at least once a year. With this type of annual review system, standards always will approximate currently attainable levels.

STANDARD COST ACCOUNTING SYSTEMS	Like cost-volume-profit analyses and direct costing, standard costing is a useful tool for management planning and control. Standard costs also are useful for product cost accounting purposes, but standard costing alone does not constitute a complete cost accounting system. Standard costing is a *feature* that can be added to an existing cost accounting system. For this reason, a standard costing system is either a standard job order cost system or a standard process cost system. With the addition of a standard costing feature, the traditional cost accounting systems become more effective for planning, control, and product costing purposes.

Accounts Affected by Standard Costing	In a standard job order system or a standard process cost system, product unit costs are expressed in terms of standard cost. The cost attachment process involves only standard material, standard labor, and standard overhead costs. For example, each filing cabinet 4H-51974 produced by the Fancy Furniture Company will be accounted for at $52.90, its total standard cost per unit. As a result, general ledger accounts for Raw Materials inventory, Work in Process inventory, Finished Goods inventory, and Cost of Goods Sold will be stated at standard cost rather than at actual cost. The Raw Materials inventory account is stated at standard prices of the raw material items on hand at the end of the accounting period.

Since a company incurs actual costs during an accounting period but records inventory transactions at standard cost, procedures must be established to account for differences between actual and standard costs. Such differences are recognized as standard cost variances, and separate ledger accounts are used for each type of variance. In the remaining portions of this chapter, specific variances are identified with illustrative journal entries used in a standard cost system, but detailed analysis of each variance is not shown. Analysis of these variances is the subject of Chapter 12.

Standard costs can be recognized in general ledger accounts and integrated into an existing cost accounting system. Standard costs and related variances also can be analyzed by worksheet procedures that are not part of a company's general ledger system. Although the worksheet approach is found in practice and does not hinder the effectiveness of standards in cost planning and control activities, emphasis in this text is placed upon integrating standard cost data into the general ledger cost accounting system.

Even though a company employs a standard cost system and records inventory transactions at standard cost, actual production costs still must be recorded in the general ledger. Raw materials are purchased at actual prices; employees are paid actual wages; and many actual overhead costs are recorded by credits to Cash and to Accounts Payable. Journal entries for these transactions follow the illustrations of cost accounting presented in Chapters 5 and 6. Standard costing, however, requires certain specialized documentation and recording techniques. Exhibit 11-4 depicts the general cost flow pattern in a standard cost accounting system. The cost flow diagram is general in nature and could represent either a job order or process cost system.

Recording Transactions at Standard Cost

EXHIBIT 11-4

COST FLOW PATTERN—STANDARD COST SYSTEM

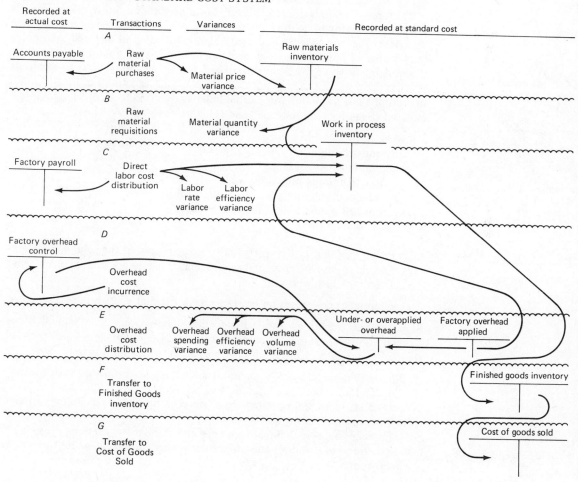

Accounting for materials Raw materials are purchased from suppliers at actual cost, which is actual quantity times actual price per unit. This amount is credited to Accounts Payable and represents the actual liability of the company. The debit to Raw Materials inventory for purchases is recorded at standard cost, which is actual quantity received times standard price per unit. Any difference between actual cost and standard cost is recorded in a Material Price Variance account. The following entry illustrates the recording of this transaction, which corresponds to transaction A in Exhibit 11-4:

Raw materials inventory (at standard)	$XXXX	
Material price variance	XX	
Accounts payable (at actual)		$XXXX
To record purchase of raw materials		

Material inventory records are maintained at standard prices, while all other documents relating to the purchase of raw materials reflect actual costs. The debit to Materials Price Variance means an unfavorable variance has been incurred. If standard costs had exceeded actual costs, the variance account would have been credited to record a favorable variance.

When raw materials are requisitioned into production, the Work in Process inventory account is debited for the standard cost of materials used. If raw materials usage exceeds the standard quantity of materials allowed to produce the number of good units produced during the period, then an unfavorable material quantity variance is recognized in the accounts. Excess materials usage is recorded in the Material Quantity Variance account. For transaction B in Exhibit 11-4, the following journal entry is required to record the total raw material usage for a period:

Work in process inventory (standard quantity × standard price)	$XXXX	
Material quantity variance	XXX	
Raw materials inventory (actual quantity used × standard price)		$XXXX
To record requisition of raw materials into production		

Accounting for labor costs Direct labor costs represent the total actual earnings of workers who are classified as direct labor personnel. Actual direct labor cost is computed as follows:

actual labor cost = actual hours worked × actual wage rate per hour

Standard cost variances applicable to labor costs occur if (1) actual hours worked differ from standard hours allowed or (2) actual wage rates differ from standard wage rates. Note the following points in relation to labor costs:

1. *Standard hours allowed* is the number of good units produced multiplied by the standard labor hours per unit of product. If actual direct labor hours exceed standard hours allowed, an unfavorable *labor efficiency variance* will be recognized in the accounts.
2. Differences between actual wage rates and standard wage rates cause *labor rate variances*. If actual rates are greater than standard rates, the variance is unfavorable.

To maintain the Work in Process inventory account at standard cost, standard direct labor cost must be debited to the Work in Process account. Standard labor cost is standard hours allowed times standard labor rates. For transaction C in Exhibit 11-4, the following entry is required to record standard labor cost and actual payroll liability for the period:

Work in process inventory
   (standard hours allowed × standard labor rate) $XXXXX
Labor rate variance   XXX
Labor efficiency variance   XXX
     Factory payroll (actual hours × actual labor rate) $XXXX
     To record standard labor cost and actual payroll

All documents relating to employee earnings are updated using actual costs, while job order cost sheets and departmental cost of production reports reflect standard costs.

Accounting for overhead costs   Manufacturing overhead costs in a standard cost system are accounted for in a manner similar to any system using predetermined overhead rates. Transactions D and E in Exhibit 11-4 illustrate this point. Actual overhead costs incurred are debited to Factory Overhead Control. Overhead is applied to Work in Process inventory as follows:

Work in process inventory $XXXX
   Factory overhead applied $XXXX
   To apply overhead costs to goods in process

Instead of using one, all-inclusive predetermined overhead rate, however, standard variable and fixed overhead rates are used. The difference between Factory Overhead Control and Factory Overhead Applied is the amount of underapplied or overapplied factory overhead for the period.

In a standard cost system, the underapplied or overapplied balance is analyzed, and three standard cost variances are recorded in the accounts. The three overhead variances are *overhead spending variance*, *overhead efficiency variance*, and *overhead volume variance*. The following entries are used to record these variances:

1. Factory overhead applied (standard cost) $XXXX
  Underapplied overhead   XXX
     Factory overhead control (actual costs) $XXXX
     To close overhead control and applied accounts
     and to recognize underapplied overhead
2. Overhead spending variance $XX
  Overhead efficiency variance   XX
  Overhead volume variance   XX
     Underapplied overhead $XXX
     To transfer underapplied overhead account
     balance to variance accounts

Determination of each overhead variance is discussed in Chapter 12. For general ledger accounting purposes, the following journal entry can be used to accomplish the same results as entries 1 and 2 above:

Factory overhead applied	$XXXX	
Overhead spending variance	XX	
Overhead efficiency variance	XX	
Overhead volume variance	XX	
Factory overhead control		$XXXX
To close overhead control and		
applied accounts and		
record overhead variances		

All standard cost variances in this chapter are shown by debit balances because variances were assumed to be unfavorable. Favorable standard cost variances have credit balances.

Inventories and Cost of Goods Sold

All cost amounts debited or credited to the Work in Process account are standard costs. As units are completed and transferred to Finished Goods inventory, the entry to record this transfer is also based on standard costs of the completed units. The related flow of standard costs is shown in transaction F of Exhibit 11-4. Consistent with the standard cost valuation of Finished Goods inventory, the cost of units sold is recognized by transferring standard cost amounts from Finished Goods inventory to Cost of Goods Sold.

FINAL NOTE

The following points summarize the principal advantages of a standard cost system used for planning, control, and product costing purposes:

1. Setting standards requires a thorough analysis of all cost functions and often discloses inefficiencies.
2. Standard cost information is more useful than historical cost for product costing and pricing purposes.
3. Standard cost variances facilitate control through the management by exception principle.
4. Standard costs are the basis of an effective budgetary control system.
5. Speed of recording regular operating data is increased.
6. Clearly defined lines of cost responsibility and authority are established by a standard cost system.
7. The setting of standards forces management to plan efficient operations.
8. Performance evaluation is enhanced through variance analysis.

There are also certain limitations regarding standard cost systems. The use of standard costing is not always practical for every company, because a standard cost system is very costly to develop. In addition, maintenance and updating requirements continue to be costly. Before making the decision to install a standard cost system, management should conduct some type of cost-benefit analysis. If the potential benefits exceed the costs, then standard costing should be introduced into the cost accounting system.

Return now to the beginning of the chapter and review the highlights section before proceeding to the review questions, exercises, and problems.

11-1. Define and illustrate the following terms and concepts:
- a. Standard cost
- b. Estimated cost
- c. Flexible budget
- d. Budgetary control
- e. Theoretical capacity
- f. Normal capacity
- g. Practical capacity
- h. Expected annual capacity
- i. Idle capacity
- j. Excess capacity
- k. Ideal standards
- l. Basic standards
- m. Currently attainable standards
- n. Standard cost variance
- o. Material price standard
- p. Material quantity standard
- q. Labor time standard
- r. Labor rate standard
- s. Favorable standard cost variance
- t. Standard hours allowed

11-2. What are the primary objectives of budgetary control?

11-3. Identify the role of standard costs in the budgetary control process.

11-4. Discuss briefly the use of standard costs in the following management activities: cost reduction, operating performance evaluation, product pricing decisions, and compiling operating budgets.

11-5. Why is the measurement of plant capacity an important consideration in the planning and control functions of management?

11-6. In selecting a measure of capacity, why is it important to distinguish between what can be produced and what will be produced?

11-7. What are the comparative advantages and disadvantages of basing standard costs upon theoretical capacity? Upon practical capacity? Upon normal capacity? Upon expected annual capacity?

11-8. "Idle capacity may be an integral part of normal capacity, but excess capacity is not." Explain this statement.

11-9. What is the difference between a static budget and a flexible budget?

11-10. State the flexible budget formula and discuss its relevance to performance measurement.

11-11. What is the role of normal capacity in determining standard overhead rates?

11-12. Why is it unrealistic to compare standard costs based upon one level of activity with actual costs incurred at a different level of activity?

11-13. "Cost behavior information is an integral part in the formulation of flexible budgets." Discuss the meaning of this statement.

11-14. How are motivational considerations important in the development of standard costs?

11-15. Compare and contrast the usefulness of ideal standards, basic standards, and currently attainable standards.

EXERCISES

11-16. *Standard Unit Cost*   Hedges Enterprises, Inc., produces desk chairs. All parts are purchased and assembled by their Thomasville plant. Standard labor cost for assembling five chairs is $18.00 (two people at $4.00/hour and two at $5.00/hour). For the current year, the standard variable overhead rate is $5.50 per direct labor hour, and the standard fixed overhead rate is $7.75 per DLH. A summary of required purchased parts follows:

PARTS PER CHAIR	STANDARD PURCHASE PRICES
1 chair housing	1,000-unit lots at $15,000 per lot
1 seat cushion	500-unit lots at $1,725 per lot
1 back cushion	500-unit lots at $950 per lot
2 arm cushions	1,000-unit lots at $750 per lot
1 base	100-unit lots at $825 per lot
4 rollers	1,000-unit lots at $250 per lot
1 raise-lower mechanism	100-unit lots at $1,375 per lot

REQUIRED: Compute the standard cost to manufacture one chair.

11-17. *Flexible Budgeting Exercise*   Mike Chrishank, controller of the Under-Par Corporation, has just prepared the following flexible budget for next month:

LEVELS OF DIRECT LABOR ACTIVITY	VARIABLE OVERHEAD EXPENSES	FIXED OVERHEAD EXPENSES	TOTAL EXPENSES
4,000 DLHs	$1,080	$3,440	$4,520
5,000 DLHs	1,350	3,440	4,790
6,000 DLHs	1,620	3,440	5,060
7,000 DLHs	1,890	3,440	5,330
8,000 DLHs	2,160	3,440	5,600
9,000 DLHs	2,430	3,440	5,870

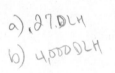

REQUIRED:

a. What did Mr. Chrishank use as a variable overhead rate per DLH?
b. What would the normal capacity be if the:
1. Fixed overhead rate equals $.43/DLH?
2. Total overhead rate is $1.13/DLH?

11-18. *Journal Entries—Standard Costing*   Isolated transactions of the Hundra Kronor Corporation for August 19X8 are listed below. The company uses a standard job order costing system.

August 6:   Purchased raw materials:
         Actual cost $13,450
         Standard cost   14,500

August 9:   Requisitioned a total of $7,500 of raw material from inventory into production. An analysis of standard quantities required indicated that $400 worth of excess materials were requisitioned and spoiled.

August 12: Paid factory wages and salaries and credited Factory Payroll account for $17,650. An analysis of factory wages disclosed the following:

         Labor rate variance $750(U)
         Labor efficiency variance $350(F)

REQUIRED: Prepare journal entries to record the above transactions.

11-19. *Standard Material Cost Determination*   L. Lightbody, comptroller of the Rational Scale Company, is in the process of establishing material cost standards for 19X7 production. In the past, scale casings have been made of sheet steel. Plans for 19X7 are to switch to an aluminum casing. Sheet aluminum will have to be purchased from three different suppliers. Supplier A will supply 40 percent of the required amount in 19X7 at $6.30 per sheet; supplier B will supply 30 percent at $6.50 per sheet; and supplier C will supply 30 percent at $7.00 per sheet.

Past experience has shown that for every 1,000 scale casings produced, 150 sheets of steel were used. Under ideal production conditions, eight steel casings can be formed from one sheet of steel. This 8 to 1 ratio will also be possible using sheet aluminum instead of sheet steel. One reason for switching to aluminum is to cut the amount of normal spoilage and scrap. Using aluminum, Lightbody anticipates that 135 sheets of aluminum will be required to produce 1,000 scale casings.

REQUIRED:
a. Compute the material price standard per sheet of aluminum and material quantity standard per scale casing for 19X7.
b. What will be the standard material cost of 100 scale casings in 19X7?

11-20. *Keeping Standards Current*   Packard Paper Company recently installed a complete standard process cost accounting system. Mr. N. A. Always, controller of the Rockford Division, is now concerned with keeping cost standards on a current basis. He is thinking about establishing a standards maintenance system and has asked Mr. I. M. Next, assistant controller, to take charge of the project and to develop a tentative outline of the system.

REQUIRED: List the suggested policies, procedures, and people that Mr. Next should include in his analysis.

11-21. Flexible Budget Formulation   Reeves Production Company is developing flexible budgets for each department as part of its plan to use standard costs. Normal monthly volume in the Milling Department is 50,000 direct labor hours. At normal volume, departmental fixed costs include $80,000 for power and $50,000 for maintenance. Allocated fixed costs from service departments are $70,000 per month. Indirect labor cost at normal volume is $125,000 which involves 25,000 hours of indirect labor at $5 per hour. Other variable costs in the Milling Department are:

Tools and supplies	$2.00 per machine hour
Maintenance	$1.40 per machine hour
Power	$3.20 per machine hour
Depreciation	$4.60 per machine hour

Normal volume is 30,000 machine hours per month. The company uses a service hours method to depreciate fixed assets.

REQUIRED:
a. Prepare a departmental flexible overhead budget for 25,000 machine hours and for 30,000 machine hours.
b. Justify your treatment of depreciation expense as a variable or fixed cost.
c. Should the flexible budget be based on direct labor hours if this measure will be used for overhead rates?

11-22. Standard Material Cost   Brown Paper Products produces a diverse line of paper products, including unprinted super-cushion egg cartons. The cartons are sold to independent egg wholesalers. Jute paper for the cartons is purchased from an outside supplier. The current supplier price for paper is $120 per 1,000 square feet (MSF), subject to a $10 quantity discount if purchased in lots over 100,000 MSF. Brown purchases f.o.b. shipper, subject to 3 percent cash discounts when paid within ten days of the invoice date. Normal freight charges on 100,000 MSF lots are $150. Brown currently purchases egg carton paper in lots of 200,000 MSF. Average production patterns yield three egg cartons per square foot of paper. Cartons are inventoried and sold by the thousand.

REQUIRED: Determine the standard material cost per 1,000 egg cartons. Present supporting analyses for standard price and quantity computations.

11-23. Standard Labor Cost   A principal product at B. J. Manufacturing Company is aluminum shelf material. Shelf forms are cut from molded sheets of metal, then trimmed and inspected. In the Molding Department, aluminum sheets are fed by hand into a molding machine that creases the standard shelf dimensions into the metal. This operation is mechanical and requires one hour of labor time per 500 good sheets. Normal spoilage, which is determined by machine rejects, averages 5 percent of good production. Thus, labor time is spent on units that are scrapped. All workers in molding are paid five dollars per hour.

In the Cutting Department, molded forms are cut, trimmed, and inspected. These highly skilled operations are subject to variation in time, but the average time to complete all three phases is five minutes per sheet. The average wage rate in cutting is eight dollars per hour.

REQUIRED: Determine the total standard labor cost per 1,000 shelves using currently attainable standards. *$677.20*

11-24. *Flexible Budget Analysis*   The following cost behavior data have been developed for the Machining Department of Jones Company:

OVERHEAD ELEMENT	COST BEHAVIOR	FIXED COST PER MONTH	VARIABLE COST PER DIRECT LABOR HOUR
Machine supplies	Variable	—	$6.00
Maintenance	Mixed	$2,000	.25
Depreciation	Fixed	4,000	—
		$6,000	$6.25

During August 19X4, the department worked 12,000 direct labor hours with actual overhead costs as stated below:

Machine supplies	$78,000
Maintenance	3,000
Depreciation	4,000
Actual overhead, August	$85,000

REQUIRED:
a. Express the monthly departmental overhead cost behavior in terms of a flexible budget formula.
b. Compare actual total overhead with the total overhead that should have been incurred during August, given 12,000 actual direct labor hours.
c. Compare each individual cost for August with the total that should have been incurred at 12,000 direct labor hours.
d. Is comparison (b) or (c) more relevant for cost control? Why?

11-25. *CPA Examination Theory Question—Standard Costing*   Standard costing procedures are used widely in manufacturing operations and, more recently, have become common in many nonmanufacturing operations.

REQUIRED:
a. What are the advantages of a standard cost system?
b. Present arguments in support of the following three methods of treating standard cost variances for purposes of financial reporting:
   1. They may be carried as deferred charges or credits on the balance sheet.
   2. They may appear as charges or credits on the income statement.
   3. They may be allocated between inventories and Cost of Goods sold.

(AICPA adapted)

11-26. *CMA Examination Question—Standard Costing and Employee Behavior* Atlas Company is expanding its Punch Press Department and wants to purchase three new punch presses from Equipment Manufacturers, Inc. Equipment Manufacturers' engineers made mechanical studies and indicate that, for Atlas's intended use, the output rate for one press should be 1,000 pieces per hour. Atlas has similar presses now in operation. At present, production from these presses averages 600 pieces per hour.

A study of the Atlas experience shows the average is derived from the following individual outputs:

WORKER	DAILY OUTPUT
L. Jones	750
J. Green	750
R. Smith	600
H. Brown	500
R. Alters	550
G. Hoag	450
Total	3,600
Average	600

Atlas management also plans to institute a standard cost accounting system in the near future. Company engineers are supporting a standard based upon 1,000 pieces per hour; the Accounting Department is arguing for 750 pieces per hour; and the department supervisor is suggesting 600 pieces per hour.

REQUIRED:

a. What argument is each proponent likely to offer to support his case?
b. Which alternative best reconciles the needs of cost control and the motivation of improved performance? Why?

(IMA adapted)

PROBLEMS

11-27. *Standard Cost per Unit* Three production departments are used by the Pleasant Toiletries Company to produce Beast, a leading men's aftershave lotion. The product requires processing in the Blending, Cooling, and Bottling departments, in that order. The following data were used to established standard materials, labor, and overhead costs for each 4-ounce unit of Beast:

RAW MATERIALS	PURCHASE QUANTITIES AND PRICES	NORMAL EVAPORATION LOSS
Sweet water	10,000 gallons at $40.00/100 gallons	20%
Herbs and spices	1,500 pounds at $180.00/100 pounds	
Bottles	1,000 bottles at $.80/bottle	

Note: Average batch size is 1,000 gallons before evaporation; 500 pounds of herbs and spices are added to each 1,000-gallon batch.

LABOR	BLENDING	COOLING	BOTTLING
Standard time per batch in each department	7 hours	2 hours	12 hours
Number of direct labor workers required per batch	2	1	4
Standard wage rate per hour	$3.40	$3.25	$3.30

$47.60 + 6.50 + $158.40 = $212.50

Manufacturing Overhead (plantwide rates):
   Standard variable overhead rate $3.46 per direct labor dollar = 735.25
   Standard fixed overhead rate   212.50× $5.94 per direct labor dollar = 1262.25

$1997.50

REQUIRED: Compute the standard production cost of:
a. One batch of Beast — TOTAL std cost $23,990
b. One 4-ounce bottle of Beast $.9371 per bottle
   (Note: 1 gallon = 128 ounces.) 32 bottles per gal.

11-28. *CPA Examination Theory Question—Standard Costing and Pricing*
   L. T. Company, the manufacturer of a single product, operated at 80 percent of normal capacity in 19X5. Since the company bases its overhead rate on normal capacity, it had a substantial amount of underapplied overhead for the period.
   Early in 19X6, L. T. Company receives an order for a substantial number of units at 30 percent off the regular $7.00 sales price. The controller wants to accept the order because $.80 of the total manufacturing cost of $5.00 per unit is fixed overhead and because the additional units can be produced within the company's practical capacity.
   The president of L. T. Company wants to know if you agree with the controller.

REQUIRED:
a. Differentiate among theoretical capacity, practical capacity, normal capacity, and expected capacity.
b. Discuss the financial considerations that the president should review before accepting or rejecting the order.
c. The financial statements of L. T. Company as of December 31, 19X6, are likely to show overapplied overhead.
   1. What is overapplied overhead?

2. What are likely to be the major causes of overapplied overhead in 19X6?

3. How, if at all, should overapplied overhead be treated in the financial statements as of December 31, 19X6?

(AICPA adapted)

11-29. *Flexible Budget—Performance Evaluation* Copeland Glassware Company manufactures a complete line of kitchen glassware items. The Denton Division specializes in 12-ounce drinking glasses. Mr. U. B. Careful, superintendent of the Denton Division, has asked the controller to prepare a performance report for April 19X9. The following analysis was handed to him a few days later:

COST CLASSIFICATION	BUDGET*	ACTUAL COSTS INCURRED DURING APRIL	VARIANCE
Raw materials (variable)	$ 5,000	$ 4,475	$ 525(F)
Direct labor (variable)	6,000	5,350	650(F)
Indirect labor (variable)	1,500	1,290	210(F)
Supplies (variable)	1,000	960	40(F)
Heat and power (30% variable)	5,000	4,825	175(F)
Other variable costs	2,500	2,340	160(F)
Depreciation (fixed)	4,200	4,200	–0–
Insurance and taxes (fixed)	1,200	1,200	–0–
Other fixed costs	1,600	1,600	–0–
Totals	$28,000	$26,240	$1,760(F)

* Based on normal capacity of 50,000 units.

Mr. Careful questioned the controller on the report, stating: "Profits have been decreasing in recent months but this report indicates that our production process is operating efficiently."

REQUIRED:

a. Prepare a flexible budget for the Denton Division using capacity levels of 40,000 units; 45,000 units; 50,000 units; and 55,000 units.

b. What is the flexible budget formula?

c. Assume the Denton Division produced 42,560 units in April. Prepare a revised performance report using actual capacity as a basis.

d. Which comparison is more meaningful for performance evaluation? Why?

11-30. *Standard Cost Formulation* Castro Company has developed material, labor, and overhead standards for its principal product, Quanto. Each unit of Quanto requires input of materials A and B plus cutting and polishing operations. Standards per unit of Quanto have been developed as follows:

MATERIALS	POUNDS	PRICE/LB.	LABOR	HOURS	RATE
A	5	$4	Cut	3	$5
B	8	$2	Polish	2	$6

Predetermined overhead rates were established at $11.50 per direct labor hour and are considered adequate for standard cost purposes.

REQUIRED:

a. Prepare a standard cost summary for one unit of Quanto.
b. If 8,000 good units of Quanto are produced during a period, what is the standard quantity allowed for material usage? What are the standard hours allowed for labor time?
c. Assume that 10,000 units of Quanto are produced during a period when the actual overhead incurred is $600,000. Determine the amount of under- or overapplied factory overhead.

11-31. *Standard Process Costing* Stonoker, Inc., uses standard absorption process costing for its east Texas plant, which manufactures a special chemical product. The standard cost per unit of finished product is:

Direct materials (4 gallons at $2.50)	$10.00
Direct labor (6 hours at $4.00)	24.00
Factory overhead (6 hours at $5.00)	30.00
Unit standard cost (4-gallon container)	$64.00

All raw materials are introduced at the start of processing, and the company uses average costing for all inventories. During April 19X3, the Processing Department transferred 300,000 units to finished goods. Work in Process inventories at the start and end of April were 20,000 and 60,000 gallons, respectively. In computing equivalent production, partly processed units are considered 50 percent complete for conversion cost purposes. Actual production costs in April were: materials—$3,400,000 at standard prices charged to Work in Process; labor—$9,700,000 at standard labor rates charged to Work in Process.

REQUIRED:

a. Prepare quantity and equivalent production schedules for April production activity.
b. Prepare a schedule that evaluates the relative efficiency of materials and labor usage.

11-32. *Standard Costs and Financial Statements* Watkins Company uses a standard absorption costing system at its plant that produces Poly-X. The standard unit cost of Poly-X is $18, consisting of the following elements:

Direct material	$ 8
Direct labor	2
Variable overhead	5
Fixed overhead	3
Standard unit cost	$18

The fixed overhead element is based on $90,000 of annual budgeted overhead and normal volume of 30,000 units. For 19X5, the company plans to produce 24,000 units and sell 20,000. The planned initial inventory is 2,000 units. Watkins Company sells the product for $30 per unit. Annual fixed costs for selling and administrative functions are $100,000. Based upon 19X4 and past experience, company management estimates that unfavorable standard cost variances for variable cost elements will amount to $11,000 in 19X5. Inventories in financial statements are valued at standard cost.

REQUIRED:
a. For 19X5 projected operations, prepare a schedule for Cost of Goods Manufactured and Sold.
b. Determine the expected amount of under- or overapplied fixed overhead for 19X5.
c. Prepare a budgeted income statement for 19X5.

11-33. *CPA Examination Theory Question—Causes of Variances* Taggson Company has a contract with a labor union that guarantees a minimum wage of $500 per month to each direct labor employee having at least twelve years of service. One hundred employees currently qualify for coverage. All direct labor employees are paid $5 per hour.

The direct labor budget for 19X0 was based on the annual usage of 400,000 hours of direct labor times $5, or a total of $2,000,000. Of this amount, $50,000 (100 employees × $500) per month (or $600,000 for the year) was regarded as fixed. Thus the budget for any given month was determined by the formula $50,000 + $3.50 × direct labor hours worked.

Data on performance for the first three months of 19X0 follow:

	JANUARY	FEBRUARY	MARCH
Direct labor hours worked	22,000	32,000	42,000
Direct labor costs budgeted	$127,000	$162,000	$197,000
Direct labor costs incurred	$110,000	$160,000	$210,000
Variance*	$ 17,000(F)	$ 2,000(F)	$ 13,000(U)

* F = favorable, U = unfavorable.

The factory manager was perplexed by the results—which showed favorable variances when production was low and unfavorable variances when production was high—because he believed his control over labor costs was consistently good.

REQUIRED:
a. Why did the variances arise? Explain and illustrate using amounts and diagrams as necessary.
b. Does this direct labor budget provide a basis for controlling direct labor cost? Explain, indicating changes that might be made to improve control over direct labor cost and to facilitate performance evaluation of direct labor employees.

c. For inventory valuation purposes, how should per-unit standard costs for direct labor be determined in a situation such as this? Explain, assuming that in some months fewer than 10,000 hours are expected to be utilized.

(AICPA adapted)

11-34. *Standard Process Costing*   D. W. Curry Cosmetics, Inc., produces Tars-off, a brand of toothpaste sold primarily to smokers. One producing department is used, and costs are accumulated through a standard process costing system. All raw materials are added at the beginning of the process with the exception of packaging tubes, which are force-filled at the end of the process. Labor and overhead costs are applied uniformly throughout the process. Cost reports for July 19X2 revealed the following data:

> Work in process inventory, July 1, 19X2:
>   400 pounds—40% completed
> Costs attached:
>   Materials $220.00
>   Conversion costs   140.80

> July 19X2 data:
>   Raw materials added:
>   Paste: 4,500 pounds at standard cost of $.50 per pound
>   Grit: 500 pounds at standard cost of $1.00 per pound
>   Tubes: 2-ounce tubes used at standard cost of $.25 per tube
>   Direct labor:
>   One standard direct labor hour allowed for each
>   5 pounds processed
>   Standard labor rate = $2.10 per standard direct labor hour
>   Manufacturing overhead:
>   Standard variable overhead rate = $1.40/DLH
>   Standard fixed overhead rate   =   .90/DLH

> Work in process inventory, July 31, 19X2:
>   900 pounds—60% completed

During the month, no spoilage occurred and no standard cost variances were incurred. Assume a FIFO process costing method.

REQUIRED:
a. Compute the standard cost per tube of toothpaste.
b. Compute the standard cost of units transferred to Finished Goods inventory during July.
c. Compute the value of ending Work in Process inventory on July 31, 19X2.
(*Note:* 16 ounces = 1 pound.)

Chapter 12: Analysis of Standard Cost Variances

CHAPTER HIGHLIGHTS

Purpose and Learning Objectives

Variance analysis is a cost control tool provided by standard cost accounting systems. This chapter illustrates and explains the techniques utilized in standard cost variance analysis. Upon completion of this chapter, students should be able to:

1. Explain the meaning of different standard cost variances
2. Compute variances for raw materials, direct labor, and factory overhead
3. Integrate variance account balances into the accounting system
4. Evaluate operating performance using variances
5. Dispose of variance balances at period-end

Relevant Concepts

The following basic concepts are introduced in this chapter:

Variance analysis   The process of computing the amount of, and isolating the causes of, variances between actual costs and budgeted or standard costs.

Raw material variance   The extent to which raw material prices and usage account for the difference between actual cost of materials and standard material cost.

Direct labor variance   The difference between actual direct labor costs and direct labor costs at standard, which is analyzed to determine influences of labor rate changes and worker efficiency.

Factory overhead variance   The differences between actual overhead costs incurred and standard overhead costs applied to good units produced, which result from spending differences, worker efficiency, or the effectiveness of capacity utilization.

Performance evaluation The assessment of job performance by linking cost variances with individuals responsible for the variances and analyzing possible causes for the variance.

Cost reduction, profit planning, and cost control are the primary reasons for installing a standard cost accounting system. The method used in standard costing to facilitate cost control is called standard cost variance analysis. The objectives of variance analysis are to pinpoint areas of operating efficiency or inefficiency, to identify persons responsible for variances, and to identify reasons for variance incurrence.

Differences between standard and actual costs of raw material are identified as either price or usage variances. Standard and actual direct labor costs may differ because of varying labor rates or worker efficiencies. Spending, efficiency, and volume variances account for the difference between actual factory overhead costs and standard overhead costs applied to production during the period.

Cost variances are isolated and analyzed internally for cost control purposes. Once the variance analysis has been completed, variance account balances in the general ledger are disposed of by allocation to Raw Materials, Work in Process, and Finished Goods inventories and Cost of Goods Sold.

Chapter Summary

Variance analysis is an integral part of standard cost accounting. As explained in Chapter 11, standard costs provide the foundation for an effective budgetary control process. The development and use of standard costs facilitate the planning phase of this process. However, budgetary control is successful only if the effectiveness of management and operating efficiency can be analyzed. Cost control is achieved through performance measurement and evaluation.

The objective of variance analysis is to measure management effectiveness and operating efficiency. Comparisons of actual operating results with budgeted or planned operating activities serve as the foundation for performance evaluation. If actual operating costs deviate from anticipated costs, a cost variance has been incurred. A variance indicates that management has failed to accomplish a stated objective. Variance analysis helps determine the reasons for unsatisfactory or superior operating results.

Variance analysis involves two phases: (1) computation of individual variances and (2) determination of the cause(s) of each variance. This chapter first concentrates on the computation of material, labor, and overhead variances. Analysis of causes, reporting variances to managers, and accounting disposition of variances conclude the study of standard cost variance analysis.

STANDARD COST VARIANCE ANALYSIS

Raw material variances result when actual material costs differ from standard material costs. The required cost analysis is a comparison of actual costs incurred with standard costs that should have been incurred. Two primary comparisons are involved in raw material variance analysis:

1. Input-output quantity comparisons: actual quantities used (inputs) versus standard quantities based on good units produced (output)
2. Price comparisons: actual price versus standard price

Input-output comparisons provide the bases for determination of *material quantity variances*, and price comparisons are used in calculating *material price variances*.

RAW MATERIAL VARIANCES

To be used effectively, variances should be determined as soon as possible after their incurrence. By isolating variances quickly, management can prevent unfavorable situations from recurring; thus, prompt recognition of material variances is important. Material quantity variances can be computed only after materials have been requisitioned and used in production. At that time, actual quantities used and standard quantities can be effectively compared and analyzed.

Material price variances can be measured at two different times: when materials are purchased or when they are requisitioned into production. Since raw materials can be stored for several months before use, timing of the variance calculation is important to cost control. Isolating material price variances *at the time of purchase* offers two advantages: (1) Price variances are known soon after purchase, and action can be taken to prevent future variances; and (2) Raw Material inventory is stated at standard price and is consistent with the Work in Process and Finished Goods inventory accounts. On the other hand, if price variances are isolated *at time of requisition*, Raw Materials inventory is carried at actual cost, and the variance information is not timely for cost control purposes.

Material Price Variance

A material price variance occurs when raw materials are purchased at a price different from standard price. *Material price variance* is the difference between actual price and standard price multiplied by the actual quantity. The first section of Exhibit 12-1 illustrates the derivation of the material price variance. Expressed as a formula,

$$\begin{aligned} \text{material price variance} &= (Q_a \times P_a) - (Q_a \times P_s) \\ &= (P_a - P_s) \times Q_a \\ &= (\text{actual price} - \text{standard price}) \\ &\quad \times \text{actual quantity} \end{aligned}$$

This variance may result from (1) price changes occurring since the standard was developed, (2) differences in quantity discounts from those anticipated, or (3) purchasing substitute raw materials that differ from original specifications. When reasons for the variance are determined, management can act to prevent similar future occurrences.

When the material price variance is isolated at the time of purchase, Raw Materials inventory is debited with an amount equal to actual quantity purchased (Q_a) times standard price (P_s). Accounts Payable must be credited with the actual liability resulting from the purchase transaction, which is actual quantity purchased (Q_a) times actual price paid per unit (P_a). The following journal entry records the purchase of raw materials and recognizes the material price variance:

Raw materials inventory $(Q_a \times P_s)$	$XXXXX	
Material price variance $(P_a - P_s) \times Q_a$	XX	
Accounts payable $(Q_a \times P_a)$		$XXXXX
To record purchase of raw materials and		
resulting material price variance		

EXHIBIT 12-1

RAW MATERIAL VARIANCE DETERMINATION

MATERIAL PRICE VARIANCE

Actual quantity at actual price/unit	Actual quantity at standard price/unit
$Q_a \times P_a$	$Q_a \times P_s$

difference equals

material price variance

$$(Q_a \times P_a) - (Q_a \times P_s) = \underline{(P_a - P_s) \times Q_a}$$

MATERIAL QUANTITY VARIANCE

Actual quantity at standard price/unit	Standard quantity at standard price/unit
$Q_a \times P_s$	$Q_s \times P_s$

difference equals

material quantity variance

$$(Q_a \times P_s) - (Q_s \times P_s) = \underline{(Q_a - Q_s) \times P_s}$$

Q_a = actual quantity purchased or used.
Q_s = standard quantity for good units produced.
P_a = actual price.
P_s = standard price.

Material Quantity Variance

A *material quantity variance* (also called *material usage variance*) results when actual quantities of raw materials used in production differ from standard quantities that should have been used to produce a specific number of good units of output; it is the difference between actual quantity of material used and standard quantity of material allowed multiplied by standard price per unit.

Derivation of the material quantity variance is shown in Exhibit 12-1. As a formula, the variance is shown as:

$$\begin{aligned}
\text{material quantity variance} &= (Q_a \times P_s) - (Q_s \times P_s) \\
&= (Q_a - Q_s) \times P_s \\
&= (\text{actual quantity} - \text{standard quantity}) \\
&\quad \times \text{standard price}
\end{aligned}$$

Possible causes of a material quantity variance include poor workmanship, faulty equipment, inferior quality of raw materials, bad material handling, and excessive spoilage or material loss during production. The journal entry to record the transfer of raw material cost into Work in Process inventory under standard cost accounting is shown below:

Work in process inventory $(Q_s \times P_s)$	$XXXXX
Material quantity variance $(Q_a - Q_s) \times P_s$	XX
Raw materials inventory $(Q_a \times P_s)$	$XXXXX

To record transfer of raw materials to Work in Process inventory and resulting material quantity variance

If the material price variance is isolated at time of purchase, all items in Raw Materials inventory are stated at standard price. For materials issued to production, Raw Materials inventory is credited with an amount equal to actual quantity of raw materials requisitioned times standard price. Work in Process inventory is debited for standard quantity of materials at a standard price. The resulting difference is recorded as the material quantity variance.

Illustrative Problem

Bornson Company manufactures utility boxes made out of wood and cardboard. Standard raw materials and price specifications follow:

Wood: 5 board feet per box at $55 per 1,000 feet
Cardboard: 2 sheets per box at 12¢ per sheet
Nails: 3 pounds per 100 boxes at 20¢ per pound

On June 1, 19X7, the following raw materials were purchased:

DESCRIPTION	QUANTITY PURCHASED	PURCHASE COST	TOTAL COST
Wood: 1 inch by ¾ inch by 12 feet	120M board feet*	$60/1,000 feet	$ 7,200
Cardboard: 4 by 6 feet	50,000 sheets	10¢ per sheet	5,000
Nails: 6-penny size	800 pounds	17¢ per pound	136
	Actual cost of materials purchased		$12,336

* M = 1,000.

During June, 17,500 boxes were produced, and actual raw materials requisitioned into production included:

Wood: 90M board feet
Cardboard: 36,000 sheets
Nails: 500 pounds

REQUIRED: Compute the material price and quantity variances for wood, cardboard, and nails for June and prepare necessary journal entries assuming material price variances are isolated at (1) time of purchase and (2) time of requisition.

SOLUTION (If material price variances are isolated at time of purchase):

Material price variances, when computed at the time of purchase, are:

Wood:	($60 − $55) × 120	= $5 × 120	= $ 600(U)
Cardboard:	(.10 − .12) × 50,000	= (.02) × 50,000 =	1,000(F)
Nails:	(.17 − .20) × 800	= (.03) × 800 =	24(F)
		Net material price variance	$ 424(F)

Full analysis of the material price variances is shown by the following schedule:

ITEM	ACTUAL PRICE			STANDARD PRICE			MATERIAL PRICE VARIANCE
	Price	Quantity	Total	Price	Quantity	Total	
Wood	$60	120M	$ 7,200	$55	120M	$ 6,600	$ 600(U)
Cardboard	.10	50,000	5,000	.12	50,000	6,000	1,000(F)
Nails	.17	800	136	.20	800	160	24(F)
Totals			$12,336			$12,760	$ 424(F)

Quantity usage analysis reveals the following material quantity variances:

Wood: $(90,000 - 87,500) \times \$55/1,000 \text{ feet} = 2.5 \quad \times \$55 = \$137.50(U)$
Cardboard: $(36,000 - 35,000) \times \$.12 \qquad\qquad = 1,000 \times .12 = 120.00(U)$
Nails: $(500 \quad - \quad 525) \times \$.20 \qquad\qquad = (25) \quad \times .20 = 5.00(F)$
$$\text{Net material quantity variance} \qquad \$252.50(U)$$

A complete analysis of the material quantity variance is presented below:

ITEM	ACTUAL QUANTITY			STANDARD QUANTITY*			MATERIAL QUANTITY VARIANCE
	Quantity	Price	Total	Quantity	Price	Total	
Wood	90M	$55	$4,950.00	87.5M	$55	$4,812.50	$137.50(U)
Cardboard	36,000	.12	4,320.00	35,000	.12	4,200.00	120.00(U)
Nails	500	.20	100.00	525	.20	105.00	5.00(F)
Totals			$9,370.00			$9,117.50	$252.50(U)

* 17,500 boxes times standard quantity of each material.

Required journal entries (trace amounts to analyses above):

June 1, 19X7:
Raw materials inventory $12,760.00
    Materials price variance .... $ 424.00
    Accounts payable 12,336.00
  To record raw material purchase and
  resulting material price variance

June 30, 19X7:
Work in process inventory .... $ 9,117.50
Material quantity variance 252.50
    Raw materials inventory .... $ 9,370.00
  To record transfer of raw materials
  to Work in Process inventory and
  resulting material quantity variance

SOLUTION (If material price variances are isolated at time of requisition):

When the material price variance is isolated at time of requisition rather than time of purchase, care should be taken to compute the variance based on *quantities requisitioned*, not on quantities purchased. Using quantities requisitioned, the material price variances would be:

Wood: ($60 − $55) × 90M   = $5   × 90M   = $450(U)
Cardboard: (.10 − .12) × 36,000 = (.02) × 36,000 =   720(F)
Nails: (.17 − .20) × 500   = (.03) × 500   =   15(F)
                          Net material price variance $285(F)

Total analysis of the material price variances is completed in the following schedule:

	ACTUAL PRICE			STANDARD PRICE			MATERIAL PRICE VARIANCE
ITEM	Price	Quantity	Total	Price	Quantity	Total	
Wood	$60	90M	$5,400	$55	90M	$4,950	$450(U)
Cardboard	.10	36,000	3,600	.12	36,000	4,320	720(F)
Nails	.17	500	85	.20	500	100	15(F)
Totals			$9,085			$9,370	$285(F)

Material quantity variance analysis yields the same results as computed in the previous solution.

Required journal entries (trace amounts to analysis above):

June 1, 19X7:
    Raw materials inventory $12,336.00
        Accounts payable $12,336.00
        To record raw material
        purchases at actual cost

June 30, 19X7:
    Work in process inventory $ 9,117.50
    Material quantity variance   252.50
        Material price variance $ 285.00
        Raw materials inventory   9,085.00
        To record transfer of raw materials
        to Work in Process inventory and
        resulting material price and
        quantity variances

The above solutions indicate that changing the time of recognition of the material price variance results in an apparent reduction in the size of the variance, from $424(F) to $285(F). This is not a correct assessment of the variance. When the material price variance is isolated at time of purchase, its amount will always be different from that computed at time of requisition, unless the quantity purchased equals the quantity requisitioned. In the case of Bornson Company, a portion of the material price variance—$139(F)—remains in raw material inventory and will be recognized when the remaining items are requisitioned into production.

DIRECT LABOR VARIANCES

Direct labor variances arise when actual labor costs are different from standard labor costs. In analyzing labor costs, the emphasis is on labor pay rates and labor hours. Analysis of labor variances parallels that of raw material variances (when the price variance is isolated at time of requisition). Timing of variance

EXHIBIT 12-2

LABOR VARIANCES—GRAPHIC ILLUSTRATION

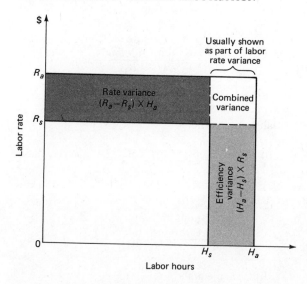

recognition involves no alternative methods for labor rate variances because labor services are paid for as they are used. Comparisons of actual and standard labor cost include:

1. Input-output labor hour comparisons: actual hours worked (inputs) versus standard hours allowed for good units produced (outputs)
2. Labor rate comparisons: actual rate versus standard rate

Labor efficiency variances are derived from input-output labor hour comparisons, and labor rate comparisons lead to *labor rate variances*.

A graphic illustration of these variances is shown in Exhibit 12-2. The vertical axis represents direct labor pay rates, and the horizontal axis denotes direct labor hours. Total standard labor cost is shown by the large unshaded box and is computed by multiplying standard direct labor rate (R_s) times standard hours allowed (H_s). Actual labor cost is actual direct labor rate (R_a) multiplied by actual hours worked (H_a) and includes the shaded and unshaded parts of the diagram. Since actual labor cost exceeds standard labor cost, the diagram illustrates unfavorable labor rate and efficiency variances. If H_s were greater than H_a, or if R_s were greater than R_a, favorable variances would result.

When actual direct labor pay rates differ from standard pay rates, the result is a *labor rate variance*, the difference between actual labor rates and standard labor rates multiplied by actual direct labor hours worked. The comparison necessary to calculate the labor rate variance is shown in the first part of Exhibit 12-3. The derivation of the variance is:

Labor Rate Variance

$$\text{labor rate variance} = (H_a \times R_a) - (H_a \times R_s)$$
$$= (R_a - R_s) \times H_a$$
$$= (\text{actual rate} - \text{standard rate}) \times \text{actual hours}$$

EXHIBIT 12-3

DIRECT LABOR VARIANCE DETERMINATION

<small>LABOR RATE VARIANCE</small>

Actual hours at actual rate/hour $H_a \times R_a$	Actual hours at standard rate/hour $H_a \times R_s$

difference equals

labor rate variance

$$(H_a \times R_a) - (H_a \times R_s) = \underline{(R_a - R_s) \times H_a}$$

<small>LABOR EFFICIENCY VARIANCE</small>

Actual hours at standard rate/hour $H_a \times R_s$	Standard hours allowed at standard rate/hour $H_s \times R_s$

difference equals

labor efficiency variance

$$(H_a \times R_s) - (H_s \times R_s) = \underline{(H_a - H_s) \times R_s}$$

R_a = actual direct labor rate.
R_s = standard direct labor rate.
H_a = actual labor hours worked.
H_s = standard labor hours allowed for good units produced.

Favorable rate variances arise whenever actual pay rates are less than standard rates; unfavorable variances occur when actual pay rates exceed standard rates. Specific causes of labor rate variances include sudden changes in overall wage rates, labor strikes that cause utilization of unskilled help, and economic conditions that cause massive labor layoffs and uneconomical usage of skilled labor retained. A significant labor rate variance indicates either mismanagement of the existing labor force or changes in management decisions regarding compensation policies and utilization of factory labor. Changes in actual pay rates that result from a revised labor contract or from a labor rate increase in an existing contract should be reflected immediately in a new set of standard direct labor rates.

Labor Efficiency Variance   The *labor efficiency variance* (also called *labor usage variance*) measures the relative efficiency of labor operations. If actual direct labor hours required to complete a job differ from the number of standard hours allowed, a labor efficiency variance results; it is the difference between actual labor hours worked and standard labor hours allowed multiplied by the standard labor rate per hour.

Standard labor hours allowed are the total standard hours that should have been used to produce a given number of good units of output. The concept of standard hours allowed (H_s) is important to both labor and overhead variance analysis. To illustrate standard hours allowed, assume that the production of 1 gallon of paint requires 1.3 standard direct labor hours. If 20,000 gallons were produced during a period, standard labor hours allowed would be:

$$20,000 \text{ gallons} \times 1.3 \text{ DLH/gallon} = 26,000 \text{ standard DLH}$$

Exhibit 12-3 illustrates the components necessary to calculate the labor efficiency variance. In formula form, the computation of the variance is:

$$\begin{aligned}
\text{labor efficiency variance} &= (H_a \times R_s) - (H_s \times R_s) \\
&= (H_a - H_s) \times R_s \\
&= (\text{actual hours} - \text{standard hours allowed}) \\
&\quad \times \text{standard rate}
\end{aligned}$$

Labor efficiency variances occur when production operations are more efficient or less efficient than standard performance. Causes of unfavorable variances include machine breakdown, inferior raw materials, poor supervision, lack of timely material handling, and poor employee performance.

Journal Entry Analysis

Labor rate and efficiency variances are recorded at the end of a payroll period. Once actual labor rates and actual hours are known, the journal entry below is recorded. Note that Work in Process inventory is charged with standard labor cost ($H_s \times R_s$), while Factory Payroll is credited with gross wages actually earned ($H_a \times R_a$).

Work in process inventory ($H_s \times R_s$)	$XXXXX	
Labor rate variance ($R_a - R_s$) $\times H_a$	XX	
Labor efficiency variance ($H_a - H_s$) $\times R_s$	XX	
Factory payroll ($H_a \times R_a$)		$XXXXX
To record standard labor cost of current production		

Illustrative Problem

DeKalb Fence Company manufactures barbed-wire fencing materials. Each completed reel of fencing material contains 1,000 feet of barbed wire and requires 2.7 standard direct labor hours to complete. During April 19X8, 47,000 reels were completed, and actual factory payroll was:

Junior machinists:	97,000 DLH at $4.10/hour	$397,700
Senior machinists:	31,500 DLH at $4.25/hour	133,875
Total labor	128,500 DLH	$531,575

Standard rate per direct labor hour is $4.20.

REQUIRED: (1) Compute the labor rate and efficiency variances and (2) Prepare a journal entry to record factory payroll for April.

SOLUTION

1a. Labor rate variance:

$$\begin{aligned}
(R_a - R_s) \times H_a &= (\$4.10 - \$4.20) \times 97,000 = (.10) \times 97,000 = \$9,700(F) \\
&+ (\$4.25 - \$4.20) \times 31,500 = .05 \times 31,500 = \underline{1,575(U)} \\
&\qquad\qquad \text{Total labor rate variance} \quad \underline{\$8,125(F)}
\end{aligned}$$

b. Labor efficiency variance:

$$(H_a - H_s) \times R_s = (128,500 - 126,900^*) \times \$4.20$$
$$= 1,600 \text{ hours} \qquad \times \$4.20 = \underline{\$6,720(U)}$$

* Standard hours allowed = 2.7 DLH/unit × 47,000 units
= 126,900 DLHs.

2. Required journal entry:

Work in process inventory†	\$532,980	
Labor efficiency variance	6,720	
Labor rate variance		\$ 8,125
Factory payroll		531,575
To record standard labor		
cost of current production		

† $H_s \times R_s$ = 126,900 DLH × \$4.20/DLH = \$532,980.

FACTORY OVERHEAD VARIANCES

Analysis of factory overhead variances is more complex than variance analysis for raw materials and direct labor. Several cost accounting concepts are involved in the analysis of overhead cost variances. A clear understanding of these concepts and their interrelationships is an important key to overhead variance analysis.

Exhibit 12-4 illustrates the conceptual factors related to standard cost variances for factory overhead. The concepts of capacity levels and the flexible budget were discussed in Chapter 11. The selection of a capacity level to use as a basis for corporate planning and control varies with companies and circumstances. For purposes of variance analysis in this text, normal capacity will be

EXHIBIT 12-4
CONCEPTUAL FOUNDATION—OVERHEAD VARIANCE ANALYSIS

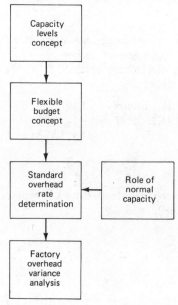

the focal point. When using the flexible budget in overhead variance analysis, the variable cost rate in the flexible budget formula will represent the *standard variable overhead rate*. An example follows:

$4.95 per DLH + $473,500 (fixed costs) = flexible budget formula

The $4.95 variable cost per labor hour is the standard variable overhead rate. Normal capacity is usually the basis used to calculate the *standard fixed overhead rate*. Assume that normal capacity in this example is 47,350 direct labor hours; the standard fixed overhead rate is computed as follows:

$$\text{standard fixed overhead rate} = \frac{\text{budgeted fixed overhead costs}}{\text{normal capacity}}$$

$$= \frac{\$473,500}{47,350 \text{ DLHs}} = \$10 \text{ per DLH}$$

The combined standard overhead rate for each direct labor hour is $14.95 ($4.95 variable + $10.00 fixed). Standard overhead rates are used to apply standard overhead costs to products.

Over- or Underapplied Overhead Versus Overhead Variances

The application of overhead costs to products in a standard cost system is identical to the use of predetermined overhead rates discussed in Chapter 5. The only difference is that standard overhead rates usually are based upon normal capacity instead of upon expected annual capacity. By using normal capacity, standard overhead rates do not fluctuate with actual capacity utilization. Actual Overhead Costs Incurred represents the debit balance in the Factory Overhead Control account. Standard Overhead Applied or Factory Overhead Applied is credited for the overhead costs charged to production. The difference between Actual Overhead Costs Incurred and Standard Overhead Applied is the total overhead variance, which equals Over- or Underapplied Overhead. The objective of overhead variance analysis is to separate the over- or underapplied overhead amount into specific types of overhead variances. Spending, efficiency, and volume variances are computed, and these variances help to explain the causes of the total overhead variance.

Key Variables in Overhead Variance Analysis

Overhead variance analysis involves the determination of three specific overhead variances. The analysis, illustrated in Exhibit 12-5, is called the *three-variance approach*. This diagram presents a general structure of overhead variance analysis and should be used for reference purposes whenever necessary. Eight key variables shown in Exhibit 12-5 provide the required data for any problem involving overhead variance analysis. These key variables are:

VARIABLE	SYMBOL
Actual variable overhead costs incurred	VC_a
Actual fixed overhead costs incurred	FC_a
Budgeted fixed overhead costs	FC_b
Actual direct labor hours worked	H_a
Standard direct labor hours allowed	H_s
Standard variable overhead rate	SR_v
Standard fixed overhead rate	SR_f
Normal capacity in labor hours	H_n

The use of symbols is not necessary, but they can make overhead variance analysis much easier.

The general analysis of overhead variances in Exhibit 12-5 shows four cost categories: actual costs incurred, standard overhead applied, a flexible overhead budget based on actual hours, and a flexible overhead budget based on standard hours allowed. Flexible budgets are used to compute cost totals so that the total overhead variance can be separated into spending, efficiency, and volume variances. These variances are computed by comparing what did happen with what should have happened in terms of overhead costs. Using direct labor hours as a measure of capacity, a flexible budget based on actual hours worked represents the overhead costs that should have been incurred during the period. Any difference between these budgeted amounts and actual overhead costs incurred is a *spending variance*.

A flexible budget based on standard hours allowed reflects the amount of overhead cost that should have been applied to good units produced during the period. Any difference between these budgeted figures and standard costs actually applied to products is caused by a difference between normal volume and standard volume. The resulting variance is called a *volume variance*.

EXHIBIT 12-5
FACTORY OVERHEAD VARIANCE ANALYSIS

		VARIABLE STANDARD COST VARIANCES		FIXED STANDARD COST VARIANCES	
OVERHEAD COST SUMMARY CATEGORIES		*Variable costs*	*Variable cost variances*	*Fixed costs*	*Fixed cost variances*
Actual costs incurred					
Variable (VC_a)	$ XXXX* →	$XXXX			
Fixed (FC_a)	XXXX*			$XXXX	
Total	$XXXXX		$XXX variable spending variance		$XXX fixed spending variance
Flexible budget based on actual hours worked					
Variable ($H_a \times SR_v$)	$ XXXX →	$XXXX			
Fixed (FC_b)	XXXX			$XXXX	
Total	$XXXXX		$XXX variable efficiency variance		
Flexible budget based on standard hours allowed					
Variable ($H_s \times SR_v$)	$ XXXX →	$XXXX			
Fixed (FC_b)	XXXX			$XXXX	
Total	$XXXXX				$XXX fixed volume variance
Standard overhead applied to good units produced					
Variable ($H_s \times SR_v$)	$ XXXX† →	$XXXX			
Fixed ($H_s \times SR_f$)	XXXX†			$XXXX	
Total	$XXXXX				

Left margin: total overhead variance (under- or overapplied overhead)

Column connectors: "difference equals"

* Debits to Factory Overhead Control.
† Credits to Factory Overhead Applied.

Standard overhead variance analysis is a function of direct labor hours and involves cost comparisons using two flexible budgets—one based on actual hours worked and one based on standard hours allowed. A portion of the total overhead variance is usually caused by efficient or inefficient utilization of labor hours. Like the labor efficiency variance, the *overhead efficiency variance* measures manpower performance by analyzing differences between actual hours worked and standard hours allowed for good units produced. The following sections illustrate the computation of each separate overhead variance.

An overhead spending variance results when actual overhead costs incurred differ from the overhead costs that should have been incurred. Overhead costs that should have been incurred are measured by a flexible budget based on actual hours worked. The term *spending variance* means that more or less overhead costs were incurred than should have been. The overhead spending variance can be divided into two parts, a variable overhead spending variance and a fixed overhead spending variance.

Overhead Spending Variance

Variable overhead spending variance   Because of market price changes and other short-term spending fluctuations, variable costs incurred may differ from budgeted variable costs measured by a flexible budget based on actual hours worked. *Variable overhead spending variance* is the difference between actual variable costs incurred and actual hours worked multiplied by the standard variable overhead rate. The formula for computing the variable overhead spending variance is developed in Exhibit 12-6 and is as follows:

variable overhead
spending variance $= VC_a - (H_a \times SR_v)$
$ =$ actual variable overhead costs
$ -$ (actual hours $\times$ standard variable overhead rate)

If VC_a is greater than $(H_a \times SR_v)$, an unfavorable variance exists because actual costs exceed the amount that should have been incurred. If VC_a is less than $(H_a \times SR_v)$, a favorable variance results.

Fixed overhead spending variance   Fixed overhead costs incurred during a period do not always equal the budgeted amount. Any difference is measured by the *fixed overhead spending variance,* which is the difference between actual fixed overhead costs incurred and budgeted or normal fixed overhead costs included in the flexible budget. The formula for this variance is derived in Exhibit 12-6, and is as follows:

fixed overhead
spending variance $= FC_a - FC_b$
$ =$ actual fixed overhead costs
$ -$ budgeted fixed overhead costs

If FC_a is greater than FC_b, an unfavorable variance results because actual costs exceed the budget.

Actual fixed overhead costs seldom equal budgeted fixed costs because property tax rates may change, insurance premiums may increase, or equipment changes may affect depreciation rates. In problem situations, this reality is often ignored; unless there is specific information concerning actual fixed costs, always assume that $FC_a = FC_b$.

EXHIBIT 12-6
OVERHEAD SPENDING VARIANCE

ACTUAL OVERHEAD COSTS INCURRED	BUDGETED OVERHEAD COSTS (BASED ON ACTUAL HOURS WORKED)

Variable costs:

actual variable costs	budgeted variable costs
VC_a	$H_a \times SR_v$

difference equals

variable overhead spending variance

$$[VC_a - (H_a \times SR_v)]$$

Fixed costs:

actual fixed costs	budgeted fixed costs
FC_a	FC_b

difference equals

fixed overhead spending variance

$$(FC_a - FC_b)$$

Overhead Efficiency Variance

The overhead efficiency variance is linked directly with the labor efficiency variance. An efficiency variance arises when actual hours worked differ from standard hours allowed for good units produced $(H_a \neq H_s)$. An *overhead efficiency variance* is the difference between actual labor hours worked and standard labor hours allowed multiplied by the standard variable overhead rate. For product costing purposes, overhead costs are charged to products by using some overhead application base, usually standard direct labor hours. If actual hours differ from standard hours allowed, an efficiency variance results. If H_a is greater than H_s, the variance is unfavorable; if H_a is less than H_s, the variance is favorable.

The overhead efficiency variance is an extension of the labor efficiency variance and indicates that variable overhead applied to production was different from the standard overhead costs that should have been incurred. Exhibit 12-7 illustrates the computations leading to the following overhead efficiency variance formula:

$$\text{overhead efficiency variance} = (H_a \times SR_v) - (H_s \times SR_v)$$
$$= (H_a - H_s) \times SR_v$$
$$= (\text{actual hours} - \text{standard hours})$$
$$\times \text{standard variable overhead rate}$$

There is never a fixed overhead efficiency variance. Fixed costs (FC_b) will

EXHIBIT 12-7

OVERHEAD EFFICIENCY VARIANCE

BUDGETED OVERHEAD COSTS (BASED ON ACTUAL HOURS WORKED)	BUDGETED OVERHEAD COSTS (BASED ON STANDARD HOURS ALLOWED)

Variable costs:

$$\text{budgeted variable costs}$$
$$H_a \times SR_v$$

$$\text{budgeted variable costs}$$
$$H_s \times SR_v$$

difference equals

overhead efficiency variance

$$(H_a \times SR_v) - (H_s \times SR_v) = \underline{(H_a - H_s) \times SR_v}$$

Fixed costs:

budgeted fixed costs
$$FC_b \longleftarrow$$

budgeted fixed costs
$$\longrightarrow FC_b$$

always equal*
(no fixed efficiency variance)

---

* The overhead efficiency variance is derived from a comparison of two flexible budgets computed for two levels of activity; by definition, the fixed portion of each flexible budget will always be identical when levels of activity are in the relevant range.

---

always be the same when comparing any two flexible budgets involving capacity measures that are in the same relevant range (see note in Exhibit 12-7).

Overhead Volume Variance

The overhead volume variance concentrates on budgeted and applied *fixed* overhead costs. As shown in Exhibit 12-8, the volume variance is measured by comparing a flexible budget based on standard hours allowed with overhead costs applied to production using standard hours allowed. Budgeted and applied variable overhead costs are the same since both amounts are computed by multiplying standard hours allowed times the standard variable overhead rate $(H_s \times SR_v)$.

The overhead volume variance formula is derived in Exhibit 12-8, and the *overhead volume variance* is defined as the difference between budgeted fixed overhead costs (FC_b) and fixed overhead applied, computed by multiplying standard hours allowed by the standard fixed overhead rate $(H_s \times SR_f)$. The overhead volume variance is favorable when fixed costs are overapplied and unfavorable when fixed costs are underapplied:

1. If $FC_b > (H_s \times SR_f)$: More fixed overhead costs were budgeted than were applied to units of production. Underapplying fixed overhead costs is an *unfavorable* variance.
2. If $FC_b < (H_s \times SR_f)$: More fixed overhead costs were applied to units of production than were required to absorb budgeted fixed costs. This results in an overapplied situation, which is *favorable*.

EXHIBIT 12-8

OVERHEAD VOLUME VARIANCE

BUDGETED OVERHEAD COSTS (BASED ON STANDARD HOURS ALLOWED)	STANDARD OVERHEAD COSTS APPLIED

Variable costs:

budgeted variable costs   variable overhead costs applied

$$H_s \times SR_v \longleftarrow \qquad \longrightarrow H_s \times SR_v$$

always equal*
(no variable volume variance)

Fixed costs:

budgeted fixed costs   fixed overhead costs applied

$$FC_b \quad \text{or} \quad H_n \times SR_f\dagger \qquad\qquad H_s \times SR_f$$

difference equals

overhead volume variance

$$(H_n \times SR_f) - (H_s \times SR_f) = \underline{(H_n - H_s) \times SR_f} \quad \text{or} \quad \underline{[FC_b - (H_s \times SR_f)]}$$

---

* Standard hours allowed (H_s) is the basis for the flexible budget and for variable overhead costs applied to good units of output. Since both computations require the use of the standard variable overhead rate (SR_v), both variable cost amounts must be equal.

† Fixed costs (FC_b) represent budgeted fixed costs. From this amount, the standard fixed overhead rate is determined as follows:

$$\frac{\text{fixed budgeted overhead}}{\text{normal capacity}} = \text{standard fixed overhead rate}$$

Using symbols, it would be expressed:

$$\frac{FC_b}{H_n} = SR_f; \quad \text{Thus,} \quad FC_b = H_n \times SR_f$$

The key to understanding the volume variance is the standard fixed overhead rate and its derivation. Using a flexible budget based on normal capacity, the standard fixed overhead rate is computed as follows:

$$\text{standard fixed overhead rate} = \frac{\text{total budgeted fixed overhead}}{\text{normal capacity}}$$

In equation form, the fixed overhead rate is:

$$SR_f = \frac{FC_b}{H_n}$$

where H_n = normal capacity expressed in labor hours. Multiplying through this equation by H_n yields the following:

$$FC_b = H_n \times SR_f$$

Since the fixed overhead rate (SR_f) is used to apply fixed overhead to production, fixed overhead costs (FC_b) will be applied to units produced *only* if normal hours of capacity (H_n) are utilized. If $H_n = H_s$, all budgeted fixed overhead costs will be applied to good units produced. A volume variance results in any period when H_n and H_s are not equal:

1. If $H_s > H_n$, volume variance is favorable and equal to credit balance of overapplied costs.
2. If $H_s < H_n$, volume variance is unfavorable and equal to debit balance of underapplied costs.

Derivation of the overhead volume variance formula in Exhibit 12-8 can now be summarized. Replacing FC_b with $H_n \times SR_f$, the volume variance formula is:

$$
\begin{aligned}
\text{overhead volume variance} &= (H_n \times SR_f) - (H_s \times SR_f) \\
&= (H_n - H_s) \times SR_f \\
&= (\text{normal hours} - \text{standard hours allowed}) \\
&\quad \times \text{standard fixed overhead rate}
\end{aligned}
$$

All volume variance analyses assume the use of absorption costing. If direct costing is used, fixed overhead is not applied to units produced, and *no* volume variance is recognized.

Illustrations of factory overhead variances have been based on the three-way or three-variance approach. The total overhead variance (under- or overapplied overhead) is separated into spending variances (both variable and fixed), efficiency variance, and volume variance. The two-variance approach involves a *budget variance* (also called a controllable variance) and a *volume variance* (or uncontrollable variance). This system is used often in practice and is required in many CPA examination problems. To convert to the two-variance approach, simply combine the spending and efficiency variances into one variance, called the *budget variance*, as follows:

Two-way Versus Three-way Approach

$$
\begin{aligned}
\text{variable spending variance} + \text{efficiency variance} &= \text{variable budget variance} \\
\text{fixed spending variance} &= \text{fixed budget variance}
\end{aligned}
$$

The budget variances can also be computed separately as follows:

Variable overhead costs incurred (VC_a)	\$XXXX
Less: Variable overhead costs applied ($H_s \times SR_v$)	XXXX
Variable budget variance [$VC_a - (H_s \times SR_v)$]	\$ XX
Fixed overhead costs incurred (FC_a)	\$XXXX
Less: Budgeted fixed overhead costs (FC_b)	XXXX
Fixed budget variance ($FC_a - FC_b$)	\$ XX

In the two-variance approach, the volume variance is computed as was explained earlier.

Factory overhead variances are not recognized in general ledger accounts and journal entries at the same time as overhead costs are incurred or applied to

Journal Entry Analysis

products. The following analysis illustrates the timing of overhead variance recognition:

Overhead cost incurrence:
1. Factory overhead control $(VC_a + FC_a)$ $XXXX
        Accounts payable and sundry accounts $XXXX
        To record the incurrence of actual
   overhead costs

Application of overhead costs to products:
2. Work in process inventory
        $(H_s \times SR_v) + (H_s \times SR_f)$ $XXXX
        Factory overhead applied $XXXX
        To record application of standard
   overhead costs to products in work
   in process

Journal entries 1 and 2 are recorded during the month based on summaries of actual costs incurred and standard hours allowed for completed production. At month end, entries 3 and 4 are required to close overhead accounts and to recognize overhead variances that are computed in a supporting schedule or report.

3. Factory overhead applied $XXXX
   Over- or underapplied overhead   XXX
        Factory overhead control $XXXX
        To close factory overhead accounts to
   over- or underapplied overhead
4. Overhead spending variance $ XX
   Overhead efficiency variance   XX
   Overhead volume variance   XX
        Over- or underapplied overhead $ XXX
        To record overhead variances making up
   over- or underapplied overhead

As an alternate journal entry procedure, entries 3 and 4 may be combined as follows:

     Factory overhead applied $XXXX
     Overhead spending variance   XX
     Overhead efficiency variance   XX
     Overhead volume variance   XX
         Factory overhead control $XXXX
         To close factory overhead accounts and to
     isolate and record overhead variances

These entries assume that variances are unfavorable as indicated by their debit balances.

Illustrative Problem   L. Rosen Publishing Company uses a standard job order cost system and has developed the following monthly flexible overhead cost budget for 19X9:

	7,000 DLH	8,000 DLH	9,000 DLH	10,000 DLH
Variable costs:				
Material handling	$10,500	$12,000	$13,500	$15,000
Indirect labor	14,000	16,000	18,000	20,000
Indirect materials	7,000	8,000	9,000	10,000
Other variable costs	3,500	4,000	4,500	5,000
Total variable costs	$35,000	$40,000	$45,000	$50,000
Fixed costs:				
Depreciation	$27,000	$27,000	$27,000	$27,000
Taxes and insurance	4,500	4,500	4,500	4,500
Other fixed costs	9,000	9,000	9,000	9,000
Total fixed costs	$40,500	$40,500	$40,500	$40,500
Total overhead costs	$75,500	$80,500	$85,500	$90,500

During June 19X9, actual overhead costs incurred were $47,450 (variable) and $40,100 (fixed). Normal capacity is 9,000 direct labor hours per month. Production reports for June indicated that 6,300 books were completed with 1.5 standard labor hours per book. Actual direct labor hours worked during the month were 9,500.

REQUIRED:
1. Compute (a) variable overhead spending variance, (b) fixed overhead spending variance, (c) overhead efficiency variance, and (d) overhead volume variance.
2. Prepare all necessary journal entries for June 19X9.

SOLUTION: Before attempting the solution, determine the values for the following eight key variables:

(1) Actual variable overhead costs incurred:

$$VC_a = \$47,450 \text{ (given)}$$

(2) Actual fixed overhead costs incurred:

$$FC_a = \$40,100 \text{ (given)}$$

(3) Budgeted fixed overhead costs:

$$FC_b = \$40,500 \text{ (given as part of flexible budget)}$$

(4) Actual hours worked:

$$H_a = 9,500 \text{ DLHs (given)}$$

(5) Standard hours allowed:

$$H_s = 6,300 \text{ products} \times 1.5 \text{ DLHs} = 9,450 \text{ DLHs}$$

(6) Standard variable overhead rate: This amount is not given in the problem but is computed from information contained in the flexible budget.

$$SR_v = \frac{\text{budgeted variable costs}}{\text{related level of capacity}} = \frac{\$35,000}{7,000} = \$5/\text{DLH}$$

Note that the standard variable overhead rate is $5 per DLH at all capacity levels shown in the flexible budget.

(7) Standard fixed overhead rate: This amount is not given but is computed from information contained in the flexible budget.

$$SR_f = \frac{\text{budgeted fixed costs}}{\text{normal capacity}} = \frac{\$40,500}{9,000} = \$4.50/\text{DLH}$$

(8) Normal capacity in labor hours:

$$H_n = 9,000 \text{ hours (given)}$$

The variance computations for Requirement 1 follow:

a. Variable overhead spending variance:

$$
\begin{aligned}
VC_a - (H_a \times SR_v) &= \$47,450 - (9,500 \times \$5) \\
&= \$47,450 - \$47,500 \\
&= \underline{\underline{\$50(F)}}
\end{aligned}
$$

b. Fixed overhead spending variance:

$$
\begin{aligned}
FC_a - FC_b &= \$40,100 - \$40,500 \\
&= \underline{\underline{\$400(F)}}
\end{aligned}
$$

c. Overhead efficiency variance:

$$
\begin{aligned}
(H_a - H_s) \times SR_v &= (9,500 - 9,450) \times \$5 \\
&= 50 \times \$5 \\
&= \underline{\underline{\$250(U)}}
\end{aligned}
$$

d. Overhead volume variance:

$$
\begin{aligned}
FC_b - (H_s \times SR_f) &= \$40,500 - (9,450 \times \$4.50) \\
&= \$40,500 - \$42,525 \\
&= \underline{\underline{\$2,025(F)}}
\end{aligned}
$$

or

$$
\begin{aligned}
(H_n - H_s) \times SR_f &= (9,000 - 9,450) \times \$4.50 \\
&= (450) \times \$4.50 \\
&= \underline{\underline{\$2,025(F)}}
\end{aligned}
$$

Here are the journal entries for Requirement 2:

1. Factory overhead control $87,550*

     Sundry accounts $87,550

    To record the incurrence of actual overhead costs

2. Work in process inventory $89,775†

     Factory overhead applied $89,775

    To record application of standard overhead costs to work in process

3. Factory overhead applied $89,775

   Overhead efficiency variance   250

     Overhead spending variance $ 450

     Overhead volume variance   2,025

     Factory overhead control   87,550

    To close factory overhead accounts and to record overhead variances

* = $VC_a + FC_a$, or $47,450 + $40,100 = $87,550.
† = $(SR_r + SR_f) \times H_s$, or ($5.00 + $4.50) × 9,450 hours = $89,775.

EXHIBIT 12-9
ROSEN COMPANY
STANDARD COST VARIANCES

OVERHEAD COST SUMMARY CATEGORIES		VARIABLE STANDARD COST VARIANCES		FIXED STANDARD COST VARIANCES	
		Variable costs	Variance	Fixed costs	Variance
Actual costs incurred					
Variable (VC_a)	$47,450	$47,450			
Fixed (FC_a)	40,100			$40,100	
Total	$87,550		$50(F) variable spending variance		$400(F) fixed spending variance
Flexible budget based on actual hours worked					
Variable ($H_a \times SR_v$)	$47,500	$47,500			
Fixed (FC_b)	40,500			$40,500	
Total	$88,000		$250(U) efficiency variance		
Flexible budget based on standard hours allowed					
Variable ($H_s \times SR_v$)	$47,250	$47,250			
Fixed (FC_b)	40,500			$40,500	
Total	$87,750				$2,025(F) volume variance
Standard costs applied to good units produced					
Variable ($H_s \times SR_v$)	$47,250				
Fixed ($H_s \times SR_f$)	42,525			$42,525	
Total	$89,775				

Solution check				
Overhead incurred	$87,550	Variable spending variance	$ 50(F)	
Less: Overhead applied	89,775	Fixed spending variance	400(F)	
Overapplied overhead		Efficiency variance	250(U)	
(also called total		Volume variance	2,025(F)	
overhead variance)	$ 2,225(F)	Total variance	$2,225(F)	

An alternative form of variance computation for this problem is presented in Exhibit 12-9. Variances computed in this alternative format correspond with the general structure of overhead variances shown in Exhibit 12-5. Note that overhead variances are the same under either procedure.

Determination of variances is only the first step in the process of standard cost variance analysis. By themselves, material, labor, and overhead variances are useless for cost control and performance evaluation. The final steps in variance analysis are to determine the person(s) responsible for each variance and to pinpoint the cause(s) for incurrence of the variances.

VARIANCES AND PERFORMANCE EVALUATION

Cost Controllability

The final phase of the budgetary control process is to formulate a basis for effective cost control. Standard cost variance analysis is a useful tool in achieving this objective. Once the variances have been computed, management personnel who are responsible for the variances are asked to give reasons for their incurrence. In addition, cost accounting personnel attempt to determine other possible causes for each variance. This review process makes managers conscious of their cost responsibilities, permits timely standard cost revisions, and leads to effective cost control through a continuous evaluation process of past and future cost incurrence.

Responsibility For Variances

Responsibility for efficient or inefficient operating results passes from the company president down the corporate hierarchy to managers in charge of divisions and smaller segments of the company. Specific titles of individuals who are responsible for each type of standard cost variance differ among companies. The analysis shown in Exhibit 12-10 indicates the managers who generally are held accountable for cost variances.

Causes of Variances

For any standard cost variance, there are many possible causes. The list in Exhibit 12-11 is not all inclusive, but it does indicate reasons commonly used to explain why variances arise. Standard cost variances are reported to various managers, the only operating personnel who can identify causes of specific variances.

EXHIBIT 12-10
RESPONSIBILITY FOR STANDARD COST VARIANCES

VARIANCE	PERSONNEL RESPONSIBLE
Material price variance	Purchasing agent or purchasing department manager
Material quantity variance	Plant superintendent, departmental supervisors, machine operators, quality control department, and material handlers
Labor rate variance	Employment department manager, departmental supervisors, and plant superintendent
Labor efficiency variance	Plant superintendent, departmental supervisors, production scheduling department, quality control department, material handlers, and machine operators
Overhead spending variance	*Variable portion* is responsibility of individual supervisors; they are expected to keep actual expenses within budget. *Fixed portion* is responsibility of top management.
Overhead efficiency variance	Same personnel responsible for labor efficiency variance
Overhead volume variance	Top management and production schedulers

EXHIBIT 12-11
POSSIBLE CAUSES OF STANDARD COST VARIANCES

Material price variance

Recent purchase price changes that have not been incorporated into the
    standard cost
Quantity purchase discount changes due to changes in ordering policies
Substitute raw materials differed from original material specifications
Freight cost changes

Material quantity variance

Poor material handling
Inferior workmanship by machine operator
Faulty equipment
Cheaper grade of raw material caused excessive scrap
Inferior quality control inspection

Labor rate variance

Recent pay rate changes within industry
Employee hired at incorrect skill and experience level
Labor strike that caused utilization of unskilled help
Labor layoff that caused skilled labor to be retained so as to prevent
    resignations and job switching
Employee sickness and vacation time

Labor efficiency variance

Machine breakdown
Inferior raw materials
Poor supervision
Lack of timely material handling
Poor employee performance
Erratic production scheduling
Inferior engineering specifications
New inexperienced employee

Overhead spending variance

Unexpected price changes
Excessive indirect labor usage
Excessive indirect material usage
Changes in employee overtime
Machine and personnel failures
Depreciation rate changes

Overhead efficiency variance

See labor efficiency variance

Overhead volume variance

Failure to utilize normal capacity
Lack of sales orders
Too much idle capacity
Inefficient or efficient utilization of existing capacity

DISPOSITION AND REPORTING OF VARIANCES

Variances are computed for both cost planning and control purposes. In the process of recording variances in the accounts, a part of actual production cost is removed from the mainstream of cost flow and is recorded in separate variance accounts. At the end of an accounting period, these variance account balances must be properly accounted for in the process of preparing financial statements. The following questions must be considered to determine the proper disposition of variance account balances:

1. What are the concepts and procedures regarding external reporting of inventories and Cost of Goods Sold when a standard costing system is employed? Do the same guidelines apply for interim reporting?
2. What type of standard cost is being utilized?
3. Are the variance balances material in amount or insignificant?
4. Was the incurrence of the variances controllable or uncontrollable?
5. Were the price and rate changes permanent or temporary?
6. What alternatives are available to account for the disposition of variance balances?

External Reporting Considerations

Chapter 4 of *Accounting Research Bulletin No. 43* contains ten statements regarding appropriate inventory pricing policies for external reporting purposes. Statement 4 reads:

Cost for inventory purposes may be determined under any one of several assumptions as to the flow of cost factors (such as first-in first-out, average, and last-in first-out); the major objective in selecting a method should be to choose the one which, under the circumstances, most clearly reflects periodic income.[1]

This statement concerns the effect of cost flow assumptions on measurement of periodic income. The following statement is made concerning the acceptability of pricing inventories at standard costs:

Standard costs are acceptable if adjusted at reasonable intervals to reflect current conditions so that at the balance-sheet date standard costs reasonably approximate costs computed under one of the recognized bases. In such cases descriptive language should be used which will express this relationship, as, for instance, 'approximated costs determined on the first-in first-out basis,' or, if it is desired to mention standard costs, 'at standard costs, approximating average costs.'[2]

Based on this generally accepted accounting principle, inventory balances can be stated at standard cost only when accurate currently attainable standards are employed. When standards are not currently attainable (basic standards or ideal standards), variance balances must be allocated to Raw Material, Work in Process, and Finished Goods inventories in order to adjust these account balances to "actual cost." If variance accounts are significant in amount, the standards used usually are not considered to be currently attainable. In such cases, inventory accounts in annual financial statements must be adjusted to approximate actual cost.

Interim Reporting of Variances

If interim financial statements for quarterly or monthly periods are not distributed for external use, the guidelines for external reporting do not have to be applied. However, large variances may cause interim operating results to be

---

[1] Committee on Accounting Procedure, American Institute of Certified Public Accountants, *Accounting Research Bulletin No. 43*, New York, 1961, p. 29.

[2] *Ibid.*, p. 30.

misleading and may affect certain management decisions. For this reason, it is suggested that rules for annual external reporting of standard cost variances also be followed when preparing interim financial statements.

Other Reporting Considerations

The controllability and permanency of variance balances are also important considerations in deciding how to dispose of the balances at year-end. Assuming the use of currently attainable standards, large variances resulting from operating efficiencies or inefficiencies should be reported as costs (losses) or credits (gains) in the current period. These variances are controllable by management; to postpone their recognition by allocating them to inventory balances would be misleading. Variances that are controllable by short-run or long-run management decisions include material quantity, labor efficiency, overhead spending, overhead efficiency, and overhead volume variances. Material price and labor rate variances may be caused by management decisions or market price changes. If the price or rate variance is caused by management decisions, the variance is controllable and should be treated as a gain or loss of the period. If the cause is traced to market price changes, the variance amount should be allocated to the appropriate inventory accounts for financial reporting purposes.

If causes of variances are temporary in nature, such variances should be treated as losses or gains of the year.[3] However, if permanent price and rate changes or permanent changes in production operating procedure caused the variance, the resulting variances should be allocated to inventory accounts and Cost of Goods Sold and not be shown as gains or losses of the period. Revisions of existing standards is also required to reflect these permanent changes.

Accounting Alternatives for Variance Disposition

Disposing of variance balances to inventories and Cost of Goods Sold prior to preparation of financial statements is generally necessary if the variances are significant in amount or if they result from using noncurrent standards. If variances are not allocated, inventory balances and Cost of Goods Sold will be stated at standard cost, and the variances will be treated as special gains or losses of the period or as adjustments to standard Cost of Goods Sold. In accounting for the disposition of variances, inventories are stated at either standard cost or approximations of actual cost.

State inventories at actual cost   Variances may be prorated or allocated to Raw Material, Work in Process, and Finished Goods inventories and to Cost of Goods Sold. The material price variance is the only one affecting all four accounts; the remaining variances affect only Work in Process, Finished Goods, and Cost of Goods Sold. Using an appropriate allocation basis, such as standard cost balances of accounts or equivalent units of production, standard cost variances are allocated to the four accounts. After the allocation, inventories are stated at approximate actual costs.

State inventories at standard cost   The second alternative to variance disposition is to assign all variance balances to Cost of Goods Sold. Since variances are not allocated, inventories are stated at standard cost. This practical approach is appropriate when inventory balances are small (most items produced during

[3] For interim external reporting purposes, *Opinion 28* of the Accounting Principles Board recommends that volume variances and price variances be deferred if they are temporary in nature and will be counterbalanced in future interim periods (paragraph 14d).

the period were sold in the same period) or when variance balances are insignificant.

Illustrative problem Operations of the Gerent Company produced the following variances during 19X2:

| | STANDARD COST VARIANCES | | |
	Favorable	Unfavorable	NET
Material price variance*	$480		$480(F)
Material quantity variance		$ 270	270(U)
Labor rate variance	20		20(F)
Labor efficiency variance		460	460(U)
Overhead spending variance		74	74(U)
Overhead efficiency variance		286	286(U)
Overhead volume variance	90		90(F)
Totals	$590	$1,090	$500(U)

* Isolated at time of requisition so that variance is not allocated to Raw Material inventory.

Of the 12,000 units started during the year, 6,000 (50 percent) were completed and sold, 4,800 (40 percent) are in Finished Goods inventory, and 1,200 (10 percent) remain in process. Using units as the basis for variance disposition, an appropriate percentage share of the net unfavorable variance is allocated to each inventory account and to Cost of Goods Sold, as follows:

Work in process	10% of $500(U) =	$ 50(U)
Finsished goods	40% of 500(U) =	200(U)
Cost of goods sold	50% of 500(U) =	250(U)
Net unfavorable variance		$500(U)

The entry to dispose of the variances would be:

Work in process inventory	$ 50	
Finished goods inventory	200	
Cost of goods sold	250	
Material price variance	480	
Labor rate variance	20	
Overhead volume variance	90	
Material quantity variance		$270
Labor efficiency variance		460
Overhead spending variance		74
Overhead efficiency variance		286
To close variance accounts at end of 19X2		

Reporting of Variances   Reporting of inventory balances and results of operations will not change when a standard cost accounting system is employed if variance balances are disposed of in the manner illustrated above. The inventory account balances and Cost of Goods Sold have been adjusted to reflect approximate actual costs. If inventory balances and Cost of Goods Sold are reported at standard cost, financial statements should contain a footnote stating that inventories are valued at standard. In addition, proper disclosure of all variances should be shown in the income statement. The following income statement of the Gerent Company reflects the alternative procedure for charging all variances to Cost of Goods Sold:

GERENT COMPANY
Income statement*
For the year ended December 31, 19X2

Sales	$474,650
Less: Cost of goods sold (at standard)	329,550
Standard gross margin	$145,100
Less: Unfavorable operating variances†	500
Actual gross margin	$144,600
Less: Selling and administrative expenses	124,600
Net income before taxes	$ 20,000
Less: Income taxes	10,000
Net income	$ 10,000

* Inventory and Cost of Goods Sold are reported at standard costs. Amounts other than variances have been inserted here for illustrative purposes.
† Supported by schedule of individual variances; no allocation to inventories.

FINAL NOTE

Standard cost variance analysis is one of the more difficult topics discussed in this text. If specific topics or concepts are still not clear to you, reread the applicable sections of the chapter. It is important that you have a strong conceptual understanding of standard cost variance analysis before attempting to solve problems in this area.

When you have completed your review of the appendix, return to the beginning of the chapter and review the highlights section before proceeding to the review questions, exercises, and problems.

APPENDIX 12-A: Mix and Yield Variances for Materials

Materials mix and product yield are two important variable factors in many manufacturing situations. Mix refers to the relative proportions of several raw materials that must be combined to produce a desired finished product. Yield is a productivity factor represented by the ratio of output quantities to material input quantities. For instance, if 600 pounds of material A and 400 pounds of material B are normally combined to produce 900 pounds of product Y, then actual materials mix is 60 percent A and 40 percent B. Product yield of 90 percent is derived from the ratio of 900 pounds of output to 1,000 pounds of input.

The purpose of this appendix is to explain and demonstrate an approach for measuring mix and yield variances for raw materials in a standard cost system. Recognition of these variances is an important supplement to the materials quantity variance that is computed in most standard cost systems. Mix and yield variances are certainly important in any production activity for which standard mix can be varied or for which product yield is a value subject to variation.

Materials Mix For certain products and processing operations, materials mix is an important operating variable. When several types or grades of materials are required to produce a product, opportunities often exist to vary the relative proportions of input materials. A mix situation involves the ability to make substitutions among direct materials within some relevant range of proportions. Typical examples include woolen goods, chemical products, and processed meats such as sausage and hamburger.

Materials substitution may result from attempts to achieve economy in resource utilization or from necessity when required input quantities are not immediately available. A standard materials mix is usually specified for the desired final product, and any deviation from these standard proportions in actual materials usage generates a mix variance.

The *mix variance* explains that portion of the total material quantity variance caused by using materials in nonstandard proportions. A mix variance arises only when materials are used in nonstandard proportions. To illustrate the variance, consider product Y, which is measured in pounds and requires the inputs of materials A, B, and C indicated in Exhibit 12-A-1.

In the most recent production run for product Y, 21,800 pounds of materials were used, and 19,350 pounds of Y were completed. The standard quantity of materials allowed to produce 19,350 pounds of Y is 21,500 pounds computed from the standard yield as follows:

$$.90 \times \text{input} = 19,350 \text{ pounds of Y}$$
$$\text{input} = 21,500 \text{ pounds}$$

Thus, actual material usage (21,800 pounds) exceeds the allowable standard (21,500 pounds). Standard materials allowed for each material input are determined by using the standard mix percentages times total standard quantity of 21,500 pounds. Exhibit 12-A-2 shows actual material usage, standard materials allowed for good production, and *normalized actual quantities* (NAQ), which are the total actual material usage distributed to each material in accordance with the standard mix percentages. Exhibit 12-A-2 summarizes the data necessary for standard cost variance analysis.

EXHIBIT 12-A-1
PRODUCT Y—STANDARD MATERIALS SPECIFICATION
(NORMAL PRODUCTION RUN = 2,000 LBS. MATERIAL)

MATERIAL	STANDARD MIX	POUNDS	STANDARD PRICE	TOTAL STANDARD COST
A	10%	200	$1.00	$ 200
B	50%	1,000	2.00	2,000
C	40%	800	1.50	1,200
Total input	100%	2,000		$3,400
Standard Yield	90%	1,800 lbs. product Y		$3,400

EXHIBIT 12-A-2
VARIANCE ANALYSIS DATA

MATERIAL	ACTUAL QUANTITY (Q_a)	NORMALIZED ACTUAL QUANTITY (NAQ)	STANDARD QUANTITY (Q_s)	STANDARD Mix	STANDARD Price
A	2,000	2,180	2,150	10%	$1.00
B	11,100	10,900	10,750	50%	$2.00
C	8,700	8,720	8,600	40%	$1.50
	21,800	21,800	21,500		

Normalized actual quantity for each material is total actual quantity (21,800 pounds) times its standard mix percentage (that is, for A, 2,180 = 10 percent of 21,800). Standard quantity for each material is total standard quantity (21,500 pounds) times its standard mix percentage. The total quantity variance for this production run is $700 unfavorable as computed below by comparing actual and standard quantities of each material shown in Exhibit 12-A-2.

MATERIAL	ACTUAL QUANTITY	STANDARD QUANTITY	$Q_a - Q_s$	STANDARD PRICE	QUANTITY VARIANCE
A	2,000	2,150	(150)	$1.00	$150(F)
B	11,100	10,750	350	2.00	700(U)
C	8,700	8,600	100	1.50	150(U)
	21,800	21,500	300		$700(U)

The total quantity variance of $700 is the combined effect of yield factors and use of materials in nonstandard proportions. Accordingly, the mix variance holds yield constant and analyzes the impact of actual versus standard mix on actual material usage. The mix variance for each material is the difference between actual quantity (Q_a) and normalized actual quantity (NAQ) as indicated in Exhibit 12-A-3.

An unfavorable mix variance of $190 was apparently caused by using a higher relative proportion of expensive material B than called for in the standard mix. Of the total quantity variance of $700 unfavorable, $190 is attributable to materials mix, and the remaining $510 is related to yield considerations.

EXHIBIT 12-A-3
MIX VARIANCE COMPUTATION

MATERIAL	ACTUAL QUANTITY	NORMALIZED ACTUAL QUANTITY	$Q_a - NAQ$	STANDARD PRICE	MIX VARIANCE
A	2,000	2,180	(180)	$1.00	$180(F)
B	11,100	10,900	200	2.00	400(U)
C	8,700	8,720	(20)	1.50	30(F)
	21,800	21,800	-0-		$190(U)

EXHIBIT 12-A-4

YIELD VARIANCE COMPUTATION

MATERIAL	NAQ	Q_s	$NAQ - Q_s$	STANDARD PRICE	YIELD VARIANCE
A	2,180	2,150	30	$1.00	$ 30(U)
B	10,900	10,750	150	2.00	300(U)
C	8,720	8,600	120	1.50	180(U)
	21,800	21,500	300		$510(U)

Product Yield

The yield variance explains the remaining portion of the total quantity variance and is caused by a yield of final product that does not correspond with the product quantity that actual inputs should have produced. In our case, 19,350 pounds of product Y were produced, and this output volume should have required 21,500 pounds of materials (19,350 ÷ .90). Since 21,800 pounds of material were actually used, there is an unfavorable quantity variance attributable to the actual yield of 88.76 percent (19,350 ÷ 21,800) which is below standard.

To isolate the impact of nonstandard yield, it is necessary to hold mix constant. The effect of mix is eliminated when normalized actual quantities are compared with standard quantities for each material. In both NAQ and Q_s for each material, the standard mix percentages have been used. Yield variances for each material are therefore computed by comparing NAQ and Q_s, as done in Exhibit 12-A-4.

When there is no mix variance, the yield variance equals the total quantity variance. Accordingly, mix and yield variances explain distinct parts of the total quantity variance and are additive:

Mix variance (Exhibit 12-A-3)	$190(U)
Yield variance (Exhibit 12-A-4)	510(U)
Total quantity variance	$700(U)

Reports on material usage can easily combine the mix and yield variances to show these individual variances for each material.

Mix-Yield Summary

To compute mix and yield variances for a production run or particular time period, follow these general guidelines:

1. Compute total standard quantity from good output data and standard yield: Q_s = output ÷ yield percentage.
2. Compute the normalized standard and actual quantities using standard mix percentages.
3. Mix variance = standard price × $(Q_a - NAQ)$.
4. Yield variance = standard price × $(NAQ - Q_s)$.
5. Total quantity variance = mix variance + yield variance.

Mix and yield variances provide useful information for production control, performance evaluation, and review of operating efficiency. Interpretation of the variances requires an understanding of a particular manufacturing process and the potential effects of nonstandard materials mix. Materials mix can often affect product yield; in such cases, the variances are not independent as their form of computation implies. The variances are summary measures that do not indicate causes of differences between actual and standard performance. For purposes of management by exception, mix and yield variances are useful in revealing operational phases of production that require investigation.

QUESTIONS

12-1. Define and illustrate the following terms and concepts:
   a. Variance analysis
   b. Material quantity variance
   c. Material price variance
   d. Labor efficiency variance
   e. Labor rate variance
   f. Standard hours allowed
   g. Normal capacity
   h. Flexible budget
   i. Over- or underapplied overhead
   j. Overhead spending variance
   k. Overhead efficiency variance
   l. Overhead volume variance
   m. Overhead budget variance
   n. Performance evaluation
   o. Cost controllability

12-2. "Variance analysis is an integral part of standard cost accounting." Explain this statement.

12-3. What two general types of comparisons are involved in raw material variance computations?

12-4. The two phases of standard cost variance analysis are (1) initial computation and (2) identification of underlying causes. Discuss the relationship between these two phases.

12-5. Parrino Company maintains a standard cost accounting system that recognizes price variances when materials are requisitioned. What is the disadvantage of this practice?

12-6. What circumstances cause a material quantity variance to be favorable?

12-7. Identify some possible causes of an unfavorable labor rate variance.

12-8. By purchasing low-grade materials, Beta Company reports favorable material price variances, but it consistently experiences unfavorable material quantity variances. What relationship may exist between these conditions? Is the price variance really favorable?

12-9. If the labor efficiency variance in Department 27 is favorable, would you also expect to find a favorable overhead efficiency variance in this department? Support your reply.

12-10. Explain the relevance of normal capacity and flexible budgets in the determination of factory overhead variances.

12-11. If factory overhead during March is underapplied, will the sum of individual factory overhead variances be favorable or unfavorable?

12-12. Identify the eight key variables used in standard overhead variance analysis.

12-13. In computing the overhead spending variance, why is the flexible budget calculation based on actual labor hours for the period?

12-14. The overhead volume variance is one measure of effectiveness in using plant capacity. Explain the conditions that lead to a favorable volume variance.

12-15. In a standard *direct* costing system, why is there no recognition of the overhead volume variance?

EXERCISES

12-16. *External Reporting of Variances*   For external reporting purposes, one of the basic issues is whether standard cost variances should be allocated or prorated to inventory accounts in the balance sheet.

REQUIRED:
a. Under what circumstances should the variances be charged entirely to Cost of Goods Sold? When should the variances also be prorated to inventory accounts?
b. What circumstances dictate that variances be reported separately in the income statement as gains or losses of the period?

12-17. *Raw Material Variances*

REQUIRED:
a. Identify the two raw material variances and state the formula used to compute each.
b. Assuming variance isolation at time of purchase, show the derivation of the formulas in part (a) through the use of journal entries.

12-18. *Raw Material Variances*   Downes Door Company manufactures fireproof doors. Each door requires two pieces of 16-gauge sheet steel measuring 94 by 50 inches. The standard cost of each piece of steel is $18. During the month of August, 2,000 doors were started and completed, and there was no beginning or ending Work in Process inventory. Accounting records revealed that 4,068 pieces of sheet steel were requisitioned during August at a cost of $71,190.

REQUIRED: Compute the material price and material quantity variances for August production assuming the price variance is isolated at time of requisition.

12-19. *Direct Labor Variances*   The Assembly Department of the Foth Corporation has established a standard time of three hours per unit of product assembled. The current standard labor rate is $4.50 per hour. During April, the department reported assembly of 740 completed units. The following entry was made to record the direct labor payroll liability for April:

Factory payroll (for 2,200 hours worked)	$10,340	
Accrued payroll		$10,340
To record payroll liability for Assembly		
Department for April		

REQUIRED:
a. Compute the labor rate and labor efficiency variances for April.
b. Prepare the journal entry for April to distribute factory payroll to production accounts.

12-20. *Overhead Variances*   Budgeted fixed factory overhead for the Jessie Manufacturing Company is $18,000 per month and variable overhead costs are budgeted at $1.40 per direct labor hour. Monthly normal capacity or volume has been established at 6,000 direct labor hours. Actual operating data for September 19X8 were as follows:

Variable overhead costs	$ 9,309
Fixed overhead costs	$18,200
Actual direct labor hours	6,420 hours
Standard hours allowed	6,350 hours

REQUIRED: Compute the following amounts, labeling your answers appropriately:
a. Total overhead applied
b. Over- or underapplied overhead
c. Variable overhead spending variance
d. Fixed overhead spending variance
e. Overhead efficiency variance
f. Overhead volume variance
g. Total overhead variance

12-21. *Direct Material Variances*   Flame Industries produces a diverse line of paper products and uses a standard cost system for all inventories. Material J15 is a chemical dye that is used in several different departments and in many products. The company has recently experienced an increasing trend of unfavorable quantity variances for material J15. The production vice president received a summary report for September operations that disclosed the following results:

Material J15 issued to production	438,000 lbs.
Standard allowance for good production	412,000 lbs.
Over standard	26,000 lbs.
Current price (Sept. 30, 19X5)	× $5.50
Unfavorable variance	$143,000

Upon inquiry, the vice president discovered that the purchase price of J15 has increased about 8 percent monthly and that standard allowances were derived by a clerical assistant who worked all day searching through completed production reports. Thus, the vice president could not readily determine either the products or the departments that accounted for this quantity variance.

REQUIRED: Write a memorandum that summarizes weaknesses in this standard cost system and that recommends appropriate changes.

12-22. *Overhead Variances* Robert Marquette Enterprises, Inc., uses a flexible budget based on the following data:

CAPACITY	BUDGETED OVERHEAD
100%	$500,000
80%	440,000

Normal capacity is considered to be 80 percent. During October, 18,000 units of product (90 percent of capacity) were produced.

REQUIRED: Compute the budget and volume variances (two-variance approach) if actual factory overhead amounted to $505,000. *Hint:* $FC_a = FC_b$.

12-23. *Direct Labor Variances* A production department supervisor receives semimonthly standard cost labor reports, the most recent report of which follows:

DEPARTMENT 214
Standard labor cost report
Period 9/1/X4–9/15/X4

Regular wages paid (gross)	$60,000
Standard wages earned (gross)	45,000
Unfavorable variance	$15,000
Actual hours worked	10,000 hours
Standard hours allowed	9,000 hours

Because of experience in past months, the supervisor has been asked to explain or comment on the unfavorable variances that have been received.

REQUIRED:
a. Prepare an analysis of the total labor variance that indicates separate amounts for rate and efficiency variances.
b. What improvements could this company make in its use of standard cost information?

12-24. *Overhead Variances* The San Angelo plant of Sludge Industries uses a standard cost system supplemented by flexible budget procedures for planning and control. The monthly flexible budget for plantwide overhead cost is $400,000 of fixed costs plus $4.80 per machine hour. Normal monthly volume is 200,000 machine hours, and this capacity was used in computing the plantwide overhead rate. During August 19X3, the plant worked 210,000 actual machine hours, although the standard hours allowed for good production were only 197,000 machine hours. Actual overhead costs incurred during August were $409,000 (fixed) and $1,082,000 (variable).

REQUIRED:
a. Determine the amount of under- or overapplied overhead during August.
b. Prepare a summary analysis, with supporting computations, for the spending, efficiency, and volume variances.

12-25. *Standard Overhead Rate Analysis*   The Shaping Department at Rudolph Manufacturing Company utilizes a flexible budget based on direct labor cost. At direct labor cost levels of $7,000 and $8,000, budgeted factory overhead is $13,200 and $14,400, respectively. Factory overhead is applied to products at a rate of 160 percent of direct labor cost.

REQUIRED:
a. The variable overhead rate per direct labor dollar is:
   1. 60 percent   4. 90 percent
   2. 70 percent   5. None of the above
   3. 80 percent
b. The budgeted fixed overhead amount is:
   1. $1,200   4. $8,000
   2. $2,500   5. None of the above
   3. $5,600
c. Normal capacity is:
   1. $7,440 direct labor dollars   4. $14,650 direct labor dollars
   2. $9,600 direct labor dollars   5. None of the above
   3. $10,000 direct labor dollars

12-26. *Raw Material and Direct Labor Variances*   M. Busch Company produces a single product from a single material. Mr. Someday, the company's cost accountant, recently installed a standard cost system. The budgeted amounts and actual operating data for June 19X7 are summarized below:

	BUDGETED		ACTUAL	
	Quantity	Dollars	Quantity	Dollars
Units produced	1,600 units		1,200 units	
Units of raw material	3,200 units	$6,400	2,600 units	$5,460
Direct labor hours	4,800 hours	6,000	4,000 hours	6,000
Factory overhead (applied on direct labor hour basis)	4,800 hours	4,800	4,000 hours	4,400

REQUIRED:
a. Compute the standard unit cost.
b. Prepare an analysis of the material and labor variances for June 19X7.

12-27. *External Reporting Using Standard Costs*   Mr. C. P. Anderson, assistant controller of the NIU-MIZZOU Corporation, has just completed the corporation's annual financial statements and has submitted them to the controller for final approval. While scrutinizing the statements, the controller noticed the following on the balance sheet:

Inventories:

Raw materials (at actual cost)	$25,000	
Plus: Unisolated favorable material price variance	5,000	$ 30,000
Work in process (at standard cost)		75,000
Finished goods (at standard cost)		70,000
Total inventories (at standard)		$175,000

The corporation employs a standard cost system in which material price variances are not isolated until the materials are requisitioned by the production department. The controller, who installed the system ten years ago, believes that all accounting reports should spotlight trends. Therefore, actual costs through the years have been compared with standard costs that have not been updated since the system was installed.

REQUIRED:

a. If you were the controller, evaluate Mr. Anderson's presentation of inventories without changing the present standard cost system.
b. Would your answer in part (a) change if the standard costs employed by the corporation were currently attainable and the unisolated material price variance were unfavorable? Give reasons for your answer.
c. Distinguish between an ideal or theoretical standard and a currently attainable standard.

12-28. *Comprehensive Variance Analysis*   Austin Powder Company produces a single product and uses a standard cost system. Its single product, Mush, requires the following inputs and cost factors:

Materials (5 gallons at $.60)	$ 3.00
Labor (2 hours at $4.00)	8.00
Overhead (2 hours at $5.00)	10.00
Standard unit cost	$21.00

The overhead element for Mush was derived from overhead budgets that estimate monthly fixed overhead of $300,000 and $450,000 of variable overhead based on normal monthly volume of 150,000 direct labor hours. Overhead is applied on the basis of standard hours allowed.

During March 19X9, Austin Powder purchased 400,000 gallons of material at total invoice cost of $270,000. Good production for the month was 70,000 units of Mush, and materials requisitioned from stores amounted to 360,000 gallons. Direct labor cost for March was $585,000 for 130,000 actual hours. Total factory overhead costs incurred were $710,000. March sales were 90,000 units of Mush at $40.

REQUIRED:

a. Prepare journal entries for all transactions and production activity during March.
b. Compute spending, efficiency, and volume variances for factory overhead and reconcile to under- or overapplied overhead.

12-29. *Total Variance Analysis*   Caldwell Fertilizer Company produces one product with a standard cost per unit of:

Raw material (3 lbs. at $.75/lb.)	$ 2.25
Direct labor (2 hrs. at $3.50/hr.)	7.00
Variable overhead (2 hrs. at $.50/hr.)	1.00
Fixed overhead (2 hrs. at $2.50/hr.)	5.00
Total	$15.25

Normal monthly production is 7,000 units. Selected transactions for November 19X8 were:

a. Produced 6,900 units
b. Direct labor: 14,100 hours; direct labor payroll: $47,940
c. Raw materials purchased—25,000 lbs. for $17,500
d. Raw materials requisitioned in production—22,080 lbs.
e. Actual factory overhead:

Variable	$ 7,450
Fixed	$36,000

REQUIRED:

a. Compute the following variances:
   1. Material price variance (at time of purchase)
   2. Material quantity variance
   3. Labor rate variance
   4. Labor efficiency variance
   5. Variable overhead spending variance
   6. Fixed overhead spending variance
   7. Overhead efficiency variance
   8. Overhead volume variance
   9. Overhead budget variance
b. Prepare journal entries to record all material, labor, and overhead transactions (use the overhead entry based on the three-variance approach).

12-30. *Overhead Variance Review*   Overhead variances are interrelated. The Needles Company and the McHugh Company both use a standard cost system and employ a single (combined) overhead rate.

REQUIRED: Fill in the unknown amounts below by analyzing the data given for each company. Capacities are expressed in direct labor hours (DLHs).

	NEEDLES COMPANY	McHUGH COMPANY
a. Combined overhead rate per DLH	$1.60	_____
b. Actual variable and fixed overhead	$13,100	_____
c. Standard hours allowed	_____	4,100 DLHs
d. Standard variable overhead rate	$.50	$2.00
e. Budgeted fixed factory overhead	_____	$12,000
f. Normal capacity in DLHs		_____
g. Actual DLHs	7,500 DLHs	_____
h. Total overhead variance	_____	$300(F)
i. Total overhead spending variance	_____	
j. Overhead efficiency variance	_____	$200(U)
k. Overhead volume variance	$220(F)	_____
l. Total overhead costs applied	$12,800	_____
m. Total budget variance	_____	$4,800(U)

12-31. *Total Variance Analysis* Varyfrum Actual Company utilizes a standard cost system and produces calibrators. All parts are purchased in sets from a foreign manufacturer. Standard costs per finished calibrator include $32.00 per set of raw materials and $9.00 for direct labor. Standard labor rate is $4.50 per hour. The total standard overhead rate for the current year is $3.50 per direct labor hour for product costing purposes. Operating data for March were as follows:

Direct material sets purchased	50,000 at $32.40
Direct materials used	62,000 sets
Direct labor	129,150 hours; total payroll is $568,260
Total overhead costs incurred	$442,000
Units produced	61,500

The applicable overhead flexible budget for the period is:

$1.40 per direct labor hour + $273,000 of fixed overhead

REQUIRED: Compute the dollar amounts of the following:
a. Material price variance (at time of purchase)
b. Material quantity variance
c. Labor rate variance
d. Labor efficiency variance
e. Overhead spending variance

f. Overhead efficiency variance
g. Overhead volume variance
h. Normal capacity in DLHs

12-32. *Total Variance Analysis—Practical Capacity* H. Billings Company makes a dehydrated liquid product called Big Herb's special. The standard variable costs for one unit of finished product are:

Direct materials (2 ounces at $.50)	$1.00
Direct labor (½ hour at $4.00)	2.00
Variable overhead ($2 per standard DLH)	1.00
Standard variable cost	$4.00

Practical monthly capacity is 15,000 units with budgeted fixed overhead of $7,500. The current selling price and variable distribution cost per unit are $6.50 and $.75, respectively. For the most recent month, 10,000 units were produced and sold. Related transactions and cost data for this period are:

Material purchases (15,000 ounces at $.40)	$ 6,000
Material usage (22,000 ounces at $.50)	$11,000
Direct labor (4,500 hours at $4.10)	$18,450
Variable overhead incurred	$11,000
Fixed overhead incurred	$ 8,200

Fixed and variable overhead is applied to production on the basis of standard hours allowed. The fixed overhead rate was computed using practical capacity.

REQUIRED: Compute the requested standard cost variances. Designate variances as favorable (F) or unfavorable (U).
a. Material price variance
b. Material quantity variance
c. Standard hours allowed
d. Labor rate variance
e. Labor efficiency variance
f. Variable overhead spending variance
g. Fixed overhead spending variance
h. Overhead efficiency variance
i. Overhead volume variance

12-33. *Multiple Choice—Standard Cost Accounting* Mifflin Company uses a standard cost system. The standard absorption cost of one gadget is:

Materials (6 lbs. at $10/lb.)	$ 60
Labor (4 hrs. at $6/hour)	24
Overhead ($10/standard labor hour)	40
Standard unit cost	$124

The company's annual flexible budget for overhead is $1,296,000 in fixed costs plus $7.00 per hour for variable overhead. The fixed portion of the overhead rate was computed by using expected annual capacity of 432,000 standard hours. Fixed overhead was budgeted uniformly for each month. In October, 9,000 gadgets were produced. Material usage during the period was 53,000 pounds, and actual labor for the period was 36,500 hours at an average hourly rate of $6.10. Actual factory overhead costs of $320,000 were incurred.

REQUIRED:

a. The standard quantity of material allowed for production in the month of October is:
   1. 53,000   3. 36,000
   2. 54,000   4. None of the above

b. The material usage or quantity variance is:
   1. $10,000(U)   3. $9,800(U)
   2. $9,800(F)   4. $10,000(F)

c. The labor rate variance for the month is:
   1. $3,600(U)   3. $3,650(U)
   2. $3,650(F)   4. $3,600(F)

d. The labor efficiency variance for the period is:
   1. $3,000(U)   3. $3,000(F)
   2. $3,050(F)   4. None of the above

e. Factory overhead applied to production is:
   1. $320,000   3. $365,000
   2. $108,000   4. $360,000

f. The volume variance for October is:
   1. $40,000(F)   3. $-0-
   2. $40,000(U)   4. Not determinable

g. The spending variance for factory overhead is:
   1. $40,000(U)   3. $43,500(F)
   2. $3,500(U)   4. None of the above

h. The efficiency variance for variable overhead is:
   1. $3,500(U)   3. $43,500(U)
   2. $-0-   4. None of the above

i. If inventories are carried at standard cost, the journal entry to record material usage should:
   1. Credit Raw Materials inventory for $540,000
   2. Debit Work in Process for $540,000
   3. Debit Work in Process for $530,000
   4. Credit Material Price Variance for $10,000

j. If all of the inventories are carried at standard cost, then the journal entry to record completion of finished units and their transfer should:
   1. Debit Finished Goods for standard cost of production
   2. Debit Finished Goods for actual cost of production
   3. Credit Work in Process for actual cost of production
   4. None of the above

12-34. *External Reporting—Standard Cost System* Harry Richard Company uses a standard direct costing system for internal planning and control purposes. Direct costing results are adjusted to standard absorption costing to satisfy external reporting requirements. A flexible budget for the production and sale of 200,000 units of product X is given below:

Sales		$2,000,000
Variable costs:		
Material and labor	$400,000	
Manufacturing overhead	600,000	
Selling and administrative	200,000	1,200,000
Contribution margin		$ 800,000
Fixed Costs:		
Manufacturing overhead	$300,000	
Selling and administrative	100,000	400,000
Income before taxes		$ 400,000

The 200,000 unit budget was adopted in 19X2 for applying manufacturing overhead to production of product X. All fixed costs are incurred uniformly during the year and correspond with budget estimates. Over- or underapplied overhead is deferred and charged or credited to Cost of Goods Sold at year-end.

REQUIRED:

a. The standard direct cost of product X for inventory purposes is _____.

b. The standard absorption cost of product X for inventory purposes is _____.

c. The breakeven point in sales dollars for product X is _____.

d. During the first nine months, 130,000 units were produced and 120,000 units were sold. Reported net income for this period under absorption costing is _____.

e. Refer to the facts in question (d). Reported net income for the first nine months under direct costing is _____.

f. Refer to the facts in question (d). With absorption costing, the amount of under- or overapplied fixed factory overhead is _____.

For parts (g) to (j), assume that in 19X2, Harry Richard Company produced 220,000 units and sold 200,000 units. Net unfavorable standard cost variances of $143,000 for material, labor, and variable overhead were deferred during the year. There was no initial inventory of product X.

g. The unfavorable variances of $143,000 and the volume variance for fixed factory overhead are to be treated as adjustments to standard Cost of Goods Sold in absorption costing reports. The adjusted Cost of Goods Sold is _____.

h. Assume that the unfavorable variances of $143,000 will be prorated between Finished Goods and Cost of Goods Sold based upon the standard cost balances of these accounts at year-end. After the proration, the adjusted balance of Finished Goods under absorption costing is _____.

i. Assume that all applicable standard cost variances will be treated as adjustments to contribution margin in direct costing reports. As adjusted, the total contribution margin reported for 19X2 is _____.

j. Following the assumption in question (i), the Finished Goods inventory valuation under direct costing will be _____.

12-35. *Income Statement Analysis Using Variances* McKeroon Company recently developed a standard cost system for material, labor, and overhead accounting. Overhead costs are charged to production on the basis of standard labor hours allowed for good production. The company uses absorption costing procedures. For the most recent month, fixed costs were budgeted at $210,000. Expected actual capacity used in establishing overhead rates was 70,000 hours monthly. The standard variable overhead rate is $4 per hour. Actual overhead costs incurred during the month were $520,000. Payroll records for the period show 75,000 actual hours and 65,000 standard hours.

REQUIRED: Complete the following report of overhead variances for the month. Indicate credit amounts and favorable variances by parentheses ( ).

Overhead costs incurred	$520,000
Overhead applied	_____
Under- or overapplied balance	════════

(1) Variable spending variance	_____
(2) Efficiency variance	_____
(3) Variable variance (1 + 2)	_____
(4) Volume variance	_____
(5) Fixed spending variance	_____
(6) Fixed variance (4 + 5)	_____
Under- or overapplied balance (3 + 6)	════════

12-36. *CMA Problem—Variance Analysis* Karberg Corporation manufactures and sells a single product and uses a standard system. The standard cost per unit of product is shown below:

Material (1 lb. plastic at $2)	$ 2.00
Direct labor (1.6 hours at $4)	6.40
Variable overhead cost	3.00
Fixed overhead cost	1.45
	$12.85

The overhead cost per unit was calculated from the following annual overhead cost budget for a volume of 60,000 units:

Variable overhead cost:

Indirect labor (30,000 hours at $4.00)	$120,000
Supplies—oil (60,000 gallons at $.50)	30,000
Allocated variable service department costs	30,000
Total variable overhead cost	$180,000

Fixed overhead cost:

Supervision	$ 27,000
Depreciation	45,000
Other fixed costs	15,000
Total fixed overhead cost	$ 87,000
Total budgeted annual overhead cost (60,000 units)	$267,000

The charges to the Manufacturing Department for November, when 5,000 units were produced, are given below:

Material (5,300 lbs. at $2.00)	$10,600
Direct labor (8,200 hours at $4.10)	33,620
Indirect labor (2,400 hours at $4.10)	9,840
Supplies—oil (6,000 gallons at $.55)	3,300
Allocated variable service department costs	3,200
Supervision	2,475
Depreciation	3,750
Other	1,250
Total	$68,035

The Purchasing Department normally buys about the same quantity as is used in production during a month. In November, 5,200 pounds were purchased at a price of $2.10 per pound.

REQUIRED:
a. Calculate the following variances from standard costs for the data given:

1. Materials purchase price   4. Direct labor efficiency
2. Materials quantity   5. Overhead budget
3. Direct labor wage rate

b. The company has divided its responsibilities such that the Purchasing Department is responsible for the price at which materials and supplies are purchased. The Manufacturing Department is responsible for the quantities of materials used. Does this division of responsibilities solve the conflict between price and quantity variances? Explain your answer.

c. Prepare a report that details the overhead budget variance. The report, which will be given to the Manufacturing Department manager, should display only that part of the variance that is the responsibility of the manager and should highlight the information in ways that would be useful to the manager in evaluating departmental performance and in considering corrective action.

d. Assume that the department manager performs the timekeeping function. From time to time analysis of overhead and direct labor variances have shown that the department manager has deliberately misclassified labor hours (by listing direct labor hours as indirect labor hours and vice versa) so that only one of the two labor variances is unfavorable. It is not feasible economically to hire a separate timekeeper. What should the company do, if anything, to resolve this problem?

(IMA adapted)

12-37. *CMA Problem—Variance Analysis* Steel Slitting Company divides 24-inch widths of rolled sheet steel into 2- and 4-inch widths. The 24-inch widths are delivered to Steel Slitting Company by its customers, and the new widths are picked up by the customers after slitting. The cut widths plus scrap loss (caused by starting and ending rolls of steel or jams on the slitters) cannot cost the customers more than acquiring the correct widths directly from steel mills. Therefore, Steel Slitting Company uses tight standard costs to stay competitive.

If bought directly from steel mills, steel would cost customers the following:

SIZE	GAGE	COST PER TON
24 inches	14	$125
24 inches	12	120
2 inches	14	136
2 inches	12	130
4 inches	12	130

The Steel Slitting Company price for slitting a ton of input steel from customers is:

SIZE	GAGE	CUSTOMER PRICE PER TON SLIT
2 inches	14	$8
2 inches	12	7
4 inches	12	6

Standard and actual slitting costs per input ton for October are as follows:

	STANDARD COST PER TON (2-INCH)	ACTUAL COST PER TON (2-INCH)	STANDARD COST PER TON (4-INCH)	ACTUAL COST PER TON (4-INCH)
Direct labor	$3.00	$3.10	$2.50	$2.60
Variable overhead	2.80	3.00	2.00	2.10
Nonvariable overhead	1.00	1.00	1.00	1.00
	$6.80	$7.10	$5.50	$5.70
Customer scrap loss (percent of input tons absorbed by customer)	1%	2%	1%	3%

Standard cost per ton is based on width of strips regardless of gage. Budgeted and actual sales for the month of October are as follows:

SIZE	GAGE	BUDGETED	ACTUAL
2 inches	14	500 input tons	300 input tons
2 inches	12	400 input tons	400 input tons
4 inches	12	100 input tons	300 input tons

REQUIRED:

a. Steel Slitting Company does not own the material, nor does it absorb any yield loss. Can a material yield variance be calculated? If so, how would you calculate it? Would it be useful to management? Explain.

b. Could the company's customers do better by purchasing steel strips directly from steel mills? Explain your answer with appropriate numbers.

(IMA adapted)

12-38. *CPA Problem—Variance Analysis* Conti Pharmaceutical Company processes a single compound product known as NULAX and uses a standard cost accounting system. The process requires preparation and blending of three materials in large batches with a variation from the standard mixture sometimes necessary to maintain quality. Conti's cost accountant became ill at the end of October 19X8, and you were engaged to determine standard costs of October production and explain any differences between actual and standard costs for the month. The following information is available for the Blending Department:

a. The standard cost card for a 500-pound batch shows the following standard costs:

	QUANTITY	PRICE	TOTAL COST	
Materials				
Mucilloid	250 pounds	$ .14	$35	
Dextrose	200 pounds	.09	18	
Ingredients	50 pounds	.08	4	
Total per batch	500 pounds			$ 57
Labor:				
Preparation and blending	10 hours	$3.00		30
Overhead:				
Variable	10 hours	1.00	$10	
Fixed	10 hours	.30	3	13
Total standard cost per 500-pound batch				$100

b. During October, 410 batches of 500 pounds each of the finished compound were completed and transferred to the Packaging Department.

c. Blending Department inventories totaled 6,000 pounds at the beginning of the month and 9,000 pounds at the end of the month (assume both inventories were completely processed but not transferred and that both consisted of materials in their standard proportions). Inventories are carried in the accounts at standard cost prices.

d. During the month of October the following materials were purchased and put into production:

	POUNDS	PRICE	TOTAL COST
Mucilloid	114,400	$.17	$19,448
Dextrose	85,800	.11	9,438
Ingredients	19,800	.07	1,386
Totals	220,000		$30,272

e. Wages paid for 4,212 hours of direct labor at $3.25 per hour amounted to $13,689.

f. Actual overhead costs for the month totaled $5,519.

g. The standards were established for a normal production volume of 200,000 pounds (400 batches) of NULAX per month. At this level of production, variable factory overhead was budgeted at $4,000 and fixed factory overhead was budgeted at $1,200.

REQUIRED:

a. Prepare a schedule presenting the computation for the Blending Department of:
   1. October production in both pounds and batches
   2. The standard cost of October production itemized by components of materials, labor, and overhead
b. Prepare schedules computing the differences between actual and standard costs and analyzing the differences as:
   1. Materials variances (for each material) caused by (a) price differences and by (b) usage differences
   2. Labor variances caused by (a) rate differences and by (b) efficiency differences
   3. Overhead variances caused by (a) controllable factors and by (b) volume factors
c. Explain how the materials variances arising from usage differences could be further analyzed (no computations are necessary).

(AICPA adapted)

12-39. *CPA Problem—Variance Analysis* Bronson Company manufactures a fuel additive that has a stable selling price of forty dollars per drum. Since losing a government contract, the company has been producing and selling 80,000 drums per month, 50 percent of normal capacity. Management expects to increase production to 140,000 drums in the coming fiscal year.

In connection with your examination of the financial statements of the Bronson Company for the year ended September 30, 19X0, you have been asked to review some computations made by Bronson's cost accountant. Your working papers disclose the following about the company's operations:

a. Standard costs per drum of product manufactured:
Materials:

8 gallons of miracle mix	$16
1 empty drum	1
	$17
Direct labor (1 hour)	$ 5
Factory overhead	$ 6

b. Costs and expenses during September 19X0:
Miracle mix:
500,000 gallons purchased at cost of $950,000;
650,000 gallons used
Empty drums:
94,000 purchased at cost of $94,000; 80,000 used
Direct labor:
82,000 hours worked at cost of $414,100
Factory overhead:

Depreciation of building and machinery (fixed)	$210,000
Supervision and indirect labor (semivariable)	460,000
Other factory overhead (variable)	98,000
	$768,000

c. Other factory overhead was the only actual overhead cost that varied from the overhead budget for the September level of production; actual other factory overhead was $98,000, and the budgeted amount was $90,000.
d. At normal capacity of 160,000 drums per month, supervision and indirect labor costs are expected to be $570,000. All cost functions are linear.
e. None of the September 19X0 cost variances are expected to occur proportionally in future months. Over the next fiscal year, the same standard usage of materials and direct labor hours are expected. The average prices expected are $2.10 per gallon of miracle mix, $1.00 per empty drum, and $5.70 per direct labor hour. The current flexible budget of factory overhead costs is considered applicable to future periods without revision.
f. The company uses the two-variance method of accounting for overhead.

REQUIRED:
a. Prepare a schedule computing the following variances for September 19X0:
1. Materials price variance
2. Materials usage variance
3. Labor rate variance
4. Labor usage (efficiency) variance
5. Controllable (budget or spending) overhead variance
6. Volume (capacity) overhead variance
Indicate whether variances were favorable or unfavorable.

b. Prepare a schedule of the actual manufacturing cost per drum of product expected at production of 140,000 drums per month using the following cost categories: materials, direct labor, fixed factory overhead, and variable factory overhead.

(AICPA adapted)

12-40. *CPA Problem—External Reporting of Variances* Last year Crowley Corporation adopted a standard cost system. Labor standards were set on the basis of time studies and prevailing wage rates. Material standards were determined from material specifications and prices then in effect. In determining its standard for overhead, Crowley estimated that a total of 6,000,000 finished units would be produced during the next five years to satisfy demand for its product. The five-year period was selected to average out seasonal and cyclical fluctuations and allow for sales trends. By dividing the annual average of 1,200,000 units into the total annual budgeted overhead, a standard cost was developed for manufacturing overhead.

On June 30, 19X9, the end of the current fiscal year, a partial trial balance revealed the following:

	DEBITS	CREDITS
Materials price variance		$25,000
Materials quantity variance	$ 9,000	
Labor rate variance	30,000	
Labor efficiency variance	7,500	
Controllable overhead variance	2,000	
Noncontrollable (capacity) overhead variance	75,000	

Standards were set at the beginning of the year and have remained unchanged. All inventories are priced at standard cost.

REQUIRED:
a. What conclusions can be drawn from each of the six variances shown in Crowley's trial balance?
b. The amount of nonvariable manufacturing overhead cost to be included in product cost depends on whether or not the allocation is based on: (1) ideal, or theoretical, capacity; (2) practical capacity; (3) normal capacity; or (4) expected annual capacity. Describe each of these allocation bases and give a theoretical principal argument for each.
c. Give the theoretical justification for each of the following methods of accounting for the net amount of all standard cost variances for year-end financial reporting:
1. Presenting the net variance as an income or expense on the income statement
2. Allocating the net variance among inventories and Cost of Goods Sold

3. Presenting the net variance as an adjustment to Cost of Goods Sold

(AICPA adapted)

12-41. *CPA Problem—Variance Analysis*   Ross Shirts, Inc., makes short- and long-sleeved men's shirts for large stores. Ross produces a single quality shirt in lots to each customer's order and attaches the store's label to each. The standard costs for a dozen long-sleeved shirts are:

Direct materials (24 yards at $.55)	$13.20
Direct labor (3 hours at $2.45)	7.35
Manufacturing overhead (3 hours at $2.00)	6.00
Standard cost per dozen	$26.55

During October 19X9, Ross worked on three orders for long-sleeved shirts. Job cost records for the month disclose the following:

LOT	UNITS IN LOT	MATERIAL USED	HOURS WORKED
30	1,000 dozen	24,100 yards	2,980
31	1,700 dozen	40,440 yards	5,130
32	1,200 dozen	28,825 yards	2,890

The following information is also available:

a. Ross purchased 95,000 yards of material during the month at a cost of $53,200. The materials price variance is recorded when goods are purchased and all inventories are carried at standard cost.

b. Direct labor incurred amounted to $27,500 during October. According to payroll records, production employees were paid $2.50 per hour.

c. Overhead is applied on the basis of direct labor hours. Manufacturing overhead totaling $22,800 was incurred during October.

d. A total of $288,000 was budgeted for overhead for the year 19X9 based on estimated production at the plant's normal capacity of 48,000 dozen shirts per year. At this level of production, overhead is 40 percent fixed and 60 percent variable.

e. There was no work in process at October 1. During October lots 30 and 31 were completed, and all material was issued for lot 32, which was 80 percent complete regarding labor.

REQUIRED:

a. Prepare a schedule computing the standard cost for October 19X9 of lots 30, 31, and 32.

b. Prepare a schedule computing the materials price variance for October 19X9 and indicate whether the variance is favorable or unfavorable.

c. Prepare schedules for each lot produced during October 19X9, computing the following (and indicating whether the variances are favorable or unfavorable):

1. Materials quantity variance in yards
2. Labor efficiency variance in hours
3. Labor rate variance in dollars

d. Prepare a schedule computing the total controllable and noncontrollable (capacity) manufacturing overhead variances for October 19X9 and indicate whether the variances are favorable or unfavorable.

(AICPA adapted)

12-42. *CPA Problem—Process Costing and Estimated Costs* Kaerwer Corporation operates a machine shop and employs an estimated cost system. In March 19X8, Kaerwer was low bidder on a contract to deliver 600 kartz by May 15 at a contract price of $200 each. Kaerwer's estimate of the costs to manufacture each kartz was:

40 pounds of materials at $1.50 per pound	$ 60
20 hours of direct labor at $2.00 per hour	40
Manufacturing overhead (40% variable)	30
Total cost	$130

Inventories on April 1 included 30 kartz that had not been transferred to Finished Goods inventory, 70 kartz 60 percent processed, and 2,000 pounds of materials at a cost of $3,000. Production during March was at estimated costs. During April, 500 kartz were started in production, 450 kartz were completed, and 480 kartz were transferred to finished goods. The Work in Process inventory on April 30 was 10 percent processed. All material was added when a kartz was started in production. The materials inventory is priced under the FIFO method at actual cost. The following information is available for the month of April:

a. Materials purchased (in sequence as shown)

POUNDS	AMOUNT
8,000	$12,000
8,000	12,800
4,000	5,600

b. Materials requisitioned and put into production totaled 21,000 pounds.
c. The direct labor payroll amounted to $18,648 for 8,880 hours.
d. Manufacturing overhead was applied on the basis of estimated direct labor hours. Actual manufacturing overhead incurred, including indirect labor, totaled $13,140 and was charged to the Overhead in Process account.
e. Accounts employed by Kaerwer Corporation include Material in Process, Labor in Process, Overhead in Process, Work in Process inventory, Finished Goods inventory, and Raw Materials inventory.

The first three accounts are closed monthly. Perpetual inventory systems are maintained for Raw Materials and Finished Goods inventories.

REQUIRED:
a. Prepare in good form:
  1. A quantity of production report that accounts both for actual units in production and for equivalent unit production for materials, labor, and overhead for April
  2. A schedule presenting the computation of the balances (before closing) of the following accounts:
    Materials inventory
    Materials in process
    Labor in process
    Overhead in process
    Work in process inventory
    Finished goods inventory
b. Kaerwer Corporation would like to install a standard cost system and requests that you prepare a schedule presenting a computation of an analysis of the material, labor, and overhead variances they could expect from such a system for production during April. Assume that the standard cost of a kartz is the same as its estimated cost. Overhead variances should be divided into controllable and noncontrollable components assuming a standard normal capacity of 400 kartz per month.

(AICPA adapted)

12-43. *CPA Problem—Variance Analysis* Jones Furniture Company uses a standard cost system in accounting for its production costs. The standard cost of a unit of furniture follows:

Lumber (100 feet at $150 per 1,000 feet)		$15
Direct labor (4 hours at $2.50 per hour)		10
Manufacturing overhead:		
Fixed (30% of direct labor)	$3	
Variable (60% of direct labor)	6	9
Total unit cost		$34

The following flexible monthly overhead budget is in effect:

DIRECT LABOR HOURS	ESTIMATED OVERHEAD
5,200	$10,800
4,800	10,200
4,400	9,600
4,000 (normal capacity)	9,000
3,600	8,400

The actual unit costs for the month of December were as follows:

Lumber used (110 feet at $120 per 1,000 feet)	$13.20
Direct labor (4¼ hours at $2.60 per hour)	11.05
Manufacturing overhead ($10,560 ÷ 1,200 units)	8.80
Total actual unit cost	$33.05

REQUIRED: Prepare a schedule that shows an analysis of each element of the total variance from standard cost for the month of December.

(AICPA adapted)

12-44. *CMA Problem—Product Mix and Variance Analysis* Arsco Company makes three grades of indoor-outdoor carpets. The sales volume for the annual budget is determined by estimating the total market volume for indoor-outdoor carpet and then applying the company's prior-year market share, adjusted for planned changes for the coming year. The volume is apportioned between the three grades based upon the prior year's product mix, again adjusted for planned changes for the coming year. Below are the company budget for 19X3 and the actual results of operations for 19X3:

BUDGET

	Grade 1	Grade 2	Grade 3	Total
Sales (units)	1,000 rolls	1,000 rolls	2,000 rolls	4,000 rolls
Sales dollars (000 omitted)	$1,000	$2,000	$3,000	$6,000
Variable expense	700	1,600	2,300	4,600
Variable margin	$ 300	$ 400	$ 700	$1,400
Traceable fixed expense	200	200	300	700
Traceable margin	$ 100	$ 200	$ 400	$ 700
Selling and administrative expense				$ 250
Net income				$ 450

ACTUAL

	Grade 1	Grade 2	Grade 3	Total
Sales (units)	800 rolls	1,000 rolls	2,100 rolls	3,900 rolls
Sales dollars (000 omitted)	$810	$2,000	$3,000	$5,810
Variable expense	560	$1,610	2,320	4,490
Variable margin	$250	$ 390	$ 680	$1,320
Traceable fixed expense	210	220	315	745
Traceable margin	$ 40	$ 170	$ 365	$ 575
Selling and administrative expense				$ 275
Net income				$ 300

Industry volume was estimated at 40,000 rolls for budgeting purposes. Actual industry volume for 19X3 was 38,000 rolls.

REQUIRED:

a. Calculate the profit impact of the unit sales volume variance for 19X3 using budgeted variable margins.
b. What portion of the variance, if any, can be attributed to the state of the carpet market?
c. What is the dollar impact on profits (using budgeted variable margins) of the shift in product mix from the budgeted mix?

(IMA adapted)

Module Four

Applications of Planning and Performance Evaluation Techniques

THIS FINAL MODULE presents concepts and techniques that extend and apply the materials covered in preceding chapters. Chapters in Module Four can be studied independently of earlier chapters. However, the authors consider the contents of Module Three to be essential foundations of the planning, decision-making, and control phases of management accounting. Cost behavior, cost-volume-profit analysis, flexible budgets, standard costs, and variance analysis are building blocks. Also, a basic understanding of unit cost determination, cost allocation, and management accounting–financial accounting relationships will add meaning to the study of Module Four.

Our basic philosophy is that responsibility accounting, operational budgeting, short-run decision analysis, capital expenditure decision analysis, and divisional performance evaluation should be viewed as applied foundations of management accounting concepts and techniques. This philosophy is particularly true for cost analysis supporting various operational decisions such as sell-or-process-further and make-or-buy decisions. In practice, the distinction between supporting foundations of management accounting and their application is difficult. This distinction, however, is useful for learning purposes so that students can visualize the relationships among various topics in management accounting.

Module Four consists of five chapters. Chapter 13 distinguishes between management and accounting functions in cost control procedures. Exception reporting and responsibility accounting are described and applied. This chapter builds upon specific standard cost materials in preceding chapters and leads logically to the study of profit planning.

Period budgeting in Chapter 14 applies many cost concepts and techniques to the formal task of quantifying management plans for an annual period. Comprehensive budgeting is illustrated, and all phases of the budgeting process are interrelated and discussed.

Short-run operating decisions and the relevant costing approach are illustrated in Chapter 15. A general approach is provided to problems involving alternative choices in a short-term time period, such as acceptance of special orders and make-or-buy decisions. The nature of project planning and techniques of capital expenditure decision analysis are presented in Chapter 16.

Chapter 17 addresses the accounting problems involved with divisional performance evaluation of decentralized organizations that have investment centers. The contribution approach is applied to formulate necessary performance measures for segments and short-run management performance. Divisional return on investment and transfer pricing are also presented and analyzed.

Chapter 13: Cost Control and Responsibility Accounting

Control by management is the general process of attempting to secure agreement between actual results and related plans. In management accounting, one important control procedure is to secure agreement between actual costs and planned amounts with the assistance of performance evaluation reports. Responsibility accounting is a system for comparing controllable costs of specific responsibility units in a company to either standard costs or budgets. This chapter analyzes the nature of cost control and demonstrates the application of cost control principles through responsibility accounting procedures.

Upon completion of this chapter, students should be able to:

1. Distinguish between management roles and related accounting functions in the cost control process
2. Utilize exception reporting criteria in specific applications of cost control
3. Identify controllable costs for organizational units when given related descriptions of authority and responsibility
4. Apply responsibility accounting and performance evaluation principles to systems design for cost control reports

The following basic concepts are introduced in this chapter:

Cost control   Comparative analysis of actual costs in relation to an appropriate base of standards or budgets to facilitate performance evaluation and specification of corrective measures.

Exception reporting   Cost control reports to managers that emphasize problem areas and reduce unnecessary detail in order to avoid information overload.

Responsibility accounting   Accumulation and comparative reporting of cost data according to specific responsibility units within an organization.

Controllable cost   A cost that can be regulated or influenced by the actions and decisions of a particular manager within a given time period.

Chapter Summary

Cost control is a basic responsibility of line managers. The function of management accounting is to measure, analyze, and communicate information to management so that good performance can be recognized or necessary corrective measures can be implemented. A prerequisite for cost control is a comparative base usually represented by standard costs or operating budgets. Planning therefore must precede control. Cost control assisted by management accounting reports is remedial in nature, since benefits are obtained only by improving future cost performance. Cost control reports do not control business operations, but they provide information that must be acted upon to obtain good control.

Responsibility accounting is a type of cost control procedure that is ideally suited for cost centers, departments, and divisional operations. These organizational units are concerned primarily with operational efficiency and cost incurrence in relation to standard costs or budgets. Responsibility accounting personalizes performance evaluation reports by identifying and reporting the costs that are controllable by each manager. In comparison with cost accounting for products, responsibility accounting is concerned with the source, or origin, of costs. Accordingly, allocation of joint costs that benefit several organizational units is unnecessary in measuring management performance.

Several practical problems must be resolved in applying responsibility accounting. Dual cost responsibility is always a complex issue, and cost controllability is usually difficult to define at lower management levels. Possible solutions to these problems are discussed along with general principles of performance evaluation.

NATURE OF COST CONTROL

Cost control is the overall process of attempting to secure conformity between actual results and related performance measures such as standard costs or operating budgets. As a basic management function, control is exercised over processes, activities, personnel, and costs incurred throughout an organization. Business organizations have many forms of "control," but each control has the common objective of directing actions so that desired results are achieved. Inventory control, internal control, cost control, and production control are examples of this basic concept. Cost control implies a comparative analysis of costs in relation to desired results and the formulation of necessary corrective actions.

Cost Control Reports

The cost control process in management accounting begins with the comparison of actual costs to an appropriate base measure of desired costs or expected actual costs. Analysis of the difference between actual costs and the related base may then lead to corrective measures that will influence future cost incurrence. Accounting reports obviously cannot change costs already incurred; benefits of control are achieved only when future costs are improved and made to correspond more closely with the desired end result.

Accounting reports for cost control purposes represent one phase in the complete cost control cycle, which involves the following procedures:

1. Establish a base measure for each cost that represents satisfactory performance
2. Accumulate actual costs incurred so that comparative reports can be assembled for each responsibility area in the firm
3. Compare actual costs with base measures by areas of responsibility and formulate corrective actions as necessary

Cost control involves performance measurement and evaluation of individual managers and company segments such as cost centers and departments.

Standards and budgets   The appropriate base measure used in cost control reports should be standard costs or operating budgets for the particular costs. As described in Chapters 11 and 12, a standard cost is a carefully predetermined estimate of costs that should be incurred under certain assumed conditions of efficiency and operating volume. Standard costs for materials, labor, and overhead represent desired cost performance and are useful in cost control reports. If standard costs are current and reasonably attainable, they are also good measures of expected actual performance. An operating or planning budget contains expected results for a future period. Currently attainable standards represent building blocks from which operating budgets can be assembled.

Operating budgets are discussed in Chapter 14, but a comparison of standard costs and budgets is useful at this point since both are related to cost control reports. Characteristics of standard costs and budgets are compared below:

CHARACTERISTICS	STANDARD COSTS	OPERATING BUDGETS
Efficiency goal	Desired results	Expected results
Functional areas	Production	All operations
Nature of data	Unit costs	Total costs

In formulating standards, management can select any desired efficiency goal. Standards based on reasonably attainable efficiency levels represent expected actual performance. If standards are based on ideal efficiency, they represent desired results. If standards are reasonably or currently attainable, operating budgets based on these measures will be fair expressions of expected actual performance.

Note also that standards usually are summarized in the form of unit cost data for various products. Budgets are essentially pro forma financial statements containing estimated revenues and expenses corresponding to underlying plans for a future period. Standard cost data are used in budgeting to determine Cost of Goods Sold, materials usage, labor cost, and various overhead amounts that can be projected by using flexible budgets. In summary, standard costs or budgeted costs provide the comparative base for cost control reports, depending upon the nature of particular costs included in a control report. For materials, labor, and overhead costs, standards are used as the comparative base. Budgeted costs are the comparative base for selling and administrative expenses.

Methods of cost control   Different cost control procedures are employed for various cost categories. Raw materials usage and factory labor costs are controlled best through periodic standard cost variance reports similar to the illustrations in Chapters 11 and 12. Factory overhead costs for a specified period are controlled by using flexible budgets to measure and report spending and efficiency variances to individual managers. Selling and administrative expenses are controlled by comparative reports based on budgeted cost amounts.

The frequency of cost control reports depends upon the variability of a given cost with volume and its sensitivity to control. In most manufacturing firms, control reports for materials usage and labor cost are prepared more frequently than control reports for production overhead. Since material and labor costs are variable with volume, weekly or even daily control reports are used to avoid lengthy periods of excessive cost incurrence. Variable overhead costs that are subject to wide variation from standard also should be analyzed frequently by flexible budget control reports. A key factor in cost control is that variable costs are caused by volume and managerial action. Costs that fluctuate with volume are often difficult to control, and they should be monitored more closely than fixed costs.

Committed fixed costs such as depreciation, supervisory salaries, insurance, and property taxes are a result of decisions to maintain a given level of plant capacity. The ideal control point for these fixed costs is the management decision to establish related capacity levels. Control reports for fixed and semivariable costs such as power and maintenance are desirable, but they are needed less frequently than control reports for variable costs.

Discretionary fixed costs for promotional efforts, research and development, and employee training usually will correspond closely with approved or budgeted expenditure levels. Since expenditure approval decisions place an upper limit on these costs, they are controlled best by guiding the underlying activities for which costs are incurred. Discretionary fixed costs often relate to efforts of professionals such as systems specialists and marketing managers. The most useful control procedure for such costs is to evaluate the quality and productivity of these professional efforts.

Exception reporting Periodic cost control reports should incorporate the principle of exception reporting. This basic concept involves *management by exception*, which holds that control reports to supervisory managers should emphasize and highlight only problem areas. Control reports serve the general purposes of performance evaluation for subordinate managers and operations review by supervisory managers. For both purposes, unnecessary detail should be omitted in order to avoid information overload.

Exception reporting calls for cost control reports that pinpoint problem areas and treat all other items "in control" with a minimum of detail. Some companies establish exception reporting criteria in relation to standard costs or operating budgets. For instance, an exception reporting format could require specific line-item comparisons for any cost that exceeds or is less than related standard by 10 percent or more. Another criterion may have a dollar limit in addition to a percentage test. Given certain criteria, cost items that are "in control" are reported in total along with total budgeted or standard costs.

As an illustration of the exception reporting concept, consider the labor cost control problems of the plant manager at Metal Products Corporation. The company uses a process cost system and incurs labor costs in eleven different departments. The plant manager is responsible for labor efficiency and reviews monthly comparisons of actual and standard labor cost for each department. For several months after joining the company, the plant manager examined a detailed report showing the actual and standard labor cost of every department. This review was time consuming, and the reports did not highlight departments with labor efficiency problems.

To facilitate this operations review, the plant manager and controller developed exception reporting criteria for each department. Based upon the absolute amount of labor costs by department and experience with past efficiency, the following labor cost reporting guidelines were developed:

DEPT.	OPERATION	REPORT EXPLANATIONS WHEN ACTUAL − STANDARD = ± X% OF STANDARD	DEPT.	OPERATION	REPORT EXPLANATIONS WHEN ACTUAL − STANDARD = ± X% OF STANDARD
1	Heating	5%	7	Unit assembly	7%
2	Molding	4%	8	Painting	2%
3	Cutting	8%	9	Testing	10%
4	Trimming	3%	10	Inspection	8%
5	Polishing	5%	11	Packing	10%
6	Drilling	3%			

EXHIBIT 13-1

EXCEPTION REPORTING FOR LABOR COSTS

Report to plant manager (developed by accounting personnel)

LABOR COST REVIEW, FOR FEBRUARY 19X3

DEPARTMENT	ACTUAL HOURS AT STANDARD RATE	STANDARD HOURS AT STANDARD RATE	OVER (UNDER) STANDARD Total	Percent of standard
1—heating*	$ 70,000	$ 65,000	$ 5,000	7.7
5—polishing*	68,500	74,000	(5,500)	7.4
9—testing*	30,100	27,000	3,100	11.5
11—packing*	25,100	22,500	2,600	11.5
Total exceptions	$193,700	$188,500	$ 5,200	
Other departments	389,300	383,800	5,500	
Total labor cost	$583,000	$572,300	$10,700	2.1

* Department manager's written commentary would be attached hereto.

Supporting cost data

DEPARTMENT	ACTUAL HOURS AT STANDARD RATE	STANDARD HOURS AT STANDARD RATE	OVER (UNDER) STANDARD
1—heating	$ 70,000	$ 65,000	$ 5,000*
2—molding	91,000	88,000	3,000
3—cutting	83,000	82,100	900
4—trimming	72,000	73,000	(1,000)
5—polishing	68,500	74,000	(5,500)*
6—drilling	43,200	42,000	1,200
7—unit assembly	51,300	50,000	1,300
8—painting	29,800	30,200	(400)
9—testing	30,100	27,000	3,100*
10—inspection	19,000	18,500	500
11—packing	25,100	22,500	2,600*
Totals	$583,000	$572,300	$10,700

Note: Supporting cost data are included above only for illustrative purposes and would not be reported to the plant manager.
* Variances over exception reporting limits.

Labor cost data for February 19X3 are summarized in Exhibit 13-1, and the exception reporting criteria are applied to develop a summary control report for review by the plant manager. With the exception reporting format, the plant manager can quickly review departments that were above or below the established percentage variances. Note that the report is to be accompanied by explanations of variance causes for the exception departments (1,5,9, and 11).

In practice, exception reporting should be applied according to the preferences of individual managers. Depending upon the number of separate cost classifications related to a particular management hierarchy, the design of cost control reports on an exception basis should recognize that some managers can review and comprehend more detail than others. In general, report design requires the cooperative efforts of report recipients and the management accountant. Exception reporting of factors controllable by an individual manager is the foundation of cost control through responsibility accounting.

Cost Control Principles

In relation to business activity, the function of management control is to obtain conformity between actual results and related plans. Performance evaluation using cost control reports is an important phase of management control activities. For a firm to be successful in its cost control efforts, certain fundamental principles should be acknowledged. Five principles are presented as guidelines for using cost control procedures.

1. Cost control is a management function. The basic responsibility of management is to plan and control organizational activities. Performance evaluation and the actual process of controlling costs are line functions. The role of management accounting in cost control is to accumulate, measure, and analyze information and to communicate these results to management.

2. Cost control requires sound planning. A comparative base of cost standards and budgets is a prerequisite to adequate cost control. Prior operating results are a poor base for evaluating current performance because prior-year results may represent inefficient operations or may not reflect current operating conditions and objectives.

3. Cost control is remedial and preventive. The ideal control device influences results before actions take place. In the "real time" dimension of process control, a digital computer is used to monitor heat and pressure in a production process. Small temperature variations are noted and corrected before the system performs adversely. In comparison with process control, cost control is more remedial than it is preventive. Cost control reports for a specified time period signal the existence of problem areas, and corrective measures then are implemented by management to avoid continuation of the problems. As a continuous cycle, cost control activities are both remedial and preventive.

4. Cost control requires a defined organization structure. An organization structure with clearly defined duties, authorities, and responsibilities provides the basic network of information flow essential for cost control. Cost control through performance evaluation depends upon clearly established areas of responsibility for each manager. Lines of communication must be defined in an organization before information can serve its cost control function. Sound organization is the key element in performance evaluation and information system design.

5. *Cost control is subject to behavioral influences.* The basic tools of cost control have been refined considerably in recent years. Accounting systems are more sophisticated; forecasting accuracy has been significantly improved; quantitative techniques are applied to numerous planning and control problems. Successful cost control depends upon how these tools are used.

Behavioral assumptions in management accounting are shifting away from traditional concepts of imposed authority, motivation by monetary reward, and lack of concern with employee goals. Cost control tools must be applied with consideration of employee response to control efforts. Modern behavioral theories view the organization as a collection of individuals, and the role of management is to maintain balance between organizational goals and opportunities for employee satisfaction.

Recognition of behavioral influences requires a participative management philosophy and understanding of the complex psychological factors affecting employee performance. Performance evaluation with cost control reports is not a science. Management must anticipate employee response to control reports and attempt to channel this response toward accomplishment of organizational goals.

THE RESPONSIBILITY ACCOUNTING SYSTEM

The basic concept of responsibility accounting is inherent in all cost control and performance evaluation procedures. *Responsibility accounting* (also called *activity*, or *profitability*, *accounting*) is an information system that personalizes control reports by accumulating and reporting cost and revenue information according to defined responsibility areas within a company. The basic control procedure is to include in performance evaluation reports only the costs and revenues that a manager *controls*. These reports provide managerial information feedback and fulfill a manager's obligation to perform assigned duties and to remain accountable for the results of personal actions and decisions. Responsibility accounting applies both to revenue control and to cost control. It involves a hierarchy of coordinated performance evaluation reports and incorporates the cost control principles discussed in the preceding section.

Responsibility Reports and Organization

A sound organizational structure is the foundation of responsibility accounting. Data accumulation and performance evaluation reports are designed to emphasize the responsibility of individual managers, and these responsibilities are defined primarily by organizational structure and supporting job descriptions. To have responsibility, managers must have sufficient authority to direct the activities for which they are accountable. In accounting control systems, then, *responsibility* means accountability for actions, decisions, and related financial consequences. To direct actual performance toward established goals, the accounting system concentrates on revenues and costs associated with activities controlled by each manager.

Responsibility accounting reports relate to particular segments of an organizational structure. Summary operating results reported to lower management levels are included in control reports prepared for higher management levels. To illustrate this point, consider the organization chart of Hardy Company shown in Exhibit 13-2. The company uses a standard cost system, and the

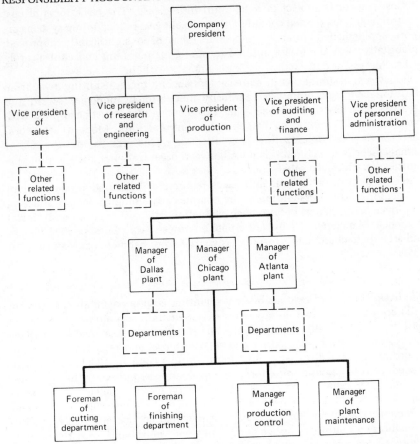

production hierarchy is shown by heavy lines. Reporting relationships in responsibility accounting generally form a pyramid, as sample cost control reports for the Hardy Company production area demonstrate in Exhibit 13-3. Reports for each department in the Chicago plant are compressed into single cost amounts for inclusion in the plant manager's report. The details of each plant manager's report then are compressed into single cost amounts for inclusion in the production vice president's cost report.

Study the pyramid profile for responsibility accounting in Exhibit 13-2. Note how detailed cost information becomes more aggregated at higher management levels in the sample reports of Exhibit 13-3. Actual monthly production costs controllable by the supervisor in the Chicago Finishing Department were $600,000. Details of these actual costs are reported to the supervisor, who is responsible for providing explanations and identifying causes of significant variances between actual and budgeted costs. In the Chicago plant manager's report, this $600,000 appears as a single amount. The plant manager is considered to control all costs that are reported as controllable by departmental supervisors. This same controllability relationship also extends to the vice president of production.

EXHIBIT 13-3

SAMPLE COST CONTROL REPORTS—HARDY COMPANY
INTERRELATIONSHIPS OF MONTHLY COST TOTALS

VICE PRESIDENT OF PRODUCTION
MONTH: JUNE

Controllable costs	Actual costs	Budget	(Over) Under budget
Vice president's office	X	X	(X)
Centralized production planning	X	X	X
Depreciation—plant buildings	X	X	—
Plants:			
Dallas	X	X	(X)
Chicago	$ 3,800,000	$ 3,900,000	$100,000
Atlanta	X	X	(X)
Total controllable	$23,400,000	$22,700,000	($700,000)

MANAGER OF CHICAGO PLANT
MONTH: JUNE

Controllable costs	Actual costs	Budget	(Over) Under budget
Chicago Plant Administration	X	X	—
Heat and power	X	X	(X)
Depreciation—equipment	X	X	—
Insurance	X	X	X
Departments:			
Cutting	X	X	X
Finishing	$ 600,000	$ 570,000	($ 30,000)
Production control	X	X	X
Plant maintenance	X	X	(X)
Total controllable	$3,800,000	$3,900,000	$100,000

FINISHING DEPARTMENT—CHICAGO PLANT
MONTH: JUNE

Controllable costs	Actual costs	Budget	(Over) Under budget
Direct material	X	X	X
Direct labor	X	X	(X)
Supplies	X	X	X
Maintenance	X	X	X
Setup—labor	X	X	(X)
Small tools	X	X	X
Supervisory salaries	X	X	—
Machine lubricants	X	X	(X)
Total controllable	$600,000	$570,000	($30,000)

The sample monthly control reports for the Hardy Company production area emphasize the controllable costs within each responsibility unit of the firm. One important characteristic of responsibility accounting is its emphasis on the source, or origin, of costs. In the Chicago plant of Hardy Company, responsibility accounting will not be concerned with overhead allocations from

Traceable and Controllable Costs

production control and plant maintenance to each producing department. Cost allocations are necessary to determine product unit costs in absorption costing, but these allocations are not useful in responsibility accounting for cost control purposes.

To control costs, management must identify the organizational units in which costs originate. Accordingly, the separable or traceable costs of each department become important for control purposes. Traceable costs are directly identified with a department's operation and are assignable to that department without proration or allocation based on some logical but arbitrary basis. Given a listing of traceable costs that originate in a particular department, responsibility accounting focuses on those traceable costs that are *controllable* by the particular department manager.

The controllable costs of a particular company segment are those traceable costs of the segment that can be regulated or influenced directly by the segment manager. Controllable costs for a particular manager are those costs which result from his or her actions and decisions. If managers have the authority to acquire, utilize, or supervise the use of particular resources or services, they control the related costs.

Cost controllability is cumulative in nature; costs that are controllable by one manager are also considered controllable by that manager's superior. The identification of controllable costs at lower management levels is often difficult, because managers seldom have absolute authority to acquire, use, or supervise resources and services. In general, managers at lower levels have only partial influence or control over particular costs. Because the identification of certain controllable costs is difficult, managers should participate in the identification of costs for which they will be held accountable in control reports.

The cumulative nature of controllability means that every cost incurred by a company is controllable by at least one manager or executive. The properly identified controllable costs of a given manager also will have several other cost characteristics. Controllable costs may be fixed or variable, and they may be direct or indirect with regard to manufactured products. All controllable costs, however, are traceable to the particular manager's activities and organizational unit.

Input phases of systems design are very important to the successful use of responsibility accounting. Appropriate coding schemes must be developed so that cost information can be processed and subsequently identified with specific responsibility areas. For a large company with centralized accounting operations, labor costs are coded to identify labor type, plant, department, cost center, employee, shift, and operation involved. Other costs—such as materials usage, individual overhead costs, and administrative expenses—are analyzed and coded similarly. Data storage and retrieval of cost information are important operational aspects of responsibility accounting. Careful coding of source documents that support business transactions and internal cost accounting operations is required to make a responsibility accounting system operational.

Issues in Responsibility Accounting

The basic concept of responsibility accounting is logical and has conceptual appeal. In processing accounting transactions, costs are initially coded to correspond with the lowest management level to which the costs are both traceable and controllable. In applying this concept, several practical problems must be resolved, such as dual cost responsibility, data aggregation, and the desire of many managers for "full cost" reports.

Dual cost responsibility In most business organizations, many costs are influenced by actions of more than one manager. Raw material cost is an example of dual cost responsibility, since materials acquisition is controlled by the purchasing officer and usage is controlled by production department supervisors. For firms using standard cost systems, responsibility accounting recognizes this dual cost responsibility. The purchasing officer is held accountable for material purchase price variances, and production supervisors are accountable for material quantity or usage variances. In this way, the independently controllable activities of the several managers are identified, and related costs are associated with these activities.

In some cases, material usage variances become the responsibility of the purchasing officer, especially when inferior grades of material are purchased. When uncertainty in assigning responsibility is encountered, it should be remembered that responsibility does not necessarily mean fault or blame. Many situations require a special assignment of "accountability" for particular costs, and the desired objective is to assign costs to managers who can best explain related cause-and-effect relationships.

Another problem in dual cost responsibility is the relationship between service departments and users of the service. In many companies, centrally managed departments provide power, maintenance services, computer services, and legal assistance to other segments of the company. Dual cost responsibility exists if services are provided to other departments on a demand or necessity basis. For example, the manager of an equipment maintenance department is responsible for most costs traceable to that department. Costs incurred by the department, however, depend partially on the volume of maintenance services, and the volume of service is controlled by user departments.

One solution to the dual cost responsibility problem for service departments is to charge user departments a standard cost rate per unit of service rendered. The standard rate should be the amount that, under normal conditions, would completely absorb the maintenance department's traceable costs. With this practice, user departments are charged a cost based on volume of service received. The maintenance department remains accountable for total traceable costs of the department that are analyzed with flexible budgets based on actual service volume.

Central service departments, such as our maintenance department case, are affected by two behavioral problems: (1) If user departments are not charged for services, the service may be abused and used inefficiently; and (2) if user departments are charged for services, some departments needing services may delay use to avoid having the related cost appear in their own cost control reports. Depending upon the circumstances, companies are known to follow both diverse policies.

Cost consciousness reports Some upper-level managers prefer to have cost control reports issued to their subordinates that include costs not directly controllable by the recipients. This practice deviates from a conceptual version of pure responsibility accounting, but it can produce desired behavioral effects. The basic idea is to include all traceable costs of a department in a manager's periodic control reports. Some of the traceable costs will not be controllable by the recipients of the report, but they are made aware of the total costs incurred to support their activities.

Cost consciousness also can be promoted by making managers aware that their actions have an impact on other departments. If costs of central maintenance services are charged to a producing department at standard rates based on volume of service rendered, then the producing department supervisor is encouraged to cooperate with maintenance and to suggest any actions that could reduce the costs incurred by the maintenance area. Responsibility accounting can be applied to promote cost consciousness, but the general guide is to distinguish clearly between controllable costs and any other costs included in performance reports to managers.

Data aggregation problems   As cost data are compressed from detailed line-item disclosures for lower-level managers to a single figure for reports to upper management, there is an obvious loss of information. The sample cost control reports in Exhibit 13-3 demonstrate this problem of data aggregation. The Finishing Department cost report discloses eight separate controllable cost categories totaling $600,000. This cost total then appears as a single item in the plant manager's report. As a general rule, managers should have access to the detailed performance reports sent to lower management levels. In addition, higher management always should be informed of significant control problems, even though summary cost data and related budget amounts for lower management fail to disclose any control problems.

Consider the exaggerated case of a plant manager supervising two production departments. A monthly cost summary to the plant manager discloses the following controllable cost amounts:

Controllable Costs	Actual	Budget	(Over) Under Budget
Department A	$500,000	$480,000	($20,000)
Department B	600,000	605,000	5,000

To investigate Department A, the plant manager could examine detailed cost reports issued to the supervisor in which numerous small variances perhaps constitute the $20,000 over-budget condition. If the plant manager decides that Department B is superior in performance to Department A, this conclusion may be unjustified.

If our plant manager is using cost control reports in this manner, significant control problems can go undetected. Assume that the detailed cost report issued to the Department B supervisor disclosed the following items:

Controllable Costs	Actual	Budget	(Over) Under Budget
Direct material	$200,000	$150,000	($50,000)
Direct labor	150,000	100,000	(50,000)
Machine supplies	50,000	10,000	(40,000)
Lubricants	80,000	100,000	20,000
Material handling labor	100,000	145,000	45,000
Maintenance labor	20,000	100,000	80,000
Total—Department B	$600,000	$605,000	$ 5,000

A glance at the detailed Department B cost report shows significant control problems not revealed by the summary data in the plant manager's report.

While the amounts are exaggerated, the point is that supervisory managers could be deceived by relying only upon summary data to disclose control problems. Summary cost reports are useful for overall evaluation only in the absence of specific line-item control problems such as those of Department B. Plant managers and other supervisory executives should receive the necessary exception reports and supporting detail to become informed about the existence of serious control problems. Aggregated data will not always disclose these control problems.

PERFORMANCE EVALUATION PRINCIPLES

The concept of performance evaluation implies that management performance is measured and analyzed to determine quality of performance and the existence of important problems or opportunities. The cost control principles discussed earlier in this chapter apply to performance evaluation; responsibility accounting is one form of performance evaluation for short-run organizational activity. Other forms of performance evaluation suitable for decentralized divisions of a company are discussed in Chapter 17.

The role of management accounting in performance evaluation is to supply necessary information to decision makers. An important factor in effective performance evaluation is appropriate information analysis of current, past, or future data. General guidelines for reporting this information to management are summarized below in five performance evaluation principles. Performance evaluation information developed for management should:

1. *Provide suitable measures of performance* Performance can be measured by input or by output of an activity or by combined input-output considerations. Examples are costs incurred, effort expended, resources employed, profitability, efficiency, and productivity. Nonfinancial measures of performance are often as useful as dollar measures.

2. *Compare actual performance to a suitable base* Performance evaluation is comparative in nature and requires actual results to be compared with goals, budgets, or standards that represent expected or desired norms.

3. *Correspond with desired segments of company operations* A segment of company operations is any organizational unit or activity for which traceable costs, revenues, or other information is desirable. If a performance objective is to segment the company according to product lines, then geographically developed sales information must be reclassified into product-line categories.

4. *Identify the responsibility of each manager* Responsibility is an obligation to remain accountable for decisions and actions. Performance evaluation information should identify the costs, revenues, and resources that are controllable by a particular manager in a given time period.

5. *Analyze important cause-and-effect relationships* In general, information for performance evaluation should be analytical and diagnostic; it should reveal cause-and-effect factors and significant interrelationships. Nonquantitative information is often useful for this purpose.

In addition to these five principles, there are other guidelines regarding the timeliness of information, its relevance, and recognition of measurement error and uncertainty. Any discussion of performance evaluation principles ultimately must conclude that the objective is to provide understandable information to management in a manner which facilitates the decision-making function. Accordingly, cost control principles and performance evaluation principles are useful in many management accounting applications.

FINAL NOTE Cost control procedures in responsibility accounting are performance evaluation tools widely used *within* a particular company. Cost control is concerned primarily with input considerations and applies mainly to cost centers, departments, and plant locations. Along with responsibility accounting, other performance evaluation techniques are useful if the business segment generates revenues and invests in capital facilities. Divisional performance evaluation is discussed in Chapter 17.

Return now to the beginning of the chapter and review the highlights section before proceeding to the review questions, exercises, and problems.

QUESTIONS

13-1. Define and illustrate the following terms and concepts:
    a. Cost control   d. Controllable cost
    b. Exception reporting   e. Traceable cost
    c. Responsibility accounting   f. Dual cost responsibility

13-2. Describe the respective roles of accounting and management personnel in the process of cost control.

13-3. "In general, cost control through performance evaluation reports is remedial in nature." Explain this statement.

13-4. Describe the basic philosophy and procedure of responsibility accounting.

13-5. What are the distinguishing characteristics of standard costs and operating budgets?

13-6. What factors determine the frequency of control reports for different types of costs?

13-7. Illustrate the following basic principle: "Cost control requires advance planning."

13-8. What tests can be applied to determine whether a given cost is controllable by a particular manager?

13-9. Why is cost controllability considered to be cumulative in nature?

13-10. What are the behavioral problems caused by dual cost responsibility between central service departments (maintenance and repair) and user departments (production)?

13-11. How is it possible to promote cost consciousness by including noncontrollable costs in a department manager's reports?

13-12. Data aggregation, in the form of summary control reports, involves a loss of information. Under what circumstances could reliance upon summary reports fail to disclose significant control problems?

13-13. What is the relationship between responsibility accounting and standard cost variance analysis?

13-14. How can a single cost accounting system function in a manner that accomplishes the objectives of both product cost accounting and responsibility reporting? (Refer to the basic cost concepts in Chapter 4 in answering this question.)

13-15. Describe and illustrate five performance evaluation principles for presenting cost control information to management.

EXERCISES AND PROBLEMS

13-16. *CMA Problem—Divisional Performance Report*   Listed below are three expense items found on the monthly performance report of a division that manufactures and sells products primarily to outside companies. Division performance is evaluation by use of return on average assets used (i.e., divisional profits ÷ average total assets).

REQUIRED: Indicate which, if any, of the report items listed below are consistent with the concept of responsibility accounting. Support your reply with a brief explanation.
a. Charge for general corporation administrative expenses equal to 10 percent of division sales
b. Charge for use of central corporate computer facility. The charge is determined by taking actual annual computer department costs and allocating an amount to each user based on the ratio of its computer use to total corporation use.
c. Charge for goods purchased from another division based upon the competitive market price of the goods

(IMA adapted)

13-17. *Organizational Structure and Responsibility*   The following job titles are used by the Patch Pocket Company:

Purchasing agent	Vice president—administration
Vice president—sales	Treasurer
Production supervisor	Personnel manager
Controller	Engineering research manager
Cashier	Marketing manager
President	Warehouse manager
Vice president— manufacturing	Supervisor—repairs and maintenance
Sales manager	Internal auditor

REQUIRED:
a. Design an organizational structure using these job titles.
b. For each position, write a one-sentence job description.
c. List some possible costs that the person holding each job would be responsible for.

13-18. *Identification of Controllable Costs* Jenkins Corporation produces gymnastic equipment. The production operation utilizes a three-tier management organizational structure as follows:

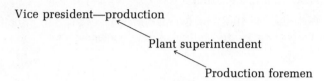

Vice president—production

Plant superintendent

Production foremen

Various production costs are accounted for each period. Examples include:

Repair and maintenance costs	Superintendent's salary
Material handling costs	Raw material costs
Direct labor	Storage—finished goods
Foremen's salaries	inventory
Plant maintenance of grounds	Property taxes—plant
Depreciation—equipment	Depreciation—plant

REQUIRED:
a. Identify each cost item as being a variable or fixed cost.
b. Identify which manager is responsible for each cost.

13-19. *Responsibility for Cost Variances* Terry Banks is plant superintendent for the Detergent Division of General Soaps Corporation. Cost variance analysis reports for April 19X6 have just been given to Banks for each of the fourteen departments under his responsibility. The report of the Mixing Department appears below:

Department: Mixing
Time period: April 19X6

CLASSIFICATION*	BUDGETED COST†	ACTUAL COST	TOTAL VARIANCE
Raw materials (V)	$47,500	$42,247	$5,253(F)
Direct labor (V)	23,800	22,900	900(F)
Indirect labor (V)	12,400	13,100	700(U)
Heat, light, & power (Fx)	2,800	2,600	200(F)
Operating supplies (V)	1,200	1,350	150(U)
Plant rent (Fx)	2,500	2,500	–0–
Depreciation—equipment (Fx)	3,250	3,400	150(U)
Miscellaneous overhead (Fx)	1,890	1,740	150(F)
Totals	$95,340	$89,837	$5,503(F)

* (V) = variable cost; (Fx) = fixed cost.
† Based on normal production of 10,000 units.

Banks found that 9,650 good units were processed by the Mixing Department during April 19X6.

REQUIRED:
a. Should Banks be happy with this report? Explain your reply.
b. Although Banks is ultimately responsible for all costs, identify the people directly responsible for each variance (after recasting the variance report to reflect proper variances).

13-20. *Managerial Conflict*   U. C. Rider is purchasing manager for Brown Vault Manufacturing Company. His job is to secure high-quality bronze, brass, and steel to be used in making vaults of sufficient size to accommodate commercial bank vault requirements. Wholesale value of finished vaults runs from $2,500 to $4,500.

"Good workmanship demands good quality raw materials," explains Mr. Jess Wright, production supervisor for the company. The comment was directed at the vice president of production, who had just blamed Wright for incurring an alarming $4,525 unfavorable raw material usage variance in the previous month.

"Blame Rider, not me!" continued Wright. "He bought that rotten bronze plate at a bargain price so that he could look good in terms of variances. His approach to purchasing sure isn't company oriented!"

"I suppose this healthy labor efficiency variance is *also* Rider's fault?" demanded the vice president.

"Of course!" shouted Wright. "Poor raw materials are bound to cause excess labor effort."

REQUIRED:
a. Identify the problem(s) in the case described above.
b. What alternatives are available to the vice president to correct the situation?
c. Which alternative would you prefer? Why?

13-21. *Data Aggregation Problems*   Avesta Stainless Steel, Inc., produces a variety of stainless steel items. Organizational structure of management is pictured below, with special emphasis placed upon the production area.

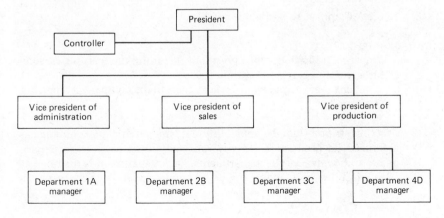

The vice president of production receives a weekly cost summary by department and has requested specifically that detailed cost items not appear on the cost summary unless actual and budgeted costs of individual items deviate by more than plus or minus 10 percent. This exception form of detail reporting is for cost control purposes.

Reports for the week ending September 9 have been distributed to management; the cost summary, as requested by the vice president of production, was as follows:

To: Vice President—Production
Date: September 12, 19X4
Period covered: 9/3/X4–9/9/X4

	BUDGET	ACTUAL	COST VARIANCE
Traceable costs:			
Department 1A	$126,500	$127,250	$ 750(U)*
Department 2B	180,400	185,925	5,525(U)
Department 3C	119,280	124,205	4,925(U)
Department 4D	94,660	93,200	1,460(F)
Totals	$520,840	$530,580	$9,740(U)
Nontraceable costs:			
Plant depreciation	$ 84,000	$ 84,000	$ -0-
Other general and administrative costs	128,800	127,225	1,575(F)
Totals	$212,800	$211,225	$1,575(F)
Total production costs	$733,640	$741,805	$8,165(U)

* Exception items from supervisor's detailed reports:

Department 1A:			
Direct labor	$37,400	$31,950	$5,450(F)
Indirect labor	19,250	25,190	5,940(U)

No other exceptions to report for period.

The vice president is puzzled by the report and asks the controller if the amounts are correct. The controller states that Department 1A is close to target and does not require exception reporting. However, Departments 2B and 3C appear to be in cost trouble.

REQUIRED:
a. Prepare a reply to the vice president including the possible reasons for any data aggregation problems.
b. What changes, if any, would you suggest in the company's reporting structure?

13-22. *Cost Centers and Dual Responsibility* A large publishing company has organized its production activity into sixty-three production departments and twelve service departments. Each department is operated as a responsibility cost center, and departmental supervisors are responsible for cost control, operating efficiency, and meeting production schedules. There is a bonus system for successful ideas and modifications that reduce costs.

The vice president of production recently established a new service department, Productivity Services. Several engineers, an operations research specialist, and a CPA were hired to staff the department. Productivity Services is to function as an advisory group to other department heads who wish to simulate new equipment sequences and other cost-saving ideas. Personnel in Productivity Services act in a consulting role to other departments and advise or implement programs as agreed upon with individual department supervisors. The expected annual budget for Productivity Services is $200,000, which includes salaries, computer usage, and materials.

Three tentative arrangements are being considered by the production vice president for encouraging effective utilization of the Productivity Services group:

Plan A: Charge user departments a cost equal to $35 per hour of consulting time and project labor time provided by Productivity Services. If the new department operated at capacity, this rate would absorb its annual $200,000 cost.

Plan B: Allow department heads to negotiate with Productivity Services concerning the "cost" charged to the using department.

Plan C: Allow departments to utilize the talents of Productivity Services without charge. Service requests would be given sequence priority based upon the amount of potential cost savings estimated by Productivity Services personnel.

REQUIRED: Evaluate the three proposed accounting policies in terms of motivation for department supervisors and the probability that Productivity Services would be utilized effectively.

13-23. *CPA Problem—Responsibility for Distribution Costs* In recent years distribution expenses of the Avey Company have increased more than other expenditures. For more effective control the company plans to provide all local managers with an income statement for each territory showing monthly and year-to-date amounts for the current and previous years. Each sales office is supervised by a local manager; sales orders are forwarded to the main office and filled from a central warehouse; billing and collections are centrally processed also. Expenses are classified first by function and then allocated to each territory in the following ways:

FUNCTION	BASIS
Sales salaries	Actual
Other selling expenses	Relative sales dollars
Warehousing	Relative sales dollars
Packing and shipping	Weight of package
Billing and collections	Number of billings
General administration	Equally

REQUIRED:
a. 1. Explain responsibility accounting and the classification of revenues and expenses under this concept.
   2. What are the objectives of profit analysis by sales territories in income statements?
b. 1. Discuss the effectiveness of Avey Company's comparative income statements by sales territories as a tool for planning and control. Include in your answer additional factors that should be considered and changes that might be desirable for effective planning by management and evaluation of the local sales managers.
   2. Compare the degree of control that can be achieved over production costs and distribution costs and explain why the degree of control differs.
   3. Criticize Avey Company's allocation and/or inclusion of (a) other selling expenses, (b) warehousing expense, and (c) general administration expense.

(AICPA adapted)

13-24. *Behavioral Aspects of Control* Maynard Rakin is manager of a wholesale cosmetics sales branch located in the Midwest. Mr. Rakin is responsible for customer contacts, sales orders, promotion, and local product warehousing operations. Inventories are obtained from regional shipping centers, and all company products are manufactured in a single plant location.

Mr. Rakin is evaluated primarily by branch profits and performance in relation to budget. He personally approves all sales budgets and expense disbursements made directly through the branch location. A comparative profit report prepared by central corporate accounting has arrived for review and is given below:

MIDWEST SALES BRANCH
Comparative profit report
($000 omitted)

	LAST MONTH		THIS MONTH	
	Actual	*Budget*	*Actual*	*Budget*
Sales	$112	$100	$125	$110
Cost of sales—standard	$ 45	$ 40	$ 48	$ 44
Salaries	19	20	19	20
Travel and entertainment	12	10	14	12
Depreciation expense	8	8	8	8
Advertising and promotion	5	6	6	7
Market survey costs	6	5	6	5
Central accounting costs	5	4	6	4
Corporate management costs	12	10	14	10
8% interest on average assets	8	8	8	8
Total expenses	$120	$111	$129	$118
Net income (loss)	($ 8)	($ 11)	($ 4)	($ 8)

The report was accompanied by a note from the vice president of sales to "watch travel and entertainment, Maynard—you'll have a profitable branch yet, someday."

Mr. Rakin asked his CPA neighbor to review the report and find out where it was wrong. According to Rakin, the monthly sales have increased every month during his three years at the Midwest branch. Rakin also expressed some disgust about the $4,000 accounting cost and $5,000 market survey cost.

The accounting charge was for central computer facilities, but all the Midwest branch receives is a sales report and monthly profit report. The computer facility can be used without limit for the $4,000 monthly charge. Rakin never uses the market survey report since he contends that it simply tells him what he already knows.

Corporate management costs in total increase every year, and the Midwest branch is allocated a larger share as sales increase. The 8 percent interest is an imputed cost based on average total assets employed by the branch. Rakin claims that nobody at corporate headquarters has ever been able to give a clear explanation of this item. According to Rakin, the accounting game for profits is a losing game. As sales increase, expenses simply keep pace. He wonders if the branch performance could be improved by reducing sales volume or by shifting sales mix.

REQUIRED:
a. Is there any justification or merit to the control report prepared by central headquarters?
b. Revise the report as necessary to accomplish corporate management objectives and to provide positive performance evaluation for Rakin.

13-25. *CMA Problem—Performance Evaluation* George Johnson was hired on July 1, 19X9, as assistant general manager of the Botel Division of Staple, Inc. It was understood that he would be elevated to general manager of the division on January 1, 19X1, when the current general manager retired; this was duly done. Besides becoming acquainted with the division and the general manager's duties, Mr. Johnson was charged specifically with the responsibility for development of the 19X0 and 19X1 budgets. As general manager in 19X1, he obviously was responsible for the 19X2 budget.

Staple, Inc., is a multiproduct company that is highly decentralized. Each division is quite autonomous. The corporation staff approves operating budgets prepared by the divisions but seldom makes major changes in them. The corporate staff actively participates in decisions requiring capital investment (for expansion or replacement) and makes the final decisions. The division management is responsible for implementing the capital investment program. The major method used by Staple, Inc., to measure division performance is contribution return on division net investment. The budgets below were approved by the corporation. (Revision of the 19X2 budget is not considered necessary, even though 19X1 actual departed from the approved 19X1 budget.)

Comparative profit report ($000 omitted)

BOTEL DIVISION	ACTUAL			BUDGET	
	19X9	19X0	19X1	19X1	19X2
Sales	$1,000	$1,500	$1,800	$2,000	$2,400
Less: Division variable costs:					
Material and labor	250	375	450	500	600
Repairs	50	75	50	100	120
Supplies	20	30	36	40	48
Less: Division managed costs:					
Employee training	30	35	25	40	45
Maintenance	50	55	40	60	70
Less: Division committed costs:					
Depreciation	120	160	160	200	200
Rent	80	100	110	140	140
Total	600	830	871	1,080	1,223
Division net contribution	$ 400	$ 670	$ 929	$ 920	$1,177
Division investment:					
Accounts receivable	100	150	180	200	240
Inventory	200	300	270	400	480
Fixed assets	1,590	2,565	2,800	3,380	4,000
Less: Accounts and wages payable	(150)	(225)	(350)	(300)	(360)
Net investment	$1,740	$2,790	$2,900	$3,680	$4,360
Contribution return on net investment	23%	24%	32%	25%	27%

REQUIRED:
a. Identify Mr. Johnson's responsibilities under the management and measurement program described above.
b. Appraise the performance of Mr. Johnson in 19X1.
c. Recommend to the president any changes in the responsibilities assigned to managers or in the measurement methods used to evaluate division management based upon your analysis.

(IMA adapted)

13-26. *Responsibility for Cost Variances* The Angelo plant of Dry Land Products developed a standard cost system for its manufacturing activities and began use of the system on September 1, 19X9. There are ten producing departments and four service departments reporting to the plant manager. In August 19X9, the plant began a two-shift operation to increase production. Previously, a single eight-hour shift was utilized six days per week. With the two-shift operation, the work week was reduced to five days.

On October 2, 19X9, the plant manager received summary standard cost reports for September operations. These reports summarized actual and standard performance by department for production output, material usage, labor, and overhead costs. The summary materials report for Department 7 is shown below. Department 7 produces construction bricks, and the standard material input per brick is three pounds of clay. A special clay is required, and the standard cost per pound is $2. Unfavorable variances are noted (U).

DEPARTMENT 7
September materials usage summary
(Material units = pounds of clay)

WEEK OF	UNITS PRODUCED	STANDARD MATERIALS	ACTUAL MATERIALS	USAGE VARIANCE
Sept. 1	10,000	30,000	34,000	$ 8,000(U)
Sept. 7	12,000	36,000	41,000	10,000(U)
Sept. 14	14,000	42,000	47,000	10,000(U)
Sept. 21	11,000	33,000	40,000	14,000(U)
				$42,000(U)

The plant manager requested explanations of the unfavorable material usage variance from the department'supervisor of each shift. Supervisor 1: "I'm not really surprised with these poor results. Our trained people have years of experience with the eight-to-five shift, and I know they do a good job. A primary reason for the unfavorable variance is the new shift; these people just don't have the experience with our equipment yet. We produced more units in September than the second shift. No telling what the results would look like without our holding things up this way." Supervisor 2: "I know the standards were developed accurately and I have no complaint there. I thought our materials efficiency was pretty good in September. Could we get a breakdown by shift to help isolate the problem?"

A review of production records disclosed the following details:

WEEK OF	SHIFT 1 (8–5 P.M.)		SHIFT 2 (6–2 A.M.)	
	Units produced	Material usage	Units produced	Material usage
Sept. 1	6,000	21,000	4,000	13,000
Sept. 7	8,000	28,000	4,000	13,000
Sept. 14	8,000	27,000	6,000	20,000
Sept. 21	6,000	26,000	5,000	14,000

REQUIRED:
a. Prepare standard cost performance reports that properly reflect the responsibility and performance of each shift and supervisor.
b. Summarize any weaknesses you detect in the use of standard cost information for responsibility reporting and offer appropriate recommendations.

13-27. *CMA Problem—Responsibility Accounting and Budgets* Argon County Hospital is located in the county seat. Argon county is a well-known summer resort area. The county population doubles during the vacation months (May to August), and hospital activity more than doubles during this time. The hospital is organized into several departments. Although it is a relatively small hospital, its pleasant surroundings have attracted a well-trained and competent medical staff.

An administrator was hired a year ago to improve the business activities of the hospital. Among the new ideas introduced is responsibility accounting. This program was announced along with quarterly cost reports to be supplied to department heads. Previously, cost data were presented to department heads infrequently. Excerpts from the announcement and the report received by the laundry supervisor are presented below:

The hospital has adopted a "responsibility accounting system." From now on you will receive quarterly reports comparing the costs of operating your department with budgeted costs. The reports will highlight the differences (variations) so that you can zero in on the departure from budgeted costs. (This is called "management by exception.") Responsibility accounting means you are accountable for keeping the costs in your department within the budget. The variations from the budget will help you identify which costs are out of line, and the size of the variation will indicate which ones are the most important. Your first such report accompanies this announcement.

ARGON COUNTY HOSPITAL
Performance report—Laundry Department
July–September, 19X3

	BUDGET	ACTUAL	(OVER) UNDER BUDGET	PERCENT (OVER) UNDER BUDGET
Patient days	9,500	11,900	(2,400)	(25)
Pounds processed—laundry	125,000	156,000	(31,000)	(25)
Costs:				
Laundry labor	$ 9,000	$12,500	($3,500)	(39)
Supplies	1,100	1,875	(775)	(70)
Water, Water heating and softening	1,700	2,500	(800)	(47)
Maintenance	1,400	2,200	(800)	(57)
Supervisor's salary	3,150	3,750	(600)	(19)
Allocated administration costs	4,000	5,000	(1,000)	(25)
Equipment depreciation	1,200	1,250	(50)	(4)
	$21,550	$29,075	($7,525)	(35)

Administrator's comments: Costs are significantly above budget for the quarter. Particular attention needs to be paid to labor, supplies, and maintenance.

The annual budget for 19X3 was constructed by the new administrator. Quarterly budgets were computed as one-fourth of the annual budget. The administrator compiled the budget from analysis of costs over the prior three years. The analysis showed that all costs increased each year and that the increases were more rapid between the second and third years. The administrator considered establishing the budget at an average of the prior three years' costs, hoping that the installation of the system would reduce costs to this level. However, in view of the rapidly increasing prices, 19X2 costs less 3 percent were finally chosen for the 19X3 budget. The activity level measured by patient days and pounds of laundry processed was set at 19X2 volume, which was approximately equal to the volume of each of the past three years.

REQUIRED:
a. Comment on the method used to construct the budget.
b. What information should be communicated by variations from budgets?
c. Does the report effectively communicate the level of efficiency of this department? Give reasons for your answer.

(IMA adapted)

13-28. *Cost Control and Collegiate Sports*[1] The department of intercollegiate athletics at North University recently employed a consulting firm to review the department's accounting system and cost control procedures. North University is a major competitor in sixteen different intercollegiate sports, and the athletic department has a staff of thirty-six people. The department is headed by the athletic director, who receives administrative assistance from the assistant director and business manager. University policy requires the department to be self-supporting in its financial affairs. The consultants' report indicated that the department should adopt responsibility reporting by function (primarily by sport) and should use the contribution approach to measure resource allocation within the athletic program. A section of the report appears below:

Effective budgetary control requires that duties of personnel and related responsibilities be clearly defined. In addition, expenses that are controllable by particular staff members must be identified and accumulated by related areas of responsibility. Functional classification systems facilitate responsibility reporting, since the expenses controllable by particular staff personnel are included within the separable expenses for each sport and other functions. As an integral part of financial control, budget estimates of controllable expenses by responsibility area must be compared with actual expenses incurred.

Expense allocation is the principal difficulty involved in identifying expenses by function because many expenses benefit a number of sports and are therefore common to several activities. Common or joint expenses can be allocated or prorated to individual sports through a number of allocation plans when some measure of full cost is necessary. To facilitate expense control and measurement of direct resource allocation, only the direct or separable expenses of each sport should be accumulated on a functional basis. Allocation of administrative and joint expenses to various sports does not improve the usefulness of internal financial reports for expense control purposes.

The most complete method of expense classification permits reporting of expenses classified by function, by activity, and by object. An example of this

[1] This problem is adapted from *Financial Reporting and Control for Intercollegiate Athletics* by Mitchell H. Raiborn (Shawnee Mission, Kansas: The National Collegiate Athletic Association, 1974).

three-part classification method demonstrates the pattern of expense grouping involved:

> Basketball (a function):
>> Recruiting (an activity):
>>> Transportation (an object) $XX
>>> Meals (an object)   XX
>>> Lodging (an object)   XX

Since the department had used general budgeting procedures for years, all the recommendations were implemented. Control reports by sport were developed for the months of September, October, and November of 19X4. Head football coach Dutch Fontenot received the following report in November:

Monthly financial summary, football
Month ending November 30, 19X4

Purpose: Detailed operating review by assistant athletic director and head coach

| | NOVEMBER | | FAVORABLE |
ACCOUNTS (SUMMARIZED)	Actual	Budget	(UNFAVORABLE)
Revenue:			
Total ticket sales	$ 68,000	$ 62,000	$6,000
Student activity fees	-0-	-0-	-0-
Guarantees and options	24,000	27,000	(3,000)
Concession rentals and sales	7,000	8,000	(1,000)
Program advertising and sales	4,000	5,000	(1,000)
Contributions for grants-in-aid	6,000	4,000	2,000
Unrestricted contributions	9,000	7,000	2,000
Broadcasting fees	8,000	9,000	(1,000)
Direct appropriations	12,000	13,000	(1,000)
Conference distribution	-0-	-0-	-0-
Other revenues	7,000	6,000	1,000
Total revenues	$145,000	$141,000	$4,000
Expense:			
Guarantees and options	$ 30,000	$ 28,000	($2,000)
Grants-in-aid	19,000	18,000	(1,000)
Coaches salaries	6,200	6,200	-0-
Wages and contractual services	8,000	6,000	(2,000)
Maintenance materials and supplies	6,000	7,000	1,000
Team travel and meals	7,000	4,800	(2,200)
Other travel expense	1,000	3,000	2,000
Athletic uniforms, equipment, and repairs	5,000	2,000	(3,000)
Printing, publicity, promotion	3,000	1,000	(2,000)
Other expenses	4,000	4,500	500
Total expenses	$ 89,200	$ 80,500	($8,700)

After reviewing the report, Dutch decided to discuss the new accounting procedures with athletic director Billy Winnum:

Bill, the new accounting procedures and cost control junk have me a little puzzled. Since football is seasonal, I'm glad to see the monthly budget figures instead of open-to-spend reports like we used to get. But now maybe you can tell me what I'm supposed to do with this report. I agree that the revenues and expenses relate to football, but my contact with some of these line items is pretty remote. What am I supposed to say if printing costs exceed the budget? You know that J. D. handles that stuff.

REQUIRED:
a. In what respects, if any, does the monthly control report for football fail to comply with the consultants' recommendations?
b. Are the reactions of the head coach justified?
c. Is it proper to apply contribution reporting and responsibility accounting to the activities of nonprofit organizations?

13-29. *CMA Problem—Analysis of Profit Performance* Sun Company, a wholly owned subsidiary of Guardian, Inc., produces and sells three main product lines. The company employs a standard cost accounting system for record-keeping purposes.

At the beginning of 19X4, the president of Sun Company presented the budget to the parent company and accepted a commitment to contribute $15,800 to Guardian's consolidated profit in 19X4. The president has been confident that the year's profit would exceed budget target, since the monthly sales reports have shown that sales for the year will exceed budget by 10 percent. The president is both disturbed and confused when the controller presents an adjusted forecast as of November 30, 19X4, indicating that profit will be 11 percent under budget. The two forecasts are presented below:

SUN COMPANY
Forecasts of operating results

	FORECASTS AS OF	
	Jan. 1, 19X4	*Nov. 30, 19X4*
Sales	$268,000*	$294,800
Cost of sales at standard	212,000*	233,200
Gross margin at standard	$ 56,000	$ 61,000
Over- or (under)absorbed fixed manufacturing overhead	–0–	(6,000)
Actual gross margin	$ 56,000	$ 55,600
Selling expenses	$ 13,400	$ 14,740
Administrative expenses	26,800	26,800
Total operating expenses	$ 40,200	$ 41,540
Earnings before tax	$ 15,800	$ 14,060

* Includes fixed manufacturing overhead of $30,000.

There have been no sales price changes or product-mix shifts since the forecast of January 1, 19X4. The only cost variance on the income statement is the underabsorbed manufacturing overhead. This arose because the company produced only 16,000 standard machine hours (budgeted machine hours were 20,000) during 19X4 as a result of a shortage of raw materials while its principal supplier was closed by a strike. Fortunately, Sun Company's inventory of finished goods was large enough to fill all sales orders received.

REQUIRED:
a. Analyze and explain why the profit declined in spite of increased sales and good control over costs.
b. What plan, if any, could Sun Company adopt during December to improve their reported profit at year-end? Explain your answer.
c. Illustrate and explain how Sun Company could adopt an alternative internal cost reporting procedure that would avoid the confusing effect of the present procedure.

(IMA adapted)

13-30. *Performance and Discretionary Costs* Rio Metal Products, Inc., is a decentralized firm with twenty-four plant locations in various states. Each plant manufactures a wide range of component steel products such as lock washers, bearings, and battery casings. A specified sales district is served by each plant, which has a company vice president who is responsible for both sales and production activity. The company uses comprehensive budget procedures, and each vice president participates in the formulation of final profit targets for his plant. Administrative personnel at each plant include the vice president, sales manager, production manager, and chief accountant. The vice president's primary responsibility is to achieve budgeted profits, and several vice presidents in recent years have been dismissed because of below-budget profit performance.

The Brownwood vice president held a management conference on Saturday, December 2, 19X5, which was attended by the sales and production managers and the chief accountant. Their conversation follows:

V. P.: Gentlemen, you've had four days to think about my memo of November 28. We now have twenty-nine days in which to find about $150,000 in order to meet our 19X5 profit target of $1,000,000. In fact, $150,000 may cut it close—give us the latest figures, Jake.

Jake: You're about right—that is, we'll be under target profit by $150,000 unless we cut some costs somewhere. I suggest we hear ideas from Sam [sales manager] and Pete [production manager].

Pete: Same story as always, men. We can postpone machinery overhauls until January—that saves $40,000 right there. Scheduled contract maintenance can also be put off—might save another $20,000 until next year. [Silence.]

Sam: In sales, I can cut client entertainment by $17,000; travel by $26,000; and eliminate product samples—probably save $3,000 on the samples.

V.P.: Good, good . . . let's see that's . . . but that's only $106,000 so far! Sam, are you still selling model Q17 at the old price?

Sam: Yea, but only to Harrison Brothers. They always buy a year's supply from us, and so I quote them a price in January and hold it firm all year.

V.P.: What shipments are scheduled to Harrison in December?

Sam: They're open on 6,000 units at $8 f.o.b. our plant.

V.P.: Good. Up the billing to $10.50, the same as we charge everybody else.

Sam: But we can't do that . . . it's against our trading policy with these people.

V.P.: I don't care who they are. I said up the billing to current price and that's it. If they don't like it, let 'em go somewhere else next year. Let's see now . . . that's $15,000 more added to the bottom line. Pete, get in here with some help!"

Pete: I've about had it with this profit game . . . no more ideas. I pass.

V.P.: This isn't bridge, Pete. For starters, you can lay off four supervisors at $1,000 each and eliminate all overtime. In total, that should save about $9,000 in December. Make sales out of inventory, Sam.

Jake: So far, that's $130,000. Our initial profit forecast included the pricing of unsold X14 models at scrap value for inventory purposes. We could, I suppose, price the units at cost, thereby reducing Cost of Goods Sold roughly $35,000.

V.P.: Sounds shaky, Jake, but do it. If that stuff won't sell, we'll take our lumps in 19X6. There it is, gentlemen: $165,000 in assured profit increases. Hold the line until January. I'll have memos on these actions to you by Monday. [All exit smiling.]

REQUIRED:

a. For profit centers such as the Brownwood plant, managers are held responsible for cost, revenue, and profit performance. Have the means and ends of budgeting and control become confused for this company?

b. How could the corporate management group revise its performance evaluation procedure and yet obtain satisfactory results without each vice president having to search for ways to achieve short-run annual profit targets?

c. Do you agree with the various decisions made by the vice president at this meeting?

Chapter 14: Period Budgets and Profit Planning

CHAPTER HIGHLIGHTS

Purpose and Learning Objectives

Period budget preparation is vital to the success of a business venture. Top management must spell out the company's goals and objectives and communicate these ideas to middle and lower management. From long-term corporate targets, yearly or period budgets (plans) are formulated. This chapter analyzes the period budget as a profit planning and control tool and illustrates the preparation of a complete master budget.

Upon completion of this chapter, students should be able to:

1. State the nature and purpose of a period budget
2. Define and prepare various types of budgets
3. Use a period budget for both planning and control purposes
4. State the advantages of budgeting
5. Interrelate the segments or parts of a master budget
6. Prepare a complete master budget

Relevant Concepts

The following basic concepts are introduced in this chapter:

Period budget   A forecast of annual operating results that represents a quantitative expression of planned activities of an organization.

Continuous budget   A perpetual twelve-month budget in which expired monthly or quarterly data are deleted and replaced by projections for a comparable future time period.

Budget data flow   The organization and implementation of departmental or functional period budgets and their integration into pro forma or forecasted financial statements.

Master budget   An integrated set of departmental or functional period budgets and forecasted financial statements for the company as a whole.

Period budgeting involves the conversion of sales and production goals into realistic cost and revenue estimates, the projection of net income (assuming plans are attained), and the integration of all proposed transactions into the firm's forecasted balance sheet. Each facet of this process is analyzed in the preparation of a master budget. A budget is a financial plan of action or a quantitative expression of planned activities. To successfully prepare a budget, many cost accounting tools are utilized, including cost-volume-profit analysis, cost accumulation methods, standard costs, flexible budgeting, and responsibility accounting. Cash budgets and capital expenditure budgets are included in a master budget; a continuous budget is a perpetual twelve-month master budget that is updated continuously.

A budget director or budget committee usually supervises the construction of a master budget. Forecasted sales and production quotas are developed in relation to long-range corporate objectives. This information is communicated to middle- and lower-level managers, who must prepare functional or departmental budgets. These departmental budgets are sent back to the budget director for coordination and integration into the company's master budget. The final master budget consists of:

1. *Detailed operating budgets*, including the sales budget, production budget, selling expense budget, raw material purchase and usage budgets, direct labor budget, factory overhead budget, general and administrative (G & A) expense budget, and capital expenditure budget.
2. *The profit plan*, made up of a Cost of Goods Sold budget and a forecasted income statement.
3. *The financial position forecast*, described by a cash budget and a forecasted balance sheet.

AN INTRODUCTION TO PERIOD BUDGETS

Establishing an effective budgeting system is the key to a successful and profitable business venture. Without a fully coordinated budgeting system, management has only a vague idea of where the company is headed financially. Monthly cash needs, raw material requirements, peak labor seasons, and timing of capital facility expenditures are examples of information supplied through the budgeting process. At the end of an accounting period, budgets help determine areas of strength and weakness within the company. Comparisons of actual operating results with projected or budgeted results are used to determine why profit expectations were not attained. Preparing period budgets and using the budgets to evaluate actual performance make up the budgetary control process. A set of coordinated period budgets is essential if the budgetary control process is to function properly.

Budgets are useful for both large corporations and smaller segments of the business community. In fact, budgets are used by individuals as well as business entities. College students often need to plan their sources and uses of monthly spending money. Families need budgets to plan their spending. Nonprofit organizations such as churches, municipalities, state and federal government agencies, community organizations, professional membership groups, and various charitable organizations all utilize some form of budgeting for planned or controlled spending. In this text, period budgets are developed and discussed from a corporate viewpoint by focusing on profit planning rather than on the expenditure or spending phase. However, many budgeting concepts and procedures are also useful for planning in nonprofit organizations.

Period budgets can be introduced at almost any point within the study of cost accounting. The budget concept can be exposed initially with little knowledge or background in cost accounting theory and practice. However, the authors believe that competence in preparing and using period budgets is obtained only after all concepts and techniques used in budgeting have been mastered.

Concepts and Techniques Used in Budgeting

Many cost accounting concepts and techniques presented earlier in this text are used in the budgeting process. Budgetary planning and control likewise are involved in many phases of cost accounting. The creation of a period budget is based on forecasts of anticipated costs and revenues for a future accounting period, which is usually one year. As shown in Exhibit 14-1, cost behavior, cost accumulation methods, cost-volume-profit analysis, flexible budgeting, the contribution margin approach, standard costs, and responsibility accounting are integrated to develop a period budget. All these areas play a role in structuring, computing, and communicating budget data.

Raw cost data include raw material, labor, factory overhead, operating expenses, and capital facility projections that provide the fundamental information needed to prepare a period budget. Specific *cost behavior patterns* are determined for each cost factor. Using *cost-volume-profit analysis*, alternative profit plans for the period can be analyzed. *Cost accumulation methods* are required to determine inventory values and projected Cost of Goods Sold. *Direct costing* and the *contribution margin approach* are useful in measuring the expected profitability of each division, department, or product line. *Flexible budgeting* is used to compile overhead budgets for production departments

EXHIBIT 14-1
THE BUDGETING PROCESS
COST ACCOUNTING TOOLS UTILIZED

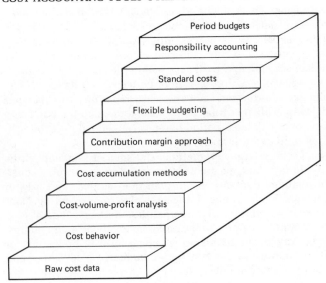

Period budgets
Responsibility accounting
Standard costs
Flexible budgeting
Contribution margin approach
Cost accumulation methods
Cost-volume-profit analysis
Cost behavior
Raw cost data

and to estimate selling and administrative expenses. If a firm has developed a set of *standard costs*, they are used throughout the budgeting process for material, labor, and overhead cost projections. *Responsibility accounting* procedures ensure that cost information is communicated throughout the organization in an orderly manner. With a proper blend of these cost accounting tools, the budget director can formulate a sound set of *period budgets*. If operating plans are based on accurate sales forecasts, the resulting cost projections will be reasonably accurate.

Budget Definition

A *budget* is a financial plan of action or a quantitative expression of planned activities. According to Professor William Vatter, "Budgets state formally—in terms of expected transactions—the decisions of all levels of management about the resources to be acquired, how they are to be used, and what ought to result. Budgets put the details of management plans for operations into money units, so that the results may be projected into expected financial statements."[1]

Types of Budgets

Various types of budgets are utilized by management. In Chapter 11, you studied the flexible or variable budget, which is geared to several potential levels of activity, and the static budget, which is based on a single level of activity. Many other types of budgets are used in corporate planning activities; some are described below:

Master budget A *master budget*, or comprehensive budget, consists of separate budgets for each functional area of activity; these are summarized to present a projection of a firm's total operations for a future period of time. The various parts of the master budget are illustrated in this chapter. In contrast to comprehensive budgeting, partial budgeting considers only part of a company's total plans, such as a sales budget not accompanied by production and inventory forecasts.

Cash budget A *cash budget* is a forecast of the cash receipts and disbursements for a future period of time. It summarizes the cash effects of planned transactions expressed in all other phases of a master budget.

Capital expenditure budget A *capital expenditure budget* includes capital expenditure plans and approved expenditures. This budget is based on long-range decisions to acquire specific items of plant and equipment in the current year. Capital expenditures related to operating plans for the forthcoming accounting period are part of the master budget. The decision-making process for these long-range investments is discussed in Chapter 16.

Continuous budget Master budgets usually are prepared for a twelve-month period based on a firm's fiscal or calendar year. In order to always have a current twelve-month master budget at any particular date, a continuous budget is maintained. A *continuous budget* is a perpetual twelve-month budget in which the current month or quarter is dropped and replaced by projections of a month or quarter one year hence. This continuous updating process is pictured on the following page. As a general budgeting procedure, continuous budgets are desirable, but they are not used by all companies.

[1] William J. Vatter, *Operating Budgets*, Wadsworth, Belmont, Calif., 1969, pp. 15–16.

Continuous budget

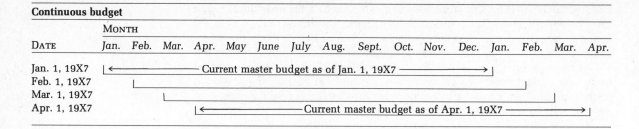

DATE	MONTH															
	Jan.	Feb.	Mar.	Apr.	May	June	July	Aug.	Sept.	Oct.	Nov.	Dec.	Jan.	Feb.	Mar.	Apr.
Jan. 1, 19X7	←			Current master budget as of Jan. 1, 19X7								→				
Feb. 1, 19X7																
Mar. 1, 19X7																
Apr. 1, 19X7				←			Current master budget as of Apr. 1, 19X7						→			

PERIOD BUDGET—A PROFIT-PLANNING VEHICLE

Budget preparation is an integral part of management activities. Long-range objectives are incorporated into long-term corporate plans. A five- or ten-year master plan usually is structured by corporations to facilitate the accomplishment of long-range objectives. Such long-range plans usually are stated in terms of profit objectives, new product lines, and anticipated capital facility expansion.

Period budgets are the vehicles that make long-term plans operational. These budgets integrate the current portion of long-range planning into a workable set of operating objectives for the forthcoming accounting period. New products, production changes, capital expenditures, sales expectations, and personnel requirements for the next year all play major roles in the period budgeting process.

Budgeting Process

Preparation of period budgets can be approached in many different ways. The budget development process and the degree of detail within individual budgets vary from company to company. In small companies, one person may prepare the entire budget. As the size of a company expands, the budgeting process becomes more complex and utilizes the talents and inputs of many people. In the large multinational companies in which a decentralized form of management is maintained, budgeting departments are created and charged with formulating and coordinating budgets for the entire company.

To illustrate the steps necessary to prepare a period budget, let us look at a medium-sized company. Rudolph Corporation is a manufacturing company with annual sales of $15,000,000. The controller, Mr. Randolph, appointed Mr. Roland as budget director. Mr. Roland created the following budget formulation policy based on a calendar-year accounting period:

May 19X4: Meeting of corporate officers and budget director to discuss major corporate plans for 19X5.

June 19X4: Meeting(s) of division managers, department heads, and budget director to communicate 19X5 corporate objectives. At this time, relevant background data is distributed to all managers, and a time schedule is established for development of 19X5 budget data.

July 19X4: Managers and department heads continue to develop budget data; finalize 19X5 monthly sales forecasts by product line and receive final sales estimates from sales vice president.

August 19X4: Finalize 19X5 monthly production activity and anticipated inventory level plans. Division managers and department heads should communicate preliminary budget figures to budget director for coordination and distribution to other operating areas.

September 19X4: Development of preliminary 19X5 master budget. Revised budget data from all functional areas to be received. Budget director will coordinate staff activities integrating manpower requirements, raw material and supply requirements, unit cost estimates, cash requirements, and profit estimates into 19X5 master budget.

October 19X4: Meeting with corporate officers to discuss preliminary 19X5 master budget; any corrections, additions, or deletions to be communicated to budget director by corporate officers; all authorized changes to be incorporated into the 19X5 master budget.

November 19X4: Submit final draft of 19X5 master budget to corporate officers for approval. Publish approved budget and distribute to all corporate officers, division managers, and department heads.

The budget development process used by the Rudolph Corporation illustrates the importance of timing and employee involvement in the preparation of a master budget. In this example, development of next year's budget begins as early as May of the current year. Planning activities begin at the top of the corporate hierarchy and are communicated systematically to all responsible personnel in middle and lower management capacities. Following the responsibility accounting format, detailed plans are formulated by lower management personnel or department heads and are given to division managers for coordination of divisional plans. Completed plans for each division are submitted to the budget director for coordination and communication to members of top management.

Profit Planning through Budgeting

A completed master budget represents estimates of *all* revenues and expenditures for a subsequent accounting period. In essence, the budget depicts a projection of all transactions for a future period. If all transactions are represented, the logical extension of the master budget is to prepare pro forma or forecasted financial statements—a balance sheet and an income statement.

The pro forma income statement expresses the planned profit for the period. If the projected profit is not adequate after all budgets have been prepared, management will request that the budget director undertake a special analysis to identify areas of excessive cost. Through interaction with various managers responsible for budget preparation, estimated costs are often reduced. Since excessive costs are not the only cause of low projected profits, sales estimates are also reviewed to determine whether they are realistic.

Need for Human Input

Human input is an important factor underlying a successful budgeting process. Management personnel develop budget goals and related estimates; these same people should be held responsible for budget implementation. Unless a company is very small, one person cannot structure and implement a complete annual profit plan. As was illustrated in Chapter 13, a corporate hierarchy consists of integrated responsibility and communication channels. A firm's success hinges on the fact that all persons in the management group know what their responsibilities are and to whom they report. This responsibility accounting concept is an important factor in the budgeting process.

Period budget preparation requires managers in every functional area of the company to communicate projected resource needs and operating plans to the budget director. Computers are used to compile and summarize these data, but computers cannot be held accountable for deviations between actual results and related plans. Likewise, a manager should not be held responsible for plans, goals, and financial estimates which he or she did not develop or approve. The need for management input and a participative approach to the budgeting process are apparent. Such input provides realistic and attainable projections and motivates responsible individuals to achieve corporate and functional goals. The basic concept is that a manager who plans and implements a specific segment of actual operations is accountable for results achieved.

Advantages of Budgeting

Several advantages of period budget determination and use have been mentioned or implied. The primary purpose of a budgeting system is to determine and to seek the most profitable course of action for the company. A fully developed budgeting or profit-planning process provides the following advantages to management:

1. Requires early consideration of corporate policies and objectives
2. Directs operating decisions toward policies of the company as a whole rather than toward policies that benefit only specific segments
3. Stresses efficiency in labor, material, facility, and capital resource utilization
4. Causes corporate policies and organizational structure to be defined and operational
5. Causes all segments to coordinate their activities and to define specific areas of responsibility
6. Guides personnel to know what is expected of them and how their efforts will be evaluated
7. Isolates operating problem areas and enables corrective action to be taken before they occur
8. Increases an awareness of the importance of cost considerations in the operations of a business
9. Forces all levels of management to work together toward a common goal
10. Requires a firm to maintain a well-defined, operational accounting system
11. Provides a vehicle for self-assessment of management and performance measurement of middle- and lower-level managers
12. Promotes the use of the concepts of management by objective and management by exception

To understand the various phases of a complete master budget, the best learning device is to actually create one. A complete master budget and its preparation phases will be illustrated for Bengtson Toys, Inc. A master budget contains an integrated set of department operating schedules, detailed budgets, and resulting forecasted financial statements. Individual companies may differ in terms of procedures and specific budgets generated, but the following individual budgets represent the type of information required to assemble a complete master budget:

THE MASTER BUDGET—A COMPREHENSIVE ILLUSTRATION

Segments of a Master Budget

1. Detailed operating budgets
   a. Unit sales forecast
   b. Dollar sales budget
   c. Unit production budget
   d. Schedule of departmental operating data
   e. Selling expense budget
   f. Material purchase and usage budgets
   g. Labor hour requirement budget
   h. Direct labor dollar budget
   i. Factory overhead budget
   j. General and administrative (G & A) expense budget
   k. Capital expenditure budget
2. The profit plan
   a. Cost of goods sold budget
   b. Forecasted income statement
3. Financial position forecast
   a. Cash budget
   b. Forecasted balance sheet

The structure and flow of data required to develop a master budget are shown in Exhibit 14-2. Each of the above budget segments is included. Note that the unit sales forecast is the cornerstone of the budgeting process. The unit production budget and all other departmental operating budgets are based on the forecasted sales volume. The arrows in Exhibit 14-2 trace the flow of information from the various operating budgets to the forecasted financial statements. As each budget is developed for our illustrative firm, it may be helpful to refer to Exhibit 14-2, which summarizes the role of each budget in the development of forecasted financial statements.

Bengtson Toys, Inc., was organized in 19X1 to manufacture a toy truck line. To date, the company has concentrated on one particular truck, a miniature 18-foot moving van. Schedule A shows the company's balance sheet on December 31, 19X5. Net income in 19X5 was $158,540, making it the most profitable year to date for Bengtson Toys, Inc. The following information pertains to the company's operations:

Bengtson Toys, Inc.

Production departments: Stamping, Assembly, Painting and decal, Packing

Service departments: Repairs and maintenance, Quality control—inspection, Material handling and storage

Full (practical) capacity—50,000 trucks per month; 60-hour work week: 6 days at 10 hours per day

Normal capacity—41,250 trucks per month; 49.5-hour work week

Storage capacity—50,000 finished trucks

Purchase and payment policies: Raw material purchases in current month equal budgeted material usage of following month; supplies are purchased every three months; raw material invoices paid in month following purchase

Cash receipts: 60% of sales collected in month of sale; 38% of sales collected in month following sale; 2% of sales are uncollectible

Standard cost per truck:

Raw material	$1.91
Direct labor	.45
Factory overhead	1.26
Total	$3.62

Standard labor hours per truck:

Stamping—.026 hours/truck
Assembly—.0416 hours/truck
Painting—.0104 hours/truck
Decals—.0104 hours/truck
Packing—.0052 hours/truck

For budget preparation purposes, it is assumed that there is no Work in Process inventory balance at month-end.

Before the master budget for Bengtson Toys, Inc., is developed, the general approach to the project needs to be discussed. The only way to learn how to prepare a master budget is to actually experience the process. Because of the complexity of the process, however, it is easy to become confused with the mass of seemingly unrelated data. The detailed operating budgets are prepared by functional managers responsible for each area. In the study of budgeting, the preparation of each operating budget or schedule should be approached as an independent project, and in many cases, one budget builds on information from previously developed budgets. An example of this would be the unit production budget, which can be developed only after the unit sales forecast has been assembled.

The integration of data from the operating budgets is necessary when preparing the forecasted financial statements. At that time, all operating budgets have been prepared; the major task remaining is to assemble the cost and revenue estimates, compute net income, and prepare the forecasted balance sheet. Exhibit 14-2 has been designed to show the data collection process for master budget preparation.

BENGTSON TOYS, INC.
Balance sheet
December 31, 19X5

A-S-S-E-T-S

Current assets:

Cash	$ 71,500	
Accounts receivable—net of uncollectible accounts	107,730	
Raw materials inventory (at standard)	71,460	
Finished goods inventory (at standard)	72,392	
Supplies inventory	789	
Total current assets		$ 323,871

Plant, equipment, and land:

Land		$ 30,000	
Buildings	$1,750,000		
Plant, equipment, and autos	940,000		
Furniture and fixtures	125,000		
	$2,815,000		
Less: Accumulated depreciation	972,500	1,842,500	
Total plant, equipment, and land			$1,872,500
Total assets			$2,196,371

L-I-A-B-I-L-I-T-I-E-S A-N-D E-Q-U-I-T-Y

Liabilities:

Current liabilities:

Accounts payable	$71,460	
Mortgage note—current	50,000	
Other payables	17,450	
Total current liabilities	$138,910	

Long-term debt (6%):

Mortgage note (19 years remaining)	950,000	
Total liabilities		$1,088,910

Stockholders' equity:

Capital stock	$700,000	
Paid in capital	86,680	
Retained earnings	320,781	
Total stockholders' equity		1,107,461
Total liabilities and equity		$2,196,371

The unit sales forecast is the initial phase of the budgeting process and perhaps the most critical. This forecast can "make or break" total company performance for a year. If it is too high, the company could produce too many units and end up with large, costly inventories. Even if the company halts production in time, it will have overspent in the areas of raw materials and personnel in anticipation of higher production volume. When the unit sales forecast is too low, a company may find itself undertooled and lacking the productive capacity needed to meet actual sales demand. The result is a possible loss of customers

Unit Sales Forecast and Sales Budget

EXHIBIT 14-2

BUDGET STRUCTURE AND DATA FLOW

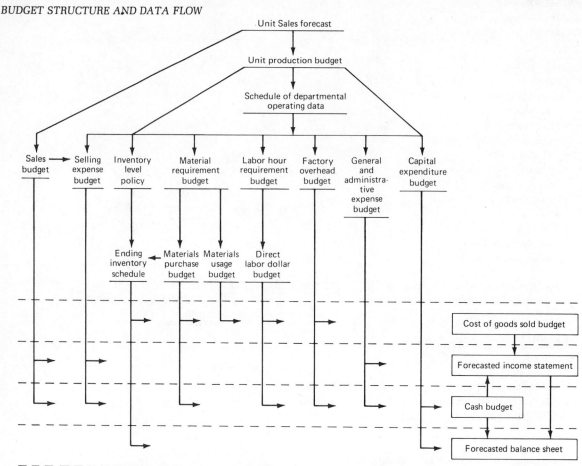

and reputation. Since the estimate of future sales volume is so important, considerable time, effort, and procedural analysis are devoted to the unit sales forecast.

Schedule B illustrates the unit sales forecast of Bengtson Toys, Inc., for 19X6. This forecast is the responsibility of the sales department and was developed by analyzing past sales trends, market growth estimates, and corporate goals for 19X6. Note that a seasonal sales pattern is recognized in the forecast. Our company has only one product, and so the task is simplified in comparison with companies such as General Motors or Texas Instruments, which have several divisions producing hundreds of products. These multiproduct organizations demand the services of a budgeting department working full-time on planning activities.

Product pricing decisions can have a significant effect on the accuracy of the unit sales forecast. Decisions on selling prices must consider (1) the costs of production and distribution, (2) selling prices of competitors, and (3) company profitability. If the selling price is too high, actual sales will be less than the unit sales forecast. Low selling prices may increase demand but reduce unit

BENGTSON TOYS, INC.
Unit sales forecast and sales budget
For year ended December 31, 19X6

MONTH	UNIT SALES FORECAST	×	UNIT SELLING PRICE	=	SALES BUDGET
January	20,000		$9.45		$ 189,000
February	30,000				283,500
March	40,000				378,000
April	50,000				472,500
May	60,000				567,000
June	50,000				472,500
July	40,000				378,000
August	30,000				283,500
September	40,000				378,000
October	50,000				472,500
November	60,000				567,000
December	30,000				283,500
Totals	500,000		$9.45		$4,725,000

Note: *Forecast* implies that sales volume is estimated based upon analysis of past trends and appraisal of current market conditions. This technical forecast is developed and then adjusted by management as necessary to represent acceptable goals for the budget period. As used here, the term *forecast* includes adjustments by management.

profitability. These general concepts are valid for products having normal price-demand relationships; as prices increase, the quantity that can be sold decreases. The toy truck produced by Bengtson Toys, Inc., is priced to its customers at $9.45. In establishing this price, top management required information from the marketing, production, and cost accounting areas.

The sales budget is a function of decisions to establish the unit sales forecast and unit selling price. As shown in schedule B, forecasted unit sales volume is multiplied times the product selling price to yield the *sales budget*. Since the sales budget represents estimated revenues for the period, it also will be used to develop the cash budget and the forecasted income statement as shown in Exhibit 14-2.

Unit Production Budget

Planning monthly production volume is influenced by unit sales forecasts, production capacity, manpower availability, and finished goods storage capacity. If a constant inventory level is desired, units produced should equal units sold during a period. However, as indicated in schedule B, the toy truck market is seasonal. There is high demand during some months and low demand during others. Under these circumstances, unit production plans must coordinate production capacity, labor availability, inventory storage capacity, and the unit sales forecast. Schedule C illustrates this point. Sixty thousand units are to be sold in May and November, but the company's maximum monthly production capacity is 50,000 units. By using its labor and production resources effectively, planned production volume is scheduled for each month to avoid slack periods, idle facilities, and employee layoffs.

In schedule C, the unit sales forecast for each month is combined with desired inventory levels to determine required production volume. Finished

BENGTSON TOYS, INC.
Unit production budget
(and related finished goods
inventory level schedule)
For year ended December 31, 19X6

MONTH	BEGINNING INVENTORY, FINISHED GOODS	+ UNIT PRODUCTION SCHEDULE	− UNIT SALES FORECAST (FROM SCHEDULE B)	= ENDING INVENTORY, FINISHED GOODS	INVENTORY LEVELS* Minimum	Maximum
January	20,000	37,500	20,000	37,500	7,500	50,000
February	37,500	37,500	30,000	45,000	10,000	50,000
March	45,000	40,000	40,000	45,000	12,500	50,000
April	45,000	45,000	50,000	40,000	15,000	50,000
May	40,000	50,000	60,000	30,000	12,500	50,000
June	30,000	50,000	50,000	30,000	10,000	50,000
July	30,000	45,000	40,000	35,000	7,500	50,000
August	35,000	40,000	30,000	45,000	10,000	50,000
September	45,000	37,500	40,000	42,500	12,500	50,000
October	42,500	37,500	50,000	30,000	15,000	50,000
November	30,000	37,500	60,000	7,500	7,500	50,000
December	7,500	37,500	30,000	15,000 (Dec. 31)	6,250	50,000
Totals	20,000 (Jan. 1)	495,000	500,000	15,000 (Dec. 31)		
January 19X7	15,000	37,500	25,000	27,500		

* Additional information:
Minimum level = 25% of following month's sales.
Maximum available storage capacity is 50,000 units.
Ending inventory level on Dec. 31, 19X6, should be relatively low for physical inventory purposes.

goods inventory cannot exceed 50,000 units because of storage capacity limitations. As a policy decision, ending inventory should not be less than 25 percent of estimated unit sales in the following month. Given these constraints, desired ending inventory levels were established for each month. The production volume for each month was then computed in the following manner, using January as an example:

JANUARY 19X6	UNITS
Sales forecast	20,000 (schedule B)
Plus: Desired inventory, Jan. 31	37,500 (determined by management)
Total units required	57,500
Less: Inventory on Jan. 1	(20,000)
Required production	37,500

As shown in schedule C, monthly production volume changes gradually during the budget period. A company with seasonal sales usually selects one of the following production-inventory policies:

1. Constant production rate with inventory levels that increase or decrease with sales volume, or
2. Constant inventory level with production rates that increase or decrease with sales volume

In the case of Bengtson Toys, the company has combined these alternatives in that both inventory levels and production output vary monthly. The effects of production and sales volumes on inventory levels is illustrated in Exhibit 14-3.

EXHIBIT 14-3
BENGTSON TOYS, INC.
COMPARISON OF SALES AND PRODUCTION BUDGETS

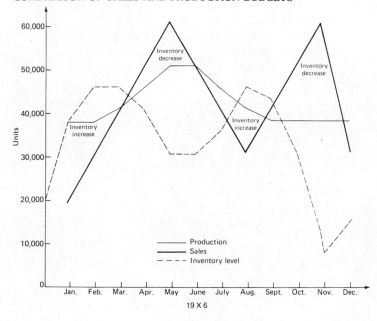

Schedule of Departmental Operating Data

Once the unit sales forecast and unit production budget have been finalized, this information is communicated to managers in each operating department so that departmental operating budgets can be prepared. The *schedule of departmental operating data* varies among companies, but its purpose is to summarize data that are used in formulating departmental budgets. Schedule D informs each production supervisor of the amounts of direct material and

BENGTSON TOYS, INC.   SCHEDULE D
Schedule of departmental operating data
For year ending December 31, 19X6

	NORMAL SPOILAGE	QUANTITY REQUIRED	STANDARD COST	COST PER TOY TRUCK
Stamping department:				
Sheets of steel (4 by 8 feet, 12 truck housings per sheet)	10%	45,375 sheets*	$10.00/sheet	$ .9167
Assembly department:				
Wire for wheel axles (12 inches per truck)	4%	515,000 feet	$15.00/roll (.015/foot)	.0156
Wheels (6 per truck)	1%	3,000,000	$10.00/1,000 (.01/wheel)	.0606
Painting and decals department:				
Paint (25 trucks per gallon)	15%	22,800 gallons	$2.50/gallon	.1150
Decals (1 set per truck)	6%	525,000 sets	$.60/set	.6360
Packing department:				
Boxes (preprinted)	1%	500,000	$.16/box	.1616
Standard material cost per truck				$1.9055
Operating supply requirements (purchased every three months):				
Lubricants (stamping)		10,000 gallons	$.90/gallon	
Fasteners (assembly)		500,000 sets	$.75/1,000 sets	
Shop rags (all departments)		2,000	$4.50/100	

Direct labor requirements:

Department	Direct labor employees	Hours required	Standard rate per hour
Stamping	5	12,870	$5.75/DLH
Assembly	8	20,592	4.50/DLH
Painting and decals:			
Painting	2	5,148	6.00/DLH
Decals	.2	5,148	3.75/DLH
Packing	1	2,574	3.00/DLH

* = planned units of production × 1.1 ÷ 12.
= 495,000 (from schedule C) × 1.1 ÷ 12.
= 45,375 sheets.

direct labor each is responsible for. In addition, the purchasing agent can determine the amount and timing of raw material and supply purchases. The personnel department and top management can also coordinate the number of direct labor employees required and the number of hours to be worked each month during the period. Standard material and labor costs are included for use by department heads in preparing their budgets.

Selling expenses such as sales commissions and automobile expenses may vary with dollar sales, or they may be fixed costs as advertising expenses and supervisory salaries are. The selling expense budget is the responsibility of the sales department and can be prepared as soon as the sales budget is completed. Bengtson's selling expense budget is illustrated in schedule E. Advertising and promotion, salaries, and other selling expenses are fixed costs each month. Sales commissions are 10 percent of expected dollar sales per month. Projected automobile expenses are computed by using a flexible budget formula. For each product sold, variable automobile costs of 5 percent of dollar sales are expected to be incurred plus $10,000 per month for auto depreciation. Decisions regarding promotional effort and efficient selling and distribution methods underlie the selling expense budget.

Selling Expense Budget

Materials purchase and usage budgets can be structured separately or together as presented in schedule F. The end result of coordinating projected purchase and usage information is the formulation of an ending inventory budget for raw materials and supplies. These budgets also can be expressed in units instead of

Materials Purchase and Usage Budgets

BENGTSON TOYS, INC.
Selling expense budget
For year ended December 31, 19X6

SCHEDULE E

Month	Advertising and Promotion	Sales Commissions*	Auto Expense— Mileage, Upkeep, and Depreciation†	Supervision and Other Salaries	Other Selling Expenses	Total
January	$ 40,000	$ 18,900	$ 19,450	$ 7,500	$ 10,000	$ 95,850
February	40,000	28,350	24,175	7,500	10,000	110,025
March	40,000	37,800	28,900	7,500	10,000	124,200
April	40,000	47,250	33,625	7,500	10,000	138,375
May	40,000	56,700	38,350	7,500	10,000	152,550
June	40,000	47,250	33,625	7,500	10,000	138,375
July	40,000	37,800	28,900	7,500	10,000	124,200
August	40,000	28,350	24,175	7,500	10,000	110,025
September	40,000	37,800	28,900	7,500	10,000	124,200
October	40,000	47,250	33,625	7,500	10,000	138,375
November	40,000	56,700	38,350	7,500	10,000	152,550
December	40,000	28,350	24,175	7,500	10,000	110,025
Totals	$480,000	$472,500	$356,250	$90,000	$120,000	$1,518,750

* Variable − 10 percent of dollar sales (see schedule B).
† Variable − 5 percent of dollar sales plus $10,000 depreciation per month.

dollar amounts as shown in schedule F. The important point is that these budgets are as accurate as the information received from the purchasing department (projected raw material and supply purchases) and from the operating department supervisors (monthly production needs). The budget director

BENGTSON TOYS, INC.   SCHEDULE F
Materials purchase and usage budgets
For year ended December 31, 19X6

RAW MATERIALS		JANUARY	FEBRUARY	MARCH	APRIL–DECEMBER	TOTALS
Sheet steel	Beginning bal.	$34,380	$34,380	$36,660	$ 41,250	$ 34,380
	Purchases	34,380	36,660	41,250	341,460	453,750
	Usage	34,380	34,380	36,660	348,330	453,750
	Ending bal.	$34,380	$36,660	$41,250	$ 34,380	$ 34,380
Wire	Beginning bal.	$ 585	$ 585	$ 630	$ 711	$ 585
	Purchases	585	630	705	5,805	7,725
	Usage	585	585	624	5,931	7,725
	Ending bal.	$ 585	$ 630	$ 711	$ 585	$ 585
Wheels	Beginning bal.	$ 2,272	$ 2,272	$ 2,424	$ 2,727	$ 2,272
	Purchases	2,272	2,424	2,727	22,577	30,000
	Usage	2,272	2,272	2,424	23,032	30,000
	Ending bal.	$ 2,272	$ 2,424	$ 2,727	$ 2,272	$ 2,272
Paint	Beginning bal.	$ 4,313	$ 4,313	$ 4,600	$ 5,175	$ 4,313
	Purchases	4,313	4,600	5,175	42,912	57,000
	Usage	4,313	4,313	4,600	43,774	57,000
	Ending bal.	$ 4,313	$ 4,600	$ 5,175	$ 4,313	$ 4,313
Decals	Beginning bal.	$23,850	$23,850	$25,440	$ 28,620	$ 23,850
	Purchases	23,850	25,440	28,620	237,090	315,000
	Usage	23,850	23,850	25,440	241,860	315,000
	Ending bal.	$23,850	$25,440	$28,620	$ 23,850	$ 23,850
Boxes	Beginning bal.	$ 6,060	$ 6,060	$ 6,464	$ 7,272	$ 6,060
	Purchases	6,060	6,464	7,272	60,204	80,000
	Usage	6,060	6,060	6,464	61,416	80,000
	Ending bal.	$ 6,060	$ 6,464	$ 7,272	$ 6,060	$ 6,060
TOTAL RAW MATERIALS						
	Beginning bal.	$71,460*	$71,460	$76,218	$ 85,755	$ 71,460
	Purchases	71,460	76,218	85,749	710,048	943,475
	Usage	71,460	71,460	76,212	724,343	943,475
	Ending bal.	$71,460	$76,218	$85,755	$ 71,460	$ 71,460
TOTAL SUPPLIES						
	Beginning bal.	$ 789*	$ 2,366	$ 1,577	$ 788	$ 789
	Purchases	2,366	—	—	7,099	9,465
	Usage	789	789	789	7,098	9,465
	Ending bal.	$ 2,366	$ 1,577	$ 788	$ 789	$ 789

* See schedule A.

assembles the information after conferring with production, purchasing, and raw material storage personnel. Decisions underlying the preparation of the materials purchase and usage budgets include the determination of raw material consumption per unit of output, inventory reorder points, delivery time, minimum and maximum inventory levels, and the most economical purchase order size. The amounts in schedule F are computed as follows:

$$purchases = subsequent\ month's\ usage\ at\ unit\ price$$
$$usage = previous\ month's\ purchases$$

For example, sheet steel purchases for January total $34,380. This amount is computed by multiplying February production of 37,500 units (from schedule C) times 110 percent (spoilage factor from schedule D) divided by 12, the number of truck housings per sheet. The result is:

$$\frac{(37,500 \times 110\%)}{12} = 3,437.5,\ or\ 3,438\ sheets$$

At ten dollars per sheet, January purchases will be $34,380.

The labor hour requirement budget may not be included in the formal master budget, but it is vital to the determination of the direct labor dollar budget. In the case of Bengtson Toys, Inc., the presence of scheduled overtime makes the schedule of hours necessary. Rather than hire and later lay off personnel following peak production periods, the company has decided to utilize a constant work force and handle peak production periods by increasing the hours of overtime per employee. As shown in schedule G, hours per week will range from a low of forty-five hours to a high of sixty hours. Monthly direct labor hour projections are computed as follows:

Labor Hour Requirement Budget

$$\frac{forecasted\ monthly\ truck\ production}{\substack{standard\ number\ of\ trucks\ produced \\ per\ hour\ by\ one\ employee}} = \substack{projected\ departmental \\ direct\ labor\ hours\ required}$$

To illustrate, let us examine the derivation of the 975 projected direct labor hours required in January in the Stamping Department. Standard labor hours per truck in this department are .026 hours. In 1 hour, an average employee is expected to stamp out 38.4615 truck housings (1 hour/.026). Using the formula to compute required labor hours,

$$\frac{37,500\ trucks}{38.4615\ trucks/hour} = 975\ stamping\ direct\ labor\ hours\ in\ January$$

Since five direct labor workers are employed in the Stamping Department, each must work 195 hours in January (an average of 45 hours per week). The remaining parts of schedule G are computed in the same manner. The average or standard time required to produce one truck was indicated by department earlier in the chapter on page 452.

Projected direct labor cost is computed by multiplying the projected direct labor hour requirement by the standard labor rate per hour. Since Bengtson Toys, Inc., plans to incur overtime premium cost, the overtime element of total

Direct Labor Dollar Budget

BENGTSON TOYS, INC.
Labor hour requirement budget
For year ended December 31, 19X6

	EMPLOYEE HOURS/WEEK	DEPARTMENTS Stamping (5 employees)	Assembly (8 employees)	Painting and decals (4 employees)	Packing (1 employee)	COMPANY TOTALS (18 employees)
January	45	975	1,560	780	195	3,510
February	45	975	1,560	780	195	3,510
March	48	1,040	1,664	832	208	3,744
April	54	1,170	1,872	936	234	4,212
May	60	1,300	2,080	1,040	260	4,680
June	60	1,300	2,080	1,040	260	4,680
July	54	1,170	1,872	936	234	4,212
August	48	1,040	1,664	832	208	3,744
September	45	975	1,560	780	195	3,510
October	45	975	1,560	780	195	3,510
November	45	975	1,560	780	195	3,510
December	45	975	1,560	780	195	3,510
Total direct labor hours		12,870	20,592	10,296	2,574	46,332

BENGTSON TOYS, INC.
Direct labor dollar budget
For year ended December 31, 19X6

SCHEDULE H

	JANUARY Straight time	JANUARY Over-time	FEBRUARY Straight time	FEBRUARY Over-time	MARCH Straight time	MARCH Over-time	APRIL–DECEMBER Straight time	APRIL–DECEMBER Over-time	TOTALS FOR YEAR Straight time	TOTALS FOR YEAR Over-time
Stamping department:										
975 hours × $5.75	$ 5,606		$ 5,606						$ 11,212	
108.33* × .5 × $5.75		$311		$311						$ 622
1,040 hours × $5.75					$ 5,980				5,980	
173.33 × .5 × $5.75						$ 498				498
9,880 hours × $5.75							$ 56,810		56,810	
2,080.35 × .5 × $5.75								$ 5,981		5,981
									$ 74,002	$ 7,101
Assembly department:										
1,560 hours × $4.50	$ 7,020		$ 7,020						$ 14,040	
173.33 × .5 × $4.50		$390		$390						$ 780
1,664 hours × $4.50					$ 7,488				7,488	
277.33 × .5 × $4.50						$ 624				624
15,808 hours × $4.50							$ 71,136		71,136	
3,328 × .5 × $4.50								$ 7,488	7,488	7,488
									$ 92,664	$ 8,892
Painting and decals department:										
390 hours × $6.00	$ 2,340		$ 2,340						$ 4,680	
43.33 × .5 × $6.00		$130		$130						$ 260
390 hours × $3.75	1,463		1,463						2,926	
43.33 × .5 × $3.75		81		81						162
416 hours × $6.00					$ 2,496				2,496	
69.33 × .5 × $6.00						$ 208				208
416 hours × $3.75					1,560				1,560	
69.33 × .5 × $3.75						130				130
3,952 hours × $6.00							$ 23,712		23,712	
832 × .5 × $6.00								$ 2,496		2,496
3,952 hours × $3.75							14,820		14,820	
832 × .5 × $3.75								1,560		1,560
Packing department:										
195 hours × $3.00	$ 585		$ 585						$ 1,170	
21.67 × .5 × $3.00		$ 33		$ 33						$ 66
208 hours × $3.00					$ 624				624	
34.67 × .5 × $3.00						$ 52				52
1,967 hours × $3.00							5,928		5,928	
415.33 × .5 × $3.00								$ 623		623
									$ 7,722	$ 741
Grand totals	$17,014	$945	$17,014	$945	$18,148	$1,512	$172,406	$18,148	$224,582	$21,550

* Overtime hours example computed as follows: January required a 45-hour work week. Therefore, 11.1% of the hours worked represent overtime hours. In the sample amount above: 975 hours × 11.1% = 108.33 overtime hours.

BENGTSON TOYS, INC.
Factory overhead budget
For year ending December 31, 19X6

	PRODUCTION				SERVICE			TOTAL
	Stamping	Assembly	Painting and decals	Packing	Repairs and maintenance	Quality control	Material handling	
Variable costs:								
Indirect materials	$ 2,535	$ 2,380	$ 950	$ 625	$ 1,700	$ 600	$ 450	$ 9,240
Indirect labor	35,000	46,300	25,000	4,000	25,000	30,000	17,000	182,300
Overtime premium (all employees $.096/L$)	10,465	13,340	7,220	1,125	2,400	2,880	1,630	39,060
Labor-related costs ($.10/L$)	10,900	13,900	7,500	1,200	2,500	3,000	1,700	40,700
Power and heat	3,500	5,000	4,000	2,000	5,000	4,500	2,000	26,000
Other	4,500	6,000	5,000	3,000	8,000	7,000	4,000	37,500
Total variable	$ 66,900	$ 86,920	$ 49,670	$11,950	$44,600	$47,980	$26,780	$334,800
Fixed costs:								
Power and heat	$ 1,000	$ 2,000	$ 900	$ 600	$ 1,200	$ 1,000	$ 600	$ 7,300
Depreciation	45,000	20,000	14,000	26,000	12,000	10,000	18,000	145,000
Supervision	20,000	24,000	18,000	9,000	16,000	20,000	14,000	121,000
Property taxes	1,000	600	500	400	700	500	200	3,900
Other	3,000	1,800	1,500	1,200	2,100	1,500	600	11,700
Total fixed	$ 70,000	$ 48,400	$ 34,900	$37,500	$32,000	$33,000	$33,400	$288,900
Total	$136,900	$135,320	$ 84,570	$49,150	$76,600	$80,980	$60,180	$623,700
To production departments (direct material $)	$ 30,090	$ 1,806	$ 22,868	$ 5,416			(60,180)	
To production departments (direct labor $)	27,533	33,202	17,816	2,429		(80,980)		
To production departments (depreciation $)	32,938	14,554	9,958	19,150	(76,600)			
					–0–	–0–	–0–	
Total	$227,461	$184,882	$135,212	$76,145				$623,700

For product costing purposes:

	Stamping	Assembly	Painting and decals	Packing
Factory overhead rate per direct labor hour Standard DLHs	12,870	20,592	10,296	2,574
Standard OH Rate	$ 17,674	$ 8,978	$ 13,132	$ 29.58

Bases for cost reapportionment (direct method):

	Stamping	Assembly	Painting and decals	Packing	Totals
DL $	74,000	92,600	50,000	7,700	224,300
%	34%	41%	22%	3%	100%
DM $	453,750	37,700	345,000	80,000	916,450
%	50%	3%	38%	9%	100%
Depreciation	45,000	20,000	14,000	26,000	105,000
%	43%	19%	13%	25%	100%

direct labor cost should be calculated separately. Such a procedure is illustrated in schedule H on page 463. Since straight time is a direct product cost and overtime is usually a factory overhead cost, separating these labor cost elements here provides necessary data for the preparation of the factory overhead budget.

Factory Overhead Budget

The budget for factory overhead shown in schedule I has two purposes. First, this budget integrates the overhead cost budgets developed by production and service department managers. Second, by reapportioning service department costs to production departments, predetermined overhead rates can be computed for the forthcoming accounting period. The development of a factory overhead budget was discussed in Chapter 5. Cost behavior patterns underlie these computations, and flexible budget information is used to prepare the factory overhead budget.

General and Administrative Expense Budget

In preparing a master budget, general and administrative expenses must be projected to provide information included in the cash budget. The general and administrative (G & A) expense budget also serves as an expense limitation for administrative functions and is a cost control vehicle. Bengtson's general and administrative expense budget is presented in schedule J; all expense elements are fixed costs each month.

Capital Expenditure Budget

Determining the capital facility needs and securing investment resources for such expenditures are very complex managerial areas. Amounts shown in the capital expenditure budget in schedule K (top of page 466) are based on a completed process of proposal preparation, proposal screening, rate-of-return calculations, and dollar resource rationing. These expenditures are important to the projected cash flows and productivity of Bengtson Toys, Inc. A complete explanation of the capital expenditure decision process is presented in Chapter 16.

BENGTSON TOYS, INC.   SCHEDULE J
General and administrative expense budget
For year ending December 31, 19X6

Month	Salaries	Depreciation	Contractual Services	Other	Annual Total
January	$ 30,000	$ 20,000	$ 10,000	$ 5,000	$ 65,000
February	30,000	20,000	10,000	5,000	65,000
March	30,000	20,000	10,000	5,000	65,000
April	30,000	20,000	10,000	5,000	65,000
May	30,000	20,000	10,000	5,000	65,000
June	30,000	20,000	10,000	5,000	65,000
July	30,000	20,000	10,000	5,000	65,000
August	30,000	20,000	10,000	5,000	65,000
September	30,000	20,000	10,000	5,000	65,000
October	30,000	20,000	10,000	5,000	65,000
November	30,000	20,000	10,000	5,000	65,000
December	30,000	20,000	10,000	5,000	65,000
Totals	$360,000	$240,000	$120,000	$60,000	$780,000

BENGTSON TOYS, INC.   SCHEDULE K
Capital expenditure budget
For year ending December 31, 19X6

Month	Capital Facility Needs	Estimated Cost
January	Sales automobile at $4,200	$ 4,200
March	74G42 stamping machine	$75,000
	Sales automobile at $4,200	4,200
Total for March		$79,200
June	Spray painting compressors (two at $940)	$ 1,880
July	Sales automobiles (two at $4,200)	$ 8,400
October	Assembly welder at $4,500	$ 4,500
Total for year		$98,180

Cost of Goods Sold Budget

The Cost of Goods Sold budget is a necessary prerequisite to the development of the forecasted income statement. At this stage of preparing the master budget, all required financial data have been compiled in departmental or functional budgets. As illustrated in schedule L and in Exhibit 14-2, information from the materials purchase and usage budget, the direct labor dollar budget, the factory overhead budget, and the ending inventory schedules are

BENGTSON TOYS, INC.   SCHEDULE L
Costs of goods sold budget
For year ending December 31, 19X6

	January	February	March	April–December	Totals
Beginning materials inventory	$ 71,460	$ 71,460	$ 76,218	$ 85,755	$ 71,460
Plus: Purchases (F)*	71,460	76,218	85,749	710,048	943,475
Materials available for use	$142,920	$147,678	$161,967	$ 795,803	$1,014,935
Less: Ending inventory (F)	71,460	76,218	85,755	71,460	71,460
Materials used (F)	$ 71,460	$ 71,460	$ 76,212	$ 724,343	$ 943,475
Direct labor (H)	17,014	17,014	18,148	172,406	224,582
Factory overhead (G & I)	47,250	47,250	50,400	478,800	623,700
Total manufacturing costs	$135,724	$135,724	$144,760	$1,375,549	$1,791,757
Plus: Beginning finished goods inventory (C)	72,392	135,735	162,882	162,882	72,392
	$208,116	$271,459	$307,642	$1,538,431	$1,864,149
Less: Ending finished goods inventory (C)	135,735	162,882	162,882	54,294	54,294
Cost of goods sold	$ 72,381	$108,577	$144,760	$1,484,137	$1,809,855

* Letters in parentheses indicate the schedules from which data are drawn.

used in formulating the Cost of Goods Sold budget. Material and labor hour usage standards were used to compute projected material, labor, and overhead costs for the period. In the master budget of Bengtson Toys, Inc., projected costs are assumed to be equal to standard costs. Monthly total manufacturing costs are adjusted for the changes in ending Finished Goods inventory to measure Cost of Goods Sold amounts on a monthly basis.

Forecasted Income Statement

Following the information flow shown in Exhibit 14-2, Cost of Goods Sold amounts for each month are transferred to the forecasted income statement in schedule M. In addition, data from the sales budget, selling expense budget, general and administrative expense budget, and cash budget (interest expense) are included in the forecasted income statement. References in schedule M indicate the source schedule for each item of information. Bad-debts expense could be included in the general and administrative expense budget, but schedule M treats it as a separate item. In 19X6, Bengtson Toys, Inc., expects to generate an after-tax net income of $226,488.

Cash Budget

The cash budget serves two purposes. Of relatively minor importance, the projected cash balance on December 31, 19X6, is used in the forecasted balance sheet. The primary purpose of a cash budget is to project periods of cash excess or deficiency. By comparing projected cash receipts and cash disbursements, the budget director can advise financial executives of months during which the

---

BENGTSON TOYS, INC.   **SCHEDULE M**
Forecasted income statement
For year ending December 31, 19X6

	JANUARY	FEBRUARY	MARCH	APRIL– DECEMBER	TOTALS
Sales (B)*	$189,000	$283,500	$378,000	$3,874,500	$4,725,000
Less: Cost of goods sold (L)	72,381	108,577	144,760	1,484,137	1,809,855
Gross profit	$116,619	$174,923	$233,240	$2,390,363	$2,915,145
Operating expenses:					
Selling expenses (E)	$ 95,850	$110,025	$124,200	$1,188,675	$1,518,750
General and administrative					
expenses (J)	65,000	65,000	65,000	585,000	780,000
Bad-debt expense (2% of sales)	3,780	5,670	7,560	77,490	94,500
Total operating expenses	$164,630	$180,695	$196,760	$1,851,165	$2,393,250
Interest expense (N)	$ 60,000	–0–	–0–	$ 8,920	$ 68,920
Net income before taxes	($108,011)	($ 5,772)	$ 36,480	$ 530,278	$ 452,975
Income taxes (50%)					226,487
Net income					$ 226,488

* Letters in parentheses indicate the schedules from which data are drawn.

BENGTSON TOYS, INC.
Cash budget
For year ending December 31, 19X6

SOURCE SCHEDULE		JANUARY	FEBRUARY	MARCH	APRIL–DECEMBER	TOTALS
	Cash receipts:					
B	Sales—previous month (38%)	$107,730	$ 71,820	$107,730	$ 143,640	$ 430,920
B	Sales—current month (60%)	113,400	170,100	226,800	3,689,280	4,199,580
	Total receipts	$221,130	$241,920	$334,530	$3,832,920	$4,630,500
	Cash disbursements:					
F	Material purchase—previous month	$ 71,460	$ 71,460	$ 76,218	$ 724,337	$ 943,475
F	Supply purchases	2,366	–0–	–0–	7,099	9,465
H	Direct labor	17,014	17,014	18,148	172,406	224,582
G and I	Factory overhead—net of depreciation and supplies	34,378	34,378	37,528	362,951	469,235
E	Selling expenses—net of depreciation	85,850	100,025	114,200	1,098,675	1,398,750
J	General and administrative expenses—net of depreciation	45,000	45,000	45,000	405,000	540,000
K	Capital facility purchases	4,200	–0–	79,200	14,780	98,180
	Income taxes	–0–	–0–	–0–	226,487	226,487
	Interest expense	60,000	–0–	–0–	8,920*	68,920
	Loan payments	50,000	–0–	–0–	165,000*	215,000
	Total disbursements	$370,268	$267,877	$370,294	$3,185,655	$4,194,094
	Cash increase (decrease)	($149,138)	($ 25,957)	($ 35,764)	$ 647,265	$ 436,406
A	Beginning cash balance	71,500	25,362	25,405	25,641	71,500
	Ending cash balance before financing	($ 77,638)	($ 595)	($ 10,359)	$ 672,906	$ 507,906
	Desired minimum cash balance	$ 25,000	$ 25,000	$ 25,000	$ 25,000	$ 25,000
	Financing required	$102,638	$ 25,595	$ 35,359	–0–	$ 163,592
	Short-term funds borrowed ($1,000 increments 12% interest)	$103,000	$ 26,000	$ 36,000	–0–	$ 165,000
	Ending cash balance after financing	$ 25,362	$ 25,405	$ 25,641	$ 672,906	$ 672,906

* Short-term borrowing:
 Interest and Principal paid at end of June
 Interest Expense   (6 months) $6,180 + (5 months) $1,300 + (4 months) $1,440 = $8,920

company will require extra short-term financing (cash deficiencies) or periods when excess cash will be available for short-term investment purposes. Other uses of the cash budget include testing the reasonableness of total company plans and pinpointing time periods in which unusual or postponable expenditures should be made.

BENGTSON TOYS, INC.
Forecasted balance sheet
December 31, 19X6

A-s-s-e-t-s

Current assets:		
Cash	$672,906	
Accounts receivable—net of		
uncollectible accounts	107,730	
Raw materials inventory (at standard)	71,460	
Finished goods inventory		
(at standard)	54,294	
Supplies inventory	789	
Total current assets		$907,179
Plant, equipment, and land:		
Land	$ 30,000	
Buildings	$1,750,000	
Plant, equipment, and autos	1,038,180	
Furniture and fixtures	125,000	
	$2,913,180	
Less: Accumulated depreciation	1,477,500	$1,435,680
Total plant, equipment, and land		1,465,680
Total assets		$2,372,859

L-i-a-b-i-l-i-t-i-e-s a-n-d E-q-u-i-t-y

Liabilities:		
Current liabilities:		
Accounts payable	$71,460	
Mortgage note—current	50,000	
Other payables	17,450	
Total current liabilities		$138,910
Long-term debt:		
Mortgage note (6%)—18 years		
remaining	900,000	
Total liabilities		$1,038,910
Stockholders' equity:		
Capital stock	$700,000	
Paid-in-capital	86,680	
Retained earnings	547,269	
Total stockholders' equity		1,333,949
Total liabilities and equity		$2,372,859

The cash budget of Bengtson Toys, Inc., is shown in schedule N. All noncash expenditures, such as depreciation expense, are excluded when determining monthly cash disbursements. Note that during January, February, and March, the company anticipates the need for short-term financing. However, by year-end, sufficient cash resources should be accumulated to allow either short-term investing or major capital expenditures in early 19X7. Information from the following source schedules is used in the cash budget of Bengtson Toys, Inc.:

Schedule	Document
A	Beginning balance sheet
B	Sales budget
E	Selling expense budget
F	Materials purchase budget
G	Labor hour requirement budget
H	Direct labor dollar budget
I	Factory overhead budget
J	General and administrative expense budget
K	Capital expenditure budget

Forecasted Balance Sheet

When all other schedules have been completed, the forecasted balance sheet in schedule O is prepared. This statement encompasses all planned financial transactions for the year and represents the company's projected financial position assuming all planned events occur. All beginning balances have been adjusted to reflect the planned transactions for the year 19X6.

PERIOD BUDGET—A CONTROL MECHANISM

Preparation of an entire budget causes all managers to visualize the goals and objectives of top management. As individual managers prepare their budgets, they also establish their goals and responsibilities. At the end of the accounting period, they are held accountable for cost variations of all cost categories under their control. In addition to its uses in planning, the period budget is a control mechanism. The accuracy of budget preparation generally is improved when managers are accountable for their personal goals and budget estimates. All significant variations between actual results and related budgets should be explained by appropriate managers.

BUDGET SIMULATION— SOPHISTICATED PROFIT PLANNING

Preparation of the master budget for Bengtson Toys, Inc., was based on a single unit sales forecast. All related departmental budgets and forecasted financial statements were structured around the sale of 500,000 toy trucks during 19X6. The end result was an estimated after-tax net income of $226,488.

If this projected net income figure becomes reality, it would be a record profit for the company. But what if top management is dissatisfied with the projected profit? What if low capacity utilization or resource usage inefficiencies caused large unfavorable cost variances? Many areas of faulty or inadequate information are possible when first putting a master budget together. If any combination of these situations could occur, an alternative approach to period budgeting, called *budget simulation*, would be superior to the single profit plan developed by Bengtson Toys, Inc.

The simulation process was discussed in Chapter 1. Management uses it to test alternative courses of action. Simulation is a method of experimentation in which planned or projected cost and other input data are systematically changed to see what effects result in forecasted net income. Simulation helps to attain the objectives of efficient resource utilization and profit maximization.

Applying the simulation process to the budgeting example of Bengtson Toys, Inc., is beyond the scope of this book. However, the following approach would be applicable:

1. To the extent practicable, distinguish all variable costs from those that are fixed for the time period under review.
2. Prepare a computer program capable of handling all parts of the master budget.
3. Using the computer, test the existing budget by generating alternative profit figures, using different sales forecasts, production plans, raw materials, and labor resource requirements.
4. Select the most profitable and practicable course of action for the forthcoming year.

FINAL NOTE

Preparing a master budget is time consuming and complex. The ability to construct an entire master budget is learned primarily by practice and experience. To develop skill in preparing a master budget, you should review each schedule in the Bengtson, Inc., master budget and recompute many of the figures. By retracing the steps taken to prepare the master budget, your technical budgeting abilities and understanding of important relationships will be enhanced.

Return now to the beginning of the chapter and review the highlights section before proceeding to the review questions, exercises, and problems.

QUESTIONS

14-1. Define and illustrate the following terms and concepts:
   a. Period budget
   b. Master budget
   c. Cash budget
   d. Capital expenditure budget
   e. Continuous budget
   f. Profit planning
   g. Static (fixed) budget
   h. Flexible (variable) budget
   i. Budget simulation
   j. Pro forma financial statements

14-2. What is the role of cost-volume-profit analysis in the preparation of period budgets?

14-3. How are standard costs employed in the process of assembling a master budget?

14-4. "A responsibility accounting system facilitates the flow of budget data through an organization." Discuss this statement in relation to the process of developing an annual selling expense budget.

14-5. What are the functions of a budget director and what conditions dictate the need for such a position?

14-6. Discuss the similarities and differences in period budgets for profit and nonprofit organizations.

14-7. "Period budgets express the current portion of long-range plans in terms of workable operating objectives for an annual accounting period." Based upon this statement, what is the implied relationship between short-run and long-run planning?

14-8. Describe the developmental sequence required to prepare a period budget.

14-9. Identify and discuss various functional or departmental budgets underlying the Cost of Goods Sold budget. What is the common characteristic of each budget?

14-10. A company with a seasonal sales pattern wants to maintain a policy of fixed inventory levels throughout the year. What are the possible effects of this policy on production scheduling and personnel management?

14-11. A company with a seasonal sales pattern wants to maintain a policy of constant production volume throughout the year. What effect may this policy have on finished goods inventory levels?

14-12. What are the principal advantages of a fully developed budgeting process?

14-13. Productive capacity limitations often cause differences between the final sales budget and the original sales forecast. What other operating factors, environmental causes, and behavioral reasons could require modifications in the original sales forecast?

14-14. How does the preparation of a cash budget facilitate the decisions required in cash management?

14-15. Brown Company operates in a highly competitive sales market and has experienced difficulty in forecasting sales accurately. Should the company continue its policy of preparing a profit plan based on its single best estimate of potential sales volume? What alternatives are available through budget simulation?

EXERCISES

14-16. *Material Purchases Budget*   Joy Cosmetics, Inc., is compiling necessary information for its comprehensive 19X4 profit plan. The company manufactures three products (A, B, and C), and each product requires units of different raw material inputs. Planned unit production of each product in 19X4 is 10,000 for A, 30,000 for B, and 20,000 for C. The raw material requirements for one unit of each product are summarized below:

	UNIT MATERIAL REQUIREMENTS			
PRODUCT/MATERIAL	P	Q	R	S
A	2	–	1	–
B	1	2	–	3
C	3	1	2	4

Unit cost and inventory for each raw material are:

	P	Q	R	S
19X4 unit cost	$2.00	$3.50	$4.00	$1.00
Inventory in units:				
Jan. 1, 19X4	10,000	5,000	3,000	20,000
Dec. 31, 19X4	8,000	2,000	6,000	30,000

Raw material unit prices as budgeted are the delivered unit costs experienced by Joy Cosmetics in 19X3.

REQUIRED: Prepare a raw materials purchase budget for 19X4.

14-17. *Sales Forecasting* Caspari Alarm Systems, Inc., had a very successful year in 19X6. Based on a $500 average unit selling price, monthly sales during 19X6 were as follows:

January	$100,000
February	90,000
March	80,000
April	70,000
May	60,000
June	50,000
July	50,000
August	60,000
September	65,000
October	75,000
November	85,000
December	95,000
	$880,000

Mr. John, vice president of sales, is preparing the sales budget for 19X7. Increased manufacturing costs will make it necessary to increase the selling price by 20 percent. Even with this price increase, sales volume is expected to increase by 40 percent. The seasonal sales pattern shown for 19X6 is expected to continue in 19X7.

REQUIRED:
a. Prepare the monthly sales budgets for 19X7.
b. Mr. John is considering the possibility of raising average sales prices

by a total of 40 percent in 19X7. He projects that sales volume will increase by only 15 percent if this action is taken. Under these conditions, what would projected sales be in 19X7?

14-18. *CMA Problem—Nature of Budgeting* The operating budget is a common instrument used by many businesses. While it usually is thought to be an important and necessary tool for management, it has been subject to some criticism from managers and researchers studying organizations and human behavior.

REQUIRED:
a. Describe and discuss the benefits of budgeting from the behavioral point of view.
b. Describe and discuss the criticisms leveled at the budgeting processes from the behavioral point of view.
c. What solutions are recommended to overcome the criticism described in part (b)?

(IMA adapted)

14-19. *Factory Labor Budget* Porth Metals Company manufactures three products in a single plant with four departments: Cutting, Grinding, Polishing, and Packing. The Company has developed standard costs for products J, K, and M and is currently analyzing direct labor hour requirements for the budget year 19X6. Routing sequence and departmental data are presented below:

UNIT OF PRODUCT	STANDARD HOURS PER UNIT				STANDARD DLH/UNIT
	Cut	Grind	Polish	Pack	
J	.3	.5	.2	.1	1.1
K	.5	—	1.4	.3	2.2
M	.8	1.5	—	.2	2.5
Hourly labor rate	$5	$4	$4.50	$3	
Annual DLH capacity	450,000	600,000	625,000	175,000	

The annual direct labor capacity for each department is practical capacity based on a normal two-shift operation. Hour requirements in excess of capacity are provided by overtime labor at 150 percent of normal hourly rates. Budgeted unit production in 19X6 for the products is 200,000 of J, 400,000 of K, and 300,000 of M.

REQUIRED: Prepare a direct labor hour requirements schedule for 19X6 and related direct labor cost budget.

14-20. *CPA Problem—Flexible Budgets and Overhead Allocation* The following annual flexible budget has been prepared for use in making decisions relating to product X:

	100,000 UNITS	150,000 UNITS	200,000 UNITS
Sales volume	$800,000	$1,200,000	$1,600,000
Manufacturing costs:			
Variable	300,000	450,000	600,000
Fixed	200,000	200,000	200,000
	500,000	650,000	800,000
Selling and other expenses:			
Variable	200,000	• 300,000	400,000
Fixed	160,000	160,000	160,000
	360,000	460,000	560,000
Income (loss)	($ 60,000)	$ 90,000	$ 240,000

The 200,000 unit budget has been adopted and will be used for allocating fixed manufacturing costs to units of product X; at the end of the first six months the following information is available:

	UNITS
Production completed	120,000
Sales	60,000

All fixed costs are budgeted and incurred uniformly throughout the year, and all costs incurred coincide with the budget. Over- and under-applied fixed manufacturing costs are deferred until year-end.

REQUIRED:

a. The amount of fixed factory costs applied to product during the first six months under absorption costing would be:
   1. Overapplied by $20,000
   2. Equal to the fixed costs incurred
   3. Underapplied by $40,000
   4. Underapplied by $80,000
   5. None of the above

b. Reported net income (or loss) for the first six months under absorption costing would be:
   1. $160,000
   2. $80,000
   3. $40,000
   4. ($40,000)
   5. None of the above

c. Reported net income (or loss) for the first six months under direct costing would be:
   1. $144,000
   2. $72,000
   3. $0
   4. ($36,000)
   5. None of the above

d. Assuming that 90,000 units of product X were sold during the first six months and that this is to be used as a basis, the revised budget estimate for the total number of units to be sold during this year would be:
   1. 360,000
   2. 240,000
   3. 200,000
   4. 120,000
   5. None of the above (80,000

(AICPA adapted)

14-21. *General and Administrative Expense Budget*   Moulton Metal Products, Inc., is made up of four divisions and uses a centralized management structure. The home office is located in Hugo, Oklahoma. General and administrative expenses of the corporation for 19X7 and expected percentage increases for 19X8 are presented below:

EXPENSE CATEGORIES	19X7 EXPENSES	EXPECTED INCREASE IN 19X8
Administrative salaries	$250,000	20%
Facility depreciation	74,000	10%
Operating supplies	49,000	20%
Insurance and taxes	12,000	10%
Computer services	400,000	40%
Clerical salaries	110,000	15%
Miscellaneous	25,000	10%
Total	$920,000	

For divisional profitability determination purposes, all general and administrative expenses are allocated to divisions on a total labor dollar basis with the exception of computer services. Computer service costs are charged directly to divisions based on usage time. Charges in 19X7 were as follows:

Division A	$100,000
Division B	88,000
Division C	72,000
Division D	60,000
Home office	80,000
Total	$400,000

REQUIRED:

a. Prepare the general and administrative expense budget for Moulton Metal Products, Inc., for 19X8.

b. Prepare a schedule of budgeted computer service cost charges to each division and the home office, assuming the percentage usage time and cost distribution in 19X8 will be the same as in 19X7.

14-22. *CPA Problem—CVP and Budgeting*   The following data relate to a year's budgeted activity for Hugh Corporation, a single-product company:

$13.50 per unit

	UNITS
Beginning inventory	30,000
Production	120,000
Available	150,000
Sales	110,000
Ending inventory	40,000

	PER UNIT	
Selling price	$5.00	6.00
Variable manufacturing costs	1.00	1.10
Variable selling costs	2.00 ✓	
Fixed manufacturing costs		
(based on 100,000 units)	.25	
Fixed selling costs		1.944
(based on 100,000 units)	.65	

Total fixed costs remain unchanged within the relevant range of 25,000 units to a total capacity of 160,000 units.

REQUIRED:

a. Projected annual breakeven sales in units for Hugh Corporation is:
   1. 30,000   3. 45,000
   2. 37,143   4. 50,000

b. Projected net income for Hugh Corporation for the year under direct (variable) costing is:
   1. $110,000   3. $130,000
   2. $127,500   4. $150,000

c. If all variances are charged to Cost of Goods Sold, projected net income for Hugh Corporation for the year under absorption costing is:
   1. $122,500   3. $130,000
   2. $127,500   4. $132,500

d. A special order is received to purchase 10,000 units to be used in an unrelated market. Given the original data, what price per unit should be charged on this order to increase Hugh Corporation's net income by $5,000?
   1. $3.50   3. $5.00
   2. $4.40   4. $6.50

e. Concerning the data for Hugh Corporation, assume selling price increases by 20 percent; variable manufacturing costs increase by 10 percent; variable selling costs remain the same; and total fixed costs increase to $104,400. How many units must now be sold to generate a profit equal to 10 percent of the contribution margin?
   1. 36,000   3. 43,320
   2. 40,000   4. 45,390

(AICPA adpated)

PROBLEMS

14-23. *Sales Budget Simulation* Jade Company plans to manufacture a new product in 19X8. The product is an addition to product lines that the company has marketed successfully for several years. Price and unit cost data for the new product are:

		$200
Selling price		
Less: Direct material	$75	
Direct labor	20	
Variable overhead	15	
Variable selling expense	10	(120)
Contribution margin		$ 80

Fixed production overhead will increase $320,000 a year as a result of adding the new product. Initial planning for this product was based on an assumed annual sales volume of 6,000 units. Sales managers now admit that sales volume could easily exceed the original estimate or fall below it. While 6,000 units is the most likely volume, sales of 10,000 units is possible. After discussion with marketing personnel, the assistant controller has assembled the following sales volume estimates and related probabilities:

POTENTIAL SALES VOLUME	CHANCE OF OCCURRENCE
10,000 units	10%
8,000	20%
6,000	40%
4,000	20%
2,000	10%

REQUIRED:

a. Determine the breakeven sales volume in units and dollars for the new product.
b. Compute the profit contribution from the product using the "expected value" of sales quantities. (Expected value or average equals the sum of each potential sales quantity multiplied by its chance of occurrence.)
c. Determine the probability of earning any profits on the new product and the probability of incurring losses.
d. What sales volume should be used for the new product when compiling the companywide profit plan for 19X8?

14-24. CPA Problem—Special-order Budget Jessie Manufacturing, Inc., is presently operating at 50 percent of practical capacity producing about 50,000 units annually of a patented electronic component. Jessie recently received an offer from a company in Yokohama, Japan, to purchase 30,000 components at six dollars per unit, f.o.b. Jessie's plant. Jessie has not previously sold components in Japan. Budgeted production costs for 50,000 and 80,000 units of output follow:

Units	50,000	80,000
Costs:		
Direct material	$ 75,000	$120,000
Direct labor	75,000	120,000
Factory overhead	200,000	260,000
Total costs	$350,000	$500,000
Cost per unit	$7.00	$6.25

The sales manager thinks the order should be accepted, even if it results in a loss of one dollar per unit, because he feels the sales may build up future markets. The production manager does not wish to have the order accepted, primarily because it would show a loss of twenty-five cents per unit when computed on the new average unit cost. The treasurer has made a quick computation indicating that accepting the order will actually increase gross margin.

REQUIRED:
a. Explain what apparently caused the drop in cost from $7.00 per unit to $6.25 per unit when budgeted production increased from 50,000 to 80,000 units. Show supporting computations.
b. 1. Explain whether (either or both) the production manager's or the treasurer's reasoning is correct.
   2. Explain why the conclusions of the production manager and the treasurer differ.
c. Explain why each of the following may affect the decision to accept or reject the special order:
   1. The likelihood of repeated special sales and/or all sales to be made at six dollars per unit
   2. Whether the sales are made to customers operating in two separate, isolated markets or whether the sales are made to customers competing in the same market

(AICPA adapted)

14-25. *Labor Dollar Budget*   (Note: This problem incorporates standard labor hours and rates as well as process costing into the budgeting procedure.) Digital clocks are manufactured by the Richardson Clock Company. A single table model is produced, with each of three production departments involved in assembly. The company utilizes one 40-hour labor shift per week. A second labor shift is not expected to be needed in the near future. Labor requirements for 19X5 have been projected as follows:

	NUMBER OF EMPLOYEES	STANDARD (CONTRACT) LABOR RATES/HOUR
Production departments:		
J: Direct labor	2	$6.00
Indirect labor	2	$4.00
K: Direct labor	4	$7.00
Indirect labor	3	$4.00
L: Direct labor	5	$7.50
Indirect labor	6	$4.50
Service departments:		
U: Indirect labor	3	$5.00
V: Indirect labor	5	$3.50

The production forecast for 19X5 is presented on the following page. Labor costs are applied uniformly within each production process.

	DEPARTMENT J		DEPARTMENT K		DEPARTMENT L	
	Units	Percent completed	Units	Percent completed	Units	Percent completed
Beginning inventory	2,500	30	1,600	25	2,100	70
Units started or transferred in	29,200		30,000		29,700	
Units completed and transferred out	30,000		29,700		30,500	
Ending inventory	1,700	80	1,900	60	1,300	50

An analysis of standard direct labor cost per clock revealed the following:

DEPARTMENT	STANDARD DIRECT LABOR HOURS	STANDARD DIRECT LABOR COST
J	.15 DLHs/clock	$ .900
K	.30 DLHs/clock	2.100
L	.35 DLHs/clock	2.625
		$5.625

REQUIRED:
a. Compute the direct labor hours and budgeted cost by department for 19X5. (Use a 40-hour work week and ignore vacation and other downtime.)
b. Compute the departmental indirect labor cost requirements for 19X5.
c. Prepare a schedule showing the projected standard direct labor hours allowed and direct labor costs applied to good units produced in 19X5.
d. Give reasons for the departmental labor cost differences between part (a) and part (c).

14-26. *CMA Problem—Budget Preparation*   Rudolph Company produces farm equipment at several plants. The business is seasonal and cyclical in nature. The company has attempted to use budgeting for planning and controlling activities, but the variable nature of the business has caused some company officials to be skeptical about the usefulness of budgeting. The accountant for the Belvidere plant has been using a system of "flexible budgeting" to help the plant's management control operations.

The company president wants to know what flexible budgeting means, how the accountant applies it at the Belvidere plant, and how it can be applied to the company as a whole. The accountant presents the following budget data for 19X3 as part of his explanation:

Normal monthly capacity of the plant in direct labor hours	10,000 hours
Material costs (6 pounds at $1.50)	$9.00 unit
Labor costs (2 hours at $3.00)	$6.00 unit

Overhead estimate at normal
monthly capacity

Variable (controllable):

Indirect labor	$ 6,650
Indirect materials	600
Repairs	750
Total variable	$ 8,000

Fixed (noncontrollable):

Depreciation	$ 3,250
Supervision	3,000
Total fixed	$ 6,250
Total fixed and variable	$14,250

Planned units for January 19X3	4,000 units
Planned units for February 19X3	6,000 units

Actual data for January 19X3

Hours worked	8,400 hours
Units produced	3,800 units

Costs incurred:

Material (24,000 pounds)	$36,000
Direct labor	25,200
Indirect labor	6,000
Indirect materials	600
Repairs	1,800
Depreciation	3,250
Supervision	3,000
Total	$75,850

REQUIRED:

a. Prepare a budget for January 19X3.
b. Prepare a report for January comparing actual and budgeted costs for the actual activity for the month.
c. Can flexible budgeting be applied to the nonmanufacturing activities of the company? Explain your answer.

(IMA adapted)

14-27. *Selling Expense Budgets* Eiteman Company uses a standard cost system for its various products and employs comprehensive period budgets for planning and control. The vice president of sales is responsible for approving the 19X7 selling expense budget. Budgeted and actual selling expenses for 19X6 are compared on the next page:

| | 19X6 AMOUNTS | |
EXPENSE ITEM	Budget	Actual
Advertising	$ 200,000	$ 190,000
Commissions	1,600,000	1,554,000
Shipping and billing	500,000	530,000
Administrative salaries	600,000	620,000
Travel—commercial	400,000	380,000
Travel—auto fleet	100,000	107,000
Printing	50,000	54,000
Premiums expense	40,000	43,000
Warranty expense	110,000	102,000
Bad debts	500,000	525,000
	$4,100,000	$4,105,000
Total sales (in thousands)	$ 200,000	$ 210,000
Standard cost of sales	(120,000)	(132,300)
Standard gross profit	$ 80,000	$ 77,700

The following costs are fixed in nature and are budgeted as follows for 19X7:

Advertising	$ 220,000
Administrative salaries	660,000
Travel—commercial	440,000
Printing	60,000
	$1,380,000

Variable and semivariable costs are estimated with flexible budget formulas as follows:

> Commissions: 2 percent of standard gross profit
> Shipping and billing: $300,000 + .1 percent of sales
> Bad debts: ¼ percent of sales
> Travel—auto fleet: $80,000 + $.20 per mile

Expected fleet auto travel in 19X7 is 120,000 miles. Premiums and warranty expenses are expected to increase 20 percent each during 19X7.

REQUIRED:

a. Prepare a selling expense budget for 19X7 based on expected sales of $240,000,000.

b. Prepare an overall flexible budget formula for total selling expenses to be expected in 19X7 at various sales volume.

c. An assistant to the vice president of sales has recommended a simplified approach: budget selling expenses at 2.1 percent of sales. Without attention to detailed expense categories, the assistant contends that ability to spend budgeted funds as needed within the overall 2.1 percent limitation will motivate personnel and improve sales volume. Discuss the potential hazards of the assistant's recommendation.

14-28. *CPA Problem—Pro Forma Financial Statements* Presto Products Corporation, a manufacturer of molded plastic containers, determined in October 19X8 that it needed cash to continue operations. The corporation began negotiating for a one-month bank loan of $100,000 to be discounted at 6 percent per annum on November 1. In considering the loan the bank requested a projected income statement and a cash budget for the month of November. The following information is available:

a. Sales were budgeted at 120,000 units per month in October 19X8, December 19X8, and January 19X9, and at 90,000 units in November 19X8. The selling price is $2 per unit. Sales are billed on the 15th and last day of each month on terms of 2/10 net 30. Past experience indicates sales are even throughout the month, and 50 percent of the customers pay the billed amount within the discount period. The remainder pay at the end of thirty days, except for bad debts, which average ½ percent of gross sales. On its income statement the corporation deducts from sales the estimated amounts for cash discounts on sales and losses on bad debts.

b. The inventory of finished goods on October 1 was 24,000 units. The finished goods inventory at the end of each month is to be maintained at 20 percent of sales anticipated for the following month. There is no work in process.

$17,400 net Inc.

c. The inventory of raw materials on October 1 was 22,800 pounds. At the end of each month the raw materials inventory is to be maintained at not less than 40 percent of production requirements for the following month. Materials are purchased as needed in minimum quantities of 25,000 pounds per shipment. Raw material purchases of each month are paid in the next succeeding month on terms of net thirty days.

d. All salaries and wages are paid on the fifteenth and last day of each month for the period ending on the date of payment.

e. All manufacturing overhead and selling and administrative expenses are paid on the tenth of the month following the month in which they were incurred. Selling expenses are 10 percent of gross sales. Administrative expenses, which include depreciation of $500 per month on office furniture and fixtures, total $33,000 per month.

f. The standard cost of a molded plastic container, based on "normal" production of 100,000 units per month, is as follows:

Materials—½ pound	$ .50	*$1.00 per lb.*
Labor	.40	
Variable overhead	.20	
Fixed overhead	.10	
Total	$1.20	

Fixed overhead includes depreciation on factory equipment of $4,000 per month. Over- or underabsorbed overhead is included in cost of sales.

g. The cash balance on November 1 is expected to be $10,000.

REQUIRED: Prepare the following for Presto Products Corporation assuming the bank loan is granted (do not consider income taxes):

a. Schedules computing inventory budgets by months for:
   1. Finished goods production in units for October, November, and December
   2. Raw material purchases in pounds for October and November
b. A projected income statement for November
c. A cash forecast for November showing the opening balance, receipts (itemized by dates of collection), disbursements, and balance at end of month

(AICPA adapted)

14-29. *CPA Problem—Preparation of Variable Budgets* Department A is one of fifteen departments in the plant and is involved in the production of all six manufactured products. The department is highly mechanized; as a result, its output is measured in direct machine hours. Variable (flexible) budgets are utilized throughout the factory in planning and controlling costs, but here the focus is upon the application of variable budgets only in Department A. The following data covering a span of approximately six months were taken from the various budgets, accounting records, and performance reports (only representative items and amounts are utilized here):

a. On March 15, 19X1, the following variable budget was approved for the department; it will be used throughout the 19X2 fiscal year, which begins July 1, 19X1. This variable budget was developed through the cooperative efforts of the department manager, his supervisor, and certain staff members from the budget department.

19X2 variable budget—Department A

CONTROLLABLE COSTS	FIXED AMOUNT PER MONTH	VARIABLE RATE PER DIRECT MACHINE HOUR
Employee salaries	$ 9,000	
Indirect wages	18,000	$.07
Indirect materials	—	.09
Other costs	6,000	.03
	$33,000	$.19

b. On May 5, 19X1, the annual sales plan and the production budget were completed. To continue preparation of the annual profit plan (which was detailed by month), the production budget was translated to planned activity for each factory department. The planned activity for Department A was:

	FOR THE 12 MONTHS ENDING JUNE 30, 19X2				
	Year	July	August	September	Etc.
Planned output in direct machine hours	325,000	22,000	25,000	29,000	249,000

Oct Sales

120,000 x 5.00 — $240,000
30th billed <120,000>
15th billed $120,000
pd disc <60,500>
60,000
<600>
$59,400

(120,000 x .005) Bad Debt

120,000
<1,200> disc
<600> BD
118,200

Nov Sales

90,000 x 2.00 = $180,000
billed 30th <90,000>
billed 15th — $90,000
less Disc A/R <44,100>
45,900

c. On August 31, 19X1, the manager of Department A was informed that the planned output for September had been revised to 34,000 direct machine hours. The manager expressed some doubt about whether this volume could be attained.

d. At the end of September 19X1, the accounting records provided the following actual data for the month for the department:

Actual output in direct machine hours	33,000
Actual controllable costs incurred:	
Employee salaries	$ 9,300
Indirect wages	20,500
Indirect materials	2,850
Other costs	7,510
	$40,160

REQUIRED: The requirements relate primarily to the potential uses of the variable budget for the period March through September, 19X1.

a. What activity base is utilized as a measure of volume in the budget for this department? How should one determine the range of the activity base in which the variable rates per direct machine hour are relevant? Explain.

b. Explain and illustrate how the variable budget should be utilized:
1. In budgeting costs when the annual sales plan and production budget are completed (about May 5, 19X1, or shortly thereafter)
2. In budgeting a cost revision based upon a revised production budget (about August 31, 19X1, or shortly thereafter)
3. In preparing a cost performance report for September 19X1.

(AICPA adapted)

14-30. *Monthly Production Forecast* Suzanne Jeans, Inc., makes and distributes women's slacks and jeans. Forty thousand slacks and/or jeans can be produced monthly if the plant operates at 90 percent of capacity for fifty hours per week. Other time schedules and related output volume utilized by the company include:

HOURS/WEEK	OUTPUT
45	36,000 slacks
40	32,000 slacks

By varying the hours per week, a constant work force can be maintained. The company tries to follow a policy of no personnel layoffs.

Capacity of 90 percent is considered full capacity, with the remaining 10 percent being made up of spare or stand-by machinery. Maximum storage capacity for finished goods inventory is 20,000 pairs of slacks and the company follows the policy of always having a minimum of 5,000 pairs on hand for special orders. Forecasted unit sales (in pairs of slacks) for 19X9 is as follows:

January	36,000	July	44,000
February	23,000	August	40,000
March	31,000	September	36,000
April	33,000	October	45,000
May	36,000	November	50,000
June	38,000	December	31,000

Beginning finished goods inventory on January 1, 19X9, consists of 5,000 pairs of slacks, and management would like 10,000 pairs on hand at year-end.

REQUIRED:

a. Complete a monthly unit production and sales budget for 19X9 using the following format:

MONTH	BEGINNING INVENTORY	UNITS PRODUCED	UNITS SOLD	ENDING INVENTORY

Assume that:
1. 36,000 pairs of slacks are produced monthly
2. 40,000 pairs of slacks are produced monthly

b. Identify the months in which minimum or maximum storage constraints are violated for each of the production plans developed in part (a).

c. Prepare a monthly production forecast that maintains company storage constraints. The company may operate at either a 40-hour, 45-hour, or 50-hour work week but can increase or decrease the work week by only 5 hours from one month to the next.

14-31. *CPA Problem—Budgets for Nonprofit Organizations* Wright College has asked for your assistance in developing its budget for the coming academic year, 19X1–19X2. You are supplied with the following data for the current year:

a.

	LOWER DIVISION (FRESHMAN-SOPHOMORE)	UPPER DIVISION (JUNIOR-SENIOR)
Average number of students per class	25	20
Average salary of faculty member	$10,000	$10,000
Average number of credit hours carried each year per student	33	30
Enrollment including scholarship students	2,500	1,700
Average faculty teaching load in credit hours per year (10 classes of 3 credit hours)	30	30

For 19X1–19X2, lower-division enrollment is expected to increase by 10 percent, while upper-division enrollment is expected to remain stable. Faculty salaries will be increased by a standard 5 percent, and additional merit increases to be awarded to individual faculty members will be $90,750 for the lower division and $85,000 for the upper division.

b. The current budget is $210,000 for operation and maintenance of plant and equipment; this includes $90,000 for salaries and wages. Experience of the past three months suggests that the current budget is realistic, but that expected increases for 19X1–19X2 are 5 percent in salaries and wages and $9,000 in other expenditures for operation and maintenance of plant and equipment.

c. The budget for the remaining expenditures for 19X1–19X2 is as follows:

Administrative and general	$240,000
Library	160,000
Health and recreation	75,000
Athletics	120,000
Insurance and retirement	265,000
Interest	48,000
Capital outlay	300,000

d. The college expects to award twenty-five tuition-free scholarships to lower-division students and fifteen to upper-division students. Tuition is $22 per credit hour, and no other fees are charged.

e. Budgeted revenues for 19X1–19X2 are as follows:

Endowments	$114,000
Net income from auxiliary services	235,000
Athletics	180,000

The college's remaining source of revenue is an annual support campaign held during the spring.

REQUIRED:

a. Prepare a schedule computing for 19X1–19X2 by division (1) the expected enrollment, (2) the total credit hours to be carried, and (3) the number of faculty members needed.

b. Prepare a schedule computing the budget for faculty salaries by division for 19X1–19X2.

c. Prepare a schedule computing the tuition revenue budget by division for 19X1–19X2.

d. Assuming that the faculty salaries budget computed in part (b) was $2,400,000 and that the tuition revenue budget computed in part (c) was $3,000,000, prepare a schedule computing the amount that must be raised during the annual support campaign in order to cover the 19X1–19X2 expenditures budget.

(AICPA adapted)

14-32. *Comprehensive Budgeting Problem*   The 19X4 year-end balance sheet of Freberg Tool and Die Company is shown on the next page:

FREBERG TOOL AND DIE COMPANY
Balance sheet
December 31, 19X4

Current assets:		
Cash	$ 48,500	
Accounts receivable	59,700	
Raw materials inventory	31,200	
Work in process inventory	49,000	
Finished goods inventory	66,700	
Total current assets		$255,100
Fixed assets:		
Machinery and equipment	$684,000	
Less: Accumulated depreciation	(136,800)	
Total fixed assets		547,200
Total assets		$802,300
Current liabilities:		
Accounts payable	$ 36,200	
Taxes payable	73,580	
Wages and salaries payable	16,000	
Total current liabilities		$125,780
Long-term debt:		
7% (20-year bonds)		100,000
Stockholders' Equity:		
Capital stock	$300,000	
Paid-in capital	48,000	
Retained earnings	228,520	
Total stockholders' equity		576,520
Total liabilities and equity		$802,300

The company's extended monthly income statement for 19X4 appears below:

Month (% of sales):	Sales	Raw Materials Used (40%)	Direct Labor (20%)	Factory Overhead* (6% + $4,000)	Selling Expenses† (4% + $3,000)	General and Administrative Expenses§ (2% + $4,000)	Net Income Before Taxes
January	$ 65,000	$ 26,000	$ 13,000	$ 7,900	$ 5,600	$ 5,300	$ 7,200
February	75,000	30,000	15,000	8,500	6,000	5,500	10,000
March	92,000	36,800	18,400	9,520	6,680	5,840	14,760
April	98,000	39,200	19,600	9,880	6,920	5,960	16,440
May	100,000	40,000	20,000	10,000	7,000	6,000	17,000
June	108,000	43,200	21,600	10,480	7,320	6,160	19,240
July	110,000	44,000	22,000	10,600	7,400	6,200	19,800
August	96,000	38,400	19,200	9,760	6,840	5,920	15,880
September	80,000	32,000	16,000	8,800	6,200	5,600	11,400
October	70,000	28,000	14,000	8,200	5,800	5,400	8,600
November	55,000	22,000	11,000	7,300	5,200	5,100	4,400
December	48,000	19,200	9,600	6,880	4,920	4,960	2,440
Totals	$997,000	$398,800	$199,400	$107,820	$75,880	$67,940	$147,160

Federal income taxes (50%) (73,580)

Net income $ 73,580

* Fixed expenses include $3,000 depreciation expense. † Fixed expenses include $1,500 depreciation expense.
§ Fixed expenses include $1,200 depreciation expense.

Additional information necessary for preparation of the 19X5 master budget follows:

a. The company maintains a minimum cash balance of $15,000. Temporary borrowing should be in $1,000 increments (ignore interest) and will be paid back as soon as possible.

b. Accounts payable are paid on the first of the following month and represent purchases of raw materials (subsequent month's usage requirement) plus $5,000 of recurring miscellaneous payables.

c. Raw material usage for January 19X6 is expected to be $30,000.

d. Federal income taxes for 19X4 will be paid in March 19X5.

e. Wages and salaries payable average $16,000 at month-end and are paid as part of the first payroll of the following month.

f. Sales are collected as follows:

> 10 percent in month of sale
> 60 percent in first month after sale
> 30 percent in second month after sale

g. Work in Process and Finished Goods inventory balances are expected to remain constant during 19X5.

h. Raw Materials inventory balance equals subsequent month's usage requirement.

i. No purchases of machinery and equipment are expected in 19X5.

j. Selling expenses and variable costs are forecasted to increase 20 percent in 19X5. Fixed expenses, other than depreciation, will increase 10 percent.

k. Sales volume will remain constant in 19X5, but selling price will be increased by 25 percent.

l. All expenses are paid in month incurred unless otherwise indicated.

REQUIRED:

a. Prepare a projected monthly income statement for 19X5.

b. Prepare a quarterly cash budget for 19X5.

c. Prepare a pro forma balance sheet for the company as of December 31, 19X5.

14-33. *CMA Problem—Forecasted Cash Flow Statement* Born Corporation uses direct costing for managerial purposes and prepared its December 31, 19X3, balance sheet on a direct costing basis as shown on the next page.

Some recent actual and forecast data are:

	ACTUAL		FORECAST			
	Nov.	Dec.	Jan.	Feb.	Mar.	Apr.
Cash sales (units)	1,200	1,200	1,000	1,000	1,000	2,000
Credit sales (units)	10,000	10,000	8,000	8,000	8,000	20,000
Selling and administrative expenses	$20,000	$20,000	$20,000	$20,000	$20,000	$20,000
Fixed manufacturing expenses*	$15,000	$15,000	$15,000	$15,000	$15,000	$15,000

* Excluding depreciation and amortization.

BORN CORPORATION
Balance sheet
As of December 31, 19X3

Current assets:

Cash		$ 10,000	
Marketable securities		50,000	
Accounts receivable		80,000	
Inventories:			
Finished goods	$ 67,500		
Work in process	45,000		
Raw materials	9,000	121,500	
Total current assets			$ 261,500

Long-term assets:

Equipment (factory)	$ 300,000		
Less: Accumulated			
depreciation	72,000	$228,000	
Plant building	$1,000,000		
Less: Accumulated			
depreciation	180,000	820,000	
Land		200,000	
Total long-term assets			$1,248,000

Other assets:

Intangibles (net)		$ 10,000	
Loan to officer of company		10,000	20,000
Total assets			$1,529,500

Current liabilities:

Accounts payable		$ 25,680	
Other payables		10,000	
Notes payable (one-month note due			
Jan. 15, 19X4)		50,000	
Current portion of long-term debt			
(due Mar. 31, 19X4)		50,000	
Total current liabilities			$ 135,680

Long-term debt (8%, 10 years;

interest payable December 31;			
repayment of principal at rate			
of $50,000 per year beginning in 19X4)			450,000
Total liabilities			$ 585,680

Owners' equity:

Common stock (issued and outstanding,			
70,000 shares, $10 per share)		$700,000	
Retained earnings		243,820	
Total owners' equity			943,820
Total equities			$1,529,500

The company manufactures a child's automobile safety seat that it sells directly to a number of automobile dealers in its four-state region and to retail customers through its own outlet. The selling price through their own outlet is thirty dollars; to dealers, the price is twenty dollars.

Since all sales through its own outlet are on a cash basis and since sales on account are to dealers with a long-standing relationship with the company, bad debts are negligible. Terms of credit sales are net 30. Of the credit sales, 60 percent are paid in the month of the sale, and the remaining 40 percent are paid in the month after the sale.

Raw materials cost five dollars per unit. All purchases of raw materials are on account. Accounts payable are on terms of net thirty days; 40 percent are paid in the month of purchase, and 60 percent are paid in the following month. Direct labor and variable manufacturing overhead costs are ten dollars per unit. Direct labor and variable manufacturing overhead costs are incurred in direct proportion to the percentage of completion and paid in cash when incurred.

At the end of each month, desired inventory levels are as follows:

> Raw materials: 20 percent of next month's requirements
> Work in process: 50 percent of next month's requirements
> Finished goods: 50 percent of next month's requirements

Work in process is assumed to be 50 percent completed at the end of the month. Raw materials are added at the beginning of production.

Depreciation on the equipment is $4,000 per month, and depreciation on the plant is $5,000 per month. Amortization of intangibles is $500 per month.

Selling and administrative expenses are all fixed; half are paid in the month incurred, and the balance is paid in the following month.

Fixed manufacturing expenses that require cash payments are paid in the month incurred.

Long-term debt principal is to be paid each March 31, starting in 19X4 at a rate of $50,000 per year.

The loan to the officer was made on December 31, 19X3, and is due March 31, 19X4; it is to be repaid on March 31, 19X4, plus interest at 6 percent per annum.

The firm requires a minimum cash balance of $10,000 at the end of each month. If the balance is less, marketable securities are sold in multiples of $5,000 at the end of the month. If necessary, cash is borrowed in multiples of $1,000 at the end of the month. Marketable securities earn 6 percent per annum, and the interest is collected at the end of each month. The short-term interest rate on notes payable is 12 percent per annum and is paid at the time the note is repaid. Taxes are to be ignored.

REQUIRED: Prepare a statement forecasting the cash balance including any necessary cash transactions to achieve company cash management objectives for January 19X4.

(IMA adapted)

14-34. *CPA Problem—Pro Forma Financial Statements*   David Construction, Inc., builds heavy construction equipment for commercial and government purposes. Because of two new contracts and the anticipated purchase of new equipment, management needs certain projections for the next three years; you have been asked to prepare these projections. You have acquired the following information from the company's records and personnel:

a. David Construction uses the completed-contract method of accounting, whereby construction costs are capitalized until the contract is completed. Since all general and administrative expenses can be identified with a particular contract, they also are capitalized until the contract is completed.

b. David's December 31, 19X3, balance sheet follows:

ASSETS		
Cash		$ 72,000
Due on contracts		—
Costs of uncompleted contracts in excess of billings		—
Plant and equipment	$2,800,000	
Less accumulated depreciation	129,600	2,670,400
Total		$2,742,400

LIABILITIES AND STOCKHOLDERS' EQUITY	
Loans payable	$ —
Accrued construction costs	612,400
Accrued income tax payable	65,000
Common stock ($10 par value)	500,000
Paid-in capital	100,000
Retained earnings	1,465,000
Total	$2,742,400

c. Two contracts will be started in 19X4—contract A and contract B. Contracts A and B are expected to be completed in December 19X5 and December 19X6, respectively. No other contracts will be started until after contracts A and B are completed. All other outstanding contracts had been completed in 19X3.

d. Total estimated revenue is $2,000,000 for contract A and $1,500,000 for contract B. The estimated cash collections per year follow:

	19X4	19X5	19X6
Contract A	$ 800,000	$1,200,000	$ —
Contract B	300,000	450,000	750,000
	$1,100,000	$1,650,000	$750,000

e. Estimated construction costs to be incurred per contract, per year follow:

	CONTRACT A	CONTRACT B
19X4	$ 720,000	$ 250,000
19X5	1,000,000	400,000
19X6	—	650,000
	$1,720,000	$1,300,000

f. Depreciation expense is included in these estimated contruction costs. For 19X4, 10 percent of the estimated construction costs represents depreciation expense. For 19X5 and 19X6, 19 percent of the estimated construction costs represents depreciation expense. The cash portion of the estimated construction costs is paid as follows: 70 percent in the year incurred and 30 percent in the following year.

g. Total general and administrative expenses (not included in construction costs) consist of a fixed portion each year for each contract and a variable portion that is a function of cash collected each year. For the two prior years, cash collected and total general and administrative expenses (based on one contract each year) were as follows:

	CASH COLLECTED	TOTAL GENERAL AND ADMINISTRATIVE EXPENSES
19X3	$1,350,000	$27,250
19X2	1,180,000	24,700

These general and administrative expenses all represent cash expenses and are paid in the year incurred.

h. Dividends are expected to be distributed as follows:

> 19X4: Stock—10 percent of common shares outstanding
> (estimated fair market value is $15 per share).
> 19X5: Stock split—two for one
> (par value to be reduced to $5 per share).
> 19X6: Cash—$1 per share.

i. David will acquire a new asset in 19X5 for $700,000 and plans to pay for it that year.

j. When the cash balance falls below $70,000, David obtains short-term loans in multiples of $10,000. For purposes of this problem, ignore interest on short-term loans and ignore any repayments on these loans.

k. Assume income taxes for each year are paid in full the *following* year.

REQUIRED:

a. Prepare projected income statements for each of the calendar years 19X5 and 19X6 (when contracts are to be completed). The income tax rate is 40 percent, and the company uses the same methods for accounting and tax purposes.

b. Prepare cash budgets for each of the calendar years 19X4, 19X5, and 19X6. The budgets should follow this format:

Cash (beginning of year)	$
Plus: Collections	
Less: Disbursements (enumerated)	
Plus: Borrowing (if any)	
Cash (end of year)	$

(AICPA adapted)

Chapter 15: Short-run Operating Decisions

The futuristic viewpoint of management accounting is most apparent in analyses supporting short-run and long-run decisions. Management decisions require the selection of a course of action from a defined set of alternatives. Concepts and techniques of management accounting have been developed to provide useful information for decision-making purposes.

This chapter introduces project-oriented planning and illustrates the application of incremental cost analysis to short-run decisions. Short-run operating decisions involve noncapital expenditure alternatives that can be implemented within a one-year period.

Upon completion of this chapter, students should be able to:

1. Distinguish between period planning and project planning activities
2. Identify information that is relevant to a variety of short-run decision problems
3. Apply the contribution approach to segment-elimination decisions, product pricing decisions, and sell or process-further decisions

The following basic concepts are introduced in this chapter:

Project planning   Formulation of plans for a specific program, process, activity, or decision alternative that may affect regular operations for several time periods.

Short-run decision analysis   Evaluation and selection of an operating decision alternative that can be implemented within a one-year period.

Incremental cost analysis   An analysis to highlight differences between costs and revenues under two or more alternative courses of action.

Relevant data   Future costs, revenues, and resources that are different between alternatives in a particular decision-making application.

CHAPTER HIGHLIGHTS

Purpose and Learning Objectives

Relevant Concepts

Chapter Summary	Period planning involves the formulation of coordinated financial and operating budgets for an annual time period. Long-term planning and strategic policy decisions provide the general framework within which period planning occurs. Project-oriented planning is different from period budgeting because the principal matter of attention is a specific project such as production processes, distribution methods, or any activity having identifiable costs, revenues, and resources.

Within an annual time period, projects affecting operations are identified and analyzed. Long-term projects requiring significant investments are called capital expenditure decisions. Short-run operating decisions involve projects with an annual time horizon and do not require capital expenditures.

Short-run operating decisions include analysis of alternatives for segment elimination, pricing special orders, sell or process-further policies, and make or buy considerations for component parts. Relevant cost analysis is the basic approach to evaluating these decision alternatives. For short-run decisions, the primary objective is to select the least costly alternative or the one offering the largest contribution to profits. Relevant costs are the cost and revenue factors that differ between alternatives; incremental or differential costs are the differences between costs and revenues related to specific decision alternatives. In practice, the terms relevant, incremental, and differential are used synonymously.

PERIOD PLANNING AND PROJECT PLANNING

Management planning and control as discussed in previous chapters have concentrated on operations for an annual time period. Product costing, inventory valuation, and income determination involve current period operations. Period planning, as illustrated in Chapter 14, requires the formulation of coordinated operating plans for an annual period and expression of these plans in a comprehensive budget. Management control is also time-period oriented and uses standard cost variance analysis and responsibility accounting to evaluate actual results and related plans for short time intervals. Recurring business activities such as sales and production occur within a short time period, and related planning and control activities concentrate on the same time span.

Long-term Planning

Strategic planning involves management decisions concerning company objectives, organizational structure, growth policies, market specialization, and other factors affecting the basic structure of the firm. Strategic planning is comparable to ship building because the basic nature and capabilities of an entity are determined by this type of planning. Strategic planning provides the basic framework within which short-run period planning is applied. Period planning with comprehensive budgeting is then analogous to charting a cruise for the ship.

Budgeting also involves long-term planning, since future operations must be considered when preparing annual profit plans. Many firms develop general operating plans for a five- or ten-year period. These plans cover total company operations but include much less detail than annual profit plans. Long-term planning anticipates operational changes in marketing and production and provides a smooth transition between business operations in consecutive annual periods. The benefit of long-term planning is that it forces management to look beyond the current year. Long-term planning is a general idea that contemplates planning over a time span longer than one year; it includes analysis of individual projects that influence operations for several years.

Period planning involves the coordination of all financial and operating activities expected to occur in a specific year or time period. A given time period will include the origination of new projects, termination of some projects, and continued operation of others. A project could involve equipment replacement, plant expansion, development of new products, changes in production processes, and other programs or capital investments having identifiable costs or revenues. Project planning involves the analysis of estimated costs and benefits of specific projects.

Project Planning

Many project-oriented decisions are concerned with significant investments that will affect productivity, cash flows, and profits for several years. The initial project cost is a *capital expenditure,* and the related analysis process is called *capital budgeting.* As discussed in Chapter 16, capital expenditure decisions involve planning, evaluating, and selecting proposed projects that will affect company operations over a relatively long time period. Specific evaluation techniques are used to measure the relative economic merits of each expenditure proposal. These evaluation techniques usually concentrate on cash flows expected to occur during the estimated project life. By concentrating on initial project investment, annual cash flows, and a time period of several years, capital expenditure decision analysis is distinctly different from analysis of short-run operating decisions.

Capital expenditure decision analysis is a form of project planning that involves long-term considerations and special forms of cost-benefit analyses. Short-run projects can be implemented within a period of one year and do not require additional capital expenditures. The economic concept of the short-run is a time period in which certain factors of production are fixed and cannot be changed. In business operations, these fixed factors of production include the basic capacities to produce and sell, such as equipment installations, a trained labor force, and channels of distribution. The time period that constitutes the short run actually varies with the production factor under consideration. For example, training of additional supervisory personnel may require only six months, while construction of a new plant may require two years.

Short-run Operating Decisions

The short-run usually is considered to be one year or less. Within an annual period, many changes in current operations can be implemented; these decision alternatives are analyzed on a project-oriented basis by concentrating on incremental costs and revenues. Short-run operating decisions involve the selection of alternatives that can be implemented within a one-year period. Examples of short-run projects include decisions (1) to make or buy component parts, (2) to sell products in a semifinished condition or to process them further, and (3) to continue or eliminate a product line or other company segment. These decisions are considered short-run in nature because the selected alternative does not require a capital expenditure and can be implemented promptly.

Project planning involves both short-term and long-term projects. Certain short-run decisions may affect operations for an indefinite number of future periods. The decision to purchase component parts from outside suppliers requires a change in firm operations if the parts are currently being manufactured within the company. This operating change will remain effective until the decision is reversed. Other short-run operating decisions present nonrecurring situations, such as the opportunity to sell products to a foreign customer at reduced prices. The decision to sell marginal output at reduced prices cannot be reversed. The general approach to short-run decisions emphasizes the contribution approach and the impact of decision alternatives on company profits. Since many factors of capacity are fixed in the short run, the basic concept is to select the decision alternative that best utilizes existing resources. Short-run decisions are analyzed with relevant cost analysis procedures.

RELEVANT COST ANALYSIS

Decision making is the process of analyzing and selecting a course of action from a number of alternatives. Accounting information supports management decision making by presenting comparative analyses of alternative actions. For each alternative, it is necessary to determine the estimated revenues, costs, and resource requirements. The principal feature of relevant cost analysis is the identification of costs, revenues, and resources that differ between alternative courses of action.

Nature of Relevant Costs

Relevant costs are estimated future costs that are different under alternative courses of action for a specific decision problem. In Chapter 4, incremental costs or differential costs were described as the difference between cost factors under two or more alternatives. The terms incremental and differential emphasize the difference between two cost amounts. Relevant, incremental, and differential apply to both costs and revenues; but for convenience, the general description of relevant cost analysis is used when analyzing both costs and revenues. Relevant cost analysis provides the basic framework for analyzing short-run decision alternatives. Alternative courses of action are evaluated, and the most desirable alternative is selected. Selection criteria for a particular decision may be the least costly alternative or the one that offers the largest increase in profits. The least costly criterion is used for projects or decisions that involve only cost incurrence without any inflow of revenues.

To illustrate the least costly criterion and relevant cost identity, assume that management is evaluating two alternative procedures to account for customer accounts receivable and sales. The present system uses manual accounting procedures, but management is considering an alternative to lease computer facilities to replace manual operations. The following analysis compares the annual costs to be incurred under each alternative:

TOTAL ANNUAL COST	(1) KEEP MANUAL SYSTEM	(2) LEASE COMPUTER TIME	BENEFIT (COST) OF LEASING $(1-2)$
Clerical salaries	$20,000	$ -0-	$20,000
Controller's salary	18,000	18,000	-0-
Computer rental	-0-	10,000	(10,000)
Accounting supplies	2,000	4,000	(2,000)
	$40,000	$32,000	$ 8,000

The $8,000 annual cost saving available under the lease alternative is a differential cost since it represents the difference between total costs to be incurred under each alternative. Relevant cost factors are computer rental, clerical salaries, and accounting supplies, because cost amounts for these items involve future costs to be incurred that are different under each alternative. The controller's salary is $18,000 in each case and is not a relevant cost. Differences between the relevant cost factors explain the $8,000 cost benefit for the leasing alternative as indicated below:

RELEVANT COST FACTOR	(1) KEEP MANUAL SYSTEM	(2) LEASE COMPUTER TIME	DIFFERENTIAL COST (1 − 2)
Clerical salaries	$20,000	$ -0-	$20,000
Computer rental	-0-	10,000	(10,000)
Accounting supplies	2,000	4,000	(2,000)
Total relevant costs	$22,000	$14,000	$ 8,000

Note that relevant costs include fixed costs (clerical salaries) and variable costs (accounting supplies). The computer rental could be fixed, variable, or semivariable in behavior. Relevance is determined by a cost that is different between alternatives, and relevance in decision analysis is independent of cost behavior patterns. This illustration highlights the subtle difference between relevant costs and differential costs. The accounting supplies are a relevant cost, but the differential cost of $2,000 is the difference between cost amounts under two alternatives.

Note that the computer leasing alternative is more desirable under the least costly criterion since $32,000 is the smaller annual cost total. When several alternatives are being evaluated, the least costly criterion is easier to apply than computation of differential costs among all the alternatives.

Role of Decision Models

The decision-making process becomes complex when numerous alternatives are to be evaluated. Another problem is that many decisions are nonrecurring in nature and cannot be resolved by relying on past experience with similar situations. General phases of decision analysis range from problem identity through selection of a specific alternative and include:

1. Selection of a measurement criterion such as minimum costs, maximum profits, or maximum rate of return. The criterion permits a quantitative comparison of alternatives in terms of goodness or desirability.
2. Preparation of forecasts of uncontrollable factors and identification of the restrictions or constraints that affect controllable factors
3. Formulation of alternative courses of action and evaluation of each alternative using the measurement criterion defined in item 1.

To facilitate this analysis, a decision model can be prepared to guide the formulation and evaluation of alternatives. A formal decision model is a symbolic or numerical representation of the variables and parameters that affect a particular decision. Variables are the factors controlled by management, and parameters are uncontrollable factors and operating constraints or limitations.

EXHIBIT 15-1

STEPS IN BUILDING A DECISION MODEL

1. Define the parameters of the project.

 2. Identify possible alternative courses
 of action and select a measurement criterion.

 3. Develop information for each alternative.

 4. Construct incremental analysis of
 alternatives.

 5. Eliminate all irrelevant information.

 6. Prepare a formal report for management;
 highlight the advantages and disadvantages
 of each alternative.

A model for a decision about product sales mix involves parameters such as customer demand, market growth, competitor actions, and production capacity limitations. Variables in this decision model are product selling price, production costs, and manufacturing methods. A decision model may be a formal mathematical representation or an informal method of organizing a decision problem.

Steps in the model-building process are outlined in Exhibit 15-1. Parameters affecting the decision are defined, and possible alternatives are identified. In steps 3 and 4, appropriate cost and revenue information is developed and analyzed. The relative benefits of each alternative then are summarized and presented to management. Output of the decision model is a comparative analysis using the measurement criterion selected for the particular decision problem. This analysis is a formal report to management that should include:

1. A brief description of the project or problem situation
2. A comparative financial analysis of each alternative
3. A summary of the relative advantages of each alternative

Cost Analysis Techniques

Short-run operating decisions involve selecting the alternative that offers the greatest increase in profits or the least costly method of accomplishing a task. Sell or process-further decisions involve alternatives that generate revenues, and the objective is to select the most profitable alternative. Make or buy decisions for component parts involve only the incurrence of costs, and the objective is to select the least costly alternative.

Incremental cost analysis is the technique used to analyze alternatives for which the objective is to minimize costs. The previous example, which compared manual accounting procedures with computer leasing, is an incremental cost analysis. Total costs of each alternative for a specific time period are compared, and incremental or differential costs are computed to determine the relative benefits of one alternative in relation to other alternatives. The analysis may be limited to relevant cost factors, since only relevant costs cause any cost differences among alternatives.

If decision alternatives involve revenues, the typical objective is to maximize annual profits. The contribution approach, which emphasizes contribution margin, is the technique used to analyze these decision problems. Revenue-generating decision problems include sell or process-further alternatives and pricing decisions for special product orders. The contribution approach can be applied by preparing a complete income statement for each alternative. The incremental approach is also suitable, since differential costs and revenues are obtained by comparing items that appear in each income statement.

The choice between selling a product at split-off or processing it further is a short-run operating decision concerning joint products. The decision to process a joint product beyond split-off rests upon an analysis of incremental or differential costs and revenues. Additional processing adds value to a product and increases its selling price above the amount for which it could be sold at split-off. The decision to process further depends upon whether the increase in total revenues exceeds the additional costs incurred for processing beyond split-off. Joint costs incurred prior to split-off have no effect on the decision, because these production costs will be incurred regardless of the point at which products are sold. Joint production costs already incurred are past costs; all past costs are defined as *sunk costs*, since these amounts cannot be changed once the cost is incurred. Only future costs that are different between alternatives are relevant for decision-making purposes.

The objective in sell or process-further decisions is to maximize annual profits as demonstrated in the following example. Frame Fertilizers, Inc., produces a variety of chemical products. "Green-Grow," "Greener-Grow," and "Super-Green" are three joint products of a particular production process. For each 10,000-pound batch of materials converted into products, $60,000 of joint production costs are incurred. At the split-off point, 50 percent of the output is Green-Grow; 30 percent is Greener-Grow; and 20 percent is Super-Green. Each product is processed beyond split-off, and the following variable costs are incurred for additional processing:

SELL OR PROCESS-FURTHER DECISIONS

PRODUCT	POUNDS	ADDITIONAL PROCESSING COSTS
Green-Grow	5,000	$ 5,000
Greener-Grow	3,000	$15,000
Super-Green	2,000	$ 5,000
	10,000	

EXHIBIT 15-2

FRAME FERTILIZER, INC.

SELL OR PROCESS-FURTHER ANALYSIS

1. Selling price information (used to compute revenue potential in part 2):

	UNIT SELLING PRICE IF SOLD	
PRODUCT	At split-off	After additional processing
Green-Grow	$ 4	$ 6
Greener-Grow	12	15
Super-Green	20	25

2. Incremental revenues and costs (per 10,000 pound batch):

		TOTAL REVENUE IF SOLD			
PRODUCT	POUNDS	After processing	At split-off	INCREMENTAL REVENUE*	INCREMENTAL COST†
Green-Grow	5,000	$30,000	$20,000	$10,000	$5,000 (A)
Greener-Grow	3,000	45,000	36,000	9,000	15,000 (B)
Super-Green	2,000	50,000	40,000	10,000	5,000 (A)

* Difference between revenue potential at split-off and after additional processing.
† Costs incurred for additional processing.
Note (A): Product should be processed beyond split-off, since incremental revenue exceeds incremental cost.
Note (B): Product should be sold at split-off, since incremental revenue is less than incremental cost.

Tillett Company has offered to buy all the joint products at split-off and will pay unit prices of $4 for Green-Grow, $12 for Greener-Grow, and $20 for Super-Green. Incremental revenue and incremental cost comparisons are presented in Exhibit 15-2. The incremental revenue and cost analysis shows that only Green-Grow and Super-Green should be sold after additional processing. If Greener-Grow is processed beyond split-off, revenues increase by $9,000 while costs increase by $15,000; additional processing is not desirable for this product. Since incremental costs exceed incremental revenues for Greener-Grow, net income can be increased by selling this product at split-off. Note that joint production costs of $60,000 per 10,000 units are not relevant to the processing decision. The analysis for a 10,000-pound batch generates the same decisions as would analysis of annual production volume.

Several technical problems are involved in measuring incremental costs incurred for additional processing beyond split-off. Costs of additional raw material usage, direct labor, and variable manufacturing overhead are incremental, since these costs are caused by additional processing. However, supervisory salaries, property taxes, insurance, and other fixed costs that will be incurred regardless of the production decision are not incremental costs. Incremental costs of additional processing should include all production costs that will be incurred only if a product is processed beyond split-off. Fixed overhead costs that are common to other production activity must be excluded from the decision analysis.

As a frame of reference for cost analysis, there are two general conditions under which a sell or process-further decision could occur:

1. The company already processes a product beyond split-off and has invested in the equipment and required personnel, or
2. The company is evaluating the possibility of processing beyond split-off and must incur certain equipment costs and other fixed costs if additional processing is to occur

In condition 1, certain fixed costs such as supervisory salaries are related to additional processing. If these production salaries would be eliminated by selling products at split-off, these costs are incremental and should be included in the decision analysis. If salaried personnel would be assigned other duties in the company when additional processing is discontinued, the salary costs are not incremental since they are incurred under either decision alternative.

If equipment used for additional processing would sit idle or be used in other processes, then it should be ignored in the decision analysis. Depreciation expense is never relevant in short-run operating decisions, since depreciation is an allocation of costs incurred in a past time period. If the equipment would be sold for cash if not used for additional processing, the annual cash equivalent cost should be included as an annual incremental cost. The annual cash equivalent cost is the annual cash flow of an annuity at a specific interest rate for which the present value equals the salvage value received upon selling old equipment. Length of the assumed annuity should correspond with the remaining useful life of the equipment. This annual cost factor is not depreciation, but it is the opportunity cost of continuing to use the equipment. The principal test in identifying incremental costs is whether a certain cost factor will be incurred only if additional processing takes place. This test is difficult to answer in many cases, and the decision analysis then must incorporate reasonable assumptions or rely on existing management policies.

Condition 2 described above is really a capital budgeting problem. If a company must expand its physical capacity to allow additional processing, it is not sufficient to determine whether incremental revenues exceed incremental costs. Since new investments in machinery and buildings are involved, rate of return on this new investment must be considered. In general, condition 2 is a problem requiring rate of return analysis on new investment opportunities as explained in Chapter 16; condition 1 is a problem of how to best use existing facilities.

ELIMINATION OF UNPROFITABLE SEGMENTS

The decision to eliminate an unprofitable division or product line is a special case of segment performance evaluation. The ordinary evaluation of segment performance using profit measures assumes continuity of the segment. To evaluate the financial consequences of eliminating a segment, it is necessary to concentrate on the incremental or differential profit effect of the decision. The basic decision is an alternative choice problem either to keep the segment or to eliminate it. Appropriate cost and profit measures must be developed for each alternative.

Assume that Dan Corporation management wants to evaluate the potential elimination of Division C. Exhibit 15-3 provides basic cost and revenue

EXHIBIT 15-3

DAN CORPORATION—YEAR 19X4

CONDENSED DIVISIONAL PROFIT SUMMARY

1. 19X4 income statements:

	DIVISIONS A AND B	DIVISION C	TOTAL COMPANY
Sales	$90,000	$10,000	$100,000
Variable expenses	(35,000)	(5,000)	(40,000)
Contribution margin	$55,000	$ 5,000	$ 60,000
Traceable fixed costs	(37,000)	(11,000)	(48,000)
Divisional income	$18,000	$ (6,000)	$ 12,000
Unallocated fixed costs			(8,000)
Income before taxes			$ 4,000

2. Comparative profits assuming the elimination of Division C and that all Division C traceable costs are avoidable (see note in item 3 below):

	TOTAL COMPANY OPERATIONS IF IT		BENEFIT OR (COST) TO ELIMINATE C
	Keeps C	Eliminates C	
Sales	$100,000	$90,000	($10,000) sales decrease
Variable expenses	40,000	35,000	5,000 cost reduction
Contribution margin	$ 60,000	$55,000	($ 5,000) contribution margin decrease
Total fixed costs*	56,000	45,000	11,000 cost reduction
Income before taxes	$ 4,000	$10,000	$ 6,000 profit increase

* $56,000 = $48,000 traceable + $8,000 unallocated; $45,000 = $56,000 total − $11,000 traceable to C.

3. *Avoidable costs* are costs that can be eliminated if a particular segment is discontinued. Avoidable costs are differential costs and can be measured by the difference between total costs under both "keep" and "eliminate" alternatives.

information and demonstrates a format for evaluating decision alternatives. All traceable costs of Division C are assumed to be avoidable and will be eliminated if Division C is discontinued. As a result, company profits will increase by $6,000 with the elimination of Division C. This analysis requires the preparation of an income statement for each alternative and the comparison of resulting profits. Knowing which costs of the division will be avoided or eliminated if the segment is discontinued is basic to the decision analysis.

An alternative form of analysis for this decision is to concentrate on the third column in part 2 of Exhibit 15-3. Revenue and cost factors that are different under each alternative can be analyzed to explain the profit difference of $6,000. The incremental factors are analyzed as follows for the decision in Exhibit 15-3:

ANALYSIS OF DAN CORPORATION INCREMENTAL COST AND REVENUE

1. Advantage to eliminate Division C:

	AMOUNT
Increase in sales	None
Decrease in costs ($5,000 + $11,000)	$16,000
Total advantage	$16,000

2. Disadvantage to eliminate Division C:

	AMOUNT
Decrease in sales	$10,000
Increase in costs	None
Total disadvantage	$10,000

3. Incremental profit to eliminate Division C (1 − 2): $ 6,000

If all fixed costs traceable to Division C are *avoidable*, then the change in company profit from eliminating the division is apparent from part 1 of Exhibit 15-3. If Division C costs are avoidable, then the operating loss of $6,000 is also avoided when the division is eliminated. The key cost concept is to isolate avoidable costs, which may not always correspond with traceable costs. Avoidable costs are incremental costs since these amounts are incurred only if the division exists.

Assume that executive and supervisory personnel in Division C will be reassigned to other divisions if Division C is eliminated. Included in the $11,000 of traceable fixed costs of Division C are $8,000 of salaries for these personnel. This assumption now changes the profit effect of eliminating Division C as indicated in the following incremental analysis:

1. Advantage to eliminate Division C:

Reduce variable expenses	$ 5,000
Reduce fixed expenses ($11,000 − $8,000)	3,000
Total benefits	$ 8,000

2. Disadvantage to eliminate Division C:

Reduce sales	$10,000

3. Decrease in profit to eliminate Division C (1 − 2): $ 2,000

Under these revised assumptions, the avoidable fixed costs of Division C are $3,000 (traceable fixed costs of $11,000 less the $8,000 cost of personnel to be reassigned to other divisions). As a general guide, it is unprofitable to eliminate any segment for which contribution margin exceeds the avoidable fixed costs. This guide is actually a condensed version of incremental profit analysis:

	DIVISION C
Contribution margin	$5,000
Avoidable fixed costs	(3,000)
Profit contribution	$2,000

Company profits would decrease $2,000 if Division C were eliminated. This conclusion is valid even though operating reports for the division disclose a loss of $6,000.

Depreciation is a cost factor that must be evaluated properly in segment disposal decisions. If equipment and other fixed assets of a discontinued segment will be used elsewhere in the company, depreciation expense is not relevant, since the annual cost amount is the same under both alternatives (continue or discontinue the segment). If the fixed assets will be sold for cash, the equivalent annual cash benefit should be added to annual profits under the discontinue alternative.

For example, assume that fixed assets of Division C will be sold for $100,000 if the division is eliminated. If the remaining useful life of these assets averages ten years, then $19,924 should be added to the annual benefits of eliminating Division C. The equivalent annual cash flow of $19,924 is computed by using Table 4 in Appendix 16-A for an assumed annuity of ten years at 15 percent with a present value of $100,000. The 15 percent interest rate is assumed to represent the return that Dan Corporation can earn on invested funds:

$$\text{cash flow} = \frac{\$100,000}{5.019} = \$19,924$$

This application involves the time value of money, a concept that is explained in Chapter 16. In general, the annuity computation provides an annual cash equivalent cost of using equipment that could be sold for $100,000 today. The equivalent annual cash flow of $19,924 is the opportunity cost of keeping Division C and, additionally, it is a benefit available from eliminating the division.

Segment-elimination decisions often involve product lines or some segment that is smaller than a company division. The general framework of analysis applied to the Division C example also applies to decisions to eliminate products and other segments. Allocated joint or common costs must be excluded from the analysis since these costs would be unchanged by a segment elimination. Investigation of fixed costs traceable to the segment is also necessary, and costs that will continue even if the segment is eliminated must be identified. Only the avoidable fixed costs are important because they are costs that could be eliminated along with the segment in question.

The decision to eliminate a particular phase of company operations involves many qualitative factors, such as customer relations, demand relationships among company products, and personnel policy. Measuring the possible effect of segment disposal on annual profits also is complicated by income tax considerations and potential uses of available plant capacity. While the effects of segment elimination are long run in nature, the basic form of analysis concentrates on changes in annual profits.

When a company has excess or idle production capacity, management can consider the possibility of selling additional products at less than normal selling prices. Units sold at the lower prices are *marginal output* and are produced in addition to regular output volume. The basic problem is to determine an acceptable price for marginal output. Decisions of this type arise when a company receives a special order from a foreign customer or from a firm that intends to resell the products under a private label or brand name. Cost analysis using the contribution approach is a useful technique to determine the short-run profit effects of special-order transactions.

The contribution margin format was used extensively in Chapters 9 and 10. This approach emphasizes the segregation of fixed and variable costs in the income statement. All variable costs, including variable selling and administrative costs, are subtracted from sales to yield contribution margin for the period. In decisions regarding the pricing of special orders where normal operations are not disturbed and where unused operating capacity exists, the accountant should not be overly concerned with attaching fixed costs to products. Pricing analysis should concentrate on the recovery of incremental costs caused by accepting the order.

Total selling price of the special order must recover variable costs incurred in order to provide a positive contribution margin. Unless fixed costs are incurred to facilitate the transaction, any contribution margin provided by the special order will increase profits. If the company attempts to include normal fixed overhead costs in the pricing analysis, the bid price may be too high, and the company could lose the entire order and any related contribution margin. By isolating the variable costs, only costs that are relevant to the decision will be used in arriving at an appropriate price. Fixed costs are relevant only if incurred to facilitate the special order.

An unusual aspect of special-order decisions is that the additional volume was not anticipated or included in period budgets. Normal capacity or expected actual capacity, excluding special orders, was used initially for budgeting and overhead rate determination. If planned capacity is attained, all fixed overhead costs will be absorbed by regular operations. Therefore, fixed overhead costs that are incurred regardless of the special-order decision are not relevant to the pricing analysis. Although special orders may be priced considerably below normal selling prices, management should exercise extreme care when accepting special orders. If the company's regular customers discover that price breaks are being granted, customer relations could be damaged severely and sales in subsequent years could be reduced. Before accepting a special order for standard products, advice should be obtained concerning the legality of any price reduction under federal price discrimination statutes.

The basic decision alternatives in special-order situations are to accept or reject a price offered by another firm. A similar cost analysis problem arises if the producing company is asked to submit tentative prices or bids to the buyer. Assume that Carvin Marlson Chair Company received an offer in October 19X4 to sell 25,000 outdoor patio chairs to the Easy Life Corporation. Easy Life would like Marlson Company to bid on the proposed sales order and indicates that this is a one-time order.

Marlson Company produces 400,000 chairs annually by operating at 80 percent of full capacity. Regular selling price for this type of chair is $33. The chairs requested are similar to those currently being produced by Marlson Company. Budgeted annual production costs and other expenses for 19X4 are:

VOLUME OF 400,000 CHAIRS	TOTAL	PER UNIT
Raw materials	$1,700,000	$4.25
Direct labor	$2,300,000	5.75
Variable factory overhead	$3,100,000	7.75
Fixed factory overhead	$2,500,000	
Variable selling costs	5% of selling price	
Fixed selling and administrative costs	$1,450,000	

EXHIBIT 15-4

MARLSON COMPANY
SPECIAL-ORDER PRICING ANALYSIS

1. Price computation (for 25,000 chairs):

Variable costs to be incurred:		
Raw materials	$	4.25
Direct labor		5.75
Variable overhead		7.75
Variable cost per unit (no selling expenses)	$	17.75
Desired unit profit		1.00
Minimum price	$	18.75
Units to be sold		× 25,000
Increase in sales		$468,750

2. Income statement analysis (19X4):

	WITHOUT SPECIAL ORDER	+ SPECIAL ORDER	= WITH SPECIAL ORDER
Sales	$13,200,000	$468,750	$13,668,750
Less: Variable costs:			
Raw materials	$ 1,700,000	$106,250	$ 1,806,250
Direct labor	2,300,000	143,750	2,443,750
Variable factory overhead	3,100,000	193,750	3,293,750
Variable selling costs*	660,000	-0-	660,000
Total variable costs	$ 7,760,000	$443,750	$ 8,203,750
Total contribution margin	$ 5,440,000	$ 25,000	$ 5,465,000
Less: Fixed costs:			
Fixed factory overhead*	$ 2,500,000	-0-	$ 2,500,000
Fixed selling and administrative costs*	$ 1,450,000	-0-	$ 1,450,000
Total fixed costs	$ 3,950,000	-0-	$ 3,950,000
Net income before taxes	$ 1,490,000	$ 25,000	$ 1,515,000

* These items are unaffected by the special order and are not relevant to the pricing decision.

Marlson Company wants to earn a minimum profit of $1 per chair, and no selling expenses will be incurred for the special-order transaction. Assume that normal operations will not be affected by the special order and that regular sales volume for the year 19X4 is 400,000 chairs as initially planned. The minimum bid price on the special order and a comparative income analysis are presented in Exhibit 15-4.

The unit price for Marlson Company is computed with the following general approach:

Total incremental costs to be incurred	
($17.75 × 25,000)	$443,750
Desired profit (25,000 × $1)	25,000
Total selling price	$468,750
Unit price ($468,750 ÷ 25,000)	$ 18.75

Since all incremental costs were variable in this case, use of unit cost data is satisfactory in computing the bid price. As a general guide, the total price is computed as the sum of all incremental costs plus desired profits. By using total costs, there is no danger that an incremental fixed cost will be treated as a variable cost. Note that the computed price of $18.75 is significantly less than the normal price of $33.00, yet the special-order transaction will increase total profits before taxes by $25,000.

Make or buy decisions arise when a company with unused production capacity considers the following alternatives:

MAKE OR BUY DECISIONS

1. Buy certain raw materials or subassemblies from outside suppliers, or
2. Use available capacity to produce the items within the company

The make or buy decision is a general problem of how best to use available capacity and should be analyzed by selecting the least costly alternative. Costs that will be incurred under both alternatives are not relevant to the analysis. Other potential uses of available capacity also should be considered, and qualitative factors must be evaluated in the decision process. These considerations include price stability from suppliers, reliability of delivery, and quality specifications of the material or component involved. Qualitative factors are not included in incremental cost analysis, but they should be used to test the reasonableness of any decision based purely on quantitative cost studies.

The following case illustrates make or buy decisions and related incremental cost analysis. McHugh Corporation produces plastic paper staplers for office use. All parts are produced internally with the exception of the metal base plate. At present, these plates are purchased from Boston Company at a price of $300 per thousand plates. Annual stapler sales have averaged 100,000 units, and no change in consumer demand is anticipated.

Boston Company has informed McHugh Corporation that the purchase price of the plates will be increased to $400 per thousand, effective immediately. McHugh Corporation has unused plant capacity that is adequate to handle production of the plates. Management has requested the controller to prepare a feasibility study of producing the plates internally instead of purchasing them from Boston Company. The controller was informed that another company in the area is willing to rent the unused plant space for storage purposes at an annual rental of $5,000. The assistant controller assembled the following cost information, which discloses that annual manufacturing costs for internal production of plates are $41,000:

McHUGH CORPORATION
Annual cost of producing plates internally

	FOR 100,000 UNITS
Raw materials	$ 8,500
Direct labor	8,000
Variable factory overhead	10,500
General fixed overhead costs	14,000
Total annual production costs	$41,000

Based upon this information, the controller prepared a comparative analysis of costs to be incurred under each alternative. Relevant cost factors are noted by (R), and incremental costs and potential savings related to the production alternative are shown in the third column:

COST DESCRIPTION	ANNUAL COSTS TO Make plates	Buy plates	COST INCREASE OR (SAVINGS) IF PLATES ARE PRODUCED
Raw materials (R)	$ 8,500	$ -0-	$ 8,500
Direct labor (R)	8,000	-0-	8,000
Variable overhead (R)	10,500	-0-	10,500
General fixed overhead	14,000	14,000	-0-
Purchase plates (R)	-0-	40,000	(40,000)
Rental revenue (R)	-0-	(5,000)	5,000
Total costs	$41,000	$49,000	$ (8,000)

In the comparative cost analysis, the less costly alternative is internal production, which offers an $8,000 annual cost saving over outside purchasing.

Note that general fixed overhead is included in the schedule; this cost is not relevant and has no effect on the decision. Rental of unused factory space provides a cash revenue if plates are purchased. This foregone rental is an opportunity cost of the production alternative and appears in the incremental cost column as an addition to incremental production costs.

If additional equipment must be purchased to permit production, the make or buy decision is no longer a short-run operating decision. Investments in additional equipment are capital expenditure decisions that should be analyzed with rate of return measures and other criteria explained in Chapter 16.

ALLOCATION OF LIMITED RESOURCES

In relevant cost analysis, an important criterion is to maximize profit contribution per unit of limited resources. Resources usually are fixed production capacities such as machine hours, storage space, or labor hours if a skilled force cannot be expanded easily.

Consider the following revenue and cost data for products A and B manufactured by Socha Company:

PER UNIT DATA	PRODUCT A	PRODUCT B
Selling price	$100	$60
Variable costs	(30)	(10)
Contribution margin	$ 70	$50
Contribution margin ratio	70%	83%
Required machine hours	2	1

Based on contribution margin per unit, product A seems more profitable, but product B has a greater contribution margin ratio. If market demand is unlimited, which product should be given priority in production and marketing?

If machine time is also unlimited, the company should produce product A, which generates a contribution margin of seventy dollars per unit. If machine time is limited, the company should maximize total contribution margin for the number of machine hours available. With limited equipment capacity, machine time is a scarce resource. Product B generates fifty dollars of contribution margin per machine hour used; product A provides only thirty-five dollars ($70 ÷ 2) of contribution margin per machine hour. Product B is more desirable because a fixed number of machine hours can be allocated to product B and this policy would maximize profits.

Assume that Socha Company can schedule only 10,000 machine hours per time period. If this machine capacity is allocated exclusively to either product, the following profits would be obtained:

	PRODUCT A	PRODUCT B
Unit contribution margin	$70	$50
Machine hours per unit	÷ 2	÷ 1
Contribution margin per hour	$35	$50
Available hours	× 10,000	× 10,000
Total contribution margin	$350,000	$500,000

Allocation of company resources is important whenever capacities are limited and alternative uses of capacities must be selected. The general concept is to select the capacity use that maximizes the cost savings or profit contribution per unit of limited resources.

FINAL NOTE

Relevant cost analysis applies to short-run operating decisions that involve alternative courses of action. The general approach is to concentrate on costs that differ between available alternatives. Specific characteristics of a decision problem indicate the particular cost analysis technique that is most useful. The contribution approach is used to analyze cases in which short-run profit maximization is the objective. Other decision problems involve alternatives in which only costs are involved; the technique in these cases is to select the least costly alternative.

Return now to the beginning of the chapter and review the highlights section before proceeding to the review questions, exercises, and problems.

QUESTIONS

15-1. Define and illustrate the following terms and concepts:
   - a. Project-oriented planning
   - b. Relevant costs
   - c. Incremental costs
   - d. Sunk costs
   - e. Long-term planning
   - f. Differential costs
   - g. Avoidable costs
   - h. Opportunity costs
   - i. Decision model

15-2. Distinguish between period planning and project-oriented planning.

15-3. What are the essential characteristics of all relevant costs?

15-4. What is the importance of the incremental cost concept in analyses for special operating decisions?

15-5. Are variable costs always relevant costs? Defend your response.

15-6. A company invests $100,000 to acquire labor-saving equipment that has a ten-year useful life. With this equipment, the company expects a $15,000 net reduction each year in cash operating expenses. Assuming straight-line depreciation, compute the cumulative ten-year increase in company profits from this investment. Is the decision to invest in this project a short-run operating decision?

15-7. Identify and discuss the steps required in building a decision model.

15-8. When pricing a special order, what is the justification for excluding fixed overhead costs from the analysis? Under what circumstances would fixed costs be relevant to the pricing decision?

15-9. What qualitative business factors affect the decision to accept or reject special orders?

15-10. What is the relationship between period planning and project planning?

15-11. Why is the term *avoidable cost* used in relation to segment-elimination alternatives?

15-12. For product-mix decisions, what criteria can be used to select products that will maximize net income?

15-13. Under what circumstances should profit contribution per machine hour be considered in a make or buy decision?

15-14. When does a sell or process-further decision problem require analysis as a capital expenditure decision alternative?

EXERCISES

15-15. *Allocation of Scarce Resources*   Watkins, Inc., manufactures two products that require both machine processing and labor operations. There is unlimited demand for both products, and Watkins could devote all capacities to a single product. Unit prices, cost data, and processing requirements are shown below:

	PRODUCT X	PRODUCT Z
Unit selling price	$80	$60
Unit variable costs	$40	$25
Machine hours per unit	.2	.7
Labor hours per unit	1	4

In 19X5, the company will be limited to 80,000 machine hours and 60,000 labor hours.

REQUIRED:
a. Determine the quantity(ies) of products to be produced in 19X5.
b. Prepare an income statement for the budgeted product volume computed in part (a).

15-16. *Relevant Costs and Revenues*   Gem Foundry manufactures a variety of household metal products such as window frames, light fixtures, and door knobs. In 19X3, the company produced 120,000 square door knobs but was able to sell only 20,000 units at $8.00 each. The remaining units cannot be sold through normal channels. Cost for inventory purposes on December 31, 19X3, included the following data on unsold units:

Direct materials	$1.00
Direct labor	2.00
Variable overhead	.50
Fixed overhead	1.50
Cost per knob	$5.00

Net Revenue $179,800

The 100,000 square knobs can be sold to a junk dealer in another state for $2.00 each. A business license for this state will cost Gem Foundry $200, and shipping expenses will average $.20 per knob.

Relevant costs $20,200

200,000
20,200
$179,800

REQUIRED:
a. Identify the relevant costs and revenues for the junk-sale alternative.
b. Assume that the square knobs can be reprocessed to produce round knobs that normally have the same $5.00 unit cost components and sell for $6.00 each. Determine the most profitable course and action.

15-17. *Pricing Marginal Output*   Hill Country Brewers, Inc., produces and distributes to wholesalers a bottled alcoholic beverage called Hill Country Ale. The product is similar to beer, and the company sells a standard case of twenty-four twelve-ounce bottles for $4.00. Variable shipping costs are $.20 per case. Hill Country has developed the following standard cost per case:

min price per case $2.90

Materials	$1.20
Direct labor—hourly	.40
Direct labor—salary	.10
Factory overhead	1.40
Case standard cost	$3.10

Standards are reasonably attainable and are based on practical capacity. The company presently operates at 80 percent of capacity and produces 640,000 cases annually. A recent cost study determined that 70 percent of the unit factory overhead cost represented fixed production costs.

Hill Country management has an opportunity to sell 100,000 cases of ale during 19X6 to a large discount retail chain. The retailer requires special labels and bottle caps that cost $.28 per case more than standard. Variable distribution expenses on this special order will be reduced 50 percent, but Hill Country must spend $50,000 to acquire special equipment that cannot be used in regular production. Repeat orders from the retail chain are not expected.

REQUIRED   (Ignore income taxes):
a. Determine the selling price per case that must be charged in order to breakeven on this special order.   fixed cost / contr. margin
b. Assume that Hill Country wishes to earn a profit contribution equal to 20 percent of sales and must use factory space that otherwise provided $20,000 of rental income. Determine the selling price per case for the special order.

15-18. *Elimination of Unprofitable Segment*   Swedish Steel Co., Inc., has three divisions, Ett, Tvo, and Tre. The divisional profit summary for 19X6 revealed the following:

SWEDISH STEEL CO., INC.
Divisional profit summary
For the year ended December 31, 19X6

loss if elim
$64,000

	DIVISIONS			TOTAL COMPANY
	Ett	Tvo	Tre	
Sales	$490,000	$533,000	$937,000	$1,960,000
Variable expenses	347,000	435,000	572,000	1,354,000
Contribution margin	$143,000	$ 98,000	$365,000	$ 606,000
Traceable fixed costs*	(96,000)	(114,000)	(175,000)	(385,000)
Segment margin	$ 47,000	($ 16,000)	$190,000	$ 221,000
Unallocated fixed costs				(82,000)
Net income before taxes				$ 139,000

* An analysis of traceable fixed costs disclosed the following:

	DIVISIONS		
	Ett	Tvo	Tre
Avoidable costs	$79,000	$100,000	$144,000
Unavoidable costs	17,000	14,000	31,000
Total	$96,000	$114,000	$175,000

REQUIRED: Determine whether it would be profitable (based on the 19X6 profit summary) for the company to eliminate one or more of its divisions. Identify the division(s) to be eliminated and state the resulting increase in net income before taxes.

15-19. CPA Problem—Make or Buy Decision Standard costs and other data for three components used by an electronics manufacturer are given below:

	PART A	PART B	PART C
Direct material	$ 9.00	$ .40	$ 8.00
Direct labor	4.00	1.00	4.70
Factory overhead	5.00	4.00	2.00
Unit standard cost	$18.00	$5.40	$14.70
Units needed per year	4,000	6,000	8,000
Machine hours per unit	5	4	2
Delivered cost if purchased	$20.00	$5.00	$15.00

In past years the company has manufactured all its required components. However, in 19X2 only a total of 30,000 hours of otherwise idle machine time can be devoted to the production of components. Accordingly, some parts will have to be purchased from outside suppliers. In producing these parts, factory overhead is applied at one dollar per standard machine hour, and 60 percent of the applied overhead represents fixed capacity costs. Fixed costs will not be affected by purchasing parts from outsiders. The 30,000 hours of available machine time are to be scheduled so that the company realizes the maximum potential cost savings.

REQUIRED: Complete the following table of purchase-production requirements. Support these amounts with orderly computations for your scheduling decision and the total cost savings to be realized by devoting machine time to production of these parts.

	ANNUAL UNIT REQUIREMENTS OF		
	Part A	Part B	Part C
To be purchased			
To be produced			
Total requirements	4,000	6,000	8,000

(AICPA adapted)

15-20. Depreciation and Segment Elimination Tech Corporation is analyzing the possible decision to eliminate its Raider Division. Fixed assets of the division on December 31, 19X4, have been classified into four groups:

GROUP	BOOK VALUE	REMAINING LIFE (YEARS)	ANNUAL DEPRECIATION
A	$600,000	10	$60,000
B	200,000	5	40,000
C	800,000	16	50,000
D	100,000	4	25,000

If Raider Division is eliminated, the fixed-asset groups will be disposed of as follows: Group A will be transferred to other divisions for use in comparable product-line production; group B assets will be disposed of without salvage value; group C will be stored in warehouse facilities at the home office and used as standby equipment during peak seasonal periods; group D assets will be sold for $50,000 cash.

REQUIRED: Company management wishes to assemble a comparative annual profit analysis showing results based upon keeping or eliminating Raider Division. What treatment do you recommend for each fixed-asset group in this analysis, and which groups are relevant to the decision? (Ignore income taxes.)

PROBLEMS

15-21. *Analysis of Special-order Alternatives*   Columbia Deluxe Can Opener Company is a subsidiary of Super Swell Appliances, Inc. The deluxe can opener produced by Columbia is in strong demand with sales during the present year, 19X7, expected to hit the 1,000,000 mark. Full plant capacity is 1,150,000 units, but the 1,000,000 unit mark was considered normal capacity for the current year. The following unit price and cost breakdown is applicable in 19X7:

	PER UNIT
Sales price	$22.50
Less: Manufacturing costs:	
Raw materials	$ 4.50
Direct labor	3.50
Overhead: Variable	2.00
Fixed	3.00
Total manufacturing costs	$13.00
Gross profit	$ 9.50
Less: Selling and administrative expenses:	
Selling: Variable	$ 1.25
Fixed	1.00
Administrative—fixed	1.50
Packaging—variable*	.75
Total selling and administrative expenses	$ 4.50
Net profit before taxes	$ 5.00

* Three types of packaging are available:

Deluxe	.75 per unit
Plain	.50 per unit
Bulk pack	.25 per unit

During November, the company received three special-order requests from large chain store companies. These orders are not part of the budgeted 1,000,000-unit sales for 19X7, but company officials feel that sufficient capacity exists so that one of the orders could be accepted.

Orders received and their terms follow:

Order 1: 75,000 can openers at $20.00 per unit, deluxe packaging
Order 2: 90,000 can openers at $18.00 per unit, plain packaging
Order 3: 125,000 can openers at $15.75 per unit, bulk packaging

Since these orders were made directly to company officials, no variable selling costs will be incurred.

REQUIRED:
a. Analyze the profitability of each of the three special orders.
b. Which special order should be accepted?

15-22. *CPA Problem—Pricing and Profit Analysis*   You have been engaged to assist the management of Stenger Corporation in arriving at certain decisions. Stenger Corporation has its home office in Philadelphia and leases factory buildings in Rhode Island, Georgia, and Illinois. The same single product is manufactured in all three factories. The following information is available regarding 19X4 operations:

	TOTAL	RHODE ISLAND	ILLINOIS	GEORGIA
Sales	$900,000	$200,000	$400,000	$300,000
Fixed costs:				
Factory	$180,000	$ 50,000	$ 55,000	$ 75,000
Administration	59,000	16,000	21,000	22,000
Variable costs	500,000	100,000	220,000	180,000
Allocated home-office expense	63,000	14,000	28,000	21,000
Total	$802,000	$180,000	$324,000	$298,000
Net profit from operations	$ 98,000	$ 20,000	$ 76,000	$ 2,000

Home-office expense is allocated on the basis of units sold. The sales price per unit is ten dollars.

Management is undecided about whether to renew the lease of the Georgia factory, which expires on December 31, 19X5, and will require an increase in rent of $15,000 per year if renewed. If the Georgia factory is shut down, the amount expected to be realized from the sale of the equipment is greater than its book value and would cover all termination expenses. The company can continue to serve customers of the Georgia factory by one of the following methods:

a. Expanding the Rhode Island factory, which would increase fixed costs by 15 percent. Additional shipping expense of $2 per unit will be incurred on the increased production.
b. Entering into a long-term contract with a competitor who will serve the Georgia-factory customers and pay Stenger Corporation a commission of $1.60 per unit.

Stenger Corporation also is planning to establish a subsidiary corporation in Canada to produce the same product. Based on estimated annual Canadian sales of 40,000 units, cost studies produced the following estimates for the Canadian subsidiary:

	TOTAL ANNUAL COSTS	PERCENT OF TOTAL ANNUAL COST THAT IS VARIABLE
Material	$193,600	100
Labor	90,000	70
Overhead	80,000	64
Administration	30,000	30

Canadian production will be sold by manufacturer's representatives who will receive a commission of 8 percent of the sales price. No portion of the United States home-office expense will be allocated to the Canadian subsidiary.

REQUIRED:
a. Prepare a schedule computing Stenger Corporation's estimated net profit from United States operations under each of the following procedures:
   1. Expansion of the Rhode Island factory
   2. Negotiation of long-term contract on a commission basis
b. Management wants to price its Canadian product to realize a 10 percent profit on the sales price. Compute the sales price per unit that would result in an estimated 10 percent profit on sales.
c. Assume that your answer to part (b) is a sales price of eleven dollars per unit. Compute the breakeven point in sales dollars for the Canadian subsidiary.

(AICPA adapted)

15-23. *CMA Problem—Sell or Process-further Decision* The management of Bay Company is considering a proposal to install a third production department within its existing factory building. With the company's present production setup, raw material is passed through Department I to produce materials A and B in equal proportions. Material A then is passed through Department II to yield product C. Material B now is sold "as is" at $20.25 per pound. Product C has a selling price of $100.00 per pound. Current per-pound standard costs used by Bay Company follow:

	DEPARTMENT I (MATERIALS A & B)	DEPARTMENT II (PRODUCT C)	(MATERIAL B)
Prior-department cost	$ —	$53.03	$13.47
Direct material	20.00	—	—
Direct labor	7.00	12.00	—
Variable overhead	3.00	5.00	—
Fixed overhead:			
Traceable	2.25	2.25	—
Allocated (⅔, ⅓)	1.00	1.00	—
	$33.25	$73.28	$13.47

These standard costs were developed by using an estimated production volume of 200,000 pounds of raw material as the standard volume. The company assigns Department I costs to materials A and B in proportion to their net sales values at the point of separation, computed by deducting subsequent standard production costs from sales prices. The $300,000 of common fixed overhead costs are allocated to the two producing departments on the basis of the space used by the departments.

The proposed Department III would be used to process material B into product D. It is expected that any quantity of product D can be sold for $30 per pound. Standard costs per pound under this proposal were developed by using 200,000 pounds of raw material as the standard volume and are as follows:

	DEPARTMENT I (MATERIALS A & B)	DEPARTMENT II (PRODUCT C)	DEPARTMENT III (PRODUCT D)
Prior-department costs	$ —	$52.80	$13.20
Direct material	20.00	—	—
Direct labor	7.00	12.00	5.50
Variable overhead	3.00	5.00	2.00
Fixed overhead:			
Traceable	2.25	2.25	1.75
Allocated (½, ¼, ¼)	.75	.75	.75
	$33.00	$72.80	$23.20

REQUIRED:

a. If (1) sales and production levels are expected to remain constant in the foreseeable future, and (2) there are no foreseeable alternative uses for the available factory space, should Bay Company install Department III and thereby produce product D? Show calculations to support your answer.

b. Instead of constant sales and production levels, suppose that under the present production setup $1,000,000 additions to the factory building must be made every ten years to accommodate growth. Suppose also that proper maintenance gives these factory additions an infinite life and that all such maintenance costs are included in the standard costs set forth in the text of the problem. How would the analysis that you performed in part (a) be changed if the installation of Department III shortened the interval at which the $1,000,000 factory additions are made from ten years to six years? Be as specific as possible in your answer.

(IMA adapted)

15-24. CPA Problem—*Relevant Costing* The management of Southern Cottonseed Company has engaged you to assist in the development of information to be used for managerial decisions. The company has the capacity to process 20,000 tons of cottonseed per year. The yield of a ton of cottonseed is as follows:

PRODUCT	AVERAGE YIELD PER TON OF COTTONSEED	AVERAGE SELLING PRICE PER TRADE UNIT
Oil	300 lbs.	$ .15 per lb.
Meal	600 lbs.	50.00 per ton
Hulls	800 lbs.	20.00 per ton
Lint	100 lbs.	3.00 per cwt.*
Waste	200 lbs.	No value

* cwt = 100 pounds.

A special marketing study revealed that the company can expect to sell its entire output for the coming year at the listed average selling prices. You have determined the company's costs to be as follows:

Processing costs
  Variable: $9 per ton of cottonseed put into process
  Fixed: $108,000 per year
Marketing costs
  All variable: $20 per ton sold
Administrative costs
  All fixed: $90,000 per year

From the above information you prepared and submitted to management a detailed report on the company's breakeven point. In view of conditions in the cottonseed market, management told you that they also would like to know the average maximum amount that the company can afford to pay for a ton of cottonseed.

Management has defined the average maximum amount that the company can afford to pay for a ton of cottonseed as the amount that would result in the company's having losses no greater when operating than when closed down under the existing cost and revenue structure. Management states that you are to assume that the fixed costs shown in your breakeven report will continue unchanged even when the operations are shut down.

REQUIRED:
a. Compute the average maximum amount that the company can afford to pay for a ton of cottonseed.
b. You also plan to mention to management the factors other than the costs that entered into your computation, which they should consider in deciding whether to shut down the plant. Discuss these additional factors.
c. The stockholders consider the minimum satisfactory return on their investment in the business to be 25 percent before corporate income taxes. The stockholders' equity in the company is $968,000. Compute the maximum average amount that the company can pay for a ton of cottonseed to realize the minimum satisfactory return on the stockholders' investment in the business.

(AICPA adapted)

15-25. *Possible Elimination of Unprofitable Segment*   B. Jack Sporting Goods, Inc., is a nationwide distributor of sporting equipment. The home office is located in Plano, Texas, and four branch distributorships are in

Reno, Nevada; Butte, Montana; Dover, Delaware, and Rome, Georgia. Operating results for 19X8 are shown below (all amounts are in thousands of dollars):

B. JACK SPORTING GOODS, INC.
Segment profit and loss summary
For the year ended December 31, 19X8

	RENO BRANCH	BUTTE BRANCH	DOVER BRANCH	ROME BRANCH	TOTAL COMPANY
Sales	$6,008	$6,712	$6,473	$8,059	$27,252
Less variable costs:					
Purchases	$3,471	$4,119	$3,970	$5,246	$16,806
Wages and salaries	694	702	687	841	2,924
Sales commissions	535	610	519	881	2,545
Selling expenses	96	102	79	127	404
Total	$4,796	$5,533	$5,255	$7,095	$22,679
Contribution margin	$1,212	$1,179	$1,218	$ 964	$ 4,573
Less traceable controllable fixed costs	405	517	470	629	2,021
Performance margin	$ 807	$ 662	$ 748	$ 335	$ 2,552
Less traceable uncontrollable fixed costs	312	290	450	510	1,562
Segment margin	$ 495	$ 372	$ 298	($ 175)	$ 990
Less nontraceable joint costs					525
Net income before taxes					$ 465

The corporate president, Mr. Rockofella, is upset with overall corporate operating results and results of the Rome branch. He has requested the controller to work up a complete profitability analysis of the four branch operations and to study the possibility of closing down the Rome branch. The controller needed the following information before the analysis could be completed:

a. Shipping costs amounted to 20 percent of the cost of goods purchased by the Rome branch.

b. Of the uncontrollable fixed costs traceable to the branch operations, the following were avoidable:

Reno	$250,000
Butte	$265,000
Dover	$394,000
Rome	$226,000

c. An analysis of sales revealed:

	AVERAGE GROWTH, LAST FIVE YEARS	GROWTH, 19X8	FUTURE AVERAGE GROWTH RATE
Reno	8%	7%	5%
Butte	7%	5%	6%
Dover	10%	13%	8%
Rome	22%	20%	10%

REQUIRED:
a. Recast the segment profit and loss summary as percentages of sales for each branch.
b. Analyze the performance of each branch president.
c. Should the corporation eliminate the Rome branch?
d. List the possible causes for the poor performance of the Rome branch in 19X8.

15-26. *CMA Problem—Special-order Analysis* George Jackson operates a small machine shop. He manufactures one standard product available from many other similar businesses, and he also manufactures products to customer order. His accountant prepared the annual income statement shown below:

	CUSTOM SALES	STANDARD SALES	TOTAL
Sales	$50,000	$25,000	$75,000
Material	$10,000	$ 8,000	$18,000
Labor	20,000	9,000	29,000
Depreciation	6,300	3,600	9,900
Power	700	400	1,100
Rent	6,000	1,000	7,000
Heat and light	600	100	700
Other	400	900	1,300
	$44,000	$23,000	$67,000
	$ 6,000	$ 2,000	$ 8,000

The depreciation charges are for machines used in the respective product lines. The power charge is apportioned on the estimate of power consumed. The rent is for the building space, which has been leased for ten years at $7,000 per year. The rent and heat and light are apportioned to the product lines based on amount of floor space occupied. All other costs are current expenses identified with the product line causing them.

A valued custom-parts customer has asked Mr. Jackson if he would manufacture 5,000 special units. Mr. Jackson is working at capacity and would have to give up some other business in order to take this business. He can't renege on custom orders already agreed to, but he could reduce the output of the standard product by about one-half for one year while producing the specially requested custom part. The customer is willing to pay $7.00 for each part. The material cost will be about $2.00 per unit, and the labor will be $3.60 per unit. Mr. Jackson will have to spend $2,000 for a special device that will be discarded when the job is finished.

REQUIRED:
a. Calculate and present the following costs related to the custom order of 5,000 units:

1. The incremental cost of the order
2. The full cost of the order
3. The opportunity cost of taking the order
4. The sunk costs related to the order

b. Should Mr. Jackson take the order? Explain your answer.

(IMA adapted)

15-27. *CPA Problem—Elimination of Unprofitable Product* The president of Eastern Company wants guidance on the advisability of eliminating product C, one of the company's three similar products, or investing in new machinery to reduce the cost of product C in the hope of reversing product C's operating loss sustained in 19X6. The three similar products are manufactured in a single plant in about the same amount of floor space, and the markets in which they are sold are very competitive.

Below is the condensed statement of operating income for the company and for product C for the year ended October 31, 19X6:

EASTERN COMPANY
Statement of operating income
For the year ended October 31, 19X6

	ALL THREE PRODUCTS	PRODUCT C
Sales	$2,800,150	$350,000
Cost of sales:		
Raw materials	565,000	80,000
Labor:		
Direct	1,250,000	150,000
Indirect	55,000	18,000
Fringe benefits (15% of labor)	195,750	25,200
Royalties (1% of product C sales)	3,500	3,500
Maintenance and repairs	6,000	2,000
Factory supplies	15,000	2,100
Depreciation (straight line)	25,200	7,100
Electrical power	25,000	3,000
Scrap and spoilage	4,300	600
Total cost of sales	$2,144,750	$291,500
Gross profit	$ 655,400	$ 58,500
Selling, general, and administrative expenses:		
Sales commissions	$ 120,000	$ 15,000
Officers' salaries	32,000	10,500
Other wages and salaries	14,000	5,300
Fringe benefits (15% of wages, salaries, and commissions)	24,900	4,620
Delivery expense	79,500	10,000
Advertising expense	195,100	26,000
Miscellaneous fixed expenses	31,900	10,630
Total selling, general, and administrative expenses	$ 497,400	$ 82,050
Operating income (loss)	$ 158,000	$ (23,550)

REQUIRED (Disregard income taxes):

a. Prepare a schedule showing the contribution of product C to the recovery of fixed costs and expenses (contribution margin) for the year ended October 31, 19X6. Assume that each element of cost and expense is entirely fixed or variable within the relevant range and that the change in inventory levels has been negligible.

b. Assume that in fiscal 19X6 the variable costs and expenses of product C totaled $297,500 and that its fixed costs and expenses amounted to $75,100. Prepare a schedule computing the breakeven point of product C in terms of annual dollar sales volume. Sales for 19X6 amounted to $350,000.

c. The direct labor costs of product C could have been reduced by $75,000, and the indirect labor costs by $4,000, by investing an additional $340,000 (financed with 5 percent bonds) in machinery with a ten-year life and an estimated salvage value of $30,000 at the end of the period. However, the company would have been liable for total severance pay costs of $18,000 (to be amortized over a five-year period), and electrical power costs would have increased $500 annually.

Assuming the information given in part (b), prepare a schedule computing the breakeven point of product C in terms of annual dollar sales volume if the additional machinery had been purchased and installed at the beginning of the year.

(AICPA adapted)

15-28. *CMA Problem—Make or Buy Decision* Vernom Corporation, which produces and sells to wholesalers a highly successful line of summer lotions and insect repellents, has decided to diversify in order to stabilize sales throughout the year. A natural area for the company to consider is the production of winter lotions and creams to prevent dry and chapped skin.

After considerable research, a winter-products line has been developed. However, because of the conservative nature of the company's management, Vernom's president has decided to introduce only one new product this coming winter. If the product is a success, further expansion in future years will be initiated.

The product selected (called Chap-off) is a lip balm that will be sold in a lipstick-type tube. The product will be sold to wholesalers in boxes of twenty-four tubes for $8 per box. Because of available capacity, no additional fixed charges will be incurred to produce the product. However, a $100,000 fixed charge will be absorbed by the product to allocate a fair share of the company's present fixed costs to the new product.

Using the estimated sales and production of 100,000 boxes of Chap-off as the standard volume, the accounting department has developed the following costs:

Direct labor	$2.00/box
Direct materials	$3.00/box
Total overhead	$1.50/box
Total	$6.50/box

Vernom has approached a cosmetics manufacturer to discuss the possibility of purchasing the tubes for Chap-off. The purchase price of the empty tubes from the cosmetics manufacturer would be $.90 per twenty-four tubes. If Vernom Corporation accepts the purchase proposal, it is estimated that direct labor and variable overhead costs would be reduced by 10 percent and that direct material costs would be reduced by 20 percent.

REQUIRED:

a. Should Vernom Corporation make or buy the tubes? Show calculations to support your answer.

b. What would be the minimum purchase price acceptable to Vernom Corporation for the tubes? Support your answer with an appropriate explanation.

c. Instead of sales of 100,000 boxes, revised estimates show sales volume at 125,000 boxes. At this new volume, additional equipment—at an annual rental of $10,000—must be acquired to manufacture the tubes. However, this incremental cost would be the only additional fixed cost required even if sales increased to 300,000 boxes. (The 300,000 level is the goal for the third year of production.) Under these circumstances should Vernom Corporation make or buy the tubes? Show calculations to support your answer.

d. The company has the option of making and buying at the same time. What would be your answer to part (c) if this alternative was considered? Show calculations to support your answer.

(IMA adapted)

15-29. *CPA Problem—Relevant Costing* Largo Manufacturing Company makes and sells a single product, VOSTEX, through normal marketing channels. You have been asked by its president to assist in determining the proper bid to submit for a special manufacturing job for Aztec Sales Company. Below is the information you have collected:

a. The special job is for MOFAC, a product unlike VOSTEC, even though the manufacturing processes are similar.

b. Additional sales of MOFAC to Aztec Sales Company are not expected.

c. The bid is for 20,000 pounds of MOFAC. Each 1,000 pounds of MOFAC requires 500 pounds of material A, 250 pounds of material B, and 250 pounds of material C.

d. Largo's materials inventory data follow:

MATERIAL	POUNDS IN INVENTORY	ACQUISITION COST PER POUND	CURRENT REPLACEMENT COST PER POUND
A	24,000	$.40	$.48
B	4,000	.25	.27
C	17,500	.90	.97
X	7,000	.80	.85

Material X may be substituted for material A in MOFAC. Material X, made especially for Largo under a patent owned by Largo, is left over from the manufacture of a discontinued product, is not usable in VOSTEX, and has a current salvage value of $180.

e. Each 1,000 pounds of MOFAC requires 180 direct labor hours at $3 per hour (overtime is charged at time and one-half). However, Largo is working near its two-shift capacity and has only 1,600 hours of regular time available. The production manager indicates that he can keep the special job on regular time by shifting the production of VOSTEX to overtime if necessary.

f. Largo's cost clerk informs you that the hourly burden rate at normal production is as follows:

Fixed element	$ .20 per direct labor hour
Variable element	.80 per direct labor hour
Total hourly burden rate	$1.00 per direct labor hour

g. The bid invitation states that a performance bond must be submitted with the bid. A local agent will bond Largo's performance for 1 percent of the total bid.

REQUIRED:

a. Prepare a schedule to compute the minimum bid (the bid that would neither increase nor decrease total profits) that Largo Manufacturing Company may submit.

b. Largo's president also wants to know what his new competitor, Melton Manufacturing Company, probably will bid. You assume that Melton's materials inventory has been acquired very recently and that Melton's cost behavior is similar to Largo's. You know that Melton has ample productive capacity to handle the special job on regular time.

Prepare a schedule to compute the minimum bid (the bid that would neither increase nor decrease total profits) that Melton Manufacturing Company might submit.

(AICPA adapted)

15-30. *CMA Problem—Unprofitable Market Segment Elimination* Justa Corporation produces and sells three products (A, B, and C), which are sold in a local market and in a regional market. At the end of the first quarter of the current year, the following income statement has been prepared:

	TOTAL	LOCAL	REGIONAL
Sales	$1,300,000	$1,000,000	$300,000
Cost of goods sold	1,010,000	775,000	235,000
Gross margin	$ 290,000	$ 225,000	$ 65,000
Selling expenses	$ 105,000	$ 60,000	$ 45,000
Administrative expenses	52,000	40,000	12,000
	$ 157,000	$ 100,000	$ 57,000
Net income	$ 133,000	$ 125,000	$ 8,000

Management has expressed special concern with the regional market because of the extremely poor return on sales. This market was entered a year ago because of excess capacity. It originally was believed that the return on sales would improve with time, but after a year no noticeable improvement can be seen from the results as reported in the above quarterly statement.

In attempting to decide whether to eliminate the regional market, the following information has been gathered:

	PRODUCTS		
	A	B	C
Sales	$500,000	$400,000	$400,000
Variable manufacturing expenses as a percentage of sales	60%	70%	60%
Variable selling expenses as a percentage of sales	3%	2%	2%

SALES BY MARKETS

Product	Local	Regional
A	$400,000	$100,000
B	300,000	100,000
C	300,000	100,000

All administrative expenses and fixed manufacturing expenses are common to the three products and to the two markets and are fixed for the period. Remaining selling expenses are fixed for the period and separable by market. All fixed expenses are based upon a prorated yearly amount.

REQUIRED:

a. Prepare the quarterly income statement showing contribution margins by markets.

b. Assuming there are no alternative uses for Justa Corporation's present capacity, would you recommend dropping the regional market? Why or why not?

c. Prepare the quarterly income statement showing contribution margins by products.

d. It is believed that a new product can be ready for sale next year if Justa Corporation decides to go ahead with continued research. The new product can be produced simply by converting equipment presently used in producing product C. This conversion will increase fixed costs by $10,000 per quarter. What must be the minimum contribution margin per quarter for the new product to make the changeover financially feasible?

(IMA adapted)

15-31. *CPA Problem—Incremental Cost Analysis* Ellford Corporation received a $400,000 low bid from a reputable manufacturer for the construction of special production equipment needed by Ellford in an expansion program. Because the company's own plant was not operating at capacity, Ellford decided to construct the equipment there and recorded the following production costs related to the construction:

Services of consulting engineer	$ 10,000
Work subcontracted	20,000
Materials	200,000
Plant labor normally assigned to production	65,000
Plant labor normally assigned to maintenance	100,000
Total	$395,000

Management prefers to record the cost of the equipment under the incremental cost method. Approximately 40 percent of the corporation's production is devoted to government supply contracts, which all are based in some way on cost. The contracts require that any self-constructed equipment be allocated its full share of all costs related to the construction.

The following information is also available:

a. The above production labor was for partial fabrication of the equipment in the plant. Skilled personnel were required and were assigned from other projects. The maintenance labor would have been idle time of nonproduction plant employees who would have been retained on the payroll whether or not their services were utilized.
b. Payroll taxes and employee fringe benefits are approximately 30 percent of labor cost and are included in manufacturing overhead cost. Total manufacturing overhead for the year was $5,630,000.
c. Manufacturing overhead is approximately 50 percent variable and is applied on the basis of production labor cost. Production labor costs for the year for the corporation's normal products totaled $6,810,000.
d. General and administrative expenses include $22,500 of executive salary cost and $10,500 of postage, telephone, supplies, and miscellaneous expenses identifiable with this equipment construction.

REQUIRED:
a. Prepare a schedule computing the amount that should be reported as the full cost of the constructed equipment to meet the requirements of the government contracts. Any supporting computations should be in good form.
b. Prepare a schedule computing the incremental cost of the constructed equipment.
c. What is the greatest amount that should be capitalized as the cost of the equipment? Why?

(AICPA adapted)

15-32. CPA Problem—Make or Buy Decision   Southwest Company, your audit client, requested assistance in deciding whether the company should continue to manufacture or should purchase mansers, a component of their major product. The annual requirement for mansers is 10,000 units, and the part is available from an outside supplier in any quantity at five dollars per unit.

The following information is available:

a. The Machining Department starts and substantially completes mansers; minor finishing is completed by the use of direct labor in the

Finishing Department. The Assembly Department places mansers in the finished product.

b. The machinery used to produce mansers could be sold for its book value of $15,000 and the proceeds invested at 6 percent per year if the mansers were purchased. Property taxes and insurance would decrease $300 per year if the machinery were sold. The machinery has a remaining life of ten years with no estimated salvage value.

c. The Machining Department is devoted about 25 percent to the production of mansers, but labor and some other costs for mansers in this department could be reduced without affecting other operations. The Finishing Department's costs include direct labor totaling $800 devoted to mansers. If mansers were not manufactured, one-half of the resulting available direct labor would be used as indirect labor, and the remaining one half would result in paid idle time of employees.

d. In 19X7, when 10,000 mansers were produced, pertinent Machining Department costs were:

	TOTAL COSTS	COSTS ALLOCATED TO MANSERS
Materials	$95,000	$24,200
Direct labor	39,400	12,200
Indirect labor	20,600	7,800
Heat and light	12,000	3,000
Depreciation	6,000	1,500
Property taxes and insurance	15,000	3,750
Production supplies	4,000	800

e. In addition, the Machining Department total costs included $18,300 in payroll taxes and other benefits.

f. Overhead allocated on the basis of 200 percent of direct labor cost was $40,000 for the Finishing Department and $20,000 for the Assembly Department in 19X7. Overhead in these departments is 25 percent fixed and 75 percent variable.

g. If mansers are purchased, Southwest will incur added costs of $.45 per unit for freight and $3,000 per year for receiving, handling, and inspection of the product.

REQUIRED:

a. Prepare a schedule comparing Southwest's total annual cost of mansers if manufactured with their annual cost if purchased. (Ignore income taxes.)

b. Without regard to your solution to part (a), assume the total annual cost of mansers if manufactured and if purchased were both $60,000. Compute the annual net cash outflow (1) if mansers are manufactured and (2) if mansers are purchased. (Ignore income taxes.)

c. Southwest's management must consider working capital requirements in deciding whether to manufacture or to purchase mansers. Explain the working capital requirements that should be considered.

(AICPA adapted)

Chapter 16: Capital Expenditure Decisions

When a company purchases a capital facility, it commits a large amount of cash resources for a long time. Capital expenditure decisions involve much uncertainty concerning their actual long-run operating results. Decision-supporting rate-of-return projections may appear favorable, but many events can prevent actual performance from reaching original objectives.

Capital expenditure decision analyses must consider all likely outcomes of proposed projects and supply realistic rate-of-return forecasts for use in selecting acceptable capital facility proposals. This chapter examines the capital expenditure decision process and illustrates various methods for evaluating proposed capital expenditures.

Upon completion of this chapter, students should be able to:

1. Identify information relevant to capital expenditure decision analysis
2. Describe the steps of the capital expenditure decision process
3. Apply the project evaluation methods of accounting rate of return, payback period, and discounted cash flow
4. Evaluate the profitability of alternative capital expenditure proposals

The following basic concepts are introduced in this chapter:

Capital expenditure decision   The process of screening, evaluating, and selecting capital expenditure projects that satisfy corporate objectives.

Time value of money   Cash flows of equal dollar amounts that are separated by a time interval will have different present values because of the effect of compound interest.

Discounted cash flow   Evaluation of capital expenditure proposals using net cash inflows weighted by the time value of money.

Capital expenditure decision analysis is a form of project-oriented planning. To select the operating revenue and expense items necessary for capital expenditure evaluations, management accountants must identify and use only information relevant to the project being analyzed. Various procedures can be used to evaluate proposed capital expenditures; the approach that best presents management with necessary information should be selected.

Because capital expenditure decisions involve large dollar outlays, management must install a decision analysis system that provides carefully developed and accurate information concerning capital expenditure requests. In deciding which alternatives to authorize, management should concentrate on project-profitability measures that utilize the concept of the time value of money. Two discounted cash flow evaluation methods, time-adjusted rate of return and net present value, provide this information. Accounting rate of return and payback period are less accurate methods, but their simplicity makes them widely used.

CAPITAL EXPENDITURE DECISION PROCESS[1]

Capital expenditure decision analysis, or capital budgeting, involves the evaluation of alternative proposals for large capital expenditures and includes considerations for financing acceptable projects. Capital budgeting is one of the most important management functions. Personnel from accounting, finance, marketing, and production may be involved in the decision analysis.

Capital expenditure decisions involve both short-term and long-term planning activities. Exhibit 16-1 illustrates the time span of the capital expenditure planning process. Long-term planning considerations shown in Exhibit 16-1 include (1) development of the ten-year plan in 1976 and (2) evaluation of alternative machines prior to the decision to purchase in 1981. Both planning activities require a ten-year forecast.

Ten-year plan   In formulating a ten-year overall corporate plan, future capital facility needs are identified, but no effort is made in this 1976 plan to develop a detailed analysis of actual expenditure amounts.

EXHIBIT 16-1
TIME SPAN OF CAPITAL EXPENDITURE PLANNING PROCESS

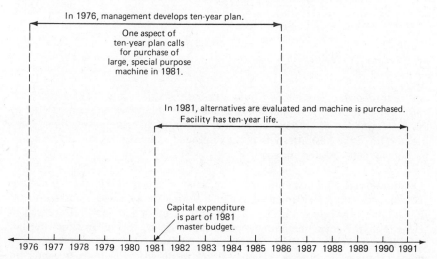

[1] The comments in this section are summarized from Henry R. Anderson and Rickard P. Schwartz, "The Capital Facility Decision," *Management Accounting*, National Association of Accountants, February 1971.

EXHIBIT 16-2
THE CAPITAL FACILITY DECISION PROCESS

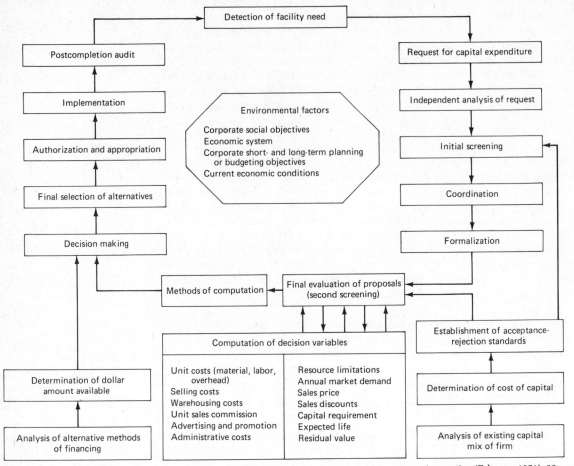

Source: Henry R. Anderson and Rickard P. Schwartz, "The Capital Facility Decision," *Management Accounting* (February 1971), 30.

Ten-year decision analysis When evaluating expenditure alternatives in 1981, a detailed ten-year analysis of related cost and revenue flows is vital to the determination of anticipated rates of return on decision alternatives. Having identified the best alternative, the approved expenditure amount becomes part of the 1981 master budget.

Evaluating capital expenditure proposals, deciding which are to be authorized, and implementing capital expenditures are long and involved procedures. Care must be exercised to invest only in profitable ventures and not to overextend the investment in tangible fixed assets during any one period. Exhibit 16-2 illustrates the total capital facility decision process. A management accountant's primary responsibilities in the decision process center on two functions: final evaluation of proposals and methods of computation. These two decision steps utilize proposal evaluation techniques, which are discussed later in the chapter. But the accountant also has related responsibilities in other areas of the decision process. Exhibit 16-2 places the various phases of capital expenditure planning in perspective, and the following sections discuss each phase of the decision process.

The capital facility decision process takes place within a defined time period and under constraints imposed by economic policies and objectives originating at corporate, industry, and/or national levels. Coordinating short- and long-term capital investment plans within this dynamic environment is management's responsibility and is vital to continued successful operations.

Environmental Factors

Identifying the need for a new capital facility is the starting point of the decision process. Ideas for capital investment opportunities may originate from past sales experience, changes in raw materials, managerial suggestions, production bottlenecks caused by obsolete equipment, new production or distribution methods, or personnel complaints. Capital facility needs also are identified within:

Detection of Facility Need

1. Proposals to add new products to the product line
2. Proposals to expand capacity in existing product lines
3. Proposals designed to reduce costs in production of existing products without altering the scale of operations[2]

A formal capital expenditure request is prepared to facilitate control over capital expenditures. The proposed expenditure request should include a complete description of the facility under review, reasons for the immediate need of the facility, alternative means of satisfying the need, estimated costs and related cost savings for each alternative, and engineering specifications.

Request for Capital Expenditure

Within highly developed capital facility decision processes, information contained in capital expenditure requests often is verified prior to initial screening of proposals. The management accountant plays a major role in this activity; the purposes are (1) to identify undesirable or nonqualifying proposals and (2) to find computational errors and deficiencies in request information.

Independent Analysis of Request

Initial screening processes are used by companies having several branch plants and a highly developed capital expenditure program. The objective of initial screening is to verify results of the independent analyses of requests.

Initial Screening

When evaluating many capital expenditure requests during a time period in which limited funds are available for capital investment purposes, some acceptance-rejection standard must be established. Such a standard may be expressed as a minimum desired rate of return or as a minimum cash flow payback period. As shown in Exhibit 16-2, acceptance-rejection standards are used in the screening processes to identify projects that offer inadequate or marginal returns; this step also identifies proposed projects with high demand and return expectations. Cost of capital information often is used to establish minimum return on investment rates.

Acceptance-Rejection Standards

Before final screening of proposed projects, various alternative proposals must be coordinated and formalized for the decision maker. Coordination involves relating the proposed projects to company objectives. Formalization is

Coordination and Formalization

[2] David G. Quirin, *The Capital Expenditure Decision*, Irwin, Homewood, Ill., 1967, p. 76.

concerned with structuring the expenditure request to highlight its advantages and to summarize cost-benefit information for top management. Department or division managers often compete for limited capital expenditure funds. The more convincing a capital expenditure request is, the more likely it is to receive final authorization.

Final Evaluation of Proposals

The management accountant is primarily responsible for this procedure. Final evaluation of proposals involves verification of decision variables and the application of capital expenditure proposal evaluation methods. The circular flow diagram, shown in Exhibit 16-2, lists several variables that could be relevant to a particular capital expenditure request. In general, the variables in capital facility decisions are (1) project life, (2) estimated cash flows, and (3) investment cost. Each variable in a proposal should be verified for accuracy.

Techniques of proposal evaluation include accounting rate of return, payback period, and discounted cash flow. Using a minimum acceptance-rejection standard as a cutoff point, the management accountant evaluates each proposal using one or more of the evaluation methods. The approach selected should be used consistently to facilitate project comparison.

Final Selection of Alternatives

After passing through the final screening process, acceptable capital expenditure requests are given to management for final review. Before deciding which requests to implement, management must consider the funds available for capital expenditures. Requests then are ranked in order of profitability or payback potential, and the final capital expenditure budget is prepared by allocating funds to selected proposals.

Authorization, Appropriation, and Implementation

Positive action by the board of directors on the proposed capital expenditure budget represents formal authorization of the projects and includes appropriation of the funds necessary to acquire, construct, or install the capital facilities. The implementation period begins with this authorization and ends when the facility is in operable condition.

Postcompletion Audit

The decision process does not end when the facility becomes operational. The accountant should perform a postcompletion audit for each project to evaluate the accuracy of forecasted results. Any weakness found in the decision process should be corrected to avoid the same problem in future decisions.

The postcompletion audit is a difficult decision step. To isolate the effects of a particular decision on a company's overall operating results requires extensive analysis. Only when an entire plant is constructed is it practical to isolate and identify relevant information and measure the performance of the facility being analyzed. The main problems in the postcompletion audit are (1) that long-term projects must be evaluated by concentrating on cash flows over the entire project life and (2) that one decision may influence the profitability of existing facilities and be difficult to identify.

CAPITAL EXPENDITURE PROPOSAL EVALUATION METHODS

Several methods are used to evaluate capital expenditure proposals; the most common ones are:

1. Accounting rate of return
2. Payback
   a. Payback period
   b. Payback reciprocal
   c. Bailout payback
3. Discounted cash flow
   a. Time-adjusted rate of return
   b. Net present value

Before discussing the capital expenditure evaluation methods listed above, we should explain the types and relevancy of information included in capital expenditure proposals.

Cost savings versus net cash flow The rate of return or the payback period of a proposed capital expenditure may be computed by using either the *annual cost savings* or the *annual net cash inflow* generated by the proposed facility. When used consistently, either amount can show the superiority of one proposal over another. In many cases, revenues are not involved, and cost savings are the only potential benefit of a project. Or revenues may be the same for each alternative and thus be irrelevant to the decision. The terms *cash flow* and *cash inflow* are used to represent actual cash inflows or cost savings related to a project.

Even versus uneven cash flows Future cost savings or net cash inflows are relevant to all evaluations of capital expenditure proposals. These cash flows may be the same for each year of the project's life, or the analysis may contain unequal annual cash flows. Unequal cash flows are not uncommon and must be analyzed on a yearly basis in the evaluation process; equal cash flows require less detailed analysis. These two approaches will be explained and illustrated in later sections.

Book value of existing assets *Book value* is the undepreciated portion of the original cost of a fixed asset. Since past or historical costs cannot be altered by a current decision, book values are irrelevant in considering capital expenditure proposals. Losses resulting from disposal or trade-in of an asset do not have a direct bearing on proposal evaluations, but tax savings arising from such a loss are relevant, as are cash proceeds from the sale and disposal of an asset.

Disposal or salvage values Disposal or salvage values represent future cash flows that are relevant to capital expenditure proposal evaluations.

Unequal lives Useful lives of alternative facilities being analyzed may not be equal. In comparing alternative proposals with unequal lives, one approach is to limit the analysis to the time period of the shortest-lived asset. Remaining alternatives then are adjusted by estimating disposal values at the end of this time period. A second approach is to use the longest time period and to assume replacement of the shorter-lived assets. Using this approach, the disposal value of the replacement must be estimated and included in the analysis. Illustrations of proposal evaluations for alternatives with unequal lives are illustrated later in the chapter.

Depreciation expense All methods of evaluating capital expenditure proposals—with the exception of accounting rate of return—utilize cash flow information. Depreciation is a *noncash expense* and is not relevant to decision analyses based on cash flow. Depreciation expense does reduce income tax expense, and so this cash savings is relevant to the evaluation analysis.

As a method of evaluating capital expenditures, the accounting rate of return is a crude but simple measure of return on investment. Several names have been used to identify this method, including unadjusted rate of return, rate of return on assets, financial statement method, and approximate rate of return. This approach measures rate of return by relating average annual net income produced by the project to its average capital investment. Accounting rate of return is computed as follows:

$$\text{accounting rate of return} = \frac{\text{increase in average annual net income}}{\text{average investment}}$$

Since the numerator of this formula deals with net income and not cash flow, fixed asset depreciation must be used to determine net income. The denominator represents average project cost over the life of the investment and is computed in the following manner:

$$\text{average investment} = \frac{\text{total investment} + \text{salvage value}}{2}$$

Assume that Mason Company is planning to purchase a machine costing $20,000; it has a salvage value of $2,000 at the end of its twelve-year life. Annual net income before depreciation is expected to increase by $3,500. Ignoring income taxes and using straight-line depreciation, the accounting rate of return on this machine would be:

$$\text{accounting rate of return} = \frac{\$3,500 - \dfrac{\$20,000 - \$2,000}{12}}{\dfrac{\$20,000 + \$2,000}{2}}$$

$$= \frac{\$3,500 - \$1,500}{\$11,000}$$

$$= \frac{\$2,000}{\$11,000}$$

$$= 18.18\%$$

The accounting rate of return can be used to measure incremental differences between two alternatives, but care should be taken to use only incremental amounts in the equation. With this approach, a positive answer shows that one alternative has a greater return on investment. Disadvantages of using the accounting rate of return are summarized below:

1. Annual averages are used in the computations, which tends to restrict the accuracy of the prediction.
2. The method is difficult to use when annual income predictions are not equal.
3. The equation's denominator can be either the total initial investment (which reflects return on investment in the first year) or an average investment, as was used above. This change in denominator amount has a significant effect on the rate of return used for decision purposes.
4. The method fails to incorporate the time-value of money concept. Future dollars are treated as being equal to present dollars.
5. Changes in depreciation methods can affect the computed rate of return.

For these reasons, the accounting rate of return yields a crude measure of a project's profit potential. Because this method is easy to apply, it is often used in practice.

Payback evaluation methods measure the time required to recover a project's total cost through cash inflow generated by the project.

Payback period   Payback period is a widely used capital expenditure evaluation method. Management is extremely interested in the time required to recover the initial project cost, and the payback period is an estimate of this time period. The payback period is computed as follows:

$$\text{payback period} = \frac{\text{project cost}}{\text{annual net cash inflow}}$$

In the Mason Company example, the payback period is:

$$\text{payback period} = \frac{\$20,000}{\$3,500} = 5.714$$

If Mason Company's maximum acceptable payback period was six years, this project would be considered acceptable. In comparing two alternative proposals, the one with the lower payback period is preferable. Note that the payback method deals with cash flow, not with net income; therefore, depreciation expense is irrelevant in payback analyses.

This method has several limitations. First, it ignores the measurement of profitability. Measuring the time period necessary to recapture initial investment does not consider the project's profit potential. The payback approach also ignores the time value of money. Unequal annual cash flows are not a problem when using this method. Instead of dividing a constant annual cash flow into the initial investment, the unequal cash flows for consecutive years are added until the cumulative cash flow equals the project cost.

Payback reciprocal   Failure to measure a project's profitability is one criticism of the payback period evaluation method. Consider the following example:

	MACHINE 1	MACHINE 2
Initial investment	$180,000	$400,000
Salvage value	-0-	-0-
Useful life	10 years	20 years
Annual net cash inflow	$20,000	$40,000
Payback period	9 years	10 years

Based on the payback periods, machine 1 should be selected. Note that after depreciation, it yields an annual net income before taxes of $2,000 for ten years, while machine 2 will produce a net income before taxes of $20,000 for twenty years.

To incorporate the profitability factor into payback computations, the payback reciprocal can be used to approximate time-adjusted rate of return:

$$\text{payback reciprocal} = \frac{1}{\text{payback period}}$$

Two conditions must exist before the payback reciprocal will yield a meaningful rate of return on investment:

1. The useful life of the asset must be at least *twice as long* as the payback period.

2. Annual net cash inflows must be constant over the life of the asset.

Because of the first factor, the payback reciprocal method cannot be used to evaluate the rate of return on machine 1. If the two required conditions are not satisfied, the payback reciprocal does not provide an accurate estimate of time-adjusted rate of return.

For the Mason Company example, the machine has a payback period of 5.714 years, useful life of 12 years, and constant net cash inflow; the payback reciprocal can be used to approximate rate of return for the project since cash flows are uniform and project life exceeds two times the payback period:

$$\text{payback reciprocal} = \frac{1}{5.714} = 17.5\%$$

Bailout payback Risk is an important consideration when investing in a speculative project. The payback period method does not indicate which alternative involves the least risk. But the bailout payback approach does identify the project with the least amount of risk. By including annual salvage values in the analysis, bailout payback answers the question, "If operations do not go as planned, which machine will provide us with the earliest recovery of invested capital?" In this case, risk is the chance of not recovering project cost.

Zick Steel Company is considering the purchase of a machine to produce long-lasting steel toothbrushes. Two alternative machines, N and O, are being analyzed:

	MACHINE N	MACHINE O
Initial capital expenditure	$200,000	$370,000
Salvage value—year 1	$170,000	$300,000
Annual decline in salvage value after year 1	$ 10,000	$ 20,000
Annual net cash inflows	$ 20,000	$ 40,000
Estimated useful life	16 years	16 years
Payback period	10 years	9.25 years

Machine O is the choice from the standpoint of payback period. The bailout payback period must be determined in order to evaluate the relative risk of each project. In the following computation schedule for each machine, cumulative cash recovery is determined for each year. Cumulative net cash flow from operations plus estimated salvage value at year-end equal total cash recovered if the equipment was sold in that year.

BAILOUT PAYBACK

Machine	End of year	Cumulative net cash inflows	+	Salvage value	=	Total cash recaptured
N	1	$ 20,000	+	$170,000	=	$190,000
	2	40,000	+	160,000	=	200,000
Bailout payback = 2 years						
O	1	$ 40,000	+	$300,000	=	$340,000
	2	80,000	+	280,000	=	360,000
	3	120,000	+	260,000	=	380,000
Bailout payback = 2½ years						

To minimize investment risk, management may select machine N because it has a shorter bailout payback period.

An important criticism of the accounting rate of return and payback period evaluation methods is that the time value of money is not considered in their computation.

Time value of money means that cash flows of equal dollar amount separated by a time interval have different values because of the effect of compound interest. For example, Bill Lings was awarded two payments of $10,000 each as a settlement in a lawsuit. One payment is due today, December 31, 19X1, and the second amount is payable on December 31, 19X4. What is the present value (value today) of the entire settlement? For purposes of our example, assume that Mr. Lings could earn 8 percent return on current funds.

Discounted Cash Flow Methods

Present value of Dec. 31, 19X1, payment	$10,000
Present value of Dec. 31, 19X4, payment	
($10,000 × .794)	7,940
Present value of settlement, Dec. 31, 19X1	$17,940

The multiplier, .794, was taken from Table 3 in Appendix 16-A and represents the discount factor for cash to be received at the end of three years assuming an 8 percent rate of return. In other words, $10,000 to be received in three years is not worth $10,000 today; if funds can be invested to earn 8 percent interest, then $1 to be received three years hence is worth $.794 today.

	DEC. 31, 19X1	DEC. 31, 19X4
Payments to be received	$10,000	$10,000
Present value on Dec. 31, 19X1:		
Dec. 31, 19X1, payment	$10,000	
Dec. 31, 19X4, payment	$ 7,940 ←	$10,000 × .794

Another way to approach this example about the time value of money is to determine the value on December 31, 19X4, of the first $10,000 payment, which is received on December 31, 19X1. Using compound interest for three years at 8 percent (see Table 1, Appendix 16-A), the future value is:

$$\$10,000 \times 1.260 = \$12,600$$

The future value of $12,600 represents the amount to which $10,000 would accumulate in three years with funds earning 8 percent compound interest. Likewise, the value today (present value) of $12,600 to be received three years hence is $10,000, since $12,600 × .794 = $10,000. Present value and future value relationships are shown in the following time-period graph:

$10,000 × 1.260 = future value three years later → $12,260

Dec. 31, 19X1	Dec. 31, 19X2	Dec. 31, 19X3	Dec. 31, 19X4

$10,000 ← present value on Dec. 31, 19X1 = .794 × $12,600

To further understand the time value of money, consider the case of Horstmann Cosmetics, Inc. Management is considering the purchase of a new machine, Model #102274, for the facial-powder production line. The machine will cost \$27,000 and will be used for fifteen years. One alternative that management should consider is investing the \$27,000 in certificates of deposit yielding 8 percent annual interest. Under this alternative, management still would have the \$27,000 at the end of fifteen years plus compound interest of \$58,644, computed [(\$27,000 × 3.172) − \$27,000], or a total cash fund of \$85,644. Several key points are derived from this comparison:

1. Management must be assured that the cost savings or increase in net cash flow from the new machine is at least \$85,644 over the fifteen-year period. If not, the \$27,000 would earn a better return in certificates of deposit.
2. \$85,644 to be received at the end of fifteen years has a *present value* of \$27,000, assuming a discount rate of 8 percent (\$85,644 × .315 = \$27,000).
3. If (a) management had to borrow funds to finance the purchase of the machine, (b) the interest rate of financing was 8 percent, and (c) the present value of future cash inflows from the machine was \$27,000, then the company would be no better off financially at the end of fifteen years by purchasing the machine than it is at present.
4. If the company has \$27,000 to invest and decides to purchase the new machine, the opportunity cost of the decision is \$58,644 of interest, which could be earned by investing in certificates of deposit. (*Opportunity cost* is defined as the earnings lost by not selecting the second-best alternative.)

At this point, it should be clear that a dollar to be received in fifteen years is not worth a dollar today. To find its present value, the technique for compounding interest is reversed. Based on a desired rate of return, the dollar is discounted back to the present using the present-value tables in Appendix 16-A. Future-value and present-value tables, along with an explanation of how to use each table, are summarized in Appendix 16-A.

Time-adjusted rate of return Unlike the accounting rate of return, the time-adjusted rate of return recognizes the time value of money. The *time-adjusted rate of return* means a constant rate of return each year based on the unrecovered project investment at start of year; it represents the rate of interest that equates discounted future cash inflows with initial project investment. Horstmann Cosmetics, Inc., described above, will illustrate time-adjusted rate of return. Assume that management has determined that the machine will increase annual net cash inflow by \$4,600 during the asset's useful life. The annual cash benefit of \$4,600 represents a cost savings that is determined by comparing the new investment proposal with the current method of operations. Thus, an incremental approach is used to measure the new machine's cash flow benefits. Using the concept of present value, which recognizes the time value of money, the following equation yields the time-adjusted rate of return:

initial project investment = present value of future cash inflows
at R percent for 15 years of useful life

\$27,000 = present value of an annuity* of
\$4,600 at R percent for 15 years

* An *annuity* is a series of equal cash flows to be received or paid at *regular* time intervals. When equal cash inflows are present, Tables 2 and 4 in Appendix 16-A based on an annuity of one dollar per period are used. If unequal cash flows are present, the present value of cash flow for each year is determined separately by using Table 3.

$$\$27{,}000 = \$4{,}600X$$

$$X = \frac{\$27{,}000}{\$4{,}600}$$

$$= 5.870$$

The 5.870 figure represents the present-value factor for the rate of return necessary to solve the equation. The process of determining time-adjusted rate of return now shifts to Table 4 in Appendix 16-A. The fifteen-year row of multipliers in Table 4 indicates that the 5.870 multiplier lies between 6.142 (14 percent) and 5.847 (15 percent). By using the process of interpolation, as shown below, the correct rate of return is calculated:

	14%	Correct %	15%
Multiplier	6.142	5.870	5.847

$$\llcorner\ .272\ \lrcorner$$

$$\llcorner \qquad .295 \qquad \lrcorner$$

difference between 14% and correct % = .272
difference between 14% and 15% = .295
correct % = 14% + (.272/.295)(1%)
= 14% + .92%
= 14.92%

If the 14.92 percent time-adjusted rate of return is above the minimum rate of return desired by Horstmann Cosmetics, Inc., the machine should be purchased.

Net present value   A second discounted cash flow approach for evaluating capital expenditure proposals is the net present value method. Instead of determining the specific time-adjusted rate of return on a proposed project, this method utilizes a minimum desired rate of return as specified by management. Using this desired rate of return, future net cash inflows are discounted back to the present. If the sum of these computed present values exceeds the total initial investment, then the time-adjusted rate of return for the proposed project exceeds the minimum desired rate of return and the expenditure request should be approved. If the sum of computed present values is less than project cost, then the project does not offer the desired minimum rate of return.

   The net present value method is superior to the time-adjusted rate of return method for the following reasons:

1. Tedious interpolations using present-value tables are not required.
2. Project evaluation is made easier by using the net present value method when unequal annual net cash inflows are involved.

The net present value method does not provide a specific rate of return that can be used for comparing decision alternatives or for ranking acceptable capital expenditure proposals. However, this disadvantage can be overcome by computing a *present value index* (also called *profitability index*) for each proposal:

$$\text{present value index} = \frac{\text{present value of cash inflows}}{\text{initial capital expenditure}}$$

In comparing two alternatives, the project having the larger present value index is more desirable. Returning to the Horstmann Cosmetics example, two sets of assumptions will be used to illustrate the net present value method. In case 1, *equal* cash inflows are assumed; case 2 is based on *unequal* cash inflows. The net present value method utilizes the same equation as used for computing the time-adjusted rate of return. However, now the rate of return is given, and the unknown variable in the equation is the present value of the future cash inflows.

Case 1—Equal Cash Inflows   Required information:

Initial investment	$27,000
Useful life	15 years
Minimum desired rate of return	14%
Annual net cash inflows	$4,600

Stated in equation format,

present value of cash inflows = present value of annuity of
$4,600 at 14% for 15 years

Using Table 4 in Appendix 16-A, the following computation is required:

present value of cash inflows = $4,600 (6.142) = $28,253

Since the present value of future cash inflows ($28,253) exceeds the amount of the initial capital expenditure ($27,000), the project is acceptable. A positive net present value of $1,253 ($28,253 − $27,000) indicates that the time-adjusted rate of return on this project exceeds the minimum desired rate of 14 percent. For purposes of ranking proposals, the present value index is:

$$\frac{\$28,253}{\$27,000} = 1.046$$

Case 2—Unequal Cash Inflows   To simplify the analysis, useful life has been reduced to five years. Required information:

Initial investment	$27,000
Useful life	5 years
Minimum desired rate of return	14%
Annual cash inflows by year:	
1	$12,000
2	$11,000
3	$10,000
4	$ 9,000
5	$ 8,000

The analysis for unequal cash inflows is based on the same equation shown above. Table 4 in Appendix 16-A no longer applies because case 2 does not involve an annuity or a series of equal cash inflows. Instead, Table 3 in Appendix 16-A must be used to determine the present value of each year's cash inflow. The following analysis is required:

Year	Cash Inflow	× 14% Multiplier	= Present Value
1	$12,000	.877	$10,524
2	11,000	.769	8,459
3	10,000	.675	6,750
4	9,000	.592	5,328
5	8,000	.519	4,152
Present value of future cash inflows			$35,213
Initial investment			(27,000)
Net present value			$ 8,213

Present value index = $35,213/$27,000 = 1.304

Since the net present value is positive, the proposed expenditure is acceptable.

Ranking Capital Expenditure Proposals

Once the acceptable capital expenditure requests have been identified by using the firm's minimum acceptance-rejection standard, management prepares the final capital budget. Since funds available for capital expenditures usually are limited, management must ration them by approving only the most desirable proposals. To aid the selection process, capital expenditure proposals are ranked or listed in order of profitability.

In ranking alternative proposals, time-adjusted rate of return, net present value, and the present value index should be used cautiously. Projected profitability is a function of the useful life of each project. Assume that three acceptable proposals are competing for the same capital expenditure funds. The projects are mutually exclusive, and only one alternative will be selected.

Project	Time-Adjusted Rate of Return	Useful Life
Y	30%	5 years
E	29%	7 years
S	28%	10 years

Using the time-adjusted rate of return as the sole criterion for ranking purposes, project Y would be selected. However, this choice would reject projects that are profitable over a longer time span. If project Y is selected, management assumes that funds generated by it can be reinvested at the end of the fifth year to yield a minimum of 30 percent. This assumption may not be valid. In general, the objective in rationing limited funds is to maximize the present value of future cash flows. Net present value and the present value index are better ranking devices than is the time-adjusted rate of return approach.

Illustrative Problem

Beta Dataflow, Inc., is a data processing company that specializes in servicing the needs of medium and small companies. Because of recent increases in customers' information demands, management is considering the purchase of a small in-house computer. Two computer companies have submitted bids to management; relevant data follow:

	COMPUTER MBI	COMPUTER IT
Cost	$75,000	$60,000
Salvage value	$12,000	$ 6,000
Useful life	5 years	5 years

The following annual cash flow information for each computer was forecasted by management:

	COMPUTER MBI			COMPUTER IT		
YEAR	Cash revenues	Cash expenses	Net cash inflow	Cash revenues	Cash expenses	Net cash inflow
1	$100,000	$75,000	$25,000	$90,000	$72,000	$18,000
2	100,000	77,000	23,000	90,000	72,000	18,000
3	100,000	79,000	21,000	90,000	72,000	18,000
4	100,000	81,000	19,000	90,000	72,000	18,000
5	100,000	82,000	18,000	90,000	72,000	18,000

The company's minimum desired rate of return is 16 percent, and the straight-line depreciation method is used.

REQUIRED:
1. Determine which computer Beta Dataflow, Inc., should purchase. Include in your analysis the following computations for each alternative:
    a. Accounting rate of return
    b. Payback period
    c. Time-adjusted rate of return
    d. Net present value
    e. Present value index
    f. Schedule comparing results of (a) through (e) for each computer
2. Prepare an incremental analysis of the two alternatives using the net present value evaluation approach.

SOLUTION

Part 1a. Accounting rate of return (average investment):

Increase in net income

	COMPUTER MBI			COMPUTER IT		
YEAR	Net cash inflow	− Depreciation =	Net income	Net cash inflow	− Depreciation =	Net income
1	$ 25,000	$12,600	$12,400	$18,000	$10,800	$ 7,200
2	23,000	12,600	10,400	18,000	10,800	7,200
3	21,000	12,600	8,400	18,000	10,800	7,200
4	19,000	12,600	6,400	18,000	10,800	7,200
5	18,000	12,600	5,400	18,000	10,800	7,200
Totals	$106,000	$63,000	$43,000	$90,000	$54,000	$36,000

Computer MBI:

$$\frac{\$43,000 \div 5}{\$87,000 \div 2} = \frac{\$8,600}{\$43,500} = 19.77\%$$

Computer IT:

$$\frac{\$36,000 \div 5}{\$66,000 \div 2} = \frac{\$7,200}{\$33,000} = \underline{\underline{21.82\%}}$$

Part 1b. Payback period:

Computer MBI:

Total cash investment		$75,000
Less: Cash flow recovery:		
Year 1	$25,000	
Year 2	23,000	
Year 3	21,000	
Year 4 (6/19 of $19,000)	6,000	(75,000)
Unrecovered investment		–0–

Payback period = 3 6/19 years, or <u>3.32 years</u>

Computer IT:

$$\frac{\text{total cash investment}}{\text{annual cash flow}} = \frac{\$60,000}{\$18,000} = \underline{\underline{3.33 \text{ years}}}$$

Part 1c. Time-adjusted rate of return:

A trial-and-error approach is required using the following formula:

capital investment = present value of future cash inflows at R percent
for n years of useful life

The time-adjusted rate of return for projects with unequal cash inflows is difficult to compute.

Computer MBI:

	NET CASH INFLOWS	TRIAL PRESENT VALUE MULTIPLIERS			TRIAL CASH INFLOW PRESENT VALUES		
YEAR	(1)	14% (2)	16% (3)	18% (4)	14% (1 × 2)	16% (1 × 3)	18% (1 × 4)
1	$ 25,000	.877	.862	.847	$21,925	$21,550	$21,175
2	23,000	.769	.743	.718	17,687	17,089	16,514
3	21,000	.675	.641	.609	14,175	13,461	12,789
4	19,000	.592	.552	.516	11,248	10,488	9,804
5	30,000*	.519	.476	.437	15,570	14,280	13,110
	$118,000				$80,605	$76,868	$73,392

* Fifth year net cash inflow plus salvage value.

	16%	?%	18%
Present values	$76,868	$75,000	$73,392

difference between 16% and correct % = $1,868
difference between 16% and 18% = $3,476
time-adjusted rate of return = 16% + ($1,868/$3,476)(2%)
= 16% + .537 (2%)
= 16% + 1.074%
= <u>17.074%</u>

Computer IT:

YEAR	NET CASH INFLOWS (1)	TRIAL PRESENT VALUE MULTIPLIERS			TRIAL CASH INFLOW PRESENT VALUES		
		14% (2)	16% (3)	18% (4)	14% (1 × 2)	16% (1 × 3)	18% (1 × 4)
1–5	$18,000*	3.433	3.274	3.127	$61,794	$58,932	$56,286
5	6,000	.519	.476	.437	3,114	2,856	2,622
					$64,908	$61,788	$58,908

* Net cash inflows for five-year period.

	16%	?%	18%
Present values	$61,788	$60,000	$58,908

difference between 16% and correct % = $1,788
difference between 16% and 18% = $2,880
time-adjusted rate of return = 16% + ($1,788/$2,880) (2%)
= 16% + .621(2%)
= 16% + 1.242%
= 17.242%

Part 1d. Net present value (desired return = 16%):

COMPUTER MBI:

Year	Net cash inflows	×	Present value multipliers (16%)	=	Present value
1	$ 25,000		.862		$21,550
2	23,000		.743		17,089
3	21,000		.641		13,461
4	19,000		.552		10,488
5	30,000		.476		14,280
Totals	$118,000				$76,868
			Cost of initial expenditure		(75,000)
			Net present value		$ 1,868

COMPUTER IT:

Year	Net cash inflows	×	Present value multipliers (16%)	=	Present value
1–5	$18,000		3.274		$58,932
5	6,000		.476		2,856
			Total present value		$61,788
			Cost of initial expenditure		(60,000)
			Net present value		$ 1,788

Part 1e. Present value index:

Computer MBI:

$$\text{present value index} = \frac{\text{present value of cash inflows}}{\text{initial capital expenditure}}$$

$$= \frac{\$76,868}{\$75,000}$$

$$= \underline{\underline{1.025}}$$

Computer IT:

$$\text{present value index} = \frac{\$61,788}{\$60,000} = \underline{\underline{1.030}}$$

Part 1f. Comparative results:

	COMPUTER MBI	COMPUTER IT	DECISION
Accounting rate of return	19.77%	21.82%	IT
Payback period	3.32 years	3.33 years	MBI
Time-adjusted rate of return	17.074%	17.242%	IT
Net present value*	$1,868	$1,788	MBI
Present value index†	1.025	1.030	IT

* Positive figures indicate that both alternatives will yield more than the desired 16 percent return.
† Present value index is a better method of evaluating profitability since it measures net present value in relationship to amount of initial capital expenditure.

Part 2:

An alternative approach to the solution in part 1d is to compute net present value of the alternatives on an incremental basis:

	NET CASH INFLOWS		DIFFERENCE (MBI − IT)	PRESENT VALUE MULTIPLIERS (16%)	PRESENT VALUE
YEAR	Computer MBI	Computer IT			
1	$25,000	$18,000	$ 7,000	.862	$ 6,034
2	23,000	18,000	5,000	.743	3,715
3	21,000	18,000	3,000	.641	1,923
4	19,000	18,000	1,000	.552	552
5 (includes salvage)	30,000	24,000	6,000	.476	2,856
Net present value of incremental cash flows (for computer MBI)					$15,080
Initial capital expenditure	$75,000	$60,000	$15,000	Incremental investment	(15,000)
Net present value (in favor of computer MBI)					$ 80

The incremental approach measures the comparative benefit of investing in computer MBI. In part 1d, the net present value of each computer project was computed separately. The difference in favor of MBI also can be determined by comparing the net present values of each alternative:

Net present value—computer MBI	$1,868
Net present value—computer IT	(1,788)
Difference in favor of MBI	$ 80

The objective of project evaluation techniques such as net present value and payback period is to measure relative benefits of a proposed capital expenditure. This measurement process concentrates on cash receipts and disbursements for a given project. Income taxes are important in capital budgeting because they affect the amount and timing of cash flows. For this reason, therefore, comprehensive project planning must include related tax considerations.

Income Tax Effects

Corporate income tax is a major consideration in business decisions. The basic corporate tax rate is 22 percent of taxable income plus 26 percent of taxable income in excess of $25,000. For problem-solving purposes, the corporate tax structure is simply expressed as 48 percent of taxable income. The effect of income taxes on cash flow can be illustrated in several ways. Consider a project that makes the following contribution to annual net income:

Cash revenues	$400,000
Cash expenses	(200,000)
Depreciation	(100,000)
Income before taxes	$100,000
Income taxes at 48%	(48,000)
Income after taxes	$ 52,000

Annual cash flow for this project can be determined by three different procedures:

1. Cash flow—receipts and disbursements

Revenues (cash inflow)	$400,000
Cash expenses (outflow)	(200,000)
Income taxes (outflow)	(48,000)
Net cash flow	$152,000

2. Cash flow—income adjustment procedure

Income after taxes	$ 52,000
Add: Noncash expenses	100,000 (depreciation)
Less: Noncash revenues	–0–
Net cash flow	$152,000

3. Cash flow—net of tax procedure

Cash revenues	$400,000	
Less: Tax increase (400,000 × .48)	192,000	
Revenues net of related taxes		$208,000
Cash expenses	$200,000	
Less: Tax reduction (200,000 × .48)	96,000	
Expenses net of related taxes		(104,000)
Tax savings: $100,000 depreciation times 48 percent		48,000
Net cash flow		$152,000

In all three computations, the net cash flow is $152,000, and the total effect of income taxes is to reduce net cash flow by $48,000.

The net of tax procedure in computation 3 is a convenient way to measure the cash flow effects of income taxes. Using this method, tax effects are related to individual revenues and expenses. Revenues and gains from the sale of equipment increase taxable income and tax payments. However, revenues are considered cash benefits only to the extent that they exceed related tax increases:

Cash revenues	$400,000
Less: 48% tax increase	(192,000)
Net cash inflow	$208,000

Gains are not cash flow items, but they do increase tax payments. If equipment with book value of $80,000 is sold for $180,000 in cash, the gain is $100,000. Assuming the gain is taxable at 48 percent, the following cash flow analysis applies:

Proceeds from sale		$180,000
Gain on sale	$100,000	
Corporate tax rate	× 48%	
Cash outflow = tax increase		(48,000)
Net cash inflow		$132,000

Taxation of gains and losses on sale of business equipment is complicated by depreciation recapture rules, investment credit recapture, and tests that must be applied to determine whether capital gains treatment is possible. Since capital gains are taxed at a lower rate than ordinary income, a proper analysis for cash flow purposes must consider the detailed provisions of Sections 1231 and 1245 of the current Internal Revenue Code.

As applied to expenses, the net of tax approach recognizes that every tax deductible expense reduces taxable income and income tax payments. Expenses reduce net income only to the extent they exceed related tax reductions. This generalization is true for cash operating expenses and losses on the sale of fixed assets. The following examples apply the net of tax approach to cash and noncash expenses:

Cash expenses:

Cash operating expenses	$100,000
Less: Tax reduction at 48%	(48,000)
Net cash outflow	$ 52,000

Noncash expenses:

Annual depreciation expense	$200,000
Corporate tax rate	× 48%
Tax reduction = cash savings	$ 96,000

Depreciation expense is not a cash flow item itself, but it provides a cash benefit equal to the available tax reduction. Losses on sale of fixed assets also are not cash flow items, but they provide a cash benefit by reducing tax payments.

After-tax Decision Analysis

The cash flow effects of income taxes provide additional data input for capital expenditure evaluation techniques such as payback, net present value, or time-adjusted rate of return. A decision concerning equipment replacement follows.

Taeley Company is considering the replacement of certain packing equipment with a newer model. The old equipment currently in operation originally cost $100,000, has accumulated depreciation of $40,000, and has a remaining life of six years. The old equipment can be sold now for $75,000, but the expected salvage value six years hence is zero. Cash operating expenses related to the old equipment are $200,000 per year.

The new equipment under consideration will cost $120,000, and it will have a six-year useful life. Expected salvage value six years hence is $6,000, and estimated annual cash operating expenses are $150,000. Straight-line depreciation is used, and salvage values are ignored for depreciation purposes.

The alternatives in this business decision are (1) to keep the old equipment or (2) to acquire the new equipment. Cash flows for each alternative are scheduled below, using the net of tax approach with an assumed 50 percent tax rate. Cash flow items appear in boxes.

ELEMENTS AFFECTING CASH OUTFLOW (INFLOW)	KEEP OLD EQUIPMENT	BUY NEW EQUIPMENT
1. Cost of new equipment	—	120,000
2. Cash operating expenses	200,000	150,000
Less: 50 percent tax reduction	(100,000)	(75,000)
After-tax cash expenses	100,000	75,000
3. Annual depreciation expense	10,000	20,000
Tax reduction at 50 percent	(5,000)	(10,000)
4. Proceeds from sale of old equipment	—	(75,000)
Less: Book value of old equipment	—	60,000
Gain on sale	—	15,000
Tax on gain at 50 percent	—	7,500
5. Proceeds from sale of new equipment	—	(6,000)
Tax on gain of $6,000	—	3,000
After-tax proceeds	—	(3,000)

From the detailed analysis of cash flow effects, the following comparative summary of cash flows is prepared for each alternative. Incremental cash flows for the replacement alternative are shown in the third column.

Timing and Amount of Cash Outflow (Inflow)	Keep Old Equipment	Buy New Equipment	Incremental Cost (Benefit) of Buy Alternative
Year 1:			
Cost of new equipment	—	$120,000 ⎫	
Proceeds from sale of old equipment	—	(75,000) ⎬	$ 52,500
Tax on gain—old equipment	—	7,500 ⎭	
Annual results—Years 1–6:			
After-tax operating expenses	$100,000	$ 75,000	
Tax reduction from depreciation	(5,000)	(10,000)	
Annual cash outflow	$ 95,000	$ 65,000	$(30,000)
Year 6:			
After-tax proceeds on sale of new equipment	—	$ (3,000)	$ (3,000)

In summary form, the cash flow schedule indicates an incremental investment of $52,500 to acquire new equipment. The new equipment offers a $30,000 cash saving or benefit each year plus a $3,000 cash inflow from its ultimate sale in year 6. The incremental cash flow data can be used to measure payback, time-adjusted rate of return, or net present value of the new equipment alternative. The specific cash flows under each alternative also could be analyzed using the techniques described earlier.

FINAL NOTE

Capital expenditure decisions are difficult to evaluate. You should remember that all decision analyses are based on estimated information. In addition, management has a tendency to doubt the more sophisticated evaluation methods and may base decisions on payback period or even personal intuition. Nevertheless, better decision criteria are made available if the time value of money is incorporated into the evaluation analysis.

When you have completed your review of the appendix, return to the beginning of the chapter and review the highlights section before proceeding to the review questions, exercises, and problems.

APPENDIX 16-A: Compound Interest and Present-value Tables

Capital expenditure decision analysis relies heavily on the concept of the time-value of money. Funds deposited today that earn a stated annual rate of interest during the deposit period will accumulate to a future value which exceeds the initial deposit. In this case, tables for the "Future Value of $1" are used to compute the future value of a deposit made today.

A different type of analysis is used to determine the present value of funds to be received in future periods. In this situation, it is necessary to determine the value of those funds if received today. Their future value is known, but the present value must be computed assuming a stated interest rate. This appendix provides four tables for use in computing the future value or present value of expected cash flows.

Table 1: Future Value of $1 after Given Number of Time Periods

Table 1 provides the multipliers necessary to compute the future value of a *single* cash deposit made at the *beginning* of year 1. Three factors must be known before the future value can be computed: (1) time period in years, (2) stated annual rate of interest to be earned, and (3) dollar amount invested or deposited.

Example Determine the future value of $5,000 deposited now that will earn 9 percent interest compounded annually for five years. From Table 1, the necessary multiplier for five years at 9 percent is 1.539, and the answer is:

$$\$5,000 \ (1.539) = \underline{\underline{\$7,695}}$$

TABLE 1

FUTURE VALUE OF $1 AFTER A GIVEN NUMBER OF TIME PERIODS

PERIODS	1%	2%	3%	4%	5%	6%	7%	8%	9%	10%	12%	14%	15%
1	1.010	1.020	1.030	1.040	1.050	1.060	1.070	1.080	1.090	1.100	1.120	1.140	1.150
2	1.020	1.040	1.061	1.082	1.103	1.124	1.145	1.166	1.188	1.210	1.254	1.300	1.323
3	1.030	1.061	1.093	1.125	1.158	1.191	1.225	1.260	1.295	1.331	1.405	1.482	1.521
4	1.041	1.082	1.126	1.170	1.216	1.262	1.311	1.360	1.412	1.464	1.574	1.689	1.749
5	1.051	1.104	1.159	1.217	1.276	1.338	1.403	1.469	1.539	1.611	1.762	1.925	2.011
6	1.062	1.126	1.194	1.265	1.340	1.419	1.501	1.587	1.677	1.772	1.974	2.195	2.313
7	1.072	1.149	1.230	1.316	1.407	1.504	1.606	1.714	1.828	1.949	2.211	2.502	2.660
8	1.083	1.172	1.267	1.369	1.477	1.594	1.718	1.851	1.993	2.144	2.476	2.853	3.059
9	1.094	1.195	1.305	1.423	1.551	1.689	1.838	1.999	2.172	2.358	2.773	3.252	3.518
10	1.105	1.219	1.344	1.480	1.629	1.791	1.967	2.159	2.367	2.594	3.106	3.707	4.046
11	1.116	1.243	1.384	1.539	1.710	1.898	2.105	2.332	2.580	2.853	3.479	4.226	4.652
12	1.127	1.268	1.426	1.601	1.796	2.012	2.252	2.518	2.813	3.138	3.896	4.818	5.350
13	1.138	1.294	1.469	1.665	1.886	2.133	2.410	2.720	3.066	3.452	4.363	5.492	6.153
14	1.149	1.319	1.513	1.732	1.980	2.261	2.579	2.937	3.342	3.798	4.887	6.261	7.076
15	1.161	1.346	1.558	1.801	2.079	2.397	2.759	3.172	3.642	4.177	5.474	7.138	8.137
16	1.173	1.373	1.605	1.873	2.183	2.540	2.952	3.426	3.970	4.595	6.130	8.137	9.358
17	1.184	1.400	1.653	1.948	2.292	2.693	3.159	3.700	4.328	5.054	6.866	9.276	10.76
18	1.196	1.428	1.702	2.026	2.407	2.854	3.380	3.996	4.717	5.560	7.690	10.58	12.38
19	1.208	1.457	1.754	2.107	2.527	3.026	3.617	4.316	5.142	6.116	8.613	12.06	14.23
20	1.220	1.486	1.806	2.191	2.653	3.207	3.870	4.661	5.604	6.728	9.646	13.74	16.37
21	1.232	1.516	1.860	2.279	2.786	3.400	4.141	5.034	6.109	7.400	10.80	15.67	18.82
22	1.245	1.546	1.916	2.370	2.925	3.604	4.430	5.437	6.659	8.140	12.10	17.86	21.64
23	1.257	1.577	1.974	2.465	3.072	3.820	4.741	5.871	7.258	8.954	13.55	20.36	24.89
24	1.270	1.608	2.033	2.563	3.225	4.049	5.072	6.341	7.911	9.850	15.18	23.21	28.63
25	1.282	1.641	2.094	2.666	3.386	4.292	5.427	6.848	8.623	10.83	17.00	26.46	32.92
26	1.295	1.673	2.157	2.772	3.556	4.549	5.807	7.396	9.399	11.92	19.04	30.17	37.86
27	1.308	1.707	2.221	2.883	3.733	4.822	6.214	7.988	10.25	13.11	21.32	34.39	43.54
28	1.321	1.741	2.288	2.999	3.920	5.112	6.649	8.627	11.17	14.42	23.88	39.20	50.07
29	1.335	1.776	2.357	3.119	4.116	5.418	7.114	9.317	12.17	15.86	26.75	44.69	57.58
30	1.348	1.811	2.427	3.243	4.322	5.743	7.612	10.06	13.27	17.45	29.96	50.95	66.21
40	1.489	2.208	3.262	4.801	7.040	10.29	14.97	21.72	31.41	45.26	93.05	188.9	267.9
50	1.645	2.692	4.384	7.107	11.47	18.42	29.46	46.90	74.36	117.4	289.0	700.2	1,084

Situations requiring the use of Table 2 are similar to those requiring Table 1 except that Table 2 is used to compute the future value of a *series* of *equal* annual deposits.

Example   What will be the future value at the end of thirty years if $1,000 is deposited each year on January 1, assuming 12 percent interest compounded annually? The required multiplier from Table 2 is 241.3, and the answer is:

$$\$1,000 \ (241.3) = \underline{\$241,300}$$

TABLE 2
FUTURE VALUE OF $1 PAID IN EACH PERIOD FOR A GIVEN NUMBER OF TIME PERIODS

PERIODS	1%	2%	3%	4%	5%	6%	7%	8%	9%	10%	12%	14%	15%
1	1.000	1.000	1.000	1.000	1.000	1.000	1.000	1.000	1.000	1.000	1.000	1.000	1.000
2	2.010	2.020	2.030	2.040	2.050	2.060	2.070	2.080	2.090	2.100	2.120	2.140	2.150
3	3.030	3.060	3.091	3.122	3.153	3.184	3.215	3.246	3.278	3.310	3.374	3.440	3.473
4	4.060	4.122	4.184	4.246	4.310	4.375	4.440	4.506	4.573	4.641	4.779	4.921	4.993
5	5.101	5.204	5.309	5.416	5.526	5.637	5.751	5.867	5.985	6.105	6.353	6.610	6.742
6	6.152	6.308	6.468	6.633	6.802	6.975	7.153	7.336	7.523	7.716	8.115	8.536	8.754
7	7.214	7.434	7.662	7.898	8.142	8.394	8.654	8.923	9.200	9.487	10.09	10.73	11.07
8	8.286	8.583	8.892	9.214	9.549	9.897	10.26	10.64	11.03	11.44	12.30	13.23	13.73
9	9.369	9.755	10.16	10.58	11.03	11.49	11.98	12.49	13.02	13.58	14.78	16.09	16.79
10	10.46	10.95	11.46	12.01	12.58	13.18	13.82	14.49	15.19	15.94	17.55	19.34	20.30
11	11.57	12.17	12.81	13.49	14.21	14.97	15.78	16.65	17.56	18.53	20.65	23.04	24.35
12	12.68	13.41	14.19	15.03	15.92	16.87	17.89	18.98	20.14	21.38	24.13	27.27	29.00
13	13.81	14.68	15.62	16.63	17.71	18.88	20.14	21.50	22.95	24.52	28.03	32.09	34.35
14	14.95	15.97	17.09	18.29	19.60	21.02	22.55	24.21	26.02	27.98	32.39	37.58	40.50
15	16.10	17.29	18.60	20.02	21.58	23.28	25.13	27.15	29.36	31.77	37.28	43.84	47.58
16	17.26	18.64	20.16	21.82	23.66	25.67	27.89	30.32	33.00	35.95	42.75	50.98	55.72
17	18.43	20.01	21.76	23.70	25.84	28.21	30.84	33.75	36.97	40.54	48.88	59.12	65.08
18	19.61	21.41	23.41	25.65	28.13	30.91	34.00	37.45	41.30	45.60	55.75	68.39	75.84
19	20.81	22.84	25.12	27.67	30.54	33.76	37.38	41.45	46.02	51.16	63.44	78.97	88.21
20	22.02	24.30	26.87	29.78	33.07	36.79	41.00	45.76	51.16	57.28	72.05	91.02	102.4
21	23.24	25.78	28.68	31.97	35.72	39.99	44.87	50.42	56.76	64.00	81.70	104.8	118.8
22	24.47	27.30	30.54	34.25	38.51	43.39	49.01	55.46	62.87	71.40	92.50	120.4	137.6
23	25.72	28.85	32.45	36.62	41.43	47.00	53.44	60.89	69.53	79.54	104.6	138.3	159.3
24	26.97	30.42	34.43	39.08	44.50	50.82	58.18	66.76	76.79	88.50	118.2	158.7	184.2
25	28.24	32.03	36.46	41.65	47.73	54.86	63.25	73.11	84.70	98.35	133.3	181.9	212.8
26	29.53	33.67	38.55	44.31	51.11	59.16	68.68	79.95	93.32	109.2	150.3	208.3	245.7
27	30.82	35.34	40.71	47.08	54.67	63.71	74.48	87.35	102.7	121.1	169.4	238.5	283.6
28	32.13	37.05	42.93	49.97	58.40	68.53	80.70	95.34	113.0	134.2	190.7	272.9	327.1
29	33.45	38.79	45.22	52.97	62.32	73.64	87.35	104.0	124.1	148.6	214.6	312.1	377.2
30	34.78	40.57	47.58	56.08	66.44	79.06	94.46	113.3	136.3	164.5	241.3	356.8	434.7
40	48.89	60.40	75.40	95.03	120.8	154.8	199.6	259.1	337.9	442.6	767.1	1,342	1,779
50	64.46	84.58	112.8	152.7	209.3	290.3	406.5	573.8	815.1	1,164	2,400	4,995	7,218

Table 3: Present Value of $1 to Be Received at the End of a Given Number of Time Periods

Table 3 is used to compute the value today of a *single* amount of cash to be received sometime in the future. To use Table 3, you must first know: (1) time period in years until funds will be received, (2) annual rate of interest, and (3) dollar amount to be received at end of time period.

TABLE 3

PRESENT VALUE OF $1 TO BE RECEIVED AT THE END OF A GIVEN NUMBER OF TIME PERIODS

PERIODS	1%	2%	3%	4%	5%	6%	7%	8%	9%	10%
1	0.990	0.980	0.971	0.962	0.952	0.943	0.935	0.926	0.917	0.909
2	0.980	0.961	0.943	0.925	0.907	0.890	0.873	0.857	0.842	0.826
3	0.971	0.942	0.915	0.889	0.864	0.840	0.816	0.794	0.772	0.751
4	0.961	0.924	0.888	0.855	0.823	0.792	0.763	0.735	0.708	0.683
5	0.951	0.906	0.883	0.822	0.784	0.747	0.713	0.681	0.650	0.621
6	0.942	0.888	0.837	0.790	0.746	0.705	0.666	0.630	0.596	0.564
7	0.933	0.871	0.813	0.760	0.711	0.665	0.623	0.583	0.547	0.513
8	0.923	0.853	0.789	0.731	0.677	0.627	0.582	0.540	0.502	0.467
9	0.914	0.837	0.766	0.703	0.645	0.592	0.544	0.500	0.460	0.424
10	0.905	0.820	0.744	0.676	0.614	0.558	0.508	0.463	0.422	0.386
11	0.896	0.804	0.722	0.650	0.585	0.527	0.475	0.429	0.388	0.350
12	0.887	0.788	0.701	0.625	0.557	0.497	0.444	0.397	0.356	0.319
13	0.879	0.773	0.681	0.601	0.530	0.469	0.415	0.368	0.326	0.290
14	0.870	0.758	0.661	0.577	0.505	0.442	0.388	0.340	0.299	0.263
15	0.861	0.743	0.642	0.555	0.481	0.417	0.362	0.315	0.275	0.239
16	0.853	0.728	0.623	0.534	0.458	0.394	0.339	0.292	0.252	0.218
17	0.844	0.714	0.605	0.513	0.436	0.371	0.317	0.270	0.231	0.198
18	0.836	0.700	0.587	0.494	0.416	0.350	0.296	0.250	0.212	0.180
19	0.828	0.686	0.570	0.475	0.396	0.331	0.277	0.232	0.194	0.164
20	0.820	0.673	0.554	0.456	0.377	0.312	0.258	0.215	0.178	0.149
21	0.811	0.660	0.538	0.439	0.359	0.294	0.242	0.199	0.164	0.135
22	0.803	0.647	0.522	0.422	0.342	0.278	0.226	0.184	0.150	0.123
23	0.795	0.634	0.507	0.406	0.326	0.262	0.211	0.170	0.138	0.112
24	0.788	0.622	0.492	0.390	0.310	0.247	0.197	0.158	0.126	0.102
25	0.780	0.610	0.478	0.375	0.295	0.233	0.184	0.146	0.116	0.092
26	0.772	0.598	0.464	0.361	0.281	0.220	0.172	0.135	0.106	0.084
27	0.764	0.586	0.450	0.347	0.268	0.207	0.161	0.125	0.098	0.076
28	0.757	0.574	0.437	0.333	0.255	0.196	0.150	0.116	0.090	0.069
29	0.749	0.563	0.424	0.321	0.243	0.185	0.141	0.107	0.082	0.063
30	0.742	0.552	0.412	0.308	0.231	0.174	0.131	0.099	0.075	0.057
40	0.672	0.453	0.307	0.208	0.142	0.097	0.067	0.046	0.032	0.022
50	0.608	0.372	0.228	0.141	0.087	0.054	0.034	0.021	0.013	0.009

Example What is the present value of $30,000 to be received twenty-five years from now assuming a 14 percent interest rate? From Table 3, the required multiplier is 0.038, and the answer is:

$$\$30,000 \ (0.038) = \underline{\underline{\$1,140}}$$

12%	14%	15%	16%	18%	20%	25%	30%	35%	40%	45%	50%
0.893	0.877	0.870	0.862	0.847	0.833	0.800	0.769	0.741	0.714	0.690	0.667
0.797	0.769	0.756	0.743	0.718	0.694	0.640	0.592	0.549	0.510	0.476	0.444
0.712	0.675	0.658	0.641	0.609	0.579	0.512	0.455	0.406	0.364	0.328	0.296
0.636	0.592	0.572	0.552	0.516	0.482	0.410	0.350	0.301	0.260	0.226	0.198
0.567	0.519	0.497	0.476	0.437	0.402	0.328	0.269	0.223	0.186	0.156	0.132
0.507	0.456	0.432	0.410	0.370	0.335	0.262	0.207	0.165	0.133	0.108	0.088
0.452	0.400	0.376	0.354	0.314	0.279	0.210	0.159	0.122	0.095	0.074	0.059
0.404	0.351	0.327	0.305	0.266	0.233	0.168	0.123	0.091	0.068	0.051	0.039
0.361	0.308	0.284	0.263	0.225	0.194	0.134	0.094	0.067	0.048	0.035	0.026
0.322	0.270	0.247	0.227	0.191	0.162	0.107	0.073	0.050	0.035	0.024	0.017
0.287	0.237	0.215	0.195	0.162	0.135	0.086	0.056	0.037	0.025	0.017	0.012
0.257	0.208	0.187	0.168	0.137	0.112	0.069	0.043	0.027	0.018	0.012	0.008
0.229	0.182	0.163	0.145	0.116	0.093	0.055	0.033	0.020	0.013	0.008	0.005
0.205	0.160	0.141	0.125	0.099	0.078	0.044	0.025	0.015	0.009	0.006	0.003
0.183	0.140	0.123	0.108	0.084	0.065	0.035	0.020	0.011	0.006	0.004	0.002
0.163	0.123	0.107	0.093	0.071	0.054	0.028	0.015	0.008	0.005	0.003	0.002
0.146	0.108	0.093	0.080	0.060	0.045	0.023	0.012	0.006	0.003	0.002	0.001
0.130	0.095	0.081	0.069	0.051	0.038	0.018	0.009	0.005	0.002	0.001	0.001
0.116	0.083	0.070	0.060	0.043	0.031	0.014	0.007	0.003	0.002	0.001	
0.104	0.073	0.061	0.051	0.037	0.026	0.012	0.005	0.002	0.001	0.001	
0.093	0.064	0.053	0.044	0.031	0.022	0.009	0.004	0.002	0.001		
0.083	0.056	0.046	0.038	0.026	0.018	0.007	0.003	0.001	0.001		
0.074	0.049	0.040	0.033	0.022	0.015	0.006	0.002	0.001			
0.066	0.043	0.035	0.028	0.019	0.013	0.005	0.002	0.001			
0.059	0.038	0.030	0.024	0.016	0.010	0.004	0.001	0.001			
0.053	0.033	0.026	0.021	0.014	0.009	0.003	0.001				
0.047	0.029	0.023	0.018	0.011	0.007	0.002	0.001				
0.042	0.026	0.020	0.016	0.010	0.006	0.002	0.001				
0.037	0.022	0.017	0.014	0.008	0.005	0.002					
0.033	0.020	0.015	0.012	0.007	0.004	0.001					
0.011	0.005	0.004	0.003	0.001	0.001						
0.003	0.001	0.001	0.001								

Table 4: Present Value of $1 Received Each Period for a Given Number of Time Periods

Table 4 is used to compute the present value of a *series* of *equal* annual cash flows.

Example   Arthur Howard won a contest on January 1, 1980, in which the prize was $30,000 payable in fifteen annual installments of $2,000 every December 31, beginning in 1980. Assuming a 9 percent interest rate, what is the present value of Mr. Howard's prize on January 1, 1980? From Table 4, the required multiplier is 8.061, and the answer is:

$$\$2,000\ (8.061) = \underline{\$16,122}$$

TABLE 4

PRESENT VALUE OF $1 RECEIVED EACH PERIOD FOR A GIVEN NUMBER OF TIME PERIODS

PERIODS	1%	2%	3%	4%	5%	6%	7%	8%	9%	10%
1	0.990	0.980	0.971	0.962	0.952	0.943	0.935	0.926	0.917	0.909
2	1.970	1.942	1.913	1.886	1.859	1.833	1.808	1.783	1.759	1.736
3	2.941	2.884	2.829	2.775	2.723	2.673	2.624	2.577	2.531	2.487
4	3.902	3.808	3.717	3.630	3.546	3.465	3.387	3.312	3.240	3.170
5	4.853	4.713	4.580	4.452	4.329	4.212	4.100	3.993	3.890	3.791
6	5.795	5.601	5.417	5.242	5.076	4.917	4.767	4.623	4.486	4.355
7	6.728	6.472	6.230	6.002	5.786	5.582	5.389	5.206	5.033	4.868
8	7.652	7.325	7.020	6.733	6.463	6.210	5.971	5.747	5.535	5.335
9	8.566	8.162	7.786	7.435	7.108	6.802	6.515	6.247	5.995	5.759
10	9.471	8.983	8.530	8.111	7.722	7.360	7.024	6.710	6.418	6.145
11	10.368	9.787	9.253	8.760	8.306	7.887	7.499	7.139	6.805	6.495
12	11.255	10.575	9.954	9.385	8.863	8.384	7.943	7.536	7.161	6.814
13	12.134	11.348	10.635	9.986	9.394	8.853	8.358	7.904	7.487	7.103
14	13.004	12.106	11.296	10.563	9.899	9.295	8.745	8.244	7.786	7.367
15	13.865	12.849	11.938	11.118	10.380	9.712	9.108	8.559	8.061	7.606
16	14.718	13.578	12.561	11.652	10.838	10.106	9.447	8.851	8.313	7.824
17	15.562	14.292	13.166	12.166	11.274	10.477	9.763	9.122	8.544	8.022
18	16.398	14.992	13.754	12.659	11.690	10.828	10.059	9.372	8.756	8.201
19	17.226	15.678	14.324	13.134	12.085	11.158	10.336	9.604	8.950	8.365
20	18.046	16.351	14.878	13.590	12.462	11.470	10.594	9.818	9.129	8.514
21	18.857	17.011	15.415	14.029	12.821	11.764	10.836	10.017	9.292	8.649
22	19.660	17.658	15.937	14.451	13.163	12.042	11.061	10.201	9.442	8.772
23	20.456	18.292	16.444	14.857	13.489	12.303	11.272	10.371	9.580	8.883
24	21.243	18.914	16.936	15.247	13.799	12.550	11.469	10.529	9.707	8.985
25	22.023	19.523	17.413	15.622	14.094	12.783	11.654	10.675	9.823	9.077
26	22.795	20.121	17.877	15.983	14.375	13.003	11.826	10.810	9.929	9.161
27	23.560	20.707	18.327	16.330	14.643	13.211	11.987	10.935	10.027	9.237
28	24.316	21.281	18.764	16.663	14.898	13.406	12.137	11.051	10.116	9.307
29	25.066	21.844	19.189	16.984	15.141	13.591	12.278	11.158	10.198	9.370
30	25.808	22.396	19.600	17.292	15.373	13.765	12.409	11.258	10.274	9.427
40	32.835	27.355	23.115	19.793	17.159	15.046	13.332	11.925	10.757	9.779
50	39.196	31.424	25.730	21.482	18.256	15.762	13.801	12.234	10.962	9.915

Table 4 applies to *ordinary annuities*, in which the first cash flow occurs one time period beyond the date for which present value is to be computed. An *annuity due* is a series of equal cash flows for N time periods, but the first payment occurs immediately. The present value of the first payment equals the face value of the cash flow; Table 4 then is used to measure the present value of N − 1 remaining cash flows.

Example   Determine the present value on January 1, 1980, of twenty lease payments; each payment of $10,000 is due on January 1, beginning in 1980. Assume an interest rate of 8 percent:

12%	14%	15%	16%	18%	20%	25%	30%	35%	40%	45%	50%
0.893	0.877	0.870	0.862	0.847	0.833	0.800	0.769	0.741	0.714	0.690	0.667
1.690	1.647	1.626	1.605	1.566	1.528	1.440	1.361	1.289	1.224	1.165	1.111
2.402	2.322	2.283	2.246	2.174	2.106	1.952	1.816	1.696	1.589	1.493	1.407
3.037	2.914	2.855	2.798	2.690	2.589	2.362	2.166	1.997	1.849	1.720	1.605
3.605	3.433	3.352	3.274	3.127	2.991	2.689	2.436	2.220	2.035	1.876	1.737
4.111	3.889	3.784	3.685	3.498	3.326	2.951	2.643	2.385	2.168	1.983	1.824
4.564	4.288	4.160	4.039	3.812	3.605	3.161	2.802	2.508	2.263	2.057	1.883
4.968	4.639	4.487	4.344	4.078	3.837	3.329	2.925	2.598	2.331	2.109	1.922
5.328	4.946	4.772	4.607	4.303	4.031	3.463	3.019	2.665	2.379	2.144	1.948
5.650	5.216	5.019	4.833	4.494	4.192	3.571	3.092	2.715	2.414	2.168	1.965
5.938	5.453	5.234	5.029	4.656	4.327	3.656	3.147	2.752	2.438	2.185	1.977
6.194	5.660	5.421	5.197	4.793	4.439	3.725	3.190	2.779	2.456	2.197	1.985
6.424	5.842	5.583	5.342	4.910	4.533	3.780	3.223	2.799	2.469	2.204	1.990
6.628	6.002	5.724	5.468	5.008	4.611	3.824	3.249	2.814	2.478	2.210	1.993
6.811	6.142	5.847	5.575	5.092	4.675	3.859	3.268	2.825	2.484	2.214	1.995
6.974	6.265	5.954	5.669	5.162	4.730	3.887	3.283	2.834	2.489	2.216	1.997
7.120	6.373	6.047	5.749	5.222	4.775	3.910	3.295	2.840	2.492	2.218	1.998
7.250	6.467	6.128	5.818	5.273	4.812	3.928	3.304	2.844	2.494	2.219	1.999
7.366	6.550	6.198	5.877	5.316	4.844	3.942	3.311	2.848	2.496	2.220	1.999
7.469	6.623	6.259	5.929	5.353	4.870	3.954	3.316	2.850	2.497	2.221	1.999
7.562	6.687	6.312	5.973	5.384	4.891	3.963	3.320	2.852	2.498	2.221	2.000
7.645	6.743	6.359	6.011	5.410	4.909	3.970	3.323	2.853	2.498	2.222	2.000
7.718	6.792	6.399	6.044	5.432	4.925	3.976	3.325	2.854	2.499	2.222	2.000
7.784	6.835	6.434	6.073	5.451	4.937	3.981	3.327	2.855	2.499	2.222	2.000
7.843	6.873	6.464	6.097	5.467	4.948	3.985	3.329	2.856	2.499	2.222	2.000
7.896	6.906	6.491	6.118	5.480	4.956	3.988	3.330	2.856	2.500	2.222	2.000
7.943	6.935	6.514	6.136	5.492	4.964	3.990	3.331	2.856	2.500	2.222	2.000
7.984	6.961	6.534	6.152	5.502	4.970	3.992	3.331	2.857	2.500	2.222	2.000
8.022	6.983	6.551	6.166	5.510	4.975	3.994	3.332	2.857	2.500	2.222	2.000
8.055	7.003	6.566	6.177	5.517	4.979	3.995	3.332	2.857	2.500	2.222	2.000
8.244	7.105	6.642	6.234	5.548	4.997	3.999	3.333	2.857	2.500	2.222	2.000
8.305	7.133	6.661	6.246	5.554	4.999	4.000	3.333	2.857	2.500	2.222	2.000

$$\text{present value} = \text{immediate payment} + \begin{array}{c} \text{present value of 19} \\ \text{subsequent payments at 8\%} \end{array}$$

$$= \$10,000 \qquad + [\$10,000 \, (9.604)]$$

$$= \underline{\underline{\$106,040}}$$

QUESTIONS

16-1. Define and illustrate the following terms and concepts:
   a. Capital expenditure
   b. Time value of money
   c. Time-adjusted rate of return
   d. Discounted cash flow
   e. Payback period
   f. Present value
   g. Net present value
   h. Accounting rate of return
   i. Acceptance-rejection standard
   j. Postcompletion audit
   k. Opportunity cost
   l. Annuity

16-2. Distinguish between cost savings and net cash flow.

16-3. Explain the relationship of compound interest in the determination of present value.

16-4. Discuss the interrelationships of the following steps in the capital facility decision process:
   a. Determination of dollar amount available
   b. Final selection of alternatives
   c. Final evaluation of proposals

16-5. "In measuring project profitability, accounting rate of return does not consider the time value of money." Explain this statement.

16-6. In evaluating equipment replacement decisions with time-adjusted rate of return measures, what is the justification for ignoring depreciation on old equipment?

16-7. What analytical adjustments must be made when evaluating two capital expenditure proposals having unequal lives?

16-8. A company uses time-adjusted rate of return in evaluating investments in new equipment.
   a. What is the justification for ignoring depreciation expense on new equipment?
   b. Explain the relevance of depreciation expense regarding income taxes.

16-9. Why are tax considerations so important in the process of evaluating proposed capital expenditures?

16-10. What is the role of cost of capital in using time-adjusted rate of return to evaluate capital expenditure proposals?

16-11. Can a company use the same project evaluation techniques (payback, discounted cash flow, rate of return, etc.) for project planning and postcompletion audit analyses? What measurement problems are involved in analyzing actual performance for projects that have been selected and implemented?

16-12. "In using discounted cash flow methods, book value of existing assets is irrelevant, but current and future salvage values are relevant." Is this statement valid? Defend your answer.

16-13. "The time-adjusted rate of return on a specific project is estimated at 18 percent." Does this statement mean that annual net cash flow will equal 18 percent of initial project cost? Explain.

16-14. What are the advantages and disadvantages of the payback period as a technique for project evaluation?

16-15. "In ranking capital expenditure proposals, profitability indicators such as time-adjusted rate of return, net present value, and the present value index should be approached with caution." Discuss this statement.

EXERCISES

16-16. *Selection of Relevant Costs* Harry R. Bunch & Sons is a scrap metal company that supplies area steel companies with recycled materials. The company collects scrap metal, sorts and cleans the material, and compresses it into 4,000-pound blocks for easy handling. Increased demand for recycled metals has caused Mr. Bunch to consider purchasing an additional metal compressing machine. He has narrowed the choice down to the two models shown below, and the accountant has gathered the information related to each model:

	MODEL 1742	MODEL 2961
Purchase price	$25,000	$30,000
Estimated useful life	10 years	10 years
Salvage value	$ 3,000	$ 5,000
Annual depreciation*	$ 2,200	$ 2,500
Resulting increases in:		
Annual sales	$43,000	$50,000
Annual operating costs:		
Raw materials	15,000	17,500
Direct labor	10,000	10,000
Operating supplies	900	1,000
Indirect labor	6,000	9,000
Insurance and taxes	400	500
Plant rental	2,000	2,000
Electrical expense	250	280
Miscellaneous overhead	1,250	1,420

* Computed by straight-line method.

REQUIRED:

a. Identify the cost and revenues relevant to the decision.

b. Prepare an incremental cash flow analysis for year one.

16-17. *Capital Expenditure Decision Analysis*

REQUIRED: Using the data from exercise 16-16, compute the following for each alternative:

a. Payback period

b. Accounting rate of return

c. Present value of cash flows (assuming 16 percent minimum desired rate of return)

16-18. *Discussion Exercise—Conflicts in Responsibilities* Overprudent Company utilizes an organizational structure containing two separate and distinct planning positions—a budget director and a long-term planning director.

Mr. S. Edwards, the budget director, is responsible for the development of the company's annual profit plan.

Mr. A. Douglas, the long-term planning director, is responsible for (a) the development and maintenance of the company's ten-year master plan and (b) the coordination and screening of proposed capital expenditure projects.

Since the inception of the program, Edwards and Douglas have been competing for staff and dollar resources. Each is trying to show top management that his department is the most important. The result has been overenlargement of staff and a burdensome supply of paper flow and memo reports to other members of the organization. In addition, Edwards is not coordinating short-term plans with the master plan.

In a recent planning strategy meeting, the president, Ms. B. Lyle, questioned the inability of the planning directors to successfully integrate their activities. Edwards continued to maintain that company resources should be directed toward short-term planning activities because they are more relevant to the current success of the company. Douglas held his ground, stating that long-term planning and implementation was the only way to keep ahead of competition.

REQUIRED: If you were the president, what would you do to ease the situation between the planning directors?

16-19. *Accounting Rate of Return* In 19X4, Sanders Company plans to replace fully depreciated equipment with new and more efficient machinery. The old equipment will be sold at a gain of $6,000, and $65,000 will be invested in machinery having a fifteen-year useful life with salvage value of $5,000. Material and labor costs with the new model will decrease $13,000 per year, but annual maintenance expenses will be $3,000 higher. Sanders Company uses straight-line depreciation with consideration of salvage values.

REQUIRED:

a. Ignoring income taxes, compute the accounting method rate of return for the investment in new machinery using both initial investment and average investment.

b. Using a 48 percent tax rate, compute the accounting method rate of return based on initial investment.

c. In part (a), which measure best approximates the time-adjusted rate of return?

16-20. *Payback Period Analysis* Greynolds Time-Sharing, Inc., is a data-processing service company. Primary emphasis of the company is on providing monthly and annual business information summaries for small and medium-sized manufacturing companies.

The company is negotiating the purchase of a deluxe card-sorting machine. Data relevant to the decision are shown below:

	MACHINE H	MACHINE M
Cost	$47,000	$52,000
Useful life	10 years	10 years
Salvage value	$ 2,000	$ 4,000
Estimated annual net cash inflow	$16,000	$16,500

REQUIRED:

a. Compute the payback period for each alternative.

b. Using the payback reciprocal approach, compute the annual rate of return for machines H and M.

c. Based on your payback analyses, which machine should the company purchase?

16-21. *Net Present Value* The final packaging operation for products of Leathers, Inc., can be performed by either labor or machinery. Labor currently is used, at an annual cost of $480,000. In addition, annual supervisory salaries of $60,000 are incurred by the packing department. Equipment to perform the packaging operation will cost $1,100,000 and will have a ten-year useful life. Estimated cash maintenance expenses for the equipment are $200,000, but the $480,000 labor cost will be eliminated if equipment is used. With labor or equipment, supervisory salaries are $60,000 annually. Minimum desired rate of return is 10 percent.

REQUIRED (Ignore income taxes):

a. Compute the present value of net cash flows for a ten-year period for both packaging alternatives.

b. Using incremental cash flows, compute the net present value of the equipment alternative.

c. Explain the relationship between your results in parts (a) and (b).

16-22. *Ranking Capital Expenditure Proposals* Management of the Prestonwood Furniture Company is ready to make final capital expenditure selections for 19X6. The following proposals and related rate of return amounts were received during the period:

PROJECT	INITIAL INVESTMENT	TIME-ADJUSTED RATE OF RETURN
A2	$ 225,000	19%
A4	250,000	34%
B2	327,000	12%
B7	400,000	28%
C2	160,000	22%
D6	120,000	18%
E5	90,000	16%
F2	200,000	26%
G1	280,000	14%
G5	600,000	23%
H9	800,000	20%
	$3,452,000	

REQUIRED: Assuming that the company's minimum desired rate of return is 15 percent and that $2,500,000 are available for capital expenditures in 19X6,
a. List the capital expenditure proposals in order of profitability.
b. Which proposals will be selected for 19X6?

16-23. *Retain Old Machine or Buy New Machine* Wakefielder Corporation purchased a large printing press five years ago at a cost of $150,000. Useful life of this machine is fifteen years, after which it will have an estimated $2,000 salvage value. During the current year, a "super" new printing press that is 50 percent more productive has come on the market. This new machine sells for $250,000, and has a useful life of ten years; its disposal value is $10,000 at the end of year ten. The old machine has a current market value of $60,000.

The controller developed the following information regarding the two machines:

	OLD MACHINE	NEW MACHINE
Annual cash revenues	$100,000	$150,000
Annual cash repair and maintenance costs	8,000	2,000
Annual cash operating costs other than repairs and maintenance	62,000	78,000

The company's minimum desired rate of return is 14 percent.

REQUIRED:
a. Using present value analysis, justify the decision to either keep the old machine or sell the old machine and purchase the new machine.
b. Compute the rate of return of the new machine, using the time-adjusted rate of return approach.

16-24. *CPA Problem—Present Value Analysis*   Madisons, Inc., has decided to acquire a new piece of equipment. It may do so by an outright cash purchase of $25,000 or by a leasing alternative of $6,000 per year for the life of the machine. Other relevant information follows:

Purchase price due at time of purchase	$25,000
Estimated useful life	5 years
Estimated salvage value if purchased	$3,000
Annual cost of maintenance contract to be acquired with either lease or purchase	$500

The full purchase price of $25,000 could be borrowed from the bank at 10 percent annual interest and could be repaid in one payment at the end of the fifth year. Additional information follows:

a. Assume a 40 percent income tax rate and use of the straight-line method of depreciation.
b. The yearly lease rental and maintenance contract fees would be paid at the beginning of each year.
c. The minimum desired rate of return on investment is 10 percent.
d. All cash flows, unless otherwise stated, are assumed to occur at the end of the year.

Selected present value factors for a 10 percent return are given below:

YEAR	PRESENT VALUE OF $1 RECEIVED AT END OF YEAR
0	1.000
1	.909
2	.826
3	.751
4	.683
5	.621

REQUIRED:
a. The present value of the purchase price of the machine is:
   1. $25,000   4. $2,500
   2. $22,725   5. None of the above
   3. $22,500
b. Under the purchase alternative the present value of the estimated salvage value is:
   1. $3,000   4. $0
   2. $2,049   5. None of the above
   3. $1,863
c. Under the purchase alternative the annual cash *inflow* (tax reduction) related to depreciation is:
   1. $5,000   4. $1,760
   2. $4,400   5. None of the above
   3. $2,640

d. Under the purchase alternative the annual after-tax cash outflow for interest and maintenance is:
   1. $3,000   4. $1,200
   2. $2,500   5. None of the above
   3. $1,800
e. If salvage value is not ignored, the before-tax interest rate implicit in the lease contract is:
   1. 20 percent or more
   2. More than 10 percent but less than 20 percent
   3. Precisely 10 percent
   4. Less than 10 percent
   5. Not determinable from the above facts

(AICPA adapted)

PROBLEMS

16-25. *Joint Products and Plant Expansion*   Saline Chemicals manufactures products X and Y, which are sold by the pound to other industrial firms. Products X and Y are joint products and become separately identifiable at the end of processing in Department 5A. In 19X4 and prior years, product X was transferred to Department 6B for additional processing, while product Y was sold at split-off for seven dollars per unit. Production and sales volumes in 19X4 were 80,000 units of X and 120,000 units of Y. Product X is not salable at split-off but sells for ten dollars per unit after additional processing. Department 6B worked only on product X in 19X4. Departmental cost summaries for 19X4 operations appear below:

TOTAL 19X4 COSTS	DEPARTMENT 5A	DEPARTMENT 6B
Direct materials	$700,000	$ 20,000
Direct labor	50,000	40,000
Factory overhead:		
Traceable to department	175,000	70,000
Allocated general	75,000	30,000
Total costs incurred	$1,000,000	$160,000

Materials added in Department 6B did not increase the units of product X.

Management believes that a more profitable market for product Y exists if certain refining operations could be performed. Additional processing of Y could be accomplished in Department 6B by expanding equipment capacity and adding supervisory personnel. Capacity expansion requires the purchase of special equipment costing $800,000. This machinery has a useful life of ten years and no expected salvage value. Straight-line depreciation is used for all machinery. The controller's staff has prepared the following 19X5 production cost budget for Department 6B, which reflects the increased costs expected from processing 120,000 pounds of product Y in addition to the normal 80,000 pound volume of product X:

19X5 Cost Budget	Department 6B
Materials	$ 90,000
Direct labor	80,000
Factory overhead:	
Traceable to department	80,000
Allocated general	60,000
Depreciation—new equipment	80,000
	$390,000

Materials used in additional processing of Y will not increase the number of units produced. Product Y can be sold for nine dollars a pound after processing in Department 6B. For inventory purposes, the company will continue to allocate joint costs in Department 5A on the basis of physical volume. Inventory levels at year-end are not significant.

REQUIRED:

a. Prepare a schedule disclosing the annual incremental costs of additional processing for product Y.
b. Prepare a pro forma income statement showing annual revenues and related costs for the two sell or process-further decision alternatives.
c. Determine whether plant expansion is desirable if the company's minimum desired return on investment is 20 percent.

16-26. *Capital Expenditure Analysis—Comparison of Methods* Horningshield Enterprises, Inc., produces firearms. Sales have been increasing at a high annual rate, and company officials are expanding productive capacity. Two stamping machines are being analyzed for possible purchase; their data follow:

	Machine ABC	Machine DEF
Cost	$155,000	$210,000
End-of-life salvage value	$ 5,000	$ 10,000
Market value during life	80% of book value	80% of book value
Estimated annual increase in sales	$100,000	$125,000
Estimated annual increase in cash operating costs:		
Raw materials	40,000	50,000
Direct labor	20,000	25,000
Other operating costs	16,000	18,000
Useful life	20 years	20 years

The company uses the straight-line depreciation method and seeks a 12 percent minimum desired rate of return.

REQUIRED:

a. Which machine should the company purchase? Include in your analysis the following computations for each alternative:
   1. Accounting rate of return
   2. Payback period
   3. Payback reciprocal
   4. Bailout payback
   5. Time-adjusted rate of return
   6. Net present value
   7. Present value index
b. Prepare an incremental analysis of the two alternatives using the present value approach.

16-27. *Projects with Unequal Lives* The Athletic Department at State University is planning to purchase an executive aircraft for use in scouting and recruiting activities. Since the department must generate all funds it spends, the director is concerned with efficiency and cost-benefit analysis supporting all capital expenditures.

Two aircraft models are under consideration. The Duke plane costs $200,000 and has a useful life of six years. Salvage value at the end of six years is $80,000, and a major overhaul costing $8,000 is needed at the end of each three-year period.

A competing model, the Viceroy, costs $230,000 and will last eight years. A major overhaul on this plane costs $10,000 and is required at the end of each four-year period. Salvage values on the Viceroy are $100,000 after six years or $90,000 after eight years.

If either plane is sold after nine years or more, expected proceeds are $50,000. The athletic department can rent either plane to other university departments for $20,000 a year. Operating expenditures for each plane are compared below:

ANNUAL OUTLAYS	DUKE	VICEROY
Maintenance	$10,000	$ 5,000
Pilot salaries	30,000	26,000
Insurance	5,000	9,000
Fuel	15,000	10,000

A 10 percent interest rate is used in all capital facility evaluations.

REQUIRED:

a. Compute the present value of net cash flows for each alternative over the six-year useful life of the Duke plane.
b. Compute the present value of net cash flows for each alternative over a common time frame of twenty-four years. Assume periodic replacements for each plane at the end of its useful life.
c. Review your analysis in parts (a) and (b) and write a brief recommendation to the departmental director specifying the minimum cost alternative.

16-28. *Even and Uneven Cash Flows* Frisbee and Newkirk, Inc., own and operate a group of apartment buildings. Management is considering selling one of its older four-family buildings and replacing it with a new facility. The old building was purchased fifteen years ago for $160,000, had a forty-year life, and has a current market value of $90,000. Annual net income before taxes on the old building is expected to average $16,000 for the remainder of its life.

The new apartment building being considered for purchase will cost $225,000 and will have a useful life of twenty-five years. Net income before taxes is expected to be as follows:

Years	Annual Net Income
1–10	$20,000
11–15	15,000
16–25	10,000

In your analysis, assume that all cash flows occur at year-end, that the company uses a straight-line depreciation method, and that the minimum desired rate of return is 16 percent.

REQUIRED:

a. What is the net present value of the future cash flows from the old building?
b. Compute the net present value of the cash flows resulting from the purchase of the new building.
c. Using an incremental approach, compute the net present value of purchasing the new facility.
d. Should the company keep the old building or purchase the new one?

16-29. *Income Taxes and Project Planning*   Western Movies Corporation is planning to construct and operate a theater in Denver. Land for the building costs $100,000, and $3,000,000 is required for equipment, seating facilities, and the theater building. The composite useful life of depreciable assets is fifteen years, and salvage value is to be ignored. Western Corporation will arrange film distribution, and the Denver theater manager will be responsible for local advertising and profitability. The Denver location is allowed to retain a working cash balance of $200,000, and excess cash balances are remitted to Western headquarters in Santa Fe.

Expected operating results for the Denver theater are presented in the following pro forma income statement:

WESTERN MOVIES, DENVER
Pro forma annual profits

Concessions and admissions		$2,000,000
Salaries and supplies	$300,000	
Film rentals	440,000	
Depreciation expense	200,000	
Other expenses	160,000	(1,100,000)
Income before taxes		$ 900,000
State and federal taxes (50%)		(450,000)
Net income		$ 450,000

Revenue growth attributable to volume and price increases is expected to equal anticipated cost increases for the Denver location.

REQUIRED:

a. Using the net of tax approach, prepare a schedule of annual operating cash flows.
b. Compute the time-adjusted rate of return for the planned Denver investment.
c. For the first year of operations, depreciation under the sum of the year's digits method would be $375,000. Determine the effect on net income and operating cash flows in year 1 using this method instead of straight-line depreciation.

16-30. *CPA Problem—Capital Expenditure Decision* During your examination of the financial statements of Benjamin Industries, the president requested your assistance in the evaluation of several financial management problems in his home appliances division, which he summarized for you as follows:

a. Management wants to determine the best sales price for a new appliance that has a variable cost of four dollars per unit. The sales manager has estimated probabilities of achieving annual sales levels for various selling prices as shown below:

| SALES LEVEL | SELLING PRICE | | | |
(UNITS)	$4	$5	$6	$7
20,000	—	—	20%	80%
30,000	—	10%	40%	20%
40,000	50%	50%	20%	—
50,000	50%	40%	20%	—

b. The division's current profit rate is 5 percent on annual sales of $1,200,000; an investment of $400,000 is needed to finance these sales. The company's basis for measuring divisional success is return on investment (net income ÷ investment).
c. Management also is considering the following two alternative plans submitted by employees for improving operations in the home appliances division:

   1. Green believes that sales volume can be doubled by greater promotional effort, but this method would lower the profit rate to 4 percent of sales and require an additional investment of $100,000.
   2. Gold favors eliminating some unprofitable appliances and improving efficiency by adding $200,000 in capital equipment. His methods would decrease sales volume by 10 percent but improve the profit rate to 7 percent.

d. Black, White, and Gray, three franchised home appliance dealers, have requested short-term financing from the company. The dealers have agreed to repay the loans within three years and to pay Benjamin Industries 5 percent of net income for the three-year period for the use of the funds. The following table summarizes by dealer the financing requested and the total remittances (principal plus 5 percent of net income) expected at the end of each year:

	BLACK	WHITE	GRAY
Financing requested	$ 80,000	$40,000	$30,000
Remittances expected at end of:			
Year 1	$ 10,000	$25,000	$10,000
Year 2	40,000	30,000	15,000
Year 3	70,000	5,000	15,000
	$120,000	$60,000	$40,000

Management believes these financing requests should be granted only if the annual before-tax return to the company exceeds the target internal rate of 20 percent on investment. Discount factors (rounded) that would provide this 20 percent rate of return are:

Year 1	.8
Year 2	.7
Year 3	.6

REQUIRED:
a. Prepare a schedule computing the expected incremental income for each of the sales prices proposed for the new product. The schedule should include the expected sales levels in units (weighted according to the sales manager's estimated probabilities), the expected total monetary sales, expected variable costs, and the expected incremental income.
b. Prepare schedules computing (1) the company's current rate of return on investment in the home appliances division, (2) the anticipated rate of return under the alternative suggested by Green, and (3) the anticipated rate of return under Gold's alternative.
c. Prepare a schedule to compute the net present value of the investment opportunities of financing Black, White, and Gray. The schedule should determine whether the discounted cash flows expected from (1) Black, (2) White, and (3) Gray would be more or less than the amounts of Benjamin Industries' investment in loans to each of the three dealers.

(AICPA adapted)

16-31. *CMA Problem—Capital Expenditure Analysis* Baxter Company manufactures toys and other short-lived items. The research and development department came up with an item that would make a good promotional gift for the office equipment dealers. Aggressive and effective effort by Baxter's sales personnel has resulted in almost firm commitments for this product for the next three years. It is expected that the product's value will be exhausted by that time.

In order to produce the quantity demanded, Baxter will need to buy additional machinery and rent some additional space. It appears that about 25,000 square feet will be needed; 12,500 square feet of presently unused, but leased, space is available now. (Baxter's present lease with ten years to run costs three dollars per foot.) There is another 12,500 square feet adjoining the Baxter facility that Baxter will rent for three years at four dollars per square foot per year if it decides to make this product.

The equipment will be purchased for about $900,000. It will require $30,000 in modifications, $60,000 for installation, and $90,000 for testing. All these activities will be done by a firm of engineers hired by Baxter. All expenditures will be paid for on January 1, 19X3. The equipment should have a salvage value of about $180,000 at the end of the third year. No additional general overhead costs are expected to be incurred.

The following estimates of revenues and expenses for this product for the three years have been developed:

	19X3	19X4	19X5
Sales	$1,000,000	$1,600,000	$800,000
Material, labor, and incurred overhead	$ 400,000	$ 750,000	$350,000
Assigned general overhead	40,000	75,000	35,000
Rent	87,500	87,500	87,500
Depreciation	450,000	300,000	150,000
	$ 977,500	$1,212,500	$622,500
Income before taxes	$ 22,500	$ 387,500	$177,500
Income tax (40%)	9,000	155,000	71,000
Net income	$ 13,500	$ 232,500	$106,500

REQUIRED:

a. Prepare a schedule that shows the incremental after-tax cash flows for this project.
b. If the company requires a two-year payback period for its investment, would it undertake this project? Show your supporting calculations clearly.
c. Calculate the after-tax accounting rate of return for the project.
d. A newly hired business school graduate recommends that the company consider the use of the net present value analysis to study this project. If the company sets a required rate of return of 20 percent after taxes, will this project be accepted? Show your supporting calculations clearly. (Assume all operating revenues and expenses occur at year-end.)

(IMA adapted)

16-32. *CMA Problem—Capital Expenditure Decision* Beta Corporation manufactures office equipment and distributes its products through wholesale distributors. The corporation recently learned of a patent on the production of a semiautomatic paper collator that can be obtained at a cost of $60,000 cash. The semiautomatic model is vastly superior to the manual model that the corporation now produces. At a cost of $40,000, present equipment could be modified to accommodate the production of the semiautomatic model. Such modifications would not affect the remaining useful life of four years or the salvage value of $10,000 that the equipment now has. Variable costs, however, would increase by one dollar per unit. Fixed costs, other than relevant amortization charges, would not be affected. If the equipment is modified, the manual model cannot be produced.

The current income statement relative to the manual collator appears below:

Sales (100,000 units at $4)		$400,000
Variable costs	$180,000	
Fixed costs*	120,000	
Total costs		300,000
Net income before income taxes		$100,000
Income taxes (40%)		40,000
Net income after income taxes		$ 60,000

* All fixed costs are directly allocable to the production of the manual collator and include depreciation on equipment of $20,000, calculated on the straight-line basis with a useful life of ten years.

Market research has disclosed three important findings relative to the semiautomatic model. First, a particular competitor will certainly purchase the patent if Beta Corporation does not. If this were to happen, Beta Corporation's sales of the manual collator would fall to 70,000 units per year. Second, if no increase in the selling price is made, Beta Corporation could sell approximately 190,000 units per year of the semiautomatic model. Third, because of the advances being made in this area, the patent will be completely worthless at the end of four years.

Because of the uncertainty of the current situation, the inventory of raw materials has been almost completely exhausted. Regardless of the decision reached, substantial and immediate inventory replenishment will be required. The engineering department estimates that if the new model is to be produced, the average monthly Raw Materials inventory will be $20,000. If the old model is continued, the inventory balance will average $12,000 per month.

REQUIRED:

a. Prepare a schedule that shows the incremental after-tax cash flows for the comparison of the two alternatives. Assume that the corporation will use the sum of the year's digits method for depreciating the costs of modifying the equipment.

b. Assuming that the incremental after-tax cash flows calculated in part (a) and the annual incomes for the two alternatives are as given in the following schedule, will Beta Corporation—if it has a cost of capital of 18 percent—decide to manufacture the semiautomatic collator? Use the net present value decision rule and assume all operating revenues and expenses occur at year-end.

| Year | Incremental Cash Flow (000s Omitted) | Annual Income (000s Omitted) | |
		Manual	Semiautomatic
1 (beginning)	− $110	—	—
1 (end)	+ 40	$24	$39
2 (end)	+ 40	24	39
3 (end)	+ 40	24	39
4 (end)	+ 50	24	39

c. Calculate the accounting rate of return for each project. Using this method, would you recommend that Beta manufacture the semiautomatic collator? Explain.

d. What additional analytical techniques, if any, would you consider before presenting a recommendation to management? Why?

e. What concerns would you have about using the information, as given in the problem, to reach a decision in this case?

(IMA adapted)

Chapter 17: Divisional Performance Evaluation

Management accounting applies concepts and techniques to formulate information used by managers in planning and controlling company operations. Many of these concepts and techniques involve the full range of company operations and related planning or control of short-run or long-run activities. Other techniques, such as responsibility accounting, focus on cost centers and other distinct company segments.

This chapter presents several concepts and techniques for evaluating the operating performance of company segments. The principal segment discussed and used in illustrations is a *division*, which generally produces and sells products and invests in capital facilities but may or may not manage its own capital structure.

Upon completion of this chapter, students should be able to:

1. Identify the characteristics of decentralized management
2. Apply the contribution approach to compute several different profit measures for divisions
3. Distinguish between proper and improper applications of return on investment for segments
4. Evaluate intracompany transfer pricing policies and related decision problems

The following basic concepts are introduced in this chapter:

Performance evaluation The application of appropriate financial measurement techniques designed to compare actual results and expectations so that performance can be evaluated and judged.

Profit center A segment of company operations that has revenue and cost responsibility.

Investment center A segment of company operations that has responsibility for revenues earned, costs incurred, and assets employed.

Relevant Concepts

Return on investment   A performance indicator for divisions that relates properly measured operating income to average assets employed during a period.

Chapter Summary   Management accounting for company segments such as profit centers and divisions is influenced strongly by the degree of decentralization. If management is highly decentralized, division managers have authority to direct operations as though each division were an independent company. Top corporate management in a decentralized company establishes strategic long-range goals and uses these guidelines to monitor divisional performance. Accounting and management must cooperate to establish desired segments, to identify traceable and controllable costs for each segment, to define suitable performance indicators, and to compare actual performance with budgets, goals, and past trends.

The contribution approach to income determination is a useful device in divisional performance evaluation. Proper analysis of traceable and controllable costs provides separate income measures for individual managers and the impersonal or tangible investments for which they are responsible. Return on investment for divisions and transfer pricing policies are two additional factors used to evaluate segment performance.

ACCOUNTING FOR DECENTRALIZED ORGANIZATIONS   For planning and control purposes, management requires cost, revenue, and asset information that pertains to particular segments of company operations. *Segments* may be product lines, geographical divisions, customer classes, or departments within a specific plant; in general, a segment is any activity or organizational unit for which *separable* costs and revenues are identified. Separable (traceable or direct) costs and revenues are clearly associated with a segment and are identifiable without allocation or proration procedures.

Responsibility accounting that uses variance analysis reports based on standard costs and operating budgets is a satisfactory control procedure for departments, cost centers, and similar business segments. In addition to these procedures, other performance evaluation techniques are needed for larger segments that have responsibility for costs, revenues, and resources (assets).

Nature of Decentralization   *Decentralization* refers to the location of decision-making authority within an organization. A company composed of several divisions is decentralized if divisional managers are given authority to direct their divisions as though they were independent companies. The manager of a decentralized division normally makes decisions concerning plant expansion, market development, product pricing, sales-mix adjustments, and other financial or operating factors concerning the division. The key element in decentralization is that operating managers are free to make business decisions within the framework of strategic policies established by top management of the entire company. Although the key factor is decision-making authority, decentralization is seldom absolute; it is a relative characteristic of management style. In a given industry, the degree of decentralization may vary among companies.

For a decentralized division that manages the production and sale of numerous products, responsibility accounting will be applied throughout the organization. However, appropriate measures of operating performance must be devised for the division as a whole. In general, a company division may be classified as a profit center or an investment center. A *profit center* is responsible for revenues and certain costs traceable to the division. In addition to revenue and cost responsibility, an *investment center* is responsible for assets and capital expenditure decisions. The function of management accounting is to develop appropriate measures of income for profit centers and investment centers. In addition, rate of return on assets employed must be measured for investment centers.

The development of financial reporting techniques for divisional performance evaluation is a cooperative project that requires the efforts of accounting and management personnel. Management must identify the responsibility areas and segments for which revenues, costs, and other financial measures are relevant. In designing a performance evaluation system for divisions, the four basic objectives are:

Basic Accounting Objectives

1. To establish desired segmentation
2. To identify separable and controllable costs of segments
3. To select desired performance indicators
4. To compare actual performance to expectations

Management accountants are involved directly with these objectives and with related systems design procedures.

Segmentation A basic management function is to identify the segments for which financial measures of performance evaluation are desired. In a decentralized firm, investment centers or divisions are the segments of primary concern. While the initial task of segmentation appears simple, two important elements should be considered: A good management reporting system should distinguish between the segment and management dimensions of performance evaluation.

Separate measures must be developed for evaluating the financial performance both of the division, which is an impersonal segment, and of the managers who are responsible for segment operations. Therefore, two types of performance evaluation reports are necessary. One type of performance evaluation should be segment or entity oriented and should concentrate on segment profitability and its economic merits as a continuing investment by the company. A second type of performance evaluation should be personal in orientation and should measure the controllable financial effects of business decisions made by segment managers.

The need for both segment and management orientation in performance measurement is most obvious if a talented manager is assigned to an unprofitable division. The long-run profit potential of the division is a segment-oriented performance evaluation problem for top management. The measurement of short-run financial improvement and performance by the division manager is a distinctly different problem. Different measures of income and operating performance are necessary to accomplish the segment and management aspects of performance evaluation.

Separable and controllable costs The proper use of cost information is an important part of segment performance evaluation. To evaluate the long-run profit potential of an investment center, all costs that are specifically traceable to division activities should be considered. Not all costs that are traceable to division operations are controllable by the division manager. The performance of segment managers should be evaluated by concentrating on the costs that are controlled by their short-run and long-run decisions. In essence, evaluation of division managers is achieved through responsibility accounting applied at the level of separate company divisions. The basic principle is that a division manager controls only some of the costs that are traceable to a specific division. Segment performance evaluation should encompass all traceable costs, and personal performance measurement for the segment manager should utilize the controllable costs.

Performance measures   Measurements in performance evaluation concentrate upon the following variables for a given division:

1. *Results achieved* in terms of revenues, units produced, orders received, or other aspects of output or accomplishment
2. *Costs incurred* in terms of period costs reported in the income statement and current expenditures for fixed assets
3. *Effort expended* in terms of nonmonetary input factors such as machine hours, labor hours, new customers, sales calls, and miles driven
4. *Resources employed* in terms of personnel, physical measures of capacity, and relative ability to generate results

As indicators of performance, these four variables can be manipulated to measure profitability, rate of return, productivity, and efficiency for any particular segment. Several performance measures may be developed for a division, and the relative emphasis placed on various performance measures is an important management decision.

Comparative performance   The quality of segment or personal performance is judged by comparing current performance with budgets, goals, standards, or trends of past performance. Financial reports for performance evaluation purposes should be comparative in nature and provide analytical commentary to facilitate interpretation.

A very significant problem in divisional performance evaluation involves *goal congruence*, which is the relative state of harmony between company goals and objectives and those of division managers. When a manager knows how performance will be measured and evaluated, he or she normally will take those actions that maximize measured performance. There is a lack of goal congruence when a manager's decisions benefit the measured performance of a division but adversely affect total company performance.

To illustrate poor goal congruence, consider a corporation composed of ten decentralized divisions. In evaluating divisional managers, corporate management emphasizes rate of return on assets. Last year Division B earned 18 percent on total assets, and this year its manager rejected an investment alternative that offered a 15 percent rate of return. For the entire corporate group, rate of return on total assets is 11 percent. In this case, the investment rejection decision in Division B benefits its performance, although total company rate of return would be improved by accepting the 15 percent project. Accordingly, the potential consequences of any performance evaluation system must be studied carefully from the standpoint of decisions and goal congruence that the system will encourage.

The contribution approach to income determination is a useful technique in divisional performance evaluation. As described in Chapter 9, the contribution approach emphasizes cost behavior by grouping income statement expense items into variable and fixed classifications. The basic contribution approach for total company operations can be expanded to provide useful income measures for segment and manager performance evaluation in divisions.

To apply the contribution approach to divisions, consider the 19X4 operating results of Guy Corporation, which are summarized in Exhibit 17-1. Total fixed expenses are $56,000 of which $8,000 represents joint fixed costs not traceable to any of the corporation's three divisions. Typical company-wide joint fixed costs include executive salaries, central accounting operations, and other administrative costs incurred by the corporate headquarters office. The remaining $48,000 of fixed costs are traceable directly to the divisions that incurred the costs.

For divisional profit evaluation, only costs that are specifically traceable to a division should be deducted from divisional revenues. The resulting *segment margin* indicates the contribution of each division to unallocated joint fixed costs and company profits. A summary divisional profit report for Guy Corporation is presented in Exhibit 17-2. The segment margin is an appropriate income measure for evaluating the long-run profit potential of each division. Note that

CONTRIBUTION APPROACH TO PERFORMANCE EVALUATION

EXHIBIT 17-1
GUY CORPORATION, 19X4
CONTRIBUTION APPROACH INCOME STATEMENT

Total sales	$100,000
Variable expenses	40,000
Contribution margin	$ 60,000
Fixed expenses (analysis below)	56,000
Income before taxes	$ 4,000

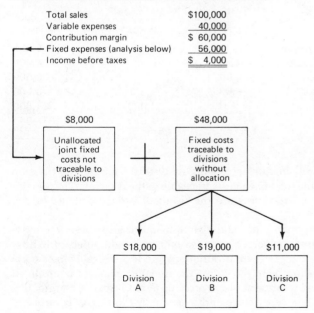

EXHIBIT 17-2
GUY CORPORATION
DIVISIONAL PROFIT REPORT, 19X4

	DIVISION A	DIVISION B	DIVISION C	TOTAL
Sales	$40,000	$50,000	$10,000	$100,000
Variable expenses	20,000	15,000	5,000	40,000
Contribution margin	$20,000	$35,000	$ 5,000	$ 60,000
Traceable fixed expenses	(18,000)	(19,000)	(11,000)	(48,000)
Segment margin*	$ 2,000	$16,000	($ 6,000)	$ 12,000
Unallocated fixed expenses not traceable to divisions				(8,000)
Income before taxes				$ 4,000

* Represents positive (or negative) contribution of the segment to recovery of unallocated fixed costs and company profits.

joint fixed costs incurred at the corporate level are not allocated to the divisions. While divisions benefit from these joint costs, the principal objective in Exhibit 17-2 is to measure the ability of segments to recover the traceable costs that result from their operations. Allocation is not desirable, since joint fixed costs are controllable for the most part at the level of corporate management.

Another refinement of the contribution approach for divisions is to separate the traceable fixed costs of each segment into controllable and uncontrollable classifications. For example, the traceable fixed costs of Division B are $19,000 as shown in Exhibit 17-2. To evaluate the personal performance of the Division B manager, the fixed costs that he or she controls must be identified. Assume that an analysis of the $19,000 produces the following subclassifications:

DIVISION B	CONTROLLABLE	UNCONTROLLABLE	TOTAL
Salary of division manager		$3,000	$ 3,000
Depreciation of equipment	$ 4,000		4,000
Salaries of division personnel	8,000		8,000
Repairs and maintenance	3,000		3,000
Advertising expenses		1,000	1,000
Traceable fixed costs	$15,000	$4,000	$19,000

According to the controllable-uncontrollable analysis, the manager of Division B controls $15,000 of the total fixed costs traceable to the division. The remaining $4,000 of traceable fixed costs are the result of decisions made by top corporate management.

To evaluate the performance of the division manager, an appropriate intermediate income measure called *performance margin* is computed in Exhibit 17-3. The performance margin is contribution margin less traceable fixed costs controlled by the division manager. Since the division manager controls all expense items deducted from revenues in arriving at performance margin, this income measure should be sensitive to improvement by proper cost control and other business decisions at the segment level.

EXHIBIT 17-3

GUY CORPORATION

DIVISION B PERFORMANCE MEASURES, 19X4

Sales	$50,000
Variable expenses	15,000
Contribution margin*	$35,000
Traceable fixed costs:	
Controllable by division manager	(15,000)
Performance margin†	$20,000
Controllable by top management	(4,000)
Segment margin§	$16,000

Use of Various Income Measures:

* *Contribution margin:* A segment measure for product lines used in CVP computations, operating budgets, and business decisions involving product promotion or sales mix.

† *Performance margin:* A managerial performance measure reflecting the income effects of divisional management decisions.

§ *Segment margin:* A segment measure used to evaluate overall profitability of a division by its contribution to unallocated company fixed costs and resulting profits.

It is possible to refine the performance margin further by concentrating on discretionary fixed costs and committed fixed costs that are controllable by the division manager. In comparison with committed costs, discretionary fixed costs can be reduced more easily. Certain situations might require computation of a *short-run performance margin* obtained by subtracting discretionary controllable fixed costs from contribution margin. This short-run performance margin is sensitive to short-run decisions implemented by division managers.

Our analysis with Guy Corporation demonstrates that several income measures can be developed to suit particular performance evaluation objectives. Similar results can be obtained with companies that use absorption costing procedures. Performance margins and segment margins for these firms are derived by deducting the appropriate traceable costs from gross profit on sales instead of the contribution margin shown in the illustrations. Since income measures under absorption costing are affected by production volume, the contribution approach is more desirable because it distinguishes between fixed and variable cost behavior.

The contribution approach to performance evaluation can be applied to segments such as divisions, sales territories, branch locations, product lines, or customer classes. For example, assume that Guy Corporation has three divisions and that each division produces three separate product lines. Within a single division, the contribution approach can be applied to each product line. The guiding principle for cost analysis is that joint costs which benefit all products should not be allocated to the various product lines. Each division will have several fixed costs that are not traceable to separate product lines. In general, as segments become smaller in scope, fewer fixed costs can be traced to each segment. In addition to appropriate profit measures, rate of return on assets employed is an important performance measure for decentralized divisions.

RETURN ON INVESTMENT FOR DIVISIONS

Rate of return on assets employed by a division or other company segment is a relative measure of profitability. For investment centers, return on investment is an important performance indicator because it considers both profits and the resources employed to produce profits. The basic formula for return on investment (ROI) is the ratio of properly measured income to investment base.

$$\text{ROI} = \frac{\text{income}}{\text{investment base}} \times 100 = XX\%$$

Both income and investment base for a division must be defined and computed in accordance with specific objectives for using ROI information.

Income Measurement Problems

Return on investment can be used to evaluate financial management and operating management functions. *Financial management* is concerned with acquisition of funds, capital structure, and debt-to-equity relationships. The appropriate ROI measure for financial management evaluation is net income after interest and taxes divided by stockholders' equity. If a division is a separately incorporated subsidiary, then this measure of ROI would be useful for evaluating financial management.

Operating management is concerned with the use of available resources to generate the largest income before interest and taxes that is consistent with long-range company policy and acceptable social standards. Evaluation of operating management must concentrate on the use of resources, and this evaluation should not be affected by capital structure policy or the costs of obtaining capital funds.

The importance of different ROI measures for financial and operating management is evident from the comparisons in Exhibit 17-4. For this illustration,

EXHIBIT 17-4
ROI MEASURES
FINANCIAL AND OPERATING MANAGEMENT

	Division X	Division Y
Current assets	$ 20,000	$ 20,000
Other assets	80,000	80,000
Total assets	$100,000	$100,000
Current liabilities	$ 10,000	$ 10,000
Long-term debt (8%)	-0-	40,000
Stockholders' equity	90,000	50,000
Total liabilities and capital	$100,000	$100,000
Net operating income	$ 25,000	$ 25,000
Interest expense (8% of debt)	-0-	3,200
Income before taxes	$ 25,000	$ 21,800
Taxes (at 50%)	12,500	10,900
Net income	$ 12,500	$ 10,900
ROI measures		
1. Net operating income ÷ total assets	25.0%	25.0%
2. Net income ÷ total assets	12.5%	10.9%
3. Net income ÷ stockholders' equity	13.9%	21.8%

we assume that a company has two separately incorporated divisions. Both divisions produce the same net operating income, but Division Y, with long-term debt in its capital structure, has an interest expense deduction and lower income taxes. Using return on investment measures, which division is more profitable? The comparative profit picture is not clear because operating managements in both divisions were equally efficient and productive. This conclusion is based on the 25 percent ROI using operating income and total assets for both divisions.

Financial management from the stockholders' viewpoint was probably superior in Division Y, which earned a 21.8 percent return on equity. The use of financial leverage in Divison Y enabled management to produce a higher return on stockholders' equity than the 8 percent return paid to suppliers of debt capital. Note that if operating management in Division Y is evaluated by net income to total assets, then ROI is 10.9 percent. In comparison with Division X, operating management performance (10.9 percent) suffers, while financial management in Division Y appears excellent. This brief analysis highlights the measurement problems that pervade financial and managerial accounting.

To resolve this apparent dilemma, the income measure for ROI computations must correspond with related performance evaluation objectives. Operating management should be evaluated by relating operating income to resources committed to operations. Interest expense and income taxes should be excluded from the operating income measure.

The segment and managerial aspects of performance evaluation also are involved in ROI analysis. For investment centers, performance margin and segment margin can be used as income measures for two separate ROI computations. Return on investment to gauge managerial performance should use performance margin and assets controllable by the division manager. To evaluate segment performance, ROI should be measured by relating segment margin to assets that are traceable to the division. By excluding interest and income taxes from the ROI analysis, operating management can be evaluated independently of division capital structure management.

The investment base used in ROI analysis must conform also to performance evaluation objectives. For operating management, some measure of assets committed to operations must be developed. There are several variations in practice, but the ideal measure is total assets traceable to a particular segment. Adjustments to reduce the total asset base are often suggested for excess and idle facilities, investments in securities and land, and for current assets such as cash and receivables. The real issue is whether ROI is measured in relation to total assets *available* or total assets *employed*. Judgment and individual preference must govern this selection. There is no single *correct* ROI measure; but once the investment base has been defined, it should be used consistently in ROI analysis. In some instances, several ROI measures can be developed for a particular segment using a different asset base for each measure. The important point is to define what the ROI seeks to measure.

Another investment measurement problem is the treatment of fixed assets and accumulated depreciation. Should tangible fixed assets be included in the investment base at historical cost or at cost less accumulated depreciation (book value)? To support either alternative, some interesting illustrations and models can be developed that generally give different results, depending upon

Investment Measurement Problems

the assumptions involved. The better alternative for company divisions is to include fixed assets at gross cost *without* deducting accumulated depreciation. A principal reason for using gross cost is to avoid the increasing ROI that otherwise occurs with the passage of time as indicated in Exhibit 17-5.

The example in Exhibit 17-5 shows a slightly decreasing ROI when the measure is based on fixed asset cost. The annual change in ROI occurs only because profits are declining each year. The logic of a constant dollar measure for particular fixed assets is sound and gives meaningful results. With fixed assets stated at gross cost, ROI will increase or decrease in the same direction as operating income. If book value of fixed assets is used, ROI increases each year simply because the ROI denominator is decreasing. If historical cost is the valuation principle used in ROI analysis, then fixed assets should be included in the asset base at gross cost.

It is also necessary to use a measure of *average* assets at gross cost. Since additional investments and asset retirements occur frequently, income for a period must be related to average assets employed during the same period. Averages can be developed from monthly or quarterly balance sheet data. Annual ROI analysis can employ an average of beginning and ending asset balances for a year if there were no significant interim changes in total assets.

As an alternative valuation principle to historical cost, some financial analysts prefer to value assets at current replacement cost. Others recommend restating historical costs to the current price level by using appropriate index number adjustments. These alternatives raise yet another measurement issue in ROI analysis. A yield ratio in the sense of economic alternatives usually is based on current market values. An ROI measure that is designed to highlight opportunity costs and the relative merits of additional investments in one division versus another should use asset replacement cost. Replacement cost of assets reflects current conditions and is useful if divisions are being compared to determine where company funds could earn the best return.

EXHIBIT 17-5
ROI AND VALUATION OF FIXED ASSETS

Case facts:
Initial fixed asset cost of $100,000. Net operating income of $15,000 decreasing $1,000 annually because of decreased efficiency. Straight-line depreciation over five-year useful life. No additional investments, and cash balances transferred to corporate headquarters.

END OF YEAR	VALUATION OF FIXED ASSETS		OPERATING INCOME	RATE OF RETURN ON	
	Cost	Book value*		Cost	Book value
1	$100,000	$80,000	$15,000	15%	18.8%
2	100,000	60,000	14,000	14%	23.3%
3	100,000	40,000	13,000	13%	32.5%
4	100,000	20,000	12,000	12%	60.0%
5	100,000	–0–	11,000	11%	†

* Cost less accumulated depreciation, which increases $20,000 per year.
† Since book value at end of year 5 is zero, ROI cannot be computed. If based on average book value for the year, ROI in year 1 is $15,000 \div [(100M + 80M) \div 2]$, or $15,000 \div 90,000 = 16.7$ percent.

If performance evaluation of operating management involves the comparison of ROI among divisions, then assets probably should be revalued for this purpose. The use of price-level adjustments to restate the historical cost of nonmonetary assets such as buildings, equipment, and land is useful. These adjustments partially compensate for the higher ROI some divisions otherwise would report on assets acquired several years ago at lower price levels.

Return on investment is a highly sensitive measure that is affected by numerous alternatives for income determination and asset valuation. These measurement problems are solved partially by a clear definition of the objective for a particular ROI computation. Another technical factor about ROI is that the ratio is an aggregate measure of many interrelationships. The basic ROI equation of income divided by assets can be expanded to show the many elements that influence the ultimate ROI number.

Return on Investment Analysis

Two important factors affecting rate of return are profit margin and asset turnover. *Profit margin,* computed as the ratio of income to sales, is the percentage of each sales dollar flowing to profits. *Asset turnover* is the ratio of sales to average assets. Turnover indicates the productivity of assets or the number of sales dollars generated by each dollar invested in assets. Return on investment is equal to profit margin times asset turnover:

$$\text{ROI} = \text{profit margin} \times \text{asset turnover}$$

or

$$\text{ROI} = \frac{\text{income}}{\text{sales}} \times \frac{\text{sales}}{\text{assets}} = \frac{\text{income}}{\text{assets}}$$

Profit margin and asset turnover are factors that explain changes in ROI for a single division or differences of ROI among divisions. The formula ROI = profit margin × asset turnover is a useful relationship for analyzing and interpreting return on investment.

Data for two divisions are summarized below to illustrate the dependency of ROI on profit margins and asset turnover:

	DIVISION A	DIVISION Z
1. Sales	$1,000,000	$2,000,000
2. Income	$ 100,000	$ 50,000
3. Average assets	$ 500,000	$ 200,000
4. Profit margin (2 ÷ 1)	10%	2½%
5. Asset turnover (1 ÷ 3)	2 times	10 times
6. Return on investment (4 × 5)	20%	25%

Division A generated the larger income, but Division Z shows a higher return on investment. While company management is concerned with total income and earnings per common share, they also are concerned with the relative profitability of invested capital. Division A could improve its comparative standing by increasing profit margin or investment turnover. Actions to increase sales, reduce costs, or reduce the assets employed would produce positive increases in ROI.

The numerous interrelationships that produce effects on the ROI measure are diagrammed in Exhibit 17-6. From this diagram, it is apparent that ROI is affected by pricing decisions, product sales mix, capital budgeting decisions

EXHIBIT 17-6
INTERRELATED FACTORS AFFECTING ROI

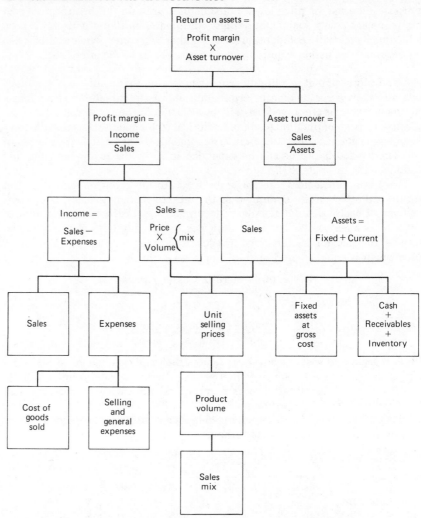

for new facilities, product sales volume, operational efficiency, and other decisions having a financial dimension. In essence, a single ROI number is a composite index of many cause-and-effect relationships and interdependent financial elements.

Because of the many factors affecting return on investment, management is advised to use this measure cautiously in performance evaluation. If ROI is overemphasized as a performance measure, division managers could react with business decisions that favor their personal ROI performance at the expense of company-wide profits or long-run success of the divisions.

A second strategy for performance evaluation systems is to develop several divisional performance indicators. Possible measures include performance margin, segment margin, one or more versions of return on investment, sales growth percentage, operating efficiency indices, share of product market, and other measures for key variables of business activity. Return on investment for divisions should be used comparatively in relation to budgeted goals and past ROI trends. Because of the technical problems in measuring ROI, changes in this percentage over time can be more revealing than the absolute number involved.

Profit measurement and return on investment for decentralized divisions are important performance evaluation problems. These problems become more complicated when divisions within a company exchange goods or services and assume the roles of customer or supplier to another company division. The pricing of intracompany transactions (transfers) affects the revenues and costs of the divisions involved. A *transfer price* is the price at which goods are exchanged among company divisions, and company transfer price policies are importantly related to performance evaluation.

PRICING INTRACOMPANY SALES

The world of transfer pricing is complex because of production capacity limitations, absence of market prices for custom products, and different degrees of decentralization among various companies. To introduce these problems, a fairly simple example with ABC Paper Company is used. As diagrammed in Exhibit 17-7, the company consists of a Paper Mill Division and a Carton Division. The Mill Division produces rolls of coarse paper that are sold to outside customers and to the Carton Division. The Carton Division manufactures corrugated boxes according to customer specification and uses a grade of paper that also is available from outside suppliers.

Since the management of ABC Paper Company believes in decentralization, the manager of each division is free to buy from any supplier and sell to any customer. Accordingly, intracompany transactions between the Mill Division

Transfer Pricing Objectives

EXHIBIT 17-7
ABC PAPER COMPANY
TRANSACTION FLOW SHOWING INTRACOMPANY TRANSFERS

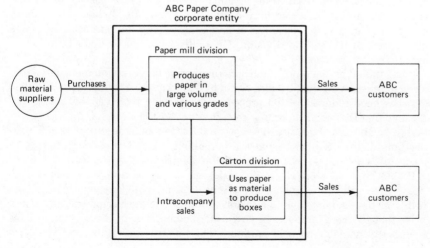

and the Carton Division are executed at the market price for Mill Division products. Under these conditions, transfer prices at market value or outside selling price accomplish three primary objectives:

1. The policy allows meaningful and realistic profit measurement for the selling division.
2. Operating results of the buying division are comparable to its being an independent company.
3. The pricing policy promotes goal congruence between company and divisional management.

Instead of this decentralized form of management, ABC Paper Company top management could make all operating decisions and require the pricing of all intracompany transfers at cost of production and distribution by the Mill Division. With transfers priced at cost, the Mill Division recognizes no profit on intracompany sales. If Carton Division costs prove to be excessive, identifying the responsibility or source of excessive costs will be difficult.

The ABC Paper Company illustrates two possible extremes in transfer pricing policy: (1) decentralized management with intracompany transfers based on market prices; or (2) centralized management with intracompany transfers priced at cost of the supplying division. If most decisions are made by top management, then realistic profit measurement for the selling division is not a strong motivational factor in performance evaluation. However, company management still could benefit from a profit analysis showing operations of the Carton Division as though it were an independent company.

Transfer pricing alternatives are internal performance evaluation measures that affect only the computed profits of the divisions. Total company profits as reported in external financial statements are not affected by using either market prices or cost. Intracompany profits are eliminated when preparing company-wide financial statements.

Transfer Pricing Methods

Two principal alternatives for transfer prices are *market price* and *cost* as described for ABC Paper Company. If custom products without widely established markets are involved, division managers in a decentralized company may agree upon a cost-plus price or some negotiated price. The *cost-plus price* is the sum of costs incurred by the producing division plus an agreed upon profit percentage. The weakness of cost-plus pricing is that cost recovery is guaranteed to the selling division. Guaranteed cost recovery fails to detect excessive cost incurrence.

A *negotiated price* could be the bargained price that division managers agree upon for custom products. It also could be a market price for standard products that has been reduced in the process of bargaining by divisional managers. Assume that Division B normally sells product X7 to Division C for $10.50 per pound. If Division C can buy the same product from outside suppliers at $10.20 per pound, then $10.20 becomes a bargained price if Division B agrees to reduce its current market price on sales to Division C.

Problems in transfer price policy arise when buying divisions elect to purchase from outside suppliers. A selling division with adequate capacity to fulfill the demand of a buying division should sell to the buying division at any price that recovers incremental costs. Incremental cost of intracompany sales includes all variable costs of production and distribution plus any fixed costs directly traceable to intracompany sales activity. If a buying division can acquire products from outside suppliers at an annual cost that is less than incremental cost to a supplying division within the company, then purchases should be made from the outside supplier.

To illustrate potential conflicts in transfer pricing decisions, consider the following case of Hawk Aircraft, Inc., and its Gauge Division. The Gauge Division manufactures an air pressure gauge used in many single-engine planes and sells this product to outside customers and to the Wizard Division of Hawk Aircraft. Annual capacity of the Gauge Division is 100,000 units, and it produced and sold 80,000 units last year (19X8). Sales to the Wizard Division were priced at $35, which is the market selling price to outside customers. Operating results of the Gauge Division for 19X8 are summarized in Exhibit 17-8.

A foreign manufacturer has offered to sell the Wizard Division its annual requirement of 10,000 gauges for $28 each. Wizard installs the gauges in small aircraft that it assembles and sells; by paying $28 per unit, Wizard could

Transfer Pricing Decisions

EXHIBIT 17-8
GAUGE DIVISION
19X8 OPERATING RESULTS

1. Income Statement (Dollar Amounts in $000)	Outside Customers	Wizard Division	Total
Sales volume in units	70,000	10,000	80,000
Sales (all at $35 per unit)	$2,450	$ 350	$2,800
Variable costs:			
Direct materials ($9 per unit)	$ 630	$ 90	$ 720
Direct labor ($10 per unit)	700	100	800
Variable overhead ($4 per unit)	280	40	320
Total variable costs	$1,610	$ 230	$1,840
Contribution margin	$ 840	$ 120	$ 960
Fixed costs:			
Manufacturing overhead—general factory operations			$ 600
Manufacturing overhead—traceable to gauge production			160
Selling and administrative expenses—allocated to gauges			100
Total fixed costs			$ 860
Net income			$ 100

2. Unit Cost Analysis

Cost factor	Unit cost
Direct materials	$ 9.00
Direct labor (2 hours at $5)	10.00
Variable overhead (2 hours at $2)	4.00
Total variable costs	$23.00
Fixed overhead ($600 + $160) ÷ 80,000 units	9.50
Average unit cost (inventory purposes)	$32.50

increase its profits by saving $7 per gauge compared with the $35 unit price paid in 19X8. The Gauge Division initially refused to sell at $28 since this price is less than average unit cost ($32.50) used for inventory purposes. If Gauge Division volume is reduced to 70,000 units, supervisory salaries will be reduced by $15,000. At sales volume of 70,000 units, Gauge Division will incur an operating loss of $5,000, determined as follows:

Sales (70,000 units at $35)	$2,450,000
Variable costs (70,000 units at $23)	(1,610,000)
Contribution margin (70,000 units at $12)	$ 840,000
Fixed costs ($860,000 − $15,000 reduction)	(845,000)
Operating loss	$ (5,000)

In comparison with this tentative operating loss, the Gauge Division would report annual profits of $30,000 if it sells to Wizard Division at $28 and incurs the additional $15,000 of supervisory salaries required to produce an annual volume of 80,000 units.

Sales to outsiders (70,000 units at $35)		$2,450,000
Sales to Wizard (10,000 units at $28)		280,000
Total sales (80,000 units)		$2,730,000
Variable costs (80,000 units at $23)		(1,840,000)
Contribution margin		$ 890,000
Annual fixed costs:		
For volume of 70,000 units	$845,000	
Additional supervisory salaries	15,000	
Total fixed costs for 80,000-unit volume		(860,000)
Net income		$ 30,000

Based upon this analysis, Gauge Division decided to sell to Wizard at $28. Annual profits of Wizard will increase $70,000, which reflects the $7 unit cost savings on 10,000 units. The $30,000 net income for Gauge Division is $70,000 less than annual profits in 19X8, when sales to Wizard were recorded at $35 per unit.

Since Gauge Division has excess capacity, it should produce and sell the 10,000 units at any price that will recover the incremental costs incurred. *Incremental costs* include all variable costs of production and distribution plus any fixed costs specifically incurred to produce and sell the additional volume. Incremental costs have exactly the same meaning as differential costs. For Gauge Division, the incremental costs for 10,000 units are $245,000 computed as follows:

Variable costs (10,000 units at $23)	$230,000
Increase in fixed costs (salaries)	15,000
Incremental costs of 10,000 units	$245,000

Incremental costs also can be determined by comparing total costs to be incurred at alternative volume levels of 70,000 and 80,000 units. The following comparison shows incremental costs in column 3.

DOLLAR AMOUNTS IN $000	(1) VOLUME OF 70,000 UNITS	(2) VOLUME OF 80,000 UNITS	(3) INCREMENTAL REVENUES AND COSTS (2 − 1)
Sales (previously computed)	$2,450	$2,730	$280
Variable costs (at $23 per unit)	(1,610)	(1,840)	(230)
Contribution margin	$ 840	$ 890	$ 40
Fixed costs	(845)	(860)	(15)
Net income (loss)	($ 5)	$ 30	$ 35

The minimum transfer price that Gauge Division should consider for the 10,000 units is $24.50, which is computed by dividing 10,000 units into incremental costs of $245,000. At a price of $24.50, Gauge Division will exactly recover the incremental costs incurred for this additional volume. Any price above $24.50 will increase Gauge Division profits in comparison with its operating results based on annual volume of 70,000 units. Note that general fixed factory overhead and fixed operating expenses allocated to the gauge product line in Exhibit 17-8 are not relevant to the transfer pricing decision. These costs will be incurred regardless of the decision concerning intracompany sales and should not be included in the group of incremental costs.

Effect of Capacity Utilization

Transfer-price analysis for the Gauge Division involves a selling division with idle capacity, since the Gauge Division could produce 100,000 units a year if necessary. If the Gauge Division can sell 100,000 units to outside customers at $35, it should not reduce its price to accommodate the needs of Wizard Division. In this case, Gauge should operate at capacity and sell to outside customers, and Wizard should purchase its requirements from outside suppliers at $28.

Incremental costs are useful in transfer pricing decisions only when the selling division has idle capacity. If the selling division operates at full capacity, the relevant cost for accepting or rejecting intracompany business is market selling price to outside customers. When products could be sold to outside customers, current market price is an opportunity cost that measures revenues foregone by selling to other company divisions at reduced prices.

In solving transfer pricing problems in a decentralized firm, there are three possible viewpoints: total company operations, selling division, and buying division. Appropriate use of incremental cost information should support any decision to purchase company-made products from outside suppliers. In relation to performance evaluation, a buy or sell decision sometimes benefits one division to the disadvantage of total company operations. To some degree, disharmony of actions in a decentralized management system cannot be avoided.

FINAL NOTE

This final chapter applies many cost accounting concepts and techniques to the general problem of performance evaluation for company segments. Divisional performance evaluation is a challenging area in which accounting information must be developed in accordance with particular management objectives. As indicated in this chapter, there are several measurement alternatives for segment income, asset or investment base, and transfer prices. Specific measures are selected to meet the information needs of a particular situation. Previous study of the subjects of cost behavior, direct costing, profit planning, and responsibility accounting will be useful in analyzing assigned problem material.

Return now to the beginning of the chapter and review the highlights section before proceeding to the review questions, exercises, and problems.

QUESTIONS

17-1. Define and illustrate the following terms and concepts:
    a. Performance evaluation   g. Segment margin
    b. Decentralized management   h. Performance margin
    c. Profit center   i. Transfer price
    d. Investment center   j. Asset turnover
    e. Return on investment   k. Cost-plus transfer price
    f. Goal congruence   l. Negotiated transfer price

17-2. What is the relationship between accounting and management in the overall process of segment performance evaluation?

17-3. Compare and contrast centralized versus decentralized management styles.

17-4. Why is there a need for both segment orientation and manager or personal orientation in divisional performance evaluation?

17-5. Identify and discuss the quantitative variables relevant to divisional performance measurement.

17-6. Why is goal congruence often a significant problem in divisional performance evaluation?

17-7. The CASB Company employs an elaborate cost allocation hierarchy for charging joint home office costs to the various corporate divisions. What is the justification for this practice? What are the negative aspects of this practice?

17-8. Give examples of costs that are traceable to a division but not controllable by the division manager.

17-9. Explain the difference in objectives for evaluating financial management and operating management.

17-10. Criticize the practice of measuring divisional return on investment in which the investment base includes fixed assets valued at cost less accumulated depreciation.

17-11. Explain the relationship between profit margin and asset turnover in connection with return on investment analysis.

17-12. What is the principal argument in favor of valuing fixed assets at replacement cost for return on investment analysis?

17-13. To facilitate segment or divisional performance measurement, transfer prices based on market value or outside selling prices are often used. What objectives are served by this practice?

17-14. Under what conditions should a division purchase from outside suppliers products that are available from other company divisions?

17-15. Under what circumstances is incremental cost not the relevant factor in setting a minimum transfer price?

17-16. What types of fixed costs should be included in the measure of incremental costs developed for transfer pricing decisions?

EXERCISES

17-17. *Cost Identification* Healthhazard Tobacco Co., Inc., operates in a single location but has four major divisions plus home-office facilities. The Smoking Pipes Division, although housed with the other three divisions, functions as an autonomous segment under the decentralized management structure of the company. The following is the profit performance report of the division for March 19X4:

Sales	$210,000
Less: Operating costs:	
Raw materials	$ 35,000
Direct labor	40,000
Operating supplies	2,500
Indirect labor	17,400
Employee fringe benefits of division personnel	32,000
Heat, light and power (divisional share)	7,100
Depreciation on equipment	12,800
Plant facility rental (divisional share)	6,400
Advertising: Pipes	8,100
Corporate (divisional share)	5,900
Computer service: Allocated portion of basic rental	2,200
Specific usage charges (fixed number of reports)	3,300
Division superintendent's salary	2,900
Miscellaneous corporate general and administrative expenses (divisional share)	6,400
Sales commissions	19,700
Fixed selling costs of division	3,800
Corporate aircraft: Allocated portion of total depreciation	1,200
Specific usage charges (variable)	2,800
Total operating costs	$209,500
Divisional net profit	$ 500

REQUIRED: Identify the above operating costs as being traceable costs (TC) and/or controllable costs of division superintendent (CC).

17-18. *Calculation of Segment and Performance Margins* Refer to the profit performance report of the Healthhazard Tobacco Co., Inc., in exercise 17-17.

REQUIRED:
a. Identify the traceable costs as being either fixed or variable.
b. Prepare a profit performance report using the contribution approach format. Within the report, identify the division's contribution margin, performance margin, and segment margin for March 19X4.

17-19. *ROI Relationships* Each independent case below presents data that are required to compute return on investment as the product of asset turnover and profit margin. Determine the numerical value of missing information. (*Note:* Use average assets to compute investment turnover.)

	CASE 1	CASE 2	CASE 3	CASE 4
Sales	$800,000	$900,000	$?	$ 600,000
Cost of goods sold	300,000	?	200,000	?
Gross margin	$500,000	$300,000	$ 300,000	$ 400,000
Expenses	400,000	?	?	?
Net income	$100,000	$100,000	$ 200,000	$ 200,000
Total assets, Jan. 1	$300,000	?	?	$1,800,000
Total assets, Dec. 31	$500,000	$400,000	$1,200,000	?
Investment turnover	?	3	?	⅓
Profit margin	?	?	?	?
Return on investment	?	33.3%	20%	?

17-20. *Minimum Transfer Price* For several years, Delta Division has manufactured a special glass container that it sells to Alpha Division at the prevailing market price of $20. Delta produced the containers only for Alpha Division and makes no sales of this product to outside customers. Annual production and sales volume is 20,000 containers. A unit cost analysis for Delta resulted in the following information:

	PER CONTAINER
Direct materials	$ 2
Direct labor (½ hour)	5
Variable overhead	4
General fixed overhead ($6 per hour)	3
Traceable fixed overhead ($40,000 ÷ 20,000)	2
Unit product cost	$16
Variable shipping expenses	1
Total unit cost	$17

General fixed overhead represents allocated joint fixed costs of production such as building depreciation, property taxes, fire insurance, and salaries of production executives. If container production were discontinued, $20,000 of the annual traceable fixed overhead could be eliminated.

REQUIRED:
a. Determine the incremental unit cost of container production.
b. If Delta Division is operating at full capacity, what is the relevant unit cost for purposes of establishing the minimum transfer price on sales to Alpha Division?

17-21. *Investment Base for ROI*   Asset measures and the 19X6 income statement for Horn Division of Royal Company are as follows:

Sales	$900,000
Depreciation expense	(200,000) (declining balance method)
Other expenses	(600,000)
Net income	$100,000
Average assets (at historical cost)	$1,000,000
Average assets (cost less depreciation)	$ 800,000

The manager of Horn Division contends that it is unfair to measure return on investment using the $800,000 base, since all other divisions use straight-line depreciation. The manager would prefer to compute ROI by using net income plus depreciation expense in relation to the $800,000 asset base.

REQUIRED:
a. Compute ROI for Horn Division using gross assets, net assets, and the manager's proposal.
b. Is there any merit to the manager's proposal?

17-22. *Measuring ROI Performance*   Breaux Division is evaluated primarily by return on investment performance in comparison with budgeted goals. For 19X3, budget data and actual results for the division included the following amounts:

	BUDGET	ACTUAL
Sales	$12,000,000	$16,000,000
Net income	$ 2,000,000	$ 2,500,000
Average total assets	$ 6,000,000	$ 7,900,000

The division manager extended credit terms from thirty to forty-five days during 19X3 and increased inventory levels to prevent stockouts and unsatisfied demand. Average total assets increased $1,500,000 over budget because of the increase in accounts receivable and inventories.

REQUIRED:
a. Compute return on investment for budget and actual results.

b. What impact did the credit and inventory decisions have on profit margin, asset turnover, and return on investment in comparison with budgeted amounts?

17-23. *Transfer Pricing Method*   Tile Products Company has two divisions involved in the production and sale of bricks. The Mining Division produces clay that is sold in 100-pound bags to the Production Division. All output of the Mining Division is shipped to the Production Division, and these transfers are priced at the average unit cost of production and distribution. A single brick is sold for $1.00 by the Production Division and requires 1 pound of clay as raw material. Operating results of the divisions for 19X7 are summarized below:

	MINING DIVISION	PRODUCTION DIVISION
Total production costs	$ 700,000	$4,500,000
Selling and general expenses	300,000	1,500,000
Total costs and expenses	$1,000,000	$6,000,000

In 19X7, the Mining Division produced and shipped 10,000,000 pounds of clay, which were billed to the Production Division at $.10 per pound. The Production Division manufactured and sold 10,000,000 bricks in 19X7. Other mines sell comparable clay material for $.30 per pound.

REQUIRED:
a. Prepare an income statement for each division assuming that intracompany transfers are priced at average cost.
b. Prepare an income statement for each division assuming that intracompany transfers are billed at market price.

17-24. *Divisional Profit Measurement*   Bellido Corporation is a decentralized firm with two divisions that produce and sell numerous products. The 19X2 income statement for company-wide operations disclosed the following results:

	DIVISION A	DIVISION B	TOTAL
Sales	$900,000	$800,000	$1,700,000
Cost of goods sold at standard variable cost	(300,000)	(400,000)	(700,000)
Contribution margin	$600,000	$400,000	$1,000,000
Fixed costs:			
Factory overhead			(360,000)
Selling and administrative			(240,000)
Income before taxes			$ 400,000
Income taxes (50%)			(200,000)
Net income			$ 200,000

Analysis of total fixed costs provided the following information concerning each division:

	DIVISION A	DIVISION B
Traceable fixed costs:		
Factory overhead	$120,000	$180,000
Selling and administrative	90,000	110,000
Traceable fixed costs controllable by division manager:		
Factory overhead	$100,000	$150,000
Selling and administrative	80,000	95,000

REQUIRED: Prepare a divisional profit analysis that discloses performance margin and segment margin for each division.

PROBLEMS

17-25. *Contribution Approach to Segment Profitability*   Missouri Mining and Metals Corporation is a diversified metal products company. Operations are divided into two major divisions, Mining and Manufacturing; the Manufacturing Division is made up of four plants—Fastener, Hardware, Locks, and Small Tools. President Joe Silverheels has requested a profit and loss summary for the year ended July 31, 19X7. He was particularly interested in a breakdown of plants in the Manufacturing Division. He received the following report from the controller, R. Gurgy:

MISSOURI MINING AND METALS CORPORATION
Profit and loss summary (in thousands)
For year ended July 31, 19X7

COST CLASSIFICATION CODE*		TOTAL COMPANY	PERCENTAGE BREAKDOWN BY DIVISION		PERCENTAGE BREAKDOWN OF PLANTS WITHIN MANUFACTURING DIVISION			
			Mining	Mfg.	Fastener	Hardware	Locks	Small tools
	Sales	$30,000	33	67	20	30	10	40
	Less: Operating costs:							
VC	Raw materials	$ 4,500	30	70	18	32	10	40
VC	Direct labor	5,000	35	65	17	30	13	40
VC	Factory overhead	3,200	40	60	19	29	10	42
VC	Selling expenses	1,500	30	70	21	28	8	43
TUFC	Salaries expense	750	33	67	16	35	12	37
TUFC	Other expenses	1,350	40	60	22	30	13	35
TCFC	Advertising expenses	1,250	40	60	22	31	11	36
TCFC	Depreciation expense	2,700	45	55	20	30	10	40
TCFC	Selling expenses	3,000	25	75	19	33	12	36
TCFC	Other expenses	550	30	70	20	30	10	40
NJC	Administrative salaries	1,200						
NJC	Other home office costs	3,450						
	Total costs	$28,450						
	Net income before taxes	$ 1,550						

* Cost classification code: VC—variable costs; TUFC—traceable uncontrollable fixed costs; TCFC—traceable controllable fixed costs; NJC—nontraceable joint costs.

Silverheels could not believe what he was seeing. "Gurgy!" he said, "We pay you for this stupidity? This is a bookkeeper's approach to segment performance evaluation! I want you back here in one hour with this mess reworked. I want to see all the figures extended and I want the report in contribution approach format showing contribution margin, performance margin, segment margin, and net income before taxes for the company as a whole. Now, get out of here!"

REQUIRED: Prepare the segment profit and loss summary that Mr. Silverheels has requested.

17-26. *Graphical ROI Analysis* Baylor, Inc., is a decentralized corporation consisting of several geographical divisions that manufacture and distribute similar product lines. Comprehensive budgeting is used by each division, and corporate management reviews the overall actual to budget performance of the divisions and their annual return on average total assets. Since operations of each division are comparable, corporate management compares ROI among divisions and has established a minimum target ROI of 12 percent for 19X5. Promotions and bonus payments to divisional managers depend upon ROI rankings among all divisions, improvement in ROI over time, and a division's ROI compared to the common target goal.

In 19X5, two divisions achieved superior performance in relation to the desired minimum ROI of 12 percent. Actual results and percentage of actual to budget are summarized below:

	WESTERN DIVISION		EASTERN DIVISION	
	Actual	% of budget	Actual	% of budget
Sales	$400,000	120	$300,000	100
Net income	$ 20,000	104	$ 24,000	102
Asset base	$100,000	105	$100,000	80
Return on investment	20%	99	24%	128

REQUIRED:
a. Compute actual and budgeted asset turnover and profit margin for each division.
b. Prepare an ROI graph in which asset turnover is on the horizontal axis and profit margin is on the vertical axis. Locate several turnover and profit margin points that yield a 12 percent ROI and construct a smooth 12 percent ROI curve.
c. Locate the asset turnover and profit margin points for each division on the ROI graph.
d. Prepare a brief summary of reasons apparently supporting the actual ROI performance of each division.

17-27. *CMA Problem—Financial Leverage and ROI* Morton Company is planning to invest $10,000,000 in an expansion program that is expected to increase earnings before interest and taxes by $2,500,000 per year. The company currently is earning $5 per share on 1,000,000 shares of outstanding common stock. The capital structure prior to the investment is:

Debt	$10,000,000
Stockholders' equity	30,000,000
Total debt and equity	$40,000,000

The expansion can be financed by sale of 200,000 common shares at $50 net or by issuing new 6 percent debt securities. The firm's most recent income statement discloses the following (in thousands):

Sales	$101,000
Variable costs	(60,000)
Fixed costs	(30,500)
Income before interest and taxes	$ 10,500
Interest expense	(500)
Income before taxes	$ 10,000
Income taxes (50%)	(5,000)
Net income	$ 5,000

REQUIRED:
a. Assume the company maintains its present income level and also achieves the anticipated earnings from the expansion project. Compute earnings per share under both debt and equity financing alternatives.
b. Determine the level of income before interest and taxes for which earnings per share under either alternative will be equal.
c. Compute return on stockholders' equity under both debt and equity financing alternatives.
d. If Morton Company is a division of a decentralized firm, which financing alternative would the Morton Company vice president prefer and why?

(IMA adapted)

17-28. *Transfer Price Determination* Two major operating divisions, the Cabinet Division and the Electronic Division, make up Dallas Industries, Inc. Utilizing a decentralized organizational structure, the company's major products are deluxe console television sets. The TV cabinets are manufactured by the Cabinet Division, while the Electronics Division produces all the electronic components and assembles the finished television sets.

The Cabinet Division supplies cabinets to the Electronics Division and also sells cabinets to other television manufacturers. Based on a normal sales order of forty cabinets, the following is a unit cost breakdown of a deluxe television cabinet:

Raw materials	$22.00
Direct labor	25.00
Variable manufacturing overhead	14.00
Fixed manufacturing overhead	16.00
Variable selling expense	9.00
Fixed selling expense	6.00
Fixed general and administrative expense	8.00
Total unit cost	$100.00

The Cabinet Division's normal profit margin is 20 percent, and the regular selling price of a deluxe cabinet is $120. Divisional management has decided recently that the $120 amount also will be the transfer price used for all intracompany transactions.

Management of the Electronics Division is unhappy with the decision. They claim that the Cabinet Division will show superior performance at the expense of the Electronics Division. Competition recently has forced the company to lower prices, and because of the newly established transfer price of the cabinet, the Electronics Division's portion of the profit margin on the deluxe television set has been lowered to 18 percent. To counteract the new intracompany transfer price, management of the Electronics Division has announced that, effective immediately, all cabinets will be purchased from an outside supplier in lots of 200 cabinets at a unit price of $110 per cabinet.

Corporate president I. M. Neutral has called a meeting of both divisional managements in order to negotiate a fair and equitable intracompany transfer price. He listed the following prices as possible alternatives:

a. Current market price $120 per cabinet
b. Current outside purchase price (This price is based on large quantity purchase discount and will cause increased storage costs for the Electronics Division.) $110 per cabinet
c. Total unit *manufacturing* costs plus normal 20 percent profit margin ($77.00 + $15.40) $92.40 per cabinet
d. Total unit cost excluding variable selling expense plus normal 20 percent profit margin ($91.00 + $18.20) $109.20 per cabinet

REQUIRED:

a. What price should be established for use in intracompany transactions? Defend your answer by showing the shortcomings of each of the other three alternatives.
b. If there was an outside market at the $120 per cabinet price for all units produced by the Cabinet Division, would your answer to part (a) change? Why?

17-29. *CMA Problem—Divisional Transfer Pricing*   A. R. Oma, Inc., manufactures a line of men's perfumes and after-shave lotions. The manufacturing process is basically a series of mixing operations with the addition of certain aromatic and coloring ingredients; the finished product is packaged in a company-produced glass bottle and packed in cases containing six bottles.

A. R. Oma feels that the sale of its product is heavily influenced by the appearance and appeal of the bottle and has, therefore, devoted considerable managerial effort to the bottle production process. This has resulted in the development of certain unique bottle production processes in which management takes considerable pride.

The two areas (perfume production and bottle manufacture) have evolved over the years in an almost independent manner; in fact, rivalry has developed between management personnel about which division is more important to A. R. Oma. This attitude is probably intensified because the bottle manufacturing plant was purchased intact ten years ago, and no real interchange of management personnel or ideas (except at the top corporate level) has taken place.

Since the Bottle Division was acquired, its entire production has been absorbed by the Perfume Division. Each area is considered a separate profit center and evaluated as such. As the new corporate controller you are responsible for the definition of a proper transfer value to use in crediting the bottle production profit center and in debiting the packaging profit center.

At your request, the general manager of the Bottle Division has asked certain other bottle manufacturers to quote a price for the quantity and sizes demanded by the Perfume Division. These competitive prices are as follows:

VOLUME	TOTAL PRICE	PRICE PER CASE
2,000,000 cases*	$ 4,000,000	$2.00
4,000,000 cases	7,000,000	1.75
6,000,000 cases	10,000,000	1.67

* Each case represents six bottles.

A cost analysis of the internal bottle plant indicates that they can produce bottles at these costs:

VOLUME	TOTAL COST	COST PER CASE
2,000,000 cases	$3,200,000	$1.60
4,000,000 cases	5,200,000	1.30
6,000,000 cases	7,200,000	1.20

(Your cost analysts point out that these costs represent fixed costs of $1,200,000 and variable costs of $1 per case.)

These figures have given rise to considerable corporate discussion about the proper value to use in the transfer of bottles to the Perfume

Division. This interest is heightened because a significant portion of a division manager's income is an incentive bonus based on profit center results.

The Perfume Division has the following costs in addition to the bottle costs:

VOLUME	TOTAL COST	COST PER CASE
2,000,000 cases	$16,400,000	$8.20
4,000,000 cases	32,400,000	8.10
6,000,000 cases	48,400,000	8.07

Market Research has furnished you with the following price-demand relationship for the finished product:

SALES VOLUME	TOTAL SALES REVENUE	SALES PRICE PER CASE
2,000,000 cases	$25,000,000	$12.50
4,000,000 cases	45,600,000	11.40
6,000,000 cases	63,900,000	10.65

REQUIRED:
a. A. R. Oma, Inc., has used market price transfer prices in the past. Using the current market prices and costs, and assuming a volume of 6,000,000 cases, calculate the income for:
   1. The Bottle Division
   2. The Perfume Division
   3. The corporation
b. This production and sales level is the most profitable volume for:
   1. The Bottle Division
   2. The Perfume Division
   3. The corporation
   Explain your answer.
c. A. R. Oma, Inc., uses the profit center concept for divisional operation.
   1. Define a profit center.
   2. What conditions should exist for a profit center to be established?
   3. Should the two divisions of A. R. Oma, Inc., be organized as profit centers?

(IMA adapted)

17-30. *Evaluation of Transfer Pricing Policy* Sunnyvale Corporation is a large enterprise with over forty profit centers. A company-wide transfer pricing rule states that a selling division always must sell to a buying division at current market prices.

Division S was asked to quote prices on 10,000 standard parts (representing 10 percent of the division's practical capacity) that Division B has ordered from time to time in past years. Division S quoted a price of $20 each, which would bring a total contribution margin of $60,000 for the 10,000 parts. However, an outside supplier quoted a price of $16, and Division S was forced by company policy to fill the order at that price.

REQUIRED:

a. How much total contribution margin will Division S earn at the price of $16? How much is the net income of Sunnyvale Corporation affected by keeping the business inside at that price rather than going outside?

b. The practical capacity of Division S is 100,000 machine hours. Suppose that it takes 1 machine hour to make one standard part. Suppose further that the order is indivisible; that is, Division S must make all 10,000 parts or none—it cannot accept a third or a half of the order. Suppose, finally, that only 10,000 machine hours of capacity were available for this production.

The S Division manager also had planned to submit a bid to an outside company for making 4,000 special parts at a selling price of $40 each, which would bring Division S a total contribution margin of $80,000 for the 4,000 parts. The manager felt virtually certain that he would get the order. It takes 2 machine hours to make one special part. However, because he could not handle both orders, he delayed submitting his bid because Division B needed the standard parts. In view of these circumstances, how were net incomes of Division S and Sunnyvale Corporation affected by the decision to keep the standard parts order inside? How would you modify the transfer pricing rule?

17-31. *CMA Problem—Professional Conduct* George Jackson has been recently "hired" by the controller of the Consumer Products Division as that division's assistant controller. This was a transfer within the corporation and represents a promotion within the total corporate accounting staff.

Since joining the divison's accounting staff, Jackson has observed two practices that do not seem in keeping with sound operating procedures and that appear to overstate division profit for the current period. The division inventory seems unusually high, and Jackson's analysis reveals that this results from failure to write down the inventory for obsolete items and from manufacture of inventory in excess of current needs.

Jackson prepared a report to the division controller containing this information, along with the dollar impact on profits and division return on investment. His recommended adjustments would materially lower the division's annual profits and its return on assets, the key numbers used to measure division performance.

The division controller orally informs Jackson that he had called these matters to the attention of the division general manager earlier in the year, although without the numerical analysis contained in the report. He states that the general manager will not authorize the write-down of the inventory and plans to continue production at current levels (which will sustain the excess inventory position through year-end). The general manager hopes that the next year's sales and profits will be large enough to absorb the excess inventory and the inventory write-down, although preliminary data gathered for next year's budget development does not support this expectation.

The corporation is organized into several autonomous divisions with a major one being the Consumer Products Division. The assistant division controller reports directly to the division controller, who in turn reports to the general manager. Division controllers have a functional responsibility to the corporate controller. The corporate controller's office develops standard accounting and reporting procedures to be followed by all divisions. Consumer Products Division is adhering to those procedures.

The assistant division controller is concerned that corporate management is not receiving proper financial information from the division. He fears that this unreliable information will lead to inappropriate decisions by corporate management to the detriment of the stockholders. As a professional management accountant he is concerned about his responsibilities to the division management, corporate management, and the stockholders.

REQUIRED:
a. What possible courses of action are available to George Jackson in resolving his problem?
b. What course of action would you recommend? Explain the basis for your answer.

(IMA adapted)

17-32. *CMA Problem—Divisional Profit Planning* Clarkson Company is a large multidivision firm with several plants in each division. A comprehensive budgeting system is used for planning operations and measuring performance. The annual budgeting process commences in August five months prior to the beginning of the fiscal year. At this time the division managers submit proposed budgets for sales, production and inventory levels, and expenses; capital expenditure requests also are formalized. The expense budgets include direct labor and all overhead items, which are separated into fixed and variable components. Direct materials are budgeted separately in developing the production and inventory schedules.

The expense budgets for each division are developed from its plants' results, as measured by the percent variation from an adjusted budget in the first six months of the current year and a target expense reduction percentage established by the corporation.

To determine plant percentages, the plant budget for the half-year period just completed is revised to recognize changes in operating procedures and costs outside the control of plant management (labor wage rate changes, product style changes, etc.). The difference between this revised budget and the actual expenses is the controllable variance, which is expressed as a percentage of the actual expenses. This percentage is added (if unfavorable) to the corporate target expense reduction percentage. A favorable plant variance percentage is subtracted from the corporate target. If a plant had a 2 percent unfavorable controllable variance and the corporate target reduction was 4 percent, the plant's budget for next year should reflect costs approximately 6 percent below this year's actual costs.

Next year's final budgets for the corporation, the divisions, and the plants are adopted after corporate analysis of the proposed budgets and a careful review with each division manager of the changes made by corporate management. Division profit budgets include allocated corporate costs, and plant profit budgets include allocated division and corporate costs.

Return on assets is used to measure the performance of divisions and plants. The asset base for a division consists of all assets assigned to the division, including its working capital, and an allocated share of corporate assets. For plants, the asset base includes the assets assigned to the plant plus an allocated portion of the division and corporate assets. Recommendations for promotions and salary increases for the executives of the divisions and plants are influenced by how well the actual return on assets compares with the budgeted return on assets.

The plant managers exercise control only over the cost portion of the plant profit budget because the divisions are responsible for sales. Only limited control over the plant assets is exercised at the plant level.

The manager of the Dexter Plant, a major plant in the Huron Division, carefully controls costs during the first six months so that any improvement appears after the target reduction of expenses is established. This is accomplished by careful planning and timing of discretionary expenditures.

During 19X3 the property adjacent to the Dexter Plant was purchased by Clarkson Company. This expenditure was not included in the 19X3 capital expenditure budget. Corporate management decided to divert funds from a project at another plant since the property appeared to be a better long-term investment.

Also during 19X3 Clarkson Company experienced depressed sales. In an attempt to achieve budgeted profit, corporate management announced in August that all plants were to cut their annual expenses by 6 percent. In order to accomplish this expense reduction, the Dexter Plant manager reduced preventive maintenance and postponed needed major repairs. Employees who quit were not replaced unless absolutely necessary. Employee training was postponed whenever possible. Inventories of raw materials, supplies, and finished goods were reduced below normal levels.

REQUIRED:
a. Evaluate the budget procedures of Clarkson Company with respect to its effectiveness for planning and controlling operations.

b. Is Clarkson Company's use of return on assets to evaluate the performance of the Dexter Plant appropriate? Explain your answer.

c. Analyze and explain the Dexter Plant manager's behavior during 19X3.

(IMA adapted)

Abnormal spoilage Unusually high spoilage rate in relation to expected or past spoilage experience; related costs are accounted for as period costs.

Absorption costing Traditional approach to product costing in which all manufacturing costs, regardless of variability with volume, are treated as product or inventoriable costs.

Acceptance-rejection standard An evaluation measure used in capital expenditure request analysis to identify projects that offer adequate versus inadequate rates of return.

Accounting rate of return Return on investment computed by relating average annual net income produced by a project to its average capital investment.

Added units The concept that accountability for units and production costs is adjusted to recognize an increase in products caused by adding new materials during processing operations.

Algebraic CVP analysis Cost-volume-profit analysis with equations using contribution margin information expressed in either percentage or per unit form.

Allocation base The base used in reapportioning costs that best measures the causal or beneficial relationship involved.

Annuity A series of equal cash flows to be received or paid at regular time intervals.

Applied factory overhead The amount of overhead costs charged to specific jobs using predetermined overhead rates.

Asset turnover The ratio of sales to average total assets.

Avoidable costs Costs that can be eliminated if a particular operating segment or activity is discontinued.

Basic standards Standards that are seldom revised or updated to reflect current operating costs and price level changes.

Breakeven point The level of operations at which total revenue is equal to total expenses.

Budgetary control The process of planning a company's operating activities and the control of operations to aid in attaining those plans.

Budget simulation A method of experimentation in which projected costs and other input data are systematically changed to see what effects these changes have on forecasted net income.

By-products Products produced simultaneously with main products that have insignificant total sales value in relation to the main products.

Capacity costs Committed costs that must be incurred if a company continues to utilize its existing capacities to produce and sell.

Capital expenditure Cost of acquiring fixed assets or investing in other projects having a useful life of several years.

Capital expenditure budget A budget that includes capital expenditure plans and approved expenditures for a particular year.

Cash budget A forecast of cash receipts and disbursements for a future time period.

Continuous budget A perpetual twelve-month budget in which expired monthly or quarterly data are deleted and replaced by projections for a comparable future time period.

Continuous production flow A system in which products completed by one department are transferred to a subsequent department for additional processing; all departments are simultaneously engaged in production activity.

Contribution approach A technique for measuring profits in which contribution margin is considered a balance available to recover fixed costs and generate profits.

Contribution margin The excess of revenues over all variable costs related to the particular sales volume.

Controllable cost A cost that can be regulated or influenced by the actions and decisions of a particular manager within a given time period.

Conversion costs The combined total of manufacturing labor and factory overhead costs incurred by a production department.

Cost accounting Internal cost data accumulation based on a set of cost concepts and related cost accumulation and other analytical techniques necessary for transforming business data into useful information for management.

Cost assignment schedule A process costing schedule within which unit costs, the cost of ending Work in Process inventory, and the cost of units transferred to subsequent departments are determined.

Cost attachment The concept that direct and indirect manufacturing costs are assigned to products as manufacturing operations are performed.

Cost behavior The manner in which costs respond to changes in volume or activity.

Cost center Any organizational segment or area of activity for which it is desirable to accumulate costs.

Cost composition The concept that costs of different types and from diverse origins may be accumulated to represent a new cost measure.

Cost control Comparative analysis of actual costs in relation to an appropriate base of standards or budgets to facilitate performance evaluation and specification of corrective measures.

Cost flow The route described by various classifications applicable to a particular cost as it progresses toward its ultimate destination as an expense in the income statement.

Cost formulation The concept that particular cost characteristics can be identified, measured, and analyzed to provide basic information needed for many purposes of management.

Cost-plus transfer price The sum of costs incurred by the producing division plus an agreed-upon profit element.

Cost reapportionment The redistribution of supporting service department overhead costs to production departments for purposes of computing predetermined overhead rates.

Currently attainable standards Standards that measure reasonable performance under average operating conditions assuming normal efficiency.

Decentralized management A system of management in which operating managers are free to make business decisions within the framework of strategic policies established by top management of the entire company.

Decision model A formal or informal representation of the variables and relationships involved in a particular decision application.

Defective units Spoiled units that are removed from the production process and reworked to a condition of being sold either as a first-line quality unit or as a factory second.

Departmental cost of production report The process costing report that summarizes the information contained in the quantity schedule, the equivalent production schedule, and the cost assignment schedule; this report yields the costs of completed production and ending Work in Process inventories.

Differential cost The difference between costs to be incurred under two or more alternative courses of action (also called *incremental cost*).

Direct costing The product costing and income measurement approach in which only variable manufacturing costs are accumulated and attached to products; fixed manufacturing costs are recorded as expenses of the period (also called *variable costing*).

Direct labor Labor cost for work performed on products that is conveniently and economically traceable to specific units of output.

Direct materials Raw materials that become an integral part of the finished product and that are conveniently and economically traceable to specific units of output.

Discounted cash flow Evaluation of capital expenditure proposals using net cash inflows weighted by the time value of money.

Discretionary costs Costs incurred because of periodic policy decisions by management.

Dual cost responsibility The concept that some costs are influenced by actions of more than one manager.

Equivalent production Production for a period of time expressed in terms of fully completed units; partially completed units are restated in terms of equivalent whole units produced.

Estimated cost A cost derived from projections based on past trends of actual costs and generally involving averages of past performance.

Exception reporting Cost control reports to managers that emphasize problem areas and reduce unnecessary detail in order to avoid information overload.

Excess capacity Production capability that will not be utilized in the foreseeable future.

Expected annual capacity The budgeted production level expected to occur in the succeeding year.

Favorable standard cost variance A variance occurring when actual costs are less than standard costs.

Financial accounting The area of accounting that is concerned primarily with the organization and preparation of reports on enterprise assets, equities, and net income and involves the recording, classifying, and summarizing of balance sheet and income statement effects of internal events and external transactions.

Finished goods inventory All fully completed products that have not been shipped to customers.

Fixed cost A cost that remains constant in total within a relevant range of activity.

Flexible budget A summary of estimated costs to be incurred at various levels of productive activity.

Function cost classification A cost classification method that emphasizes the business purpose for which costs were incurred.

Goal congruence The relative state of harmony between company goals and objectives and those of individual managers.

Graphic CVP analysis Cost-volume-profit analysis using a graph that shows the relationship between total costs and total revenues over a range of activity.

High-low cost analysis A mathematical method used to measure cost behavior by analyzing paired data for the high point and low point of paired cost and volume observations.

Ideal standards Perfection standards that allow

minimum materials, labor time, and cost constraints for manufacturing a particular product.

Idle capacity Facilities to be used only during peak production periods or during downtime of similar equipment.

Incremental cost *See* **Differential cost.**

Incremental cost analysis An analysis to highlight differences between costs and revenues under two or more alternative courses of action.

Indirect labor Labor costs of production-related activities that cannot be associated with or conveniently and economically traceable to end products.

Indirect materials Production supplies and other materials that cannot conveniently or economically be assigned to specific units of output.

Initial spoilage Spoilage that occurs at or near the start of processing in a particular department; costs of these spoiled units are allocated to completed units and final Work in Process inventories.

Inventoriable cost Manufacturing costs that are assigned to products and are carried from one accounting period to another in inventory accounts until the products are sold (also called *product cost*).

Inventory valuation concept Process of selecting and applying a particular basis for measuring inventories in monetary terms.

Investment center A segment of company operations that has responsibility for revenues earned, costs incurred, and assets employed.

Job order cost system A product costing system applicable to unique or special-order products in which material, labor, and manufacturing overhead costs are assigned to specific job orders or batches of products.

Job order cost sheet The document that accumulates the total costs assigned to each job in a job order cost system. It also serves as the subsidiary ledger for the Work in Process inventory control account.

Job time ticket The document used in a job order cost system to record the hours worked on particular jobs by direct labor personnel.

Joint cost A cost that collectively applies or relates to several products or costing objects and that can be assigned to those costing objects only by means of arbitrary allocation.

Joint products Two or more products produced

simultaneously having major revenue-producing potential that appear for the first time as individual products at the split-off point.

Labor efficiency variance The difference between actual hours worked and standard hours allowed multiplied by the standard labor rate per hour.

Labor rate standard The hourly labor cost expected to prevail during the next twelve-month period.

Labor rate variance The difference between actual labor rates and standard rates multiplied by actual direct labor hours worked.

Labor time standard A realistic estimate of the labor time required to complete each specific phase in the production of a product.

Linear approximation The assumption in cost-volume-profit analysis that cost and revenue functions are linear in nature over the relevant range.

Linear regression analysis A statistical method for fitting a straight line to paired observations of an independent variable and a dependent variable.

Long-term planning General operating plans for a five- or ten-year period that anticipate operational changes in marketing and production and provide a smooth transition between business operations in consecutive annual periods.

Lost units Product loss resulting from spoilage, shrinkage, or evaporation of the materials employed so that completed output yields a smaller volume than the total of basic inputs.

Management accounting The application of appropriate techniques and concepts in processing the historical and projected economic data of an entity to assist management in establishing plans for reasonable economic objectives and in the making of rational decisions with a view toward achieving these objectives. It includes the methods and concepts necessary for effective planning, for choosing among alternative business actions, and for control through the evaluation and interpretation of performance.

Management accounting cycle An interrelated set of cost and managerial accounting concepts and techniques that aid in servicing the informational requirements of management.

Management cycle The collective efforts of a team of experienced business managers who together establish the objectives and goals of the organization and guide various segments of the firm to the eventual attainment of those goals.

Manufacturing costs All production costs incurred to bring manufactured products to a salable condition, including direct materials, direct labor, and indirect manufacturing overhead costs.

Manufacturing overhead All manufacturing costs (except direct material and direct labor costs) that have the common characteristic of not being directly identifiable with or traceable to specific units of output.

Master budget An integrated set of departmental or functional period budgets and forecasted financial statements for a company as a whole.

Material price standard A predetermined cost reflecting the current market price per unit of raw material used in production.

Material price variance The difference between actual price paid for materials and standard price multiplied by the actual quantity purchased.

Material quantity standard A predetermined measure that expresses expected normal usage of raw materials per unit of finished product.

Material quantity variance The difference between actual quantity of material used and standard quantity of material allowed multiplied by standard price per unit.

Material requisition The primary document used by a production department to request items stored in inventory that lists the items required and the quantity required of each; it is signed by an authorized person in the production department.

Mixed cost A semivariable cost that demonstrates both fixed and variable characteristics.

Negotiated transfer price The bargained price that division managers agree upon for custom products.

Net present value The difference between future net cash inflows of a project discounted at the minimum acceptable return on investment and estimated cost of the project.

Net realizable value Product selling price less estimated costs of completion and disposal.

Nonlinear cost behavior Costs that are variable in nature but do not vary in direct proportion to changes in volume.

Normal capacity   Average annual capacity required to satisfy anticipated sales volume based on consideration of seasonal factors and cyclical business fluctuations.

Normal costing   An approach to cost accounting for products in which factory overhead costs are charged to Work in Process by using a predetermined overhead rate.

Normal spoilage   Product loss that is unavoidable and uncontrollable; related costs are accounted for as product costs.

Object cost classification   A cost classification method that uses as its basis the description of what is obtained in exchange for cash disbursements or liabilities incurred.

Opportunity cost   The earnings lost by not selecting the second-best alternative use of particular resources.

Overhead allocation   The systematic assignment of manufacturing overhead costs to batches of products or other cost objects.

Overhead budget variance   The difference between actual overhead costs incurred and a flexible budget amount for overhead costs based on standard hours allowed.

Overhead efficiency variance   The difference between actual labor hours worked and standard labor hours allowed multiplied by the standard variable overhead rate.

Over- or underapplied overhead   The amount by which overhead costs assigned to goods worked on during the period either exceeds or is less than actual overhead costs incurred.

Overhead spending variance   The difference between actual overhead costs incurred and the overhead costs that should have been incurred based on actual hours worked.

Overhead volume variance   The difference between budgeted fixed overhead costs and fixed overhead applied on the basis of st ndard hours allowed.

Overtime premium   The extra hourly earnings (extra half-time) commonly paid to employees who work more than forty hours per week.

Payback period   The time period required to recover the initial cost of a capital expenditure project.

Performance evaluation   The assessment of job per-

formance by linking cost variances with individuals responsible for the variances and analyzing possible causes for the variance.

Performance margin   Contribution margin of a division less traceable fixed costs controlled by the division manager.

Period budget   A forecast of annual operating results that represents a quantitative expression of planned activities of an organization.

Period cost   A cost that is incurred to maintain the enterprise's selling and administrative functions during the period, cannot be deferred, and must be charged against revenue as an expense of the accounting period in which it is incurred. All expired costs that are reported as expenses in the income statement are period costs.

Periodic inventory method   A system of accounting for inventory in which costs are not routed through inventory accounts in the general ledger. Instead, end-of-period inventory values are determined from physical counts of units in storage.

Perpetual inventory method   A system of accounting for inventories in which on-hand inventory balances and costs are readily available upon request because general ledger inventory accounts with continuous balances are maintained for Raw Materials, Work in Process, and Finished Goods inventories.

Physical unit flow   Unit flow from one department to another department engaged in continuous production.

Postcompletion audit   A procedure used to evaluate the accuracy of forecasted results in capital expenditure decisions.

Practical capacity   Theoretical capacity reduced by allowances for unavoidable facility downtime due to anticipated machine repairs, retooling, and other stoppages caused by employee, raw material, or power failure.

Predetermined overhead rate   An overhead cost factor used for overhead cost assignment to specific units or jobs based on estimated overhead costs and production volume for a specific future period.

Present value   The value today of funds to be paid or received sometime in the future.

Prior department costs   Costs of products completed in one department that are transferred to the Work in Process inventory account of the next department.

Process cost accounting A product costing system applicable to production situations involving a large volume of similar products or a continuous production flow where manufacturing costs are accumulated by department or process rather than by batches of goods.

Product cost *See* **Inventoriable cost.**

Production flow concept Arrangement of the phases of a production process to facilitate an orderly flow of goods and efficient use of available resources.

Pro forma financial statements Forecasted financial statements based on estimated data.

Profit center A segment of company operations that has revenue and cost responsibility.

Profit planning The analysis of planned profits for a period based on estimates of revenues, costs, and related operating decisions.

Project planning Formulation of plans for a specific program, process, activity, or decision alternative that may affect regular operations for several time periods.

Quantity schedule A process costing schedule that summarizes the flow of physical units.

Raw materials The materials that became a part of the finished product.

Raw materials inventory All purchased raw materials and supplies that have not been issued to production or service departments.

Relative sales value method A method of allocating joint production costs to joint products in proportion to their relative sales values at the point of split-off; cost allocation is based on a product's ability to generate revenues rather than on physical measures.

Relevant data Future costs, revenues, and resources that are different between alternatives in a particular decision-making application.

Relevant range A band or range of potential volume levels within which actual operations are likely to occur.

Resource allocation concept Efficient resource usage to achieve cost savings while still producing a quality product.

Responsibility accounting Accumulation and comparative reporting of cost data according to specific responsibility units within an organization.

Return on investment A performance indicator for divisions that relates properly measured operating income to average assets employed during a period.

Sales mix analysis CVP analysis that considers the relative proportions of different products making up total sales.

Segment margin The contribution of each division to unallocated joint fixed costs and company profits.

Separable costs *See* **Traceable costs.**

Simulation A system of testing proposed changes in operations through experimentation using different operating variables in repeated trials to determine optimal courses of action.

Split-off point The stage in a joint production process where separate products are first identifiable.

Spoilage loss The product loss resulting from the removal of units from production that do not meet product specifications.

Standard cost A carefully predetermined estimate of what material, labor, and overhead costs should be on a per unit basis, given product specifications and desired operating efficiency.

Standard cost variance The difference between actual and standard costs.

Standard hours allowed The number of good units produced multiplied by the standard labor hours per unit of product.

Static budget A budget based on a single level of activity (also called *fixed budget*).

Step-variable cost A cost that varies or changes in relation to volume over wide volume ranges; within a narrow range of planned activity, the cost will remain constant.

Sunk cost Past costs that have been incurred already.

Supporting service departments All necessary manufacturing activities of a firm that are connected indirectly with the production process.

Terminal spoilage Spoilage that occurs at or near the end of a process; related costs are allocated only to units completed and transferred out.

Theoretical capacity Maximum productive output assuming that all facilities operate at optimum speed without production interruptions.

Time-adjusted rate of return A rate of return that equates discounted future cash inflows with the initial cost of a capital expenditure project.

Time value of money The concept that cash flows of equal dollar amounts which are separated by a time interval will have different present values because of the effect of compound interest.

Traceable cost Costs that are directly identified with a segment's operations and are assignable to a product or a segment without proration or allocation (also called *separable cost*).

Transfer price The price at which goods and services are exchanged among company divisions.

Value added The concept that costs of raw materials and other manufacturing costs are traceable to or allocated to a product, adding value as it progresses through the production process.

Variable cost A cost that varies in direct proportion to an appropriate volume or activity base.

Variable costing *See* **Direct costing.**

Variance analysis The process of computing the amount of, and isolating the causes of, variances between actual costs and standard costs.

Work in process inventory Partially completed units of output at period end.

Cost of Goods Manufactured, 46, 47
  and by-product accounting, 246
  and closing entries, 68
  in conversion to direct costing, 311
  and direct costing procedures, 305, 307
  and direct vs. absorption costing, 301–302
  and financial statements, 141
  and job order cost flow, 140
  process cost system, 174
  total, 63, 64
Cost of Goods Sold, 46, 307
  and approximate sales value method, 242
  budgets, 445, 446, 451, 466–467
  components of, 63
  computation of, 62, 63–65
  in cost accounting systems, 101, 116
  defined, 47
  in direct and absorption costing, 302
  as expense category, 92, 97
  and financial statements, 141
  and labor costs, 53
  and overapplied overhead, 301
  and perpetual inventory cost flow, 119, 140
  and standard cost accounting, 329, 342, 346, 417
  and underapplied overhead, 133–134, 301
  and unit costs, 136, 141
  and variance account balances, 359, 383, 384, 385
Cost of production report, 101
  and added units at end, 213, 214, 215
  phases of analysis, 162
  and units started and completed method, 179
  see also Departmental cost of production report
Cost of units sold, 346
Cost-plus price, 586
Cost recovery
  and by-product accounting method, 244–245
  and contribution approach, 272
  and spoiled units sales, 207
  and transfer pricing, 586
Cost reduction, 359
Cost savings, 535, 540
Cost summaries, 9
  in process cost accounting systems, 199–200
  in production process, 34–36
Cost-volume-profit analyses (CVP)
  assumptions, 262, 264, 279
  and budgeting process, 445, 446
  and capacity levels, 332
  and contribution approach, 272–279
    algebraic method, 273–275

graphic method, 275–276
    sales mix analysis, 276–279
  and cost behavior, 264, 298
  and direct costing, 307–310, 313
  nature of, 261–264
Currently attainable standards
  and cost control, 417
  defined, 337
  and inventory balances, 382
  updated, 342
  and variance balances, 383

Data accumulation, 17
Data aggregation, 426–427
Data processing, 5, 17–18, 19
Decentralization
  accounting for, 574–577
  and transfer prices, 585, 586, 589
Decision information, as cost accounting objectives, 89, 96
Decision making, 45, 99, 100
  alternatives and contribution approach, 262
  and decentralization, 574
  divisional management performance evaluation, 575, 576, 578, 579
  long-range strategic, 496, 497
  and management accounting, 3, 5–6, 7, 12, 495
  and material purchase and usage budget, 461
  product pricing, 454–455
  and ROI analysis, 583
  and selling expense budget, 459
  to sell or process-further, 246–248
  techniques, 16
  and transfer prices, 586, 587–589
  see also Capital expenditure decisions; Short-run decision analysis
Decision models, 499–500
Demand, market, 329, 331
Departmental cost of production report
  and added units, 211, 212, 213, 215
  and cost allocation schedule, 238
  format and phases, 171–172
  and prior departmental costs, 201
  purpose, 162, 163, 166, 167, 168
  stages, 169
  and standard costs, 345
  Work in Process inventory, ending, 172–173
Departments
  budgets, 445, 470
  cost accumulation, 163, 164, 174, 218

Incremental costs (*cont.*)
  and transfer pricing, 586–587, 588, 589
Incremental profit analysis, 503, 505–506
Incremental revenues
  analysis, 247
  and capital budgeting, 503
  and relevant cost analysis, 498
  and short-run operating decisions, 497, 501–503, 504
Indirect costs, 46
  and controllable costs, 424
  and cost attachment, 92
  and cost classifications, 98–99
  and direct costing, 299
Indirect labor costs, 46, 53, 61, 139, 335
Indirect manufacturing costs. *See* Overhead costs
Indirect material costs, 46, 49, 61, 139
Initial inventory balances. *See* Beginning inventory balances
Initial investment. *See* Capital expenditure decisions
Institute of Management Accounting (IMA), 19
Insurance premiums, 122, 247, 267, 371, 418, 502
Interest
  and discounted cash flow, 539, 540
  and ROI measures, 580, 581
  tables, 551–557
  and time-adjusted rate of return, 540
Internal reporting, 298, 303, 311, 313, 314
Inventoriable costs, 46, 48, 97, 298
Inventory. *See* Periodic inventory method; Perpetual inventory method; *and under specific names*
Inventory cost flow, 198, 218–220
Inventory pricing methods, 51, 52, 94. *See also* Average cost method; FIFO; LIFO
Inventory valuation
  and actual costs, 383
  and cost accumulation methods, 446
  and cost flow assumptions, 218–220
  defined, 198, 218
  and direct costing, 299, 311
  and joint production costs, 236, 237, 247
  and period planning, 496
  in process cost accounting, 162, 198, 199
  in product costing, 94
  and standard cost accounting, 336, 337, 342, 346, 383
Investment center
  defined, 573, 575

  and ROI measures, 581
  and segment performance evaluation, 576

Job order cost sheet
  and job order cost system, 134, 135–136, 239
  and standard costing, 345
Job order cost system, 134–141
  and cost accumulation, 101
  defined, 115, 116–117
  and joint production costs, 236, 239
  and overhead rates, 102
  and perpetual inventory cost flows, 118–119, 137–141
  and process cost system, 164
  and standard cost accounting, 329, 343
Job time tickets, 134, 135, 139
Joint fixed costs, 577, 578, 579
Joint production costs, 98, 99, 245, 279, 329
  allocation of, 243, 247, 416
    and physical volume method, 237–240
    and relative sales value method, 240–241
  defined, 235, 236
  nature of, 236–237
  and short-run operating decisions, 246–248, 506
Joint products, 235
  accounting for, 236, 237–244
  defined, 236
  and cost recovery method, 245
  and decision making, 246–248
  and short-run operating decisions, 501, 502
Journal entry analysis
  direct costing and absorption costing, 300–301
  in job order cost system, 137–141
  and overhead variances, 375–378
  periodic, 67
  periodic and perpetual inventories, 119–120

Labor costs
  accounting for, 53–57, 61, 62, 65, 67
  actual, 330, 331, 333, 344, 359, 364, 365
  algebraic CVP analysis, 275
  and cost classification, 97
  cost control, 57, 418
  and cost flows, 92
  and direct costing, 297, 298, 299, 304, 305
  indirect, 46, 53, 61, 139, 335
  in job order cost system, 115, 116–117, 134–135, 139

Work in Process inventory (*cont.*)
and perpetual inventory system, 117, 118, 119, 135, 137–139, 140
and prior department costs, 199, 200, 201
in process cost accounting, 162–184 *passim*
and product costing, 94, 97, 115, 117
and spoilage, 202, 203, 205–207
and standard cost accounting, 329, 340, 342, 344, 345, 346

and unprocessed materials and delayed transfers, 216–218
and variances, 359, 362, 367, 382, 383
Worksheet
and by-product accounting, 246
format, 68
illustrative analysis, 69–76, 141–148
and standard costs, 342